MICHAEL ARMSTRONG
WITH STEPHEN TAYLOR

14TH EDITION

ARMSTRONG'S HANDBOOK OF HUMAN RESOURCE MANAGEMENT PRACTICE

KoganPage

Publisher's note

Every possible effort has been made to ensure that the information contained in this book is accurate at the time of going to press, and the publishers and authors cannot accept responsibility for any errors or omissions, however caused. No responsibility for loss or damage occasioned to any person acting, or refraining from action, as a result of the material in this publication can be accepted by the editor, the publisher or the author.

First edition published in 1977 as *A Handbook of Personnel Management Practice* by Kogan Page
Seventh edition published in 1999 as *A Handbook of Human Resource Management Practice*
Eleventh edition published in 2009 as *Armstrong's Handbook of Human Resource Management Practice*
Fourteenth edition 2017

2nd Floor, 45 Gee Street	c/o Martin P Hill Consulting	4737/23 Ansari Road
London EC1V 3RS	122 W 27th St, 10th Floor	Daryaganj
United Kingdom	New York, NY 10001	New Delhi 110002
www.koganpage.com	USA	India

© Michael Armstrong, 1977, 1984, 1988, 1991, 1995, 1996, 1999, 2001, 2003, 2006, 2009, 2012, 2014, 2017

ISBN   978 0 7494 7411 9
E-ISBN   978 0 7494 7412 6

British Library Cataloguing-in-Publication Data

A CIP record for this book is available from the British Library.

Library of Congress Cataloging-in-Publication Data

Names: Armstrong, Michael, 1928- author.
Title: Armstrong's handbook of human resource management prac[...]
    Armstrong.
Other titles: Handbook of human resource management practice
Description: 14th Edition. | New York : Kogan Page Limited, 2017. | Revised
    edition of the author's Armstrong's handbook of human resource management
    practice, 2014.
Identifiers: LCCN 2016037277 (print) | LCCN 2016038041 (ebook) | ISBN
    9780749474119 (pbk.) | ISBN 9780749474126 (ebook)
Subjects: LCSH: Personnel management–Handbooks, manuals, etc.
Classification: LCC HF5549.17 .A76 2017 (print) | LCC HF5549.17 (ebook) | DDC
    658.3–dc23
LC record available at https://lccn.loc.gov/2016037277

Typeset by Graphicraft Ltd
Print production managed by Jellyfish
Printed and bound in Great Britain by Henry Ling Limited, at the Dorset Press, Dorchester DT1 1HD

To Clarissa

CONTENTS IN BRIEF

CONTENTS

PART VII Learning and development 315

32 Strategic learning and development 319

33 How people learn 327

34 The process of learning and development 335

35 Workplace learning 349

36 Social learning 355

PART XI Employee well-being 509

PART XII International HRM 527

60   Managing expatriates   557

PART XIII   HRM Practices   569

61   HR information systems   571

62   Employment law   577

LIST OF FIGURES

LIST OF TABLES

PREFACE TO THE 14TH EDITION

The 14th edition of the *Handbook of Human Resource Management Practice* includes greatly extended sections dealing with employee resourcing, learning and development and reward management. The impact of social networks in a number of HR areas has been covered for the first time. The handbook has been brought up to date by reference to the findings of a number of significant research projects and other investigations of how HRM operates in practice.

The plan of the book is illustrated in the 'route map' shown in Figure 0.1. The logic of the sequence of parts is as follows. Part I contains a conceptual framework for the rest of the handbook by providing a general introduction to the concept of human resource management (HRM) and the associated concepts of human capital management and strategic HRM. Part II describes how HRM strategies, policies and practices are delivered through the HR function and its members. It also examines the contribution made by HRM to improving organizational performance. Part III deals with the HRM practices such as HR strategies, policies, procedures and analytics that affect the whole organization. Part III also covers other general and important aspects of HRM such as HR analytics, knowledge management, the ethical dimension of HRM and corporate social responsibility. Following the initial framework provided by Parts I to III, Parts IV and V together act as a bridge between the general considerations dealt with in the previous three parts and the specific areas of HRM covered in Parts VI to XIII. The aim of Parts IV and V is to explain the basis of organizational and individual behaviour to inform how the different aspects of HRM practice should be managed and the approaches that can be used to develop the organization and design the work and jobs which enable it to function. The last part of the book is devoted to describing the key skills that HR professionals have to use.

The companion website at **www.koganpage. com/ArmstrongHRMPractice** provides extensive additional resources for lecturers and students. These comprise:

- A lecturers' manual containing notes on how teaching could be organized by reference to the chapters in the main text and the supplementary material in the manual. Suggestions are made on various kinds of semesters and guidance is provided on the links between the handbook text and CIPD programmes. The manual includes sections for each chapter containing a summary of the main learning points, an outline of the subject matter, discussion points and questions with comments on the points to be considered. In many chapters there are multiple-choice questions, case studies and role-playing exercises. Most of the chapters contain supplementary abstracts from relevant HRM.

- Additional material for lecturers in the shape of PowerPoint slides, with notes covering all the chapters.

- A students' manual consisting of material that can be used to reinforce the contents of the main book. Summaries of each chapter are provided and, in addition, most of the chapters include supplementary abstracts from relevant HRM literature. To assist in revision, the extra material includes multiple choice questions and 'flash' cards containing questions and answers about key aspects of the subject matter. There are also a number of case studies.

- Summaries of recent HRM research findings.

- A set of toolkits providing guidance on developing key HR processes.

- A glossary of HRM terms.

- An HRM bibliography.

FIGURE 0.1   Handbook route map

II Delivering HRM

4 HR architecture – the HR system
5 The role of the HR function
6 The role of HR professionals
7 HRM and performance

III Human resource management processes

8 HR strategies
9 HR policies
10 HR procedures
11 HR analytics
12 Knowledge management
13 Competency-based HRM
14 The ethical dimension of HRM
15 Corporate social responsibility

I Fundamentals of human resource management

1 Human resource management (HRM)
2 Human capital management
3 Strategic HRM

IV People and organizations

16 Organizational behaviour
17 Work, organization and job design
18 Organization development

V Factors influencing employee behaviour

19 Motivation
20 Commitment
21 Employee engagement

VI People resourcing

22 Strategic resourcing
23 Workforce planning
24 Recruitment and selection
25 Talent management
26 Introduction to the organization
27 Release from the organization
28 Managing employee retention
29 Absence management
30 Managing diversity and inclusion
31 Managing flexibility

VII Learning and development (L&D)

32 Strategic L&D
33 How people learn
34 The process of L&D
35 Workplace learning
36 Social learning
37 E-learning
38 Training
39 Leadership and management development
40 The role of the L&D function

VIII Performance management

41 Performance management fundamentals
42 The process of performance management

IX Rewarding people

43 Reward management
44 Market pricing
45 Job evaluation
46 Grade and pay structures
47 Contingent pay
48 Managing reward for special groups
49 Managing reward systems

X Employee relations

50 The basis of employee relations
51 The employment relationship
52 The psychological contract
53 The practice of industrial relations
54 Employee voice
55 Employee communications

XI Employee well-being

56 The practice of employee well-being
57 Health and safety

XII International HRM

58 International HRM framework
59 The practice of international HRM
60 Managing expatriates

XIII HRM practices

61 HR information systems
62 Employment law

XIV HR skills

63 Strategic HRM skills
64 Business skills
65 Problem-solving skills
66 Analytical and critical skills
67 Research skills
68 Statistical skills
69 Selection interviewing skills
70 Job, role and skills analysis and competency modelling
71 Learning and development skills
72 Negotiating skills
73 Leading and facilitating change
74 Leadership skills
75 Influencing skills
76 Handling people problems
77 Handling challenging conversations
78 Managing conflict
79 Political skills
80 Investigating a business issue from an HR perspective

PART I

Fundamentals of human resource management

Introduction

Human resource management (HRM) is about how people are managed and employed. It can be regarded as a philosophy about the ways in which people should be dealt with at work, which is underpinned by a number of theories relating to the behaviour of people and organizations. It is concerned with making a contribution to the improvement of organizational effectiveness through people, but it is, or should be, equally concerned with the ethical dimension – how people should be treated in accordance with a set of moral values. HRM involves the application of policies and practices in the fields of organization design and development, employee resourcing, learning and development, performance and reward and the provision of services that enhance the well-being of employees. These are based on human resource (HR) strategies which are integrated with one another and aligned to the business strategy.

The term 'human resources' can be criticized because it implies that people can be manipulated like any other factor of production. It's increasingly being replaced by 'people management'. But HRM is most common.

Whatever term is adopted, the approach should be based on the principle laid down by Schneider (1987: 450) that: 'Organizations are the people in them; that people make the place'. He went on to explain that 'Positive job attitudes for workers in an organization can be expected when the natural inclinations of the persons there are allowed to be reflected in their behaviours by the kinds of processes and structures that have evolved there.'

As Keegan and Francis (2010: 873) noted, HR work is now 'largely framed as a business issue'. The emphasis is on business alignment and strategic fit. These are important requirements, but focusing on them can lead HR professionals to place less emphasis on employee needs and motivations when developing HR policy and practice. A simplistic view of the business imperative permits little room for considering how HR strategy should impact on individual employees. HRM indeed aims to support the achievement of business goals but equally, it should aim to build a relationship based on trust, openness and personal fulfilment.

This part of the handbook covers the conceptual basis of HRM, including the various HRM models, the associated concept of human capital management, and the strategic framework within which HRM activities take place.

References

Keegan, A and Francis, H (2010) Practitioner talk: the changing textscape of HRM and emergence of HR business partnership, *International Journal of Human Resource Management*, **21** (6), pp 873–98

Schneider, B (1987) The people make the place, *Personnel Psychology*, **40** (3), pp 437–53

01
Human resource management (HRM)

KEY CONCEPTS AND TERMS

Added value

Contextual model of HRM

European model of HRM

5-P model of HRM

Hard HRM

Harvard framework

HRM architecture

HR philosophy

Human resource management (HRM)

Matching model of HRM

Resource-based theory

Soft HRM

Strategic alignment

Strategic human resource management
   (SHRM)

LEARNING OUTCOMES

On completing this chapter you should be able to define these key concepts. You should also know about:

- The fundamental concept of HRM and how it developed
- The goals and beliefs of HRM
- The theoretical base of HRM
- Models of HRM
- HRM today

Introduction

Human resource management (HRM) is concerned with all aspects of how people are employed, managed and developed in organizations. This definition is expanded in the first section of the chapter which then covers in turn how the concept of HRM emerged, its goals, philosophy and theoretical base. The chapter concludes with a description of the various models of HRM.

Human resources defined

As Boxall (2007: 13) explained: 'Human resources include the knowledge, skills, networks and energies of people and, underpinning them, their physical and emotional health, intellectual capabilities, personalities and motivations.'

Some people criticize the notion of referring to people as resources. Osterby and Coster (1992: 31) argued that: 'The term "human resources" reduces people to the same category of value as materials, money and technology – all resources, and resources are only valuable to the extent they can be exploited or leveraged into economic value.'

Human resource management defined

Human resource management (HRM) can be described as a strategic, integrated and coherent approach to the employment, development and well-being of the people working in organizations. HRM was defined pragmatically by Boxall and Purcell (2003: 1) as 'all those activities associated with the management of employment relationships in the firm'. A more comprehensive definition was offered by Watson (2010: 919):

> HRM is the managerial utilization of the efforts, knowledge, capabilities and committed behaviours which people contribute to an authoritatively co-ordinated human enterprise as part of an employment exchange (or more temporary contractual arrangement) to carry out work tasks in a way which enables the enterprise to continue into the future.

HRM is delivered through the HR architecture of systems and structures, the HR function and, importantly, line management.

The emergence of HRM

HRM emerged in the 1980s as a philosophy of how people should be managed. As Hendry and Pettigrew (1990: 20) observed: 'What HRM did at this point was to wrap around some of the observable changes, while providing a focus for challenging deficiencies – in attitudes, scope, coherence and direction – of existing personnel management.' They also commented (ibid: 25) that HRM can be perceived as a 'perspective on personnel management and not personnel management itself.'

The concept of HRM

HRM as originally conceived had a conceptual framework consisting of a philosophy underpinned by a number of theories drawn from the behavioural sciences and from the fields of strategic management, human capital management and industrial relations. The HRM philosophy has been heavily criticized by some academics as being managerialist and manipulative, but this criticism has subsided, perhaps because it became increasingly evident that the term HRM had been adopted as a synonym for what used to be called personnel management, without paying much attention to the philosophy of its founding fathers. As noted by Storey (2007: 6): 'In its generic broad and popular sense it [HRM] simply refers to any system of people management'. HRM practice today is no longer governed by the original philosophy, if it ever was. It is just what HR people and line managers do.

The goals and beliefs of HRM

The goals of HRM are to:

- support the organization in achieving its objectives by developing and implementing human resource (HR) strategies which are integrated with the business strategy (strategic HRM);
- contribute to the development of a high-performance culture;

- ensure that the organization has the talented, skilled and engaged people it needs;
- create a positive employment relationship between management and employees, as well as a climate of mutual trust;
- encourage the application of an ethical approach to people management.

The beliefs of HRM as defined by Storey (2001: 7) include 'the assumptions that it is the human resource which gives competitive edge, that the aim should be to enhance employee commitment, that HR decisions are of strategic importance and that therefore HR policies should be integrated into the business strategy'.

The theoretical base of HRM

The original notion of HRM had a strong theoretical base. Guest (1987: 505) commented that: 'Human resource management appears to lean heavily on theories of commitment and motivation and other ideas derived from the field of organizational behavior.' The main theories underpinning the HRM concept are summarized below.

Motivation

Motivation theory, especially expectancy theory and goal theory, explains the factors that affect goal-directed behaviour. It therefore influences the approaches used in HRM to enhance engagement, reward people and manage performance.

The resource-based view

Resource-based theory expressed as 'the resource-based view' states that competitive advantage is achieved if a firm's resources are valuable, rare and costly to imitate. HRM can play a major part in ensuring that the firm's human resources meet these criteria.

Social exchange theory

Social exchange theory suggests that social beings feel obliged to return favours. Feelings of loyalty and commitment and discretionary effort are in some form a social reciprocation by employees to a good employer. Employees will reciprocate their contribution to the organization if they perceive that the organization has treated them well. This theory is related to the leader-member exchange (LMX) theory of leadership as formulated by Graen (1976), which focuses on the two-way (dyadic) relationship between leaders and the people they lead.

Stakeholder theory

A number of different groups are stakeholders in organizations, including shareholders, managers, employees, customers and the public at large. Organizations must take account of these various interests when formulating and implementing policies.

Models of HRM

Over the years a number of models have defined what HRM is and how it operates. Of these, the matching model and the Harvard framework which provided the first descriptions of HRM have been the most influential.

The matching model of HRM

Fombrun *et al* (1984) proposed the 'matching model' which indicated that HR systems and the organization structure should be managed in a way that is congruent with organizational strategy. This point was made in their classic statement that: 'The critical management task is to align the formal structure and human resource systems so that they drive the strategic objectives of the organization' (ibid: 37). Thus they took the first steps towards the concept of strategic HRM.

The Harvard model of HRM

Beer *et al* (1984) produced what has become known as the 'Harvard framework'. They started with the proposition that: 'Human resource management (HRM) involves all management decisions and actions that affect the nature of the relationship between the organization and employees – its human resources' (ibid: 1). They believed that: 'Today... many pressures are demanding a broader, more comprehensive and more strategic perspective with regard to the organization's human resources' (ibid: 4). They also stressed that it was necessary to adopt 'a longer-term perspective in managing people and consideration of people as a potential asset rather than merely a variable cost' (ibid: 6). Beer and his colleagues were the first to underline the HRM tenet that it belongs to line managers. They suggested that HRM had two characteristic features: 1) line managers accept more responsibility for ensuring the alignment of competitive strategy and HR policies, and 2) HR has the mission of setting policies that govern how HR activities are developed and implemented in ways that make them more mutually reinforcing.

Contextual model of HRM

The contextual model of HRM refers to the importance of environmental factors that affect the practice of HRM such as the influence of the social, institutional and political forces that have been underestimated in other models. The model advocates integrating the human resource management system in the environment in which it is developed. According to Martin-Alcázar *et al* (2005: 638): 'Context both conditions and is conditioned by the HRM strategy.' A broader set of stakeholders is involved in the formulation and implementation of human resource strategies. This is referred to by Schuler and Jackson (2000: 229) as a 'multiple stakeholder framework'. These stakeholders may be external as well as internal and both influence and are influenced by strategic decisions.

The 5-P model of HRM

As formulated by Schuler (1992) the 5-P model of HRM describes the way HRM operates under the five headings of:

1 *HR philosophy* – a statement of how the organization regards its human resources, the role they play in the overall success of the business, and how they should be treated and managed.

2 *HR policies* – these provide guidelines for action on people-related business issues and for the development of HR programmes and practices based on strategic needs.

3 *HR programmes* – these are shaped by HR policies and consist of coordinated HR efforts intended to initiate and manage organizational change efforts prompted by strategic business needs.

4 *HR practices* – these are the activities carried out in implementing HR policies and programmes. They include resourcing, learning and development, performance and reward management, employee relations, and administration.

5 *HR processes* – these are the formal procedures and methods used to put HR strategic plans and policies into effect.

European model of HRM

Brewster (1993) described a European model of HRM as follows:

- Environment – established legal framework.
- Objectives – organizational objectives and social concern – people as a key resource.
- Focus – cost/benefits and environment analysis.
- Relationship with employees – union and non-union.
- Relationship with line managers – specialist/ line liaison,
- Role of HR specialist – specialist managers: ambiguity, tolerance, flexibility.

The main distinction between this model and what Brewster referred to as 'the prescribed model' was that the latter involves deregulation (no legal framework), no trade unions and a focus on organizational objectives but not on social concern.

The hard and soft models of HRM

Storey (1989: 8) distinguished between the 'hard' and 'soft' versions of HRM. He wrote that: 'The hard one emphasizes the quantitative, calculative and business-strategic aspects of managing human resources in as "rational" a way as for any other economic factor. By contrast, the soft version traces its roots to the human-relations school; it emphasizes communication, motivation and leadership.'

However, it was pointed out by Keenoy (1997: 838) that 'hard and soft HRM are complementary rather than mutually exclusive practices'. Research in eight UK organizations by Truss *et al* (1997) indicated that the distinction between hard and soft HRM was not as precise as some commentators have implied.

HRM today

As a description of people management activities in organizations the term HRM is generally accepted even if it is only used as a label to describe traditional personnel management practices without paying much attention to the original philosophy. Emphasis is now placed on the need for HR to be strategic and business-like and to add value, ie to generate extra value (benefit to the business) by the expenditure of effort, time and money on HRM activities. There have been plenty of new interests and developments, including human capital management, engagement, talent management, competency-based HRM, e-HRM, high-performance work systems, and performance and reward management. But these have not been introduced under the banner of the HRM concept as originally defined.

The practice of HRM can be diverse. Dyer and Holder (1988) pointed out that HRM goals vary according to competitive choices, technologies, characteristics of employees (eg could be different for managers) and the state of the labour market. Boxall (2007: 48) observed that: 'Human resource management covers a vast array of activities and shows a huge range of variations across occupations, organizational levels, business units, firms, industries and societies.'

HRM has largely become something that organizations do when they manage people rather than an aspiration or a philosophy. A convincing summary of what HRM means today, which focuses on what HRM is rather than on its philosophy, was provided by Peter Boxall, John Purcell and Patrick Wright.

Source review

The meaning of HRM – Boxall *et al* (2007:1)

Human resource management (HRM), the management of work and people towards desired ends, is a fundamental activity in any organization in which human beings are employed. It is not something whose existence needs to be radically justified: HRM is an inevitable consequence of starting and growing an organization. While there are a myriad of variations in the ideologies, styles, and managerial resources engaged, HRM happens in some form or other. It is one thing to question the relative performance of particular models of HRM in particular contexts... It is quite another thing to question the necessity of the HRM process itself, as if organizations cannot survive or grow without making a reasonable attempt at organizing work and managing people.

Key learning points: Human resource management

HRM defined

Human resource management (HRM) is concerned with all aspects of how people are employed and managed in organizations.

Goals of HRM

The goals of HRM are to:

- support the organization in achieving its objectives by developing and implementing human resource (HR) strategies which are integrated with the business strategy (strategic HRM);

- contribute to the development of a high-performance culture;

- ensure that the organization has the talented, skilled, and engaged people it needs;

- create a positive employment relationship between management and employees and a climate of mutual trust;

- encourage the application of an ethical approach to people management.

Beliefs of HRM

The beliefs of HRM included the assumptions that it is the human resource which gives competitive edge, that the aim should be to enhance employee commitment, that HR decisions are of strategic importance and that therefore HR policies should be integrated into the business strategy (Storey, 2001: 7).

Underpinning theories

'Human resource management appears to lean heavily on theories of commitment and motivation and other ideas derived from the field of organizational behaviour' (Guest, 1987: 505).

The diversity of HRM

Many HRM models exist, and practices within different organizations are diverse, often only corresponding to the conceptual version of HRM in a few respects.

References

Beer, M, Spector, B, Lawrence, P, Quinn Mills, D and Walton, R (1984) *Managing Human Assets*, New York, The Free Press

Boxall, P F (2007) The goals of HRM, in (eds) P Boxall, J Purcell and P Wright, *Oxford Handbook of Human Resource Management*, Oxford, Oxford University Press, pp 48–67

Boxall, P F and Purcell, J (2003) *Strategy and Human Resource Management*, Basingstoke, Palgrave Macmillan

Boxall, P F, Purcell, J and Wright, P (2007) Human resource management: scope, analysis and significance, in (eds) P Boxall, J Purcell and P Wright, *Oxford Handbook of Human Resource Management*, Oxford, Oxford University Press, pp 1–16

Brewster, C (1993) Developing a 'European' model of human resource management, *The International Journal of Human Resource Management*, 4 (4), pp 765–84

Dyer, L and Holder, G W (1988) Strategic human resource management and planning, in (ed) L Dyer *Human Resource Management: Evolving roles and responsibilities*, Washington DC, Bureau of National Affairs, pp 1–46

Fombrun, C J, Tichy, N M and Devanna, M A (1984) *Strategic Human Resource Management*, New York, Wiley

Graen, G (1976) Role-making processes within complex organizations, in (ed) M D Dunnette, *Handbook of Industrial and Organizational Psychology*, Chicago IL, Rand-McNally

Guest, D E (1987) Human resource management and industrial relations, *Journal of Management Studies*, 24 (5), pp 503–21

Hendry, C and Pettigrew, A (1990) Human resource management: an agenda for the 1990s, *International Journal of Human Resource Management*, 1 (1), pp 17–44

Keenoy, T (1997) HRMism and the images of re-presentation, *Journal of Management Studies*, 34 (5), pp 825–41

Martin-Alcázar, F, Romero-Fernandez, P M and Sánchez-Gardey, G (2005) Strategic human resource management: integrating the universalistic, contingent, configurational and contextual perspectives, *International Journal of Human Resource Management*, 16 (5), pp 633–59

Osterby, B and Coster, C (1992) Human resource development – a sticky label, *Training and Development*, April, pp 31–32

Schuler, R S (1992) Strategic HRM: linking people with the needs of the business, *Organizational Dynamics*, 21, pp 19–32

Schuler, R S and Jackson, S E (2000) *Strategic Human Resource Management*, Oxford, Blackwell

Storey, J (1989) From personnel management to human resource management, in (ed) J Storey, *New Perspectives on Human Resource Management*, London, Routledge, pp 1–18

Storey, J (2001) Human resource management today: an assessment, in (ed), J Storey, *Human Resource Management: A critical text*, London, Thompson Learning, pp 3–20

Storey, J (2007) What is human resource management? in (ed) J Storey, *Human Resource Management: A critical text*, London, Thompson Learning, pp 3–19

Truss, C, Gratton, L, Hope-Hailey, V, McGovern, P and Stiles, P (1997) Soft and hard models of human resource management: a re-appraisal, *Journal of Management Studies*, 34 (1), pp 53–73

Watson, T J (2010) Critical social science, pragmatism and the realities of HRM, *The International Journal of Human Resource Management*, 21 (6), pp 915–31

02
Human capital management

LEARNING OUTCOMES

On completing this chapter you should be able to define these key concepts. You should also understand:

- The nature of human capital management
- The concept of human capital
- Characteristics of human capital
- Constituents of human capital
- Significance of human capital theory

Human capital management defined

Human capital management is concerned with the knowledge, skills, abilities and capacity to develop and innovate possessed by people in an organization and the added value they therefore provide. It regards them as assets to be invested in through resourcing and learning and development policies. It also stresses the need to assess the contribution of people and to measure the effectiveness of the HR practices used to manage them. The latter process of measurement makes use of HR analytics as described in Chapter 11.

This chapter starts with a definition of the concept of human capital and continues with an analysis of its constituents. The chapter concludes with a description of the approaches to people management raised by human capital theory.

The concept of human capital

Human capital consists of the knowledge, skills and abilities of the people employed in an organization. Adam Smith, cited by Schultz (1981: 140), originated the idea of human capital (like so many other economic concepts) when he wrote that: 'The acquired wealth of nations derives from the acquired abilities of people – their education, experience, skills and health.' Individuals generate, retain and use knowledge and skill (human capital) and create intellectual capital. Their knowledge is enhanced by the interactions between them (social capital) and generates the institutionalized knowledge possessed by an organization (organizational capital).

The significance of the term was emphasized by Schultz (1961: 1) who defined it as follows:

> Although it is obvious that people acquire useful skills and knowledge, it is not obvious that these skills and knowledge are a form of capital, that this capital is in substantial part a product of deliberate investment, that it has grown in Western countries at a much faster rate than conventional (non-human) capital, and that its growth may well be the most distinctive feature of the economic system.

He also noted that: 'Attributes... which are valuable and can be augmented by appropriate investment will be treated as human capital... Consider all human abilities to be either innate or acquired' (ibid: 21).

Scarborough and Elias (2002: ix) commented that: 'The concept of human capital is most usefully viewed as a bridging concept – that is, it defines the link between HR practices and business performance in terms of assets rather than business processes.' They pointed out that human capital is to a large extent 'non-standardized, tacit, dynamic, context dependent and embodied in people.' These characteristics make it difficult to evaluate human capital, bearing in mind that 'the features of human capital that are so crucial to firm performance are the flexibility and creativity of individuals, their ability to develop skills over time and to respond in a motivated way to different contexts' (ibid: ix).

It is indeed the knowledge, skills and abilities of individuals that create value, which is why the focus has to be on means of attracting, retaining, developing and maintaining the human capital they represent.

The constituents of human capital

Human capital consists of intellectual, social and organizational capital.

Intellectual capital

The concept of human capital is associated with the overarching notion of intellectual capital, which is defined as the stocks and flows of knowledge available to an organization. These can be regarded as the intangible resources associated with people that, together with tangible resources (money and physical assets), comprise the market or total value of a business.

Social capital

Social capital is another element of intellectual capital. It consists of the knowledge derived from networks of relationships within and outside the organization. Social capital has been defined by Putnam (1996: 66) as 'the features of social life – networks, norms and trust – that enable participants to act together more effectively to pursue shared objectives'. It is important to take into account social capital considerations, that is, the ways in which knowledge is developed and learning takes place (social learning) through interaction between people. Bontis *et al* (1999) commented that it is flows as well as stocks that matter. Intellectual capital develops and changes over time and a significant part is played in these processes by people acting together.

Organizational capital

Organizational capital is the institutionalized knowledge possessed by an organization that is stored in databases, manuals, etc (Youndt, 2000). It is often called 'structural capital' (Edvinson and Malone, 1997), but the term 'organizational capital' is preferred by Youndt because, he argues, it conveys more clearly that this is the knowledge that the organization actually owns.

Approaches to people management raised by human capital theory

An approach to people management based on human capital theory involves obtaining answers to these questions:

- What are the key performance drivers that create value?
- What skills do we have?
- What skills do we need now and in the future to meet our strategic aims?
- How are we going to attract, develop and retain these skills?
- How can we develop a culture and environment in which organizational and individual learning takes place that meets both our needs and the needs of our employees?
- How can we provide for both the explicit and tacit knowledge created in our organization to be captured, recorded and used effectively?

Key learning points: Human capital management

The concept of human capital

Individuals generate, retain and use knowledge and skill (human capital) and create intellectual capital. Human capital 'defines the link between HR practices and business performance in terms of assets rather than business processes' (Scarborough and Elias, 2002).

Characteristics of human capital

Human capital is non-standardized, tacit, dynamic, context dependent and embodied in people (Scarborough and Elias, 2002).

Constituents of human capital

Human capital consists of intellectual capital, social capital and organizational capital.

Significance of human capital

Human capital theory regards people as assets and stresses that investment by organizations in people will generate worthwhile returns.

References

Bontis, N, Dragonetti, N C, Jacobsen, K and Roos, G (1999) The knowledge toolbox: a review of the tools available to measure and manage intangible resources, *European Management Journal*, **17** (4), pp 391–402

Edvinson, L and Malone, M S (1997) *Intellectual Capital: Realizing your company's true value by finding its hidden brainpower*, New York, Harper Business

Putnam, R D (1996) The strange disappearance of civic America, *The American Prospect*, Winter, pp 34–48

Scarborough, H and Elias, J (2002) *Evaluating Human Capital*, London, CIPD

Schultz, T W (1961) Investment in human capital, *American Economic Review*, **51**, March, pp 1–17

Schultz, T W (1981) *Investing in People: The economics of population quality*, Los Angeles, CA, University of California Press

Youndt, M A (2000) Human resource considerations and value creation: the mediating role of intellectual capital, Paper delivered at National Conference of US Academy of Management, Toronto, August

03
Strategic HRM

LEARNING OUTCOMES

On completing this chapter you should be able to define these key concepts. You should also understand:

- The conceptual basis of strategic HRM
- How strategy is formulated
- The aims of strategic HRM
- The resource-based view and its implications
- The meaning of strategic fit
- The three HRM 'perspectives' of Delery and Doty
- The significance of bundling
- The significance of the concepts of 'best practice' and 'best fit'
- The significant features of strategic HRM

Introduction

Strategic human resource management (strategic HRM or SHRM) is an approach to the development and implementation of HR strategies that are integrated with business strategies and support their achievement.

This chapter starts with an analysis of the nature of SHRM and next deals with how it is linked to the processes of strategic management and human resource management. Its underpinning concepts – the resource-based view and strategic fit – are then described and this is followed by an examination of how strategic HRM works, namely the universalistic, contingency and configurational perspectives defined by Delery and Doty (1996) and the three approaches associated with those perspectives – best practice, best fit and bundling.

The nature of strategic human resource management

As defined by Cascio (2015: 423) SHRM is 'the choice, alignment, and integration of an organization's HRM system so that its human capital resources most effectively contribute to strategic business objectives'. It has been described by Boxall (1996) as the interface between HRM and strategic management. Schuler and Jackson (2007: 5) stated that SHRM is fundamentally about 'systematically linking people with the firm'.

One of the earlier but still most helpful descriptions of SHRM was made by Hendry and Pettigrew (1986: 4) who suggested that it had four meanings:

1 The use of planning.
2 A coherent approach to the design and management of HR systems based on an employment policy and manpower strategy and often underpinned by a 'philosophy'.
3 Matching HRM activities and policies to some explicit business strategy.
4 Seeing the people of the organization as a 'strategic resource' for the achievement of 'competitive advantage'.

In essence, strategic HRM is conceptual; it is concerned with how integration or 'fit' between HR and business strategies is achieved, the benefits of taking a longer-term view of where HR should be going and how to get there, and how coherent and mutually supporting HR strategies should be developed and implemented. Importantly, it is also about how members of the HR function should adopt a strategic approach on a day-to-day basis. This means that they operate as part of the management team to ensure that HR activities support the achievement of business strategies on a continuous basis and add value.

The rationale for SHRM is the perceived advantage of having an agreed and understood basis for developing and implementing approaches to people management which takes into account the business plans and priorities of the firm and the changing context in which it operates. As Dyer and Holder (1988: 13) remarked, SHRM should provide 'unifying frameworks which are at once broad, contingency based and integrative'.

Strategic HRM and strategic management

Strategic HRM takes the notion of HRM as a strategic, integrated and coherent process and associates it with the process of strategic management as described below.

Strategic management

Strategic management is an approach to management that takes a broad and long-term view of where the business is going and manages it in ways that ensure that this strategic thrust is maintained.

As stated by Boxall and Purcell (2003: 44): 'Strategic management is best defined as a process. It is a process of strategy making, of forming and, if the firm survives, reforming its strategy over time.' The purpose of strategic management was expressed by Kanter (1984: 288) as being to 'elicit the present actions for the future and become action vehicles – integrating and institutionalizing mechanisms for change'. Truss *et al* (2014: 49) also emphasized the action-orientated nature of strategic management. They defined it as 'the process that enables organizations to turn strategic intent into action'.

The focus is on identifying the organization's mission and strategies, but attention is also given to the resource base required to make it succeed. Managers who think strategically will have a broad and long-term view of where they are going. But they will also be aware that they are responsible, first, for planning how to allocate resources to opportunities that contribute to the implementation of strategy, and second, for managing these opportunities in ways that will add value to the results achieved by the firm.

To summarize, strategic management deals with both ends and means. As an end, it describes a vision of what something will look like in the future. As a means, it shows how it is expected that this vision will be realized. To understand how strategic management functions, it is necessary to appreciate the meaning of strategy as discussed below.

The meaning of strategy

Strategy is the approach selected to achieve specified aims in the future. As defined by Chandler (1962: 13) it is: 'The determination of the long-term goals and objectives of an enterprise, and the adoption of courses of action and the allocation of resources necessary for carrying out those goals.' The formulation and implementation of corporate strategy is a process for developing a sense of direction, making the best use of resources and ensuring strategic fit. It is also about business model innovation, as explained later.

Characteristics of strategy

Strategy has three fundamental characteristics. First, it is forward looking. It is about deciding where you need to go and how you mean to get there. In this sense a strategy is a declaration of intent: 'This is what we want to do and this is how we intend to do it.' Strategies define longer-term goals but they also cover how those goals will be attained. They guide purposeful action to deliver the required result. A good strategy is one that works, one that in Abell's (1993: 1) phrase, ensures that organizations adapt to changing demands and circumstances by 'mastering the present and pre-empting the future'. As Boxall (1996: 70) explained: 'Strategy should be understood as a framework of critical ends and means.'

Second, strategy recognizes that the organizational capability of a firm (its capacity to function effectively) depends on its resource capability (the quality and quantity of its resources and their potential to deliver results). This is called the resource-based view.

Third, strategy aims to achieve strategic fit – the need when developing functional strategies such as HR to achieve congruence between them and the organization's business strategies within the context of its external and internal environment.

The content of strategy

Hambrisk and Fredrickson (2001) explained that a complete business strategy needs to cover five points:

1 Where the organization will be active – what type of products and services it will offer, what markets it will serve.

2 How it will function – where it will operate or get its products and services.

3 How it will win – what its competitive advantage will be.

4 What its moves will be – how it will change and grow.

5 How it will be profitable – what business model it will follow, as discussed below.

Strategy and business model innovation

Strategy is concerned with defining and developing the business model of an organization – a picture of the business that explains how it achieves competitive advantage and makes money. Business model innovation is the process followed by an organization to introduce a new business model or change an existing one in order to improve its performance.

Critical evaluation of the concept of strategy

The development of corporate strategy is often assumed to be a logical, step-by-step affair, the outcome of which is a formal written statement that provides a definitive guide to the organization's intentions. Many people still believe and act as if this were the case, but it is a misrepresentation of reality. In practice, the formulation of strategy may not be as rational and linear a process as some writers describe it or as some managers attempt to make it. There are limitations to the totally logical model of management that underpins the concept of strategic human resource management. In the words of Mabey *et al* (1998: 74): 'The reality is... that strategies may not always be easy to discern, that the processes of decision making may be implicit, incremental, negotiated and compromised.'

Sparrow *et al* (2010: 4) asserted succinctly that: 'Strategy is not rational and never has been'. Strategy formulation can best be described as 'problem solving in unstructured situations' (Digman, 1990: 53) and strategies will always be formed under conditions of partial ignorance. Quinn (1980: 9) stated that a strategy may simply be 'a widely held understanding resulting from a stream of decisions'. He believed that strategy formulation takes place by means of 'logical incrementalism', ie it evolves in several steps rather than being conceived as a whole. Pettigrew and Whipp (1991: 26) observed that: 'Strategy does not move forward in a direct linear way, nor through easily discernible sequential phases. Quite the reverse; the pattern is much more appropriately seen as continuous, iterative and uncertain.'

Another difficulty is that strategies are often based on the questionable assumption that the future will resemble the past. Some years ago, Heller (1972: 150) had a go at the cult of long-range planning: 'What goes wrong' he wrote, 'is that sensible anticipation gets converted into foolish numbers: and their validity always hinges on large loose assumptions.' Faulkner and Johnson (1992: 17–18) said of long-term planning that it:

> ... was inclined to take a definitive view of the future, and to extrapolate trend lines for the key business variables in order to arrive at this view. Economic turbulence was insufficiently considered, and the reality that much strategy is formulated and implemented in the act of managing the enterprise was ignored. Precise forecasts ending with derived financials were constructed, the only weakness of which was that the future almost invariably turned out differently.

Strategy formulation is not necessarily a deterministic, rational and continuous process, as was emphasized by Mintzberg (1987). He noted that, rather than being consciously and systematically developed, strategy reorientation happens in what he called brief 'quantum loops.' A strategy, according to Mintzberg, can be deliberate – it can realize the intentions of senior management, for example to attack and conquer a new market. But this is not always the case. In theory, he says, strategy is a systematic process: first we think, then we act; we formulate then we implement. But we also 'act in order to think'. In practice, 'a realized strategy can emerge in response to an evolving situation' (ibid: 68) and the strategic planner is often 'a pattern organizer, a learner if you like, who manages a process in which strategies and visions can emerge as well as be deliberately conceived' (ibid: 73). This concept of 'emergent strategy' conveys the essence of how in practice organizations develop their business and HR strategies.

Boxall and Purcell (2003: 34) suggested that 'it is better if we understand the strategies of firms as sets of strategic choices, some of which may stem from planning exercises and set-piece debates in senior management, and some of which may emerge in a stream of action.'

Research conducted by Tyson (1997: 280) confirmed that, realistically, strategy:

- has always been emergent and flexible – it is always 'about to be', it never exists at the present time;
- is not only realized by formal statements but also comes about by actions and reactions;
- is a description of a future-oriented action that is always directed towards change;
- is conditioned by the management process itself.

Strategic HRM and HRM

One of the characteristics of HRM is that it is strategic, so what's the difference between HRM and strategic HRM? An answer to this question was provided by Truss and Gratton (1994: 666) who wrote that: 'We should perhaps regard SHRM as an overarching concept that links the management and development of people within the organization to the business as a whole and its environment, while HRM could be viewed as an organizing activity that takes place under this umbrella.'

Strategic HRM and HRM strategies

What's the difference, if any, between SHRM and HRM strategy? The answer to this question is that SHRM is an overall approach that provides guidance on how key issues of human resource management can be dealt with strategically in the sense that they support the achievement of corporate goals. But SHRM only becomes real when it produces actions and reactions that can be regarded as strategic, either in the form of overall or specific HR strategies or strategic behaviour on the part of HR professionals working alongside line managers. SHRM provides the conceptual framework within which individual strategies can be devised and implemented.

CASE STUDY

The Peabody Trust

This is how the chief executive of the Peabody Trust explained the organization's approach to strategic HRM:

> First of all you have your business strategy, which includes at management team level a review of what we expect our HR to deliver. We define what the strategy means in terms of its implications for us as individuals and for our employees. We decide what changes we have to effect and how we are going to communicate with and motivate the staff group to achieve those changes. The management team needs to be clear on what our vision for our people is, what we see our people doing, what we think they have to learn and what practices they need to change to effect the strategy we want. When you have answered those questions, then you can start to decide what the strategy is. The key to this is that all our directors have to contribute. The most important thing is the corporate understanding and responsibility for HR strategy.
>
> A good HR strategy is one which actually makes people feel valued. It makes them knowledgeable about the organization and makes them feel clear about where they sit as a group, a team, or an individual. It must show that what they do either together or individually fits into the strategy. Importantly, it should indicate how people are going to be rewarded for their contribution and how they might be developed and grow in the organization.

Critical evaluation of the concept of SHRM

The whole concept of SHRM is predicated on the belief that HR strategies should be integrated with corporate or business strategies. Vertical integration (strategic fit between business and HR strategies) may be desirable but it is not easy to achieve for the following reasons.

Diversity of strategic processes, levels and styles

The different levels at which strategy is formulated and the different styles adopted by organizations may make it difficult to develop a coherent view of what sort of HR strategies will fit the overall strategies and what type of HR contributions are required during the process of formulation.

The complexity of the strategy formulation process

Business strategy formulation and implementation is a complex, interactive process heavily influenced by a variety of contextual and historical factors. In these circumstances, as Guest (1991) asked, how can there be a straightforward flow from the business strategy to the HR strategy? It has been pointed out by Truss (1999: 44) that the assumption of some matching models of strategic HRM is that there is a simple linear relationship between business strategy and human resource strategy, but this assumption 'fails to acknowledge the complexities both between and within notions of strategy and human resource management... [It] is based on a rational model of organizations and individuals which takes no account of the significance of power, politics and culture.'

The evolutionary nature of business strategy

The evolutionary and incremental nature of strategy making may make it difficult to pin down the HR issues that are likely to be relevant. Hendry and Pettigrew (1990) suggest that there are limits to the extent to which rational HR strategies can be drawn up if the process of business strategic planning is itself irrational.

The absence of articulated business strategies

If, because of its evolutionary nature, the business strategy has not been clearly articulated, this would add to the problems of clarifying the business strategic issues that human resource strategies should address.

The qualitative nature of HR issues

Business strategies tend, or at least aim, to be expressed in the common currency of figures and hard data on portfolio management, growth, competitive position, market share, profitability, etc. HR strategies may deal with quantifiable issues such as resourcing and skill acquisition but are equally likely to refer to qualitative factors such as engagement, commitment, motivation, good employee relations and high employment standards. The relationship between the pursuit of policies in these areas and individual and organizational performance may be difficult to establish.

Integration with what?

The concept of SHRM implies that HR strategies must be totally integrated with corporate/business strategies in the sense that they both flow from and contribute to such strategies. But as Brewster (2004) argued, HR strategy will be subjected to considerable external pressure; for example, in Europe, legislation about involvement. This may mean that HR strategies cannot be entirely governed by the corporate/business strategy.

The question, 'To what extent should HR strategy take into account the interests of all the stakeholders in the organization, employees in general as well as owners and management?' also needs to be answered.

Conclusions

The difficulties mentioned above are real, but they are frequently glossed over in rhetorical statements about the need for integration. Too often the outcome is a platitudinous statement such as: 'Our HR strategy is to develop a performance culture' or: 'Our HR strategy is to ensure that the organization has the talented people it needs'. These are perfectly laudable broad objectives but they need to be more specific about how the aims will be achieved and how they will support the achievement of business goals.

Matching HR and business strategies is a problematic process but this doesn't mean that the attempt to do so should be abandoned. HR strategists must make every effort to understand the business model of their organization (ie a picture of an organization that explains how it achieves competitive advantage and makes money) and the plans for business model innovation (the process followed by an organization to develop a new business model or change an existing one). They have to take into account the difficulties mentioned above but they need to overcome these by persistent efforts designed to obtain insight into the real issues facing the organization, leading to plans for practical interventions that address those issues.

However, SHRM is best understood against the background of the various concepts as described below that influence its philosophy and application.

The resource-based view of SHRM

To a very large extent, the philosophy of SHRM is underpinned by the resource-based view. This states that it is the range of resources in an organization, including its human resources, that produces its unique character and creates competitive advantage. The resource-based view is founded on the ideas of Penrose (1959: 24–25), who wrote that the firm is 'an administrative organization and a collection of productive resources' and saw resources as 'a bundle of potential services'. It was expanded by Wernerfelt (1984: 172), who explained that strategy 'is a balance between the exploitation of existing resources and the development of new ones'. Resources were defined by Hunt (1991: 322) as 'anything that has an enabling capacity'.

The concept was developed by Barney (1991: 102), who stated that: 'A firm is said to have a competitive advantage when it is implementing a value-creating strategy not simultaneously being implemented by any current or potential competitors and when these other firms are unable to duplicate the benefits of this strategy.' This will happen if their resources are valuable, rare, inimitable and non-substitutable. He noted later (Barney 1995: 49) that an environmental analysis of strengths, weaknesses, opportunities and threats (SWOT analysis) was only half the story: 'A complete understanding of sources of a firm's competitive advantage requires the analysis of a firm's internal strengths and weaknesses as well.' He emphasized that:

> Creating sustained competitive advantage depends on the unique resources and capabilities that a firm brings to competition in its environment. To discover these resources and capabilities, managers must look inside their firm for valuable, rare and costly-to-imitate resources, and then exploit these resources through their organization. (ibid: 60)

The following rationale for resource-based strategy was produced by Grant (1991: 13):

> The resources and capabilities of a firm are the central considerations in formulating its strategy: they are the primary constants upon which a firm can establish its identity and frame its strategy, and they are the primary sources of the firm's profitability. The key to a resource-based approach to strategy formulation is understanding the relationships between resources, capabilities, competitive advantage and profitability – in particular, an understanding of the mechanisms through which competitive advantage can be sustained over time. This requires the design of strategies which exploit to maximum effect each firm's unique characteristics.

Resource-based SHRM can produce what Boxall and Purcell (2003) referred to as 'human resource advantage'. The aim is to develop strategic capability. This means strategic fit between resources and opportunities, obtaining added value from the effective deployment of resources, and developing managers who can think and plan strategically in the sense that they understand the key strategic issues and ensure that what they do enables the strategic goals of the business to be achieved. In line with human capital theory, the resource-based view emphasizes that investment in people increases their value to the firm. It proposes that sustainable competitive advantage is attained when the firm has a human resource pool that cannot be imitated or substituted by its rivals.

Boxall (1996: 66) suggested that: 'The resource-based view of the firm provides a conceptual basis, if we needed one, for asserting that key human resources are sources of competitive advantage.' He noted that human resource advantage is achieved by a combination of 'human capital advantage', which results from employing people with competitively valuable knowledge and skills, and 'human process advantage', which follows from the establishment of 'difficult to imitate, highly evolved processes within the firm, such as cross-departmental cooperation and executive development'. Accordingly, 'human resource advantage', the superiority of one firm's labour management over another's, can be thought of as the product of its human capital and human process advantages. He also observed (ibid: 66) that the strategic goal emerging from the resource-based view was to 'create firms which are more intelligent and flexible than their competitors' by hiring and developing more talented staff and by extending their skills base. Resource-based strategy is therefore concerned with the enhancement of the human or intellectual capital of the firm. As Ulrich (1998: 126) commented: 'Knowledge has become a direct competitive advantage for companies selling ideas and relationships. The challenge to organizations is to ensure that they have the capability to find, assimilate, compensate and retain the talented individuals they need.'

This is the basis of resource dependence theory (Pfeffer and Davis-Blake, 1992) which suggests that HR strategies such as those concerned with reward are strongly influenced by the need to attract, retain and energize high-quality people.

Critical evaluation of the resource-based view

The resource-based view has had considerable influence on thinking about human resource management. It provides a justification for attaching importance to resourcing activities, especially those concerned with talent management. It can also be used to enhance the value of the HR contribution in achieving competitive advantage. But it has the following limitations:

- it may be difficult to find resources that satisfy all the criteria;
- external factors such as product market pressures are ignored;
- it provides only generalized guidance on what resources are suitable;
- different resource configurations can provide the same value for firms;
- as Priem and Butler (2001) pointed out, the theory is tautological because valuable resources and competitive advantage are defined in the same terms.

Strategic fit

The concept of strategic fit stresses that when developing HR strategies, it is necessary to achieve congruence between them and the organization's business strategies within the context of its external and internal environment. This notion is fundamental to SHRM, as was stressed by Wright and Snell (1998: 758) who wrote: 'The primary role of strategic HRM should be to promote a fit with the demands of the competitive environment.' In more detail, Schuler (1992: 18) stated that:

> Strategic human resource management is largely about integration and adaptation. Its concern is to ensure that: (1) human resources (HR) management is fully integrated with the strategy and strategic needs of the firm (vertical fit); (2) HR policies cohere both across policy areas and across hierarchies (horizontal fit); and (3) HR practices are adjusted, accepted and used by line managers and employees as part of their everyday work.

Perspectives on SHRM

Taking into account the concepts of the resource-based view and strategic fit, Delery and Doty (1996: 802) contended that 'organizations adopting a particular strategy require HR practices that are different from those required by organizations adopting different strategies' and that organizations with 'greater congruence between their HR strategies and their (business) strategies should enjoy superior performance' (ibid: 803). They identified three HRM perspectives:

1 The universalistic perspective – some HR practices are better than others and all organizations should adopt these best practices. There is a universal relationship between individual 'best' practices and firm performance.

2 The contingency perspective – to be effective an organization's HR policies must be consistent with other aspects of the organization. The primary contingency factor is the organization's strategy. This can be described as 'vertical fit.'

3 The configurational perspective – this is a holistic approach that emphasizes the importance of the pattern of HR practices and is concerned with how this pattern of independent variables is related to the dependent variable of organizational performance.

This typology provided the basis for what has become the most commonly used classification of approaches, which is to adopt the terms 'best practice' and 'best fit' for the universalistic and contingency perspectives, and 'bundling' as the third approach (Richardson and Thompson, 1999). This follows the classifications made by Guest (1997) of fit as an ideal set of practices, fit as contingency and fit as bundles.

The best practice model

This model is based on the assumption that there is a set of best HRM practices that are universal in the sense that they are best in any situation, and that adopting them will lead to superior organizational performance.

A number of lists of 'best practices' have been produced, the most quoted being by Pfeffer (1998):

- employment security;
- selective hiring;
- self-managed teams;
- high compensation contingent on performance;
- training to provide a skilled and motivated workforce;
- reduction of status differentials;
- sharing information.

The best fit model

The best fit model is in line with contingency theory. It emphasizes that HR strategies should be congruent with the context and circumstances of the organization. 'Best fit' can be perceived in terms of vertical integration or alignment between the organization's business and HR strategies. There are three models: life cycle, competitive strategy and strategic configuration.

The life cycle model

The life cycle model is based on the theory that the development of a firm takes place in four stages: start-up, growth, maturity and decline. This is in line with product life cycle theory. The basic premise of this model was expressed by Baird and Meshoulam (1988: 117) as follows:

Human resource management's effectiveness depends on its fit with the organization's stage of development. As the organization grows and develops, human resource management programmes, practices and procedures must change to meet its needs. Consistent with growth and development models it can be suggested that human resource management develops through a series of stages as the organization becomes more complex.

Best fit and competitive strategies

Three strategies aimed at achieving competitive advantage were identified by Porter (1985):

1 Innovation – being the unique producer.
2 Quality – delivering high-quality goods and services to customers.
3 Cost leadership – the planned result of policies aimed at 'managing away' expense.

It was argued by Schuler and Jackson (1987) that to achieve the maximum effect it is necessary to match the role characteristics of people in an organization with the preferred strategy.

Strategic configuration

Another approach to best fit is the proposition that organizations will be more effective if they adopt a policy of strategic configuration (Delery and Doty, 1996). This means matching their strategy to one of the ideal types defined by theories such as those produced by Miles and Snow (1978), who identified the following four types of organizations, classifying the first three types as 'ideal' organizations:

1 Prospectors, which operate in an environment characterized by rapid and unpredictable changes. Prospectors have low levels of formalization and specialization and high levels of decentralization. They have relatively few hierarchical levels.

2 Defenders, which operate in a more stable and predictable environment than prospectors and engage in more long-term planning. They have more mechanistic or bureaucratic structures than prospectors and obtain coordination through formalization, centralization, specialization and vertical differentiation.

3 Analysers, which are a combination of the prospector and defender types. They operate

in stable environments, like defenders, and also in markets where new products are constantly required, like prospectors. They are usually not the initiators of change, like prospectors, but they follow the changes more rapidly than defenders.

4 Reactors, which are unstable organizations existing in what they believe to be an unpredictable environment. They lack consistent, well-articulated strategies and do not undertake long-range planning.

Critical evaluation of the best practice and best fit models

The best practice model

The notion of best practice assumes that there are universally effective HR practices that can readily be transferred. This rubric has been attacked by a number of commentators. Cappelli and Crocker-Hefter (1996: 7) commented that the notion of a single set of best practices has been overstated: 'There are examples in virtually every industry of firms that have very distinctive management practices... Distinctive human resource practices shape the core competencies that determine how firms compete.'

Purcell (1999: 26) noted that 'the search for best practice tends to take on the flavour of a moral crusade'. He also criticized the best practice or universalist view by pointing out the inconsistency between a belief in best practice and the resource-based view, which focuses on the intangible assets, including HR, that allow the firm to do better than its competitors. He asked how can 'the universalism of best practice be squared with the view that only some resources and routines are important and valuable by being rare and imperfectly imitable?' and stated that: 'The claim that the bundle of best practice HRM is universally applicable leads us into a utopian cul-de-sac' (ibid: 36). Boxall (2007: 5) concluded that he was 'deeply sceptical about claims for universal applicability for particular HRM practices or clusters of practices [but] this does not rule out the search for general principles in the management of work and people.'

However, a knowledge of what is assumed to be best practice can be used to inform decisions on what practices are most likely to fit the needs of the organization, as long as it is understood why a particular practice should be regarded as a best practice and what needs to be done to ensure that it will work in the context of the organization. Becker and Gerhart (1996) argued that the idea of best practice might be more appropriate for identifying the principles underlying the choice of practices, as opposed to the practices themselves.

The best fit model

The best fit model seems to be more realistic than the best practice model. As Dyer and Holder (1988: 31) observed: 'The inescapable conclusion is that what is best depends.' But there are limitations to the concept. Paauwe (2004: 37) emphasized that: 'It is necessary to avoid falling into the trap of "contingent determinism" (ie claiming that the context absolutely determines the strategy). There should be room for making strategic choices.'

There is a danger of mechanistically matching HR policies and practices with strategy. It is not credible to claim that there are single contextual factors that determine HR strategy, and internal fit cannot therefore be complete. Purcell (1999: 35) pointed out that: 'Each firm has to make choices not just on business and operational strategies but on what type of HR system is best for its purposes.' As Boxall (2007: 61) asserted: 'It is clearly impossible to make all HR policies reflective of a chosen competitive or economic mission.' They may have to fit with social legitimacy goals. And Purcell (1999: 37) commented that: 'The search for a contingency or matching model of HRM is also limited by the impossibility of modelling all the contingent variables, the difficulty of showing their interconnection, and the way in which changes in one variable have an impact on others.'

Best fit models tend to be static and don't take account of the processes of change. They neglect the fact that institutional forces shape HRM – it cannot be assumed that employers are free agents able to make independent decisions.

Conclusions

It is often said that best fit is better than best practice, but this statement can only be accepted with reservations. As Stavrou et al (2010: 952–53) argued:

There may be merit in both approaches where the debate is between general principles/bundles (training and development, staffing, compensation and benefits, communication and participation, and planning) and the manner in which they are carried out... It seems that the 'best fit' and 'best practice' approaches of the HR–performance relationship are not necessarily mutually exclusive. On the contrary, they may be combined to provide a more holistic picture.

This is particularly the case if the term 'best practice' is replaced by 'good practice', thus avoiding the notion of universality implied by the former term. For example, the meta-analysis carried out by Schmidt and Hunter (1998) established conclusively that when selecting people, the best levels of predictive validity are achieved by a combination of structured interviews and intelligence tests. But a decision on what sort of structured interview should be adopted and whether or not to use intelligence tests would depend on the situation in which the decision was made.

Bundling

'Bundling' is the development and implementation of several HR practices together so that they are interrelated and therefore complement and reinforce each other. This is the process of horizontal integration, which is also referred to as the use of 'complementarities'. Richardson and Thompson (1999) suggested that a strategy's success turns on combining vertical or external fit and horizontal or internal fit. They concluded that a firm with bundles of associated HR practices should have a higher level of performance, provided it also achieves high levels of fit with its competitive strategy.

Dyer and Reeves (1995: 656–57) noted that: 'The logic in favour of bundling is straightforward... Since employee performance is a function of both ability and motivation, it makes sense to have practices aimed at enhancing both.' Thus there are several ways in which employees can acquire needed skills (such as careful selection and training) and multiple incentives to enhance motivation (different forms of financial and non-financial rewards). Their study of various models listing HR practices that create a link between HRM and business performance found that the activities appearing in most of the models were involvement, careful selection, extensive training and contingent pay.

The process of bundling HR strategies is an important aspect of the concept of strategic HRM. In a sense, SHRM is holistic: it is concerned with the organization as a total system or entity and addresses what needs to be done across the organization as a whole. It is not interested in isolated programmes and techniques, or in the ad hoc development of HR strategies and practices.

Bundling can take place in a number of ways. Competency frameworks (a set of definitions of the competencies that describe the types of behaviour required for the successful performance of a role) can be devised that have a variety of uses, for example to specify recruitment standards, provide a framework for structured interviews, identify learning and development needs and indicate the standards of behaviour or performance required. Job evaluation can also be used to clarify and define levels in an organization. Grade structures can define career ladders in terms of competency requirements (career family structures) and thus provide the basis for learning and development programmes. Total reward approaches 'bundle' financial and non-financial rewards together. High-performance systems are in effect based on the principle of bundling because they group a number of HR practices together to produce synergy and thus increase their impact.

Critical evaluation of bundling

Bundling sounds like a good idea. The research by MacDuffie (1995) and others has shown that bundling can improve performance. But there are a number of inhibiting factors, namely:

- deciding which bundles are likely to be best – there is no evidence that one bundle is generally better than another;
- actually linking practices together – it is always easier to deal with one practice at a time;
- managing the interdependencies between different parts of a bundle;
- convincing top management and line managers that bundling will benefit the organization and them.

These can be overcome by dedicated HR professionals, but it is hard work. What can be done, with difficulty, is to find ways in which different HR practices can support one another, as in the examples given above.

The conceptual basis of strategic HRM

Strategic HRM is the 'interface between HRM and strategic management'. It takes the notion of HRM as a strategic, integrated and coherent approach and develops that in line with the concept of strategic management (Boxall, 1996).

The fundamental characteristics of strategy

- Forward looking.

- The organizational capability of a firm depends on its resource capability.

- Strategic fit – the need when developing HR strategies to achieve congruence between them and the organization's business strategies within the context of its external and internal environment.

How strategy is formulated

An emergent and flexible process of developing a sense of direction, making the best use of resources and ensuring strategic fit.

The aim of SHRM

To generate organizational capability by ensuring that the organization has the skilled, engaged, committed and well-motivated employees it needs to achieve sustained competitive advantage.

Implications of the resource-based view (RBV)

The RBV emphasizes the importance of creating firms that are 'more intelligent and flexible than their competitors' (Boxall, 1996) by hiring and developing more talented staff and by extending the skills base.

Implications of the concept of strategic fit

The concept of strategic fit means developing HR strategies that are integrated with the business strategy and support its achievement (vertical integration or fit), and the use of an integrated approach to the development of HR practices.

Best practice

There is a set of best HRM practices that are universal in the sense that they are best in any situation and adopting them will lead to superior organizational performance. The notion of best practice incorrectly assumes that there are universally effective HR practices that can readily be transferred.

Best fit

HR strategies should be congruent with the context and circumstances of the organization. More realistic than best practice, but there is a danger of mechanistically matching HR policies and practices with strategy.

The significance of bundling

The process of bundling HR strategies is an important aspect of the concept of SHRM, which is concerned with the organization as a total system or entity and addresses what needs to be done across the organization as a whole.

References

Abell, D F (1993) *Managing with Dual Strategies: Mastering the present, pre-empting the future*, New York, Free Press

Baird, L and Meshoulam, I (1988) Managing two fits of strategic human resource management, *Academy of Management Review*, **13** (1), pp 116–28

Barney, J B (1991) Firm resources and sustained competitive advantage, *Journal of Management Studies*, **17** (1), pp 99–120

Barney, J B (1995) Looking inside for competitive advantage, *Academy of Management Executive*, **9** (4), pp 49–61

Becker, B E and Gerhart, S (1996) The impact of human resource management on organizational performance: progress and prospects, *Academy of Management Journal*, **39** (4), pp 779–801

Boxall, P F (1996) The strategic HRM debate and the resource-based view of the firm, *Human Resource Management Journal*, **6** (3), pp 59–75

Boxall, P F (2007) The goals of HRM, in (eds) P Boxall, J Purcell and P Wright, *The Oxford Handbook of Human Resource Management*, Oxford, Oxford University Press, pp 48–67

Boxall, P F and Purcell, J (2003) *Strategy and Human Resource Management*, Basingstoke, Palgrave Macmillan

Brewster, C (2004) European perspectives of human resource management, *Human Resource Management Review*, **14** (4), pp 365–82

Cappelli, P and Crocker-Hefter, A (1996) Distinctive human resources are firms' core competencies, *Organizational Dynamics*, Winter, pp 7–22

Cascio, W F (2015) *Strategic HRM: Too important for an insular approach*, **54** (3), pp 423–26

Chandler, A D (1962) *Strategy and Structure*, Boston, MA, MIT Press

Delery, J E and Doty, H D (1996) Modes of theorizing in strategic human resource management: tests of universality, contingency and configurational performance predictions, *Academy of Management Journal*, **39** (4), pp 802–35

Digman, L A (1990) *Strategic Management: Concepts, decisions, cases*, Georgetown, Ontario, Irwin

Dyer, L and Holder, G W (1988) Strategic human resource management and planning, in (ed) L Dyer, *Human Resource Management: Evolving roles and responsibilities*, Washington, DC, Bureau of National Affairs

Dyer, L and Reeves, T (1995) Human resource strategies and firm performance: what do we know

and where do we need to go?, *The International Journal of Human Resource Management*, **6** (3), pp 656–70

Faulkner, D and Johnson, G (1992) *The Challenge of Strategic Management*, London, Kogan Page

Grant, R M (1991) The resource-based theory of competitive advantage: implications for strategy formulation, *California Management Review*, **33** (3), pp 114–35

Guest, D E (1991) Personnel management: the end of orthodoxy, *British Journal of Industrial Relations*, **29** (2), pp 149–76

Guest, D E (1997) Human resource management and performance: a review of the research agenda, *The International Journal of Human Resource Management*, **8** (3), pp 263–76

Hambrisk, D C and Fredrickson, J W (2001) Are you sure you have a strategy? *Academy of Management Executive*, **15** (4), pp 48–59

Heller, R (1972) *The Naked Manager*, London, Barrie & Jenkins

Hendry, C and Pettigrew, A (1986) The practice of strategic human resource management, *Personnel Review*, **15** (5), pp 2–8

Hunt, S (1991) The resource-advantage theory of competition, *Journal of Management Inquiry*, **4** (4), pp 317–22

Kanter, R M (1984) *The Change Masters*, London, Allen & Unwin

Mabey, C, Salaman, G and Storey, J (1998) *Human Resource Management: A strategic introduction*, 2nd edn, Oxford, Blackwell

MacDuffie, J P (1995) Human resource bundles and manufacturing performance, *Industrial Relations Review*, **48** (2), pp 199–221

Miles, R E and Snow, C C (1978) *Organizational Strategy: Structure and process*, New York, McGraw-Hill

Mintzberg, H (1987) Crafting strategy, *Harvard Business Review*, July–August, pp 66–74

Paauwe, J (2004) *HRM and Performance: Achieving long-term viability*, Oxford, Oxford University Press

Penrose, E (1959) *The Theory of the Growth of the Firm*, Oxford, Blackwell

Pettigrew, A and Whipp, R (1991) *Managing Change for Strategic Success*, Oxford, Blackwell

Pfeffer, J (1998) *The Human Equation*, Boston, MA, Harvard Business School Press

Pfeffer, J and Davis-Blake, A (1992) Understanding organizational wage structures: a resource dependence approach, *Academy of Management Journal*, 30, pp 437–55

Porter, M E (1985) *Competitive Advantage: Creating and sustaining superior performance*, New York, The Free Press

Priem, R L and Butler, J E (2001) Is the resource-based theory a useful perspective for strategic management research?, *Academy of Management Review*, 26 (1), pp 22–40

Purcell, J (1999) Best practice or best fit: chimera or cul-de-sac, *Human Resource Management Journal*, 9 (3), pp 26–41

Quinn, J B (1980) *Strategies for Change: Logical incrementalism*, Georgetown, Ontario, Irwin

Richardson, R and Thompson, M (1999) *The Impact of People Management Practices on Business Performance: A literature review*, London, IPD

Schmidt, F L and Hunter, J E (1998) The validity and utility of selection methods in personnel psychology: practical and theoretical implications of 85 years of research findings, *Psychological Bulletin*, 124 (2), pp 262–74

Schuler, R S (1992) Strategic human resource management: linking people with the strategic needs of the business, *Organizational Dynamics*, 21 (1), pp 18–32

Schuler, R S and Jackson, S E (1987) Linking competitive strategies with human resource management practices, *Academy of Management Executive*, 9 (3), pp 207–19

Schuler, R S and Jackson, S E (2007) *Strategic Human Resource Management*, 2nd edn, Oxford, Blackwell

Sparrow, P, Hesketh, A, Hird, M and Cooper, C (2010), Introduction: Performance-led HR, in (eds) P Sparrow, A Hesketh, M Hird, and C Cooper, *Leading HR*, pp 1–22, Basingstoke, Palgrave Macmillan

Stavrou, E T, Brewster, C and Charalambousa, C (2010) Human resource management and firm performance in Europe through the lens of business systems: best fit, best practice or both? *The International Journal of Human Resource Management*, 21 (7), pp 933–62

Truss, C (1999) Soft and hard models of HRM, in (eds) L Gratton, V H Hailey, P Stiles and C Truss, *Strategic Human Resource Management*, Oxford, Oxford University Press

Truss, C, Deldridge, R, Alfes, K, Shantz, A and Soane, E (2014) Introduction, *Employee Engagement in Theory and Practice*, London, Routledge

Truss, C and Gratton, L (1994) Strategic human resource management: a conceptual approach, *International Journal of Human Resource Management*, 5 (3), pp 663–86

Tyson, S (1997) Human resource strategy: a process for managing the contribution of HRM to organizational performance, *International Journal of Human Resource Management*, 8 (3), pp 277–90

Ulrich, D (1998) A new mandate for human resources, *Harvard Business Review*, January–February, pp 124–34

Wernerfelt, B (1984) A resource-based view of the firm, *Strategic Management Journal*, 5 (2), pp 171–80

Wright, P M and McMahan, G C (1992) Theoretical perspectives for SHRM, *Journal of Management*, 18 (2), pp 295–320

Wright, P M and Snell, S A (1998) Towards a unifying framework for exploring fit and flexibility in strategic human resource management, *Academy of Management Review*, 23 (4), pp 756–72

PART II

Delivering HRM

PART II CONTENTS

Introduction

HR is delivered by means of the framework provided by the HR architecture of an organization, which consists of the HR system and HR practices and the HR model adopted for the organization – the provision of advice and services by HR professionals in the HR function working in conjunction with line management.

HR techniques such as organization development, selection interviewing and testing, talent management, performance management and total reward play an important part in the delivery of HR. But there is the danger that new and seemingly different techniques become 'flavours of the month', only to be quickly forgotten when they fail to deliver. Some time ago McLean (1981: 4) observed that:

The history of the management of human resources is littered with examples of widely acclaimed techniques enthusiastically introduced by managers who are keen to find solutions to their 'people' problems, only to be discarded and discredited by the same disillusioned and increasingly cynical managers some time later.

Times have not changed. The effective delivery of HR depends on using techniques which are tried, tested and appropriate, not ones which have been promoted vigorously as 'best practice' without supporting evidence.

This part includes chapters on the HR architecture and system, the role of the HR function and the role of the HR professional. It also deals with a key aspect of HR delivery: the impact HR makes on performance.

Reference

McLean, A (1981) Organization development: a case of the emperor's new clothes? *Personnel Review*, **4** (1), pp 3–14

04
HR architecture – the HR system

KEY CONCEPTS AND TERMS

HR architecture

HR delivery model

HR system processes and programmes

LEARNING OUTCOMES

On completing this chapter you should be able to define these key concepts. You should also understand the meaning of HR architecture and the components of an HR system.

HR architecture

HR architecture consists of the HR systems, processes and structure of an organization, and employee behaviours. It is a comprehensive representation of all that is involved in HR, not simply the structure of the HR function. As explained by Becker *et al* (2001: 12): 'We use the term HR architecture to broadly describe the continuum from the HR professionals within the HR function, to the system of HR-related policies and practices, through the competencies, motivation and associated behaviours of the firm's employees.' It was noted by Hird *et al* (2010: 25) that: 'this architecture is seen as a unique combination of the HR function's structure and delivery model, the HR practices and system, and the strategic employee behaviours that these create.'

Purcell (1999: 38) suggested that the focus should be on 'appropriate HR architecture and the processes that contribute to organizational performance'. Becker and Huselid (2006: 899) stated that: 'It is the fit between the HR architecture and the strategic capabilities and business processes that implement strategy that is the basis of HR's contribution to competitive advantage.'

FIGURE 4.1   The HRM system

The HR system

The HR system contains the interrelated and jointly supportive HR activities and practices which together enable HR goals to be achieved. Becker and Huselid (1998: 95) observed that: 'The HR system is first and foremost a vehicle to implement the firm's strategy'. Later (2006), they argued that it is the HR system that is the key HR asset. Boselie *et al* (2005: 73) pointed out that in its traditional form, HR can be viewed as 'a collection of multiple discrete practices with no explicit or discernible link between them. The more strategically minded system approach views HR as an integrated and coherent bundle of mutually reinforcing practices.'

As illustrated in Figure 4.1, an HR system brings together HR philosophies that describe the overarching values and guiding principles adopted in managing people.

Taking account of the internal and external environments in which the organization operates, the system incorporates:

- HR strategies, which define the direction in which HR intends to take each of its main areas of activity.

- HR policies, which set out what HR is there to do and provide guidelines defining how specific aspects of HR should be applied and implemented.

- HR practices, which consist of the HR activities involved in managing and developing people and in managing the employment relationship.

Key learning points: HR architecture – the HR system

HR delivery

HR is delivered through the HR architecture of an organization, which includes the HR system, HR practices and the HR delivery model adopted by the HR function.

HR architecture

HR architecture includes the HR systems and processes and employee behaviours as well as the structure of the HR function.

The HR system

The HR system as part of the HR architecture consists of the interrelated and jointly supportive HR activities and practices, which together enable HR goals to be achieved.

References

Becker, B E and Huselid, M A (1998) High performance work systems and firm performance: a synthesis of research and managerial implications, *Research on Personnel and Human Resource Management*, **16**, pp 53–101

Becker, B E and Huselid, M A (2006) Strategic human resource management: where do we go from here? *Journal of Management*, **32** (6), pp 898–925

Becker, B E, Huselid, M A and Ulrich, D (2001) *The HR Score card: Linking people, strategy, and performance*, Boston, MA, Harvard Business School Press

Boselie, P, Dietz, G and Boon, C (2005) Commonalities and contradictions in HR and performance research, *Human Resource Management Journal*, **15** (3), pp 67–94

Hird, M, Sparrow, P and Marsh, C (2010) HR structures: are they working?, in (eds) P Sparrow, A Hesketh, M Hird, and C Cooper, *Leading HR*, Basingstoke, Palgrave Macmillan, pp 23–45

Purcell, J (1999) Best practice or best fit: chimera or cul-de-sac, *Human Resource Management Journal*, **9** (3), pp 26–41

05

The role of the HR function

KEY CONCEPTS AND TERMS

Three-legged stool model of HR

Transactional HR activities

Transformational HR activities

LEARNING OUTCOMES

On completing this chapter you should be able to define these key concepts. You should also understand:

- The contribution of HR
- The role and organization of the HR function
- Evaluating the HR function
- HRM in SMEs

Introduction

The HR function specializes in matters relating to the employment, management, development and performance of people in organizations. The members of the function may be involved in strategic or transformational activities although the function will also have the transactional role of providing the HR services the organization requires. The 'clients' of the HR function are not just the management of the organization; they also include line managers and employees generally.

The remit of the HR function will vary in different organizations. It may be concerned with all or any the following areas of HRM: organization design and development, workforce planning, recruitment and selection, learning and development, knowledge management, performance management, reward management, employment relations, employee well-being, managing diversity and inclusion, health and safety, fulfilment of statutory requirements, dealing with employment law issues, and HR administration. HR functions are sometimes given other responsibilities such as managing the car fleet or providing catering facilities.

The contribution of HR

The contributions that HR can make are to:

- *Provide insight* – seek understanding of the issues affecting the organization and its employees, explore the implications of these issues for business and people management and convey these messages to management. The aim is to help organizations 'to find new ways of meeting current and future challenges' (CIPD, 2010a: 5).

- *Contribute to the formulation and implementation of business strategy* – as Lawler and Mohrman (2003: 16) commented: 'HR can play an important role in the formulation of strategy by making explicit the human capital resources required to support various strategies and strategic initiatives, by playing a leadership role in helping the organization develop the necessary capabilities to enact the strategy, and by playing a strong role in implementation and change management.'

- *Improve organizational effectiveness (the ability of an organization to achieve its goals by making effective use of the resources available)* – plan and implement organization development programmes. As emphasized by the CIPD (2010: 7): 'HR has a unique role to play in helping an organization succeed today in a way that lays the foundations for future, sustainable success.'

- *Facilitate change* – fulfil the role of change agent, leading and advising senior and line managers how best to manage organizational change. Ulrich (1998: 125) suggested that HR should become 'an agent of continuous transformation'.

- *Deliver HR services* – provide effective and efficient services in such fields as recruitment, learning and development, reward management and employee relations which meet the needs of the organization, its management and its employees.

- *Provide expertise* – in contributing to the achievement of the organization's strategy, developing HR strategies and delivering advice and services in accordance with good practice in each aspect of HRM.

- *Provide advice* – improve the quality of employment relationships by advising managers on the implementation of HR policies and procedures, on employment issues and on handling people problems.

- *Develop the employee value proposition* – take action to improve the value of what the organization offers to prospective or existing employees in order to persuade them to join or remain with the business.

- *Promote the well-being of employees* – help to improve the quality of the work environment, covering how people are treated at work in such areas as health and safety, reduction of stress and work–life balance issues.

- *Promote social responsibility* – formulate socially responsible HR policies on such issues as equal opportunity, the management of diversity, flexible working, harassment, and bullying and ensure they are implemented. Act as the guardian of the organization's values and ethical standards concerning people, pointing out when behaviour conflicts with those values or where proposed actions will be inconsistent with them. Ulrich (1998) called this the 'employee champion' role.

- *Ensure compliance with employment law* – develop and implement policies and procedures which ensure that the provisions of employment law are fully taken into account.

The role of the HR function

Members of the HR function provide insight, leadership, advice and services on matters affecting the management, employment, learning and development, reward and well-being of people, and the relationships between management and employees. Importantly, they contribute to the achievement of organizational effectiveness and success (the impact of HRM on performance is dealt with in Chapter 7).

Although the basic role of HR is to deliver HRM services, it does much more than that. It plays a key part in the creation of an environment that enhances employee engagement by enabling people to make the best use of their capacities, to realize their potential to the benefit of both the organization and themselves, and to achieve satisfaction through their work.

Increasingly, the role of HR is seen to be business-oriented – contributing to the achievement of sustained competitive advantage. Becker and Huselid (1998: 97) argued that HR should be 'a resource that solves real business problems'. But one of the issues explored by Francis and Keegan (2006) through their research is the tendency for a focus on business performance outcomes to obscure the importance of employee well-being in its own right. They quoted the view of Ulrich and Brockbank (2005: 201) that 'caring, listening to, and responding to employees remains a centrepiece of HR work'. The HR function and its members have to be aware of the ethical dimensions of their work (the ethical dimension of HRM is considered in Chapter 14).

The organization of the HR function

HR activities can be divided into two broad categories: 1) transformational (strategic) activities that are concerned with developing organizational effectiveness and the alignment and implementation of HR and business strategies; 2) transactional activities, which cover the main areas of HR service delivery – resourcing, learning and development, reward and employee relations.

The HR operating model

Operating models for the organization of the HR function vary immensely. As Sisson (1990) commented, HR management is not a single homogeneous occupation – it involves a variety of roles and activities that differ from one organization to another and from one level to another in the same organization. Tyson (1987) claimed that the HR function is often 'balkanized' – not only is there a variety of roles and activities but these tend to be relatively self-centred, with little passage between

them. Hope-Hailey *et al* (1997: 17) believed that HR could be regarded as a 'chameleon function' in the sense that the diversity of practice established by their research suggests that 'contextual variables dictate different roles for the function and different practices of people management'.

A chief executive's view on the HR agenda as quoted by Hesketh and Hird (2010: 105) was that it operates on three levels: 'There's the foundation level, which we used to call personnel, it's just pay and rations, recruitment, all that sort of stuff that makes the world go round, transactional work. Level two to me is tools, it could be engagement, reward, development, those sort of things. Level three is the strategic engagement.'

The operating model for the HR function depends on the size of the business, the extent to which operations are decentralized, the type of work carried out, the kind of people employed and the role assigned to the HR function. A survey by Incomes Data Services (IDS, 2010) found that the overall median number of HR staff in the responding organizations was 14: in companies with up to 499 employees the median number was 3.5, and in companies with 500 or more employees it was 20. While, as would be expected, large organizations employed more staff than small- and medium-sized companies, they had on average fewer HR staff per employee. For smaller companies the median ratio of employees to HR staff was 62:1; in large employers it was 95:1. The overall ratio was 80:1. The IRS 2012 survey of HR roles and responsibilities found that the median ratio of employees to HR practitioners was 80:1.

A traditional organization might consist of an HR director responsible directly to the chief executive, with functional heads dealing with recruitment and employment matters including talent management, learning and development, and reward management. Crail (2006: 15) used the responses from 179 organizations to an IRS survey of the HR function to produce a model of an HR department. He suggested that this 'might consist of a team of 12 people serving a workforce of around 1,200. The team would have a director, three managers, one supervisor, three HR officers and four assistants. It would include a number of professionally qualified practitioners, particularly at senior level.' However, there is no such thing as a typical HR function, although the 'three-legged stool' model as described below has attracted a lot of attention.

The three-legged stool model

The notion of delivering HRM through three major areas – centres of expertise, business partners and HR shared service centres – emerged from the HR delivery model produced by Ulrich (1997, 1998), although Ulrich has stated that the three-part structure was not his idea but an interpretation of his writing. The first reference to the three-legged stool was in an article by Johnson (1999: 44), two years after Ulrich published his delivery model. In this article Johnson quoted David Hilborn, an associate of William Mercer, management consultants, as follows:

> The traditional design [of an HR department] typically includes a vice president of HR, then a manager of compensation and benefits, a manager of HRIS and payroll, a manager of employment and so on. However, the emerging model is more like a three-legged stool. One leg of the stool includes an administrative service centre which processes payroll, benefits and the like and focuses on efficiency in transaction functions. The second leg is a centre of excellence (or expertise) in which managers and specialists work. These employees concentrate on design rather than transactions and will have line managers as their customers. HR business partners make up the third leg. They are generalists who usually report to line managers and indirectly to HR. These employees don't get involved in transactions, but instead act as consultants and planners, linking the business with appropriate HR programmes.

This exposition provided the blueprint for all subsequent versions of the model, which has evolved in its three-part form as follows:

- *Centres of expertise* – these specialize in the provision of high-level advice and services on key HR activities. The CIPD survey on the changing HR function (CIPD, 2007) found that they existed in 28 per cent of respondents' organizations. The most common expertise areas were learning and development (79 per cent), recruitment (67 per cent), reward (60 per cent) and employee relations (55 per cent).
- *Strategic business partners* – these work with line managers to help them reach their goals through effective strategy formulation and execution. They are often 'embedded' in business units or departments.
- *HR shared service centres* – these handle all the routine 'transactional' services across the business, which include such activities as recruitment, absence monitoring and advice on dealing with employee issues such as discipline and absenteeism.

Critical evaluation of the three-legged stool model

Although this model has attracted a great deal of attention, the 2007 CIPD survey found that only 18 per cent of respondents had implemented all three 'legs', although 47 per cent had implemented one or two elements, with business partners being the most common (29 per cent).

Moreover, there are difficulties with the notion. Gratton (2003: 18) pointed out that: 'This fragmentation of the HR function is causing all sorts of unintended problems. Senior managers look at the fragments and are not clear how the function as a whole adds value.' And as Reilly (2007) commented, respondents to the CIPD survey mentioned other problems in introducing the new model. These included difficulties in defining roles and accountabilities, especially those of business partners, who risk being 'hung, drawn and quartered by all sides', according to one HR director. At the same time, the segmented nature of the structure gives rise to 'boundary management' difficulties, for example when it comes to separating out transactional tasks from the work of centres of expertise. The model can also hamper communication between those engaged in different HR activities. Other impediments were technological failure, inadequate resources in HR and skills gaps.

Hird *et al* (2010: 31) drew attention to the following issues:

- An 'off-the-shelf' introduction of a new HR structure without careful thought as to how the model fits the organization's requirements.
- A lack of care in dealing with the boundary issues between elements of the HR structure which can easily be fragmented.

- A lack of attention to the new skill sets needed by business partners to ensure they can play at the strategic level.

- A lack of understanding on the part of managers as to the value of a new HR structure.

- A lack of skill on the part of line managers to make the required shift to greater responsibility for people issues implied by the new model.

- What is referred to as the 'polo' problem: a lack of provision of the execution of HR services as the business partner shifts to strategic work, and the centre of expertise to an advisory role.

However, some benefits were reported by respondents to the CIPD (2007) survey. Centres of expertise provide higher-quality advice. Business partners exercise better business focus, line managers are more engaged, and the profile of HR is raised. Also, the introduction of shared services results in improved customer service and allows other parts of HR to spend more time on value-adding activities. It can also cut costs by reducing the number of HR staff required.

Dealing with structuring issues

The following approach, incorporating recommendations by Holley (2009: 8–9), can be used to deal with HR structuring issues:

- ensure that top management are behind the changes;

- involve line managers and the whole of HR in planning and implementation;

- work out exactly who will do what in each area – HR and the line – avoid overlaps and ambiguities, taking particular care in defining the respective responsibilities of business partners and members of shared services centres and centres of expertise;

- ensure that the right balance is achieved between HR strategic (transformational) activities and HR service delivery (transactional) activities;

- ensure that the right people are in the right roles (don't simply switch job titles);

- let everyone know about the changes – why they are taking place, how they will work and any differences in responsibilities;

- define the skills required by both HR staff and line managers and help in their development;

- plan the implementation, phasing it as required to avoid any disruption;

- monitor implementation to ensure that it is going according to plan.

Power of the HR function

Research by Sheehan *et al* (2014) established that the amount of power possessed by the HR function – the amount of influence it exerts – depends on three dimensions:

1 Power of resources:
   - HR functional expertise;
   - in-house HRM (ie not significantly outsourced).
2 Power of processes:
   - HR works closely with top management team;
   - HR function as facilitator.
3 Power of meaning:
   - support from the chief executive;
   - use of business language in communicating with line managers;
   - use of HR analytics.

Evaluating the HR function

It is necessary to evaluate the contribution of the HR function to establish how effective it is at both the strategic level and in terms of service delivery and support. The prime criteria for evaluating the work of the function are its ability to operate strategically and its capacity to deliver the levels of services required.

Research conducted by the Institute for Employment Studies (Hirsh, 2008) discovered that the factors that correlated most strongly with line managers' and employees' satisfaction with HR were:

- being well supported in times of change;
- HR giving good advice to employees;
- being well supported when dealing with difficult people or situations;
- HR getting the basics right.

But the results showed that HR could do better in each of these areas. The conclusions reached were that HR must find out what its customers need and what their experiences of HR services are. HR has to be responsive – clear about what it is there for and what services it offers – and easy to contact.

The IRS 2012 survey of HR roles and responsibilities established that the main measures used by respondents to assess HR effectiveness were:

- absence management data – 79 per cent;
- staff turnover data – 75 per cent;
- exit interview feedback – 66 per cent;
- discipline and grievance data – 60 per cent;
- results of employee surveys – 60 per cent;
- anecdotal/informal feedback – 59 per cent;
- number of tribunal cases – 50 per cent;
- benchmarking – 47 per cent;
- spending against budget – 46 per cent;
- time-to-fill vacancies data – 34 per cent;
- cost per hire – 30 per cent.

CASE STUDIES

HR organization at the National Australia Bank Group

HR at the National Australia Bank Group has a number of centres of expertise, business partners, solutions consultants, project managers, a shared services centre, and telephone advisory service for employees (the people advisory helpline).

Centres of expertise

Centres of expertise cover areas such as reward, employment policy, talent management, culture management, diversity and performance. The staff in the centres are specialists in their respective fields, while the other parts of HR can be found in the HR service centre, with the exception of recruitment, which is conducted by line managers.

Business partners

Business partners attend business unit leadership team meetings, set the company's people strategies and deliver the HR requirements emerging from various projects. They tend to work in the areas of talent, performance, leadership, diversity and culture, and their job is to facilitate the implementation of corporate people initiatives with the relevant specialist HR partners. Unlike shared services staff, they only get involved in HR's daily operational matters if projects escalate and extra help is required.

Solutions consultants

Solutions consultants deal with operational queries referred to them from the people advisory helpline – mainly issues of case management and other more complex enquiries. They are a key point of contact for people leaders on matters of policy and procedure, although they do participate in some transaction work as well.

Project staff

Project staff work on projects that emerge from strategic discussions.

The HR shared services model at PricewaterhouseCoopers (PwC)

The HR shared services model at PwC consists of transactional and professional areas. Transactional functions include payroll, benefits administration and the joiners/leavers process department. The transactional functions also provide services for their professional counterparts. In contrast, professional areas organized into centres of expertise include functions such as recruitment, learning and development, reward, diversity, and legal and advisory.

The centres of expertise sit within the central human capital services centre but there are definite lines between them. Every centre of expertise is a cost centre, but for the annual budgeting process all are looked at together as part of the HR shared services function.

The result of introducing the centres of expertise has been that specialist knowledge is now organized into discrete units enabling know-how and experience to be more easily shared. The new structure means there is less duplication and the improved efficiencies allow more time to be dedicated to strategic issues. Additionally, a decrease in costs has been achieved via a combination of reductions in headcount, economies of scale and related efficiencies.

Reorganizing HR in the Greater Manchester Fire Service

Following major changes in operations, it was decided by senior management that the role of the fire service's HR function was to provide high-level, strategic advice from advisers who could work closely with them, backed up by specialists. In other words, a business partner model. So the brigade began to recruit business partners – placing a special emphasis on those with expertise in employee relations – and specialists to cover areas such as occupational health, equality and diversity, reward, pensions and recruitment. Finding candidates with sufficient gravitas to act as top-level strategic advisers was difficult. There weren't many true business partners about. A lot of people calling themselves business partners were really HR advisers.

When the team was in place, the major developments were:

- to introduce a more transparent promotions process;

- to work on the organizational climate and leadership – a series of away days for leaders using organizational climate tools such as 360-degree feedback and the Belbin Team Inventory;

- the recruitment process was also modernized by putting together a resourcing team, building a microsite and developing an applicant tracking system;

- to reorganize training;

- a departmental competency framework was put in place to ensure HR staff would be able to move easily within the organization rather than becoming bogged down in specialist areas.

The role of HRM in small- and medium-sized organizations (SMEs)

SMEs are usually defined as companies with up to 250 employees. The approach to HR they adopt varies even more widely than in larger organizations. There may be no HR function at all, or in some larger or more sophisticated SMEs there may be a fully formed HR department, albeit a small one. However, people management activities tend generally tend to be more informal, at least in the early stages of development. Research conducted by Miller (2015) established that there were four stages of SME growth. As a company moves through each change, different HR requirements emerge which may lead to the appointment of full-time or part-time HR professionals or the extended use of external agencies and consultants.

Stage 1: Start-up. In this initial stage, people matters tend to be dealt with by the owner, with no formal HR role. Overall the business is characterized by informality, with an emergent strategy, fluid structures and flexible job roles. The owner takes responsibility for hiring, looking for someone who 'fits' with what the company is all about. The people-related requirements tend to be minimal, centred on pay and contracts, with the rate for the job set by the owner.

Stage 2: Emerging enterprise. In a growing business, the owner will have to delegate more and people issues become more important. Someone may be appointed to look after HR matters, possibly on a part-time basis for any of the following reasons:

● The business has reached a size where policies and procedures are needed to guide work and create a sense of fairness.

● The owner feels that people issues are taking up too much of their time.

● People management is seen as vital for growth and to achieve the company's vision.

● There is a specific people issue that needs to be addressed, for example tribunal cases, skills shortages, high turnover.

But the owner may decide simply to outsource HR work such as recruitment and seek advice from consultants on any serious people problem.

Stage 3: Consolidation. As the business develops and expands it may appoint a full-time HR specialist who will introduce more sophisticated practices in areas such as recruitment, talent management, or reward or performance management to meet the needs of the business for talented high-performing employees.

Stage4: Established business. Fully established businesses will set up an HR department under a generalist manger with specialized assistants, for example one focusing on recruitment and talent management and another dealing with learning and development.

The research by Miller found that attaching workforce numbers to the stages did not reveal any particular pattern. SMEs tended to develop more formal HR practices and a dedicated HR manager or function at different workforce sizes, depending on the people requirements of the business, the leader's view on people management and the industry the business operates in.

However, Marlow *et al* (2010) established through their research in six growing SMEs that although there was some formalization of HR, many owners still retained informal control over employment matters. They commented that SMEs did not necessarily move from informality to formality and that it could be argued that in a small firm there may be advantages in maintaining an informal approach to people management.

Key learning points: The role of the HR function

The HR delivery model

The HR delivery model describes how those services are delivered by the HR function.

The 'three-legged stool' model of the HR function

This model identifies three areas of HR activity: centres of expertise, strategic business partners and shared service centres.

Evaluating the HR function

It is necessary to evaluate the contribution of the HR function to establish how effective it is at both the strategic level and in terms of service delivery and support.

The role of HRM in small- and medium-sized organizations (SMES)

The approach to HR adopted by SMEs varies even more widely than in larger organizations. There may be no HR function at all, or in some larger or more sophisticated SMEs there may be a fully formed HR department, albeit a small one. However, people management activities generally tend to be more informal, at least in the early stages of development.

References

Becker, B E and Huselid, M A (1998) High performance work systems and firm performance: a synthesis of research and managerial implications, *Research on Personnel and Human Resource Management*, **16**, pp 53–101

Chartered Institute of Personnel and Development (2007) *The Changing HR Function*, London, CIPD

Chartered Institute of Personnel and Development (2010) *Next Generation HR*, London, CIPD

Crail, M (2006) HR roles and responsibilities 2006: benchmarking the HR function, *IRS Employment Review*, **839**, 20 January, pp 9–15

Francis, H and Keegan, A (2006) The changing face of HRM: in search of balance, *Human Resource Management Journal*, **16** (3), pp 231–49

Gratton, L (2003) The Humpty Dumpty effect: a view of a fragmented HR function, *People Management*, 5 January, p 18

Hesketh, A and Hird, M (2010) Using relationships between leaders to leverage more value from people: building a golden triangle, in (eds) P Sparrow, A Hesketh, M Hird and C Cooper, *Leading HR*, Basingstoke, Palgrave Macmillan, pp 103–21

Hird, M, Sparrow, P and Marsh, C (2010) HR structures: are they working?, in (eds) P Sparrow, A Hesketh, M Hird, and C Cooper, *Leading HR*, Basingstoke, Palgrave Macmillan, pp 23–45

Hirsh, W (2008) What do people want from you?, *People Management*, 18 September, pp 23–6

Holley, N (2009) *HR Models: Lessons from best practice*, Henley, Henley Business School http://www.henleyhktest.reading.ac.uk [accessed 26 February 2013]

Hope-Hailey, V, Gratton, L, McGovern, P, Stiles, P and Truss, C (1997) A chameleon function? HRM in the '90s, *Human Resource Management Journal*, **7** (3), pp 5–18

IDS (2010) HR Function Survey, HR Study 928, October, London, IDS

IRS (2012) HR Roles and Responsibilities Survey, http://www.xperthr.co.uk/article/106943/hr-role-and-responsibilities-the- 2012-survey [accessed 24 February 2013]

Johnson, C (1999) Changing shapes: trends in human resource reorganizations, *HR Magazine*, **44** (3), pp 40–48

Lawler E E and Mohrman S A (2003) What does it take to make it happen? *Human Resource Planning*, **26** (3), pp 15–29

Marlow, S, Taylor, S and Thompson, A (2010) Informality and formality in medium-sized companies: contestation and synchronization, *British Journal of Management*, **21**, pp 954–66

Miller, J (2015) *What Does the Future of HR in an SME Look Like?* London, CIPD

Reilly, P (2007) Facing up to the facts, *People Management*, 20 September, pp 43–45

Sheehan, C, De Cieri, H and Cooper, C (2014) Exploring the power dimensions of the human resource function, Human Resource Management Journal 24 (2), pp 193–210

Sisson, K (1990) Introducing the Human Resource Management Journal, *Human Resource Management Journal*, **1** (1), pp 1–11

Tyson, S (1987) The management of the personnel function, *Journal of Management Studies*, **24** (5), pp 523–32

Ulrich, D (1997) *Human Resource Champions*, Boston, MA, Harvard Business School Press

Ulrich, D (1998) A new mandate for human resources, *Harvard Business Review*, January–February, pp 124–34

Ulrich, D and Brockbank, W (2005) *The HR Value Proposition*, Cambridge, MA, Harvard Press

06
The role of HR professionals

KEY CONCEPTS AND TERMS

Business partnering

Change agent

HR business partner

HR strategic partner

Transactional role

Transformational role

LEARNING OUTCOMES

On completing this chapter you should be able to define these key concepts. You should also understand:

- The various roles of HR professionals including the Ulrich model
- The role of business partners
- The partnership role of HR professionals
- Competency and behavioural requirements for HR professionals
- Carrying out the role of an HR professional
- The HR role of line managers

The overall role of the HR professional

The CIPD Profession Map (2013: 9) states that the HR profession is 'an applied business discipline with a people and organization specialism'.

HR professionals provide advice, guidance and services on all matters concerning the employment of people. The role can be transactional, dealing with basic HR matters such as recruitment and selection, or transformational, operating strategically in order to make significant changes in how the organization functions or how its employees are treated.

The roles of HR professionals vary according to the extent to which they are generalist (eg HR director, HR manager, HR officer), or specialist (eg head of learning and development, head of talent management, head of reward), the level at which they work (strategic, executive or administrative), the needs of the organization, the view of senior management about their contribution, the context within which they work and their own capabilities. They can act as strategists, business partners, innovators, internal consultants, facilitators, coaches or service providers. Tyson and Fell (1986: 7) explained that they were 'specialists in managing the employment relationship'. The best-known summary of the roles of HR professionals is the Ulrich model as described below.

The Ulrich model

In his influential *Harvard Business Review* article (1998:124) Dave Ulrich wrote that: 'HR should not be defined by what it does but by what it delivers – results that enrich the organization's value to customers, investors, and employees.' More specifically, he suggested that HR can deliver in four ways: as a strategic partner, an administrative expert, an employee champion and a change agent. This first model was later modified by Ulrich and Brockbank (2005), who defined five roles as follows:

1 *Employee advocate* – focuses on the needs of employees through listening, understanding and emphasizing.

2 *Human capital developer* – focuses on preparing employees to be successful in the future.

3 *Functional expert* – concerned with the HR practices that are central to HR value on the basis of the body of knowledge they possess.

4 *Strategic partner* – combines the multiple dimensions of business expert, change agent, strategic HR planner, knowledge manager and consultant to align HR systems to help accomplish the organization's vision and mission, helping managers to get things done and disseminating learning across the organization.

5 *Leader* – leading the HR function, collaborating with other functions and providing leadership to them, setting and enhancing the standards for strategic thinking and ensuring corporate governance.

They commented on the importance of the employee advocate role, noting that HR professionals spend about one-fifth of their time on employee relations issues and that caring for, listening to and respond-ing to employees remains a centrepiece of HR work. Their model draws attention to the multifaceted nature of the role, although most attention has been paid to the notion of the strategic nature of HR work and the concept of the strategic business partner. These are discussed below, as are the other aspects of the role not referred to specifically in the latest version of the Ulrich model, namely the innovation role, the change agent role and the service delivery role.

The strategic role of the HR professional

Sparrow *et al* (2010: 88) observed that: 'HR must be fully responsive to the strategy and business model of the business. HR is not a rule to itself. It is not "HR for HR", but HR (as broadly defined across the competing stakeholders whom HR has to satisfy) for the business.'

HR professionals have a strategic role when they are operating at a transformational level as HR directors, heads of HR centres of expertise or main HR functions, or strategic business partners. As such, they take part in conjunction with their line manager colleagues in the development and implementation of innovative HR strategies that are aligned with business strategies and thus help to achieve them. At a transactional level (as an HR officer, adviser or assistant providing basic HR services, possibly in an HR shared service centre) their role is not primarily strategic but they can make a contribution to the formulation and implementation of HR strategy.

Clearly, the extent to which HR roles are strategic depends on the level of the role and its primary purpose, and summaries of what this involves for directors, heads or senior members of functions or centres of expertise are given below. This is followed by an analysis of the role of business partners who, conceptually at least, function strategically.

Restructuring the organization is an area where, as pointed out by Hardman and Mookherjee (2015), to be successful, HR needs to be involved in strategic conversations right from the start, and right at the top. To earn a place in those conversations, HR professionals need to have credibility within their organization. They can achieve this by developing their ability to think and work strategically and, in particular, being able to ask good questions.

The strategic role of HR directors

The strategic role of HR directors is to promote the achievement of the organization's goals and values by: 1) developing and implementing HR strategies that are integrated with the business strategy and are coherent and mutually supportive; 2) ensuring that a strategic approach is adopted that ensures HR activities support the business and add value; and 3) taking into account the ethical dimension of HRM. To carry out this role, HR directors need to:

- understand the strategic goals of the organization;
- appreciate the business imperatives and performance drivers relative to these goals;
- understand the business model of the organization (how it makes money) and play a part in business model innovation;
- comprehend how sustainable competitive advantage can be obtained through the human capital of the organization and know how HR practices can contribute to the achievement of strategic goals;
- contribute to the development of the business strategy on an 'outside-in' basis (Wright *et al*, 2004), starting from an analysis of the customer, competitor and business issues that the organization faces – the HR strategy then derives directly from these challenges to create solutions, add value and ensure that the organization has the distinctive human capital required to make an impact;
- contribute to the development for the business of a clear vision and a set of integrated values;
- ensure that senior management understands the HR implications of its business strategy;
- see the big picture, including the broader context (the competitive environment and the business, economic, social and legal factors that affect it) in which the organization operates;
- think in the long term of where HR should go and how to get there;
- understand the kinds of employee behaviour required to execute the business strategy successfully;
- take time to identify business issues and their implications for HR strategy (see Chapter 80);

- believe in and practise evidence-based management;
- be capable of making a powerful business case for any proposals on the development of HR strategies;
- fully embrace ethical considerations when developing and implementing HR strategy.

The strategic role of heads of HR functions

The strategic role of heads of HR functions or centres of expertise is fundamentally the same for their function as that of HR directors for the whole organization. They promote the achievement of the organization's business goals by developing and implementing functional strategies that are aligned with the business strategy and integrated with the strategies for other HR functions, and adopt a strategic approach in the sense of ensuring that HR activities support the business, add value and are ethical. To carry out this role, heads of HR functions should:

- understand the strategic goals of the organization as they affect their function;
- appreciate the business imperatives and performance drivers relative to these goals;
- help senior management to understand the implications of its strategy for the HR function;
- take time to identify business issues and their implications for HR strategy (see Chapter 80);
- know how HR practices in the function can contribute to the achievement of the strategic goals;
- ensure that their activities provide added value for the organization;
- be aware of the broader context (the competitive environment and the business, economic, social and legal factors that affect it) in which the function operates;
- think in terms of the bigger and longer-term picture of where HR strategies for the function should go and how to get there;
- believe in and practise evidence-based management;

- be capable of making a powerful business case for any proposals on the development of HR strategies for the function;
- fully embrace ethical considerations when developing and implementing HR strategy for the function.

The HR business partner role

HR business partners work alongside their line management colleagues in order to develop and implement an HR agenda which contributes to achieving the business goals of the organization or function. They share responsibility with their line management colleagues for the success of the enterprise and get involved with them in implementing business strategy and running the business. They may be 'embedded' in an operational division or department or be part of a centralized HR function.

The CIPD (2015a: 1) defined HR business partnering as: 'A model whereby HR professionals work closely with business leaders and/or line managers to achieve shared organizational objectives, in particular designing and implementing HR systems and processes that support strategic business aims. This can involve the formal designation of HR business partners – HR professionals who are embedded within specific areas of the business.'

An earlier definition by Ulrich and Beatty, (2001: 294) stated that the strategic business partner 'represented a "player" whose aim is to add value through acting as a "coach, architect, builder, facilitator, leader and conscience".'

But there are many different definitions of HR business partnering and the role of HR business partners can vary widely from one organization to another. In some cases, it may involve an entirely new approach to HR. At the opposite extreme, the title may simply be a re-badging of a traditional generalist HR role. Pritchard (2010: 176) noted that the strategic partner role 'appears to be something of a moving target, rather loosely defined and precariously positioned with respect to changing relationships both internal and external to the HR function', and that being a business partner can be a 'fragmented experience'.

The term originated in the concept of the strategic business partner as defined by Ulrich (1998). He advocated that HR should become a partner with senior and line managers in strategy execution. Ever since then the focus has been on the strategic nature of the business partner's role, although it is not always made clear what being strategic really means. But research conducted by Hirsh (2008) found that the word strategic itself was hardly used by the line manager participants. They talked much more about HR helping them to solve the key people problems they faced. And this is essentially what business partners are there to do, bearing in mind that business strategy is devised and implemented by people.

However, as Keegan and Francis (2010: 236) observed: 'The business partner term seems to have become the title of choice for ambitious HR practitioners.'

Research by Burroughs (2015) established that over 50 per cent of the organizations surveyed had introduced some form of HR business partner.

Conceptually, HR business partners have to:

- understand the business as a whole as well as its competitive environment;
- understand the goals of their part of the business and its plans to attain them;
- see the broad picture of how HR contributes to business success;
- ensure that their activities support the strategic activities of their colleagues;
- be proactive, anticipating requirements, identifying HR issues and problems and producing innovative and evidence-based solutions to them which are aligned with business requirements;
- respond to the needs of managers and ensure that the transactional HR services required by them are provided by colleagues in shared services departments or by outsourcing;
- build relationships founded on trust and demonstrated expertise with their line management clients.

Reilly (2015) observed that research conducted by the CIPD and the IES in 2007 established that the business partner concept had helped HR to become a more strategic contributor, to increase its business focus and to improve the credibility of the function. It also encouraged greater line engagement with people management and put people management issues higher on the agenda. But the research revealed the following problems:

- Business partners get drawn into 'wrong' activities – usually lower-level tasks than they should, given their role (and pay grade).

- A tension arises between responding to corporate and business unit needs (often manifested by business partners 'going native' as they pursue parochial objectives at what the corporate centre regards as the expense of the whole organization).

- Difficulties are apparent in finding staff of the right calibre.

- The failure of those in the role to be strategic (rather than operational in their contribution).

The following practical advice on carrying out the role was given by two strategic business partners in a London-based US investment bank interviewed by Pritchard (2010: 182, 184):

- I think the way you change their [the business clients'] behaviours in the longer term is by getting to be a trusted advisor, and the way to become a trusted advisor is to know your individual, to know your client and to know how to hook the individual.

- If you don't know the little things, they'll [the business leaders] never trust you with the bigger things. . . you survive by doing the little things and doing them right; and then building up that trust and that relationship with them.

Critical evaluation of the business partner concept

Achieving success in the deployment of business partners is hard. Research by Sparrow *et al* (2015: 6) led to the conclusion that the following difficulties need to be overcome to make the concept work:

- problems of capability (upskilling, building business acumen, cultural insight and relational skills);

- problems of expectations (selling the proposition, educating the line about how to use the expertise and building the line capability to actually do it);

- aligning the resources behind the business partner (aligning them to the business, avoiding role overload and providing necessary support);

- regulating the relationships they have so they can be aligned to potential differences between business unit and corporate agendas;

- avoiding role drift back into reactive, operational or residual transactional work;

- managing the boundaries between the business partners and their connections back to work in centres of expertise and service centres.

Holley (2015: 12) noted that:

> Historically a lot of HR work has been about delivering processes to the business, administering payroll, keeping out of tribunals, writing terms and conditions, and so on, so HR has attracted people with the requisite skills and mindset. The HR business partner role is very different. It's about delivering innovative ways of developing organizational and people capability, building on deep data-driven insights into the strategic and commercial direction of the business. This requires a different level of thinking, as the complexity and degree of ambiguity inherent in the role, and in the environment in which organizations are operating, has increased exponentially. In some cases, the issue has been that no one has actually articulated to the newly rebadged business partners how the role is different or the new level it is operating at.

It can be argued that too much has been made of the business partner model. Perhaps it is preferable to regard the role of HR professionals as being part of the business rather than merely being partners. There is a risk of overemphasizing the seemingly glamorous role of business or strategic partner at the expense of the service delivery aspect of the HR practitioner's role. Syrett (2006) noted that whatever strategic aspirations senior HR practitioners have, they will amount to nothing if the function they represent cannot deliver the essential transactional services their internal line clients require. As an HR specialist commented to Caldwell (2004): 'My credibility depends on running an extremely efficient and cost-effective administrative machine... If I don't get that right, and consistently, then you can forget about any big ideas.' Another person interviewed during Caldwell's research referred to personnel people as 'reactive pragmatists', a realistic situation in many organizations.

The danger is that if business partners do focus too much on strategy (without appreciating what that means or how to do it) they will exist in some sort of strategic stratosphere, remote from everyday people management concerns. Perhaps it would be preferable to emphasize the transformational as distinct from the transactional nature of a business manager's role. They are there to make a difference to business performance through applications of HRM such as organization development and talent management.

The problem of making too much of the strategic business partner role has been influenced by the erroneous belief that Ulrich was simply focusing on HR executives as business partners. This has had the unfortunate effect of implying that it was their only worthwhile function. But Ulrich cannot be blamed for this. In 1998 he gave equal emphasis to the need for HR people to be administrative experts, employee champions and change agents.

CASE STUDY

Business partnering at the Automobile Association (AA)

The key competencies required by the AA for its business partners are concerned with commercial decision making, commerciality, influencing people and facilitating change. They have to:

- understand the key factors affecting overall costs and profits;

- understand and interpret financial data;

- understand the connectivity between functional areas of the business;

- understand the impact of actions on cash flow and profitability.

The partnership role of HR professionals

It is not just business partners who need to adopt a partnership approach with line managers. This applies to all HR professionals. Partnership means working with line managers to deal jointly with issues, people problems and, importantly, implementing HR strategies and new HR policies and practices. Traditionally, some HR specialists have tended to lay down the law to their line manager clients: 'This is the policy, this is what you have to do about it, this is how I am going to help you'. In a partnership mode, they will still explain what the policy is and what the responsibilities of the manager are in implementing it, and they will still provide guidance and advice. But in adopting a partnership approach, the HR professional will be focused on understand-ing the particular preoccupations and concerns of individual managers and working alongside them to produce a joint agreement on how to proceed based on that understanding. It will be a matter of agreeing rather than prescribing.

When acting as partners, HR specialists need to demonstrate to line managers that they understand the situation in which the latter operate and the pressures they face. HR people need to be appreciated as colleagues who understand the business and will listen to managers when they make suggestions or express doubts about a new policy. They will discuss possible approaches and even agree modifications to fit particular circumstances, as long as these do not fundamentally affect the policy. They will work alongside line managers when a new policy is being introduced, not as a prescriptive trainer but as, in effect, a coach.

The innovation role

A strategic and therefore proactive approach to HRM will mean that HR specialists will need to innovate – to introduce new processes and procedures they believe will increase organizational effectiveness.

The case for innovation should be established by processes of analysis and diagnosis using an evidence-based management approach to identify the business need and the issues to be addressed. 'Benchmarking' can be used to identify 'best practice' in other organizations. But 'best fit' is more important than 'best practice' – in other words, the innovation should meet the particular needs of the business, which are likely to differ from those of other 'best practice' organizations. It has to be demonstrable that the innovation is appropriate, beneficial, practical in the circumstances and can be implemented without too much difficulty in the shape of opposition from those affected by it or the unjustifiable use of resources – financial and the time of those involved.

The danger, according to Marchington (1995), is that HR people may go in for 'impression management' – aiming to make an impact on senior managers and colleagues through publicizing high-profile innovations. HR specialists who try to draw attention to themselves simply by promoting the latest flavour of the month, irrespective of its relevance or practicality, are falling into the trap that Drucker (1955: 243), anticipating Marchington by 40 years, described as follows: 'The constant worry of all personnel administrators is their inability to prove that they are making a contribution to the enterprise. Their preoccupation is with the search for a "gimmick" which will impress their management colleagues.'

As Marchington points out, the risk is that people believe 'all can be improved by a wave of the magic wand and the slaying of a few evil characters along the way'. This facile assumption means that people can too readily devise elegant solutions that do not solve the problem because of the hazards encountered during implementation – for example, the indifference or even open hostility of line managers. These have to be anticipated and catered for.

The guidelines for HR innovations are:

- Be clear on what has to be achieved and why.
- Ensure that what you do fits the strategy, culture and circumstances of the organization.

- Don't follow fashion – do your own thing as long as it is relevant and fits the organization's needs.
- Keep it simple – over-complexity is a common reason for failure.
- Define the innovation in language and using terms that line managers use.
- Don't rush – it will take longer than you think.
- Don't try to do too much at once – an incremental approach is generally best.
- Assess resource requirements and costs.
- Pay close attention to project planning and management.
- Remember that the success of the innovation rests as much on the effectiveness of the process of implementation (line manager buy-in and skills are crucial) as it does on the quality of the concept, if not more so.
- Focus on change management approaches – communicate, involve and train.

The change agent role

The implementation of strategy means that HR specialists have to act as change agents, facilitating change by providing advice and support on its introduction and management. Caldwell (2001) categorized HR change agents in four dimensions:

1 *Transformational change* – a major change that has a dramatic effect on HR policy and practice across the whole organization.

2 *Incremental change* – gradual adjustments of HR policy and practices which affect single activities or multiple functions.

3 *HR vision* – a set of values and beliefs that affirm the legitimacy of the HR function as a strategic business partner.

4 *HR expertise* – the knowledge and skills that define the unique contribution the HR professional can make to effective people management.

The service delivery role

The role of HR professionals operates at a transformational level when HR strategies, programmes and policies are devised and implemented which further the achievement of business goals and help to meet the needs of employees. But for many HR people, the emphasis is on transactional activities such as recruitment, training, handling day-to-day employment matters, helping to solve people problems and dealing with employment law issues. The latter is one of the most demanding and time-consuming areas in which they give advice and provide services. A 2002 survey by the CIPD found that two-thirds of HR specialists were spending in excess of 20 per cent of their time coping with employment law issues, while a quarter reported that over 40 per cent of their working days were being spent in this way.

For many HR practitioners, service delivery is what they do. The importance of this aspect of their work should not be underestimated by focusing too much on strategic or business partner roles. Line managers tend to judge HR professionals on the quality and efficiency of the services they provide rather than on their strategic capabilities.

HR professionals: role requirements

The role requirements of HR professionals are exacting. They are described below in terms of levels of competency and expected behaviours.

HR competencies

Research conducted by Brockbank *et al* (1999) led to a definition of the key HR competency 'domains' and their components, as set out in Table 6.1.

A competency framework for the strategic partner role in an investment bank as reported by Pritchard (2010) emphasized three key areas: organizational effectiveness, personal impact and business insight. The additional competencies identified included trusted advisor, leading change, critical thinking, financial acumen and strategy formulation.

TABLE 6.1   Key HR specialist competency areas

Competency domains	Components definition
1 Personal credibility	Live the firm's values, maintain relationships founded on trust, act with an 'attitude' (a point of view about how the business can win, backing up opinion with evidence).
2 Ability to manage change	Drive change: ability to diagnose problems, build relationships with clients, articulate a vision, set a leadership agenda, solve problems and implement goals.
3 Ability to manage culture	Act as 'keepers of the culture', identify the culture required to meet the firm's business strategy, frame culture in a way that excites employees, translate desired culture into specific behaviours, encourage executives to behave consistently with the desired culture.
4 Delivery of human resource practices	Expert in the speciality, able to deliver state-of-the-art innovative HR practices in such areas as recruitment, employee development, compensation and communication.
5 Understanding of the business	Strategy, organization, competitors, finance, marketing, sales, operations and IT.

HR behaviours

The CIPD's HR profession map (CIPD, 2013) lists the following behaviours needed by HR professionals to carry out their role:

- *Curious* – Shows an active interest in the internal and external environment and in the continuous development and improvement of self and others at both organization and individual levels. Is open minded with a bias and willingness to learn and enquire.

- *Decisive thinker* – Demonstrates the ability to analyse and understand data and information quickly. Is able to use information, insights and knowledge in a structured way using judgement wisely to identify options and make robust and defendable decisions.

- *Skilled influencer* – Demonstrates the ability to influence across a complex environment, to gain the necessary commitment, consensus and support from a wide range of diverse stakeholders in pursuit of organization benefit.

- *Driven to deliver* – Demonstrates a consistent and strong bias to action, taking accountability for delivery of results both personally and/or with others. Actively plans, prioritizes and monitors performance, holding others accountable for delivery.

- *Collaborative* – Works effectively and inclusively with colleagues, clients, stakeholders, customers, teams and individuals both within and outside of the organization.

- *Personally credible* – Builds a track record of reliable and valued delivery using relevant technical expertise and experience and does so with integrity and in an objective manner.

- *Courage to challenge* – Shows courage and confidence to speak up and challenge others even when confronted with resistance or unfamiliar circumstances

- *Role model* – Consistently leads by example. Acts with integrity, impartiality and independence, applying sound personal judgement in all interactions.

Carrying out the role of the HR professional

How HR professionals carry out their roles depends on the context in which they work (the size and culture of the organization, the types of activities it carries out and the requirements of senior management), their skills and disposition and, importantly, the values they adopt. They will be affected by ambiguity and questions on the status of the profession and what is involved in being a professional. It can be a difficult job to do well and the criteria for success are demanding.

The values of HR

The most important aspect of HR values is the ethical stance HR people take in promoting people management policies and practices that are just, fair and take account of the interests of employees as well as those of the business. The pressure on HR practitioners in the private sector is to promote the interests of the business and thus increase shareholder value. In the public sector, the pressure is to promote the aims of the organization. The problem is that, as observed by Parkes and Davis (2013: 2413): 'HR seems wedded to its allegiance to profitability and distancing itself from any connections with welfare.' They also note that: 'The economic drivers for organizations are important but the danger of relying only on the business case is that ethics and responsibility become optional.'

Ambiguities in the role of HR practitioners

The activities and roles of HR specialists and the demands made upon them as described above appear to be quite clear cut, but Thurley (1981) pointed out that HR practitioners can be specialists in ambiguity. This continues in the age of Ulrich. As Hope-Hailey *et al* (2005: 51) commented: 'Ulrich highlighted that HR professionals must be both strategic and operational, yet the potential role conflict this could engender was not addressed.' Caldwell (2004: 212) reached the following conclusions on the basis of his research:

There is the issue of 'powerlessness' or the marginality of HR practitioners in management decision-making processes, especially at a strategic level. The HR function has an inward-looking tendency to identify professional expertise mainly with administrative concerns over who controls HR activities, rather than questions of HR practices or who has responsibility for implementing HR policy.

The difficulties that HR professionals face in dealing with ambiguity were well described by Guest and King (2004: 421):

> Much management activity is typically messy and ambiguous. This appears to apply more strongly to people management than to most other activities. By implication, the challenge lies not in removing or resolving the ambiguities in the role [of HR professionals] but in learning to live with them. To succeed in this requires skills in influencing, negotiating and learning when to compromise. For those with a high tolerance for ambiguity, the role of HR specialist, with its distinctive opportunity to contribute to the management of people in organizations, offers unique challenges; for those only comfortable if they can resolve the ambiguities, the role may become a form of purgatory.

The status of HR

Over the years, the HR profession has suffered from an inferiority complex. This may arise because the role of HR professionals is ill-defined (they are unsure of where they stand), their status is not fully recognized, or top management and line managers have equivocal views about their value to the organization. Tyson and Fell (1986: 68) remarked that 'the ambiguous character of their work contributes to the problems of convincing others of its value'.

Long ago Drucker (1955: 243) observed that: 'The constant worry of all personnel administrators is their inability to prove that they are making a contribution to the organization.' Skinner (1981: 106) in his *Harvard Business Review* article, 'Big hat no cattle', stated that 'the corporate role of personnel has always been problematic'; and Tyson and Fell (1986: 136) argued that: 'Classical personnel management has not been granted a position in decision-making circles because it has frequently not earned one. It has not been concerned with the totality of the organization but often with issues which have not only been parochial but esoteric to boot.'

Watson (1996) referred to the 'perpetual marginality' of the HR function and Caldwell (2004: 212)

raised the 'issue of "powerlessness" or the marginality of HR practitioners in management decision-making processes'.

Traditionally, the HR practitioner's reaction to this problem has been, in the words of Drucker (1955: 243) to 'search for a "gimmick" that will impress their management colleagues'. This was later called adopting 'the flavour of the month'. HR professionals have now become more sophisticated. They have enthusiastically supported approaches that appeal to management such as engagement policies and talent management. And in the UK, the CIPD spends a lot of time attempting to boost the status of the HR profession by stressing the strategic and business partner role of practitioners.

But research conducted by Guthrie *et al* (2011: 1681) confirmed that: 'HR departments are still often viewed, collectively, as a function that is more bureaucratic than strategic.' They noted previous research, which has shown that 'it is this role – the strategic role – in which line executives believe that HR is particularly deficient' (ibid: 1682). The following perceptive comment was made on this trend by Keegan and Francis (2010: 878):

> Bearing in mind the history of HR practitioners' struggles for acceptance as key organizational players it is hardly surprising that a way of discursively modelling the concept of HR as 'hard' and relating it to others concepts such as 'business driven agendas' and 'strategic management', has become so popular. It offers perhaps a way out of the dualism when they seek to claim a share of strategic decision making while at the same time struggling to attend to the employee-centred and administrative aspects of the role.

They also commented that: 'Exhortations for HR practitioners to pursue strategic roles and downplay their historically embedded administrative and employee championing pose a serious threat to the integrity of HR work and claims to professional expertise' (ibid: 894). And Farndale and Brewster (2005: 35) observed that: 'HR has largely relied on attempting to develop a strategic role to enhance its professional standing.'

What it means to be an HR professional

Professionalism in HR, as in other fields, can be defined generally as the conduct exhibited by people who are providing advice and services that require expertise and who meet defined or generally accepted standards of behaviour. Work done by a professional is usually distinguished by its reference to a framework of fundamental concepts that reflect the skilful application of specialized education, training and experience. It is accompanied by a sense of responsibility and an acceptance of recognized standards. HR professionals who are members of the Chartered Institute of Personnel and Development (CIPD) are required to uphold the standards laid down by that body. More loosely, people can be described as acting 'professionally' when they do their work well and act with integrity.

The CIPD (2015b: 12) advocates the following approach to professionalism:

> Rather than focusing on the activities it delivers, the (HR) profession should build its credibility and trust by showing its capability and courage to challenge accepted practice and offer business leaders a range of critical perspectives on how to create sustainable organizational value through people, underpinned by a body of fundamental and internationally relevant knowledge rather than anecdotal 'best practice.' We propose that a principles-based approach to HR practice can elevate the definition of 'good' from practice to the systems level, while giving freedom to individual people management professionals to apply their professional judgement in designing bespoke 'good' practices in real-life scenarios.

But it was argued by Farndale and Brewster (2005: 35, 46), following a world-wide study of professional HR associations, including the CIPD, that there was:

> a paradox at the heart of HR professionalism: one of the hallmarks of HRM is the attempt to align it with business strategy and to follow the interest of the owners of the business; one of the hallmarks of a profession is having its own standards that override those of the business. Most of the time, of course, these will be complementary, but the professional associations have no mechanisms in place to deal with the situations where they are not... There is no mandatory requirement for specialists to be certified, and national associations do not apply common standards of entry and performance monitoring to members. Indeed, practitioners are not legally required to be members of these professional bodies.

Criteria for success as an HR professional

1 Understand fundamental concepts explaining organizational and individual behaviour and take action accordingly.

2 Develop and apply HR expertise and skills (generalist or specialist as appropriate).

3 Understand the business model of the organization and the context in which it operates and appreciate the key factors that affect organizational performance.

4 Be insight-driven, clearly perceiving issues or problems which need to be tackled in order to improve organizational capability and effectiveness.

5 Adopt an evidence-based approach to innovation – support proposals on HR developments with hard data derived from HR analytics, research, benchmarking and the analysis and evaluation of the organizational context and HR practice.

6 Define and offer HR innovations and practices in language that clients or customers, eg line managers, can understand.

7 Understand the concerns of managers and employees generally by keeping in touch (conversing with them regularly).

8 Respond eagerly and promptly to requests for help or advice.

9 Deliver the deal – generate trust by doing what was promised.

10 Act with integrity in accordance with firm principles relating to veracity, reliability, uprightness and honesty.

The HR role of line managers

HR can initiate new policies and practices but it is line managers that have the main responsibility for implementing them. In other words, HR proposes but the line disposes. As Guest (1991: 159) observed: 'HRM is too important to be left to personnel managers.'

If line managers are not inclined favourably towards what HR wants them to do, they won't do it, or, if compelled to, they will be half-hearted about it. On the basis of their research, Guest and King (2004: 421) noted that 'better HR depended not so much on better procedures but better implementation and ownership of implementation by line managers.'

As pointed out by Purcell *et al* (2003), high levels of organizational performance are not achieved simply by having a range of well-conceived HR policies and practices in place. What makes the difference is how these policies and practices are implemented. That is where the role of line managers in people management is crucial: 'Managers... play a vital role in making involvement happen, in communicating, in being open to allow employee concerns to be raised and discussed, in allowing people space to influence how they do their job, and in coaching, guiding and recognizing performance and providing help for the future' (ibid: 40). Purcell and his colleagues noted that dealing with people is perhaps the aspect of their work in which line managers can exercise the greatest amount of discretion and they can use that discretion by not putting HR's ideas into practice. As they observed, it is line managers who bring HR policies to life.

A further factor affecting the role of line managers is their ability to do the HR tasks assigned to them. People-centred activities such as defining roles (job design), interviewing, reviewing performance, providing feedback, coaching, and identifying learning and development needs all require special skills. Some managers have them; many don't. Performance management systems often fail because too much is expected of line managers by HR. They are required to conduct demanding annual performance reviews which have multiple purposes, but they do not get adequate training or support. They are immersed in HR-led bureaucracy and subject to a barrage of jargon. Performance pay arrangements can easily fail because managers are not given the help and guidance they require. The implementation of policies to enhance engagement levels (as described in Chapter 21) depends largely on line managers.

Hutchinson and Purcell (2003) made the following recommendations on how to improve the quality of the contribution line managers make to people management.

Source review

Improving the quality of line managers as people managers – Hutchinson and Purcell (2003)

- Provide them with time to carry out their people management duties, which are often superseded by other management duties.

- Select them carefully, with much more attention being paid to the behavioural competencies required.

- Support them with strong organizational values concerning leadership and people management.

- Encourage the development of a good working relationship with their own managers.

- Ensure they receive sufficient skills training to enable them to perform their people management activities such as performance management.

To which can be added that better implementation and better ownership by line managers of HR practices is more likely to be achieved if: 1) the practice demonstrably benefits them; 2) they are involved in the development and, importantly, the testing of the practices; 3) the practice is not too complicated, bureaucratic or time-consuming; 4) their responsibilities are defined and communicated clearly; and 5) they are provided with the guidance, support and training required to implement the practice.

Key learning points: The role of HR professionals

HR professionals

HR professionals provide advice, guidance and services on all matters concerning the employment of people. The role can be mainly transactional, dealing with basic HR matters such as recruitment and selection, or largely transformational, operating strategically in order to make significant changes in how the organization functions or how its employees are treated.

The Ulrich model

The most celebrated delivery model was produced by Dave Ulrich. He wrote that: 'HR should not be defined by what it does but by what it delivers – results that enrich the organization's value to customers, investors, and employees'. More specifically, he suggested that HR can deliver in four ways: as a strategic partner, an administrative expert, an employee champion and a change agent. This first model was later modified by Ulrich and Brockbank (2005), who defined five roles as follows:

1 Employee advocate.

2 Human capital.

3 Functional expert.

4 Strategic partner.

5 Leader.

The strategic role

HR professionals have a strategic role when they are operating at a transformational level as HR directors, heads of HR centres of expertise or main HR functions, or strategic business partners.

The HR business partner role

HR business partners work alongside their line management colleagues in order to develop and implement an HR agenda which contributes to achieving the business goals of the organization or function. They share responsibility with their line management colleagues for the success of the enterprise and get involved with them in implementing business strategy and running the business.

The partnership role of HR professionals

It is not just business partners who need to adopt a partnership approach with line managers. This applies to all HR professionals. Partnership means working with line managers to deal jointly with issues, people problems and, importantly, implementing HR strategies and new HR policies and practices.

The innovation role

A strategic and therefore proactive approach to HRM will mean that HR specialists will need to innovate – to introduce new processes and procedures they believe will increase organizational effectiveness.

The change agent role

The implementation of strategy means that HR specialists have to act as change agents, facilitating change by providing advice and support on its introduction and management.

The service delivery role

For many HR people the emphasis is on transactional activities such as recruitment, training, handling day-to-day employment matters, helping to solve people problems and dealing with employment law issues.

Carrying out the role of the HR professional

How HR professionals carry out their roles depends on the context in which they work (the size and culture of the organization, the types of activities it carries out and the requirements of senior management), their skills and disposition and, importantly, the values they adopt. They will be affected by ambiguity and questions on the status of the profession and what is involved in being a professional. It can be a difficult job to do well and the criteria for success are demanding.

What it means to be an HR professional

Professionalism in HR, as in other fields, can be defined generally as the conduct exhibited by people who are providing advice and services that require expertise and who meet defined or generally accepted standards of behaviour.

HR role of line managers

HR can initiate new policies and practices but it is line managers that have the main responsibility for implementing them.

References

Brockbank, W, Ulrich, D and Beatty, D (1999) HR professional development: creating the future creators at the University of Michigan Business School, *Human Resource Management*, 38, Summer, pp 111–17

Burroughs, A (2015) The future is 'centres of expertise', in CIPD *Changing HR Operating Models*, pp 8–11 [online] http://www.cipd.co.uk/binaries/changing-operating-models.pdf [accessed 17 October 2015]

Caldwell, R (2001) Champions, adapters, consultants and synergists: the new change agents in HRM, *Human Resource Management Journal*, 11 (3), pp 39–52

Caldwell, R (2004) Rhetoric, facts and self-fulfilling prophesies: exploring practitioners' perceptions of progress in implementing HRM, *Industrial Relations Journal*, 35 (3), pp 196–215

Chartered Institute of Personnel and Development (2002) *Employment Law: Survey report*. London, CIPD

Chartered Institute of Personnel and Development (2013) *HR Profession Map*, http://www.cipd.co.uk/hr-profession-map-download.aspx [accessed 25 January 2013]

Chartered Institute of Personnel and Development (2015a) Business partnering [online] http://www.cipd.co.uk/hr-resources/factsheets/hr-business-partnering.aspx [accessed 17 October 2015]

Chartered Institute of Personnel and Development (2015b) *From best to good practice HR: developing principles for the profession*, [online] http://çhttp://www.cipd.co.uk/hr-resources/research/best-good-practice-hr-developing-principles-profession.aspx [accessed 28 December 2015]

Drucker, P (1955) *The Practice of Management*, London, Heinemann

Farndale, E and Brewster, C (2005) In search of legitimacy: personnel management associations worldwide, *Human Resource Management Journal*, 15 (3), pp 33–48

Francis, H and Keegan, A (2006) The changing face of HRM: in search of balance, *Human Resource Management Journal*, 16 (3), pp 231–49

Guest, D E (1991) Personnel management: the end of orthodoxy, *British Journal of Industrial Relations*, 29 (2), pp 149–76

Guest, D E and King, Z (2004) Power, innovation and problem-solving: the personnel managers' three steps to heaven? *Journal of Management Studies*, 41 (3), pp 401–23

Guthrie, J P, Flood, P C, Liu, W, MacCurtain, S and Armstrong, C (2011) Big hat no cattle? The relationship between the use of high-performance work systems and managerial perceptions of HR departments, *The International Journal of Human Resource Management*, 22 (8), pp 1672–85

Hardman, P and Mookherjee, D (2015) How to make a restructuring go smoothly, *People Management*, November, p 58

Hirsh, W (2008) What do people want from you? *People Management*, 18 September, pp 23–26

Holley, N (2015) 'You can't put in what God left out.' Not everyone can be a strategic HR business partner, in CIPD, *Changing HR Operating Models*, pp 12–14 [online] http://www.cipd.co.uk/binaries/changing-operating-models.pdf [accessed 16 October 2015]

Hope-Hailey, V, Farndale, E and Truss, C (2005) The HR department's role in organizational performance, *Human Resource Management Journal*, 15 (3), pp 49–66

Hutchinson, S and Purcell, J (2003) *Bringing Policies to Life: The vital role of front line managers in people management*, London, CIPD

Keegan, A and Francis, H (2010) Practitioner talk: the changing textscape of HRM and emergence of HR business partnership, *The International Journal of Human Resource Management*, 21 (6), pp 873–98

Marchington, M (1995) Fairy tales and magic wands: new employment practices in perspective, *Employee Relations*, Spring, pp 51–66

Parkes, C and Davis, A J (2013) Ethics and social responsibility – do HR professionals have 'the courage to challenge' or are they set to be permanent 'bystanders'? *International Journal of Human Resource Management*, 23 (12), pp 2411–34

Pritchard, K (2010) Becoming an HR strategic partner: tales of transition, *Human Resource Management Journal*, 20 (2), pp 175–88

Purcell, J, Kinnie, K, Hutchinson, R, Rayton, B and Swart, J (2003) *Understanding the People and Performance Link: Unlocking the black box*, London, CIPD

Reilly, P (2015) HR business partners: yes please or no thanks? [online] http://www.employment-studies.co.uk/system/files/resources/files/mp110.pdf [accessed 28 December 2015]

Skinner, W (1981) Big hat no cattle: managing human resources, *Harvard Business Review*, September–October, pp 106–14

Sparrow, P, Hesketh, A, Hird, Marsh, C and Balain, S (2010) Using business model change to tie HR into strategy: reversing the arrow, in (eds) P Sparrow, A Hesketh, M Hird, and C Cooper, *Leading HR*, Basingstoke, Palgrave Macmillan, pp 68–89

Sparrow, P, Hird, M and Cooper, C (2015) *Do we need HR?* Basingstoke, Palgrave Macmillan

Syrett, M (2006) *Four Reflections on Developing a Human Capital Measurement Capability: What's the future for human capital?* London, CIPD

Thurley, K (1981) Personnel management: a case for urgent treatment, *Personnel Management*, August, pp 24–29

Tyson, S and Fell, A (1986) *Evaluating the Personnel Function*, London, Hutchinson

Ulrich, D (1998) A new mandate for human resources, *Harvard Business Review*, January–February, pp 124–34

Ulrich, D and Beatty, D (2001). From partners to players: extending the HR playing field, *Human Resource Management*, **40** (4), pp 293–307

Ulrich, D and Brockbank, W (2005) *The HR Value Proposition*, Cambridge, MA, Harvard Press

Watson, T (1996) *Management, Organisation and Employment Strategy*, London, Routledge

Wright, P M, Snell, S A and Jacobsen, H (2004) Current approaches to HR strategies: inside-out versus outside-in, *Human Resource Planning*, **27** (4), pp 36–46

07
HRM and performance

LEARNING OUTCOMES

On completing this chapter you should be able to define these key concepts. You should also understand:

- What impact HRM can make on performance
- How HRM makes that impact
- The nature of a high-performance culture

- How a high-performance work system functions
- The role of performance management
- How HR can contribute

Introduction

All organizations are under an obligation to their stakeholders to perform well. To do this they depend on the quality, dedication, enthusiasm, expertise and skill of the people working in them at every level. The message of the resource-based view is that HRM delivers added value and helps to achieve sustainable competitive advantage through the stra-

tegic development of the organization's rare, hard-to-imitate and hard-to-substitute human resources. As Guest (1997: 269) argued: 'The distinctive feature of HRM is its assumption that improved performance is achieved through the people in the organization.' If, therefore, appropriate HR policies and practices are introduced, it can also be assumed that HRM will impact on firm performance.

The chapter begins with a review of the evidence that HRM makes an impact on performance and of the problems met by researchers in establishing what the link is and how it works. It continues with a description of the concept of a high-performance culture and how it can be achieved through a high-performance work system and performance management.

The impact of HR

Much research has been carried out showing that good HRM practice and firm performance are correlated; notable examples in the UK are Guest *et al* (2000a), Patterson *et al* (1997), Purcell *et al* (2003), Thompson (2002), West *et al* (2002) and Birdi *et al*, summarized in Table 7.1.

The link between HRM and performance

Storey *et al* (2009: 4) observed that: 'The premise is that, in some shape or form, HR policies have an effect on HR practices and these in turn influence staff attitudes and behaviours which will, in turn again, impact on service offerings and customer perceptions of value.' The assumption is that good HRM practices will enhance performance. This is supported by the notion of 'best practice HRM', which, as noted in Chapter 3, is illustrated by lists such as Pfeffer's (1998).

Bowen and Ostroff (2004) argued that the link between HRM and performance is likely to be greater where what they describe as a 'strong' HR system is in place. Core characteristics of their 'strong' system are high levels of distinctiveness, consistency and consensus. Where these are present there will be an organizational climate that supports HR implementation. But they also made the obvious suggestion that it is not enough to have good practices if they are not properly implemented. As Guest (2011: 6) commented: 'What this does is switch the focus to line management.' Nishii *et al* (2008) argued that it is not just the presence of practices that is important but 'perceptions about the intentions behind the practices'.

An extensive research project conducted by Guest and Conway (2011) led to the finding that consensus on HR effectiveness did not support Bowen and Ostroff's (2004) proposition that a strong HR system would have a significant association with outcomes. Guest and Conway commented

that their study revealed very low levels of agreement about HR effectiveness. They concluded that: 'There are three elements in a logical model of HR effectiveness. HR practices must be present, they must be effective and they must be effectively implemented' (ibid: 1700).

Uncertainties about the link between HRM and performance

As noted earlier, much research has demonstrated an association between HRM and performance. But Guest *et al* (2000b) observed that it left uncertainties about cause and effect. Ulrich (1997: 304) pointed out that: 'HR practices seem to matter; logic says it is so; survey findings confirm it. Direct relationships between performance and attention to HR practices are often fuzzy, however, and vary according to the population sampled and the measures used.' Guest (2011: 11) summed up his article on HRM and performance with the comment that: 'After hundreds of research studies we are still in no position to assert with any confidence that good HRM has an impact on organization performance.'

There are two issues that affect the determination of a link between HRM and firm performance: 'causal ambiguity' and 'contingency factors'. These contribute to what is known as the 'black box' phenomenon.

Causal ambiguity

The term causal ambiguity refers to the numerous, subtle and often hidden interconnections between the factors influencing cause and effect. Boselie *et al* (2005: 75) referred to the causal distance between an HRM input and an output such as financial performance: 'Put simply, so many variables and events, both internal and external, affect organizations that this direct linkage strains credibility.'

A basic reason for ambiguity is multiple causation, which exists when there is more than one possible cause for an effect. HRM may have caused an improvement in performance but there may be many other economic or business factors that did so, and it could be difficult to unravel them. Another factor is the possibility of reversed causality (a situation where A might have caused B but B might well have caused A). As Purcell *et al* (2003: 2) expressed it: 'Although it is nice to believe that more HR practices leads to higher economic return, it is just as possible that it is successful firms that can afford more extensive (and expensive) HRM practices.'

TABLE 7.1   Research on the link between HRM and firm performance

Researcher(s)	Methodology	Outcomes
Patterson *et al* (1997)	The research examined the link between business performance and organization culture and the use of a number of HR practices.	HR practices explained significant variations in profitability and productivity (19% and 18% respectively). Two HR practices were particularly significant: 1) the acquisition and development of employee skills, and 2) job design including flexibility, responsibility and variety.
Guest *et al* (2000a)	An analysis of the 1998 WERS survey which sampled some 2,000 workplaces and obtained the views of about 28,000 employees.	A strong association exists between HRM and both employee attitudes and workplace performance.
Thompson (2002)	A study of the impact of high-performance work practices such as teamworking, appraisal, job rotation, broad-banded grade structures and sharing of business information in UK aerospace establishments.	The number of HR practices and the proportion of the workforce covered appeared to be the key differentiating factor between more and less successful firms.
West *et al* (2002)	Research conducted in 61 UK hospitals obtaining information on HR strategy, policy and procedures from chief executives and HR directors and mortality rates.	An association between certain HR practices and lower mortality rates was identified. As noted by West: 'If you have HR practices that focus on effort and skill; develop people's skills; encourage cooperation, collaboration, innovation and synergy in teams for most, if not all employees, the whole system functions and performs better.'
Purcell *et al* (2003)	A University of Bath longitudinal study of 12 companies to establish how people management impacts on organizational performance.	The most successful companies had 'the big idea.' They had a clear vision and a set of integrated values. They were concerned with sustaining performance and flexibility. Clear evidence existed between positive attitudes towards HR policies and practices, levels of satisfaction, motivation and commitment, and operational performance. Policy and practice implementation (not the number of HR practices adopted) is the vital ingredient in linking people management to business performance and this is primarily the task of line managers.
Birdi *et al* (2008)	A longitudinal research study by the Institute of Work Psychology, University of Sheffield covering 308 companies over 22 years designed to establish the impact of various HRM and operational practices on company productivity.	It was found that the impact of empowerment (job enrichment) was to produce a gain of nearly 7 per cent of value added per employee, while the gain for extensive training was nearly 6 per cent. But teamwork did not make a significant impact, neither did total quality management or just-in-time.

Contingency factors

Causation will additionally be affected by the organization's context, ie the internal and external environmental factors that influence what happens within the organization.

The black box phenomenon

Causal ambiguity also stems from the black box phenomenon, as illustrated in Figure 7.1. This is the situation in which, while it may be possible to observe HRM inputs in the form of HR practices and to measure firm performance outputs, it may be difficult to ascertain, through research, what happened in between – what the HRM outcomes were that converted the input of HR practices into firm performance outputs. Alvesson (2009: 56) suggested that: 'Research does not proceed beyond attempts to find an empirical association between HR practices and organizational performance. The phenomena are in a black box, only input and output are registered and what is happening remains clouded in the dark.'

Explanations of how HRM makes an impact

Guest (1997: 268) stated that: 'The assumption is that "appropriate" HRM practices tap the motivation and commitment of employees.' He explained how expectancy theory might help to explain the HR/performance link as follows:

> The expectancy theory of motivation provides one possible basis for developing a more coherent rationale about the link between HRM practices and performance. Although expectancy theory is concerned primarily with motivation, it is also a theory about the link between motivation and performance. Specifically, it proposes that high performance, at the individual level, depends on

high motivation plus possession of the necessary skills and abilities and an appropriate role and understanding of that role. It is a short step to specify the HRM practices that encourage high skills and abilities, for example careful selection and high investment in training; high motivation, for example employee involvement and possibly performance-related pay; and an appropriate role structure and role perception, for example job design and extensive communication and feedback.

Following this contribution from Guest, any explanation of the impact of HRM on organizational performance is likely to be based on three propositions: 1) that HR practices can make a direct impact on employee characteristics such as engagement, commitment, motivation and skill; 2) if employees have these characteristics it is probable that organizational performance in terms of financial results, productivity, quality and the delivery of high levels of customer service will improve; and 3) if such aspects of organizational performance improve, the financial results achieved by the organization will improve. This can be described as the HR value chain.

The propositions highlight the existence of an intermediate factor between HRM and financial performance. This factor consists of the HRM outcomes in the shape of employee characteristics affected by HR practices. Therefore, HRM does not make a direct impact. A model of the impact of HRM, taking into account the considerations of reverse causation and contingency effects mentioned earlier, is shown in Figure 7.2.

But high performance is not just about HR practices. The case-based research by Purcell *et al* (2003) showed that the key to activating what they called the 'people-performance' link lies not only in well-crafted 'bundles' of HR practices, but in their conjunction with a powerful and cohering organizational vision (or 'big idea') and corporate leadership, together with front-line leadership's action and use of its discretionary power.

FIGURE 7.1   The black box phenomenon

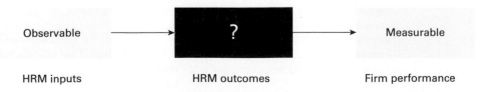

FIGURE 7.2   Impact of HRM on organizational performance (based on Paauwe, 2004)

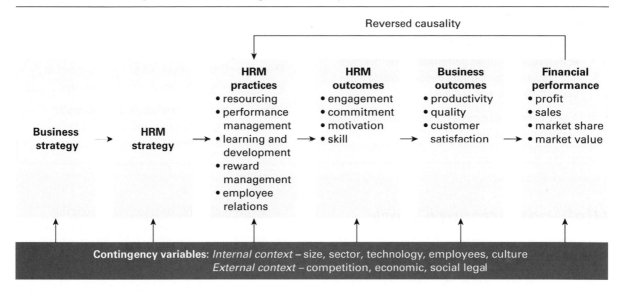

Developing a high-performance culture

Organizations achieve sustained high performance through the systems of work they adopt, but these systems are managed and operated by people. Ultimately, therefore, high-performance working is about improving performance through people.

This can be done through the development and implementation of a high-performance culture involving high-performance work systems in which performance management plays an important part.

High-performance cultures are ones in which the achievement of high levels of performance is a way of life. The characteristics of such cultures are set out below.

Characteristics of a high-performance culture

- Management defines what it requires in the shape of performance improvements, sets goals for success and monitors performance to ensure that the goals are achieved.

- Alternative work practices are adopted such as job redesign, autonomous work teams, improvement groups, team briefing and flexible working.

- People know what is expected of them – they understand their goals and accountabilities.

- People feel that their job is worth doing, and there is a strong fit between the job and their capabilities.

- People are empowered to maximize their contribution.

- There is strong leadership from the top that engenders a shared belief in the importance of continuing improvement.

- There is a focus on promoting positive attitudes that result in an engaged, committed and motivated workforce.

- Performance management processes are aligned to business goals to ensure that people are engaged in achieving agreed objectives and standards.

- Capacities of people are developed through learning at all levels to support performance improvement and they are provided with opportunities to make full use of their skills and abilities.

- A pool of talent ensures a continuous supply of high performers in key roles.

- People are valued and rewarded according to their contribution.

- People are involved in developing high-performance practices.

- There is a climate of trust and teamwork, aimed at delivering a distinctive service to the customer.

- A clear line of sight exists between the strategic aims of the organization and those of its departments and its staff at all levels.

High-performance work systems

High-performance work systems (HPWS) are bundles of HR practices that facilitate employee involvement, skill enhancement and motivation. An HPWS was described by Becker and Huselid (1998: 55) as: 'An internally consistent and coherent HRM system that is focused on solving operational problems and implementing the firm's competitive strategy'. The approach used in an HPWS is sometimes referred to as 'high-performance working'.

Performance cultures are created by high-performance work systems that embody ways of thinking about performance in organizations and how it can be improved. They are concerned with developing and implementing bundles of complementary practices that, as an integrated whole, will make a much more powerful impact on performance than if they were dealt with as separate entities. Appelbaum *et al* (2000) stated that they facilitate employee involvement, skill enhancement and motivation.

Features of an HPWS

There is no generally accepted definition of an HPWS and there is no standard list of the features or components of such a system. In spite of this problem of definition, an attempt to describe the basic components of an HPWS was made by Shih *et al* (2005) as follows:

- *Job infrastructure* – workplace arrangements that equip workers with the proper abilities

to do their jobs, provide them with the means to do their jobs, and give them the motivation to do their jobs. These practices must be combined to produce their proper effects.

- *Training programmes to enhance employee skills* – investment in increasing employee skills, knowledge and ability.

- *Information sharing and worker involvement mechanisms* – to understand the available alternatives and make correct decisions.

- *Reward and promotion opportunities that provide motivation* – to encourage skilled employees to engage in effective discretionary decision making in a variety of environmental contingencies.

Many descriptions of high-performance systems include lists of desirable features and therefore embody the notion of 'best practice'. However, Gephart (1995) noted that research has not clearly identified any single set of high-performance practices. Becker *et al* (1997) pointed out that high-performance work systems were highly idiosyncratic and had to fit the organization's individual circumstances. The lists that have been compiled vary considerably, as is shown in the selection set out in Table 7.2.

Examples

The examples in Table 7.3 of firms that adopt high-performance working policies and practices illustrate the variety and generalized nature of approaches.

TABLE 7.2 Components of an HPWS

US Department of Labor (1993)	Appelbaum *et al* (2000)	Sung and Ashton (2005)	Thompson and Heron (2005)
• Careful and extensive systems for recruitment, selection and training. • Formal systems for sharing information with employees. • Clear job design. • High-level participation processes. • Monitoring of attitudes. • Performance appraisals. • Properly functioning grievance procedures. • Promotion and compensation schemes that provide for the recognition and reward of high-performing employees.	• Work is organized to permit front-line workers to participate in decisions that alter organizational routines. • Workers require more skills to do their jobs successfully, and many of these skills are firm-specific. • Workers experience greater autonomy over their job tasks and methods of work. • Incentive pay motivates workers to extend extra effort on developing skills. • Employment security provides front-line workers with a long-term stake in the company and a reason to invest in its future.	• High-involvement work practices – eg self-directed teams, quality circles, and sharing/access to company information. • Human resource practices – eg sophisticated recruitment processes, performance appraisals, work redesign and mentoring. • Reward and commitment practices – eg various financial rewards, family-friendly policies, job rotation and flexi hours.	• Information sharing. • Sophisticated recruitment. • Formal induction programme. • Five or more days of off-the-job training in the last year. • Semi or totally autonomous work teams; continuous improvement teams; problem-solving groups. • Interpersonal skill development. • Performance feedback. • Involvement – works council, suggestion scheme, opinion survey. • Team-based rewards, employee share ownership scheme, profit-sharing scheme.

TABLE 7.3   Examples of high-performance working ingredients

Organization	High-performance working ingredients
Halo Foods	A strategy that maintains competitiveness by increasing added value through the efforts and enhanced capability of all staff.
	The integration of technical advance with people development.
	Continuing reliance on teamworking and effective leadership, with innovation and self- and team-management skills.
Land Registry	Organizational changes to streamline processes, raise skill levels and release talents.
	Managers who could see that the problems were as much cultural as organizational.
	Recruitment of people whose attitudes and aptitudes match the needs of high-performance work practices.
Meritor Heavy Vehicle Braking Systems	Skill enhancement, particularly of management and self-management skills using competence frameworks.
	Teamworking skills and experience used on improvement projects.
	Linking learning, involvement and performance management.
Orangebox	A strategy that relies on constant reinvention of operational capability.
	Engagement and development of existing talent and initiative in productivity improvement.
	Increasing use of cross-departmental projects to tackle wider opportunities.
Perkinelmer	A vision and values worked through by managers and supervisors.
	Engagement of everyone in the organization and establishment of a continuous improvement culture.
	Learning as a basis for change.
United Welsh Housing Association	Linking of better employment relations with better performance.
	Using staff experience to improve customer service.
	Focusing management development on the cascading of a partnership culture.

Critical evaluation of the high-performance work system approach

Research conducted by Ramsay *et al* (2000) aimed to explore linkages from HPWS practices to employee outcomes, and via these to organizational performance. They referred to the existence of the 'black box', meaning that while the introduction of an HPWS may be associated with improved performance, no researchers have yet established how this happens. They commented that 'the widely held view that positive performance outcomes from HPWS flow via positive employee outcomes has been shown to be highly questionable' (ibid: 521).

Godard (2001) concluded, following his research in Canada, that the actual effects of high-performance work systems can vary considerably and many have a limited lifespan. Following further research, he commented in 2004 that:

> The full adoption of this (high-performance) paradigm may not yield outcomes that are appreciably more positive than those yielded by practices that have long been associated with good management, including professional personnel practices (eg job ladders, employment security, grievance systems, formal training, above-market pay), group work organization, information sharing and accommodative union relations policies... There may be positive effects in some workplaces. However, these effects may be inherently more limited than assumed and, in a great many workplaces, may not be sufficient to justify full adoption.

But research conducted by Sung and Ashton (2005), Combs *et al* (2006) and Ericksen (2007) indicated that an HPWS can significantly improve performance. Even so, it is still possible to have reservations about causality and there seems to be no agreement on what constitutes an HPWS except for variable lists of 'best practices' – a dubious concept. As Godard (2004) commented, these lists are no more than bundles of long-accepted good personnel practices. Perhaps the virtue of the HPWS model is simply that it makes people think about what can be done to improve performance and how the various approaches can be linked together in a cohesive action programme.

Performance management

Performance management can contribute to the development of a high-performance culture in an organization by delivering the message that high performance is important. The management of organizational performance is the continuing responsibility of top management who, with the help and advice of HR, plan, organize, monitor and control activities and provide leadership to achieve strategic objectives and satisfy the needs and requirements of stakeholders. Individual and team performance management systems play an important part, but they function within the context of what is done to manage organizational performance and to develop effective work systems.

The strategic approach adopted by Johnson & Johnson was described by Wortzel-Hoffman and Boltizar (2007) as follows:

> As we embarked on developing an integrated performance and development process into the organization, we knew that driving change and an enhanced process requires a cultural shift within an organization. The best performance management becomes a continuous process and is not a one-time event; it takes time and effort and a dedication to developing people. We also knew that from a business standpoint it was critical to build and develop the talent pipeline of the organization to meet the aggressive business goals and dynamically changing marketplace.

Performance management at organizational, team and individual levels defines what high performance is and how managers and their teams should achieve it. It explains how performance should be measured and the steps that should be taken to monitor results in comparison with expectations. The means of achieving high performance are provided by defining the performance expectations implicit in the psychological contract, creating high levels of engagement, motivating people and enhancing skills and competencies through feedback, coaching and personal development planning. Performance management systems are described more fully in Chapters 41 and 42.

The contribution of HR

HR contributes to enhancing organizational performance by providing insights on the performance issues affecting the organization and its employees. This means identifying the reasons for the issues, exploring their implications for business and people management and conveying these messages to management. The aim is to find new ways of meeting performance challenges.

HR can advise management on the development of a high-performance strategy supported by performance and reward initiatives. Additionally, HR can review policies and practices such as those concerned with organizational development, engagement, resourcing, learning and development, and employee relations. Decisions can then be made to enhance existing policies and practices or introduce new ones. Importantly, consideration needs to be given to how integration of these policies and practices can be achieved by linking them together in a 'bundle' so that they are mutually supportive.

HR has then to prepare a business case for any developments or innovations and persuade management to accept it. Line managers and employees should be involved in the development programme and a communications strategy should be created to inform people about what is going on and how it will affect them.

HR will also be involved in producing and project managing an implementation programme and this will involve facilitating change. As necessary, learning and development activities and events will be conducted to ensure that line managers and employees have the skills required.

Key learning points: HRM and performance

The impact of HRM

Much research has been carried out showing that good HRM practice and firm performance are correlated; notable examples in the UK are Guest *et al* (2000a), Patterson *et al* (1997), Purcell *et al* (2003), Thompson (2002) and West *et al* (2002).

How HRM makes an impact

Storey *et al* (2009: 4) observed that: 'The premise is that, in some shape or form, HR policies have an effect on HR practices and these in turn influence staff attitudes and behaviours which will, in turn again, impact on service offerings and customer perceptions of value.'

Explanations of how HRM makes an impact

Guest (1997: 268) stated that: 'The assumption is that "appropriate" HRM practices tap the motivation and commitment of employees.'

An explanation of the impact of HRM is based on three propositions: 1) that HR practices can make a direct impact on employee characteristics such as engagement, commitment, motivation and skill; 2) if employees have these characteristics it is probable that organizational performance in terms of productivity, quality and the delivery of high levels of customer service will improve; and 3) if such aspects of organizational performance improve, the financial results achieved by the organization will improve.

Developing a high-performance culture

Organizations achieve sustained high performance through the systems of work they adopt, but these systems are managed and operated by people. Ultimately, high-performance working is about improving performance through people. This can be done through the development and implementation of a high-performance culture involving HPWS in which performance management plays an important part.

High-performance work systems

HPWS are bundles of HR practices that facilitate employee involvement, skill enhancement and motivation. HPWS provide the means for creating a performance culture.

Performance management

Performance management can contribute to the development of a high-performance culture by delivering the message in an organization that high performance is important.

The contribution of HR

HR can contribute to enhancing organizational performance by providing insight on the performance issues affecting the organization and its employees.

References

Alvesson, M (2009) Critical perspectives on strategic HRM, in (eds) J Storey, P M Wright and D Ulrich, *The Routledge Companion to Strategic Human Resource Management*, Abingdon, Routledge, pp 53–68

Appelbaum, E, Bailey, T, Berg, P and Kalleberg, A L (2000) *Manufacturing Advantage: Why high-performance work systems pay off*, Ithaca, NY, ILR Press

Becker, B E and Huselid, M A (1998) High performance work systems and firm performance: a synthesis of research and managerial implications, *Research on Personnel and Human Resource Management*, 16, pp 53–101

Becker, B E, Huselid, M A, Pickus, P S and Spratt, M F (1997) HR as a source of shareholder value: research and recommendations, *Human Resource Management*, Spring, 36 (1), pp 39–47

Birdi, K, Clegg, C, Patterson, M, Robinson, A, Stride, C B, Wall, T D and Wood, S J (2008) The impact of human resource and operational management practices on company productivity: a longitudinal study, *Personnel Psychology*, 61 (3), pp 467–501

Boselie, P, Dietz, G and Boon, C (2005) Commonalities and contradictions in HRM and performance research, *Human Resource Management Journal*, 15 (3), pp 67–94

Bowen, D and Ostroff, C (2004) Understanding HRM – firm performance linkages: the role of the 'strength' of the HRM system, *Academy of Management Review*, 29 (2), pp 203–21

Combs, J, Liu, Y, Hall, A and Ketchen, D (2006) How much do high-performance work practices matter? A meta-analysis of their effects on organizational performance, *Personnel Psychology*, 59 (3), pp 501–28

Ericksen, J (2007) High performance work systems: dynamic workforce alignment and firm performance, *Academy of Management Proceedings*, pp 1–6

Gephart, M A (1995) The road to high performance: steps to create a high performance workplace, *Training and Development*, June, p 29

Godard, J (2001) Beyond the high performance paradigm? An analysis of variation in Canadian managerial perceptions of reform programme effectiveness, *British Journal of Industrial Relations*, 39 (1), pp 25–52

Godard, J (2004) A critical assessment of the high performance paradigm, *British Journal of Industrial Relations*, 42 (2), pp 349–78

Guest, D E (1997) Human resource management and performance; a review of the research agenda, *The International Journal of Human Resource Management*, 8 (3), pp 263–76

Guest, D E (2011) Human resource management and performance: still searching for some answers, *Human Resource Management Journal*, 21 (1), pp 3–13

Guest, D E and Conway, N (2011) The impact of HR practices, HR effectiveness and a 'strong HR system' on organizational outcomes: a stakeholder perspective, *The International Journal of Human Resource Management*, 22 (8), pp 1686–702

Guest, D E, Michie, J, Sheehan, M and Conway, N (2000a) *Employee Relations, HRM and Business Performance: An analysis of the 1998 Workplace Employee Relations Survey*, London, CIPD

Guest, D E, Michie, J, Sheehan, M, Conway, N and Metochi, M (2000b) *Effective People Management: Initial findings of Future of Work survey*, London, CIPD

Nishii, L, Lepak, D and Schneider, B (2008) Employee attributions of the 'why' of HR practices: their effects on employee attitudes and behaviours, and customer satisfaction, *Personnel Psychology*, 61 (3), pp 503–45

Paauwe, J (2004) *HRM and Performance: Achieving long-term viability*, Oxford, Oxford University Press

Patterson, M G, West, M A, Lawthom, R and Nickell, S (1997) *Impact of People Management Practices on Performance*, London, CIPD

Pfeffer, J (1998) *The Human Equation*, Boston, MA, Harvard Business School Press

Purcell, J, Kinnie, K, Hutchinson, R, Rayton, B and Swart, J (2003) *Understanding the People and Performance Link: Unlocking the black box*, London, CIPD

Ramsay, H, Scholarios, D and Harley, B (2000) Employees and high-performance work systems: testing inside the black box, *British Journal of Industrial Relations*, 38 (4), pp 501–31

Shih, H-A, Chiang, Y-H and Hsu, C-C (2005) Can high performance work systems really lead to better performance? Academy of Management Conference Paper, pp 1–6

Storey, J, Wright, P M and Ulrich, D (2009) Introduction, in (eds) J Storey, P M Wright and D Ulrich, *The Routledge Companion to Strategic Human Resource Management*, Abingdon, Routledge, pp 3–13

Sung, J and Ashton, D (2005) *High Performance Work Practices: Linking strategy and skills to performance outcomes*, DTI in association with CIPD [online] http://www.cipd.co.uk/subjects/corpstrtgy/

Thompson, M (2002) *High Performance Work Organization in UK Aerospace*, London, The Society of British Aerospace Companies

Thompson, M and Heron, P (2005) Management capability and high-performance work organization, *International Journal of Human Resource Management*, **16** (6), pp 1029–48

Ulrich, D (1997) *Human Resource Champions*, Boston, MA, Harvard Business School Press

US Department of Labor (1993) *High Performance Work Practices and Work Performance*, Washington, DC, US Government Printing Office

West, M A, Borrill, C S, Dawson, C, Scully, J, Carter, M, Anclay, S, Patterson, M and Waring, J (2002) The link between the management of employees and patient mortality in acute hospitals, *International Journal of Human Resource Management*, **13** (8), pp 1299–310

Wortzel-Hoffman, N and Boltizar, S (2007) Performance and development planning: a culture shift perspective, *Organization Development Journal*, **25** (2), pp 195–200

PART III

Human resource management processes

PART III CONTENTS

Introduction

The HR processes covered in this part are those which deal with aspects of HRM that affect how it operates generally, such as HR strategies and policies, rather than the practices such as employee resourcing and learning and development that are concerned with particular HR activities.

08
HR strategies

KEY CONCEPTS AND TERMS

High-commitment management   High-performance management

High-involvement management   Strategy

LEARNING OUTCOMES

On completing this chapter you should be able to define these key concepts. You should also know about:

- The nature of HR strategies
- Types of HR strategies
- Criteria for an effective HR strategy
- Developing and implementing HR strategies

Introduction

HR strategies specify what the organization is proposing to do about people management generally or in particular areas of HRM. They may be defined formally as part of a strategic human resource management process, which leads to the development of overall or specific HR strategies for implementation by HR *and*, vitally, line managers. But it should be noted that an organization which has developed an HR strategy will not be practising strategic human resource management unless that HR strategy has relevance to the organization's success. Wright and McMahan (1999: 52) stated that HRM can only be considered to be strategic if 'it enables an organization to achieve its goals'.

HR strategies are governed or at least influenced by the overall approach adopted to strategic HRM. They could be regarded as the manifestation of SHRM in action. However, HR strategies can come into existence through an emergent, evolutionary and possibly unarticulated process influenced by the business strategy as it develops and changes in the internal and external environment. Pettigrew and Whipp (1991: 30) emphasized that strategy '... far from being a straightforward, rational phenomenon, is in fact interpreted by managers according to their own frame of reference, their particular motivations and information.' But there are still strong arguments for a systematic approach to identifying strategic directions, which can provide a framework for decision making, and action.

What are HR strategies?

HR strategies set out what the organization intends to do about its human resource management policies and practices and how they should be integrated with the business strategy and each other. Tyson and Witcher (1994: 21) defined HR strategies as 'the intentions and plans for using human resources to achieve business objectives'. HRM strategies were described by Dyer and Reeves (1995: 656) as 'internally consistent bundles of human resource practices', and in the words of Boxall (1996: 61) they provide 'a framework of critical ends and means'. Richardson and Thompson (1999: 3) suggested that: 'A strategy, whether it is an HR strategy or any other kind of management strategy must have two key elements: there must be strategic objectives (ie things the strategy is supposed to achieve), and there must be a plan of action (ie the means by which it is proposed that the objectives will be met).' HR strategy sets out aspirations, which have to be expressed as intentions, which then have to be converted into actions. Purcell (2001: 72) made the point that: 'Strategy in HR, like in other areas, is about continuity and change, about appropriateness in the circumstances, but anticipating when the circumstances change. It is about taking strategic decisions.'

HR strategies may set out intentions and provide a sense of purpose and direction, but they are not just long-term plans. They can be immediately relevant. It is necessary to bear in mind the dictum of Fombrun *et al* (1984) that businesses and managers should perform well in the present to succeed in the future.

HR strategies should be distinguished from HR policies. Strategies are dynamic. They provide a sense of direction and answer the question, 'How are we going to get from here to there?' Policies are more about the here and now. They define 'the way things are done around here'. Of course they evolve but this may not be a result of a strategic choice. It is when a deliberate decision is made to change policies that a strategy for achieving this change has to be formulated.

Perhaps the main argument for articulating HR strategies is that unless you know where you are going, you will not know how to get there or when you have arrived.

Because all organizations are different, all HR strategies are different. There is no such thing as a standard strategy. Research into HR strategy conducted by Armstrong and Long (1994) and Armstrong and Baron (2002) revealed many variations. Some strategies are simply very general declarations of intent. Others go into much more detail. The two types of HR strategies are: 1) general strategies such as high-performance working; 2) specific strategies relating to the different aspects of HRM such as learning and development and reward.

General HR strategies

General strategies describe the overall system or bundle of complementary HR practices that the organization proposes to adopt or puts into effect in order to improve organizational performance. The three main approaches are summarized below.

High-performance management

High-performance management aims, through high-performance work systems (bundles of practices that enhance employee performance and facilitate their engagement, motivation and skill enhancement), to make an impact on the performance of the organization in such areas as productivity, quality, levels of customer service, growth and profits. High-performance working practices include rigorous recruitment and selection procedures, extensive and relevant training and management development activities, incentive pay systems and performance management processes.

High-commitment management

One of the defining characteristics of HRM is its emphasis on the importance of enhancing mutual commitment (the concept of mutuality formulated by Walton, 1985). High-commitment management has been described by Wood (1996) as: 'A form of management which is aimed at eliciting a commitment so that behaviour is primarily self-regulated rather than controlled by sanctions and pressures external to the individual, and relations within the organization are based on high levels of trust.'

High-involvement management

The term 'high involvement' was first used by Lawler (1986) to describe management systems based on commitment and involvement, as opposed to the old bureaucratic model based on control. As defined by Benson *et al* (2006: 519): 'High-involvement work practices are a specific set of human resource practices that focus on employee decision-making, power, access to information, training and incentives.' Camps and Luna-Arocas (2009: 1057) observed that: 'High-involvement work practices aim to provide employees with the opportunity, skills and motivation to contribute to organizational success in environments demanding greater levels of commitment and involvement.'

Examples of general HR strategies

- A local authority: As expressed by the chief executive of this borough council, its HR strategy is about 'having a very strong focus on the overall effectiveness of the organization, its direction and how it's performing; there is commitment to, and belief in, and respect for individuals, and I think that these are very important factors.'

- A public utility: 'The only HR strategy you really need is the tangible expression of values and the implementation of values... unless you get the human resource values right you can forget all the rest' (managing director).

- A manufacturing company: 'The HR strategy is to stimulate changes on a broad front aimed ultimately at achieving competitive advantage through the efforts of our people. In an industry of fast followers, those who learn quickest will be the winners' (HR director).

- A retail stores group: 'The biggest challenge will be to maintain [our] competitive advantage and to do that we need to maintain and continue to attract very high-calibre people. The key differentiator on anything any company does is fundamentally the people, and I think that people tend to forget that they are the most important asset. Money is easy to get hold of, good people are not. All we do in terms of training and manpower planning is directly linked to business improvement' (managing director).

Specific HR strategies

Specific HR strategies set out what the organization intends to do in areas such as:

- *HR analytics* – obtaining, analysing and reporting on data that informs the direction of value adding and people management.

- *Knowledge management* – creating, acquiring, capturing, sharing and using knowledge to enhance learning and performance.

- *Corporate social responsibility* – a commitment to managing the business ethically in order to make a positive impact on society and the environment.

- *Engagement* – the development and implementation of policies designed to increase the level of employees' engagement with their work and the organization.

- *Organization development* – the planning and implementation of programmes designed to enhance the effectiveness with which an organization functions and responds to change.

- *Resourcing* – attracting and retaining high-quality people.

- *Diversity and inclusion* – managing the diverse elements of the workforce and ensuring that that people with disabilities and special needs should be employed by organizations without restrictions or limitations of any kind related to those disabilities or needs.

- *Talent management* – how the organization ensures that it has the talented people it needs to achieve success.

- *Employee well-being* – meeting the needs of employees for a healthy, safe and supportive work environment.

- *Learning and development* – providing an environment in which employees are encouraged to learn and develop.

- *Reward* – defining what the organization wants to do in the longer term to develop and implement reward policies, practices and processes that will further the achievement of its business goals and meet the needs of its stakeholders.

● *Employee relations* – defining the intentions of the organization about what needs to be done and what needs to be changed in the ways in which the organization manages its relationships with employees and their trade.

The following are some examples of specific HR strategies.

The Children's Society

● Implement the rewards strategy of the society to support the corporate plan and secure the recruitment, retention and motivation of staff to deliver its business objectives.

● Manage the development of the human resources information system to secure productivity improvements in administrative processes.

● Introduce improved performance management processes for managers and staff of the society.

● Implement training and development that supports the business objectives of the society and improves the quality of work with children and young people.

Diageo

There are three broad strands to the *Organization and People Strategy*:

● *Reward and recognition*: use recognition and reward programmes to stimulate outstanding team and individual performance contributions.

● *Talent management*: drive the attraction, retention and professional growth of a deep pool of diverse, talented employees.

● *Organizational effectiveness*: ensure that the business adapts its organization to maximize employee contribution and deliver performance goals.

The strategy provides direction to the company's talent, operational effectiveness and performance and reward agendas. The company's underlying thinking is that the people strategy is not for the human resource function to own but is the responsibility of the whole organization, hence the title 'Organization and People Strategy'.

A government agency

The key components of the HR strategy are:

● Investing in people – improving the level of intellectual capital.

● Performance management – integrating the values contained in the HR strategy into performance management processes and ensuring that reviews concentrate on how well people are performing those values.

● Job design – a key component concerned with how jobs are designed and how they relate to the whole business.

● The reward system – in developing reward strategies, taking into account that this is a very hard-driven business.

A local authority

The focus is on the organization of excellence. The strategy is broken down into eight sections: employee relations, recruitment and retention, training, performance management, pay and benefits, health and safety, absence management and equal opportunities.

Criteria for an effective HR strategy

An effective HR strategy is one that works, in the sense that it achieves what it sets out to achieve. Its criteria are that it:

● will satisfy business needs;

● is founded on detailed analysis and study and is evidence-based – it is not just wishful thinking;

● can be turned into actionable programmes that anticipate implementation requirements and problems;

● is coherent and integrated, being composed of components that fit with and support each other;

● takes account of the needs of line managers and employees generally as well as those of the organization and its other stakeholders.

Formulating HR strategies

Research conducted by Wright *et al* (2004) identified two approaches that can be adopted by HR to strategy formulation: 1) the inside-out approach begins with the status quo HR function (in terms of skills, processes, technologies, etc.) and then attempts (with varying degrees of success) to identify linkages to the business (usually through focusing on 'people issues'), making minor adjustments to HR activities along the way; 2) the outside-in approach, in which the starting point is the business and the customer, competitor and business issues it faces. The HR strategy then derives directly from these challenges to add real value.

Wright *et al* commented that HR strategies are more likely to flow from business strategies dominated by product/market and financial considerations. But there is still room for HR to make an essential contribution at the stage when business strategies are conceived, for example by focusing on resource issues. This contribution may be more significant when strategy formulation is an emergent or evolutionary process – HR strategic issues will then be dealt with as they arise during the course of formulating and implementing the corporate strategy.

Implementing HR strategies

As Gratton (2000: 30) commented: 'There is no great strategy, only great execution.' Strategies cannot be left as generalized aspirations or abstractions. But getting strategies into action is not easy: intent does not always lead to action. Too often, strategists act like Charles Dickens' character Mr Pecksmith, who was compared by Dickens (*Martin Chuzzlewit*, Penguin Classics, 2004: 23) to 'a direction-post which is always telling the way to a place and never goes there.' It is necessary to avoid saying, in effect: 'We need to get from here to there but we don't care how.'

If, in Kanter's (1984) phrase, HR strategies are to be action vehicles, they must be translated into HR policies that provide guidelines on decision-making and HR practices that enable the strategy to work. These can be the basis for implementation programmes with clearly stated objectives and deliverables.

To a large extent, HR strategies are implemented by line managers. As Purcell *et al* (2003: *x*) stressed, it is front-line managers who 'bring policies to life'. They pointed out that:

> Implementing and enacting policies is the task of line managers. It is necessary first to involve line managers in the development of HR strategy – bearing in mind that things done *with* line managers are much more likely to work than things done *to* line managers. Second, ensure

that the HR policies they are expected to put into practice are manageable with the resources available. Third, provide managers with the training, supporting processes and on the spot guidance they need.

Ensuring the effective delivery of HR strategy

To provide for the effective delivery of HR strategy it necessary to adopt the approaches described below.

Formulate practical strategies

A practical strategy is one that can be put into effect without too much difficulty.

The aims should be to: 1) keep it simple; 2) spell out *how* the strategy is to be implemented as well as *what* is to be implemented; and 3) ensure that support is given to line managers in the shape of advice, guidance and training.

Involve

Involve as many line managers and other employees as possible in formulating the strategy – people support what they help to create.

Communicate

It is essential to communicate details of the strategy to line managers and employees.

Build skills

New strategies may require the use of new skills or the development of existing ones. This applies to employees generally as well as line managers, who should be trained in what they have to do to implement the strategy. Skills can be built through formal off-the-job training courses but there is much to be said for coaching.

Monitor and evaluate

The introduction of HR strategy should be carefully monitored in order to evaluate its effectiveness.

Manage change

The implementation of HRM strategy requires close attention to the management of change, which can be hard to introduce and may be resisted.

Key learning points: HR strategies

The nature of HR strategies

- HR strategies set out what the organization intends to do about its human resource management policies and practices and how they should be integrated with the business strategy and each other.

- HR strategies are governed or at least influenced by the overall approach adopted to strategic HRM. They could be regarded as the manifestation of SHRM in action.

- The main argument for articulating HR strategies is that unless you know where you are going, you will not know how to get there or when you have arrived.

General HR strategies

General strategies describe the overall system or bundle of complementary HR practices that the organization proposes to adopt or puts into effect in order to improve organizational performance. The three types of general strategies are:

1 High-performance management.

2 High-commitment management.

3 High-involvement work.

Specific HR strategies

Specific HR strategies set out what the organization intends to do in areas such as: HR analytics, knowledge management, corporate social responsibility, engagement, organization development, resourcing, diversity and inclusion, talent management, learning and development, reward, employee relations and employee well-being.

Criteria for an effective HR strategy

An effective HR strategy is one that works in the sense that it achieves what it sets out to achieve. Its criteria are that it:

- will satisfy business needs;

- is founded on detailed analysis and study and is evidence-based – it is not just wishful thinking;

- can be turned into actionable programmes that anticipate implementation requirements and problems;

- is coherent and integrated, being composed of components that fit with and support each other;

- takes account of the needs of line managers and employees generally as well as those of the organization and its other stakeholders.

Formulating HR strategies

Research conducted by Wright *et al* (2004) identified two approaches that can be adopted by HR to strategy formulation: 1) the inside-out approach begins with the status quo HR function and then attempts to identify linkages to the business; 2) the outside-in approach in which the starting point is the business and the customer, competitor and business issues it faces. The HR strategy then derives directly from these challenges to add real value.

Implementing HR strategies

Implementing strategy can be much harder than formulating it. To provide for the effective delivery of HR strategy it is necessary to adopt the following approaches:

- formulate practical strategies;

- involve;

- communicate;

- build skills;

- monitor and evaluate;

- manage change.

References

Armstrong, M and Baron, A (2002) *Strategic HRM: The route to improved business performance*, London, CIPD

Armstrong, M and Long, P (1994) *The Reality of Strategic HRM*, London, IPM

Benson, G S, Young, S M and Lawler, E E (2006) High involvement work practices and analysts' forecasts of corporate performance, *Human Resource Management*, **45** (4), pp 519–27

Boxall, P F (1996) The strategic HRM debate and the resource-based view of the firm, *Human Resource Management Journal*, **6** (3), pp 59–75

Camps, J and Luna-Arocas, R (2009) High-involvement work practices and firm performance, *International Journal of Human Resource Management*, **20** (5), pp 1056–77

Dickens, C (1843) *Martin Chuzzlewit*, London, Chapman & Hall (Penguin Classics, 2004)

Dyer, L and Reeves, T (1995) Human resource strategies and firm performance: what do we know and where do we need to go? *The International Journal of Human Resource Management*, **6** (3), pp 656–70

Fombrun, C J, Tichy, N M and Devanna, M A (1984) *Strategic Human Resource Management*, New York, Wiley

Gratton, L A (2000) Real step change, *People Management*, 16 March, pp 27–30

Kanter, R M (1984) *The Change Masters*, London, Allen & Unwin

Lawler, E E (1986) *High Involvement Management*, San Francisco, CA, Jossey-Bass

Pettigrew, A and Whipp, R (1991) *Managing Change for Strategic Success*, Oxford, Blackwell

Purcell, J (2001) The meaning of strategy in human resource management, in (ed) J Storey, *Human Resource Management: A critical text*, 2nd edn, London, Thompson Learning, pp 59–77

Purcell, J, Kinnie, K, Hutchinson, R, Rayton, B and Swart, J (2003) *People and Performance: How people management impacts on organizational performance*, London, CIPD

Richardson, R and Thompson, M (1999) *The Impact of People Management Practices on Business Performance: A literature review*, London, CIPD

Tyson, S and Witcher, M (1994) Human resource strategy emerging from the recession, *Personnel Management*, August, pp 20–23

Walton, R E (1985) From control to commitment in the workplace, *Harvard Business Review*, March–April, pp 77–84

Wood, S (1996) High commitment management and organization in the UK, *The International Journal of Human Resource Management*, **7** (1), pp 41–58

Wright, P M and McMahan, G C (1999) Theoretical perspectives for human resource management, in (eds) R S Schulker and S E Jackson, *Strategic Human Resource Management*, Blackwell, Oxford, pp 49–72

Wright, P M, Snell, S A and Jacobsen, H H (2004) Current approaches to HR strategies: inside-out versus outside-in, *Human Resource Planning*, **27** (4), pp 36–46

References

09
HR policies

KEY CONCEPTS AND TERMS

Diversity

Equal opportunities

LEARNING OUTCOMES

On completing this chapter you should be able to define these key concepts. You should also know about:

- The reasons for having HR policies
- Overall HR policy
- Specific HR policies
- Formulating HR policies
- Implementing HR policies

Introduction

HR policies set out the approaches that the organization adopts to dealing with key aspects of HRM and provide continuing guidelines on how these approaches should be applied. They define the philosophies and values of the organization on how people should be treated, and from these are derived the principles upon which managers are expected to act when dealing with HR matters.

HR policies should be distinguished from HR procedures. A policy provides generalized guidance on how HR issues should be dealt with. A procedure spells out precisely what steps should be taken to deal with major employment issues such as grievances, discipline, capability and redundancy.

Why have HR policies?

HR policies define how the organization wants to handle key aspects of people management. As guidelines, the aim is to ensure that any HR issues are dealt with consistently in accordance with the values of the organization and in line with certain defined principles. All organizations have HR policies. Some, however, exist implicitly as a philosophy of management and an attitude to employees that is expressed in the way in which HR issues are handled; for example, the introduction of a new grade and pay structure. The advantage of explicit policies in terms of consistency and understanding may appear to be obvious, but there are disadvantages: written policies can be inflexible, constrictive, platitudinous, or all three. To a degree, policies have often to be expressed in abstract terms and managers do not generally care for abstractions. But they do want to know where they stand – people like structure – and formalized HR policies can provide the guidelines they need.

Formalized HR policies can be used in induction, team leader and management training to help participants understand the philosophies and values of the organization and how they are expected to behave within that context. They are a means for defining the employment relationship and the psychological contract. HR policies can be expressed formally as overall statements of the values of the organization or in relation to specific areas, as discussed in this chapter.

Overall HR policy

The overall HR policy defines how the organization fulfils its social responsibilities for its employees and sets out its attitudes towards them. It is an expression of its values or beliefs about how people should be treated. The values expressed in an overall statement of HR policies may explicitly or implicitly refer to the following concepts:

- *Equity* – treating employees fairly and justly by adopting an 'even-handed' approach. This includes protecting individuals from any unfair decisions made by their managers, providing equal opportunities for employment and promotion, and operating an equitable payment system.
- *Consideration* – taking account of individual circumstances when making decisions that affect the prospects, security or self-respect of employees.
- *Organizational learning* – a belief in the need to promote the learning and development of

all the members of the organization by providing the processes and support required.
- *Performance through people* – the importance attached to developing a performance culture and to continuous improvement; the significance of performance management as a means of defining and agreeing mutual expectations; the provision of fair feedback to people on how well they are performing.
- *Quality of working life* – consciously and continually aiming to improve the quality of working life. This involves increasing the sense of satisfaction that people obtain from their work by – so far as possible – reducing monotony; increasing variety, autonomy and responsibility; avoiding placing people under too much stress; providing for an acceptable balance between work and life outside work.
- *Working conditions* – providing healthy, safe and – so far as practicable – pleasant working conditions.

These values are espoused by many organizations in one form or another. But to what extent are they practised when making 'business-led' decisions (which can, of course, be highly detrimental to employees if, for example, they lead to redundancy)? One of the dilemmas facing all those who formulate HR policies is: how can we pursue policies focusing on business success and at the same time fulfil our obligations to employees in such terms as equity, consideration, quality of working life, security and working conditions? To argue, as some do, that HR policies should be entirely business-led implies that human considerations are unimportant. Yet organizations have obligations to all their stakeholders, not just their owners.

It may be difficult to express these overall policies in anything but generalized terms, but employers increasingly have to recognize that they are subject to external as well as internal pressures and moral imperatives, which act as constraints on the extent to which they can disregard the higher standards of behaviour towards their employees that are expected of them. What needs to be done to avoid accusations that general HR policy statements are mere rhetoric is to convert them into reality through specific HR policies and enforce their application.

Specific HR policies

The most common areas in which specific HR policies exist are age and employment, AIDS, bullying, discipline, diversity management, e-mails and the internet, employee development, employee relations, employee voice, the employment relationship, equal opportunity, grievances, health and safety, new technology, promotion, redundancy, reward, sexual harassment, substance abuse, whistle-blowing and work–life balance.

Age and employment

The policy on age and employment should take into account the UK legislation on age discrimination and the following facts:

- Age is a poor predictor of job performance.
- It is misleading to equate physical and mental ability with age.
- More of the population are living active, healthy lives as they get older.

AIDS

An AIDS policy could include the following points:

- The risk through infection in the workplace is negligible.
- Where the occupation does involve blood contact – as in hospitals, doctors' surgeries and laboratories – the special precautions advised by the Health and Safety Commission will be implemented.
- Employees who know that they are infected with AIDS will not be obliged to disclose the fact to the company, but if they do it will remain completely confidential.
- There will be no discrimination against anyone with or at risk of acquiring AIDS.
- Employees infected with HIV or suffering from AIDS will be treated no differently from anyone else suffering a severe illness.

Bullying

An anti-bullying policy will state that bullying will not be tolerated by the organization and that those who persist in bullying staff will be subject to disciplinary action, which could be severe in particularly bad cases. The policy will make it clear that individuals who are being bullied should have the right to discuss the problem with another person, a representative or a member of the HR function, and to make a complaint. The policy should emphasize that if a complaint is received it will be thoroughly investigated.

Discipline

The disciplinary policy should state that employees have the right to know what is expected of them and what could happen if they infringe the organization's rules. It should also make the point that, in handling disciplinary cases, the organization will treat employees in accordance with the principles of natural justice. It should be supported by a disciplinary procedure (see Chapter 10).

Diversity and inclusion

A policy on managing diversity and inclusion sets out the ways in which the organization, while recognizing the differences between people, ensures that those of different ethnic backgrounds, religions, gender and age groups are brought together to work in cohesive and productive organizational units. The policy will indicate how a culture is developed and maintained in which individuals of all backgrounds are fairly treated and valued for who they are. This is considered in more detail in Chapter 30.

E-mails and use of the internet

The policy on e-mails could state that the sending or downloading of offensive e-mails is prohibited and that the senders or downloaders of such messages are subject to normal disciplinary procedures. The policy may also prohibit internet browsing, for example of social networks, or downloading material not related to the business, although this can be difficult to enforce. Some companies have always believed that reasonable use of the telephone is acceptable and that policy may be extended to the internet.

If it is decided that employees' e-mails should be monitored to check on excessive or unacceptable use, this should be included in an e-mail policy, which would therefore be part of the contractual arrangements. A policy statement could be included to the effect that: 'The company reserves the right to access and monitor all e-mail messages created, sent, received or stored on the company's system.'

Employee development

The employee development policy could express the organization's commitment to the continuous development of the skills and abilities of employees in order to maximize their contribution and to give them the opportunity to enhance their skills, realize their potential, advance their careers and increase their employability, both within and outside the organization. The policy could also express the belief that age should not be a barrier to learning opportunities from which everyone can benefit, irrespective of how old they are.

Employee relations

The employee relations policy will set out the organization's approach to the rights of employees to have their interests represented to management through trade unions, staff associations or some other form of representative system. It will also cover the basis upon which the organization works with trade unions, eg emphasizing that this should be regarded as a partnership.

Employee voice

The employee voice policy should spell out the organization's belief in giving employees an opportunity to have a say in matters that affect them. It should define the mechanisms for employee voice such as joint consultation and suggestion schemes.

The employment relationship

Employment policies should be concerned with fundamental aspects of the employment relationship. They should take account of the requirements of relevant UK and European legislation and case law, as covered in Chapter 62.

Equal opportunity

The equal opportunity policy should spell out the organization's determination to give equal opportunities to all, irrespective of sex, sexual orientation, race, creed, disability, age or marital status. The policy should also deal with the extent to which the organization wants to take 'affirmative action' to redress imbalances between the numbers employed according to sex or race or to differences in the levels of qualifications and skills they have achieved. The policy could be set out as follows:

1 We are an equal opportunity employer. This means that we do not permit direct or indirect discrimination against any employee on the grounds of race, nationality, sex, sexual orientation, disability, religion, marital status or age.

2 Direct discrimination takes place when a person is treated less favourably than others are or would be treated in similar circumstances.

3 Indirect discrimination takes place when, whether intentional or not, a condition is applied that adversely affects a considerable proportion of people of one race, nationality, sex, sexual orientation, religion or marital status, or those with disabilities or older employees.

4 The firm will ensure that equal opportunity principles are applied in all its HR policies and in particular to the procedures relating to the recruitment, training, development and promotion of its employees.

5 Where appropriate and where permissible under the relevant legislation and codes of practice, employees of under-represented groups will be given positive training and encouragement to achieve equal opportunity.

Grievances

The policy on grievances could state that employees have the right to raise their grievances with their manager, to be accompanied by a representative if they so wish, and to appeal to a higher level if they feel that their grievance has not been resolved satisfactorily. The policy should be supported by a grievance procedure (see Chapter 10).

Health and safety

Health and safety policies cover how the organization intends to provide healthy and safe places and systems of work (see Chapter 57).

New technology

A new technology policy statement could state that there will be consultation about the introduction of new technology and the steps that would be taken by the organization to minimize the risk of compulsory redundancy or adverse effects on other terms and conditions or working arrangements.

Promotion

A promotion policy could state the organization's intention to promote from within wherever this is appropriate as a means of satisfying its requirements for high-quality staff. The policy could, however, recognize that there will be occasions when the organization's present and future needs can only be met by recruitment from outside. The point could be made that a vigorous organization needs infusions of fresh blood from time to time if it is not to stagnate. In addition, the policy might state that employees will be encouraged to apply for internally advertised jobs and will not be held back from promotion by their managers, however reluctant the latter may be to lose them. The policy should define the approach that the organization adopts to engaging, promoting and training older employees. It should emphasize that the only criterion for selection or promotion should be ability to do the job.

Redundancy

The redundancy policy should state that the aim of the organization is to provide for employment security. It is the organization's intention to use its best endeavours to avoid involuntary redundancy through its redeployment and retraining programmes. However, if redundancy is unavoidable, those affected will be given fair and equitable treatment, the maximum amount of warning and every help that can be provided to obtain suitable alternative employment. The policy should be supported by a redundancy procedure (see Chapter 10).

Reward

The reward policy could cover such matters as:

- providing an equitable pay system;
- equal pay for work of equal value;
- paying for performance, competence, skill or contribution;
- sharing in the success of the organization (gain sharing or profit sharing);
- the relationship between levels of pay in the organization and market rates;
- the provision of employee benefits, including flexible benefits, if appropriate;
- importance attached to the non-financial rewards resulting from recognition, accomplishment, autonomy and the opportunity to develop.

Sexual harassment

The sexual harassment policy should state that:

- Sexual harassment will not be tolerated.
- Employees subjected to sexual harassment will be given advice, support and counselling as required.
- Every attempt will be made to resolve the problem informally with the person complained against.
- Assistance will be given to the employee to complain formally if informal discussions fail.
- A special process will be available for hearing complaints about sexual harassment. This will provide for employees to bring their complaint to someone of their own sex if they so wish.
- Complaints will be handled sensitively and with due respect for the rights of both the complainant and the accused.

Sexual harassment is regarded as gross misconduct and, if proved, makes the individual liable for instant dismissal. Less severe penalties may be reserved for minor cases, but there will always be a warning that repetition will result in dismissal.

Substance abuse

A substance abuse policy could include assurances that:

- employees identified as having substance abuse problems will be offered advice and help;
- any reasonable absence from work necessary to receive treatment will be granted under the organization's sickness scheme, provided there is full cooperation from the employee;
- an opportunity will be given to discuss the matter once it has become evident or suspected that work performance is being affected by substance-related problems;
- the right to be accompanied by a friend or employee representative in any such discussion;
- agencies will be recommended to which the employee can go for help if necessary;
- employment rights will be safeguarded during any reasonable period of treatment.

Whistle-blowing

Whistle-blowing takes place when someone reports a suspected wrongdoing at work. Dismissal of an employee for whistle-blowing is deemed in law as automatic unfair dismissal if a 'protected disclosure', for example referring to a criminal offence by the employer, is made and the employee 'reasonably believes' that the disclosure is in the 'public interest'. Obviously employers want to avoid that situation and employees need guidance on what they can and can't do and how they should act. Hence the need for a whistle-blowing policy that will:

- Explain that the organization believes that it is important to deal with any wrongdoing, especially those malpractices specifically referred to in the Public Interest Disclosure Act 1998, including criminal offences, risks to health and safety, failure to comply with a legal obligation, a miscarriage of justice and environmental damage. Specific examples of unacceptable behaviour could be given.
- Indicate that if anyone becomes aware of an issue that needs to be dealt with they should raise the matter inside the organization, either with their line manager or, if the allegation is about their line manager, to a more senior manager.
- State that employees will not be penalized for informing management about a malpractice.

Work–life balance

Work–life balance policies define how the organization intends to allow employees greater flexibility in their working patterns so that they can balance what they do at work with the responsibilities and interests they have outside work. The policy will indicate how flexible work practices can be developed and implemented. It will emphasize that the numbers of hours worked must not be treated as a criterion for assessing performance. It will set out guidelines on the specific arrangements that can be made, such as flexible hours, compressed working week, term-time working contracts, working at home, special leave for parents and carers, career breaks and various kinds of child care.

A flexibility policy will need to take account of the Work and Families Act 2006, as described in Chapter 62.

Formulating HR policies

HR policies need to address the key HR issues that have been identified in the organization. They must also take account of external factors such as legislation. The maximum amount of consultation should take place with managers, employees and their representatives and the policies should be communicated widely with guidelines on their application. The following steps should be taken when formulating HR policies:

- Gain understanding of the corporate culture and its shared values.
- Analyse existing policies – written and unwritten. HR policies will exist in any organization, even if they are implicit rather than expressed formally.
- Analyse external factors. HR policies are subject to the requirements of UK employment legislation, European Commission employment regulations, and the official Codes of Practice issued by bodies in the UK such as ACAS (the Advisory, Conciliation and Arbitration Service), the Commission for Equality and Human Rights, and the Health and Safety Executive. The Codes of Practice issued by relevant professional institutions, such as the CIPD, should also be consulted.

- Assess any areas where new policies are needed or existing policies are inadequate.
- Check with managers, preferably starting at the top, on their views about HR policies and where they think they could be improved.
- Seek the views of employees about the HR policies, especially the extent to which they are inherently fair and equitable and are implemented fairly and consistently. Consider doing this through an attitude survey.
- Seek the views of union representatives.
- Analyse the information obtained in the first seven steps and prepare draft policies.
- Consult, discuss and agree policies with management and union representatives.
- Communicate the policies with guidance notes on their implementation as required

(although they should be as self-explanatory as possible). Supplement this communication with training.

Implementing HR policies

The aim will be to implement policies fairly and consistently. Line managers have an important role in doing this. It is they who will be largely responsible for policy implementation. Members of the HR function can give guidance, but it is line managers who are on the spot and have to make decisions about people. The role of HR is to communicate and interpret the policies, convince line managers that they are necessary, and provide training and support that will equip managers to implement them. As Purcell *et al* (2003) emphasized, it is line managers who bring HR policies to life.

Key learning points: HR policies

The reasons for having HR policies

HR policies provide guidelines on how key aspects of people management should be handled. The aim is to ensure that any HR issues are dealt with consistently in accordance with the values of the organization and in line with certain defined principles.

Overall HR policy

The overall HR policy defines how the organization fulfils its social responsibilities for its employees and sets out its attitudes towards them. It is an expression of its values or beliefs about how people should be treated.

Specific HR policies

The internet, employee development, diversity management, employee relations, employee voice, the employment relationship, equal opportunity, grievances, health and safety, new technology, promotion, redundancy, reward, sexual harassment, substance abuse and work–life balance.

Formulating HR policies

HR policies need to address the key HR issues that have been identified in the organization. They must also take account of external factors such as legislation. The maximum amount of consultation should take place with managers, employees and their representatives, and the policies should be communicated widely with guidelines on their application.

Implementing HR policies

The aim will be to implement policies fairly and consistently. Line managers have a key role in doing this.

Reference

Purcell, J, Kinnie, K, Hutchinson, S, Rayton, B and Swart, J (2003) *Understanding the People and Performance Link: Unlocking the black box*, London, CIPD

10
HR procedures

KEY CONCEPTS AND TERMS

Capability   HR procedure

Discipline   Redundancy

Grievance

LEARNING OUTCOMES

On completing this chapter you should be able to define these key concepts. You should also:

- Be able to define what HR procedures are
- Know about the main HR procedures

What are HR procedures?

HR procedures set out the ways in which certain actions concerning people should be carried out by the management or individual managers. In effect, they constitute a formalized approach to dealing with specific matters of policy and practice.

They should be distinguished from HR policies, as described in Chapter 9, which serve as guidelines on people management practices but do not necessarily lay down precisely the steps that should be taken in particular situations. Procedures are more exacting. They state what must be done as well as spelling out how to do it.

It is desirable to have the key HR procedures written down in order to ensure that related HR policies are applied consistently and in accordance with both legal requirements and ethical considerations. The existence of a written and well-publicized procedure ensures that everyone knows precisely what steps need to be taken when dealing with certain significant and possibly recurring employment issues.

The introduction or development of HR procedures should be carried out in consultation with employees and their representatives. It is essential to brief everyone on how the procedures operate and they should be published either in an employee handbook or as a separate document. Line managers may need special training on how they should apply the procedures, and the HR department should provide guidance wherever necessary. HR will normally have the responsibility of ensuring that procedures are followed consistently.

Procedures are required to deal with capability and disciplinary issues, grievances and redundancy, as discussed below.

Capability procedure

Some organizations deal with matters of capability under a disciplinary procedure, but there is much to be said for dealing with poor performance issues separately, leaving the disciplinary procedure to be invoked for misconduct cases. An example of a capability procedure is given below.

Example: Capability procedure

Policy

The company aims are to ensure that performance expectations and standards are defined, performance is monitored and employees are given appropriate feedback, training and support to meet these standards.

Procedure

1 If a manager/team leader believes that an employee's performance is not up to standard, an informal discussion will be held with the employee to try to establish the reason and to agree the actions required to improve performance by the employee and/or the manager/team leader. If, however:

   – it is agreed that the established standards are not reasonably attainable, they will be reviewed;

   – it is established that the performance problems are related to the employee's personal life, the necessary counselling/support will be provided;

   – it is decided that the poor performance emanates from a change in the organization's standards, those standards will be explained to the employee and help will be offered to obtain conformity with the standards;

   – it is apparent that the poor performance constitutes misconduct, the disciplinary procedure will be invoked.

2 Should the employee show no (or insufficient) improvement over a defined period (weeks/months), a formal interview will be arranged with the employee (together with a representative if so desired). The aims of this interview will be to:

   – explain clearly the shortfall between the employee's performance and the required standard;

   – identify the cause(s) of the unsatisfactory performance and to determine what – if any –

remedial treatment (training, retraining, support, etc) can be given;

   – obtain the employee's commitment to reaching that standard;

   – set a reasonable period for the employee to reach the standard and agree on a monitoring system during that period;

   – tell the employee what will happen if that standard is not met.

3 The outcome of this interview will be recorded in writing and a copy will be given to the employee.

4 At the end of the review period a further formal interview will be held, at which time:

   – if the required improvement has been made, the employee will be told of this and encouraged to maintain the improvement;

   – if some improvement has been made but the standard has not yet been met, the review period will be extended;

   – if there has been no discernible improvement and performance is still well below an acceptable standard this will be indicated to the employee and consideration will be given to whether there are alternative vacancies that the employee would be competent to fill; if there are, the employee will be given the option of accepting such a vacancy or being considered for dismissal;

   – if such vacancies are available, the employee will be given full details of them in writing before being required to make a decision;

   – in the absence of suitable alternative work, the employee will be informed and invited to give his or her views on this before the final decision is taken.

5 Employees may appeal against their dismissal. The appeal must be made within three working days.

Disciplinary procedure

A disciplinary procedure sets out the stages through which any disciplinary action should proceed. An example is given below.

Example: Disciplinary procedure (part 1)

Policy

It is the policy of the company that if disciplinary action has to be taken against employees it should:

- be undertaken only in cases where good reason and clear evidence exists;
- be appropriate to the nature of the offence that has been committed;
- be demonstrably fair and consistent with previous action in similar circumstances;
- take place only when employees are aware of the standards that are expected of them or the rules with which they are required to conform;
- allow employees the right to be represented by a representative or colleague during any formal proceedings;
- allow employees the right to know exactly what charges are being made against them and to respond to those charges;
- allow employees the right of appeal against any disciplinary action.

Disciplinary rules

The company is responsible for ensuring that up-to-date disciplinary rules are published and available to all employees. These will set out the circumstances in which an employee could be dismissed for gross misconduct.

Procedure

The procedure is carried out in the following stages:

1   *Informal warning.* A verbal or informal warning is given to the employee in the first instance or instances of minor offences. The warning is administered by the employee's immediate manager or team leader.

2   *Formal warning.* A written formal warning is given to the employee in the first instance of more serious offences or after repeated instances of minor offences. The warning is administered by the employee's immediate manager or team leader. It states the exact nature of the offence and indicates any future disciplinary action that will be taken against the employee if the offence is repeated within a specified time limit. A copy of the written warning is placed in the employee's personal record file but is destroyed 12 months after the date on which it was given, if the intervening service has been satisfactory. The employee is required to read and sign the formal warning and has the right to appeal to higher management if he or she thinks the warning is unjustified. The HR manager should be asked to advise on the text of the written warning.

3   *Further disciplinary action.* If, despite previous warnings, an employee still fails to reach the required standards in a reasonable period of time, it may become necessary to consider further disciplinary action. The action taken may be up to three days' suspension without pay, or dismissal. In either case the departmental manager should discuss the matter with the HR manager before taking action. Staff below the rank of departmental manager may only recommend disciplinary action to higher management, except when their manager is not present (for example, on night shift), when they may suspend the employee for up to one day pending an inquiry on the following day. Disciplinary action should not be confirmed until the appeal procedure has been carried out.

Example: Disciplinary procedure (part 2)

Summary dismissal

An employee may be summarily dismissed (ie given instant dismissal without notice) only in the event of gross misconduct, as defined in company rules. Only departmental managers and above can recommend summary dismissal, and the action should not be finalized until the case has been discussed with the HR manager and the appeal procedure has been carried out. To enable this review to take place, employees should be suspended pending further investigation, which must take place within 24 hours.

Appeals

In all circumstances, an employee may appeal against suspension, dismissal with notice, or summary dismissal. The appeal is conducted by a member of management who is more senior than the manager who initially administered the disciplinary action. The HR manager should also be present at the hearing. If he or she wishes, the employee may be represented at the appeal by a fellow employee of his or her own choice. Appeal against summary dismissal or suspension should be heard immediately. Appeals against dismissal with notice should be held within two days. No disciplinary action that is subject to appeal is confirmed until the outcome of the appeal.

If an appeal against dismissal (but not suspension) is rejected at this level, the employee has the right to appeal to the chief executive. The head of HR and, if required, the employee's representative should be present at this appeal.

Grievance procedure

A grievance procedure spells out the policy on handling grievances and the approach to dealing with them. An example of a grievance procedure is given below.

Example: Grievance procedure

Policy

It is the policy of the company that employees should:

- be given a fair hearing by their immediate supervisor or manager concerning any grievances they may wish to raise;

- have the right to appeal to a more senior manager against a decision made by their immediate supervisor or manager;

- have the right to be accompanied by a fellow employee of their own choice when raising a grievance or appealing against a decision.

The aim of the procedure is to settle the grievance as nearly as possible to its point of origin.

Procedure

The main stages through which a grievance may be raised are as follows:

1 The employee raises the matter with his or her immediate manager or team leader and may be accompanied by a fellow employee of his or her own choice.

2 If the employee is not satisfied with the decision, the employee requests a meeting with a member of management who is more senior than the manager or team leader who initially heard the grievance. This meeting takes place within five working days of the request and is attended by the manager, an HR manager or business partner, the employee appealing against the decision, and, if desired, his or her representative. The HR manager records the results of the meeting in writing and issues copies to all concerned.

3 If the employee is still not satisfied with the decision, he or she may appeal to the appropriate director. The meeting to hear this appeal is held within five working days of the request and is attended by the director, the head of HR, the employee making the appeal and, if desired, his or her representative. The manager responsible for HR records the result of this meeting in writing and issues copies to all concerned. No further appeal can be made beyond this stage.

Redundancy procedure

A redundancy procedure aims to meet statutory, ethical and practical considerations when dealing with this painful process. An example of a procedure is given below.

Example: Redundancy procedure (part 1)

Definition

Redundancy is defined as the situation in which management decides that an employee or employees are surplus to requirements in a particular occupation and cannot be offered suitable alternative work.

Employees may be surplus to requirements because changes in the economic circumstances of the company mean that fewer employees are required, or because changes in methods of working mean that a job no longer exists in its previous form. An employee who is given notice because he or she is unsuitable or inefficient is not regarded as redundant and would be dealt with in accordance with the usual disciplinary or capability procedure.

Objectives

The objectives of the procedure are to ensure that:

- employees who may be affected by the discontinuance of their work are given fair and equitable treatment;

- the minimum disruption is caused to employees and the company;

- as far as possible, changes are effected with the understanding and agreement of the unions and employees concerned.

Principles

The principles governing the procedure are as follows:

- The trade unions concerned will be informed as soon as the possibility of redundancy is foreseen.

- Every attempt will be made to:
  - absorb redundancy by the natural wastage of employees;
  - find suitable alternative employment within the company for employees who might be affected, and provide training if this is necessary;
  - give individuals reasonable warning of pending redundancy in addition to the statutory period of notice.

- If alternative employment in the company is not available and more than one individual is affected, the factors to be taken into consideration in deciding who should be made redundant will be:
  - length of service with the company;
  - value to the company;
  - other things being equal, length of service should be the determining factor.

- The company will make every endeavour to help employees find alternative work if that is necessary.

Example: Redundancy procedure (part 2)

The procedure for dealing with employees who are surplus to requirements is set out below.

Review of employee requirements

Management will continuously keep under review possible future developments that might affect the number of employees required, and will prepare overall plans for dealing with possible redundancies.

Measures to avoid redundancies

If the likelihood of redundancy is foreseen, the company will inform the union(s), explaining the reasons, and in consultation with the union(s) will give consideration to taking appropriate measures to prevent redundancy.

Departmental managers will be warned by the management of future developments that might affect them so that detailed plans can be made for running down the numbers of employees by allowing natural wastage to take place without replacements, retraining, or transfers.

Departmental managers will be expected to keep under review the work situation in their departments so that contingency plans can be prepared and the HR manager is informed of any likely surpluses.

Consultation on redundancies

If all measures to avoid redundancy fail, the company will consult the union(s) at the earliest opportunity in order to reach agreement.

Selection of redundant employees

In the event of impending redundancy, the individuals who might be surplus to requirements should be selected by the departmental manager with the advice of the HR manager on the principles that should be adopted.

The HR manager should explore the possibilities of transferring affected employees to alternative work. The HR manager should inform management of proposed action (either redundancy or transfer) to obtain approval.

The union(s) will be informed of the numbers affected, but not of individual names.

The departmental manager and the HR manager will jointly interview the employees affected either to offer a transfer or, if a suitable alternative is not available, to inform them that they will be redundant. At this interview, full information should be available to give to the employee on the following, as appropriate:

- the reasons for being surplus;
- the alternative jobs that are available;
- the date when the employee will become surplus (that is, the period of notice);
- the entitlement to redundancy pay;
- the employee's right to appeal to an appropriate director;
- the help the company will provide.

Example: Redundancy procedure (part 3)

An appropriate director will hear any appeals with the HR manager.

The HR manager will ensure that all the required administrative arrangements are made.

If the union(s) have any points to raise about the selection of employees or the actions taken by the company, these should be discussed in the first place with the HR manager. If the results of these discussions are unsatisfactory, a meeting will be arranged with an appropriate director.

Alternative work within the company

If an employee is offered and accepts suitable alternative work within the company, it will take effect without a break from the previous employment and will be confirmed in writing. Employees will receive appropriate training and will be entitled to a four-week trial period to see if the work is suitable. This trial period may be extended by mutual agreement to provide additional training. During this period, employees are free to terminate their employment and, if they do, would be treated as if they had been made redundant on the day their old job ended. They would then receive any redundancy pay to which they are entitled.

Alternative employment

Employees for whom no suitable work is available in the company will be given reasonable opportunities to look for alternative employment.

Key learning points: HR procedures

- HR procedures set out the ways in which certain actions concerning people should be carried out by the management or individual managers. In effect, they constitute a formalized approach to dealing with specific matters of policy and practice.

- They should be distinguished from HR policies, which serve as guidelines on people management practices but do not necessarily lay down precisely the steps that should be taken in particular situations. Procedures are more exacting: they state what must be done as well as spelling out how to do it.

- It is desirable to have the key HR procedures written down to ensure that HR policies are applied consistently and in accordance with both legal requirements and ethical considerations.

- The existence of a written and well-publicized procedure ensures that everyone knows precisely what steps need to be taken when dealing with certain significant and possibly recurring employment issues.

- The introduction or development of HR procedures should be carried out in consultation with employees and, where appropriate, their representatives.

- It is essential to brief everyone on how the procedures operate, and they should be published either in an employee handbook or as a separate document.

- Line managers may need special training on how they should apply the procedures and the HR department should provide guidance wherever necessary. HR will normally have the responsibility of ensuring that procedures are followed consistently.

- Procedures are required to deal with capability and disciplinary issues, grievances and redundancy.

11
HR analytics

LEARNING OUTCOMES

On completing this chapter you should be able to define these key concepts. You should also know about:

- The nature of HR analytics
- The purpose of HR analytics
- The three levels of HR analytics

Introduction

It has been said (Rousseau and Barends 2011: 221) that: 'Blind faith has no place in professional practice.' Human resource management needs to be evidence-based, which means making use of appropriate information derived from the analysis of the messages delivered by the data available in organizations.

Pfeffer and Sutton (2006: 70) stated that evidence-based management 'features a willingness to put aside belief and conventional wisdom – the dangerous half-truths that many embrace – and replace these with an unrelenting commitment to gather the necessary facts to make more intelligent and informed decisions.' HR analytics as discussed in this chapter is the necessary process of gathering and analysing that data.

HR analytics defined

HR analytics uses metrics to provide the basis for assessing the impact of HRM practices and the contribution made by people to organizational performance, and for indicating approaches to future developments. It is about 'data mining' – getting as much out of HR data as possible and then going on to find links, correlations and, ideally, causation, between different sets of the data, using statistical techniques.

The analytical process may involve the handling of 'big data' – extremely large data sets that may be analysed computationally to reveal patterns, trends and associations. The term was originated by McAfee and Brynjolfsson (2012: 63), who, in a *Harvard Business Review* article, described it as data characterized by sheer volume, velocity (speed with which it can be collected) and variety (number of different sources, for example, social media). They claimed that: 'Data-driven decisions are better decisions – it's as simple as that. Using big data enables managers to decide on the basis of evidence rather than intuition. For that reason, it has the potential to revolutionize management.'

The purpose of HR analytics

HR analytics provides a basis for people management decision making. The process of identifying metrics or measures and collecting and analysing information relating to them focuses the attention of the organization on what needs to be done to find, keep, develop and make the best use of its human capital. Measurements can be used to monitor progress in achieving strategic HR goals and generally to evaluate the effectiveness of HR practices. This in accordance with the principle that 'you cannot manage what you cannot measure'.

As expressed by the CIPD (2015: 1): 'HR analytics enables better decision making by providing an organization with insights about the workforce and the HR policies and practices that support them. Analytics may be used to look at the traits of the workforce, in particular its human capital: the value of individual knowledge, skills and experience of individuals and teams.'

The need is to develop a framework within which reliable information can be collected and analysed, such as added value per employee, productivity and measures of employee behaviour (eg attrition and absenteeism rates, engagement levels, performance figures and accident rates).

In more detail, the purposes to which HR analytics can be put include:

- measuring levels of engagement;
- improving employee retention rates;
- reducing absenteeism;
- evaluating the effectiveness of different sources of recruits;
- evaluating the effectiveness of learning and development activities;
- investigating the effectiveness of performance management or performance-related pay in improving performance;
- measuring the impact of organizational development interventions;
- reducing accident rates;
- providing guidance on future HR strategy.

In each area, the analysis would investigate trends and, whenever possible, the interrelationships between different types of data and between the data and performance. This evidence could be used to reach conclusions about any action required or to evaluate the effectiveness of action already taken.

HR analytics levels

There are three levels of HR analytics:

1 *Descriptive analytics*: The use of data to record a particular aspect of HR and provide information on what has been happening to, for example, labour turnover or absence rates.

2 *Multidimensional analytics*: The combination of different sets of data to establish any relationships (correlations) between them and, hopefully, indicate causation (eg that a particular HR initiative has caused an improvement in performance).

3 *Predictive analytics*: The most advanced form of HR analytics is to use the data to predict trends and therefore provide guidance on future HR strategy.

Descriptive analytics

Descriptive analytics cover the following types of data:

- Basic workforce data – demographic data (numbers by job category, sex, race, age, disability), working arrangements, absence and sickness, turnover, health and safety, pay.
- People development and performance data – learning and development programmes,

performance management/potential assessments, skills and qualifications.

- Employee engagement data – engagement surveys.
- Perceptual data – opinion surveys, focus groups, exit interviews.
- Performance data – financial, operational and customer.

A summary of HR data and their possible uses is given in Table 11.1.

TABLE 11.1   A summary of HR data and their possible uses

Data	Possible use: analysis leading to action
Workforce composition – gender, race, age, full-time, part-time	Analyse the extent of diversity Assess the implications of a preponderance of employees in different age groups, eg extent of losses through retirement Assess the extent to which the organization is relaying on part-time staff
Length of service distribution	Indicate level of success in retaining employees Indicate preponderance of long- or short-serving employees Enable analyses of performance of more experienced employees to be assessed
Skills analysis/assessment – graduates, professionally/technically qualified, skilled workers	Assess skill levels against requirements Indicate where steps have to be taken to deal with shortfalls
Attrition – employee turnover rates for different categories of management and employees	Indicate areas where steps have to be taken to increase retention rates Provide a basis for assessing levels of commitment
Attrition – cost of	Support business case for taking steps to reduce attrition
Absenteeism/sickness rates	Identify problems and need for more effective attendance management policies
Average number of vacancies as a percentage of total workforce	Identify potential shortfall problem areas
Total payroll costs (pay and benefits)	Provide data for productivity analysis

TABLE 11.1 *continued*

Data	Possible use: analysis leading to action
Compa-ratio – actual rates of pay as a percentage of policy rates	Enable control to be exercised over management of pay structure
Percentage of employees in different categories of contingent pay or payment-by-result schemes	Demonstrate the extent to which the organization believes that pay should be related to contribution
Total pay review increases for different categories of employees as a percentage of pay	Compare actual with budgeted payroll increase costs Benchmark pay increases
Average bonuses or contingent pay awards as a percentage of base pay for different categories of managers and employees	Analyse cost of contingent pay Compare actual and budgeted increases Benchmark increases
Employee surveys of engagement levels	Record outcome of engagement enhancement programmes and indicate direction of future plans
Outcome of equal pay reviews	Reveal pay gap between male and female employees
Personal development plans completed as a percentage of employees	Indicate level of learning and development activity
Training hours per employee	Indicate actual amount of training activity (note that this does not reveal the quality of training achieved or its impact)
Percentage of managers taking part in formal management development programmes	Indicate level of learning and development activity
Internal promotion rate (percentage of promotions filled from within)	Indicate extent to which talent management programmes are successful
Succession planning coverage (percentage of managerial jobs for which successors have been identified)	Indicate extent to which talent management programmes are successful
Percentage of employees taking part in formal performance reviews	Indicate level of performance management activity
Distribution of performance ratings by category of staff and department	Indicate inconsistencies, questionable distributions and trends in assessments
Accident severity and frequency rates	Assess health and safety programmes
Cost savings/revenue increases resulting from employee suggestion schemes	Measure the value created by employees

Multidimensional analytics

Multidimensional analytics combines different sets of data to show the extent to which there is any relationship between them. Thus it could be interesting to find out if an increase in the engagement levels of sales staff (as measured in an engagement survey) produced higher sales.

Regression analysis is a typical method of doing this. Regression is the relationship between two variables indicating how changes in levels of X relate to changes in levels of Y. A regression line (a trend line or line of best fit) can be traced on a scattergram expressing values of one variable on one axis and values of the other variable on the other axis as shown in Figure 11.1.

The scattergram in Figure 11.1 shows that as engagement levels go up, labour turnover rates go down. This means that they are correlated, which is interesting. But the conclusion cannot be reached that higher engagement levels cause lower turnover. There may be other factors such as fewer employment opportunities elsewhere or significant increases in pay.

However, even if causation cannot be established with confidence, the existence of correlation can be revealing. At least it can prove that a positive relationship does exist between an HR initiative and desirable outcomes. This can be used to justify the investment and point the way to further developments.

FIGURE 11.1 A scattergram with regression (trend) line showing relationship between levels of engagement and labour turnover

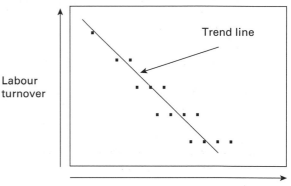

Predictive analytics

Some HR data can be analysed and used to predict future trends. This enables HR to make evidence-based decisions on strategy and to obtain information on the financial benefits of innovations which can be used to justify them. For example, an extrapolation of the trend line in Figure 11.1 would forecast further reductions in labour turnover. The resulting cost savings could be calculated and used to support continued expenditures on practices such as improving employee voice arrangements designed to enhance engagement.

CASE STUDIES

Nationwide Building Society

Nationwide feeds its HR capital information into an intranet-based information system that gives users an assessment of how they're doing against a number of indicators. It uses a dashboard of red, amber and green indicators to give each business unit an idea of how they are faring on a number of key drivers of employee commitment. This is backed up with advice on how improvement might be made.

Standard Chartered Bank

Standard Chartered Bank uses a human capital scorecard to analyse its data. This is produced on a quarterly and annual basis with various cuts of the same data produced for different business segments and countries, in addition to a global report. This comprises a series of slides with commentary to enable managers to understand the data.

The data is also included in twice-yearly board reviews on people strategy and forms part of the annual strategy planning process. The scorecard data is reviewed within each global business by a top team 'People Forum'. At country level, each local chief executive and his or her management committee reviews key trends in order to specify areas they need to focus on.

In addition, the bank uses qualitative analysis to examine trends and this has led it to identify the role of the manager as mediating the relationship between engagement and performance. In turn, this has led to a focus on qualitative research to identify what raises the bank's best managers above the rest. A further example is a qualitative analysis of high performance in selected customer-facing roles to determine the key behaviours that continue to drive customer loyalty.

Key learning points: HR analytics

HR analytics defined

HR analytics uses metrics to provide the basis for assessing the impact of HRM practices and the contribution made by people to organizational performance.

The purpose of HR analytics

HR analytics provides a basis for people management decision making.

HR analytics levels

There are three levels of HR analytics:

1   Descriptive analytics.

2   Multidimensional analytics.

3   Predictive analytics.

References

CIPD (2015) Fact sheet: HR analytics [online] http://www.cipd.co.uk/hr-resources/factsheets/hr-analytics.aspx [accessed 12 November 2015]

McAfee, A and Brynjolfsson, E (2012) Big Data: the management revolution, *Harvard Business Review*, October, pp 60–68

Pfeffer, J and Sutton, R I (2006) Evidence-based management, *Harvard Business Review*, January, pp 62–74

Rousseau, D M and Barends, E G (2011) Becoming an evidence-based HR practitioner, *Human Resource Management Journal*, **21** (3), pp 221–35

12
Knowledge management

KEY CONCEPTS AND TERMS

Communities of practice

Data

Explicit knowledge

Information

Knowledge

Knowledge management

Tacit knowledge

LEARNING OUTCOMES

On completing this chapter you should be able to define these key concepts. You should also know about:

- The purpose and significance of knowledge management
- Knowledge management strategies
- Knowledge management systems
- Knowledge management issues
- The contribution HR can make to knowledge management

Introduction

Knowledge management is concerned with storing and sharing the wisdom, understanding and expertise accumulated in an enterprise about its processes, techniques and operations. It treats knowledge as a key resource. It was defined by Tan (2000: 10) as: 'The process of systematically and actively managing and leveraging the stores of knowledge in an organization.' As Ulrich (1998: 126) remarked: 'Knowledge has become a direct competitive advantage for companies selling ideas and relationships.'

There is nothing new about knowledge management. Hansen *et al* (1999: 106) observed that: 'For hundreds of years, owners of family businesses have passed on their commercial wisdom to children, master craftsmen have painstakingly taught their trades to apprentices, and workers have exchanged ideas and know-how on the job.' But they also commented that: 'As the foundation of industrialized economies has shifted from natural resources to intellectual assets, executives have been compelled to examine the knowledge underlying their business and how that knowledge is used' (ibid: 106).

Knowledge management is more concerned with people and how they acquire, exchange and spread knowledge than it is about information technology. That is why it has become an important area for HR practitioners, who are in a strong position to exert influence in this aspect of people management. It is associated with intellectual capital theory (see Chapter 2), in that it refers to the notions of human, social and organizational or structural capital. It is also linked to organizational learning (see Chapter 32).

Knowledge management should be based on an understanding of the concept of knowledge; this is therefore dealt with in the first section of this chapter. In subsequent sections, knowledge management is described in more detail, strategies for developing its practice are described, and consideration is given to the role of HR.

The concept of knowledge

Knowledge is defined as what people understand about things, concepts, ideas, theories, procedures and practices. It can be described as know-how or, when it is specific, expertise. A distinction was made by Ryle (1949) between 'knowing how' and 'knowing that'. 'Knowing how' is the ability of a person to perform tasks, and 'knowing that' is holding pieces of knowledge in one's mind. According to Blackler (1995: 1023): 'Rather than regarding knowledge as something that people have, it is suggested that knowing is better regarded as something that they do.' He also noted that: 'Knowledge is multifaceted and complex, being both situated and abstract, implicit and explicit, distributed and individual, physical and mental, developing and static, verbal and encoded' (ibid: 1032–33).

Nonaka (1991) suggested that knowledge is held either by individuals or collectively. In Blackler's (1995) terms, embodied or embraced knowledge is

individual and embedded, and cultural knowledge is collective. It can be argued (Scarborough and Carter, 2000) that knowledge emerges from the collective experience of work and is shared between members of a particular group or community.

Explicit and tacit knowledge

Nonaka (1991) and Nonaka and Takeuchi (1995) stated that knowledge is either explicit or tacit. Explicit knowledge can be codified – it is recorded and available and is held in databases, in corporate intranets and intellectual property portfolios. Tacit knowledge exists in people's minds. It is difficult to articulate in writing and is acquired through personal experience. As suggested by Hansen *et al* (1999), it includes scientific or technological expertise, operational know-how, insights about an industry and business judgement. The main challenge in knowledge management is how to turn tacit knowledge into explicit knowledge.

Data, information and knowledge

A distinction can be made between data, information and knowledge:

- Data consist of the basic facts – the building blocks – for information and knowledge.

- Information is data that have been processed in a way that is meaningful to individuals; it is available to anyone entitled to gain access to it. As Drucker (1988: 46) put it: 'Information is data endowed with meaning and purpose.'

- Knowledge is information used productively; it is personal and often intangible and it can be elusive – the task of tying it down, encoding it and distributing it is tricky.

Knowledge management defined

Knowledge management is about getting knowledge from those who have it to those who need it in order to improve organizational effectiveness. It was defined by Scarborough *et al* (1999: 1) as 'any process or practice of creating, acquiring, capturing, sharing and using knowledge, wherever it resides, to enhance learning and performance in organizations'. They suggested that it focuses on the development of firm-specific knowledge and skills that are the result of organizational learning processes. Knowledge management deals with both stocks and flows of knowledge. Stocks include expertise and encoded knowledge in computer systems. Flows represent the ways in which knowledge is transferred from people to people or from people to a knowledge database.

Knowledge management identifies relevant information and then disseminates it so that learning can take place. It promotes the sharing of knowledge by linking people with people and by linking them to information so that they learn from recorded experiences. As explained by Blake (1988), the purpose of knowledge management is to capture a company's collective expertise and distribute it to wherever it can achieve the biggest payoff. This is in accordance with the resource-based view of the firm, which suggests that the source of competitive advantage lies within the firm (ie in its people and their knowledge), not in how it positions itself in the market. A successful company is a knowledge-creating company.

Knowledge is possessed by organizations and people in organizations. Organizational operational, technical and procedural knowledge can be stored in databanks and found in reports, libraries, policy documents, manuals and presentations. It can also be moved around the organization through information systems and by meetings, workshops, courses, 'master classes', written publications and 'communities of practice', defined by Wenger and Snyder (2000: 139) as 'groups of people informally bound together by shared expertise and a passion for joint enterprise'. The intranet provides an additional and very effective medium.

People possess knowledge that has been acquired through their own experiences at work. But it will not necessarily be shared formally or even informally with their colleagues, and crucial knowledge could be lost if it remains locked up in the minds of employees, or taken elsewhere by them if they leave the organization. An important issue in knowledge management is how knowledge can be identified and distributed.

In the information age, knowledge rather than physical assets or financial resources is the key to competitiveness. Knowledge management allows companies to make the best use of their employees' creativity and expertise (Mecklenburg *et al*, 1999). As Boxall and Purcell (2000: 197) noted: 'Managing knowledge inevitably means managing both the company's proprietary technologies and systems (which don't walk out of the door at the end of the day) and the people (who do)'.

Knowledge management strategies

Two approaches to knowledge management strategy have been identified by Hansen *et al* (1999): the codification strategy and the personalization strategy.

The codification strategy

Knowledge is carefully codified and stored in databases where it can be accessed and used easily by anyone in the organization. Knowledge is explicit and is codified using a 'people-to-document' approach. The strategy is therefore document-driven. Knowledge is extracted from the person who developed it, made independent of that person and reused for various purposes. It is stored in an electronic repository for people to use, and allows people to search for and retrieve codified knowledge without having to contact the person who originally developed it. This strategy relies largely on information technology to manage databases and also on the use of the intranet.

The personalization strategy

Knowledge is closely tied to the person who has developed it and is shared mainly through direct person-to-person contacts. This 'person-to-person' approach means providing for tacit knowledge to be passed on. The exchange is achieved by creating networks and encouraging face-to-face communication between people by informal conferences, workshops, communities of practice, brainstorming and one-to-one sessions.

Hansen *et al* (1999) proposed that the choice of strategy should be contingent on the organization: what it does and how it does it. Thus consultancies such as Ernst & Young, using knowledge to deal with recurring problems, may rely on codification so that recorded solutions to similar problems are easily retrievable. Strategy consultancy firms such as McKinsey or Bains, however, rely on a personalization strategy to help them to tackle the high-level strategic problems they are presented with that demand the provision of creative, analytically rigorous advice. They need to channel individual expertise and they find and develop people who are able to use a person-to-person knowledge-sharing approach. Experts can be identified who can be approached by e-mail, telephone or personal contact.

The research conducted by Hansen *et al* (1999) established that companies that use knowledge well adopt either the codification or the personalization strategy predominantly and use the other strategy to support their first choice. They pointed out that those who try to excel at both strategies risk failing at both.

Knowledge management issues

The strategies referred to above do not provide easy answers. The issues that need to be addressed in developing knowledge management practices are discussed below.

The pace of change

One of the main issues in knowledge management is how to keep up with the pace of change and identify what knowledge needs to be captured and shared.

Relating knowledge management strategy to business strategy

As Hansen *et al* (1999) showed, it is not knowledge per se but the way it is applied to strategic objectives that is the critical ingredient in competitiveness. They suggested that 'competitive strategy must drive knowledge management strategy' and that management have to answer the question: 'How does knowledge that resides in the company add value for customers?' (ibid: 114).

Technology and people

Technology may be central to companies adopting a codification strategy, but for those following a personalization strategy, IT is best used in a supportive role. Hansen *et al* (1999: 113) commented that:

> In the codification model, managers need to implement a system that is much like a traditional library – it must contain a large cache of documents and include search engines that allow people to find and use the documents they need. In the personalization model, it's more important to have a system that allows people to find other people.

Scarborough *et al* (1999) suggested that technology should be viewed as a means of communication rather than as a means of storing knowledge. Knowledge management is more about people than technology. Research by Davenport (1996) established that managers get two-thirds of their information from face-to-face or telephone conversations.

There is a limit to how much tacit knowledge can be codified. In organizations relying more on tacit than explicit knowledge, a person-to-person approach works best, and IT can only support this process; it cannot replace it.

The significance of process

Blackler (1995) emphasized that a preoccupation with technology may mean that too little attention is paid to the processes (social, technological and organizational) through which knowledge combines and interacts in different ways. The key processes are the interactions between people. This is the social capital of an organization – 'the network of relationships [that] constitute a valuable resource for the conduct of social affairs' (Nahpiet and Ghoshal, 1998: 243). Social networks can be particularly important in ensuring that knowledge is shared. Trust is also required – people are not willing to share knowledge with those they do not trust.

The culture of the company may inhibit knowledge sharing. The norm may be for people to keep knowledge to themselves as much as they can because 'knowledge is power'. An open culture will encourage people to share their ideas and knowledge.

Knowledge workers

Knowledge workers, as defined by Drucker (1993), are individuals who have high levels of education and specialist skills combined with the ability to apply these skills to identify and solve problems. As Argyris (1991: 100) commented, they are: 'The nuts and bolts of management... increasingly consist of guiding and integrating the autonomous but interconnected work of highly skilled people.' Knowledge management is about the management and motivation of knowledge workers who create knowledge and will be the key players in sharing it.

The contribution of HR to knowledge management

HR can make an important contribution to knowledge management simply because knowledge is shared between people; it is not just a matter of capturing explicit knowledge through the use of IT. The role of HR is to see that the organization has the intellectual capital it needs. The resource-based view of the firm emphasizes, in the words of Cappelli and Crocker-Hefter (1996: 7), that 'distinctive human resource practices help to create unique competences that differentiate products and services and, in turn, drive competitiveness'.

HR can contribute by providing advice on culture management, organization design and development, and by establishing learning and communication programmes and systems. There are 10 ways of doing this:

1 Help to develop an open culture in which the values and norms emphasize the importance of sharing knowledge.

2 Promote a climate of commitment and trust.

3 Advise on the design and development of organizations that facilitate knowledge sharing through networks, teamwork and communities of practice.

4 Advise on resourcing policies and provide resourcing services that ensure that valued employees who can contribute to knowledge creation and sharing are attracted and retained.

5 Advise on methods of motivating people to share knowledge and rewarding those who do so.

6 Help in the development of performance management processes that focus on the development and sharing of knowledge.

7 Develop processes of social learning, ie learning from other people by social interaction, that will generate and assist in disseminating knowledge.

8 Set up and organize workshops, conferences, seminars, communities of practice and symposia that enable knowledge to be shared on a person-to-person basis.

9 In conjunction with IT, develop systems for capturing and, as far as possible, codifying explicit and tacit knowledge.

10 Generally, promote the cause of knowledge management with senior managers to encourage them to exert leadership and support knowledge management initiatives.

Key learning points: Knowledge management

The purpose and significance of knowledge management

Knowledge management is about getting knowledge from those who have it to those who need it in order to improve organizational effectiveness.

Knowledge management strategies

The codification strategy – knowledge is carefully codified and stored in databases where it can be accessed and used easily by anyone in the organization. Knowledge is explicit and is codified using a 'people-to-document' approach.

The personalization strategy – knowledge is closely tied to the person who has developed it and is shared mainly through direct person-to-person contacts. This is a 'person-to-person' approach that involves ensuring that tacit knowledge is passed on.

Knowledge management systems

- Creating an intranet.

- Creating 'data warehouses'.

- Using decision support systems.

- Using 'groupware', ie information communication technologies such as e-mail or discussion bases.

- Creating networks or communities of practice or interest of knowledge workers.

Knowledge management issues

- The pace of change.

- Relating knowledge management strategy to business strategy.

- IT is best used in a supportive role.

- Attention must be paid to the processes (social, technological and organizational) through which knowledge combines and interacts in different ways.

- The significance of knowledge workers must be appreciated.

The contribution HR can make to knowledge management

- Help to develop an open culture that emphasizes the importance of sharing knowledge.

- Promote a climate of commitment and trust.

- Advise on the design and development of organizations that facilitate knowledge sharing.

- Ensure that valued employees who can contribute to knowledge creation and sharing are attracted and retained.

- Advise on methods of motivating people to share.

- Help in the development of performance management processes that focus on the development and sharing of knowledge.

- Develop processes of social learning that will generate and assist in disseminating knowledge.

- Set up and organize workshops, conferences and communities of practice and symposia that enable knowledge to be shared on a person-to-person basis.

- In conjunction with IT, develop systems for capturing and, as far as possible, codifying explicit and tacit knowledge.

- Generally, promote the cause of knowledge management with senior managers.

References

Argyris, C (1991) Teaching smart people how to learn, *Harvard Business Review*, May–June, pp 54–62

Blackler, F (1995) Knowledge, knowledge work and experience, *Organization Studies*, **16** (6), pp 16–36

Blake, P (1988) The knowledge management explosion, *Information Today*, **15** (1), pp 12–13

Boxall, P and Purcell, J (2000) Strategic human resource management: where have we come from and where are we going? *International Journal of Management Reviews*, **2** (2), pp 183–203

Cappelli, P and Crocker-Hefter, A (1996) Distinctive human resources are firms' core competencies, *Organizational Dynamics*, **24** (3), pp 7–22

Davenport, T H (1996) Why re-engineering failed: the fad that forgot people, *Fast Company*, Premier Issue, pp 70–74

Drucker, P (1988) The coming of the new organization, *Harvard Business Review*, January–February, pp 45–53

Drucker, P (1993) *Post-capitalist Society*, Oxford, Butterworth-Heinemann

Hansen, M T, Nohria, N and Tierney, T (1999) What's your strategy for managing knowledge? *Harvard Business Review*, March–April, pp 106–16

Mecklenberg, S, Deering, A and Sharp, D (1999) Knowledge management: a secret engine of corporate growth, *Executive Agenda*, **2**, pp 5–15

Nahpiet, J and Ghoshal, S (1998) Social capital, intellectual capital and the organizational advantage, *Academy of Management Review*, **23** (2), pp 242–66

Nonaka, I (1991) The knowledge-creating company, *Harvard Business Review*, November–December, pp 96–104

Nonaka, I and Takeuchi, H (1995) *The Knowledge-Creating Company*, New York, Oxford University Press

Ryle, G (1949) *The Concept of Mind*, Oxford, Oxford University Press

Scarborough, H and Carter, C (2000) *Investigating Knowledge Management*, London, CIPD

Scarborough, H, Swan, J and Preston, J (1999) *Knowledge Management: A literature review*, London, IPD

Tan, J (2000) Knowledge management – just more buzzwords? *British Journal of Administrative Management*, March–April, pp 10–11

Ulrich, D (1998) A new mandate for human resources, *Harvard Business Review*, January–February, pp 124–34

Wenger, E and Snyder, W M (2000) Communities of practice: the organizational frontier, *Harvard Business Review*, January–February, pp 33–41

13
Competency-based HRM

LEARNING OUTCOMES

On completing this chapter you should be able to define these key concepts. You should also understand:

- The meaning of competency-based HRM
- The different types of competencies
- The contents of competency frameworks
- Reasons for using competencies
- Coverage of competencies
- Applications of competency-based HRM
- How to develop a competency framework
- Keys to success in using competencies
- Competencies and emotional intelligence

Introduction

Competency-based HRM is about using the notion of competency and the results of competency analysis to inform and improve HR processes, especially those concerned with recruitment and selection, learning and development, and performance and reward management. It has an important part to play in a number of HR activities.

Competency defined

The term 'competency' refers to an underlying characteristic of a person that results in effective or superior performance. The leading figure in defining and popularizing the concept of competency was Boyatzis (1982). He conducted research that established that there was no single factor but a range of factors that differentiated successful from less successful performance. These factors included personal qualities, motives, experience and behavioural characteristics. Since his contribution, three types of competencies have been identified: behavioural competencies, technical competencies and NVQs/SNVQs.

Behavioural competencies

Behavioural competencies define behavioural expectations, ie the type of behaviour required to deliver results under such headings as teamworking, communication, leadership and decision making, and are sometimes known as 'soft skills'. Criterion referencing, ie comparing one measure or situation with a criterion in the form of another measure or outcome, may be used to determine the relationship between them. They can be set out in a 'competency framework', which contains definitions of the behavioural competencies used for all employees in an organization or for particular occupations such as managers. Guidelines on defining behavioural competencies are provided in Chapter 70.

Technical competencies

Technical competencies define what people have to know and be able to do (knowledge and skills) in order to carry out and meet performance expectations, and are sometimes known as 'hard skills'. They are related to either generic roles (groups of similar roles), or to individual roles ('role-specific competencies'). They are not usually part of a behavioural-based competency framework, although the two are linked when considering and assessing role demands and requirements.

The terms 'technical competencies' and 'competences' are closely related, although the latter has a particular and more limited meaning when applied to NVQs/SNVQs, as discussed below. Guidelines on defining technical competencies are provided in Chapter 70.

NVQ/SNVQ competences

The concept of competence was conceived in the UK as a fundamental part of the process of developing standards for NVQs/SNVQs. These specify minimum standards for the achievement of set tasks and activities expressed in ways that can be observed and assessed with a view to certification. An element of competence in NVQ language is a description of something that people in a work area should be able to do. They are assessed on being competent or not yet competent. No attempt is made to assess the level of competence.

Competency headings

The most common competencies included in frameworks are people skills, although outcome-based skills, such as focusing on results and solving problems, are also popular. The more common competency headings included in the frameworks of organizations responding to a Competency and Emotional Intelligence survey in 2006/7 are shown in Table 13.1.

The first seven of these were used in over 50 per cent of the respondent organizations. The 49 frameworks included 553 competency headings. No doubt many of these overlapped. The typical number of competencies was seven, rising to eight where the frameworks applied solely to managers.

Competency frameworks

Competency frameworks provide the basis for the use of competencies in areas such as recruitment and selection, learning and development, and performance management. They may simply contain definitions of each competency heading as in the example given in Table 13.2.

Some frameworks illustrate these definitions with descriptions of acceptable or unacceptable behaviour, which may be expressed as positive or negative indicators, as shown in Table 13.3.

TABLE 13.1   Incidence of different competency headings

Competency heading	Summary definition	% used
Team orientation	The ability to work cooperatively and flexibly with other members of the team with a full understanding of the role to be played as a team member.	86
Communication	The ability to communicate clearly and persuasively, orally or in writing.	73
People management	The ability to manage and develop people and gain their trust and cooperation to achieve results.	67
Customer focus	The exercise of unceasing care in looking after the interests of external and internal customers to ensure that their wants, needs and expectations are met or exceeded.	65
Results orientation	The desire to get things done well and the ability to set and meet challenging goals, create own measures of excellence and constantly seek ways of improving performance.	59
Problem-solving	The capacity to analyse situations, diagnose problems, identify the key issues, establish and evaluate alternative courses of action and produce a logical, practical and acceptable solution.	57
Planning and organizing	The ability to decide on courses of action, ensuring that the resources required to implement the action will be available and scheduling the programme of work required to achieve a defined end result.	51
Technical skills	Possession of the knowledge, understanding and expertise required to carry out the work effectively.	49
Leadership	The capacity to inspire individuals to give of their best to achieve a desired result and to maintain effective relationships with individuals and the team as a whole.	43
Business awareness	The capacity to continually identify and explore business opportunities, understand the business needs and priorities of the organization and constantly to seek methods of ensuring that the organization becomes more business-like.	37
Decision making	The capacity to make sound and practical decisions which deal effectively with the issues and are based on thorough analysis and diagnosis.	37

TABLE 13.1 *continued*

Competency heading	Summary definition	% used
Change orientation	The ability to manage and accept change.	33
Developing others	The desire and capacity to foster the development of members of his or her team, providing feedback, support, encouragement and coaching.	33
Influence and persuasion	The ability to convince others to agree on or to take a course of action.	33
Initiative	The capacity to take action independently and to assume responsibility for one's actions.	29
Interpersonal skills	The ability to create and maintain open and constructive relationships with others, to respond helpfully to their requests and to be sensitive to their needs.	29
Strategic orientation	The capacity to take a long-term and visionary view of the direction to be followed in the future.	29
Creativity	The ability to originate new practices, concepts and ideas.	26
Information management	The capacity to originate and use information effectively.	26
Quality focus	The focus on delivering quality and continuous improvement.	24
Self-confidence and assertiveness	Belief in oneself and standing up for one's own rights.	24
Self-development	Managing one's own learning and development.	22
Managing	Managing resources, people, programmes and projects.	20

TABLE 13.2   Example of a basic competency framework

- *Achievement/results orientation.* The desire to get things done well and the ability to set and meet challenging goals, create own measures of excellence and constantly seek ways of improving performance.
- *Business awareness.* The capacity continually to identify and explore business opportunities, understand the business opportunities and priorities of the organization and constantly to seek methods of ensuring that the organization becomes more business-like.
- *Communication.* The ability to communicate clearly and persuasively, orally or in writing.
- *Customer focus.* The exercise of unceasing care in looking after the interests of external and internal customers to ensure that their wants, needs and expectations are met or exceeded.
- *Developing others.* The desire and capacity to foster the development of members of his or her team, providing feedback, support, encouragement and coaching.
- *Flexibility.* The ability to adapt to and work effectively in different situations and to carry out a variety of tasks.
- *Leadership.* The capacity to inspire individuals to give of their best to achieve a desired result and to maintain effective relationships with individuals and the team as a whole.
- *Planning.* The ability to decide on courses of action, ensuring that the resources required to implement the actions will be available and scheduling the programme of work required to achieve a defined end result.
- *Problem solving.* The capacity to analyse situations, diagnose problems, identify the key issues, establish and evaluate alternative courses of action and produce a logical, practical and acceptable solution.
- *Teamwork.* The ability to work cooperatively and flexibly with other members of the team with a full understanding of the role to be played as a team member.

TABLE 13.3   Example of competency framework definition with positive and negative indicators

Competency heading	Manage continuous improvement
Competency definition	Constantly seeking ways of improving the quality of services, the relevance and appeal of those services to the needs of customers and clients, and their effectiveness.
Competency requirement	Set targets for improvement. Develop and implement programmes for managing change. Contribute to the development of quality assurance and control processes and ensure that they are implemented.
Positive indicators	Encourages the development of new ideas and methods, especially those concerned with the provision of quality. Conscious of the factors that enable change to take place smoothly. Discusses ideas with colleagues and customers and formulates views on how to improve services and processes.
Negative indicators	Doesn't try anything that hasn't been done before. Complacent, believes that there is no room for improvement. Follows previous practices without considering whether there is any need to change.

Using competencies

A number of approaches to using competencies are adopted, as described below.

The 'menu' approach

A 'menu' approach selects competencies that are relevant to generic or individual roles. Some organizations provide guidelines on the number of competencies to be selected (eg four to eight) and others combine their core framework with a menu so that users are required to select the organization-wide core competencies but can add a number of optional ones.

Role-specific competencies

Role-specific competencies are also used by some organizations for generic or individual roles. These may be incorporated in a role profile in addition to a statement of key result areas. This approach is adopted in performance management processes, in recruitment person specifications and in the preparation of individual learning programmes.

Graded competencies

A further, although less common, application of competencies is in graded career or job family structures (career or job families consist of jobs in a function or occupation such as marketing, operations, finance, IT, HR, administration or support services that are related through the activities carried out and the basic knowledge and skills required, but in which the levels of responsibility, knowledge, skill or competence needed differ). In such families, the successive levels in each family are defined in terms of competencies as well as the key activities carried out.

Applications of competency-based HRM

The Competency and Emotional Intelligence 2006/7 survey found that 95 per cent of respondents used behavioural competencies and 66 per cent used technical competencies. It was noted that because the latter deal with specific activities and tasks they inevitably result in different sets of competencies for groups of related roles, functions or activities. The three top areas where competencies were applied are:

- Recruitment and selection: 85 per cent.
- Learning and development: 82 per cent.
- Performance management: 76 per cent.

Only 30 per cent of organizations linked competencies to reward. The ways in which these competencies are used are described below.

Recruitment and selection

Competencies are used in many organizations as a basis for person specifications set out under competency headings developed through role analysis. The competencies defined for a role are used as the framework for recruitment and selection, and competency-based interviews are structured around the competencies listed in the specification.

Learning and development

Role profiles, which are either generic (covering a range of similar jobs) or individual (role-specific), can include statements of the competencies required. These are used to assess the levels of competency achieved by individuals and so identify their learning and development needs. Learning events can be based on competency analysis related to an organization's competency framework.

Competencies are also used in development centres, which help participants build up their understanding of the competencies they require now and in the future so that they can plan their own self-directed learning programmes.

Performance management

Competencies in performance management are used to ensure that performance reviews do not simply focus on outcomes but also consider the behavioural aspects of how the work is carried out that determine those outcomes. Performance reviews conducted on this basis are used to inform personal improvement and development plans and learning programmes.

Reward management

Competency-related pay relates additional awards to assessments of competency but it has never become popular. However, more frequent use is made of contribution-related pay, which provides for people to be rewarded according to both the results they achieve and their level of competence.

Developing a competency framework

A competency framework should be as simple to understand and use as possible. The language should be clear and jargon-free. Without clear language and examples it can be difficult to assess the level of competency achieved. When defining competencies, especially if they are used for performance management or competency-related pay, it is essential to ensure that they can be assessed. They must not be vague or overlap with other competencies and they must specify clearly the sort of behaviour that is expected and the level of technical or functional skills (competencies) required to meet acceptable standards. It is helpful to address the user directly ('you will...') and to give clear and brief examples of how the competency needs to be performed.

Developing a behavioural competency framework that fits the culture and purpose of the organization and provides a sound basis for a number of key HR processes is not to be undertaken lightly. It requires a lot of hard work, much of it concerned with involving staff and communicating with them to achieve understanding and buy-in. The steps required are described below.

Step 1. Programme launch

Decide on the purpose of the framework and the HR processes for which it will be used. Make out a business case for its development, setting out the benefits to the organization in such areas as improved performance, better selection outcomes, more focused performance management, employee development and reward processes. Prepare a project plan that includes an assessment of the resources required and the costs.

Step 2. Involvement and communication

Involve line managers and employees in the design of the framework (Steps 3 and 4) by setting up a task force. Communicate the objectives of the exercise to staff.

Step 3. Framework design – competency list

First, get the task force to draw up a list of the core competencies and values of the business – what it should be good at doing and the values it believes should influence behaviour. This provides a foundation for an analysis of the competencies required by people in the organization. The aim is to identify and define the behaviours that contribute to the achievement of organizational success, and there should be a powerful link between these people competencies and the organization's core competencies.

The list can be drawn up by brainstorming. The list should be compared with examples of other competency frameworks, to avoid replicating other lists. It is essential to produce a competency framework that fits and reflects the organization's own culture, values, core competencies and operations, but referring to other lists will help to clarify the conclusions reached in the initial analysis and serve to check that all relevant areas of competency have been included. When identifying competencies, care must be taken to avoid bias because of sex or race.

Step 4. Framework design – definition of competencies

Care needs to be exercised to ensure that definitions are clear and unambiguous and that they will serve their intended purpose. If, for example, one of the purposes is to provide criteria for conducting performance reviews, then it is necessary to be certain that the way the competency is defined, together with supporting examples, will enable fair assessments to be made. The following four questions have been produced by Mirabile (1998) to test the extent to which a competency is valid and can be used:

1 Can you describe the competency in terms that others understand and agree with?

2 Can you observe it being demonstrated or failing to be demonstrated?

3 Can you measure it?

4 Can you influence it in some way, eg by training, coaching or some other method of development?

It is also important at this stage to ensure that definitions are not biased.

Step 5. Define uses of the competency framework

Define exactly how it is intended that the competency framework should be used, covering such applications as recruitment and selection, learning and development, performance management and reward.

Step 6. Test the framework

Test the framework by gauging the reactions of a balanced selection of line managers and other employees to ensure that they understand it and believe that it is relevant to their roles. Also, pilot-test the framework in live situations for each of its proposed applications.

Step 7. Finalize the framework

Amend the framework as necessary following the tests and prepare notes for guidance on how it should be used.

Step 8. Communicate

Let everyone know the outcome of the project – what the framework is, how it will be used and how people will benefit. Group briefings and any other suitable means should be used.

Step 9. Train

Give line managers and HR staff training in how to use the framework.

Step 10. Monitor and evaluate

Monitor and evaluate the use of the framework and amend it as required.

Keys to success in using competencies

- The competencies should reflect the organization's values and its needs, as established by analysis, to determine the behaviours that will lead to high performance.
- Frameworks should not be over-complex.
- There should not be too many headings in a framework – seven or eight will often suffice.
- The language used should be clear and jargon-free.
- Competencies must be selected and defined in ways that ensure that they can be assessed by managers – the use of 'behavioural indicators' is helpful.
- Frameworks should be regularly updated.

Competencies and emotional intelligence

Emotional intelligence is a combination of skills and abilities such as self-awareness, self-control, empathy and sensitivity to the feelings of others. It covers many of the interpersonal skills included in competency frameworks.

But as Dulewicz and Higgs (1998) pointed out, the concept of emotional intelligence overlaps with that of competency.

Key learning points: Competency-based HRM

Competency-based HRM is about using the notion of competency and the results of competency analysis to inform and improve HR processes, especially those concerned with recruitment and selection, learning and development, and performance and reward management.

Competency defined

The term 'competency' refers to an underlying characteristic of a person that results in effective or superior performance. The different types of competencies are:

- Behavioural competencies define behavioural expectations, ie the type of behaviour required to deliver results under such headings as teamworking, communication, leadership and decision making.

- Technical competencies define what people have to know and be able to do (knowledge and skills) to carry out their roles effectively.

- NVQ/SNVQ competences specify minimum standards for the achievement of set tasks and activities expressed in ways that can be observed and assessed with a view to certification.

The contents of competency frameworks (the 10 most popular headings)

1 team orientation;

2 communication;

3 people management;

4 customer focus;

5 results orientation;

6 problem solving;

7 planning and organizing;

8 technical skills;

9 leadership;

10 business awareness.

Uses of competencies

- Learning and development: 82 per cent.

- Performance management: 76 per cent.

- Selection: 85 per cent.

- Recruitment: 55 per cent.

- Reward: 30 per cent.

How to develop a competency framework

- Decide on the purpose of the framework and the HR processes for which it will be used.

- Make out a business case for its development, setting out the benefits.

- Prepare a project plan that includes an assessment of the resources required and the costs.

- Involve line managers and employees in the design of the framework.

- Communicate the objectives of the exercise to staff.

- Draw up a list of the core competencies of the business.

- Define the competencies for inclusion in a competency framework.

- Test and finalize and communicate framework.

Keys to success in using competencies

- The competencies should reflect the organization's values and its needs, as established by analysis, to determine the behaviours that will lead to high performance.

- Frameworks should not be over-complex.

- There should not be too many headings in a framework – seven or eight will often suffice.

- The language used should be clear and jargon-free.

- Competencies must be selected and defined in ways that ensure they can be assessed by managers – the use of 'behavioural indicators' is helpful.

- Frameworks should be regularly updated.

Competencies and emotional intelligence

The emotional intelligence elements of self-awareness, emotional management, empathy, relationships, communication and personal style correspond to competencies such as sensitivity, flexibility, adaptability, resilience, impact, listening, leadership, persuasiveness, motivating others, energy, decisiveness and achievement motivation.

References

Boyatzis, R (1982) *The Competent Manager*, New York, Wiley

Competency and Emotional Intelligence (2006/7) *Raising Performance Through Competencies: The annual benchmarking survey*, London, Competency and Emotional Intelligence

Dulewicz, V and Higgs, M (1999) The seven dimensions of emotional intelligence, *People Management*, 28, October, p 53

Mirabile, R J (1998) Leadership competency development, competitive advantage for the future, *Management Development Forum*, **1** (2), pp 1–15

14
The ethical dimension of HRM

LEARNING OUTCOMES

On completing this chapter you should be able to define these key concepts. You should also understand:

- The meaning of ethics
- The nature of ethical decisions and judgements
- The ethical concepts of deontology, utilitarianism, stakeholder theory and discourse theory
- The significance of the concepts of equity, justice and fair dealing
- HRM ethical guidelines
- How to resolve ethical dilemmas
- The ethical role of HR

Introduction

The theme of this chapter is the importance of recognizing that there is an ethical dimension to human resource management. As Boxall *et al* (2007: 5) pointed out: 'While HRM does need to support commercial outcomes (often called "the business case"), it also exists to serve organizational needs for social legitimacy.' This means exercising social responsibility, ie being concerned for the interests (well-being) of employees and acting ethically with regard to the needs of people in the organization and the community.

To grasp this ethical dimension, it is necessary to understand the nature and principles of ethics, the ethical role of HR and the ethical guidelines they can use. It is also necessary to know about approaches to resolving ethical dilemmas.

The meaning and concerns of ethics

Ethics is defined by the *Compact Oxford Dictionary* as being 'related to morals, treating of moral questions', and ethical is defined as 'relating to morality'. Morality is defined as 'having moral qualities or endowments' and moral is defined as 'of or pertaining to the distinction between right and wrong'. Petrick and Quinn (1997: 42) wrote that ethics 'is the study of individual and collective moral awareness, judgement, character and conduct'. Hamlin *et al* (2001: 98) noted that ethics is concerned with rules or principles that help us to distinguish right and wrong.

Ethics and morality are sometimes treated as being synonymous, although Beauchamp and Bowie (1983: 1–2) suggested that they are different: 'Whereas morality is a social institution with a history and code of learnable rules, ethical theory refers to the philosophical study of the nature of ethical principles, decisions and problems.' Clearly, ethics is concerned with matters of right and wrong and therefore involves moral judgements. Even if ethics and morality are not the same, the two are closely linked. As Clegg *et al* (2007: 111) put it: 'We understand ethics as the social organizing of morality.' Simplistically, ethics could be described as being about behaviour while morality is about beliefs.

Ethics is concerned with making decisions and judgements about what is the right course of action to take. It can be described in terms of a framework that sets out different approaches and can be extended to embrace particular concepts that affect and guide ethical behaviour, namely equity, justice and fair dealing. These approaches and concepts are discussed below.

The nature of ethical decisions and judgements

As defined by Jones (1991: 367), an ethical decision is one that is morally acceptable to the larger community. He also noted that: 'A moral issue is present where a person's actions, when freely performed, may harm or benefit others. In other words, the action or decision must have consequences for others and must involve choice, or volition, on the part of the actor or decision maker' (ibid: 367).

Winstanley and Woodall (2000a: 8–9) observed that:

> Ethics is not about taking statements of morality at face value; it is a critical and challenging tool. There are no universally agreed ethical frameworks... Different situations require ethical insight and flexibility to enable us to encapsulate the grounds upon which competing claims can be made. Decisions are judgements usually involving choices between alternatives, but rarely is the choice between right and wrong... Moral disagreement and judgements are concerned with attitudes and feelings, not facts.

Clegg *et al* (2007: 112) emphasized that: 'Ethical decisions emerge out of dilemmas that cannot be managed in advance through rules.' People have to make choices. Foucault (1997: 284) asked: 'What is ethics, if not the practice of freedom?'

Ethical frameworks

The ethical concepts of deontology, utilitarianism, stakeholder theory and discourse theory, as described below, provide frameworks that can be used to evaluate HRM policies and practices.

Deontological theory

Deontological (from the Greek for 'what is right') theory maintains that some actions are right or wrong irrespective of their consequences. It is associated with Kant's notion of the categorical imperative, which contains two main propositions: a) that one should follow the principle that what is right for one person is right for everyone, and thus you must do to others as you would be done by; and b) in the words of Rawls (1973: 183): 'We must treat persons solely as ends and not in any way as means.'

Utilitarianism

Utilitarianism is the belief that the highest principle of morality is to maximize happiness, the overall balance of pleasure against pain. Actions are justified when they result in the greatest good to the greatest number. As Sandel (2010: 33) explained, utilitarianism says that 'the morality of an action depends solely on the consequences it brings about; the right thing to do will be whatever brings about the best state of affairs.' In other words, actions should be judged in terms of their results. This can be interpreted as supporting the dubious principle that the end justifies the means – torture is all right as long as it prevents terrorism (NB even if this argument were accepted, the effectiveness of torture as a means of preventing terrorism is highly questionable). Utilitarianism has been criticized first because it fails to respect individual rights and second because, as Michael Sandel explained, it implies that all moral judgements can be translated into a single currency of value, but there is no such thing as a 'util'.

Stakeholder theory

In accordance with the ideas of Freeman (1984), stakeholder theory states that the organization should be managed on behalf of its stakeholders: its owners, employees, customers, suppliers and local communities. As Legge (1998: 22) described it, management must act in the interests of the stakeholders as their agent, and also act in the interests of the organization to ensure the survival of the firm, safeguarding the long-term stakes of each group.

Discourse ethics

Foucault (1972) defined discourse as the taken-for-granted ways that people are collectively able to make sense of experience. Discourse ethics, as explained by Winstanley and Woodall (2000a: 14), suggests that 'the role of ethicists is not to provide solutions to ethical problems, but rather to provide a practical process and procedure which is both rational and consensus enhancing, through which issues can be debated and discourse can take place.'

Equity theory

Equity theory, as formulated by Adams (1965), is concerned with the perceptions people have about how they are being treated as compared with others. To be dealt with equitably is to be treated fairly in comparison with another group of people (a reference group) or a relevant other person. Equity involves feelings and perceptions and it is always a comparative process. It is not synonymous with equality, which means treating everyone the same and which would be inequitable if they deserve to be treated differently.

Justice

Justice is the process of treating people in a way that is inherently fair, right and proper. The concept of 'justice as fairness' proposed by Rawls (1973: 348) states that 'natural duties and obligations arise only in virtue of ethical principles'. These principles were expressed by Rawls as follows:

> First: every person is to have the equal right to the most extensive basic liberty comparable with a similar liberty for others.
> Second: social and economic inequalities are to be arranged so that they are both (a) reasonably expected to be to everyone's advantage, and (b) attached to positions and offices open to all. (ibid: 60)

There are four types of justice: procedural justice, distributive justice, social justice and natural justice.

Procedural justice

Procedural justice (Adams, 1965; Leventhal, 1980) involves treating people in ways that are fair, consistent, transparent and properly consider their views and needs. In organizations, it is concerned with fair process and the perceptions employees have about the fairness with which company procedures in such areas as performance appraisal, promotion and discipline are being operated. The five factors that affect perceptions of procedural justice, as identified by Tyler and Bies (1990), are:

- Adequate consideration of an employee's viewpoint.
- Suppression of personal bias towards an employee.
- Applying criteria consistently across employees.
- Providing early feedback to employees about the outcome of decisions.
- Providing employees with an adequate explanation of decisions made.

Distributive justice

Distributive justice (Adams, 1965; Leventhal, 1980) means ensuring that people are rewarded equitably in comparison with others in the organization and in accordance with their contribution, and that they receive what was promised to them (management 'delivers the deal').

Social justice

Social justice is based on the concepts of human rights and equality. Rawls (1973: 3–4) rejected the principle of utilitarianism when he asserted that in society: 'Each person possesses an inviolability founded on justice that even the welfare of society as a whole cannot override. For this reason, justice denies that the loss of freedom for some is made right by a greater good shared by others.' In organizations, social justice means relating to employees generally in ways that recognize their natural rights to be treated justly, equitably and with respect.

Natural justice

According to the principles of natural justice, employees should know the standards they are expected to achieve and the rules to which they are expected to conform. They should be given a clear indication of where they are failing or what rules have been broken and, except in cases of gross misconduct, they should be given a chance to improve before disciplinary action is taken.

HRM ethical guidelines

The guidelines set out below relate to how employees are treated in general and to the major HRM activities of organization development, recruitment and selection, learning and development, performance management, reward management and employee relations. They also relate to employment practices concerning the work environment, employee well-being, equal opportunities, managing diversity, handling disciplinary matters and grievances, job security and redundancy.

General guidelines

- Recognize that the strategic goals of the organization should embrace the rights and needs of employees as well as those of the business.
- Recognize that employees are entitled to be treated as full human beings with personal needs, hopes and anxieties.
- Do not treat employees simply as means to an end or mere factors of production.
- Relate to employees generally in ways that recognize their natural rights to be treated justly, equitably and with respect.

Organization development (OD)

- Agree in advance with clients and individuals the goals, content and risks of an OD programme.
- Make explicit any values or assumptions used in the programme.
- Obtain the maximum involvement of all concerned in the programme so that they understand the processes involved and how they can benefit from them.

- Work with clients to plan and implement change to the benefit of all stakeholders.
- Enable individuals to continue with their development on completing the programme.
- Protect confidentiality.

Recruitment and selection

- Treat candidates with consideration – applications should be acknowledged, candidates should be kept informed without undue delay of decisions made about their application, and they should not be kept waiting for the interview.
- Avoid intrusive or hectoring questioning in interviews.
- Do not put candidates under undue stress in interviews.
- Do not criticize any aspect of the candidate's personality or experience.
- Use relevant selection criteria based on a proper analysis of job requirements.
- Give candidates reasonable opportunity to present their case and to ask questions.
- Avoid jumping to conclusions about candidates on inadequate evidence or as a result of prejudice.
- Give accurate and complete information to candidates about the job, prospects, security and terms and conditions of employment.
- Only use properly validated tests administered by trained testers.
- Do not use discriminating or biased tests.
- Monitor tests for impact and unintended bias.
- Ensure that candidates are not unfairly disadvantaged by testing processes.
- Give candidates feedback on test results unless there are compelling reasons why feedback should not be given.
- Ensure that selection decisions are free of discrimination or bias on the grounds of sex, sexual orientation, race, age or disability.
- Give unsuccessful candidates the reason for the decision if they request it.

Learning and development

- Respect individual rights for dignity, self-esteem, privacy and autonomy.
- Recognize that it is necessary and legitimate to provide individuals with learning opportunities that enable them to gain the knowledge and skills required to perform well in their jobs and develop their potential. But note that individuals should still be allowed autonomy to choose the extent to which they pursue learning and development programmes beyond this basic requirement.
- Accept that while the organization has the right to conduct learning and development activities that enhance performance, individuals also have the right to be provided with opportunities to develop their own knowledge, skills and employability.
- Ensure that people taking part in learning events feel 'psychologically safe' in accordance with the view expressed by Schein (1993: 91) that: 'To make people feel safe in learning, they must have a motive, a sense of direction, and the opportunity to try out new things without the fear of punishment.'
- Avoid manipulating people to accept imposed organizational values.

Performance management

Performance management ethical principles have been defined by Winstanley and Stuart-Smith (1996) as follows:

- *Respect for the individual* – people should be treated as 'ends in themselves' and not merely as 'means to other ends'.
- *Mutual respect* – the parties involved in performance management should respect each other's needs and preoccupations.
- *Procedural fairness* – the procedures incorporated in performance management should be operated fairly in accordance with the principles of procedural justice.
- *Transparency* – people affected by decisions emerging from performance management processes should have the opportunity to scrutinize the basis upon which decisions were made.

Reward management

- Generally apply the principles of procedural and distributive justice.
- Ensure that reward policies and practices are fair, equitable and transparent and that they are applied consistently.
- Reward people according to their contribution.
- Ensure that people know in general the basis upon which rewards are provided and in particular how their own reward package is determined.
- Maintain reasonable and defensible pay differentials.
- Ensure that equal pay is provided for work of equal value.
- Base decisions about performance pay or bonuses on fair and equitable criteria.
- Avoid bonus schemes that encourage undesirable behaviour.
- Do not pay less than the living wage.

Employee relations

- Deliver the deal.
- Be open to employees' input and responsive to justifiable questions and concerns about employment policies and practices.
- Provide genuine opportunities and channels for employees to express their views and influence decisions on matters that affect them.
- Negotiate in good faith.
- Recognize that the interests of management and employees do not necessarily coincide and develop, and implement employee relations policies accordingly.

Employment practices

- Create a healthy, safe and fulfilling work environment.
- Promote the well-being of employees by improving the quality of working life

provided for them, enhancing work–life balance and developing family-friendly policies.

- Take particular care to minimize the stress to which employees may be subjected.
- Provide equal opportunities for all with regard to recruitment and selection, learning and development, talent management, career progression and promotion.
- Manage diversity by recognizing the differences between people and ensuring that everyone feels valued and that the talents of all employees will be properly utilized.
- Handle disciplinary matters according to the principles of natural justice.
- Recognize that people may have legitimate grievances and respond to them promptly, fully and sympathetically.
- Preserve job security as far as possible and take alternative action to avoid compulsory redundancies.
- If compulsory redundancy is unavoidable, do whatever is possible to alleviate the distress by, for example, helping people to find work.
- Do not allow whistle-blowers who expose wrongdoing to be penalized.

Ethical dilemmas

'Ethics will be enacted in situations of ambiguity where dilemmas and problems will be dealt with without the comfort of consensus or certitude' (Clegg *et al*, 2007: 109). Bauman, quoted in Bauman and Tester (2001: 44), commented that: 'Morality concerns choice first of all – it is the predicament human beings encounter when they must make a selection amongst various possibilities.' And Derrida (1992) observed that ethical responsibility can exceed rational calculation.

Resolving ethical dilemmas

As Adam Smith (1759) wrote in *The Theory of Modern Sentiments* (quoted by Harrison, 2009: 246): 'When ethically perplexed, the question we should always ask is: would a disinterested observer, in full possession of the relevant facts, approve or disapprove of our actions?' This guidance is just as compelling and relevant today.

Woodall and Winstanley (2000: 285) suggested that 'being ethical is not so much about finding one universal principle to govern all action, but more about knowing how to recognize and mediate between often unacknowledged differences of view.' By definition, an ethical dilemma is one that will be difficult to resolve. There may be all sorts of issues surrounding the situation, some of which will be unclear or contentious. The extent to which people react or behave rationally may be limited by their capacity to understand the complexities of the situation they are in and affected by their emotional reactions to it (the concept of bounded rationality). As Harrison (2009: 331) explained:

> Some of the factors that militate against a purely 'rational' approach include confused, excessive,

incomplete or unreliable data, incompetent processing or communicating of information, pressures of time, human emotions, and differences in individuals' cognitive processes, mental maps and reasoning capacity.

Faced with factors such as these the process of ethical dilemma resolution can be hard going.

There is no 'one right way' to deal with an ethical issue, but an approach based on systematic questioning, analysis and diagnosis to get at the facts and establish the issues involved is more likely to produce a reasonably satisfactory outcome than one relying purely on 'gut feeling'. The following checklist – used judiciously and selectively according to the circumstances – can provide a basis for such questioning and analysis.

Checklist – dealing with ethical issues

- What are the known facts about the situation and is it possible that there are facts or circumstances that have not come to light, and if so what can be done to uncover them?

- In disciplinary or conduct cases, to what extent does the conduct contravene the organization's code of ethical conduct (if one exists) or any other relevant organizational policy guidelines and rules?

- In disciplinary cases, are there any mitigating circumstances?

- Have different versions or interpretations of the facts and circumstances been offered and, if so, what steps can be taken to obtain the true and full picture?

- Do the facts as established and confirmed justify the proposed action?

- Is the proposed action in line with both the letter and the spirit of the law?

- Is the proposed action and any investigations leading to it consistent with the principles of natural, procedural or distributive justice?

- Will the proposed action benefit the organization and if so how?

- Is there any risk of the proposed action doing harm to the organization's reputation for fair dealing?

- Will the proposed action be harmful to the individual affected or to employees generally in any way and if so how?

The ethical role of HR

Legge (1998: 20–21) commented that: 'In very general terms I would suggest that the experience of HRM is more likely (but not necessarily) to be viewed positively if its underlying principles are

ethical.' HR professionals have a special responsibility for guarding and promoting core values in the organization on how people should be managed and treated. They need to take action to achieve fair dealing. This means treating people according to the principles of procedural, distributive, social and natural justice, and seeing that decisions or policies that affect them are transparent in the sense that they are known, understood, clear and applied consistently.

Kochan (2007: 600) suggested that: 'HR derives its social legitimacy from its ability to serve as an effective steward of a social contract in employment relationships capable of balancing and integrating the interests and needs of employers, employees and the society in which these relationships are embedded.' But he also noted that most HR professionals have 'lost any semblance of credibility as stewards of the social contract because most HR professionals have lost their ability to seriously challenge or offer an independent perspective on the policies and practices of the firm' (ibid: 604). And, Parkes and Davis (2013: 2427) pointed out the risk that the HR role can become 'rather passive, favouring communicating standards rather than actively promoting ethical behaviour'.

To overcome this problem and thus fulfil an ethical role Winstanley and Woodall (2000b: 7) remarked that: 'HR professionals have to raise awareness of ethical issues, promote ethical behaviour, disseminate ethical practices widely among line managers, communicate codes of ethical conduct, ensure people learn about what constitutes ethical behaviours, manage compliance and monitor arrangements.'

There are three approaches that HR can adopt. The first is to ensure that HR policies and the actions taken to implement them meet acceptable ethical standards. HR can press for the production of a value statement that sets out how the organization intends to treat its employees. Value statements may be set out under such headings as care and consideration for people, belief that people should be treated justly and equitably and belief that the views of employees about matters that concern them should be listened to.

This requires advocacy skills to persuade management to adopt and act on these policies and the courage and determination to make out the ethical case even when management favours a conflicting business case. But value statements are meaningless until the values are put into practice; the ethical role of HR involves helping to ensure that this takes place.

Second, HR practitioners can act as role models, leading by example and living and breathing good ethical behaviour. As a respondent to the survey conducted by Parkes and Davis (2013: 2426) commented: 'If HR does not act ethically, how can it expect employees to do so?'

The third approach, and the hardest, is to challenge unethical behaviour on the part of management. Such behaviour can take many forms, including management tolerance for exploitation and bullying; the lack of a whistle-blowing policy that provides routes for reporting malpractice, and performance management criteria that emphasize organizational gain over all else. The latter was the case at the Royal Bank of Scotland (RBS) before the financial crisis, where the performance management concentrated on target achievement, ignoring behaviour. The courage to challenge is less likely to be forthcoming in organizations where the culture is one of command and control – and obedience is expected to whatever is dictated by management (features of the pre-crash RBS culture). Power, politics and culture shape norms of behaviour and, as Herb Kelleher (the CEO of Southwest Airlines) put it, culture is 'what people do when no one is looking' (reported by Lee, 1994). One respondent to the Parkes and Davis survey (2013: 2425) commented: 'It can be difficult on a personal level to be speaking out – HR do not have the power'. Another said: 'Speaking out can be career suicide'. It is too easy in these circumstances for HR to be mere bystanders. Neil Roden, former head of HR at RBS, explained HR's position in relation to the financial debacle at the bank as follows: 'I'm not absolving myself totally... (but) I can't see what HR could have done... I wasn't running the bank... the CEO makes the decisions, not me. HR is a support function, no more, no less important than sales or IT.'

An HR director who is a member of an executive board can question decisions from an ethical viewpoint but if the comments are not heeded then the director will either have to accept the decision or resign. It is important to challenge – and the courage to do so is listed by the CIPD as one of the qualities required by an HR professional. But it is difficult and there may be limits to what HR can do. If HR professionals cannot do anything about the way their organization does things they either have to carry on and do whatever they can in other less confrontational ways, or they must leave.

Key learning points: The ethical dimension of HRM

Ethics and morality defined

Ethics is defined by the *Compact Oxford Dictionary* as being 'related to morals, treating of moral questions', and ethical is defined as 'relating to morality'. Morality is defined as 'having moral qualities or endowments' and moral is defined as 'of or pertaining to the distinction between right and wrong'. Simplistically, ethics could be described as being about behaviour while morality is about beliefs.

Ethics is concerned with making ethical decisions and judgements. It can be described in terms of an ethical framework that sets out different approaches and can be extended to embrace particular concepts that affect and guide ethical behaviour, namely equity, justice and fair dealing. An ethical decision is one that is morally acceptable to the larger community.

Ethical concepts

The ethical concepts of deontology, utilitarianism, stakeholder theory and discourse theory provide frameworks that can be used to evaluate HRM policies and practices.

An important role for HR professionals is to do whatever they can to embed the consistent application of ethical values in the organization so that they can become values in use rather than simply professed values in a code of practice or values statement.

Ethical guidelines

Ethical guidelines relate to how employees are treated in general, and to the major HRM activities of organization development, recruitment and selection, learning and development, performance management, reward management, employee relations and employment practices concerning the work environment, employee well-being, equal opportunities, managing diversity, handling disciplinary matters and grievances, job security and redundancy.

Handling ethical dilemmas

There is no 'one right way' to deal with an ethical dilemma but an approach based on systematic questioning, analysis and diagnosis to get at the facts and establish the issues involved is more likely to produce a reasonably satisfactory outcome than one relying purely on 'gut feeling'. An ethical dilemma is one that will be difficult to resolve. There may be all sorts of issues surrounding the situation, some of which will be unclear or contentious.

The role of HR

HR professionals have a special responsibility for guarding and promoting core values in the organization on how people should be managed and treated generally. They are particularly concerned with values relating to just and fair treatment. They can act as role models and challenge unethical practices. But challenging can be difficult.

References

Adams, J S (1965) Injustice in social exchange, in (ed) L Berkowitz, *Advances in Experimental Psychology*, New York, Academic Press

Bauman, Z and Tester, K (2001) *Conversations with Zygmunt Bauman*, Cambridge, Polity Press

Beauchamp, T L and Bowie, N E (1983) *Ethical Theory and Business*, 2nd edn, Englewood Cliffs, NJ, Prentice Hall

Boxall, P F, Purcell, J and Wright, P (2007) Human resource management; scope, analysis and significance, in (eds) P Boxall, J Purcell and P Wright, *The Oxford Handbook of Human Resource Management*, Oxford, Oxford University Press, pp 1–18

Clegg, S, Kornberger, M and Rhodes, C (2007) Business ethics as practice, *British Journal of Management*, **18** (2), pp 107–22

Derrida, J (1992) Forces of law: the mystical foundation of authority, in (eds) D Cornell, M Rosenfeld and D G Carlson, *Deconstruction* and the Possibility of Justice, London, Routledge, pp 3–68

Foucault, M (1972) *The Archaeology of Knowledge and the Discourse on Language*, New York, Pantheon Books

Foucault, M (1997) *Ethics, Subjectivity and Truth. Essential Works of Foucault, 1954–1984*, ed P Rabinow, New York, The New Press

Freeman, R E (1984) *Strategic Management: A stakeholder perspective*, Englewood Cliffs, NJ, Prentice Hall

Hamlin, B, Keep, J and Ash, K (2001) *Organizational Change and Development: A reflective guide for managers*, London, FT Pitman

Harrison, R (2009) *Learning and Development*, 5th edn, London, CIPD

HR Magazine (2010) Interview with Neil Roden, former HR Director of RBS, available at http://www.hrmagazine.co.uk/hr/opinion/105196/interview-neil-roden-hr-director-royal-bank-scotland [accessed 6 July 2013]

Jones, T M (1991) Ethical decision making by individuals in organizations: an issue-contingent model, *Academy of Management Review*, 16 (2), pp 366–95

Kochan, T A (2007) Social legitimacy of the HRM profession: a US perspective, in (eds) P Boxall, J Purcell and P Wright, *The Oxford Handbook of Human Resource Management*, Oxford, Oxford University Press, 599–619

Lee, W G (1994) A conversation with Herb Kelleher, *Organizational Dynamics*, 23 (2), pp 64–74

Legge, K (1998) The morality of HRM, in (eds) C Mabey, D Skinner and T Clark, *Experiencing Human Resource Management*, London, Sage, pp 14–32

Leventhal, G S (1980) What should be done with equity theory? in (eds) G K Gergen, M S Greenberg and R H Willis, *Social Exchange:*

Advances in theory and research, New York, Plenum

Parkes, C and Davis, A J (2013) Ethics and social responsibility – do HR professionals have 'the courage to challenge' or are they set to be permanent 'bystanders'? *International Journal of Human Resource Management*, 23 (12), pp 2411–34

Petrick, J A and Quinn, J F (1997) *Management Ethics: Integrity at work*, London, Sage

Rawls, J (1973) *A Theory of Justice*, Oxford, Oxford University Press

Sandel, M J (2010) *Justice: What's the right thing to do?* London, Penguin Books

Schein, E (1993) How can organizations learn faster? The challenge of entering the green room, *Sloan Management Review*, 34 (2), pp 85–92

Tyler, T R and Bies, R J (1990) Beyond formal procedures: the interpersonal context of procedural justice, in (ed) J S Carrol, *Applied Social Psychology and Organizational Settings*, Hillsdale, NJ, Lawrence Erlbaum

Winstanley, D and Stuart-Smith, K (1996) Policing performance: the ethics of performance management, *Personnel Review*, 25 (6), pp 66–84

Winstanley, D and Woodall, J (2000a) Introduction, in (eds) D Winstanley and J Woodall, *Ethical Issues in Contemporary Human Resource Management*, Basingstoke, Macmillan, pp 3–22

Winstanley, D and Woodall, J (2000b) The ethical dimension of human resource management, *Human Resource Management Journal*, 10 (2), pp 5–20

Woodall, J and Winstanley, D (2000) Concluding comments: ethical frameworks for action, in (eds) D Winstanley and J Woodall, *Ethical Issues in Contemporary Human Resource Management*, Basingstoke, Macmillan, pp 3–22

15
Corporate social responsibility

LEARNING OUTCOMES

On completing this chapter you should be able to define these key concepts. You should also understand:

- The meaning of corporate social responsibility (CSR)
- CSR activities

- CSR strategy
- Developing a CSR strategy
- The rationale for CSR

Introduction

The notion that businesses should act in a socially responsible way by practising 'corporate social responsibility' (CSR) has been around for some time. J M Keynes wrote in 1923 that: 'The business man is only tolerable so long as his gains can be held to bear some relation to what, roughly and in some sense, his activities have contributed to society.' The aim of this chapter is to explore what CSR means as a concept and a strategy. The rationale for CSR is also considered – the arguments in favour of CSR

are overwhelming, but reference is made also to powerful opposing views.

HR professionals, because of the ethical dimension of their function (as described in Chapter 14), have an important role to play in furthering CSR. CSR was justified by the CIPD (2009: 1) as a relevant and important HR activity because:

> CSR needs to be embedded in an organization's culture to make a change to actions and attitudes, and the support of the top team is critical to success. HR already works at communicating and implementing ideas, policies, cultural and

Key learning points: Corporate social responsibility

The meaning of CSR

CSR activities include incorporating social characteristics or features into products and manufacturing processes, adopting progressive HRM practices, achieving higher levels of environmental performance through recycling and pollution abatement, and advancing the goals of community organizations.

The rationale for CSR

There are two arguments for CSR (Hillman and Keim, 2001): first, there is a moral imperative for businesses to 'do the right thing' without regard to how such decisions affect firm performance (the social issues argument); second, firms can achieve competitive advantage by tying CSR activities to primary stakeholders (the stakeholders argument).

Developing a CSR strategy

- Identify the areas in which CSR activities might take place by reference to their relevance in the business context of the organization and an evaluation of their significance to stakeholders.

- Prioritize as necessary on the basis of an assessment of the relevance and significance of CSR to the organization and its stakeholders, and the practicalities of introducing the activity or practice.

- Draw up the strategy and make the case for it to top management and the stakeholders to obtain their approval.

- Communicate information on the strategy, comprehensively and regularly.

- Provide training to employees on the skills they need to use in implementing the CSR strategy.

References

Baron, D (2001) Private policies, corporate policies and integrated strategy, *Journal of Economics and Management Strategy*, **10** (1), pp 7–45

Business for Social Responsibility (2007) Annual Report [online] www.BSR.org [accessed 5 October 2008]

Business in the Community (2007) Benchmarking Responsible Business Practice [online] bitc.org.uk [accessed 5 October 2008]

CIPD (2003) *Corporate Social Responsibility and HR's Role*, London, CIPD

CIPD (2009) *Corporate Social Responsibility*, London, CIPD

CSR Academy (2006) *The CSR Competency Framework*, Norwich, Stationery Office

Egan, J (2006) Doing the decent thing: CSR and ethics in employment, *IRS Employment Review*, 858, 3 November, pp 9–16

Freeman, R E (1984) *Strategic Management: A stakeholder perspective*, Englewood Cliffs, NJ, Prentice Hall

Friedman, M (1962) *Capitalism and Freedom*, Chicago, IL, University of Chicago Press

Friedman, M (1970) The social responsibility of business is to increase its profits, *New York Times Magazine*, September, p 13

Hillman, A and Keim, G (2001) Shareholder value, stakeholder management and social issues: what's the bottom line? *Strategic Management Journal*, **22** (2), pp 125–39

Husted, B W and Salazar, J (2006) Taking Friedman seriously: maximizing profits and social performance, *Journal of Management Studies*, **43** (1), pp 75–91

Keynes, J M (1923) *A Tract on Monetary Reform*, London, Macmillan

Levitt, T (1958) The dangers of social responsibility, *Harvard Business Review*, September–October, pp 41–50

McWilliams, A, Siegal, D S and Wright, P M (2006) Corporate social responsibility: strategic implications, *Journal of Management Studies*, **43** (1), pp 1–12

Moran, P and Ghoshal, S (1996) Value creation by firms, Academy of Management Best Paper Proceedings, pp 41–45

Porter, M E and Kramer, M R (2006) Strategy and society: the link between competitive advantage and corporate social responsibility, *Harvard Business Review*, December, pp 78–92

Russo, M V and Fouts, P A (1997) A resource-based perspective on corporate environmental performance and profitability, *Academy of Management Review*, 40 (3), pp 534–59

Wood, D J (1991) Corporate social performance revisited, *Academy of Management Review*, 16 (4), pp 691–718

PART IV

People and organizations

PART IV CONTENTS

Introduction

Human resource management policies and practices need to be based on an understanding of the factors that affect the behaviour of people in organizations. The purpose of this part of the book is to outline a basic set of concepts and to provide analytical tools that will enable HR specialists to diagnose organizational behaviour and to take appropriate actions.

The part starts in Chapter 16 with a general analysis of the concept of organizational behaviour, the term used to describe: 1) how organizations function with regard to their structure, processes and culture; 2) the characteristics of people and how they act in organizations, individually or in groups. Organizational behaviour theory is based on the main behavioural science theories, which have been proved by research. Like all proven theories it provides insights into good practice. Thus it provides guidance on the design of work systems, organizations and jobs, as discussed in Chapter 17, and approaches to organization development (the systematic process of improving organizational capability, which is concerned with process – how things get done) in Chapter 18. It also provides the conceptual framework for approaches to achieving the motivation, commitment and engagement of people, as considered in Part V of this handbook.

16
Organizational behaviour

LEARNING OUTCOMES

On completing this chapter you should be able to define these key concepts. You should also know about:

● What is meant by organizational behaviour
● The sources and applications of organizational behaviour theory
● How organizations function
● Organizational culture
● Organizational climate
● Organizational processes
● Characteristics of people
● Implications for HR specialists

Introduction

An understanding of how organizations function and how people behave in them is important to HR professionals, indeed to all managers, as pointed out by Nadler and Tushman (1980).

Source review

The significance of organizational behaviour theory – Nadler and Tushman (1980: 30)

Managers perform their jobs within complex social systems called organizations. In many senses, the task of the manager is to influence behaviour in a desired direction, usually towards the accomplishment of a specific task or performance goal. Given this definition of the managerial role, skills in the diagnosis of patterns of organizational behaviour become vital. Specifically, the manager needs to understand the patterns of behaviour that are observed, predict in what direction behaviour will move (particularly in the light of managerial action), and to use this knowledge to control behaviour over the course of time.

Source review

Characteristics of organizational behaviour – Ivancevich *et al* (2008: 11)

● It is a way of thinking – about individuals, groups and organizations.

● It is multidisciplinary – it uses principles, models, theories and methods from other disciplines.

● There is a distinctly humanistic orientation – people and their attitudes, perceptions, learning capacities, feelings and goals are of major importance.

● It is performance-oriented – it deals with the factors affecting performance and how it can be improved.

● The use of scientific method is important in studying variables and relationships.

● It is applications-oriented in the sense of being concerned with providing useful answers to questions that arise when managing organizations.

Organizational behaviour defined

Organizational behaviour was defined by Huczynski and Buchanan (2007: 843) as the term used to describe 'the study of the structure, functioning, and performance of organizations and the behaviour of groups and individuals within them'. The following are the characteristics of organizational behaviour theory.

The sources and applications of organizational behaviour theory

Organizational behaviour theory is based on the main behavioural science disciplines. These are defined as the fields of enquiry dedicated to the study of human behaviour through sophisticated and rigorous methods. The ways in which they contribute to different aspects of organizational behaviour theory and how they in turn influence HRM practices are summarized in Figure 16.1.

FIGURE 16.1   The sources and applications of organization behaviour theory

Discipline	Contribution to theory	Application
Psychology	• individual differences • personality • attitudes • perceptions • self-concept • attributions • motivation • engagement and commitment • learning • leadership	• job/work design • selection processes and tests • learning and development programmes • performance management • reward management • attitude measurement
Social psychology	• group processes • attitude change • behavioural change • communication	• organization development • organization design • change management • communication systems
Sociology	• group dynamics • power • politics • conflict • organization culture • leadership	• organization development • organization design • job design • leadership development • employee relations

How organizations function

An organization is an entity that exists to achieve a purpose through the collective efforts of the people who work in or for it. Organizing is the process of making arrangements in the form of defined or understood responsibilities and relationships to enable those people to work cooperatively together. Organizations can be described as systems that, as affected by their environment, have a structure that has both formal and informal elements.

Organization structures are frameworks for getting things done. Traditional formal structures were based on laid-down hierarchies (lines of command) represented in organization charts, and use was made of closely defined job descriptions. But to varying extents, organizations operate informally as well as formally by means of a network of roles and relationships that cut across formal organizational boundaries and lines of command. Organization structures can evolve almost spontaneously as circumstances change and new activities have to be carried out.

Factors affecting how organizations function

The processes that take place in organizations – interaction and networking, leadership, group behaviour, the exercise of power and the use of politics – may well have much more effect on how organizations function than can be shown in a defined organization chart supported by elaborate job descriptions and an organization manual. Moreover, the way in which an organization functions will be largely contingent on its purpose, technology, methods of working and external environment. A number of theories have been developed, summarized in Table 16.1, to explain how organizations function, culminating in the contingency and post-bureaucratic schools that now predominate.

Types of organization

The main types of organization are described briefly below:

- Line and staff – a traditional organization based on the military model in which a hierarchy of 'line managers' carry out the fundamental operations such as manufacturing, sales or customer service while the 'staff' functions such as finance and personnel provide them with services, advice and support.

- Mechanistic – a formal organization that is hierarchical with rigid chains of command and control, distinct departments and tightly defined and specialized jobs (usually a characteristic of a line and staff organization).

- Organic – a relatively informal organization with a non-hierarchical, flat structure where the emphasis is on horizontal processes, the elimination of boundaries between functions, teamwork and flexible roles (also known as a lattice organization).

TABLE 16.1   Schools of organization theory

School	Leading exponents	Summary of theory
The classical school	Taylor (1911), Fayol (1916), Urwick (1947)	Organizations need control, measurement, order and formality to function well. They have to minimize the opportunity for unfortunate and uncontrollable informal relations, leaving room only for the formal ones.
The human relations school	Barnard (1938), Roethlisberger and Dickson (1939)	Barnard emphasized the importance of the informal organization – the network of informal roles and relationships that, for better or worse, strongly influences the way the formal structure operates. In their analysis of the Hawthorne studies, Roethlisberger and Dickson stressed the importance of informal groups and decent, humane leadership.
The behavioural science school	Argyris (1957), Herzberg *et al* (1957), McGregor (1960), Likert (1961), Schein (1965)	A humanistic point of view is adopted that is concerned with what people can contribute and how they can best be motivated.

TABLE 16.1   *continued*

School	Leading exponents	Summary of theory
The bureaucratic model	Weber (1908) translated in 1947	Max Weber coined the term 'bureaucracy' as a label for a type of formal organization in which impersonality and rationality are developed to the highest degree. Bureaucracy, as he conceived it, was the most efficient form of organization because it was logical and because personalized relationships and non-rational, emotional considerations do not get in its way.
The socio-technical model	Emery (1959), Trist *et al* (1963)	In any system of organization, technical or task aspects are interrelated with the human or social aspects. The emphasis is on interrelationships between, on the one hand, the technical processes of transformation carried out within the organization and, on the other hand, the organization of work groups and the management structures of the enterprise.
The systems school	Miller and Rice (1967)	Organizations should be treated as open systems that are continually dependent upon and influenced by their environments. The basic characteristic of the enterprise as an open system is that it transforms inputs into outputs within its environment.
The contingency school	Burns and Stalker (1961), Woodward (1965), Lawrence and Lorsch (1969)	Members of the contingency school analysed a variety of organizations and concluded that their structures and methods of operation are a function of the circumstances in which they exist. They do not subscribe to the view that there is one best way of designing an organization or that simplistic classifications of organizations as formal or informal, bureaucratic or non-bureaucratic are helpful.
The post-bureaucratic school	Pascale (1990), Ghoshal and Bartlett (1995)	Rather than seeing organizations as a hierarchy of static jobs, members of the post-bureaucratic school think of them as a portfolio of dynamic processes that overlay and often dominate the vertical, authority-based processes of the hierarchical structure. The emphasis is on 'horizontal tasks', collaboration and networking across units rather than on 'vertical tasks' within functional units. Hence the concept of the 'boundaryless organization'.

- Matrix organization – an organization that consists of a functional structure with a number of different disciplines and a project structure consisting of project teams drawn from the disciplines.

- Network organization – a collection of interrelated organizations that extends beyond the boundaries of any single organization.

- Virtual organization – an organization that mainly uses electronic means for its members to interact with one another, thus minimizing face-to-face contacts.

Organizational culture

The culture of an organization has been described by Deal and Kennedy (2000: 4) as 'the way we do things around here'. It is more complex than that, as other definitions given below indicate. But this simplistic definition at least demonstrates that it is an all-pervading notion that affects the way in which people behave and has to be taken into account as a contingency factor in any programme for developing organizations and HR policies and practices. Organizational culture offers a shared system of meanings which is the basis for communications and mutual understanding. If these functions are not fulfilled in a satisfactory way, culture may significantly reduce the effectiveness of an organization. This is why it is important for HR specialists to understand the concept of organizational culture and how it affects organizations.

Organizational culture defined

Organizational or corporate culture is the pattern of values, norms, beliefs, attitudes and assumptions that may not have been articulated but shape the ways in which people in organizations behave and things get done. 'Values' refer to what is believed to be important about how people and organizations behave. 'Norms' are the unwritten rules of behaviour.

This definition emphasizes that organizational culture is concerned with the subjective aspect of what goes on in organizations. It refers to abstractions such as values and norms that pervade the whole or part of a business, which may not be defined, discussed or even noticed. Nevertheless, culture can have a significant influence on people's behaviour. The following are some other definitions of organizational culture:

- A strong culture is a system of informal rules that spells out how people are to behave most of the time. (Deal and Kennedy, 2000: 15)

- The culture of an organization refers to the unique configuration of norms, values, beliefs and ways of behaving that characterize the manner in which groups and individuals combine to get things done. (Eldridge and Crombie, 1974: 89)

- Organizational culture offers a shared system of meanings that is the basis for communications and mutual understanding (Furnham and Gunter, 1993: 70–71).

- Culture is a pattern of basic assumptions – invented, discovered or developed by a given group as it learns to cope with the problems of external adaptation and internal integration – that has worked well enough to be considered valid and, therefore, to be taught to new members as the correct way to perceive, think and feel in relation to these problems. (Schein, 1990: 110)

How organizational culture develops

The values and norms that are the basis of culture are formed in four ways. First, by the leaders in the organization, especially those who have shaped it in the past. Schein (1990) indicates that people identify with visionary leaders – how they behave and what they expect. They note what such leaders pay attention to and treat them as role models. Second, as Schein also points out, culture is formed around critical incidents – important events from which lessons are learnt about desirable or undesirable behaviour. Third, culture develops from the need to maintain effective working relationships among organization members that establish values and expectations. Finally, culture is influenced by the organization's environment, which may tend to be dynamic or unchanging.

Culture evolves over time as a result of shared experiences. Schein (1984) suggested that this is a learning process which takes place either through the trauma model, in which members of the organization learn to cope with some threat by the erection of defence mechanisms, or by means of the positive reinforcement model, where things that seem to work become embedded and entrenched. Learning takes place as people adapt to and cope with external pressures, and as they develop successful approaches and mechanisms to handle the internal challenges, processes and technologies in their organization. Where culture has developed over long periods of time and has become firmly embedded, it may be difficult to change quickly, if at all, unless a traumatic event occurs.

The diversity of culture

The development process described above may result in a culture that characterizes the whole organization. But there may be different cultures within organizations. For example, the culture of an outward-looking marketing department may be substantially different from that of an internally focused manufacturing function. There may be some common organizational values or norms, but in some respects these will vary between different work environments.

The components of culture

Organizational culture can be described in terms of values, norms, artefacts and management or leadership style.

Values

Values are beliefs in what is best or good for the organization and what should or ought to happen. The 'value set' of an organization may only be recognized at top level, or it may be shared throughout the business, in which case the business could be described as value-driven.

The stronger the values the more they will influence behaviour. This does not depend upon their having been articulated. Implicit values that are

deeply embedded in the culture of an organization and are reinforced by the behaviour of management can be influential, while espoused values that are mere rhetoric and are not reflected in managerial behaviour may have little or no effect. When values are acted on they are called 'values in use'. Examples are listed below.

Areas in which values may be expressed – explicitly or implicitly

- Care and consideration for people.
- Competence.
- Competitiveness.
- Customer service.
- Innovation.
- Performance.
- Quality.
- Teamwork.

Values may be expressed through norms and artefacts, as described below. They may also be expressed through the media of language (organizational jargon), rituals, stories and myths.

Norms

Norms are the unwritten rules of behaviour, the 'rules of the game' that provide informal guidelines on how to behave. Norms tell people what they are supposed to be doing, saying, believing, even wearing. They are never expressed in writing – if they were, they would be policies or procedures. They are passed on by word of mouth or behaviour and can be enforced by the reactions of people if they are violated. They can exert very powerful pressure on behaviour because of these reactions – we control others by the way we react to them.

Typical norms

- How managers treat the members of their teams (management style) and how the latter relate to their managers. The prevailing work ethic, eg 'work hard, play hard', 'come in early, stay late', 'if you cannot finish your work during business hours you are obviously inefficient', 'look busy at all times', 'look relaxed at all times'.

- Status – how much importance is attached to it; the existence or lack of obvious status symbols.

- Ambition – naked ambition is expected and approved of, or a more subtle approach is the norm.

- Performance – exacting performance standards are general; the highest praise that can be given in the organization is to be referred to as 'very professional'.

- Power – recognized as a way of life; executed by political means, dependent on expertise and ability rather than position; concentrated at the top; shared at different levels in different parts of the organization.

- Politics – rife throughout the organization and treated as normal behaviour; not accepted as overt behaviour.

- Loyalty – expected, a cradle-to-grave approach to careers; discounted, the emphasis is on results and contribution in the short term.

- Anger – openly expressed; hidden, but expressed through other, possibly political, means.

- Approachability – managers are expected to be approachable and visible; everything happens behind closed doors.

- Formality – a cool, formal approach is the norm; forenames are/are not used at all levels; there are unwritten but clearly understood rules about dress.

Artefacts

Artefacts are the visible and tangible aspects of an organization that people hear, see or feel and which contribute to their understanding of the organization's culture. Artefacts can include such things as the working environment, the tone and language used in e-mails, letters or memoranda, the manner in which people address each other at meetings or over the telephone, the welcome (or lack of welcome) given to visitors and the way in which receptionists deal with outside calls. Artefacts can be very revealing.

Management style

The approach managers use to deal with people – their management or leadership style – is a significant part of the culture of an organization. Management style can be described in terms of the following extremes:

charismatic	↔	non-charismatic
autocratic	↔	democratic
controller	↔	enabler
transactional	↔	transformational

Most managers adopt an approach somewhere between the extremes. Some will vary it according to the situation or their feelings at the time; others will stick to the same style whatever happens. Every manager has his or her own style but this will be influenced by the organizational culture, which may produce a prevailing management style that represents a behavioural norm for managers that is generally expected and adopted.

Classifying organizational culture

There have been many attempts to classify or categorize organizational cultures as a basis for analysis and for taking action to support or change them. Most of these classifications are expressed in four dimensions; three of the best-known ones are summarized below. Note that following the lead of Harrison (1972), there is much common ground between them.

Harrison (1972) – organization ideologies

- Power-oriented – competitive, responsive to personality rather than expertise.

- People-oriented – consensual, management control rejected.

- Task-oriented – focus on competency, dynamic.

- Role-oriented – focus on legality, legitimacy and bureaucracy.

Handy (1981) – culture typology

- The power culture is one with a central power source that exercises control. There are few rules or procedures and the atmosphere is competitive, power-oriented and political.

- The role culture in which work is controlled by procedures and rules and the role, or job description, is more important than the person who fills it. Power is associated with positions not people.

- The task culture in which the aim is to bring together the right people and let them get on with it. Influence is based more on expert power than on position or personal power. The culture is adaptable and teamwork is important.

- The person culture in which the individual is the central point. The organization exists only to serve and assist the individuals in it.

Appropriate cultures

It is not possible to say that one culture is better than another, only that a culture is to a greater or lesser extent appropriate in the sense that it is relevant to the needs and circumstances of the organization and helps rather than hinders its performance. However, embedded cultures can exert considerable influence on organizational behaviour. If there is an appropriate and effective culture it would therefore be desirable to take steps to support or reinforce it. If the culture is inappropriate, attempts should be made to determine what needs to be changed and to develop and implement plans for change. A culture will be more effective if it is consistent in its components and shared amongst organizational members, and if it makes the organization unique, thus differentiating it from other organizations.

Schein (1984) – classification of cultures

- Power culture in which leadership resides in a few and rests on their ability and tends to be entrepreneurial.

- Role culture in which power is balanced between the leader and the bureaucratic structure. The environment is likely to be stable and roles and rules are clearly defined.

- Achievement culture in which personal motivation and commitment are stressed and action, excitement and impact are valued.

- Support culture in which people contribute out of a sense of commitment and solidarity.

Organizational climate

As defined by Harrison and Shirom (1999: 263), organizational climate refers to 'members' perceptions of organizational features such as decision making, leadership and norms about work'. Ivancevich *et al* (2008: 528) described organizational climate as: 'A set of properties of the work environment, perceived directly or indirectly by the employees, that is assumed to be a major force in influencing employee behaviour.'

The term 'organizational climate' is sometimes confused with 'organizational culture' and there has been much debate on what distinguishes them from one another. In Denison's (1996) analysis of this issue, he suggested that 'culture' refers to the deep structure of organizations, which is rooted in the values, beliefs and assumptions held by organizational members. In contrast, 'climate' refers to those aspects of the environment that are consciously perceived by organizational members. Rousseau (1988) stated that climate is a perception and is descriptive. Perceptions are sensations or realizations experienced by an individual. Descriptions are what a person reports of these sensations.

The debate about the meanings of these terms can become academic. It is easiest to regard organizational climate as how people perceive (see and feel about) the culture existing in their organization. French *et al* (1985) distinguish between the actual situation (ie culture) and the perception of it (ie climate).

Organizational processes

A number of social processes take place in organizations that affect how they function. These are: interaction and networking, communication, group behaviour, leadership, power, politics and conflict.

Interaction and networking

Interactions between people criss-cross the organization, creating networks for getting things done and exchanging information that is not catered for in the formal structure. 'Networking' is an increasingly important process in flexible and delayered organizations where more fluid interactions across the structure are required between individuals and teams. Networking means that people canvass opinion and enlist support to promote their projects or ideas. In this way they may get more done than by going through formal channels. People also get things done in organizations by creating alliances – getting agreement on a course of action with other people and joining forces to put the proposed action into effect.

Communications

The communications processes used in organizations have a marked effect on how it functions, especially if they take place through the network, which can then turn into the 'grapevine'. E-mails encourage the instant flow of information (and sometimes produce information overload) but may inhibit face-to-face interactions, which are often the best ways of doing things.

Group behaviour

Organizations consist of groups or teams of people working together. They may be set up formally as part of the structure or they may be informal gatherings. A group can be a permanent or a temporary feature in an organization. Interactions take place within and between groups and the degree to which these processes are formalized varies according to the organizational context.

Formal groups or teams are created by organizations to achieve a defined purpose. People are brought together with the necessary skills to carry out the tasks and a system exists for directing, coordinating and controlling the group's activities. Informal groups are set up by people in organizations who have some affinity for one another. It could be said that formal groups satisfy the needs of the organization while informal groups satisfy the needs of their members.

Groups develop an ideology that affects the attitudes and actions of their members and the degree of satisfaction they feel. If the group ideology is strong and individual members identify closely with the group, it will become increasingly cohesive. Group norms or implicit rules will be evolved that define what is acceptable behaviour and what is not. This is described as a 'reference group', which consists of the group of people with whom an individual identifies. The individual accepts the group's norms and, if in doubt about what to do or say, reference is made to these norms or to other group members before action is taken. Most people in organizations belong to a reference group and this can significantly affect the ways in which they behave.

Four stages of group development were identified by Tuckman (1965):

1 Forming, when there is anxiety, dependence on the leader and testing to find out the nature of the situation and the task, and what behaviour is acceptable.

2 Storming, where there is conflict, emotional resistance to the demands of the task, resistance to control and even rebellion against the leader.

3 Norming, when group cohesion is developed, norms emerge, views are exchanged openly, mutual support and cooperation increase and the group acquires a sense of its identity.

4 Performing, when interpersonal problems are resolved, roles are flexible and functional, there are constructive attempts to complete tasks and energy is available for effective work.

Leadership

Organizations largely function by means of managers and supervisors who exercise leadership in order to get their teams into action and ensure that they achieve the results expected of them. Goleman (2000) reported that a study by Hay McBer of 3,871 executives, selected from a database of more than 20,000 executives worldwide, established that leadership had a direct impact on organizational climate, and that climate in turn accounted for nearly one-third of the financial results of organizations. The conclusion from research conducted by Higgs (2006) was that leadership behaviour accounts for almost 50 per cent of the difference between change success and failure. Research by Northouse (2006) into 167 US firms in 13 industries established that over a 20-year period leadership accounted for more variations in performance than any other variable. Leadership skills are described in Chapter 74.

Power

Organizations exist to get things done; in the process of doing this, people or groups exercise power. Directly or indirectly, the use of power in influencing behaviour is a pervading feature of organizations, whether it is exerted by managers, specialists, informal groups or trade union officials. It is a way of achieving results, but it can be misused.

Politics

Political behaviour is an inevitable feature of organizational life. The aim of organizational politicians is to get their own way by influencing people to accept their point of view without going through the usual channels or relying on their authority. Some individuals genuinely believe that the best way to get something done is by using political means, especially when they are frustrated by the normal decision processes. Others unashamedly pursue their own ends. Political behaviour can be harmful when it is underhand and devious, but it can sometimes help to enlist support and overcome obstacles to getting results. All managers need political skills, as described in Chapter 79, but, because of the nature of their role, such skills are particularly important for HR specialists.

Conflict

Conflict is also inevitable in organizations because they function by means of adjustments and compromises among competitive elements in their structure and membership. Conflict also arises when there is change, because it may be seen as a threat to be challenged or resisted, or when there is frustration. Conflict is not always deplorable. It can be a result of progress and change and it can be used constructively.

Characteristics of people

To manage people effectively, it is necessary to take into account the factors that affect how they behave at work. The development of HR processes and the design of organizations are often predicated on the belief that everyone is the same and that they will behave rationally when faced with change or other demands. But the behaviour of people differs because of their characteristics and individual differences and it is not always rational.

The management of people would be much easier if everyone were the same, but they are not. As discussed below, they are, of course, different because of variations in personal characteristics and the influence of their background (the way in which they were brought up). Some people also consider sex, race or disability as factors that affect people's behaviour at work, although holding this view readily leads to discrimination. In addition, there will be differences in ability, intelligence and personality.

Variations in personal characteristics

The headings under which personal characteristics can vary have been classified by Mischel (1968) as follows.

Source review

Variations in personal characteristics – Mischel (1968)

- Competencies – abilities and skills.

- Constructs – the conceptual frameworks which govern how people perceive their environment.

- Expectations – what people have learnt to expect about their own and others' behaviour.

- Values – what people believe to be important.

- Self-regulatory plans – the goals people set themselves and the plans they make to achieve them.

These characteristics are affected by environmental or situational variables, which include the type of work individuals carry out; the culture, climate and management style in the organization; the social group within which they work; and the 'reference groups' individuals use for comparative purposes (eg comparing conditions of work or pay between one category of employee and another).

The personal characteristics that affect people's behaviour at work, as discussed below, are their ability, intelligence, personality, attitudes, emotions and emotional intelligence.

Ability

Ability is the quality possessed by people that makes an action possible. Abilities have been analysed by Burt (1954) and Vernon (1961). They classified them into two major groups: V:ed – verbal, numerical, memory and reasoning abilities; and K:m –

spatial and mechanical abilities, as well as perceptual (memory) and motor skills relating to physical operations such as eye/hand coordination and mental dexterity.

They also suggested that overriding these abilities there is general mental ability (GMA), which accounts for most variations in performance. Following a meta-analysis of 85 years of research findings, Schmidt and Hunter (1998) established that GMA was the most valid predictor of future performance and learning for selecting people without previous experience.

Intelligence

Intelligence has been variously defined as:

- The capacity to solve problems, apply principles, make inferences and perceive relationships (Argyle, 1989: 53).

- The capacity for abstract thinking and reasoning with a range of different contents and media (Toplis *et al*, 2004: 20).

- What is measured by intelligence tests (Wright and Taylor, 1970: 31).

The last, tautological definition is not facetious. As an operational definition, it can be related to the specific aspects of reasoning, inference, cognition (ie knowing, conceiving) and perception (ie understanding, recognition), which intelligence tests attempt to measure.

General intelligence (GI) consists of a number of mental abilities that enable a person to succeed at a wide variety of intellectual tasks that use the faculties of knowing and reasoning. It can be measured by an intelligence test and is sometimes expressed as an intelligence quotient (IQ), which is the ratio of an individual's mental age to the individual's actual age as measured by an intelligence test.

The concept of emotional intelligence (as described later) stresses that emotional maturity – in the sense of the ability to identify, assess and manage the emotions of one's self and others – is also important.

Personality

Personality has been defined by Huczynski and Buchanan (2007: 138) as: 'The psychological qualities that influence an individual's characteristic behaviour patterns in a stable and distinctive manner.' As noted by Ivancevich *et al* (2008), personality appears to be organized into patterns that are, to some degree, observable and measurable and involves both common and unique characteristics – every person is different from every other person in some respects but similar to other people in other respects. Personality is a product of both nature (hereditary) and nurture (the pattern of life experience). Personality can be described in terms of traits or types.

Traits

Traits are predispositions to behave in certain ways in a variety of different situations. The leading model of personality traits is the following 'big five' classification (Costa and McRae, 1992; Digman, 1990):

1 Openness – inventive/curious or consistent/cautious.

2 Conscientiousness – efficient/organized or easy-going/careless.

3 Extraversion – outgoing/energetic or solitary/reserved.

4 Agreeableness – friendly/compassionate or cold/unkind.

5 Neuroticism – sensitive/nervous or secure/confident.

The assumption that people are consistent in the ways they express these traits is the basis for making predictions about their future behaviour. We all attribute traits to people in an attempt to understand why they behave in the way they do. But people do not necessarily express the same trait across different situations or even the same trait in the same situation. Different people may exhibit consistency in some traits and exhibit considerable variability in others.

Types

Type theories of personality identify a number of types of personality that can be used to categorize people and may form the basis of a personality test. The types may be linked to descriptions of various traits. One of the most widely used type theories is that of Jung (1923). He identified four major preferences:

- relating to other people – extraversion or introversion;

- gathering information – sensing (dealing with facts that can be objectively verified), or intuitive (generating information through insight);

- using information – thinking (emphasizing logical analysis as the basis for decision making), or feeling (making decisions based on internal values and beliefs);

- making decisions – perceiving (collecting all the relevant information before making a decision), or judging (resolving the issue without waiting for a large quantity of data).

This is the basis of personality tests such as the Myers-Briggs Types Indicator.

Types should be distinguished from traits. As Huczynski and Buchanan (2007: 142) put it: 'Type approaches fit people into categories possessing common behaviour patterns. A personality trait, on the other hand, is an enduring behaviour that occurs in a variety of settings. While individuals belong to types, traits belong to individuals.'

Attitudes

An attitude can broadly be defined as a settled mode of thinking. Attitudes are evaluative. They are developed through experience but they are less stable than traits and can change as new experiences are gained or influences absorbed. Within organizations they are affected by cultural factors (values and norms); the behaviour of management (management style); policies such as those concerned with pay, recognition, promotion and the quality of working life; and the influence of the 'reference group' (the group with whom people identify). Sometimes there may be a discrepancy between attitudes and behaviour, ie someone may believe in one thing – such as being fair to people – but act differently. This is called 'cognitive dissonance'.

Emotions

Emotions are feelings that arouse people and therefore influence their behaviour, such as anger, fear, sadness, joy, anticipation and acceptance. The mildest forms of emotions are called 'moods', which are low-intensity, long-lasting emotional states.

Emotional intelligence

The notion of emotional intelligence was first defined by Salovey and Mayer (1990), who proposed that it involves the capacity to perceive emotion, integrate emotion in thought, understand emotion and manage emotions effectively. Goleman (1995) popularized the concept. He defined emotional intelligence as: 'The capacity for recognizing our own feelings and those of others, for motivating ourselves, for managing emotions well in ourselves as well as others.'

He suggested that its four components are:

1 Self-management – the ability to control or redirect disruptive impulses and moods and regulate own behaviour coupled with a propensity to pursue goals with energy and persistence. The six competencies associated with this component are self-control, trustworthiness and integrity, initiative, adaptability – comfort with ambiguity, openness to change and a strong desire to achieve.

2 Self-awareness – the ability to recognize and understand your moods, emotions and drives as well as their effect on others. This is linked to three competencies: self-confidence, realistic self-assessment and emotional self-awareness.

3 Social awareness – the ability to understand the emotional make-up of other people, and skill in treating people according to their emotional reactions. This is linked to six competencies: empathy, expertise in building and retaining talent, organizational awareness, cross-cultural sensitivity, valuing diversity, and service to clients and customers.

4 Social skills – proficiency in managing relationships and building networks to get the desired result from others and reach personal goals, and the ability to find common ground and build rapport. The five competencies associated with this component are: leadership, effectiveness in leading change, conflict management, influence/communication, and expertise in building and leading teams.

According to Goleman, it is not enough to have a high IQ; emotional intelligence is also required.

Since Goleman's contribution, three major models of emotional intelligence, as summarized by Clarke (2007), have dominated thinking in this area:

1 Personality models have become the most popular theory of emotional intelligence following Goleman. Here, emotional intelligence is viewed as comprising a range of emotional dispositions as well as competencies, from individual traits to a number of learnt capabilities. These are all contained within the components of emotional intelligence listed above.

2 Mixed models comprise aspects of personality as well as abilities to perceive emotional intelligence and manage emotions.

3 The ability model views emotional intelligence more narrowly as a set of four cognitive abilities that involve the capacity to identify, reason with, and utilize emotions effectively.

As Clarke comments, the first two models have come under criticism in terms of the ambiguity associated with the areas included and the measurement approaches employed. The ability model has received more positive commentary as possessing greater validity.

Critical evaluation of the concept of emotional intelligence

The notion that there is more to being effective as a manager or working with people than having a high IQ is persuasive. What matters is how that intelligence is used, especially when relating to people. The term 'emotional intelligence' has become a convenient and recognizable label for this requirement: someone who is poor at dealing with people is described as lacking in emotional intelligence.

Instruments are available for measuring emotional intelligence such as the Trait Emotional Intelligence Questionnaire (Petrides and Furnham, 2000). On the basis of such questionnaires, learning and development programmes can be created for individuals or groups, which focus on any weaknesses revealed.

But doubts have been expressed about the notion of emotional intelligence. Locke (2005: 426), a well-respected occupational psychologist, made the following observation:

The concept of emotional intelligence has now become so broad and the components so variegated that no one concept could possibly encompass or integrate all of them, no matter what the concept was called; it is no longer even an intelligible concept. What is the common or integrating element in a concept that includes: introspection about emotions, emotional expression, non-verbal communication with others, empathy, self-regulation, planning, creative thinking and the direction of attention? There is none.

He suggested that emotional intelligence should be renamed as a skill.

Goleman's mixed model of emotional intelligence, although the most popular, has been heavily criticized. Mayer *et al* (2008) described it as mere 'pop psychology'. There is also the question of whether the concept of emotional intelligence adds anything significant to that of behavioural competencies. Dulewicz and Higgs (1999) have produced a detailed analysis of how the emotional intelligence elements of self-awareness, emotional management, empathy, relationships, communication and personal style correspond to competencies such as sensitivity, flexibility, adaptability, resilience, impact, listening, leadership, persuasiveness, motivating others, energy, decisiveness and achievement motivation. They conclude that there are distinct associations between competency modes and elements of emotional intelligence. There is a danger of confusion if emotional intelligence notions and competency frameworks overlap.

Implications for HR specialists

The main implications of organizational behaviour theory for HR specialists are summarized below.

How organizations function

When involved in organization design, bear in mind that, while the highly structured classical model with clearly defined roles and lines of control and communication may appear to be the ideal solution, in practice, organizations function differently. It is necessary to take into account the post-bureaucratic

school and think of the organization as a portfolio of dynamic processes that overlay and often dominate the vertical, authority-based processes of the hierarchical structure. Similarly, organizational development activities should be based on an analysis and understanding of these dynamic processes.

Organizational culture

While it may not be possible to define an ideal culture or to prescribe how it can be developed, it can at least be stated with confidence that embedded cultures exert considerable influence on organizational behaviour and therefore performance. If there is an appropriate and effective culture it is desirable to take steps to support or reinforce it. If the culture is inappropriate, attempts should be made to determine what needs to be changed and to develop and implement plans for change (approaches to culture management are described in Chapter 18). HR innovations need to take account of the culture in which they will operate. They are likely to fail if they are countercultural.

Organizational climate

The perceptions of employees about the organization, which form the organization climate, need to be assessed and understood so that action can be taken to deal with negative factors. Diagnostic tools, as described in Chapter 18, can be used for this purpose.

Organizational processes

The social processes of interaction and networking, communication, group behaviour, leadership, power, politics and conflict need to be understood and considered when considering ways of improving organizational effectiveness (the ability of an organization to achieve its goals by making effective use of the resources available to it). Social and political factors can affect how HR decisions are made and how well they are implemented.

Individual differences

When designing jobs, preparing learning and development programmes, assessing and counselling staff, developing reward systems and dealing with grievances and disciplinary problems, it is necessary to remember that all people are different. What fulfils or motivates one person may not fulfil or motivate another. Abilities, aptitudes and intelligence differ widely and it is necessary to take particular care in fitting the right people in the right jobs and giving them the right training. Personalities, attitudes and emotions also differ. It is important to focus on how to manage diversity. This should take account of individual differences, which will include any issues arising from the employment of women, people from different ethnic groups, those with disabilities and older people. The predictive effectiveness of GMA tests as selection aids should be noted.

Judgements on personality

Personality should not be judged or measured simplistically in terms of stereotyped traits. People are complex and they change, and account has to be taken of this. The problem for HR specialists and managers in general is that, while they have to accept and understand these differences and take full account of them, they have ultimately to proceed on the basis of fitting them to the requirements of the situation, which are essentially what the organization needs to achieve. There is always a limit to the extent to which an organization that relies on collective effort to achieve its goals can adjust itself to the specific needs of individuals. But the organization has to appreciate that the pressures it places on people can result in stress and therefore can become counterproductive.

Key learning points: Organizational behaviour

People perform their roles within complex systems called organizations. The study of organizational behaviour focuses on how this happens.

Organizational behaviour defined

Organizational behaviour was defined by Huczynski and Buchanan (2007) as the term used to describe 'the study of the structure, functioning, and performance of organizations and the behaviour of groups and individuals within them'.

The sources and applications of organizational behaviour theory

Organizational behaviour theory is based on the main behavioural science disciplines. These are defined as the fields of enquiry dedicated to the study of human behaviour through sophisticated and rigorous methods.

How organizations function

- An organization is an entity that exists to achieve a purpose through the collective efforts of the people who work in or for it.

- Organizing is the process of making arrangements in the form of defined or understood responsibilities and relationships to enable those people to work cooperatively together.

- Organizations can be described as systems that, as affected by their environment, have a structure that has both formal and informal elements.

- Organization structures are frameworks for getting things done.

- Traditional formal structures were based on laid-down hierarchies (lines of command) represented in organization charts, and use was made of closely defined job descriptions. But to varying extents, organizations operate informally as well as formally by means of a network of roles and relationships that cut across formal organizational boundaries and lines of command.

Organizational culture

The culture of an organization has been described by Deal and Kennedy (2000: 4) as 'the way we do things around here'. Organizational or corporate culture is the pattern of values, norms, beliefs, attitudes and assumptions that may not have been articulated but shape the ways in which people in organizations behave and the ways in which things get done.

How organizational culture develops

The values and norms that are the basis of culture are formed in four ways:

- By the leaders in the organization, especially those who have shaped it in the past.

- Around critical incidents – important events from which lessons are learnt about desirable or undesirable behaviour.

- From the need to maintain effective working relationships among organization members; this establishes values and expectations.

- Influenced by the organization's environment. The external environment may be relatively dynamic or unchanging.

The components of culture

Organizational culture can be described in terms of values, norms, artefacts and management style.

Classifying organizational culture (Harrison, 1972)

- Power-oriented – competitive, responsive to personality rather than expertise.

- People-oriented – consensual, management control rejected.

- Task-oriented – focus on competency, dynamic.

- Role-oriented – focus on legality, legitimacy and bureaucracy.

Appropriate cultures

It is not possible to say that one culture is better than another, only that a culture is to a greater or lesser extent appropriate in the sense that it is relevant to the needs and circumstances of the organization and helps rather than hinders its performance.

Organizational climate

As defined by Harrison and Shirom (1999), organizational climate refers to 'members' perceptions of organizational features such as decision making, leadership and norms about work'.

Organizational processes

A number of social processes take place in organizations that affect how they function. These are: interaction and networking, communication, group behaviour, leadership, power, politics and conflict.

Personal characteristics

The personal characteristics that affect people's behaviour at work are their ability, intelligence, personality, attitudes, emotions and emotional intelligence.

Emotional intelligence

Emotional intelligence is a combination of skills and abilities such as self-awareness, self-control, empathy and sensitivity to the feelings of others. Someone with high levels of emotional intelligence should be able to relate to people effectively.

References

Argyle, M (1989) *The Social Psychology of Work*, Harmondsworth, Penguin

Argyris, C (1957) *Personality and Organization*, New York, Harper & Row

Barnard, C (1938) *The Functions of an Executive*, Boston, MA, Harvard University Press

Burns, T and Stalker, G (1961) *The Management of Innovation*, London, Tavistock

Burt, C (1954) The differentiation of intellectual ability, *British Journal of Educational Psychology*, **24**, pp 45–67

Clarke, N (2007) Be selective when choosing emotional intelligence training, *People Management*, 3 May, p 47

Costa, P and McRae, R R (1992) *NEO PI-R: Professional manual*, Odessa, FL, Psychological Assessment Resources

Deal, T and Kennedy, A (2000) *Corporate Cultures*, New York, Perseus Books

Denison, D R (1996) What is the difference between organizational culture and organizational climate? A native's point of view on a decade of paradigm wars, *Academy of Management Review*, **21** (3), pp 619–54

Digman, J M (1990) Personality structure: emergence of the five-factor model, *Annual Review of Psychology*, **41**, pp 417–40

Dulewicz, V and Higgs, M (1999) The seven dimensions of emotional intelligence, *People Management*, 28 October, p 53

Eldridge, J and Crombie, A (1974) *The Sociology of Organizations*, London, Allen & Unwin

Emery, F E (1959) *Characteristics of Socio-technical Systems*, London, Tavistock Publications

Fayol, H (1916) *Administration Industrielle et General*, translated by C Storrs (1949) as *General and Industrial Management*, London, Pitman

French, W L, Kast, F E and Rosenzweig, J E (1985) *Understanding Human Behaviour in Organizations*, Harper & Row, New York

Furnham, A and Gunter, B (1993) *Corporate Assessment*, London, Routledge

Ghoshal, S and Bartlett, C A (1995) Changing the role of top management: beyond structure to process, *Harvard Business Review*, January–February, pp 86–96

Goleman, D (1995) *Emotional Intelligence*, New York, Bantam

Goleman, D (2000) Leadership that gets results, *Harvard Business Review*, March–April, pp 78–90

Handy, C (1981) *Understanding Organizations*, Harmondsworth, Penguin Books

Harrison, M and Shirom, A (1999) *Organizational Diagnosis and Assessment*, Thousand Oaks, CA, Sage

Harrison, R (1972) Understanding your organization's character, *Harvard Business Review*, September–October, pp 119–28

Herzberg, F W, Mausner, B and Snyderman, B (1957) *The Motivation to Work*, New York, Wiley

Higgs, M (2006) *Change and its Leadership*, New York, Rowland, Fisher, Lennox Consulting

Huczynski, A A and Buchanan, D A (2007) *Organizational Behaviour*, 6th edn, Harlow, FT Pitman

Ivancevich, J M, Konopaske, R and Matteson, M T (2008) *Organizational Behaviour and Management*, 8th edn, New York, McGraw-Hill/Irwin

Jung, C (1923) *Psychological Types*, London, Routledge Kegan Paul

Lawrence, P R and Lorsch, J W (1969) *Developing Organizations*, Reading, MA, Addison-Wesley

Likert, R (1961) *New Patterns of Management*, New York, Harper & Row

Locke, E A (2005) Why emotional intelligence is an invalid concept, *Journal of Organizational Behaviour*, **26** (4), pp 425–31

Mayer, J D, Salovey, P and Caruso, D R (2008) Emotional intelligence: new ability or eclectic traits? *American Psychologist*, **63** (6), pp 503–17

McGregor, D (1960) *The Human Side of Enterprise*, New York, McGraw-Hill

Miller, E and Rice, A (1967) *Systems of Organization*, London, Tavistock

Mischel, W (1968) *Personality and Assessment*, New York, Wiley

Nadler, D A and Tushman, M L (1980) A congruence model for diagnosing organizational behaviour, in (ed) R H Miles, *Resource Book in Macro-organizational Behaviour*, Santa Monica, CA, Goodyear Publishing, pp 30–49

Northouse, P G (2006) *Leadership: Theory and practice*, 4th edn, Thousand Oaks, CA, Sage

Pascale, R (1990) *Managing on the Edge*, London, Viking

Petrides, K V and Furnham, A (2000) On the dimensional structure of emotional intelligence, *Personality and Individual Differences*, **29**, pp 313–20

Roethlisberger, F and Dickson, W (1939) *Management and the Worker*, Cambridge, MA, Harvard University Press

Rousseau, D M (1988) The construction of climate in organizational research, in (eds) L C Cooper and I Robertson, *International Review of Industrial and Organizational Psychology*, Chichester, Wiley

Salovey, P and Mayer, J D (1990) *Emotional Intelligence, Imagination, Cognition and Personality*, **9**, pp 185–211

Schein, E H (1965) *Organizational Psychology*, Englewood Cliffs, NJ, Prentice-Hall

Schein, E H (1984) Coming to a new awareness of culture, *Sloan Management Review*, **25** (2), pp 1–15

Schein, E H (1990) Organizational culture, *American Psychologist*, **45**, pp 109–19

Schmidt, F L and Hunter, J E (1998) The validity and utility of selection methods in personnel psychology: practical and theoretical implications of 85 years of research findings, *Psychological Bulletin*, **124** (2), pp 262–74

Taylor, F W (1911) *Principles of Scientific Management*, New York, Harper

Toplis, J, Dulewicz, V and Fletcher, C (2004) *Psychological Testing*, Institute of Personnel Management, London

Trist, E L, Higgin, G W, Murray, H and Pollock, A B (1963) *Organizational Choice*, London, Tavistock Publications

Tuckman, B (1965) Development sequences in small groups, *Psychological Bulletin*, **63**, pp 123–56

Urwick, L F (1947) *Dynamic Administration*, London, Pitman

Vernon, P E (1961) *The Structure of Human Abilities*, London, Methuen

Weber, M (1908) *The Theory of Social and Economic Organization*, translated by A M Henderson and T Parsons, 1947, Oxford, Oxford University Press

Woodward, J (1965) *Industrial Organization*, Oxford, Oxford University Press

Wright, D S and Taylor, A (1970) *Introducing Psychology*, Harmondsworth, Penguin

17
Work, organization and job design

LEARNING OUTCOMES

On completing this chapter you should be able to define these key concepts. You should also understand:

- Work design methodology
- Changes in the nature of work
- Work system design
- Process planning
- Smart working

- Flexible working
- High-performance working
- Lean manufacturing
- Organization design
- Job design

Introduction

Work, organization, and job design are three distinct but closely associated processes that establish what work is done in organizations and how it is done. HR can and should make an important contribution to each of the processes, ensuring that they take account of human factors.

Work design deals with the ways in which things are done in the work system of a business by teams and individuals. Organization design is concerned with deciding how organizations should be structured. Job design is about establishing what people in individual jobs or roles are there to do. Although these three activities are dealt with separately in this chapter they share one purpose – to ensure that the organization's work systems and structure operate effectively, make the best use of people in their jobs and roles, and take account of the needs of people at work.

In theory, to achieve that purpose, work, organization and job design function sequentially. The work system is designed to meet the specific needs of the business and to deliver value to its customers or clients. An organization structure or system (not all organizations are rigidly structured) has to be developed to enable the work system to operate. The structure is made up of jobs or roles (there is a distinction, which will be explained later) that have to be designed in ways that will maximize the extent to which they can be carried out effectively and provide intrinsic motivation, ie motivation from the work itself.

In practice, the processes involved can run concurrently – the work system will involve deciding how the work should be organized, and both the work system and organization design processes will define what sort of jobs or roles are required. At the same time, job design considerations will affect how the work is organized and how the work system functions. This chapter deals with each aspect of design separately, but it should be remembered that the processes interlink and overlap.

Work design

Work design is the creation of systems of work and a working environment that enhance organizational effectiveness and productivity, ensure that the organization becomes 'a great place in which to work' and are conducive to the health, safety and well-being of employees. Work involves the exertion of effort and the application of knowledge and skills to achieve a purpose. Systems of work are the combined processes, methods and techniques used to get work done. The work environment comprises the design of jobs, working conditions and the ways in which people are treated at work by their managers and co-workers as well as the work system. Work design is closely associated with organization and job design in that the latter is conducted within the context of the system of work and the work environment.

To understand the meaning of work design it is necessary first to appreciate what is happening to the world of work and next to review its history.

What is happening to work

The nature of work is changing. Organizations are functioning more flexibly. They tend to specialize more and are organized organically, ie they are relatively informal with the emphasis on lateral processes and interaction (networking) and the structure is flat, ie non-hierarchical without many layers of management. These developments have taken place against the background of the following changes in the contextual and external environment surrounding the world of work as identified by Parker *et al* (2001):

- a shift away from large-scale industrial production, with a dramatic decline in manufacturing jobs and rise in service work;

- partly as a consequence of this, an increase in customer-facing roles involving some form of emotional behaviour – the requirement for employees to express positive emotions in the way in which they interact with customers;

- significant shifts in the demographics of the workforce in the shape of an increased proportion of women, greater ethnic diversity, better-educated employees and an ageing workforce;

- growth in the number of employees engaged in 'knowledge work' – for example, professional services and new product and service development;

- the requirement for a greater variety of products and services and flexibility and agility in responding to customer needs and increased global competition;

- developments in technology affecting the degree to which jobs are involved in IT and become dependent on it;

- shifts from traditional, office or factory-based working to more flexible alternatives, including homeworking;

- a significant increase in the number of employers that an individual employee expects to work for during his or her career.

Work design – a short history

Work design began with the concept of the division of labour originated by Adam Smith (1776). Much later came 'Taylorism', the scientific management movement pioneered by Taylor (1911), which was based on the belief that the most efficient way to do tasks was to remove the responsibility for how to do the work from the individual employee to engineers or managers. The next step was 'Fordism', the moving assembly line introduced by Henry Ford in 1914. Thereafter, the practice of work simplifica-tion became embedded in organizations and to a large extent still exists.

The first move away from this situation was provided by the concept of job enrichment popularized by Herzberg (1968: 83), who referred to it as 'vertical job loading'. His definition of the principles and motivators involved is set out in Table 17.1. This was reinforced by job design theory (Hackman and Oldham, 1974).

More recently, the notion of 'smart working' has emerged. Essentially, this means managing the work environment in order to release employees' energy and drive business performance. Smart working, as described in detail later, has been the subject of extensive research conducted by the CIPD (2008).

However, before examining the notion of smart working it is necessary to remember that it takes place within the system of work, and approaches to work system design are therefore examined first.

Work system design

A system is a set of practices or activities that fit together and interact to achieve a purpose. Work system design is concerned with how the various processes required to make a product or provide a service should operate. It deals with the set of

TABLE 17.1   Vertical job loading (job enrichment) principles and motivators involved

Principles	Motivators involved
Removing some controls while retaining accountability	Responsibility and personal achievement
Increasing the accountability of individuals for own work	Responsibility and personal achievement
Giving a person a complete natural unit of work (module, division, area, and so on)	Responsibility and recognition
Granting additional authority to employees in their activity; job freedom	Responsibility, achievement and recognition
Making periodic reports directly available to the workers themselves rather than to supervisors	Internal recognition
Introducing new and more difficult tasks not previously handled	Growth and learning
Assigning individuals specific or specialized tasks, enabling them to become experts	Responsibility, growth and advancement

(**SOURCE:** Herzberg, 1968: 83)

related activities that combine to give a result that customers want. The structure of the system describes the relations between different operations.

A work system may be centred on activities such as manufacturing, chemical processing, information processing, supply, distribution, transport, the provision of public services or customer service. There is usually a choice between different processes within the work system. As the design of the work system affects costs, quality and productivity, it is important to provide the best match between the product or service and the process used to make or deliver it.

Process-centred organizations

Process-centred organizations avoid focusing too closely on the design of a rigid work system but instead concentrate on the stream of products or services required and the processes required to ensure that work flows smoothly to the ultimate satisfaction of the customer or client. They have the following features:

- The focus is on horizontal processes that cut across organizational boundaries.

- The overriding objective will be to maintain a smooth flow of work between functions and to achieve synergy by pooling resources from different functions in task forces or project teams.

- The organization will not be based on the old hierarchical 'command and control' structure, ie one that consists of a functional structure with a number of different disciplines. Instead it will be a 'lattice', or 'matrix' organization (a lattice organization is one with a non-hierarchical, flat structure where the emphasis is on horizontal processes, the elimination of boundaries between functions and teamwork; a matrix organization is one that consists of a functional structure with a number of different disciplines and a project structure consisting of project teams drawn from the disciplines);

- There may still be designated functions for, say, manufacturing, sales and distribution, but the emphasis will be on how these areas work together on multifunctional projects to deal with demands such as product/market development.

- Belief in and reliance on teamwork.

- Expansion of traditional jobs and increased emphasis on flexible roles, with employees making decisions and dealing with all types of customer issues.

- Access to all types of information and knowledge throughout the organization.

- Quality and continuous improvement will be regarded as a common responsibility shared between managers and staff from each function.

Process planning

Work system design covers the planning of processes such as flexible manufacturing systems (computer numerical control machines controlled by a central computer that allows fast and easy changes between products), and supply chain management (the control of products from the original suppliers of materials through to the final customers). It may involve facility layout – the physical arrangement of equipment, offices, rooms, work stations (including 'hot-desks' – individual desks shared between several people) and other resources.

Process planning may determine how manufacturing or the provision of a service should be divided into a series of stages such as machines in a production line, each of which uses resources and adds value.

Requirements to be met in work system design

When designing a work system, it is necessary to see that it will:

- fit work requirements for efficiency and flexibility;

- ensure the smooth flow of processes or activities, or of materials from supplier to customer;

- facilitate the effective use of resources and the control of waste;

- as far as possible enable employees to gain fulfilment from their work by providing scope for variety, challenge and autonomy;

- encourage cooperative effort through teamworking;

- provide a good work environment in terms of working conditions;
- take account of the need to provide a healthy and safe system of work ('build safety into the system') bearing in mind the need to minimize stress and pay attention to ergonomic considerations in the design of equipment and work stations to eliminate or at least significantly reduce the risk of such conditions as repetitive strain injury;
- take account of environmental considerations;
- operate generally in accordance with the principles of 'smart working' as described below.

Smart working

As defined by the CIPD (2008: 4), smart working is: 'An approach to organizing work that aims to drive greater efficiency and effectiveness in achieving job outcomes through a combination of flexibility, autonomy and collaboration, in parallel with optimizing tools and working environments for employees.' The characteristics of smart working as established by the CIPD research were:

- self-management – a high degree of autonomy and a philosophy of empowerment;
- the use of virtual teams or work groups;
- focus on outcome-based indicators of performance;
- high-performance working;
- flexibility in work locations and hours;
- use of more advanced communications technology;
- hot-desking and working from home;
- ways of working that are underpinned by or drive high-trust working relationships;
- alignment of smart working with business objectives.

Typical smart working arrangements identified by the CIPD include flexible working, high-performance working, 'lean' production and designing jobs in which there is a higher degree of freedom to act. The role of each of those arrangements in work design is described below.

Flexible working

Flexible working is a pattern of working practice or working hours that deviates from the standard or normal arrangement. The aim is to provide for greater operational flexibility, improve the use of employees' skills and capacities, increase productivity and reduce employment costs. Flexible working has become increasingly important as a means of enhancing operational effectiveness. It is examined in detail in Chapter 31.

High-performance working

High-performance working was defined by Combs *et al* (2006) as the sum of the processes, practices and policies put in place by employers to enable employees to perform to their full potential. They referred to employee participation and flexible working arrangements as examples of such systems that have a direct impact on ways of working and therefore flow through to job design.

Sung and Ashton (2005) defined high-performance work practices as a set or 'bundle' of 35 complementary work practices covering three broad areas:

1 High employee involvement work practices – eg self-directed teams, quality circles and sharing/access to company information.

2 Human resource practices – eg sophisticated recruitment processes, performance appraisals, mentoring and work redesign.

3 Reward and commitment practices – eg various financial rewards, family-friendly policies, job rotation and flexible hours.

Lean manufacturing

Lean manufacturing or lean production, often known simply as 'Lean', is a process improvement methodology developed by Toyota in Japan. Lean focuses on reducing waste and ensuring the flow of production in order to deliver value to customers. It concentrates initially on the design of the process so that waste can be minimized during manufacture. It then examines operations in order to identify opportunities to improve the flow of production, remove wasteful practices and engage in continuous improvement. Various tools are available such as 'FiveS', which is a workplace methodology that uses a list of five words starting with the letter 'S' (sorting, straightening, systematic cleaning, standardizing and sustaining). Reference to these enables a dialogue to take place with employees on how work should be done.

But, as noted by the CIPD (2008: 11), the success of Lean depends not so much on the tools but on its approach to work. Lean is implemented by communities of people who carry out and supervise the work and may include stakeholders such as customers. Lean team members are encouraged to think flexibly and be adaptable to change. They have a sense of ownership of what they do and achieve.

CASE STUDY

Work organization: W L Gore

As described by the CIPD (2008: 25–26), W L Gore, which is best known for its GORE-TEX® fabrics, has a non-hierarchical, flat organization structure (a 'lattice' structure). There are no traditional organization charts, no ranks or job titles and no chains of command nor predetermined channels of communication. What is important when recruiting new people is that they have the right fit with Gore's culture. There are no rigid job specifications. Instead, associates make a commitment to contribute individually and collectively to work areas or projects according to their skills. Individuals are encouraged to take an interest in a wide variety of job areas or projects. Provided the core responsibilities within their role are carried out, associates can then stretch and build on their role to suit their interests, aspirations and the business needs. Gore's 'lattice' structure gives associates the opportunity to use their own judgement, take ownership of work areas and access the resources they need for projects to be successful. Gore's core values and ways of working are built on the principles of 'smart working'. Its unique culture, which fosters creativity, self-motivation, participation and equality, has proved to be a key contributor to associate satisfaction and retention.

Organization design

Organization design is the process of deciding how organizations should be structured in terms of the ways in which the responsibility for carrying out the overall task is allocated to individuals and groups of people and how the relationships between them function. The aim is to ensure that people work effectively together to achieve the overall purpose of the organization. The basic question of 'Who does what?' is answered by line managers but HR specialists are also involved in their capacity of helping the business to make the best use of its people. HR professionals can contribute to organization design or redesign activities by using their understanding of the factors affecting organizational behaviour and their knowledge of the business as a whole.

It is generally assumed that organization design is a logical and systematic affair, based on accepted principles and using analytical techniques that produce an inevitable 'best' result. But, as explained below, there is always organizational choice. There are certain guidelines to which consideration needs to be given, and organization reviews should be based on analysis, as also discussed below. But, ultimately, the ways in which an organization functions and therefore its structure (or sometimes its lack of structure) are contingent on the context. This consists of the business model, the people who work in the organization and the systems and techniques it uses to achieve its purpose.

Organizational choice

There is never one best way of organizing anything. There is always a choice. It is necessary to bear in mind that structural requirements in organizations or organizational units will vary widely according to what they are there to do and the activities they have to carry out. That is why there are no absolute principles such as the traditional precepts of 'unity of command' (one person, one boss) or the need to limit spans of control (the number of functions or people for which a manager is responsible). It all depends. Burns and Stalker (1961) established in their study of electronic companies in Scotland that in stable conditions, a highly structured or 'mechanistic' organization will emerge that has specialized functions, clearly defined jobs, strict administrative routines and a hierarchical system of exercising control. However, when the environment is volatile, a rigid system of ranks and routine will inhibit the organization's speed and sensitivity of response. In these circumstances the structure is, or should be, 'organic' in the sense that it is a function of the situation in which the enterprise finds itself rather than conforming to any predetermined and rigid view of how it should operate.

As explained by Cummings and Worley (2005: 516), this means that there are two different types of organization design – mechanistic and organic – the characteristics of which are shown in Table 17.2.

Organization reviews

In exercising organizational choice, an organizational review, as described below, will help in the evaluation of the alternatives, but the law of the situation, as described originally by Mary Parker Follett (1924), should prevail. This states that the work that people are required to do depends on the objective requirements of the situation. The final choice will depend upon the context and circumstances of the organization – as Lupton (1975) pointed out, it is important to achieve best fit.

Organizations may evolve organically without any conscious attempt to design them. But if a deliberate design programme is planned this should be based on the evidence that can be produced by a formal organization review conducted in the following stages:

1 *Activity analysis* to establish what work is done and what needs to be done. Two questions need to be answered: 1) are all the activities required properly catered for?; 2) are any unnecessary activities being carried out?

2 *Structural analysis* to determine how activities are grouped together; the number of levels in the hierarchy; the extent to which authority is decentralized to divisions and strategic business units (SBUs); where functions such as finance, HR, IT and research and development are placed in the structure (eg as central functions or integrated into divisions or SBUs); the relationships that exist between different units and functions (with particular attention being given to the way in which they communicate and cooperate with one another). Attention would be paid to such issues as the logic of the way in which activities are grouped and decentralized; the span of control of managers (the number of separate functions or people they are directly responsible for); any overlap between functions or gaps leading to the neglect of certain activities; the existence of unnecessary departments, units, functions or layers of management; the clarity with which individual responsibilities and accountabilities are defined.

TABLE 17.2   Mechanistic and organic design

	Mechanistic design	Organic design
Structure	Formal	Informal
	Hierarchical (command and control)	Flat, lean and flexible-horizontal processes
	Distinct functional units	Lattice structure
Work	Tightly defined jobs	Flexible roles
	Minimal scope in jobs for decision making	Enriched roles with more autonomy
	Closely controlled work groups	Self-managed teams

customer service unit, or strung along an assembly line. In more complex jobs, individuals may carry out a variety of connected tasks (multitasking), each with a number of functions, or these tasks may be allocated to a team of workers or be divided between them. In the latter case, the tasks may require a variety of skills that have to be possessed by all members of the team (multiskilling) in order to work flexibly. Complexity in a job may be a reflection of the number and variety of tasks to be carried out, the different skills or competencies to be used, the range and scope of the decisions that have to be made, or the difficulty of predicting the outcome of decisions.

The internal structure of each task consists of three elements: planning (deciding on the course of action, its timing and the resources required), executing (carrying out the plan) and controlling (monitoring performance and progress and taking corrective action when required). A completely integrated job includes all these elements for each of the tasks involved. The worker, or group of workers, having been given objectives in terms of output, quality and cost targets, decides on how the work is to be done, assembles the resources, performs the work, and monitors output, quality and cost standards. Responsibility in a job is measured by the amount of authority that someone has to do all of these things.

The ideal arrangement from the point of view of engagement and motivation is to provide for fully integrated jobs containing all three task elements. In practice, management and team leaders are often entirely responsible for planning and control, leaving the worker responsible for execution. To a degree, this is inevitable, but one of the aims of job design is often to extend the responsibility of workers into the functions of planning and control. This can involve empowerment – giving individuals and teams more responsibility for decision making and ensuring that they have the training, support and guidance to exercise that responsibility properly.

Intrinsic motivation

The case for using job design techniques is based on the premise that effective performance and genuine satisfaction in work follow mainly from the intrinsic content of the job. This is related to the fundamental concept that people are motivated when they are provided with the means to achieve their goals.

Work enables people to earn money, which as an extrinsic reward satisfies basic needs and is instrumental in providing ways of satisfying higher-level needs. But work also provides intrinsic rewards related to achievement, responsibility and the opportunity to use and develop skills that are more under the control of the worker.

The job characteristics model

The most influential model for job design is the job characteristics model developed by Hackman and Oldham (1974). They identified five core job characteristics:

1 *Skill variety*: the degree to which a job requires an employee to perform activities that challenge his or her skills and abilities.

2 *Task identity*: the degree to which the job requires completion of an identifiable piece of work.

3 *Task significance*: the degree to which the job outcome has a substantial impact on others.

4 *Autonomy*: the degree to which the job gives an employee discretion in scheduling work and determining how it is performed. The concept of 'supported autonomy' refers to the provision of freedom for employees to manage their work within certain boundaries (policies and expected behaviours) but with support available as required.

5 *Feedback*: the degree to which an employee gets information about the effectiveness of his or her efforts – with particular emphasis on feedback directly related to the work itself rather than from a third party (for example, a manager).

Hackman and Oldham explained that if the design of a job satisfied the core job characteristics, the employee would perceive that the work was worthwhile, would feel responsible for the work, and would know if the work had been completed satisfactorily. The outcome of this would be high-quality work performance and high job satisfaction as a result of intrinsic motivation.

The implications of group activities

Jobs should never be considered in isolation. All job holders belong to formal or informal groups and the interrelationships that exist in such groups should be considered when looking at the content of an individual job.

Approaches to job design

Job design starts with an analysis of task requirements, using the job analysis techniques described in Chapter 70. These requirements will be a function of the system of work and the organization structure. As described by Robertson and Smith (1985), the method can be based on the job characteristics model as follows:

- Influence skill variety by providing opportunities for people to do several tasks and by combining tasks.
- Influence task identity by combining tasks to form natural work units.
- Influence task significance by forming natural work units and informing people of the importance of their work.
- Influence autonomy by giving people responsibility for determining their own working systems.
- Influence feedback by establishing good relationships and opening feedback channels.

These methods influence the four approaches to job design described below.

Job rotation

This is the movement of employees from one task to another to reduce monotony by increasing variety.

Job enlargement

This means combining previously fragmented tasks into one job, again to increase the variety and meaning of repetitive work.

Job enrichment

This goes beyond job enlargement to add greater autonomy and responsibility to a job. Job enrichment aims to maximize the interest and challenge of work by providing the employee with a job that has these characteristics:

- it is a complete piece of work in the sense that the worker can identify a series of tasks or activities that end in a recognizable and definable product;
- it affords the employee as much variety, decision-making responsibility and control as possible in carrying out the work;
- it provides direct feedback through the work itself on how well the employee is doing his or her job.

As described by Herzberg (1968), job enrichment is not just increasing the number or variety of tasks, nor is it the provision of opportunities for job rotation. These approaches may relieve boredom, but they do not result in positive increases in motivation.

Self-managing teams (autonomous work groups)

These are self-regulating teams who work largely without direct supervision. The philosophy on which this approach is founded is that of job enrichment but it is also influenced by socio-technical systems theory, which suggests that because the technical aspects of work are interrelated with the social aspects, both should be considered when designing jobs.

A self-managing team enlarges individual jobs to include a wider range of operative skills (multiskilling); decides on methods of work and the planning, scheduling and control of work; distributes tasks itself among its members; and monitors its own performance, taking corrective action when required.

The advocates of self-managing teams or autonomous work groups claim that they represent a more comprehensive view of organizations than the rather simplistic individual motivation theories that underpin job rotation, enlargement and enrichment. Be that as it may, the strength of this system is that in line with socio-technical theory, it takes account of the social or group factors and the technology, as well as the individual motivators.

In a study of customer service representatives in a telecommunications company, Batt (1999) found that work organized into self-managed teams led to better service and sales performance (an increase of 9.2 per cent per employee) than traditional work designs, and that the interactive effect of self-managed teams and new technology raised sales by an additional 17.4 per cent.

Choice of approach

Of the four approaches described above, it is generally recognized that, although job rotation and job enlargement have their uses in developing skills and relieving monotony, they do not go to the root of the requirements for intrinsic motivation and for meeting the various motivating characteristics of jobs. These are best satisfied by using, as appropriate, job enrichment, autonomous work groups, or high-performance work design.

High-performance work design

This concentrates on setting up working groups in environments where high levels of performance can be achieved. As described by Buchanan (1987), this requires management to define what it needs in the form of methods of production and the results expected from its introduction. It involves multiskilling – job demarcation lines are eliminated as far as possible and encouragement and training are provided for employees to acquire new skills. Self-managed teams are set up with full responsibility for planning, controlling and monitoring the work.

Role development

Role development is the continuous process through which roles are defined or modified as work proceeds and evolves. Job design as described above takes place when a new job is created or an existing job is changed, often following a reorganization or the introduction of a new work system. But the parts that people play in carrying out their roles can evolve over time as people grow into their roles and grow with them, and as incremental changes take place in the scope of the work and the degree to which individuals have freedom to act (their autonomy). Roles will be developed as people develop in them – responding to opportunities and changing demands, acquiring new skills and developing competencies.

Role development takes place in the context of day-to-day work and is therefore a matter between managers and the members of their teams. It means agreeing definitions of accountabilities, objectives and competency requirements as the roles evolve. When these change – as they probably will in all except the most routine jobs – it is desirable to achieve mutual understanding of new expectations.

The process of understanding how roles are developing, and agreeing the implications, can take place through performance management in which the regularly updated performance agreement spells out agreed outcomes (key result areas) and competency requirements. It is necessary to ensure that managers and team leaders define roles within the performance management framework, taking into account the principles of job design set out above.

Key learning points: Work, organization and job design

Work, organization and job design

These are three distinct but closely associated processes that establish what work is done in organizations and how it is done.

Work design

Work design is the creation of systems of work and a working environment that enhance organizational effectiveness and productivity, ensure that the organization becomes 'a great place in which to work' and are conducive to the health, safety and well-being of employees.

Work system design

Work system design is concerned with how the processes required to make a product or provide a service should operate. It deals with the set of related activities that combine to give a result that customers want. The structure of the system describes the relations between different operations.

Smart working

The CIPD (2008: 4) defined smart working as:
'An approach to organizing work that aims to

drive greater efficiency and effectiveness in achieving job outcomes through a combination of flexibility, autonomy and collaboration, in parallel with optimizing tools and working environments for employees.'

Flexible working

Flexible working is a pattern of working practice or working hours that deviates from the standard or normal arrangement.

High-performance working

High-performance working was defined by Combs *et al* (2006) as the sum of the processes, practices and policies put in place by employers to enable employees to perform to their full potential.

Lean manufacturing

A process improvement methodology developed by Toyota. 'Lean' focuses on minimizing waste and ensuring the flow of production in order to deliver value to customers.

Aims of organization design

The overall aim of organization design is to optimize the arrangements for conducting the affairs of the business or function and thus achieve the 'best fit' between the structure and what the business or function is there to do.

Organization analysis

The starting point for an organization review is an analysis of the existing circumstances, structure and processes of the organization and an assessment of the strategic issues that might affect it in the future.

Organization diagnosis

The aim of the diagnosis is to establish, on the basis of the analysis, the reasons for any structural problems facing the organization or function.

Organizational choice

There is never one best way of organizing anything. There is always a choice.

Job design

Job design specifies the contents of jobs in order to satisfy work requirements and meet the personal needs of the job holder, thus increasing levels of employee engagement.

Jobs and roles

A job is an organizational unit consisting of a group of defined tasks or activities to be carried out or duties to be performed. A role is the part played by individuals and the patterns of behaviour expected of them in fulfilling their work requirements. Jobs are about tasks; roles are about people.

The job characteristics model

The job characteristics model was developed by Hackman and Oldham (1974). They identified five core job characteristics: skill variety, task identity, task significance, autonomy and feedback.

Approaches to job design

Job design starts with an analysis of task requirements, using job analysis techniques.

Role development

Role development is the continuous process through which roles are defined or modified as work proceeds and evolves.

References

Batt, R (1999) Work organization, technology and performance in customer service and sales, *Industrial and Labor Relations Review*, **52** (4), pp 539–64

Buchanan, D A (1987) Job enrichment is dead: long live high-performance work design! *Personnel Management*, May, pp 40–43

Burns, T and Stalker, G (1961) *The Management of Innovation*, London, Tavistock

Child, J (1972) Organizational structure, environment and performance: the role of strategic choice, *Sociology*, **6** (1), pp 1–22

CIPD (2008) *Smart Working: How smart is UK PLC? Findings from organizational practice*, London, CIPD

Combs, J, Liu, Y and Hall, A (2006) How much do high-performance work practices matter? A meta-analysis of their effects on organizational performance, *Personnel Psychology*, **59** (3), pp 501–28

Cummings, T G and Worley, C G (2005) *Organization Development and Change*, Mason, OH, South Western

Follett, M P (1924) *Creative Experience*, New York, Longmans Green

Hackman, J R and Oldham, G R (1974) Motivation through the design of work: test of a theory, *Organizational Behaviour and Human Performance*, **16** (2), pp 250–79

Herzberg, F (1968) One more time: how do you motivate employees? *Harvard Business Review*, January–February, pp 109–20

Huczynski, A A and Buchanan, D A (2007) *Organizational Behaviour*, 6th edn, Harlow, FT Prentice Hall

Lupton, T (1975) Best fit in the design of organizations, *Personnel Review*, **4** (1), pp 15–22

Parker, S K, Wall, T D and Cordery, J L (2001) Future work design research and practice: towards an elaborated model of work design, *Journal of Occupational and Organizational Psychology*, **74** (4), pp 413–40

Robertson, I T and Smith, M (1985) *Motivation and Job Design*, London, IPM

Smith, A (1776) *The Wealth of Nations*, Harmondsworth, Penguin Books, 1986

Sung, J and Ashton, D (2005) *High Performance Work Practices: Linking strategy and skills to performance outcomes*, London, DTI

Taylor, F W (1911) *Principles of Scientific Management*, New York, Harper

Wall, T D and Clegg, C (1998) Job design, in (ed) N Nicholson, *Blackwell's Encyclopaedic Dictionary of Organizational Behaviour*, Oxford, Blackwell, pp 265–68

Whittington, R and Molloy, E (2005) *HR's Role in Organizing: Shaping change*, London, CIPD

Wilson, N A B (1973) *On the Quality of Working Life*, London, HMSO

18
Organization development

KEY CONCEPTS AND TERMS

Action research

Behaviour modelling

Behavioural science

Business model innovation

Change management

Diagnostics

Force-field analysis

Group dynamics

Humanism

Integrated strategic change

Intervention

Neurolinguistic programming

Organization capability

Organization development

Organizational/corporate culture

Organizational transformation

Process

Process consultation

Survey feedback

T-groups

Transactional analysis

LEARNING OUTCOMES

On completing this chapter you should be able to define these key concepts. You should also understand:

- The meaning of organization development
- The contents of traditional organization development (OD) programmes
- The criticisms made of the original OD concept
- How OD has moved on since it was first introduced
- The nature of organization development today, including the processes of diagnosis and programming

Introduction

Work, organization and job design provide the basic ingredients for operating a business. But it is necessary to see that these processes work well, which is the aim of organization development. In this chapter, organization development is defined and its somewhat chequered history is described, from its origins as 'OD' to the more focused and business-like approaches adopted today. This leads to a discussion of organization development strategy and an examination of organization development in practice, involving the use of diagnostics as the basis for preparing organization development programmes.

Organization development defined

Organization development is a systematic approach to improving organizational capability, which is concerned with process – how things get done. As expressed by Beer (1980: 10), OD operates as: 'A system-wide process of data collection, diagnosis, action planning, intervention and evaluation.'

Organization development in its traditional form as OD was later defined by Rowlandson (1984: 90) as 'an intervention strategy that uses group processes to focus on the whole culture of an organization in order to bring about planned change'. More recently, the CIPD (2010: 1) defined it broadly as a 'planned and systematic approach to enabling sustained organization performance through the involvement of its people'.

The nature of organization development

Organization development in its original version as OD was based on behavioural science concepts, ie the field of enquiry dedicated to the study of human behaviour through sophisticated and rigorous methods. OD was practised through what were called 'interventions'.

However, during the 1980s and 1990s a number of other approaches were introduced. Further changes occurred in the following decade during

which a more strategic focus was adopted and more business-focused activities such as smart working and high-performance working came to the fore. It is these changes that led to the broader definition produced by the CIPD.

Organization development used to be the province of specialized consultants who tended to practise it as a mystery, with HR playing a supporting role if it played any role at all. But *HR Magazine* spelt out the close relationship between HR and organization development as follows.

Source review

HR and organization development – *HR Magazine* (2007: 1)

To remain competitive in today's global marketplace, organizations must change. One of the most effective tools to promote successful change is organization development (OD). As HR increasingly focuses on building organizational learning, skills and workforce productivity, the effective use of OD to help achieve company business goals and strategies is becoming a broad HR competency as well as a key strategic HR tool. While there are variations regarding the definition of OD, the basic purpose of organization development is to increase an organization's effectiveness through planned interventions related to the organization's processes (often company-wide), resulting in improvements in productivity, return on investment and employee satisfaction.

The CIPD (2010: 3) stated that: 'We place considerable importance on OD, seeing it as one of the ten professional areas within the HR profession map which emphasizes its importance as an HR skill.' The CIPD also commented that:

OD is not a new discipline and has always had a focus on people but has only relatively recently become considered as a mainstream discipline of HR. Supporters of OD argue that its strength is its ability to understand the whole organization and as such it may be inhibiting to root it too firmly in the HR function. However, given the increasing need for the HR profession to act as a business partner, OD and its methods have a part to play in developing HR's strategic role and its involvement in organizational change, organizational culture and employee engagement (ibid: 3).

The strategic nature of organization development as an integral part of HRM arises because it can play a part in the implementation of business strategy. For example, a strategy for business model innovation (the process followed by an organization to develop a new business model or change an existing one) could result in the need for new organization structures and processes. This would include organization development and change management activities. The aim of this chapter is to explain the purpose of organization development in the light of an analysis of the history of the concept and how it can be applied as part of a strategic HRM approach.

The story of organization development

There are three chapters in the story of organizational development: the original version of the 1960s and '70s, the extensions and modifications to the original approach in the 1980s and '90s, and the new look at organization development of the 2000s.

The first chapter – the original version

Organization development emerged as the 'OD' movement in the 1960s. It was based on the strong humanistic values of its early founders, who wanted to improve the conditions of people's lives in organizations by applying behavioural science knowledge. Its origins can be traced to the writings of behavioural scientists such as Lewin (1947, 1951) on group dynamics (the improvement of group processes through various forms of training, eg team building, interactive skills training, T-groups) and change management. Other behavioural scientists included Maslow (1954) who produced his needs theory of motivation, Herzberg *et al* (1957) who wrote about the motivation to work, and Argyris (1957) who emphasized the need to plan for integration and involvement. McGregor (1960) produced his 'Theory Y', which advocates the recognition of the needs of both the organization and the individual on the basis that, given the chance, people will not only accept but seek responsibility. Likert (1961) added his theory of supportive relationships.

The two founders of the organization development movement were Beckhard (1969) who probably coined the term, and Bennis (1969) who, according to Buchanan and Huczynski (2007: 575), described OD as a 'truth, trust, love and collaboration approach'. Ruona and Gibson (2004: 53) explained that:

> Early OD interventions can be categorized as primarily focusing on individuals and interpersonal relations. OD was established as a social philosophy that emphasized a long-term orientation, the applied behavioural sciences, external and process-oriented consultation, change managed from the top, a strong emphasis on action research and a focus on creating change in collaboration with managers.

The objectives, assumptions and values of the original version of OD

As originally conceived, OD programmes aimed to increase the effectiveness of the various processes that take place in organizations, especially those relating to the ways in which people work together. It was also concerned with improving the quality of people's working lives. The original OD philosophy was that of humanism – the belief that human factors are paramount in the study of organizational behaviour. This had its roots in the conclusions reached from the Hawthorne studies of 1924 to 1932 (Mayo, 1933; Roethlisberger and Dickson, 1939) that the productivity of workers increases when someone they respect takes an interest in them. The focus then turned to the needs of people as individuals and in groups with an emphasis on process – how people worked together and how this could be improved. The assumptions and values of OD were that:

- Most individuals are driven by the need for personal growth and development as long as their environment is both supportive and challenging.

- The work team, especially at the informal level, has great significance for feelings of satisfaction, and the dynamics of such teams have a powerful effect on the behaviour of their members.

- Organizations can be more effective if they learn to diagnose their own strengths and weaknesses.
- Managers often do not know what is wrong and need special help in diagnosing problems, although the outside 'process consultant' ensures that decision making remains in the hands of the client.

Traditional OD programmes

OD during this time was practised predominantly by external consultants working with senior managers. Personnel specialists were not involved to any great extent. OD programmes consisted then of 'interventions' such as those listed below. In OD jargon an intervention is a planned activity designed to improve organizational effectiveness or manage change. The following are the traditional OD interventions; they still feature in current programmes:

- Process consultation – helping clients to generate and analyse information that they can understand and, following a thorough diagnosis, act upon. The information relates to organizational processes such as inter-group relations, interpersonal relations and communications.
- Change management – often using the techniques advocated by Lewin (1951), which consisted of processes of managing change by unfreezing, changing and freezing, and force-field analysis (analysing and dealing with the driving forces that affect transition to a future state).
- Action research – collecting data from people about process issues and feeding it back in order to identify problems and their likely causes as a basis for an action plan to deal with the problem.
- Appreciative enquiry – a methodology that does not focus entirely on finding out what is wrong in order to solve problems. Instead it adopts the more positive approach of identifying 'best practices' – what is working well – and using that information as a basis for planning change. It can be associated with action research.
- Survey feedback – a variety of action research in which data is systematically collected about the system through attitude surveys and workshops leading to action plans.

- Group dynamics – improving the ways in which people work together by means of programmes that aim to increase the effectiveness of groups through various forms of training, eg team building, interactive skills training and T-groups ('training groups', which aim to increase sensitivity, diagnostic ability and action skills).
- Personal interventions – developing interpersonal skills through such processes as transactional analysis (an approach to understanding how people behave and express themselves through transactions with others), behaviour modelling (the use of positive reinforcement and corrective feedback to change behaviour) and neurolinguistic programming or NLP (teaching people to programme their reactions to others and develop unconscious strategies for interacting with them).

The second chapter – criticisms of the original version of OD and new approaches

The OD movement as originally conceived and practised was characterized by what Buchanan and Huczynski (2007: 559) called 'quasi-religious values' with some of the features of a religious movement, which, they claimed, is one reason why it has survived as a concept in spite of the criticisms that began to be levelled at it in the 1980s. Weidner (2004: 39) wrote that: 'OD was something that practitioners felt and lived as much as they *believed*' (original emphasis).

Criticisms of OD

One of the earliest critics was McLean (1981: 4) who noted 'the moral and ethical misgivings concerned with the development of what might be regarded as a sophisticated science of manipulation'. He cited a comment by Strauss (1976) that at times OD is little more than abstract moralization and asserted that:

> It is becoming increasingly apparent that there exists a considerable discrepancy between OD as practised and the prescriptive stances taken by many OD writers... The theory of change

and change management which is the foundation of most OD programmes is based on over-simplistic generalizations which offer little specific guidance to practitioners faced with the confusing complexity of a real change situation (ibid: 13).

Armstrong (1984: 113) commented that: 'Organization development has lost a degree of credibility in recent years because the messianic zeal displayed by some practitioners has been at variance with the circumstances and real needs of the organization.' Burke (1995: 8) stated that 'in the mid-1970s, OD was still associated with T-groups, participative management and consensus, Theory Y, and self-actualization – the soft human, touchy-feely kinds of activities'.

An even more powerful critic was Legge (1995: 212), who observed that the OD rhetoric fitted the era of 'flower power' and that: 'OD was seen, on the one hand as a form of devious manipulation, and on the other as "wishy-washy" and ineffectual.' She noted 'the relative lack of success of OD initiatives in effecting major and lasting cultural change, with the aim of generating commitment to new values in the relatively small number of organizations in which it was tried' (ibid: 213), and produced the following devastating critique.

Source review

A critique of organization development – Legge (1995: 213)

In order to cope with an increasingly complex and changing environment, many of the initiatives were, in retrospect, surprisingly inward looking, involving schemes of management development, work system design, attempts at participation, almost as a good in their own right, without close attention as to how they were to deliver against market-driven organizational success criteria. The long-term nature of OD activities, together with difficulties to clearly establishing to sceptics their contribution to organizational success criteria (and within a UK culture of financial short-termism) rendered the initiatives at best marginal... and at worst to be treated with a cynical contempt.

The main criticisms of OD, as noted by Marsh *et al* (2010: 143), were that it was: 'Oriented to process and tools rather than results... where techniques are considered to be ends in themselves rather than a means to deliver organizational performance.'

New approaches

During the 1980s and '90s an alternative approach emerged, that of culture management, which aimed at achieving cultural change as a means of enhancing organizational capability. Culture change or culture management programmes start with an analysis of the existing culture, which may involve the use of a diagnostic such as the 'Organizational Culture Inventory' devised by Cooke and Lafferty (1989). The desired culture is then defined – one that enables the organization to function effectively and achieve its strategic objectives. As a result, a 'culture gap' is identified, which needs to be filled. This analysis of culture identifies behavioural expectations so that HR processes can be used to develop and reinforce them. This sounds easier than it really is. Culture is a complex and often hard-to-define notion and it is usually strongly embedded and therefore difficult to change. Anthony (1990: 4) argued that: 'The management of culture... purports to define the meaning of people's lives so that they become concomitant with the organization's view of itself. [It is] the adjustment of human meaning for organizational ends.' He also observed that: 'Published cases do exist of organizations within which major changes in culture have been successfully accomplished and shown to persist but they are rare' (ibid: 5). However, culture management became a process in its own right and OD consultants jumped on the bandwagon.

Culture management involves change management, another important item in the OD toolkit. But as Caldwell (2003: 132) argued: 'It is assumed within most OD models that change can be planned in a "rational" or linear manner, and that the change agent can facilitate this group process, although there is little evidence to support this illusion of "manageability".'

Other movements in this period that could be described as organization development activities but exist as distinct entities included total quality management (TQM) and quality circles. TQM aims to ensure that all activities within an organization happen in the way they have been planned in order to meet the defined needs of customers. Its approach is holistic – quality management is not a separate function to be treated in isolation, but is an integral part of all operations. Quality circles are groups of volunteers engaged in related work who meet regularly to discuss and propose ways of improving working methods under a trained leader.

Another approach more closely related to OD that emerged at this time was organizational transformation. This was defined by Cummings and Worley (2005: 752) as: 'A process of radically altering the organization's strategic direction, including fundamental changes in structures, processes and behaviours.'

Holistic approaches to improving organizational capability emerging in this period, which were not part of what was conventionally known as OD, included high-performance working, high-commitment management, high-involvement management and performance management. The development of these systems in the 2000s led to a radically changed view of what constituted organization development.

The third chapter– changing the focus

The most significant change in the 2000s was the shift to a strategic perspective. As noted by Cummings and Worley (2005: 12): 'Change agents have proposed a variety of large-scale or strategic-change models; each of these models recognizes that strategic change involves multiple levels of the organization and a change in its culture, is driven from the top by powerful executives, and has important effects on performance.' They also commented that the practice of organization development therefore went far beyond its humanistic origins. Another development was the emergence of the concept of 'smart working', as described in Chapter 17. This could be described as an OD intervention because it involves taking a fundamental look at methods of improving organizational effectiveness.

There was also more emphasis on associating organization design with organization development. Marsh *et al* (2010) suggested that organization design and organization development need to be merged into one HR capability, with organization design taking precedence. They considered that this should all be brought in-house as a necessary part of the business model innovation process. But as they observed: 'We do not believe that the field of organization development has passed its sell-by date. Far from it. It just needs to be repositioned as an HR capability' (ibid: 143).

However, Weidner (2004: 37) made the following more pessimistic comment about OD: 'Unfortunately, after sixty years – despite the best efforts and intentions of many talented people – OD finds itself increasingly at the margins of business, academe, and practice. The field continues to affirm its values, yet has no identifiable voice.' OD 'interventions' still have a role to play in improving performance but as part of an integrated business and HR strategy planned and implemented by HR in conjunction with senior management, with or without outside help.

The main change that has taken place in the move from traditional OD to organizational development as practised currently is the focus on improving organizational performance and results through organization-wide initiatives. These do encompass the behaviour of people, especially when this relates to their levels of engagement (the degree to which people are committed to their work and the organization and motivated to achieve high levels of performance). But they are also concerned with the organizational processes that affect behaviour and engagement, namely, strategic HRM, work system design, smart working, high-performance working, organization design and job design.

Organization development strategy

Organization development strategy is founded on the aspiration to improve organizational capability, which is broadly the capacity of an organization to function effectively in order to achieve desired results. It has been defined more specifically by Ulrich and Lake (1990: 40) as 'the ability to manage people for competitive advantage'. It is concerned with mapping out intentions on how the work system should be developed in line with the concept of smart working, on how the organization should be structured to meet new demands, on system-wide change in fields such as reward and performance management, on how change should be managed, on what needs to be done to improve organizational processes involving people such as teamwork, communications and participation, and how the organization can acquire, retain, develop and engage the talent it needs. These intentions will be converted into actions on work systems development, structure design, the redesign of jobs and, possibly, OD-type interventions. The latter could take the form of action research, survey feedback and programmes for improving group processes and interpersonal skills, as described earlier in this chapter. The strategy can involve processes of integrated strategic change, as described below, and will be based on organizational diagnosis leading to the design of an organization development programme, as considered in the following sections.

Integrated strategic change

The process of integrated strategic change as conceived by Worley *et al* (1996) can be used to formulate and implement organization development strategies. The steps required are:

1 Strategic analysis, a review of the organization's strategic orientation (its strategic intentions within its competitive environment) and a diagnosis of the organization's readiness for change.

2 Develop strategic capability – the ability to implement the strategic plan quickly and effectively.

3 Integrate individuals and groups throughout the organization into the processes of analysis, planning and implementation to maintain the firm's strategic focus, direct attention and resources to the organization's key competencies, improve coordination and integration within the organization and create higher levels of shared ownership and commitment.

4 Create the strategy, gain commitment and support for it and plan its implementation.

5 Implement the strategic change plan, drawing on knowledge of motivation, group dynamics and change processes, dealing with issues such as alignment, adaptability, teamwork and organizational and individual learning.

6 Allocate resources, provide feedback and solve problems as they arise.

Organizational diagnosis

The practice of organization development is based on an analysis and diagnosis of the circumstances of the organization, the strategic, operational or process issues that are affecting the organization and its ability to perform well. As defined by Manzini (1988: ix): 'An organizational diagnosis is a systematic process of gathering data about a business organization – its problems, challenges, strengths and limitations – and analysing how such factors influence its ability to interact effectively and profitably with its business environment.' This involves the use of the diagnostic cycle with associated analytical and diagnostic tools, which enable those concerned with development to identify areas of concern that can be dealt with in an organization development programme.

The diagnostic cycle

The diagnostic cycle as described by Manzini (1988: 11) consists of:

- data gathering;
- analysis;
- feedback;
- action planning;
- implementation;
- evaluation.

Analytical tools

The two most used analytical tools are SWOT analysis and PESTLE analysis. A SWOT analysis is a 'looking in' and 'looking out' approach that covers the internal organizational factors of strengths and weaknesses and the external factors of opportunities and threats. PESTLE analysis is an environmental scanning tool that covers the following factors: political, economic, social, technological, legal and environmental.

Diagnostics

Diagnostics are tools such as questionnaires or checklists that gather information about a business or on the opinions and attitudes of employees in order to identify issues and problems that can be dealt with in an organization development programme. They enable those concerned with organization development to understand what is happening and why it is happening so that they can do something about it. Diagnostics can be used to assess overall organizational effectiveness in the shape of general strategic, business and operational issues, or they can deal with more specific areas of concern such as a review of the organization's ideology, culture or climate, or a survey of levels of engagement or commitment. Examples of the approaches used by various diagnostic instruments are given below.

Organizational ideology questionnaire (Harrison, 1972)

This questionnaire deals with the four orientations defined by Harrison (power, role, task and self). The questionnaire is completed by ranking statements according to views on what is closest to the organization's actual position. The following are examples of statements:

- a good boss is strong, decisive and firm but fair;
- a good subordinate is compliant, hard-working and loyal;
- people who do well in the organization are shrewd and competitive, with a strong need for power;
- the basis of task assignment is the personal needs and judgements of those in authority;
- decisions are made by people with the most knowledge and expertise about the problem.

Organizational culture inventory (Cooke and Lafferty, 1989)

This instrument assesses organizational culture under 12 headings:

1 *Humanistic-helpful* – organizations managed in a participative and person-centred way.

2 *Affiliative* – organizations that place a high priority on constructive relationships.

3 *Approval* – organizations in which conflicts are avoided and interpersonal relationships are pleasant – at least superficially.

4 *Conventional* – conservative, traditional and bureaucratically controlled organizations.

5 *Dependent* – hierarchically controlled and non-participative organizations.

6 *Avoidance* – organizations that fail to reward success but punish mistakes.

7 *Oppositional* – organizations in which confrontation prevails and negativism is rewarded.

8 *Power* – organizations structured on the basis of the authority inherent in members' positions.

9 *Competitive* – a culture in which winning is valued and members are rewarded for out-performing one another.

10 *Competence/perfectionist* – organizations in which perfectionism, persistence and hard work are valued.

11 *Achievement* – organizations that do things well and value members who set and accomplish challenging but realistic goals.

12 *Self-actualization* – organizations that value creativity, quality over quantity, and both task accomplishment and individual growth.

Typical dimensions of organizational climate questionnaires (Koys and De Cotiis, 1991)

- *Autonomy* – the perception of self-determination with respect to work procedures, goals and priorities.

- *Cohesion* – the perception of togetherness or sharing within the organization setting.

- *Trust* – the perception of freedom to communicate openly with members at higher organizational levels about sensitive or personal issues with the expectation that the integrity of such communications will not be violated.

- *Resource* – the perception of time demands with respect to task completion and performance standards.

- *Support* – the perception of the degree to which superiors tolerate members' behaviour, including willingness to let members learn from their mistakes without fear of reprisal.
- *Recognition* – the perception that members' contributions to the organization are acknowledged.
- *Fairness* – the perception that organizational policies are non-arbitrary or capricious.
- *Innovation* – the perception that change and creativity are encouraged, including risk-taking into new areas where the member has little or no prior experience.

Employee surveys

A number of organizations conduct employee surveys, also known as attitude or opinion surveys, on behalf of their clients. Apart from the advantage of being well tested and professionally administered they also facilitate benchmarking. Surveys provided by such organizations include the CIPD People and Performance employee questionnaire, the IES engagement survey, the Gallup engagement survey and the Saratoga engagement and commitment matrix.

Organization development programmes

The traditional OD programme was behavioural science-based and almost entirely devoted to inter-personal relationships, organizational processes and culture change in the broadest sense. There may still be a need for such interventions today but organization development is a more eclectic affair – anything can be included under the organization development heading as long as it contributes to organizational effectiveness. As explained below, there is a choice of activities and some examples are given of approaches to a major organization development initiative, namely culture change.

Organization development activities

The choice is from activities such as those set out in Table 18.1.

These activities can be combined in many ways so that they become mutually supporting. Ones such as culture change and team building can include traditional OD interventions such as action learning, survey feedback and group dynamics. It can be argued that change management is not a separate organization development activity but is a fundamental part of all such activities. Each of those listed above involves change, which has to be managed using the sort of change management skills described in Chapter 73. The following examples of culture change activities drawn from research conducted by the CIPD (2011) illustrate the range of activities covered under the broad heading of culture change:

- Arts Council England Interventions focused on the organizational structure, embedding the new values and demonstrating leadership commitment for the culture change.
- Children's Trust Southampton Interventions focused on the organization's structure, developing values to support the strategy and structure.
- London Borough of Barnet Interventions centred on establishing a Lean team to drive the project. Front-line staff were at the heart of the process, which involved them identifying what's wrong with the service and how things could be improved.
- National Police Improvements Agency activities include a restructuring of the top management team, a review of existing processes, the involvement of stakeholders and a focus on retaining respect for past ways of working.
- NP Paribas focused activities on the organization's structure, processes, values and the importance of leadership.
- Visa Europe established a culture change programme that was called 'peak performance'. The process focused on the individual and helping each individual to recognize how their own values and aspirations could be connected with those of the organization in a mutually beneficial way.

TABLE 18.1   Organization development activities

Organization development activity	Brief description	Objective
Business model innovation	The process followed by an organization to develop a new business model or change an existing one.	To obtain insight into the business issues facing the organization, leading to plans for practical interventions that address those issues.
Change management	The process of planning and introducing change systematically, taking into account the likelihood of it being resisted.	To achieve the smooth implementation of change.
Culture change	The process of changing the organization's culture in the shape of its values, norms and beliefs.	To improve organizational effectiveness – the ability of an organization to achieve its goals by making effective use of the resources available to it.
Engagement, enhancement of	The development of improved levels of job and organizational engagement.	To ensure that people are committed to their work and the organization and motivated to achieve high levels of performance.
High-performance working	Developing work system processes, practices and policies to enable employees to perform to their full potential.	To impact on the performance of the organization through its people in such areas as productivity, quality, levels of customer service, growth and profits.
Knowledge management	Storing and sharing the wisdom, understanding and expertise accumulated in an organization about its processes, techniques and operations.	To get knowledge from those who have it to those who need it in order to improve organizational effectiveness.
Lean	A process improvement methodology that focuses on continuous improvement, reducing waste and ensuring the flow of production	To deliver value to customers.
Organizational learning	The acquisition and development of knowledge, understanding, insights, techniques and practices.	To facilitate performance improvement and major changes in strategic direction.

TABLE 18.1 *continued*

Organization development activity	Brief description	Objective
Organization design	The process of deciding how organizations should be structured in terms of the ways in which the responsibility for carrying out the overall task is allocated to individuals and groups of people and how the relationships between them function.	To ensure that people work effectively together to achieve the overall purpose of the organization.
Performance management	A systematic process involving the agreement of performance expectations and the review of how those expectations have been met.	To improve organizational performance by developing the performance of individuals and teams.
Smart working	An approach to organizing work through a combination of flexibility, autonomy and collaboration, in parallel with optimizing tools and working environments for employees.	To drive greater efficiency and effectiveness in achieving job outcomes.
Team building	Using interactive skills and training techniques to improve the ways in which people in teams work together.	To increase group cohesion, mutual support and cooperation.
Total rewards	The combination of financial and non-financial rewards available to employees. It involves integrating the various aspects of reward.	To blend the financial and non-financial elements of reward into a cohesive whole so that together they make a more powerful and longer-lasting impact on job satisfaction and performance.

Conclusions on organization development

Organization development is no longer solely the preserve of external process consultants with behavioural science backgrounds. Instead it is a territory frequently inhabited by business-oriented people based in the organization and acting, in effect, as internal consultants. They include HR specialists who are there not just because they know about HRM but because they are familiar with how businesses operate and where people management fits in.

The organization development processes with which internal specialists and their colleagues are concerned will be determined by the outcome of diagnostic reviews. Because these outcomes will always be different, organizational development programmes will always be different. There is no such thing as a standard 'OD' approach, as was formerly the case. A number of approaches are available, but which to use and how to use it is a matter of choice depending on the facts of the situation. This is why the initial analysis and diagnosis is so important. An analytical toolkit for organization development, along with extensive other resources, can be found on the companion website to this book: **www. koganpage.com/ArmstrongHRMPractice**

Key learning points: Organization development

Organization development defined

Organization development in its traditional form as 'OD' was defined by Rowlandson (1984: 90) as 'an intervention strategy that uses group processes to focus on the whole culture of an organization in order to bring about planned change'. The CIPD (2010: 1) defined organization development as a 'planned and systematic approach to enabling sustained organization performance through the involvement of its people'.

Strategic nature of organization development

The strategic nature of organization development as an integral part of HRM arises because it can play a significant role in the implementation of business strategy.

Assumptions and values of OD

The assumptions and values of OD as originally conceived were that:

- Most individuals are driven by the need for personal growth and development as long as their environment is both supportive and challenging.

- The work team, especially at the informal level, has great significance for feelings of satisfaction and the dynamics of such teams have a powerful effect on the behaviour of their members.

- OD programmes aim to improve the quality of working life of all members of the organization.

- Organizations can be more effective if they learn to diagnose their own strengths and weaknesses.

- Managers often do not know what is wrong and need special help in diagnosing problems, although the outside 'process consultant' ensures that decision making remains in the hands of the client.

OD interventions

OD interventions include process consultation, change management, action research, survey feedback, group dynamics and personal interventions.

Criticisms of OD

The main criticisms of OD, as noted by Marsh *et al* (2010: 143), were that it was 'Oriented to process and tools rather than results... where techniques are considered to be ends in themselves rather than a means to deliver organizational performance.'

Organization development strategy

Organization development strategy is based on the aspiration to improve organizational capability, which is broadly the capacity of an organization to function effectively in order to achieve desired results.

The practice of organization development

The practice of organization development is based on an analysis and diagnosis of the circumstances of the organization, the strategic, operational or process issues that are affecting the organization and its ability to perform well. This involves the use of diagnostic tools.

Organization development programmes

The traditional OD programme was behavioural science-based and almost entirely devoted to interpersonal relationships, organizational processes and culture change in the broadest sense. There may still be a need for such interventions today but the emphasis now is on much more focused activities to do with high-performance working, Lean manufacturing, smart working and the enhancement of levels of engagement.

References

Argyris, C (1957) *Personality and Organization*, New York, Harper & Row

Anthony, P D (1990) The paradox of managing culture or 'he who leads is lost', *Personnel Review*, **19** (4), pp 3–8

Armstrong, M (1984) *A Handbook of Personnel Management Practice*, 2nd edn, London, Kogan Page

Beckhard, R (1969) *Organization Development: Strategy and models*, Reading, MA, Addison-Wesley

Beer, M (1980) *Organization Change and Development: A systems view*, Santa Monica, CA, Goodyear

Bennis, W G (1969) *Organization Development: Its nature, origin and prospects*, Reading, MA, Addison-Wesley

Buchanan, D and Huczynski, A (2007) *Organizational Behaviour*, Harlow, FT Prentice-Hall

Burke, W W (1995) Organization development: then, now and tomorrow, *Organization Development Journal*, **13** (4), pp 7–17

Caldwell, R (2003) Models of change agency: a fourfold classification, *British Journal of Management*, **14** (2), pp 131–42

Chartered Institute of Personnel and Development (2010) *Organization Development*, London, CIPD

Chartered Institute of Personnel and Development (2011) *Developing Organisation Culture: Six case studies*, London, CIPD

Cooke, R and Lafferty, J (1989) *Organizational Culture Inventory*, Plymouth, MI, Human Synergistic

Cummings, T G and Worley, C G (2005) *Organization Development and Change*, Mason, OH, South Western

Harrison, R (1972) Understanding your organization's character, Harvard Business Review, 5, pp 119–28

Herzberg, F, Mausner, B and Snyderman, B (1957) *The Motivation to Work*, New York, Wiley

HR Magazine (2007) *Organization development: a strategic HR tool*, **52** (9), pp 1–10

Koys, D and De Cotiis, T (1991) Inductive measures of organizational climate, *Human Relations*, **44**, pp 265–85

Legge, K (1995) *Human Resource Management: Rhetorics and realities*, London, Macmillan

Lewin, K (1947) Frontiers in group dynamics, *Human Relations*, **1** (1), pp 5–42

Lewin, K (1951) *Field Theory in Social Science*, New York, Harper & Row

Likert, R (1961) *New Patterns of Management*, New York, Harper & Row

Manzini, A O (1988) *Organizational Diagnosis*, New York, AMACOM

Marsh, C, Sparrow, P and Hird, M (2010) Improving organization design: The new priority for HR directors, in (eds) P Sparrow, A Hesketh, M Hird and C Cooper, *Leading HR*, Basingstoke, Palgrave Macmillan, pp 136–61

Maslow, A (1954) *Motivation and Personality*, New York, Harper & Row

Mayo, E (1933) *The Human Problems of an Industrial Civilisation*, London, Macmillan

McGregor, D (1960) *The Human Side of Enterprise*, New York, McGraw-Hill

McLean, A (1981) Organization development: a case of the emperor's new clothes? *Personnel Review*, **4** (1), pp 3–14

Roethlisberger, F and Dickson, W (1939) *Management and the Worker*, Cambridge, MA, Harvard University Press

Rowlandson, P (1984) The oddity of OD, *Management Today*, November, pp 91–93

Ruona, W E A and Gibson, S K (2004) The making of twenty-first century HR: the convergence of HRM, HRD and OD, *Human Resource Management*, **43** (1), pp 49–66

Strauss, G (1976) Organization development, in (ed) R Dubin, *Handbook of Work*, Organization and Society, Chicago, IL, Rand MacNally

Ulrich, D and Lake, D (1990) *Organizational Capability: Competing from the inside out*, New York, Wiley

Weidner, C K (2004) A brand in dire straits: organization development at sixty, *Organization Development Journal*, **22** (2), pp 37–47

Worley, C, Hitchin, D and Ross, W (1996) *Integrated Strategic Change: How organization development builds competitive advantage*, Reading, MA, Addison-Wesley

PART V

Factors influencing employee behaviour

Introduction

A preoccupation shared by all those involved in managing people is how to get the best out of them. 'The best' may be difficult to define. It could be high performance. Or it could be discretionary behaviour (the choice made by people to exercise additional effort, care, innovation and productive behaviour in their jobs). It could be doing more than is contracted for so that the words 'it's not in my job description' or 'this is above my pay grade' are seldom if ever heard. It could be cooperating fully with managers and colleagues or showing loyalty to the organization. It could be any combination of these.

Getting the best out of people is primarily the responsibility of managers and team leaders by exercising effective leadership. But it is also the concern of HR specialists who can help to create a work environment conducive to high performance and can introduce policies and practices that encourage people to do everything expected of them if not more. HR can also provide any advice and help managers to fulfil their people management responsibilities.

To do this, managers and HR specialists need to take into account the general factors that affect how people behave at work, as described in Chapter 16 – namely, ability, intelligence, personality, attitudes, emotions and emotional intelligence. But they should also be aware of the following more specific factors that influence behaviour and therefore performance:

- Motivation – the strength and direction of behaviour and the factors that influence people to behave in certain ways.
- Commitment – the strength of an individual's identification with, and involvement in, an organization.
- Engagement – a situation in which people are committed to their work and the organization and are motivated to achieve high levels of performance.

These are examined in the three chapters of this part.

Of the three constructs (a construct is a conceptual framework that explains how people perceive and react to their environment), motivation is a long-standing one that has been extensively researched and written about since the earlier part of the 20th century. Motivation theory has been used and is still used to inform decisions on how to get more effort and better performance from employees, for example the use of performance-related pay. The importance of the construct of commitment emerged later, notably in the contribution of Richard Walton (1985) whose seminal article in the *Harvard Business Review* advocated the adoption of a commitment strategy rather than one based on control. The most recent construct is that of engagement, which was first presented in a 1990 *Academy of Management Journal* article by William Kahn. He defined engagement as 'the harnessing of organization members' selves to their work roles' (1990: 694).

The construct of engagement contains elements of motivation and commitment. It also embraces the notion of organizational citizenship behaviour (OCB), which is positive discretionary behaviour at work that goes beyond role requirements.

However, it is difficult to disentangle the concepts of motivation, commitment and engagement, although an attempt to do so is made in the three chapters of this part. Simplistically, it could be argued that when motivation is extrinsic, ie when things are done to or for people in order to motivate them, such as through pay or recognition, the aim is to make a direct impact on individual performance. In contrast, both commitment and engagement are states of being that can be affected by managerial actions. They are not so direct or immediate as the direct instruments used in the motivation strategies aimed at individuals. Engagement and commitment strategies may be more about taking action that affects employees collectively such as improvements in the work environment.

Three other aspects of the behaviour of people at work are considered in this part. The first of these is job satisfaction, ie the attitudes and feelings that people have about their jobs. This is associated with motivation and engagement but it could be regarded as an outcome of engagement rather than a constituent of it. Whether or not job satisfaction improves performance is considered in Chapters 19 and 21. Second, the relationship between money and motivation is examined in Chapter 19. This is important because it affects policies and practices concerned with the use of pay as an incentive or reward. Third, reference is made in Chapter 21 to the dark side of engagement – burnout – how it happens and what can be done about it.

References

Kahn, W A (1990) Psychological conditions of personal engagement and disengagement at work, *Academy of Management Journal*, **33** (4), pp 692–724

Walton, R E (1985) From control to commitment in the workplace, *Harvard Business Review*, March–April, pp 77–84

19
Motivation

LEARNING OUTCOMES

On completing this chapter you should be able to define these key concepts. You should also understand:

- The meaning of motivation
- Types of motivation
- The different motivation theories
- Motivation and job satisfaction
- Approaches to developing a motivation strategy

Introduction

Motivation is the force that energizes, directs and sustains behaviour. High performance is achieved by well-motivated people who are prepared to exercise discretionary effort, ie independently do more than is expected of them. Even in fairly basic roles, Hunter *et al* (1990) found through their research that the difference in value-added discretionary performance between 'superior' and 'standard' performers was 19 per cent. For highly complex jobs it was 48 per cent. The aims of this chapter are to explore the meaning of motivation, define the two main types of motivation – intrinsic and extrinsic – describe and critically evaluate the main theories of motivation, discuss two related aspects of motivation – its relationship to job satisfaction and money – and outline approaches to motivation strategy.

The meaning of motivation

The term 'motivation' derives from the Latin word for movement (*movere*). A motive is a reason for doing something. Motivation is the strength and direction of behaviour and the factors that influence people to behave in certain ways. People are motivated when they expect that a course of action is likely to lead to the attainment of a goal and a valued reward – one that satisfies their needs and wants. The term 'motivation' can refer variously to the goals that individuals have, the ways in which individuals choose their goals and the ways in which others try to change their behaviour. Locke and Latham (2004: 388) observed that: 'The concept of motivation refers to internal factors that impel action and to external factors that can act as inducements to action.'

As described by Arnold *et al* (1991) the three components of motivation are:

1 *Direction* – what a person is trying to do.
2 *Effort* – how hard a person is trying.
3 *Persistence* – how long a person keeps on trying.

Well-motivated people engage in positive discretionary behaviour – they decide to make an effort. Such people may be self-motivated, and as long as this means they are going in the right direction to attain what they are there to achieve, then this is the best form of motivation. But additional motivation provided by the work itself – the quality of leadership, and various forms of recognition and reward – builds on self-motivation and helps people to make the best use of their abilities and to perform well.

There are two types of motivation and a number of theories explaining how it works, as discussed below.

Types of motivation

Intrinsic motivation

Intrinsic motivation takes place when individuals feel that their work is important, interesting and challenging and that it provides them with a reasonable degree of autonomy (freedom to act), opportunities to achieve and advance, and scope to use and develop their skills and abilities. It can be described as motivation by the work itself. It is not created by external incentives. Deci and Ryan (1985) suggested that intrinsic motivation is based on the need to be competent and self-determining (that is, to have a choice). Michael Sandel (2012: 122) remarked that: 'When people are engaged in an activity they consider intrinsically worthwhile, offering money may weaken their motivation by "crowding out" their intrinsic interest or commitment.'

Intrinsic motivation can be enhanced by job design. Katz (1964) suggested that jobs should in themselves provide sufficient variety, complexity, challenge and skill to engage the abilities of the worker. Hackman and Oldham (1974) in their job characteristics model identified the five core characteristics of jobs that result in intrinsic motivation, namely: skill variety, task identity, task significance, autonomy and feedback. Pink (2009) stated that there are three steps that managers can take to improve motivation:

1 *Autonomy* – encourage people to set their own schedule and focus on getting work done, not how it is done.
2 *Mastery* – help people to identify the steps they can take to improve and ask them to identify how they will know they are making progress.
3 *Purpose* – when giving instructions, explain the why as well as the how.

Intrinsic motivation is associated with the concept of employee engagement, as explained in Chapter 21.

Extrinsic motivation

Extrinsic motivation occurs when things are done to or for people in order to motivate them. These include rewards such as incentives, increased pay, praise or promotion, and punishments such as disciplinary action, withholding pay, or criticism.

Extrinsic motivators can have an immediate and powerful effect, but it will not necessarily last long. The intrinsic motivators, which are concerned with the 'quality of working life' (a phrase and movement that emerged from this concept), are likely to have a deeper and longer-term effect because they are inherent in individuals and the work – and are not imposed from outside in such forms as incentive pay.

Motivation theory as described below explains the ways in which intrinsic and extrinsic motivation take place.

Motivation theory

As mentioned by Steers *et al* (2004: 379) the earliest approaches to understanding human motivation date from the time of the Greek philosophers and focus on the concept of hedonism as a principle driving force in behaviour. Individuals were seen as directing their efforts to seeking pleasure and avoiding pain. This principle was later refined and further developed in the works of philosophers such as John Locke and Jeremy Bentham in the 17th and 18th centuries. Motivation theory has moved on from then. It started in the earlier part of the 20th century with the contributions of the exponents of scientific management (instrumentality theory). In the middle years of that century the behavioural scientists entered the field and began to develop the 'content' or 'needs' theory of motivation. The main process theories such as expectancy theory emerged in the 1960s and '70s, although the first formulation of the process theory of reinforcement took place in 1911. The three main areas of motivation theory – instrumentality, content and process – are examined below.

Instrumentality theory

Instrumentality theory states in effect that rewards and punishments are the best instruments with which to shape behaviour. It assumes that people will be motivated to work if rewards and penalties are tied directly to their performance; thus the awards are contingent upon effective performance. Instrumentality theory has its roots in the scientific management methods of Taylor (1911: 121) who wrote: 'It is impossible, through any long period of time, to get workmen to work much harder than the average men around them unless they are assured a large and a permanent increase in their pay.'

This theory provides a rationale for financial incentives such as performance-related pay, albeit a dubious one. Motivation using this approach has been and still is widely adopted. It may be successful in some circumstances, eg piece work, but – for reasons explained in Chapter 47 – merit or performance pay is flawed.

Instrumentality theory relies exclusively on a system of external controls and does not recognize a number of other human needs. It also fails to appreciate the fact that the formal control system can be seriously affected by the informal relationships existing between workers.

Content theory

The aim of the content or needs theory produced by Maslow, Alderfer, McClelland, Herzberg, and Deci and Ryan was to identify the factors associated with motivation. The theory focuses on the content of motivation in the shape of needs. Its basis is the belief that an unsatisfied need creates tension and a state of disequilibrium. To restore the balance, a goal is identified that will satisfy the need, and a behaviour pathway is selected that will lead to the achievement of the goal and the satisfaction of the need. Behaviour is therefore motivated by unsatisfied needs. A content theory model is shown in Figure 19.1. Content theory, as the term implies, indicates the components of motivation but it does not explain how motivation affects performance – a necessary requirement if the concept is to provide guidance on HR policy and practice. This was the role of expectancy theory, as will be discussed later.

Maslow's hierarchy of needs

The most famous classification of needs is the one formulated by Maslow (1954). He suggested that there are five major need categories that apply to people in general, starting from the fundamental physiological needs and leading through a hierarchy of safety, social and esteem needs to the need for self-fulfilment, the highest need of all. When a lower need is satisfied the next highest becomes dominant and the individual's attention is turned to satisfying this higher need. The need for self-fulfilment, however, can never be satisfied. 'Man is a wanting animal'; only an unsatisfied need can motivate

FIGURE 19.1   The process of motivation according to content theory

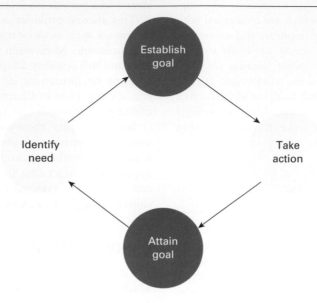

behaviour and the dominant need is the prime motivator of behaviour. Psychological development takes place as people move up the hierarchy of needs, but this is not necessarily a straightforward progression. The lower needs still exist, even if temporarily dormant as motivators, and individuals constantly return to previously satisfied needs.

Maslow's needs hierarchy has an intuitive appeal and has been very popular. But it has not been verified by empirical research such as that conducted by Wahba and Bridwell (1979), and it has been criticized for its apparent rigidity – different people may have different priorities and the underpinning assumption that everyone has the same needs is invalid. It is difficult to accept that needs progress steadily up the hierarchy and Maslow himself expressed doubts about the validity of a strictly ordered hierarchy. But he did emphasize that the higher-order needs are more significant.

ERG theory (Alderfer)

Alderfer (1972) produced a more convincing and simpler theory, which postulated three primary categories of needs:

1 *Existence needs* such as hunger and thirst – pay, fringe benefits and working conditions are other types of existence needs.

2 *Relatedness needs*, which acknowledge that people are not self-contained units but must engage in transactions with their human environment – acceptance, understanding, confirmation and influence are elements of the relatedness process.

3 *Growth needs*, which involve people in finding the opportunities to be what they are most fully and to become what they can. This is the most significant need.

McClelland's achievement motivation

An alternative way of classifying needs was developed by McClelland (1961), who based it mainly on studies of managers. He identified three needs, of which the need for achievement was the most important:

1 The need for *achievement*, defined as the need for competitive success measured against a personal standard of excellence.

2 The need for *affiliation*, defined as the need for warm, friendly, compassionate relationships with others.

3 The need for *power*, defined as the need to control or influence others.

Herzberg's two-factor model

The two-factor model of motivation developed by Herzberg *et al* (1957) and Herzberg (1966) was based on an investigation into the sources of job satisfaction and dissatisfaction of accountants and engineers, who were asked what made them feel exceptionally good or exceptionally bad about their jobs. According to Herzberg, this research established that there were two factors that affected feelings of satisfaction or dissatisfaction. Motivating factors or 'satisfiers' relate to the job content and consist of the need for achievement, the interest of the work, responsibility and opportunities for advancement. These needs are the intrinsic motivators. He summed this up in the phrase 'motivation by the work itself'.

Hygiene factors relate to the job context, including such things as pay and working conditions. 'Hygiene' is used in the medical use of the term, meaning preventative and environmental. In themselves, hygiene factors neither satisfy nor motivate and they serve primarily to prevent job dissatisfaction, while having little effect on positive job attitudes. Pay is not a satisfier but if it is inadequate or inequitable it can cause dissatisfaction. However, its provision does not provide lasting satisfaction.

Herzberg's two-factor theory in effect identifies needs but it has been attacked by, for example, Opsahl and Dunnette (1966). The research method has been criticized because no attempt was made to measure the relationship between satisfaction and performance. It has been claimed that the two-factor nature of the theory is an inevitable result of the questioning method used by the interviewers. It has also been suggested that wide and unwarranted inferences have been drawn from small and specialized samples and that there is no evidence to suggest that the satisfiers do improve productivity. The underpinning assumption that everyone has the same needs is invalid. Denise Rousseau (2006: 263), in her presidential address to the US Academy of Management, summed up these views as follows: 'Herzberg's long-discredited two-factor theory is typically included in the motivation section of management textbooks, despite the fact that it was discredited as an artefact of method bias over thirty years ago.'

In spite of these objections, the Herzberg two-factor theory continues to thrive; partly because it is easy to understand and seems to be based on real-life rather than academic abstractions, and partly because it convincingly emphasizes the positive value of the intrinsic motivating factors and highlights the need to consider both financial and non-financial factors when developing reward systems. It is also in accord with a fundamental belief in the dignity of labour and the Protestant ethic – that work is good in itself. Herzberg's strength as a proselytizer rather than a researcher meant that he had considerable influence on the job enrichment movement, which sought to design jobs in a way that would maximize the opportunities to obtain intrinsic satisfaction from work and thus improve the quality of working life. Herzberg famously remarked that if you want people to do a good job then give them a good job to do (quoted by Dowling, 1971).

Self-determination theory

As formulated by Deci and Ryan (2000), this theory states that individuals are motivated by the need to achieve three fundamental goals: striving for competence, autonomy and relatedness.

Comment on content theories

Shields (2007: 74) observed that content theories share some common shortcomings. His criticisms were that they incorrectly assume:

- the existence of a universally applicable set of human needs;
- that according to Maslow (1954), needs conform to a simple ordered hierarchy of need importance, when in reality, needs seem to operate in a more flexible, less ordered and predictable way;
- that the link between needs and behaviours is direct and automatic, rather than mediated by human consciousness, values and choice.

In addition, he pointed out that content theories 'underestimate the motivational potency of extrinsic rewards, including financial rewards'.

Process theory

In process theory, the emphasis is on the psychological or mental processes and forces that affect motivation, as well as on basic needs. It is also known as cognitive theory because it refers to people's perceptions of their working environment and the ways in which they interpret and understand it. The main process theories are concerned with reinforcement, expectancy, goals, equity, and cognitive evaluation.

Reinforcement theory

This is the oldest and least complex of the process theories. It is based on 'the law of effect' as formulated by Thorndike (1911), which states that over time, people learn about the relationships between their actions and the consequences of them and this understanding guides their future behaviour. In other words, if they believe that something has worked previously, then they will do it again. It was later developed by Hull (1943, 1951).

Skinner (1953) and others later built on these principles with the notion of 'operant conditioning', which was influenced by the work of Pavlov and his salivating dogs. As Shields (2007: 76) put it: 'Positive reinforcement of desired behaviour elicits more of the same; punishment of undesired behaviour (negative reinforcement) elicits less of the same.' Reinforcement models continue to thrive today as explanatory vehicles for understanding work motivation and job performance, and as a justification of performance pay.

But reinforcement theory can be criticized for taking an unduly mechanistic view of human nature. It implies that people can be motivated by treating them as machines – by pulling levers. In assuming that the present choices of individuals are based on an understanding of the outcomes of their past choices, reinforcement theory ignores the existing context in which choices are made. In addition, motivational theories based on the principle of reinforcement pay insufficient attention to the influence of expectations – no indication is given of how to distinguish in advance which outcomes would strengthen responses and which would weaken them. Above all, they are limited because they imply, in Allport's (1954) vivid phrase, a hedonism of the past.

Expectancy theory

Expectancy theory states that motivation will be high when people know what they have to do in order to get a reward, expect that they will be able to get the reward and expect that the reward will be worthwhile.

The concept of expectancy was originally contained in the valency-instrumentality-expectancy (VIE) theory that was formulated by Vroom (1964). Valency stands for value; instrumentality is the belief that if we do one thing it will lead to another; and expectancy is the probability that action or effort will lead to an outcome.

The strength of expectations may be based on past experiences (reinforcement), but individuals are frequently presented with new situations – a change in job, payment system, or working conditions imposed by management – where past experience is an inadequate guide to the implications of the change. In these circumstances, motivation may be reduced.

Motivation is only likely when a clearly perceived and usable relationship exists between performance and outcome, and the outcome is seen as a means of satisfying needs. This explains why extrinsic financial motivation – for example, an incentive or bonus scheme – works only if the link (line of sight) between effort and reward is clear and the value of the reward is worth the effort. It also explains why intrinsic motivation arising from the work itself can be more powerful than extrinsic motivation. Intrinsic motivation outcomes are more under the control of individuals, who can place greater reliance on their past experiences to indicate the extent to which positive and advantageous results are likely to be obtained by their behaviour.

This theory was developed by Porter and Lawler (1968) into a model shown in Figure 19.2, which follows Vroom's ideas by suggesting that there are two factors determining the effort that people put into their jobs: first, the value of the rewards to individuals in so far as they satisfy their needs for security, social esteem, autonomy and self-actualization; second, the probability that rewards depend on effort, as perceived by individuals – in other words, their expectations about the relationships between effort and reward. Thus, the greater the value of a set of awards and the higher the probability that receiving each of these rewards depends upon effort, the greater the effort that will be put forth in a given situation.

But, as Porter and Lawler emphasized, mere effort is not enough. It has to be effective effort if it is to produce the desired performance. The two

FIGURE 19.2   Expectancy motivation model (Porter and Lawler, 1968)

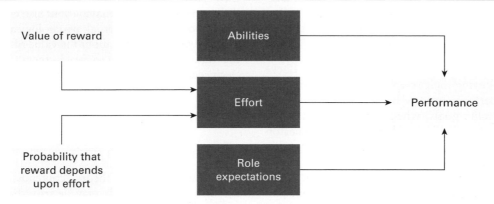

variables additional to effort that affect task achievement are: 1) ability – individual characteristics such as intelligence, knowledge, skills; 2) role perceptions – what the individual wants to do or thinks they are required to do. These are good from the viewpoint of the organization if they correspond with what it thinks the individual ought to be doing. They are poor if the views of the individual and the organization do not coincide.

Alongside goal theory (see below), expectancy theory has become the most influential motivation theory, particularly as it affects performance and reward management. But reservations have been expressed about it. House *et al* (1974) remarked that: 'Evidence for the validity of the theory is very mixed.' They also established that there were a number of variables affecting expectations that make it difficult to predict how they function. These are:

- Leadership behaviour – the function of the leader in clarifying expectations, guiding, supporting and rewarding subordinates.

- Individual characteristics – the subjects' perception of their ability to perform the required task.

- Nature of the task – whether accomplishing the task provides the necessary reinforcements and rewards.

- The practices of the organization – its reward and control systems and how it functions.

Research conducted by Behling and Starke (1973) established that individuals:

- make crucial personal decisions without clearly understanding the consequences;

- do not in practice consistently evaluate their order of preference for alternative actions;

- have to assign two values when making a decision – its desirability and its achievability – but they tend to be influenced mainly by desirability – they let their tastes influence their beliefs;

- may be able to evaluate the extrinsic rewards they expect but may find it difficult to evaluate the possibility of achieving intrinsic rewards;

- may find it difficult to distinguish the benefits of one possible outcome from another.

They concluded that: 'Expectancy theory can account for some of the variations in work effort but far less than normally attributed to it' (ibid: 386).

Shields (2007: 80) commented that a problem with expectancy theory is that it assumes that 'behaviour is rational and premeditated when we know that much workplace behaviour is impulsive and emotional'.

However, in spite of these objections, the simple message of expectancy theory – that people will be motivated if they expect that their behaviour will produce a worthwhile reward – is compelling.

And it provides a useful tool to assess the effectiveness of motivating devices such as performance-related pay.

Goal theory

Goal theory as developed by Latham and Locke (1979) following their research, states that motivation and performance are higher when individuals are set specific goals, when goals are demanding but accepted, and when there is feedback on performance. Goals must be clearly defined. Participation in goal setting is important as a means of getting agreement to the setting of demanding goals. Feedback is vital in maintaining motivation, particularly towards the achievement of even higher goals.

However, the universality of goal theory has been questioned. For example, Pintrich (2000) noted that people have different goals in different circumstances and that it is hard to justify the assumption that goals are always accessible and conscious. And Harackiewicz et al (2002) warned that goals are only effective when they are consistent with and match the general context in which they are pursued. But support for goal theory was provided by Bandura and Cervone (1983) who emphasized the importance of self-efficacy (a belief in one's ability to accomplish goals).

Equity theory

Equity theory, as defined by Adams (1965), is concerned with the perceptions people have about how they are being treated as compared with others. He proposed that employees assess the fairness or otherwise of their rewards (outcomes) in relation to their effort or qualifications (inputs) and that they do this by comparing their own input/output ratio against that of other individuals. If the input/output ratio is perceived to be unfavourable, they will feel that there is reward inequity.

Equity theory explains only one aspect of the processes of motivation and job satisfaction, although it may be significant in terms of morale and, possibly, of performance.

Social learning theory

Social learning theory as developed by Bandura (1977) combines aspects of both reinforcement and expectancy theory. It recognizes the significance of the basic behavioural concept of reinforcement as a determinant of future behaviour but also emphasizes the importance of internal psychological factors, especially expectancies about the value of goals and the individual's ability to reach them. The term 'reciprocal determinism' is used to denote the concept that while the situation will affect individual behaviour, individuals will simultaneously influence the situation.

Cognitive evaluation theory

Cognitive evaluation theory contends that the use of extrinsic rewards may destroy the intrinsic motivation that flows from inherent job interest. It was formulated by Deci and Ryan (1985). Referring to their research, they stated that: 'Rewards, like feedback, when used to convey to people a sense of appreciation for work well done, will tend to be experienced informationally and will maintain or enhance intrinsic motivation. But when they are used to motivate people, they will be experienced controllingly and will undermine intrinsic motivation.'

Deci et al (1999) followed up this research by carrying out a meta-analysis of 128 experiments on rewards and intrinsic motivation to establish the extent to which intrinsic motivation was undermined by rewards. The results of the study indicated that for high-interest tasks, rewards had significant negative effects on what the researchers called 'free-choice measures', which included the time spent on the task after the reward was removed.

But as noted by Gerhart and Rynes (2003: 52): 'The vast majority of research on this theory has been performed in school rather than work settings, often with elementary school-aged children.' But that did not stop other commentators assuming that the results were equally significant for working adults. It is interesting to note that while research in industry conducted by Deci and Ryan (1985) found that financial incentives did decrease intrinsic motivation in high-control organizational cultures, it also established that in organizations with the opposite high-involvement culture, intrinsic and extrinsic motivation were both increased by monetary incentives. Context is all important. Moreover, a meta-analysis of 145 studies conducted by Cameron et al (2001) led to the conclusion that rewards do not inevitably have negative effects on intrinsic motivation.

Flow

The concept of flow was originated by Mihály Csíkszentmihályi (1990) who described it as the mental state of someone who is fully focused and immersed in an activity and enjoys doing it. It can be described as fully focused motivation. According to Csikszentmihályi, the flow experience is characterized by immediate feedback, feeling that you have the potential to succeed, and feeling so engrossed in the experience that other needs become negligible. Schaffer (2013) proposed seven flow conditions:

1 Knowing what to do.
2 Knowing how to do it.
3 Knowing how well you are doing.
4 Knowing where to go.
5 High perceived challenges.
6 High perceived skills.
7 Freedom from distractions.

The notion of flow usefully encapsulates a number of familiar concepts from the fields of motivation, engagement and job design theory

Purposeful work behaviour

A more recent integrated motivation theory formulated by Barrick and Mount (2013) focused on the impact on motivation of individual factors, such as personality and ability, and situational factors, such as job characteristics. The motivation to engage in purposeful work behaviour depends on both these factors.

Comment on process theories

Process theories are not based on suspect assumptions about the universality of needs, as are content theories. Process theories emphasize the importance of individual decision making on work behaviour. As pointed out by Shields (2007: 85) they 'acknowledge the importance of social and job context as co-determinants of motivational strength while those other than reinforcement theory also high-light the importance of self-efficacy, task or goal clarity and motivational learning'.

Summary of motivation theories

A summary of motivation theories is set out in Table 19.1.

Conclusions on motivation theory

All the theories referred to above make some contribution to an understanding of the processes that affect motivation. But instrumentality theory provides only a simplistic explanation of how motivation works. Needs and content theories are more sophisticated but have their limitations. As Gerhart and Rynes (2003: 53) commented:

> Although the ideas developed by Maslow, Herzberg and Deci have had considerable appeal to many people, the prevailing view in the academic literature is that the specific predictions of these theories is not supported by empirical evidence. On the other hand, it would be a mistake to underestimate the influence that these theories have had on research and practice. Pfeffer, Kohn and others continue to base their argument regarding the ineffectiveness of money as a motivator on such theories.

But, bearing in mind the reservations set out earlier, needs theory still offers an indication of the factors that motivate people and content theory provides useful explanations of how motivation takes place. And while instrumentality and reinforcement theories may be simplistic, they still explain some aspects of how rewards affect motivation and performance and they continue to exert influence on the beliefs of some people about the power of incentives to motivate people. Herzberg's research may be flawed but he still contributed to the recognition of the importance of job design.

Motivation theory can explain what makes people tick at work but it is also necessary to consider two other aspects of the impact of motivation – its relationship with job satisfaction and the effect of money on motivation. Strategies for motivation based on the lessons learnt from motivation theory are considered at the end of this chapter.

TABLE 19.1   Summary of motivation theories

Category	Theory	Summary of theory	Implications
Instrumentality	Taylorism Taylor (1911)	If we do one thing it leads to another. People will be motivated to work if rewards and punishments are directly related to their performance.	Basis of crude attempts to motivate people by incentives. Often used as the implied rationale for performance-related pay, although this is seldom an effective motivator.
Content or needs	Hierarchy of needs Maslow (1954)	A hierarchy of needs exists: physiological, safety, social, esteem, self-fulfilment. Needs at a higher level only emerge when a lower need is satisfied.	Focuses attention on the various needs that motivate people and the notion that a satisfied need is no longer a motivator. The concept of a hierarchy has no practical significance.
	ERG Alderfer (1972)	A non-hierarchical theory identifying three basic needs: existence, relatedness and growth.	A simpler and more convincing categorization of needs.
	Achievement motivation McClelland (1961)	Identified three needs for managers: achievement, affiliation and power. Of these, achievement is the most important.	Emphasized the importance to managers of achievement as a motivating factor.
	Two-factor model Herzberg (1957, 1966)	Two groups of factors affect job satisfaction: 1) those intrinsic to the work itself; 2) those extrinsic to the job such as pay and working conditions. The factors that affect positive feelings (the motivating factors) are quite different from those that affect negative feelings (the hygiene factors).	The research methodology has been strongly criticized (it does not support the existence of two factors) and the underpinning assumption that everyone has the same needs is invalid. But it has influenced approaches to job design (job enrichment) and it supports the proposition that reward systems should provide for both financial and non-financial rewards.
	Self-determination Deci and Ryan (2000)	Individuals are motivated to achieve three fundamental goals: striving for competence, autonomy, and relatedness.	Provides an alternative and simpler classification of needs.

TABLE 19.1   *continued*

Category	Theory	Summary of theory	Implications
Process	Reinforcement Thorndike (1911) Skinner (1953)	As experience is gained in satisfying needs, people perceive that certain actions help to achieve goals while others are unsuccessful. The successful actions are repeated when a similar need arises.	Provide feedback that positively reinforces effective behaviour.
	Expectancy Vroom (1964) Porter and Lawler (1968)	Effort (motivation) depends on the likelihood that rewards will follow effort and that the reward is worthwhile.	The key theory informing approaches to rewards, ie that there must be a link between effort and reward (line of sight), the reward should be achievable and it should be worthwhile.
	Goal Latham and Locke (1979)	Motivation will improve if people have demanding but agreed goals and receive feedback.	Influences performance management and learning and development practices.
	Equity Adams (1966)	People are better motivated if treated equitably, ie treated fairly in comparison with another group of people (a reference group) or a relevant other person.	Need to have equitable reward and employment practices.
	Social learning Bandura (1977)	Recognizes the significance of reinforcement as a determinant of future behaviour but also emphasizes the importance of expectancies about the value of goals and the individual's ability to reach them.	The emphasis is on expectancies, individual goals and values and the influence of both person and situational factors as well as reinforcement.
	Cognitive evaluation Deci and Ryan (1985)	The use of extrinsic rewards may destroy the intrinsic motivation that flows from inherent job interest.	Emphasizes the importance of non-financial rewards. The conclusions reached from Deci and Ryan's research have been questioned.
	Flow Csikszentmihályi (1990)	The mental state of someone who is fully focused and immersed in an activity and enjoys doing it. It can be described as fully focused motivation.	Encapsulates approaches to motivation, such as an emphasis on feedback and setting goals. Also refers to principles of job design and the factors that contribute to high levels of engagement.

Motivation and job satisfaction

Job satisfaction can be defined as the attitudes and feelings people have about their work. Positive and favourable attitudes towards the job indicate job satisfaction. Negative and unfavourable attitudes towards the job indicate job dissatisfaction. It can be distinguished from morale, which is a group rather than individual variable, related to the degree to which group members feel attracted to their group and want to remain a member of it.

The factors that affect job satisfaction

Levels of job satisfaction or dissatisfaction are influenced by:

- The intrinsic motivating factors. These relate to job content, especially the five dimensions of jobs identified by Hackman and Oldham (1974): skill variety, task identity, task significance, autonomy and feedback (the job characteristics model).

- The quality of supervision. The Hawthorne studies (Roethlisberger and Dixon, 1939) resulted in the claim that supervision is the most important determinant of worker attitudes. Elton Mayo (1933) believed that a man's desire to be continuously associated in work with his fellows is a strong, if not the strongest human characteristic.

- Success or failure. Success obviously creates satisfaction, especially if it enables individuals to prove to themselves that they are using their abilities to the full. And it is equally obvious that the reverse is true of failure.

Job satisfaction and performance

It is a commonly held and not unreasonable belief that an increase in job satisfaction results in improved performance. The whole human relations movement led by Mayo (1933) and supported by the Roethlisberger and Dixon (1939) research was based on the belief that productivity could be increased by making workers more satisfied, primarily through pleasant and supportive supervision and by meeting their social needs. But research by Katz et al (1950) and Katz et al (1951) found that the levels of satisfaction with pay, job status or fellow workers in high productivity units were no different to those in low productivity units.

Meta-analysis by Brayfield and Crockett (1955) of a number of studies concluded that there was little evidence of any simple or appreciable relationship between satisfaction and performance. A later review of research by Vroom (1964) found that the median correlation between job satisfaction and job performance for all these studies was only 0.14, which is not high enough to suggest any marked relationship between them. Spector (1997) came to the same conclusion. Indeed, it can be argued that it is not increases in satisfaction that produce improved performance but improved performance that increases satisfaction. This was confirmed by data on the link between job satisfaction and performance for 177 store managers, analysed by Christen et al (2006). It was established that store managers' performance increased their job satisfaction but that job satisfaction had no impact on job performance.

Motivation and money

Money, in the form of pay or some other sort of remuneration, is regarded by many people as the most obvious extrinsic reward. Money seems to provide the carrot that most people want.

Doubts were cast on the effectiveness of money by Herzberg (1968), which although unsupported by his research have some degree of face validity. He claimed that while the lack of money can cause dissatisfaction, its provision does not result in lasting satisfaction. There is something in this, especially for people on fixed salaries or rates of pay who do not benefit directly from an incentive scheme. They may feel good when they get an increase; apart from the extra money, it is a highly tangible form of recognition and an effective means of helping people to feel that they are valued. But this feeling of euphoria can rapidly die away. Other causes of dissatisfaction from Herzberg's list of hygiene factors, such as working conditions or the quality of management, can loom larger in some people's minds when they fail to get the satisfaction they need from the work itself. However, it must be re-emphasized that different people have different needs and wants. Some will be much more motivated by money than others. What cannot be assumed is that money motivates everyone in the same way and to the same extent. Thus it is naive to think that the introduction of a performance-related pay scheme will miraculously transform everyone overnight into well-motivated, high-performing individuals.

Nevertheless, money is a powerful force because it is linked directly or indirectly to the satisfaction of many needs. Money may in itself have no intrinsic meaning, but it acquires significant motivating power because it comes to symbolize so many intangible goals. It acts as a symbol in different ways for different people, and for the same person at different times.

But do financial incentives motivate people? The answer is yes, for those people who are strongly motivated by money and whose expectations are that they will receive a worthwhile financial reward. But less confident employees may not respond to incentives that they do not expect to achieve. It can

also be argued that extrinsic rewards may erode intrinsic interest – people who work just for money could find their tasks less pleasurable and may not, therefore, do them so well. What we do know is that a multiplicity of factors is involved in performance improvements and many of those factors are interdependent.

Money can therefore provide positive motivation in the right circumstances not only because people need and want money but also because it serves as a highly tangible means of recognition. But badly designed and managed pay systems can demotivate. Another researcher in this area was Jaques (1961), who emphasized the need for such systems to be perceived as being fair and equitable. In other words, the reward should be clearly related to effort or level of responsibility and people should not receive less money than they deserve compared with their fellow workers. Jaques called this the 'felt-fair' principle.

Motivation strategies

Motivation strategies aim to create a working environment and to develop policies and practices that will provide for higher levels of performance from employees. The factors affecting them and the HR contribution are summarized in Table 19.2.

TABLE 19.2   Factors affecting motivation strategies and the HR contribution

Factors affecting motivation strategies	The HR contribution
The complexity of the process of motivation means that simplistic approaches based on instrumentality or needs theory are unlikely to be successful.	Avoid the trap of developing or supporting strategies that offer prescriptions for motivation based on a simplistic view of the process or fail to recognize individual differences.
People are more likely to be motivated if they work in an environment in which they are valued for what they are and what they do. This means paying attention to the basic need for recognition.	Encourage the development of performance management processes that provide opportunities to agree expectations and to recognize accomplishments.

TABLE 19.2   *continued*

Factors affecting motivation strategies	The HR contribution
Extrinsic motivators such as incentive pay can have an immediate and powerful effect, but it will not necessarily last long. The intrinsic motivators, which are concerned with the 'quality of working life' (a phrase and movement that emerged from this concept), are likely to have a deeper and longer-term effect because they are inherent in individuals and the work they do and not imposed from outside in such forms as performance-related pay.	Develop total reward systems that provide opportunities for both financial and non-financial rewards to recognize achievements. Bear in mind, however, that financial rewards systems are not necessarily appropriate and the lessons of expectancy, goal and equity theory need to be taken into account in designing and operating them. Pay particular attention to recognition as a means of motivation. Develop intrinsic motivation by paying attention to job design, ensuring that managers are aware of its importance and their role in designing intrinsically motivating jobs.
Some people will be much more motivated by money than others. It cannot be assumed that money motivates everyone in the same way and to the same extent.	Avoid the introduction of a performance-related pay scheme in the belief that it will miraculously transform everyone overnight into well-motivated, high-performing individuals.
The need for work that provides people with the means to achieve their goals, a reasonable degree of autonomy, and scope for the use of skills and competences.	Advise on processes for the design of jobs that take account of the factors affecting the motivation to work, providing for job enrichment in the shape of variety, decision-making responsibility and as much control as possible in carrying out the work.
The need for the opportunity to grow by developing abilities and careers.	Provide facilities and opportunities for learning through such means as personal development planning processes as well as more formal training. Develop career planning processes.
The cultural environment of the organization in the shape of its values and norms will influence the impact of any attempts to motivate people by direct or indirect means.	Advise on the development of a culture that supports processes of valuing and rewarding employees.
Motivation will be enhanced by leadership, which sets the direction, encourages and stimulates achievement and provides support to employees in their efforts to reach goals and improve their performance generally.	Devise competency frameworks that focus on leadership qualities and the behaviours expected of managers and team leaders. Ensure that leadership potential is identified through performance management and assessment centres. Conduct leadership development programmes.
Achievement motivation is important for managers and those who aspire to greater responsibility.	Pay attention to job design to ensure that people are given the scope to achieve. Develop talent management processes to provide people with opportunities to achieve and performance management processes to provide them with feedback on how well they are achieving and what they must do to achieve more.

Key learning points: Motivation

The process of motivation

Motivation is goal-directed behaviour. People are motivated when they expect that a course of action is likely to lead to the attainment of a goal and a valued reward – one that satisfies their needs and wants.

Types of motivation

The two basic types are intrinsic and extrinsic motivation.

Motivation theories

There are a number of motivation theories that, in the main, are complementary to one another. The most significant theories are those concerned with expectancy, goal setting, equity and cognitive evaluation, which are classified as process or cognitive theories.

Motivation strategies

Motivation strategies aim to create a working environment and to develop policies and practices that will provide for higher levels of performance from employees. They include the design of intrinsically motivating jobs and leadership development programmes and the development of total reward systems and performance management processes.

References

Adams, J S (1965) Injustice in social exchange, in (ed) L Berkowitz, *Advances in Experimental Psychology*, New York, Academic Press

Alderfer, C (1972) *Existence, Relatedness and Growth*, New York, The Free Press

Allport, G (1954) The historical background of modern social psychology, in (ed) G Lindzey, *Theoretical Models and Personality*, Cambridge MA, Addison-Wesley

Arnold, J, Robertson, I T and Cooper, C L (1991) *Work Psychology*, London, Pitman

Bandura, A (1977) *Social Learning Theory*, Englewood Cliffs, NJ, Prentice-Hall

Bandura, A and Cervone, D (1983) Self-evaluation and self-efficacy mechanisms governing the motivational effects of goal systems, *Journal of Personality and Social Psychology*, **45** (5), pp 1017–28

Barrick, M R and Mount, M K (2013) The theory of purposeful work behavior: the role of personality, higher-order goals, and job characteristics, *Academy of Management Review*, **38**, (1), pp 132–53

Behling, O and Starke, F A (1973) The postulates of expectancy theory, *Academy of Management Journal*, **16** (3), pp 375–88

Brayfield, A H and Crockett, W H (1955) Employee attitudes and employee performance, *Psychological Bulletin*, **52**, pp 346–424

Cameron, J, Banko, K M and Pierce, W D (2001) Pervasive negative effects of rewards on intrinsic motivation: the myth continues, *The Behavior Analyst*, **24** (1), pp 1–44

Christen, M, Iyler, G and Soberman, D (2006) Job satisfaction, job performance, and effort: a reexamination using agency theory, Journal of Marketing, **70**, pp 137–50

Csikszentmihályi, M (1990) *Flow: The psychology of optimal experience*, New York, Harper & Row

Deci, E L and Ryan, R M (1985) *Intrinsic Motivation and Self-determination in Human Behaviour*, New York, Plenum

Deci, E L and Ryan, R M (2000) The 'what' and 'why' of goal pursuits: human needs and the self-determination of behaviour, *Psychological Inquiry*, **11**, pp 227–68

Deci, E L, Koestner, R and Ryan, R M (1999) A meta-analytic review of experiments examining the effects of extrinsic rewards on intrinsic motivation, *Psychological Bulletin*, **25**, pp 627–68

Dowling, W E (1971) An interview with Frederick Herzberg, Management Review, **60**, pp 2–15

Gerhart, B and Rynes, S L (2003) *Compensation: Theory, evidence and strategic implications*, Thousand Oaks CA, Sage

Hackman, J R and Oldham, G R (1974) Motivation through the design of work: test of a theory,

Organizational Behaviour and Human Performance, **16** (2), pp 250–79

Harackiewicz, J M, Barron, P R, Pintrich, P R, Elliot, A J and Thrash, T M (2002) Revision of goal theory: necessary and illuminating, *Journal of Educational Psychology*, **94** (3), pp 638–45

Herzberg, F (1966) *Work and the Nature of Man*, New York, Staple Press

Herzberg, F (1968) One more time: how do you motivate employees? *Harvard Business Review*, January–February, pp 109–20

Herzberg, F W, Mausner, B and Snyderman, B (1957) *The Motivation to Work*, New York, Wiley

House, R J, Shapiro, H J and Wahba, M A (1974) Expectancy theory as a predictor of work behaviour and attitude: a re-evaluation of empirical evidence, *Decision Science*s, **5** (3), pp 481–506

Hull, C L (1943) *Principles of Behaviour*. New York, Appleton-Century-Crofts

Hull, C (1951) *Essentials of Behaviour*, New Haven CT, Yale University Press

Hunter, J E, Schmidt, F L and Judiesch, M K (1990) Individual differences in output variability as a function of job complexity, *Journal of Applied Psychology*, **75** (1), pp 28–42

Jaques, E (1961) *Equitable Payment*, London, Heinemann

Katz, D (1964) The motivational basis of organizational behaviour, *Behavioural Science*, **9**, pp 131–36

Katz, D, Maccoby, N, Gurin, G and Floor, L G (1951) *Productivity, Supervision and Morale in an Office Situation*, Ann Arbor, MI, University of Michigan

Katz, D, Maccoby, N and Morse, N C (1950) *Productivity, Supervision and Morale among Railway Workers*, Ann Arbor, MI, University of Michigan

Latham, G and Locke, E A (1979) Goal setting – a motivational technique that works, *Organizational Dynamics*, Autumn, pp 68–80

Locke, E A (1976) The nature and causes of job satisfaction, in (ed) M D Dunnette, *Handbook of Industrial and Organizational Psychology*, Chicago, Rand McNally, pp 1297–349

Locke, E A and Latham, G (2004) What should we do about motivation theory? Six recommendations for the twenty-first century, *Academy of Management Review*, **29** (3), pp 398–403

Maslow, A (1954) *Motivation and Personality*, New York, Harper & Row

Mayo, E (1933) *The Human Problems of an Industrial Civilisation*, London, Macmillan

McClelland, D C (1961) *The Achieving Society*, New York, Van Nostrand

Opsahl, R C and Dunnette, M D (1966) The role of financial compensation in individual motivation, *Psychological Bulletin*, **56**, pp 94–118

Pink, D H (2009) *Drive: The surprising truth about workplace motivation*, New York, Riverhead Books

Pintrich, P R (2000) An achievement goal perspective on issues in motivation technology, theory and research, *Contemporary Educational Psychology*, **25**, pp 92–104

Porter, L W and Lawler, E (1968) *Managerial Attitudes and Performance*, Homewood IL, Irwin-Dorsey

Roethlisberger, F and Dickson, W (1939) *Management and the Worker*, Cambridge, MA, Harvard University Press

Rousseau, D M (2006) Is there such a thing as evidence-based management? *Academy of Management Review*, **31** (2), pp 256–69

Sandel, M (2012) *The Moral Limits of Markets: What money cannot buy*, London, Allen Lane

Schaffer, O (2013), *Crafting Fun User Experiences: A method to facilitate flow*, London, Human Factors International

Shields, J (2007) Managing Employee Performance and Reward, Port Melbourne, Cambridge University Press

Skinner, B F (1953) *Science and Human Behavior*, New York, The Free Press

Spector, P E (1997) *Job Satisfaction: Application, assessment, causes and consequences* (Vol 3), London, Sage

Steers, R M, Mowday, R T and Shapiro, D L (2004) Call for papers: the future of work motivation theory, *Academy of Management Review*, **29** (3), pp 379–87

Taylor, F W (1911) *Principles of Scientific Management*, New York, Harper (republished Norton, 1967)

Thorndike, E L (1911) *Animal Intelligence*, New York, Macmillan

Vroom, V (1964) *Work and Motivation*, New York, Wiley

Wahba, M A and Bridwell, L G (1979) Maslow reconsidered: a review of research on the need hierarchy theory, in (eds) R M Sters and L W Porter, *Motivation and Work Behaviour*, New York, McGraw-Hill

20
Commitment

LEARNING OUTCOMES

On completing this chapter you should be able to define these key concepts. You should also understand:

- The meaning of organizational commitment

- The importance of commitment

- Commitment and engagement

- Problems with the concept of commitment

- The impact of high commitment

- Factors affecting commitment

- Developing a commitment strategy

Introduction

Commitment represents the strength of an individual's identification with, and involvement in, an organization. It is a concept that has played an important part in HRM philosophy. As Guest (1987: 503) suggested, HRM policies are designed to 'maximize organizational integration, employee commitment, flexibility and quality of work'. Beer *et al* (1984: 20) identified commitment in their concept of HRM as a key dimension because it 'can result not only in

more loyalty and better performance for the organization, but also in self-worth, dignity, psychological involvement, and identity for the individual'.

The meaning of organizational commitment

Commitment refers to attachment and loyalty. It is associated with the feelings of individuals about

21
Employee engagement

LEARNING OUTCOMES

On completing this chapter you should be able to define these key concepts. You should also understand:

- The meaning of employee engagement
- Job engagement
- Organizational engagement
- The theory of engagement
- The components of engagement
- The drivers of engagement
- Outcomes of engagement
- Enhancing engagement
- The significance of burnout

Introduction

Engagement takes place when people are committed to their work and the organization and are motivated to achieve high levels of performance. According to the CIPD (2012: 13): 'Engagement has become for practitioners an umbrella concept for capturing the various means by which employers can elicit additional or discretionary effort from employees –

People resourcing

Introduction

People resourcing, often called 'employee resourcing', or simply 'resourcing', is the term used to describe the employment activities of workforce planning and recruitment and selection that ensure the organization has the people it needs. It is also concerned with the employment issues of employee retention and absenteeism, flexible working and the management of diversity and inclusion.

Resourcing is a vital organizational activity that recognizes that the strategic capability of a firm depends on its resource capability in the shape of people (the resource-based view).

Employee resourcing is not just about recruitment and selection. It is concerned with any means

22
Strategic resourcing

LEARNING OUTCOMES

On completing this chapter you should be able to define these key concepts. You should also know about:

- The meaning of strategic resourcing
- The strategic HRM approach to resourcing
- Strategic fit in resourcing
- The components of resourcing strategy
- The importance of the employer brand and the employee value proposition

Strategic resourcing defined

Strategic resourcing is the process of ensuring that the organization has the people it needs to achieve its goals. It involves the development and implementation of employee resourcing strategies which contribute to the achievement of the business strategy.

The concept that the strategic capability of a firm depends on its resource capability in the shape of people (the resource-based view) provides the rationale for strategic resourcing. The objective is therefore to ensure that a firm achieves competitive advantage by recruiting, retaining and developing more capable people than its rivals. The organization attracts such people by being 'the employer of choice'. It retains them by providing better opportunities, rewards and conditions of employment than others and by developing a positive psychological contract (the set of reciprocal but unwritten expectations that exist between individual employees and their employers), which increases engagement and commitment and creates mutual trust. Furthermore, the organization deploys its people in ways that maximize the added value they supply and develops their talents and skills.

The strategic HRM approach to resourcing

The philosophy behind the strategic approach to resourcing is that it is people who implement the strategic plan. As Quinn Mills (1983) put it, the process is one of 'planning with people in mind'.

Strategic resourcing includes specific strategies for:

- workforce planning;
- developing the organization's employer brand and employee value proposition;
- resourcing plans;
- retention;
- flexibility;
- talent management.

It involves the integration of business and resourcing strategies and is based on an understanding of the direction in which the organization is going and the determination of:

- the numbers of people required to meet business needs;
- the skills and behaviours required to support the achievement of business strategies;
- the need to create a talent pool of people with high potential as part of a talent management strategy;
- the impact of organizational restructuring as a result of rationalization, decentralization, delayering, acquisitions, mergers, product or market development, or the introduction of new technology – for example, cellular manufacturing;
- plans for changing the culture of the organization in such areas as ability to deliver, performance standards, quality, customer service, teamworking and flexibility, which indicate the need for people with different attitudes, beliefs and personal characteristics.

Strategic resourcing emphasizes the need to find people whose attitudes and behaviours are likely to be what management believes to be conducive to success. This tendency has its dangers. Innovative and adaptive organizations need non-conformists, even mavericks, who can 'buck the system'. If managers recruit people 'in their own image', there is the risk of staffing the organization with conformist clones and of perpetuating a dysfunctional culture – one that may have been successful in the past but is no longer appropriate in the face of new challenges.

The resourcing strategies that emerge from the process of strategic resourcing exist to provide the people and skills required to support the business strategy, but they should also contribute to the formulation of that strategy. HR directors have an obligation to point out to their colleagues the human resource opportunities and constraints that will affect the achievement of strategic plans. In mergers or acquisitions, for example, the ability of management within the company to handle the new situation and the quality of management in the new business will be important considerations.

Strategic resourcing is concerned with defining the numbers and types of people required to meet present and future business needs and planning how to satisfy those requirements (workforce planning), as dealt with in Chapter 23. It also involves the preparation of employee retention and flexibility plans and talent management programmes, as covered in later chapters.

The foundation for strategic resourcing is provided by the organization's employer brand, as described below.

Employer brand

An employer brand is the image presented by an organization as a good employer – 'a great place to work'. A positive brand will help the business to become an employer of choice, thus attracting better applicants for jobs. The key feature of the brand will be the reputation of the company as an employer – the way people are treated, the provision of a fair deal, opportunities for growth, work–life balance, leadership, the quality of management and involvement with colleagues. But the reputation of the organization in terms of how it does business, the quality of its products or services, its core values as revealed by its actions, and how and why it is successful are also important.

To develop an employer brand, it is necessary to:

- define the desirable features of the brand on the basis of an examination and review of each of the areas that are likely to affect people's perceptions of the organization;

- analyse what the best candidates need and want and take this into account in deciding what should be offered and how it should be offered;

- develop an employer value proposition which conveys what the company has to offer people (described in more detail below);

- use social media to present information on what the company is like to work for that is linked to company websites and career sites and which can be made available through mobile apps – the aim is to steer people to the company's career website so that they click on it and apply for relevant jobs;

- use what is called 'recruitment content marketing' to create and maintain the social media presentations – this means: 1) defining objectives, eg increase brand awareness, increase traffic to career site by x per cent; 2) identifying the target audience in terms of job titles and skills and locations; and 3) deciding on content such as images, photographs, video and written text, which will achieve objectives for the target audience;

- benchmark the approaches of other organizations (*The Sunday Times* list of the 100 best companies to work for is useful) to obtain ideas about what can be done to enhance the brand but focus on developing a unique proposition rather than replicating what other organizations offer.

Employee value proposition

An organization's employee value proposition consists of what it offers to prospective or existing employees that they will value and that will persuade them to join or remain with the business. It will include remuneration – which is important but can be overemphasized compared with non-financial factors. The latter may be crucial in attracting and retaining people and may include the reputation of the organization, the degree to which it acts responsibly, respects diversity and inclusion, and provides work–life balance and opportunities for personal and professional growth. The aim is to become a firm that people want to work for and stay with. The conclusions of John Purcell and his colleagues on this subject were as follows.

Source review

On being an employer of choice – Purcell *et al* (2003)

What seems to be happening is that successful firms are able to meet people's needs both for a good job and to work 'in a great place'. They create good work and a conducive working environment. In this way they become an 'employer of choice'. People will want to work there because their individual needs are met – for a good job with prospects linked to training, appraisal and working with a good boss who listens and gives some autonomy but helps with coaching and guidance.

To develop an employee value proposition it is necessary to analyse what the organization has to offer people by reference to:

- its reputation as a business and as an employer;

- its working environment;

- its approach to diversity;

- its approach to work–life balance;

- its location;

- the career opportunities available;

- the scope that it provides for learning new skills;

- the terms and conditions of employment it offers.

It is advisable to monitor how the employer brand is being perceived. This can be done by listening to and recording any comments by applicants. It is worth keeping an eye on Glassdoor, the employee review site, to see how the organization is regarded by its staff.

CASE STUDIES

Developing an employer brand at the Ordnance Survey

The Ordnance Survey was finding it difficult to recruit technological and commercial staff of the right calibre and it was therefore decided to deal with the problem by conducting an employer branding exercise.

Objectives

The objectives of the exercise were to:

- improve external perceptions of Ordnance Survey as an employer;

- get recruitment campaigns 'right first time';

- reduce recruitment costs;

- attract and recruit high-quality people, especially in technology and commercial areas;

- unlock people's potential to deliver great performance;

- match the employee experience to the organization's strong corporate brand.

The research programme

The employee-research company ORC was engaged to conduct internal and external research and consultation. The external research covered four other large employers with which Ordnance Survey compared well. It also included in-depth interviews with recruitment consultants, short-service leavers and those who had been offered a post but not taken it up. Internal research took the form of focus groups, interviews and consultation with recent joiners. The key messages from this external and internal research were fed into the brand development workshop.

The brand development workshop

The workshop consisted of a cross-section of staff who discussed the attributes of Ordnance Survey and the ways in which it presented them. Action groups met to consider particular aspects of the organization and its policies and how the brand could be developed. The focus was on the 'touch points' at which existing and potential employees engaged with the organization. The aim was to create something compelling and achievable with regard to each of these key elements. A leadership development programme was conducted that included looking at the employer brand.

Outcome

The employer brand created by this process was used as a centre point to inform and shape the people strategy and is aligned to the business strategy.

Recruitment and retention strategy at Buckingham County Council

Attracting and retaining high-quality staff is considered key to the corporate strategy of Buckingham County Council, which employs around 14,000 people. Resourcing is one of the most important things the council does to improve performance.

Resourcing and people strategy

The resourcing strategy complements and reinforces the people strategy, which has five targets:

- being the best employer;

- bringing in additional talent;

- developing existing talent;

- championing diversity;

- transforming the organization.

The people strategy dashboard

A people strategy dashboard has been created to ensure that human resources are managed more effectively. This extends the people strategy targets and is used to monitor progress in achieving them.

Improving recruitment and selection

This involved:

- strengthening the employer brand;

- developing a better recruitment website;

- developing a talent bank to ensure that vacancies were filled quickly;

- streamlining processes to reduce the time to fill vacancies;

- the development of a competency framework used for competency-based selection.

Retaining talent

A holistic approach is adopted to retaining talent. This involves paying attention to every aspect of the employment relationship and setting a best-employer target. A staff survey is used to measure employee engagement.

Total reward strategy

A total reward approach is adopted, including the use of total reward statements.

Talent management

A talent management toolkit is used to identify and develop potential high performers at every level in the organization.

Key learning points: Strategic resourcing

Employee resourcing defined

Employee resourcing, generally known simply as 'resourcing', is the term used to describe activities concerned with the acquisition, retention and development of human resources.

Strategic resourcing defined

- Strategic resourcing is concerned with ensuring that the organization obtains and retains the people it needs and employs them effectively. It is a key part of the strategic human resource management process, which is fundamentally about matching human resources to the strategic and operational needs of the organization and ensuring the full utilization of those resources.

- The aim of strategic resourcing is therefore to ensure that a firm achieves competitive advantage by employing more capable people than its rivals. These people will have a wider and deeper range of skills and will behave in ways which will maximize their contribution.

- Strategic resourcing places more emphasis than traditional personnel management on finding people whose attitudes and behaviour are likely to

be congruent with what management believes to be appropriate and conducive to success.

- The philosophy behind the strategic HRM approach to resourcing is that it is people who implement the strategic plan. Resourcing strategies exist to provide the people and skills required to support the business strategy, but they should also contribute to the formulation of that strategy.

- Strategic resourcing is not just about recruitment and selection. It is concerned with any means available to meet the needs of the firm for certain skills and behaviours.

- The overarching component of strategic resourcing is the integration of resourcing and business plans. Within this framework, strategic resourcing includes specific strategies for:

  - workforce planning;

  - developing the organization's employee value proposition and its employer brand;

  - resourcing plans;

  - retention;

  - flexibility;

  - talent management.

- It involves the integration of business and resourcing strategies and is based on an understanding of the direction in which the organization is going and the determination of:

  - the numbers of people required to meet business needs;

  - the skills and behaviours required to support the achievement of business strategies;

  - the impact of organizational restructuring;

  - changing the organization's culture.

Employer brand

- An employer brand is the image presented by an organization as a good employer – 'a great place to work'.

- A positive brand will help the business to become an employer of choice, thus attracting better applicants for jobs.

- The key feature of the brand will be the reputation of the company as an employer – the way people are treated, the provision of a fair deal, opportunities for growth, work–life balance, leadership, the quality of management and involvement with colleagues.

Employee value proposition

An organization's employee value proposition consists of what it offers to prospective or existing employees that they will value and that will persuade them to join or remain with the business.

Reference

Purcell, J, Kinnie, K, Hutchinson, N, Rayton, B and Swart, J (2003) *People and Performance: How people management impacts on organizational performance*, London, CIPD

Quinn Mills, D (1983) Planning with people in mind, *Harvard Business Review*, November–December, pp 97–105

23
Workforce planning

KEY CONCEPTS AND TERMS

Demand forecasting

Hard human resources planning

Human resources planning

PESTLE analysis

Ratio-trend analysis

Scenario planning

Soft human resources planning

Supply forecasting

SWOT analysis

LEARNING OUTCOMES

On completing this chapter you should be able to define these key concepts. You should also understand:

- The nature of workforce planning
- The link between workforce and business planning
- The rationale for workforce planning
- Workforce planning issues
- Approaches to workforce planning

Introduction

Organizations have to know how many people and what sort of people they need to meet present and future business requirements. As noted by Peter Reilly (2015: 1): 'Workforce planning is in essence a simple concept: it is about matching the organization's demand for labour with the supply of labour over time.'

The purpose of this chapter is to describe how workforce planning operates, bearing in mind that it is not as straightforward as it was presented when

the notion of 'manpower planning' became popular in the 1960s and '70s. Workforce planning, or human resource planning as it used to be called, may be well established in the HRM vocabulary but it does not seem to be embedded as a key HR activity.

This chapter starts with a definition of workforce planning and continues with a discussion of its aims and the issues involved, including its link with business planning. The final section of the chapter describes the processes used, namely scenario planning, demand and supply forecasting and action planning.

Workforce planning defined

The process of workforce planning is to establish an organization's people requirements so that plans can be made to satisfy them. The following definition was produced by the CIPD (2010a: 4): 'Workforce planning is a core process of human resource management that is shaped by the organizational strategy and ensures the right number of people with the right skills, in the right place at the right time to deliver short- and long-term organizational objectives.'

Workforce planning may be conducted as an overall approach to establishing and satisfying people requirements covering all major employee categories and skills. However, it frequently concentrates on key categories of staff, for example, doctors, nurses and other health workers in the National Health Service, skilled operatives in a manufacturing company, sales staff in a retail store or drivers in a transport company.

Rothwell (1995: 194) distinguished between HR planning in the hard sense – 'to serve as an indicator of the likely match or mismatch of the supply and demand for the right number of people with appropriate skills' – and HR planning in the soft sense – 'to alert the organization to the implications of business strategy for people development, culture and attitudes as well as numbers and skills.' The CIPD (2010a: 4) made a similar distinction between 'hard' and 'soft' workforce planning. As the report on their research commented:

> Hard workforce planning is about numbers. In the past this often revolved around using past trends to predict the future, matching supply and demand for labour with the result that plans were often out of date before the ink was dry. Now there is more emphasis on management information that can help understand cause and effect of certain phenomena.

Soft workplace planning focuses on general issues relating to the supply of and demand for people and how they are deployed.

The precursor to workforce planning – manpower planning as conceived in the 1960s – was almost entirely about numbers in the shape of quantitative demand and supply forecasts. It was the failure in many organizations to produce accurate forecasts and therefore prepare meaningful plans that led to its decline if not fall. Workforce planning today covers a wider range of activities such as succession planning, smart working, flexible working and talent planning, and is not such a numbers game.

Incidence of workforce planning

The CIPD *Annual Survey of Resourcing and Talent Planning* (2010b) found that 61 per cent of organizations conducted workforce planning, although it was most common in the public services sector and in larger organizations: 20 per cent of organizations planned for less than one year, 41 per cent for one to two years and only 2 per cent for more than five years. The CIPD (2010a) research established that the top five planning activities were:

1 Succession planning – 62 per cent.
2 Flexible working – 53 per cent.
3 Demand/supply forecasting – 53 per cent.
4 Skills audit/gap analysis – 49 per cent.
5 Talent management – 42 per cent.

The link between workforce and business planning

Workforce planning is an integral part of business planning. The strategic planning process defines projected changes in the types of activities carried out by the organization and the scale of those activities. It identifies the core competencies that the organization needs to achieve its goals and therefore its skill and behavioural requirements.

Workforce planning interprets these plans in terms of people requirements. But it may influence the business strategy by drawing attention to the ways in which people could be developed and deployed more effectively to further the achievement of business goals. It will also address issues concerning the supply of suitable people which might affect the achievement of business objectives.

Reasons for workforce planning

Research conducted by the Institute for Employment Studies (Reilly, 1999) established that there were three main reasons why organizations engaged in workforce planning:

1 Planning for substantive reasons, that is, to have a practical effect by optimizing the use of resources and/or making them more flexible, acquiring and nurturing skills that take time to develop, identifying potential problems and minimizing the chances of making a bad decision.

2 Planning because of the process benefits, which involves understanding the present in order to confront the future, challenging assumptions and liberating thinking, making explicit decisions that can later be challenged, standing back and providing an overview and ensuring that long-term thinking is not driven out by short-term focus.

3 Planning for organizational reasons, which involves communicating plans so as to obtain support/adherence to them, linking HR plans to business plans so as to influence them, (re) gaining corporate control over operating units and coordinating and integrating organizational decision making and actions.

Workforce planning issues

The main difficulties faced by those involved in quantitative (hard) workforce planning are the impact of change and trying to predict the future. Many organizations therefore adopt a short-term approach and deal with deficits or surpluses of people as they arise. This problem is compounded by what Rothwell (1995) referred to as the shifting kaleidoscope of policy priorities and strategies within organizations. It sounds like a good idea to adopt an integrated approach to workforce and business planning but it won't work well if business plans are volatile, vague, misleading or non-existent, as they easily can be. Beardwell (2007: 62) commented that HR plans should be treated as 'tentative, flexible, and reviewed and modified on a regular basis.' Cappelli (2009: 10) noted that: 'The competitive environment for businesses is so changeable, and firms adjust their own strategies and practices so frequently that these estimates [of the demand for talent] are rarely accurate and they get much worse the farther out one goes.'

This problem will not be so acute in a stable marketplace, with largely passive (and static) customers, and with scope for long-term forecasting. But these are rare conditions today, even in the public sector where for a long time workplace planning has thrived.

It can be said that workforce planning is more art than science. Perhaps the accuracy of demand and supply forecasts is less important than the overall understanding of what the organization needs in the way of people, which can be generated by a systematic approach to planning.

Systematic workforce planning

A flow chart of the process of workforce planning is shown in Figure 23.1. This identifies the main planning activities described below. Although these are referred to as separate areas, they are interrelated and can overlap. For example, demand forecasts may be prepared on the basis of assumptions about the productivity of employees. But a forecast of the supply of suitable people will also have to consider productivity trends and how they might affect the supply.

Business planning

The business plan provides the basis for the workforce plan insofar as it sets out what the organization intends to do in terms of activities and the scale of those activities.

Forecast activity levels

Forecasts of future activity levels flow from the business plan, which will have implications for the demand for people. Activity level forecasts will also be affected by external factors, for example demographic and political policy trends, especially in the public sector. Data will need to be collected and analysed for this purpose.

FIGURE 23.1   Workforce planning flow chart

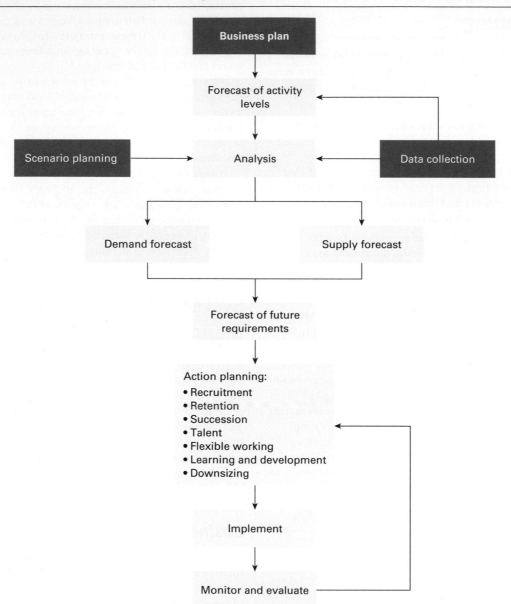

Scenario planning

Scenario planning involves an assessment of changes in the business and its environment which are likely to affect the organization so that a picture is produced of where the organization might be heading and a prediction made of the possible situations that may have to be dealt with in the future.

Data collection

The information used in workforce planning can be collected under the following headings:

- *Qualitative internal data*: business information on product/market developments, proposed work system and organizational changes; HR information on people (skills, performance, etc).

- *Quantitative internal data*: workforce data on turnover, absence, demographics, skills audits, etc.

- *Qualitative external data*: PESTLE analysis covering the following factors: political, economic, social, technological, legal and environmental.

- *Quantitative external data*: labour market – demographics, skills availability.

Analysis

The analysis stage brings all the information together from the business plan, the activity forecast, scenarios and internal and external data to provide the basis for demand and supply forecasts.

Demand forecasting

Demand forecasting is the process of estimating the future numbers of people required and the likely skills and competences they will need. The basis of the forecast is the annual budget and longer-term business plan, translated into activity levels for each function and department. In a manufacturing company the sales budget would be translated into a manufacturing plan, giving the numbers and types of products to be made in each period. From this information the number of hours to be worked by each skill category to make the quota for each period would be computed.

Details are required of any organizational and work plans that would result in increased or decreased demands for employees. Examples are setting up a new regional organization, creating a new sales department, decentralizing a head office function to the regions, plans for new methods of working, additional outsourcing, increasing productivity and reducing employment costs. The demand forecasting methods for estimating the numbers of people required are described below.

Managerial judgement

The most typical method of forecasting used is managerial judgement. This simply requires managers to sit down, think about their future workloads, and decide how many people they need. It may be quite unscientific and misleading.

Forecasting might be done on a 'bottom-up' basis, with line managers submitting proposals for agreement by senior management. Alternatively, a 'top-down' approach can be used, in which company and departmental forecasts are prepared by top management, possibly acting on advice from the personnel departments. These forecasts are reviewed and agreed with departmental managers. A less directive approach is for top management to prepare planning guidelines for departmental managers, setting out the planning assumptions and the targets they should try to meet.

Perhaps the best way of using managerial judgement is to adopt both the 'bottom-up' and 'top-down' approaches. Guidelines for departmental managers should be prepared, indicating broad company assumptions about future activity levels that will affect their departments. Targets are also set where necessary. Armed with these guidelines, departmental managers prepare their forecasts to a laid-down format. They are encouraged to seek help at this stage from the personnel or work study departments. Meanwhile, the HR department, in conjunction as necessary with planning and work study departments, prepares a company forecast. The two sets of forecasts can then be reviewed by a human resource planning committee consisting of functional heads. This committee reconciles with departmental managers any discrepancies between the two forecasts and submits the final amended forecast to top management for approval. This is sometimes called the 'right-angle method'.

Ratio-trend analysis

Ratio-trend analysis is carried out by analysing existing ratios between an activity level and the number of employees working on that activity. The ratio is applied to forecast activity levels to determine an adjusted number of people required. Account can be taken of possible improvements in productivity that would affect the ratio. The analysis may be extended to cover employees connected to but not directly involved in the activity – the indirect workers who provide support to the direct workers responsible for carrying out the activity. The existing ratio of directs to indirects would be applied to the forecast number of directs needed to deal with the new activity levels to forecast the number of indirects needed.

Work study techniques

Work study techniques are used in association with activity level forecasts to calculate how long operations should take and the number of people required. Work study techniques for direct workers can be combined with ratio-trend analysis to calculate the number of indirect workers needed.

Forecasting skill and competency requirements

Forecasting skill and competency requirements is largely a matter of managerial judgement. This judgement should, however, be exercised on the basis of an analysis of the impact of projected product/market developments and the introduction of new technology, either information technology or computerized manufacturing.

Supply forecasting

Supply forecasting measures the number of people likely to be available from within and outside the organization. The internal supply analysis covers the following areas:

- existing number of people employed by occupation, skill and potential;
- potential losses to existing resources through attrition (employee turnover);
- potential changes to existing resources through internal promotions;
- changes to the organization structure, new methods of working (including flexible working) more part-time working and different working hours;
- effect of increases in productivity;
- sources of supply from within the organization – existing employees and the outputs of talent management or training programmes.

The external supply analysis examines the local and national labour markets to assess implications for the availability of future people requirements. It will also take account of environmental changes as revealed by scenario planning.

Forecast of future requirements

To forecast future requirements, it is necessary to analyse the demand and supply forecasts to identify any deficits or surpluses. The analysis can be made with the help of spreadsheets. The basic data can be set out as follows:

1	Current number employed	700
2	Annual level of turnover	10 per cent
3	Expected losses during year	70
4	Balance at end year	630
5	Number required at end year	750
6	Number to be obtained	(5 – 4) = 120 during year

The data on the number of employees required may be modified by reference to the impact of any productivity plans, organizational changes, new methods of working or revision of role responsibilities.

Action planning

Action plans to satisfy future requirements are derived from the broad resourcing strategies and the more detailed analysis of demand and supply factors. However, the plans often have to be short term and flexible because of the difficulty of making firm predictions about workforce requirements in times of rapid change. The planning activities start with the identification of internal resources available now or that could be made available through learning and development programmes. They continue with plans for recruitment and retention, succession and talent management, the reduction of employee turnover and absenteeism, flexible working, outsourcing, productivity improvement and the revision of role responsibilities. Learning and development programmes may be prepared to provide for future skill requirements. Regrettably, but sometimes inevitably, plans for downsizing may be necessary, but these can aim to avoid compulsory redundancies by such means as recruitment freezes.

Implementation

The implementation of the action plans will provide a challenge. A flexible approach involving quick responses is needed to cope with unforeseeable changes in people requirements.

Monitoring and evaluation

Because of unpredictable events, the implementation of action plans does not always run smoothly. It is necessary to monitor progress carefully, evaluate the effects and, as required, amend the action plan.

Approach to workforce planning

Peter Reilly (2015) suggested that the real problem with workforce planning is its execution. Organizations get the concept but find it hard to put into practice. He believes that HR should keep workforce planning as simple as possible, concentrating on the essential data needed for the task. HR should identify important business problems (such as expansion, downsizing or relocation) and work backwards from there as to what it is necessary to know to plan the resource implications. The focus of workforce planning should be on key employment groups determined by their labour market scarcity and impact on organizational performance.

CASE STUDIES

Buckinghamshire County Council

Business need drove the workforce planning project at Buckinghamshire County Council. This recognized that current workforce planning practices would not meet the challenge of the Care Standards Act 2000, or of future service delivery. One of the main issues in working with children and families was recruiting and retaining qualified social workers. There were insufficient numbers of social workers in post. Turnover levels among established and new employees were high.

The council therefore decided to align strategy and workforce planning in social care for children and families. The workforce plan was developed with the input of a team of representatives from social care for children and families. It was recognized that workforce planning was essential to anticipate future areas of skills shortages. This council is now in a position to anticipate skills shortages and has dealt with them innovatively and immediately.

The workforce plan looked at short- and long-term planning. Short-term planning covered immediate action on recruitment and promotion. Long-term planning covered activities that may span the next five years. Workforce planning allowed for an assessment of skills and an exploration of the levels employees need to work at.

Plymouth Primary Care Trust

The trust set up a multidisciplinary team drawn from the workforce planning and development department, finance and public health teams within the organization to introduce workforce planning across the whole organization. The trust's 230 managers and budget holders were then invited to an awareness programme to introduce the Six Steps Workforce Planning Methodology developed by the NHS Workforce Projects Team (2009). The steps are:

1   Define the plan.

2   Map service change.

3   Define the required workforce.

4   Understand workforce availability.

5   Plan to deliver the required workforce.

6   Implement, monitor and refresh.

Managers were informed that, using this framework, they would be required to produce plans over one-year, two-year and five-year timescales. The guide was applied by asking each manager to define their workforce plan, outline forces for change, assess demand, assess supply, undertake a gap analysis and subsequent action planning and carry out implementation and a review of the plans.

It was found that while some managers were skilled in workforce planning, the majority needed support to link together the financial, workforce and planning elements of the process. The outcomes were:

● trust-wide workforce planning, using electronic staff record and planning tools;

● workforce planning is now part of day-to-day trust business;

● detailed workforce plans across clinical and non-clinical directorates;

Key learning points: Workforce planning

Workforce planning defined

The following definition of workplace planning was produced by the CIPD (2010a: 4): 'Workforce planning is a core process of human resource management that is shaped by the organizational strategy and ensures the right number of people with the right skills, in the right place at the right time to deliver short- and long-term organizational objectives.'

Incidence of workforce planning

The CIPD (2010a) research revealed that workforce planning in one form or another is taking place in many organizations.

Link to business planning

Workforce planning is an integral part of business planning.

The rationale for workforce planning

Workforce planning provides a basis for a systematic approach to assessing the number and type of people needed and, having taken into account information on the supply of labour and environmental scanning, for the preparation of recruitment, retention, management succession and talent management plans. Workforce planning is important because it encourages employers to develop clear and explicit links between their business and HR plans and to integrate the two more effectively.

Workforce planning issues

The main difficulties faced by those involved in workforce planning are the impact of change and predicting the future.

● Approaches to workforce planning.

● Business planning.

● Forecast activity levels.

● Scenario planning.

● Data collection.

● Analysis.

● Demand forecasting.

● Supply forecasting.

● Forecast of future requirements.

● Action planning.

● Implementation.

● Monitoring and evaluation.

References

Beardwell, J (2007) Human resource planning, in (eds) J Beardwell and T Claydon, *Human Resource Management: A contemporary approach*, 5th edn, Essex, Pearson, pp 189–224

Cappelli, P (2009) A supply chain approach to workforce planning, *Organizational Dynamics*, 38 (1), pp 8–15

CIPD (2010a) *Workforce Planning: Right people, right time, right skills*, London, CIPD

CIPD (2010b) *Annual Survey of Resourcing and Talent Planning*, London, CIPD

Reilly, P (1999) *The Human Resource Planning Audit*, Cambridge, Cambridge Strategy Publications

Reilly, P (2105) Workforce planning: A framework for thinking about your own approach, *Institute for Employment Studies* [online] http://www.employment-studies.co.uk/system/files/resources/files/mp112_0.pdf [accessed 25 December 2015]

Rothwell, S (1995) Human resource planning, in (ed) J Storey, *Human Resource Management: A critical text*, London, Routledge

Workforce Projects Team (2009) *Skills for Health*, http://www.healthcareworkforce.nhs.uk/resource/latest _resources/introduction_to_workforce_planning.html [accessed 29 July 2011]

24
Recruitment and selection

KEY CONCEPTS AND TERMS

Biodata

Candidate relationship management
    system

Criterion measure

Employer brand

Employer of choice

Intelligence quotient (IQ)

Job board

Knowledge, skills and abilities (KSAs)

Person specification

Predictive ability

Psychological test

Psychometric test

Recruitment

Recruitment process outsourcing (RPO)

Reliability (test)

Role profile

Selection

Social media

Validity (test)

LEARNING OUTCOMES

On completing this chapter you should be able to define these key concepts. You should also understand:

- The recruitment and selection process
- Defining requirements
- Attracting candidates
- Processing applications

- Selection methods – interviewing and tests
- Making the decision
- References and offers
- Dealing with recruitment problems

Introduction

Recruitment is the process of finding and engaging the people the organization needs. Selection is that part of the recruitment process concerned with deciding which applicants or candidates should be appointed to jobs. Recruitment can be costly, especially for senior staff. The 2015 CIPD *Survey of Resourcing and Talent Planning* found that the average recruitment cost of filling a vacancy for a director or senior manager was £7,250 while for other employees it was £2,000.

The recruitment and selection process

The stages of recruitment and selection are:

1 Defining requirements
2 Attracting candidates
3 Sifting applications
4 Interviewing
5 Testing
6 Assessing candidates
7 Obtaining references
8 Checking applications
9 Offering employment
10 Following up

Defining requirements

The number and categories of people required may be set out in formal workforce plans from which are derived detailed recruitment plans. More typically, requirements are expressed as ad hoc demands for people because of the creation of new posts, expansion into new activities or areas, or the need for a replacement. These short-term demands may put HR under pressure to deliver candidates quickly.

Requirements should be defined in the form of role profiles and person specifications. These provide the information required to post vacancies on the company's website, the internet or a social network site such as LinkedIn, draft advertisements, brief agencies or recruitment consultants and assess candidates by means of interviews and selection tests.

Role profiles

Role profiles define the overall purpose of the role, its reporting relationships and the key result areas. For recruiting purposes, the profile is extended to include information on terms and conditions (pay, benefits and hours of work); special requirements such as mobility, travelling or unsocial hours; and learning, development and career opportunities. The recruitment role profile provides the basis for a person specification.

Person specification

A person specification, also known as a recruitment or job specification, defines the knowledge, skills and abilities (KSAs) required to carry out the role, the types of behaviour expected from role holders (behavioural competencies) and the education, qualifications, training and experience needed to acquire the necessary KSAs. It also lists *specific demands* – anything that the role holder will be expected to achieve in specified areas, eg develop new markets or products; improve sales, productivity or levels of customer service; introduce new systems or processes, and *special requirements* – travelling, unsocial hours, mobility, etc.

It is advisable not to overstate the requirements. Perhaps it is natural to go for the best, but setting an unrealistically high level for candidates increases the problems of attracting applicants and results in dissatisfaction among recruits when they find their talents are not being used. Understating requirements can, of course, be equally dangerous, but it happens less frequently.

The KSAs and competencies defined in the role profile form a fundamental feature of the selection process, which becomes more of a person-based than a job-based approach. They are used as the basis for structured interviews and provide guidance on which selection techniques, such as psychological testing or assessment centres, are most likely to be useful.

The following is an example of the key KSA and competencies parts of a person specification for an HR recruitment adviser.

KSA and competency requirements for a recruitment adviser

1 Knowledge of:
   - all aspects of recruitment;
   - sources of recruits;
   - different media for use in recruiting;
   - relevant test instruments (OPQ qualified).

2 Skills and abilities in:
   - interviewing techniques;
   - test administration;
   - role analysis;
   - use of social media.

3 Behavioural competencies:
   - able to relate well to others and use interpersonal skills to achieve desired objectives;
   - able to influence the behaviour and decisions of people on matters concerning recruitment and other HR or individual issues;
   - able to cope with change, to be flexible and to handle uncertainty;
   - able to make sense of issues, identify and solve problems and 'think on one's feet';
   - focus on achieving results;
   - able to maintain appropriately directed energy and stamina, to exercise self-control and to learn new behaviours;
   - able to communicate well, orally and on paper.

Attracting candidates

Attracting candidates is primarily a matter of identifying, evaluating and using the most appropriate sources of applicants. However, in cases where difficulties in attracting or retaining candidates are being met or anticipated, it may be necessary to carry out a study of the factors that are likely to attract or deter candidates – the strengths and weaknesses of the organization as an employer.

The study could make use of an attitude survey to obtain the views of existing employees. The analysis should cover such matters as the national or local reputation of the organization, pay, employee benefits and working conditions, the intrinsic interest of the job, security of employment, opportunities for education and training, career prospects, and the location of the office or plant.

Candidates are, in a sense, selling themselves, but they are also buying what the organization has to offer. If, in the latter sense, the labour market is a buyer's market, then the company selling itself to candidates must study their wants and needs in relation to what it can provide. The study can be used to develop the employee brand (the image presented by an organization as a good employer) and the employee value proposition (what an organization has to offer that prospective employees would value and that would help to persuade them to join the business). They can contribute to the recruitment material used on corporate websites and in advertisements and brochures to help make the organization 'an employer of choice'.

Analyse the requirements

First, it is necessary to establish what jobs have to be filled and by when. Then turn to an existing role profile and person specification or, if not available or out of date, draw up new ones that set out information on responsibilities and competency requirements. This information can be analysed to determine the required education, qualifications and experience.

The next step is to consider where suitable candidates are likely to come from: within the organization, from other organizations or from education establishments, and the parts of the country where they can be found. Next, define the terms and conditions of the job (pay and benefits).

Finally, refer to the analysis of strengths and weaknesses to assess what it is about the job or the organization that is likely to attract good candidates, so that the most can be made of these factors when advertising the vacancy or reaching potential applicants in other ways. Consider also what might put them off, for example the location of the job, so that objections can be anticipated. Analyse previous successes or failures to establish what does or does not work.

Identify sources of candidates

The main sources, as established by the 2013 CIPD resourcing survey, were:

- corporate website – 62 per cent;
- recruitment agencies – 49 per cent;
- employee referral scheme – 33 per cent;
- social media – 32 per cent;
- commercial job boards – 32 per cent;
- local newspaper advertisements – 29 per cent;
- specialist journals – 24 per cent;
- Jobcentre Plus – 19 per cent;
- search consultants – 17 per cent;
- links with educational establishments – 14 per cent;
- national newspaper advertisements – 12 per cent.

The 2015 CIPD resourcing survey provided data on the sources used by respondents for different employee groups. The six most important sources for each category are shown in Table 24.1.

As might be expected, there are considerable differences between the different groups. However, corporate websites are the leading method except for senior executives. Local newspapers are useful for more junior jobs while national newspapers only appear in the top six for senior executives.

Consideration should first be given to internal candidates. In addition, it is always worth trying to persuade former employees to return to the organization or obtain suggestions from existing employees (referrals). These can be encouraged by offering rewards when a vacancy has been filled through a referral. Talent banks that record candidate details can be maintained and referred to at this stage.

Candidate relationship management systems can also be used. These allow recruiters to maintain a pool of potential candidates that can be brought in for consideration at short notice. While this can be done manually through phone calls or e-mails, dedicated candidate relationship management

TABLE 24.1   Most effective methods for attracting applications from different groups (percentage of respondents)

Senior managers	Middle management	Specialist technical/ professional	Administration/ secretarial employees	Manual and shop floor workers
Search consultants (43%)	Corporate website (52%)	Corporate website (48%)	Corporate website (58%)	Corporate website (54%)
Recruitment consultants (39%)	Recruitment consultants (46%)	Recruitment consultants (46%)	Commercial job boards (33%)	Local newspaper (33%)
Corporate website (36%)	Commercial job boards (29%)	Commercial job boards (31%)	Recruitment consultants (31%)	Encourage speculative applications (25%)
Networking site eg LinkedIn (28%)	Networking site eg LinkedIn (27%)	Networking site eg LinkedIn (23%)	Local newspaper (22%)	Commercial job boards (21%)
Specialist journals (17%)	Search consultants (10%)	Specialist journals (23%)	Jobcentre Plus (13%)	Jobcentre Plus (21%)
National newspapers (17%)	Local newspaper (10%)	Search consultants (9%)	Encourage speculative applications (!4%)	Recruitment consultants (21%)
			Networking site eg LinkedIn (12%)	

(**SOURCE**: CIPD recruitment and talent planning survey 2015)

systems can automate the process, making it easier to aggregate candidates from various channels, know each candidate's level of interest and sort candidates for specific jobs.

If these approaches do not work, the sources of candidates as examined below are online recruiting, social media, advertising, recruitment agencies, job centres, consultants, recruitment process outsourcing providers and direct approaches to educational establishments.

There is usually a choice between different methods or combinations of them. The criteria to use when making the choice are: 1) the likelihood that it will produce good candidates; 2) the speed with which the choice enables recruitment to be completed; and 3) the costs involved, bearing in mind that there may be direct advertising costs or consultants' fees.

Online recruitment

Online or e-recruitment uses the internet to advertise or 'post' vacancies, provides information about jobs and the organization, and enables e-mail communications to take place between employers and candidates. The latter can apply for jobs online and can e-mail application forms and CVs to employers or agencies. Tests can be completed online. The main types of online recruitment sites are corporate websites, commercial job boards and agency sites. Social media as described below is also used extensively.

The advantages of online recruiting are that it can reach a wider range of possible applicants. It is quicker and cheaper than traditional methods of advertising, more details of jobs and firms can be supplied on the site, and CVs can be matched and applications submitted electronically. More than four-fifths of respondents to the CIPD's 2013 survey reported that online recruiting helped them to increase the strength of their employer brand. The disadvantages are that it may produce too many irrelevant or poor applications and it is still not the first choice of many job seekers. Consider using it in conjunction with other recruitment methods to maximize response.

Corporate websites are a very effective source. They may simply list vacancies and contact details. A more elaborate approach would consist of a dedicated website area that gives details of vacancies, person specifications, benefits and how to apply for jobs, for example by completing online application forms and tests. Such areas may be linked directly to an organization's home page so that general browsers can access them. An intranet link may be available to enable internal staff to access the website. Some organizations are building their own professional communities or talent networks. The management of websites can be outsourced to recruitment consultants or specialized web agencies. The following are guidelines on the use of websites:

- Keep the content of the site up to date.
- Ensure the site is accessible directly or through search engines.
- Provide contact numbers for those with technical problems.
- Take care over the wording of online copy – the criteria for good copy in conventional advertisements apply.

Commercial job boards are operated by specialized firms such as Monster.co.uk and Fish4jobs.com and consist of large databanks of vacancies. Companies pay to have their jobs listed on the sites. Information about vacancies may reproduce an advertisement so that the site is simply an additional form of communication, but some vacancies are only found online. Links may be provided to the organization's website. As recommended by Syedain (2012):

- Go for specialized sites rather than generalist.
- Stick to one or two sites rather than spreading your vacancy everywhere.
- If you are unsure about the best site, Google the job and browse the sites that come up in order to see which is most authoritative.
- Pay to obtain a prominent site.
- Bear in mind that people who look at the site are seeking a job. Job sites are not like print advertisements, which have to attract casual readers.
- Ensure that the information you provide is clear about what you are offering and the achievements, qualifications and experience you are looking for.

Agency sites are run by established recruitment agencies. Candidates register online but may be expected to discuss their details in person before these are forwarded to a prospective employer.

Social media

The use of social media means applying Web 2.0 technologies to search for recruits and find out more about them online. Social media is defined as any online platform for networking or sharing information or opinions, such as Facebook, LinkedIn, Twitter or blogs, but not e-mail.

By far the most popular site for recruiters is LinkedIn, which provides the LinkedIn Recruiter tool, enabling employers to search for potential candidates by sector, job level, specialism and location, and then to contact them directly. The LinkedIn advanced search function can be used to identify and provide details of possible recruits from the target audience by entering the job title, company name and key words. A Boolean search, which combines key words with operators such as AND, NOT and OR, can be used to produce more specific and relevant results. LinkedIn is most effective when the target audience and the key words appropriate for that audience are known. It is best to personalize direct approaches, whether in e-mails or invitations to connect. It is also necessary to be selective about the number and type of jobs that are publicized – it is easy to overwhelm people's feeds and inboxes.

But other social media sites such as Facebook and Twitter can also be used to promote the employer brand and make contacts. As Headworth (2015: 23) comments: 'Social networks can be very powerful when used on their own, but are sometimes more effective when combined together. This is particularly relevant for cross-platform sharing and messaging, as each social network has a slightly different audience and therefore a different objective from a recruiting perspective.'

Another approach is provided by 'matching' technology, which takes the principles of online dating into job searching. Candidates are asked to make a list of the values that matter to them, which are then matched by the service provider to potential employers for whom those values are important.

Examples of use of social media

At CERN, the world's largest particle physics laboratory, extensive use has been made of social media for recruiting purposes. All job vacancies are advertised on LinkedIn, Facebook and Twitter. These networks provide much more than simple job boards in that they are used as communication tools to interact with the audience; with candidates and with people who are not necessarily candidates but may know people who may want to apply. Appropriate use is made of each medium. For example, Facebook is used to host a weekly question and answer session between one of CERN's recruiters and anyone who wants to submit a question, whereas the professional network on LinkedIn provides a forum for more specialized discussions.

T-Mobile International has created a Facebook site for graduate recruitment. Potential graduate recruits established an individual presence on this invitation-only site. The site was used to provide information on selection procedures and processes, for example criteria and timetables, and to allow the potential recruits to communicate with each other. As well as T-Mobile's IT department, an internal 'brand ambassador' was involved in design throughout.

Advertising

Advertising has traditionally been the most obvious method of attracting candidates and it is still fairly important, especially at local level and in specialized journals. However, many organizations now prefer to use online recruitment, agencies or consultants. A conventional advertisement will have the following aims:

- Generate candidates – attract a sufficient number of good candidates at minimum cost.
- Attract attention – it must compete for the attention of potential candidates against other employees.
- Create and maintain interest – it has to communicate, in an attractive and interesting way, information about the job, the company and the terms and conditions of employment.
- Stimulate action – the message needs to be conveyed in a way that will prompt a sufficient number of replies from candidates with the right qualifications for the job.

To achieve these aims, it is necessary to carry out the actions set out below. A recruitment advertisement should start with a compelling headline and then contain information on the following:

- the organization;
- the job;

- the person required – qualifications, experience, etc;
- the pay and benefits offered;
- the location;
- the action to be taken.

The headline is all important. The simplest and most obvious approach is to set out the job title in bold type. To gain attention, it is advisable to quote the rate of pay and key benefits such as a company car. Applicants are suspicious of clauses such as 'salary will be commensurate with age and experience' or 'salary negotiable'. This often means either that the salary is so low that the company is afraid to reveal it, or that pay policies are so incoherent that the company has no idea what to offer until someone tells them what he or she wants.

The name of the company should be given. Do not use box numbers – if you want to be anonymous, use a consultant. Add any selling points, such as growth or diversification, and any other areas of interest to potential candidates, such as career prospects. The essential features of the job should be conveyed by giving a brief description of what the job holder will do and, as far as space permits, the scope and scale of activities. Create interest in the job but do not oversell it.

The qualifications and experience required should be stated as factually as possible. There is no point in overstating requirements and seldom any point in specifying exactly how much experience is wanted. Be careful about including a string of personal qualities such as drive, determination and initiative. These have no real meaning to candidates. Phrases such as 'proven track record' and 'successful experience' are equally meaningless. No one will admit to not having either of them.

The advertisement should end with information on how the candidate should apply. 'Brief but comprehensive details' is a good phrase. Candidates can be asked to write or e-mail their response, but useful alternatives are to ask them to telephone or to come along for an informal chat at a suitable venue.

Remember the anti-discrimination legislation set out in the Equality Act (2010). This makes it unlawful to discriminate in an advertisement by favouring either sex, the only exceptions being a few jobs that can be done only by one sex. Advertisements must therefore avoid sexist job titles such as 'salesman' or 'stewardess'. They must refer to a neutral title such as 'sales representative', or amplify the description to cover both sexes by stating 'steward or stewardess'. Potential respondents should be referred to only as the 'candidate' or the 'applicant', otherwise you must specify 'man or woman' or 'he or she'. It is accepted, however, that certain job titles are unisex and therefore non-discriminatory, including director, manager, executive and officer.

It is also unlawful to place an advertisement that discriminates against any particular race. As long as race is never mentioned or even implied in an advertisement, you should have no problem in keeping within the law. The Equality Act also makes it unlawful to discriminate against employees on account of their age. Age limits should therefore not be included in advertisements and the wording should not indicate that people below or above a certain age are not wanted.

It is essential to measure the response to advertisements to provide guidance on the relative cost-effectiveness of different media. Cost per reply is the best ratio.

Recruitment agencies

Most recruitment agencies deal with secretarial and office staff who are registered with them. They are usually quick and effective but quite expensive. Agencies can charge a fee for finding someone of 15 per cent or more of the first year's salary. It can be cheaper to advertise or use the internet, especially when the company is in a buyer's market. Shop around to find the agency that suits the organization's needs at a reasonable cost.

Agencies should be briefed carefully on what is wanted. They can produce unsuitable candidates but the risk is reduced if they are clear about the requirements.

Jobcentre Plus

The job centres operated by the government are mainly useful for manual and clerical workers and sales or call centre assistants.

Recruitment consultants

Recruitment consultants advertise, interview and produce a shortlist. They provide expertise and reduce workload. The organization can be anonymous if it wishes. Most recruitment consultants charge a fee based on a percentage of the basic salary for the job, usually ranging from 15 to 20 per cent.

When choosing a recruitment consultant, check their reputation and expertise, compare fees and meet the person who will work on the assignment to assess his or her quality. To use them effectively:

- Agree terms of reference.
- Brief them on the organization, where the job fits in, why the appointment is to be made, terms and conditions and any special requirements.
- Give them every assistance in defining the job and the person specification – they will do much better if they have comprehensive knowledge of what is required and what type of person is most likely to fit into the organization well.
- Check carefully the proposed programme and the draft text of the advertisement.
- Clarify the arrangements for interviewing and shortlisting.
- Clarify the basis upon which fees and expenses will be charged.
- Ensure that arrangements are made to deal directly with the consultant who will handle the assignment.

Executive search consultants

Use an executive search consultant or 'headhunter' for senior jobs where there is only a limited number of suitable people and a direct lead to them is wanted. Headhunters are not cheap. They charge a fee of 30 to 50 per cent or so of the first year's salary, but they can be quite cost-effective.

Executive search consultants first approach their own contacts in the industry or profession concerned. The good ones have an extensive range of contacts and their own data bank. They will also have researchers who will identify suitable people who may fit the specification or can provide a lead to someone else who may be suitable. The more numerous the contacts, the better the executive search consultant. When a number of potentially suitable and interested people have been assembled, a fairly relaxed and informal meeting takes place and the consultant forwards a shortlist to the client with full reports on candidates.

There are some good and some not so good executive search consultants. Do not use one unless a reliable recommendation is obtained.

Educational and training establishments

Many jobs can, of course, be filled by school leavers. For some organizations, the main source of recruits for training schemes will be universities and colleges as well as schools. Graduate recruitment is a major annual exercise for some companies, which go to great efforts to produce glossy brochures, visit campuses on the 'milk run' and use elaborate sifting and selection procedures to vet candidates, including 'biodata' and assessment centres.

Recruitment process outsourcing

Recruitment process outsourcing (RPO) is the term used when an organization commissions a provider to take responsibility for the end-to-end delivery of the recruitment process, covering all vacancies or a selection of them. This involves liaising with hiring managers to define requirements and specifications, deciding on the best ways to attract candidates, processing applications, and setting up and facilitating interviews. Some companies do not hand over all recruitment, using RPO only for high-volume vacancies. They may retain responsibility for senior and specialist jobs.

The advantage of RPO is that it can save time, bring outside expertise to bear on recruitment problems and free up HR for more value-adding activities. The disadvantage is the perception by some HR people and line managers that the provider is too remote to deal with the real issues and that there is a danger of losing control.

Comparison of sources

A summary of sources and an analysis of their advantages and disadvantages is given in Table 24.2.

Dealing with applications

If recruitment agencies or consultants are used they will deliver their client a shortlist of candidates for interview. If not, the organization has to sift the applications itself. This means examining the information supplied by applicants, sorting them and drawing up a shortlist of applicants to be interviewed.

TABLE 24.2 Comparison of sources of candidates

Source	Description	Advantages	Disadvantages
Online recruitment	Company websites, job boards, social media.	Generally, can reach a wider range of possible applicants, and it is quicker and cheaper than traditional methods of advertising. More details of jobs and firms can be supplied on the site and CVs can be matched and applications submitted electronically. Websites can use an organization's brand to attract candidates. Job boards are keyword searchable. Job details can be changed and CVs managed electronically. Social media are good for reach – LinkedIn currently has 100 million members worldwide.	Generally, may produce too many irrelevant or poor applications and it is still not the first choice of many job seekers. Websites are expensive and still need other media to drive traffic to the site. Job boards are bad for 'passive seekers'. Social media – employer/ recruiter has to manage own profile.
Social media	Social media, especially LinkedIn.	Can reach a wide audience, which in the case of LinkedIn is receptive to the idea of changing jobs.	May not be sufficient in themselves
Advertising	Display or classified advertisements in national or local newspapers or journals.	Attract 'passing trade' – people who are not actively looking for a job.	Soon become irrelevant.
Recruitment agencies	Mainly recruit office and sales staff who are registered with them.	Convenient, save time and trouble, draw on an established pool of candidates.	Can produce unsuitable candidates. Pool may be limited.
Job centres	Mainly for manual workers and clerical and sales staff.	No cost; usually plenty of choice.	Limited to relatively routine jobs.
Recruitment consultants	Advertise, interview and produce a shortlist.	Provide expertise and reduce workload.	Can be expensive.
Executive search consultants	Conduct searches for senior executives.	Can find top-level people who might not otherwise be interested.	Expensive, limited to top jobs.
Educational establishments	Universities, colleges and schools.	Major source of future talent.	Recruitment campaigns can be costly.
Recruitment process outsourcing	Deliver complete recruiting process.	Save time, bring outside expertise to bear on recruitment problems and free up HR for more value-adding activities.	Feeling that provider is too remote to deal with the real issues and that there is a danger of losing control.

Examining information from candidates

Candidates may respond to an online notice or an advertisement with a formal application (by e-mail or letter), usually supported by a CV. Applicants may be asked to provide information about their education, qualifications, training and experience in a standardized format to provide a structured basis for drawing up shortlists, the interview itself and for the subsequent actions in offering an appointment and in setting up records. This ensures that all applicants are considered on the same basis against the person specification.

An application form, as illustrated in Figure 24.1 which sets out the information required, can be completed online or on paper. To use application forms more effectively:

- Decide what the criteria for selection are and how these will be assessed by use of the application form.
- Keep questions clear, relevant and non-discriminatory.
- Ask for only the bare minimum of personal details.
- Widen your pool of applicants by offering different options and guidance for completing and viewing application forms.

Employers may also refer for further information to social networks or the candidate's own blog.

Processing applications

When the vacancy or vacancies have been posted or advertised and a fair number of replies received, the initial step is to list the applications on the recruitment database, setting out name, date application was received and actions taken (reject, hold, interview, shortlist, offer). A standard acknowledgement letter should be sent to each applicant unless an instant decision can be made to interview or reject. The next steps are to sift applications prior to drawing up a shortlist and arranging interviews.

Sorting applications

Applications are sifted by comparing the information available about them with the key criteria in the person specification. The criteria should be analysed with care so that they are fully understood. The criteria can be classified under the following three headings so that they can be applied consistently to guide sifting decisions:

- *Essential* – applicants will not be considered unless this criterion is satisfied.
- *Very desirable* – preference will be given to applicants who meet this criterion.
- *Desirable* – applicants who meet this criterion will be given favourable consideration but it is not an essential requirement. However, if a number of applicants meet the first two criteria, satisfying desirable criteria would be a factor in making a choice.

A highly structured method of sifting applications is provided by the use of biodata. These are items of biographical data that are criterion-based (ie they relate to established criteria in such terms as qualifications and experience which indicate that individuals are likely to be suitable). These are objectively scored and, by measurements of past achievements, predict future behaviour.

Following the analysis, applicants can be sorted initially into three categories: possible, marginal and unsuitable. The more information made available and the clearer the criteria the easier this process is. When there is a large field of applicants with many 'possibles', sifting may have to be repeated against more stringent criteria until a shortlist for interview is identified.

Ideally, the numbers on the shortlist should be between four and eight. Fewer than four leaves relatively little choice (although such a limitation may be forced on the recruiter if an insufficient number of good applications have been received). More than eight will mean that too much time is spent on interviewing and there is a danger of diminishing returns setting in.

Draw up an interviewing programme

The time allowed for an interview will vary according to the complexity of the job. For a fairly routine job, 30 minutes or so should suffice. For a more senior job, 60 minutes or more is required. It is best

FIGURE 24.1   Example of application form (compressed)

APPLICATION FORM			
Surname:		**First name:**	
Address:			
Tel. (home)	**Tel. (work)**	**e-mail (personal)**	
Position applied for:			

Education

Dates		Name of secondary school, college or university	Main subjects taken	Qualifications
From	**To**			

Specialized training received

Other qualifications and skills (languages, keyboard skills, current driving licence, etc)

Employment history

(Give details of all positions held since completing full-time education, start with your present or most recent position and work back)

Dates		Name of employer, address and nature of business including any service in the Armed Forces	Position and summary of main duties	Starting and leaving rate of pay	Reasons for leaving or wanting to leave
From	**To**				

Add any comments you wish to make to support your application

I confirm that the information given on this application form is correct

Signature of applicant..**Date**.......................

not to schedule too many interviews for senior jobs in a day – interviewers who try to conduct more than four or five exacting interviews will quickly run out of steam and do neither the interviewee nor the organization any justice. It is advisable to leave 15 to 30 minutes between interviews to write up notes and prepare for the next one.

Administering the selection programme

When the interviewing programme has been drawn up, shortlisted candidates can be invited for interview, using a standard letter where large numbers are involved. Candidates should be asked to complete an application form if they have not already done so. There is a lot to be said at this stage for sending candidates more details of the organization and the job so that too much time is not spent in going through this information at the interview.

Review the remaining 'possibles' and 'marginals' and decide if any are to be held in reserve. Send reserves a standard 'holding' letter and send the others a standard rejection letter. The latter should thank candidates for the interest shown and inform them briefly, but not too brusquely, that they have not been successful. A typical reject letter might read as follows:

> Since writing to you on... we have given careful consideration to your application for the above position. I regret to inform you, however, that we have decided not to ask you to attend for an interview. We should like to thank you for the interest you have shown.

Selection methods

The aim of selection is to assess the suitability of candidates by predicting the extent to which they will be able to carry out a role successfully. It involves deciding on the degree to which the characteristics of applicants in terms of their knowledge, skills and abilities (KSAs), competencies, experience, qualifications, education and training match the person specification and then using this assessment to make a choice between candidates. The so-called 'classic trio' of selection methods consists of application forms, interviews and references. To these should be added selection tests and assessment centres.

Interviews are normally conducted by means of a face-to-face discussion. But, as established by the CIPD's 2013 survey, a considerable proportion of employers (56 per cent) conduct interviews by telephone. Nearly a third (30 per cent) use video or Skype interviews, rising to 42 per cent of those who recruit from overseas.

Interviewing

The interview is the most familiar method of selection. The aim is to elicit information about candidates that will enable a prediction to be made about how well they will do the job and thus lead to a selection decision.

An interview involves face-to-face discussion. When it is an individual rather than a panel interview, it provides the best opportunity for the establishment of close contact – rapport – between the interviewer and the candidate, thus easing the acquisition of information about the candidate's suitability and how well he or she would fit into the organization. As described below, interviews should be structured (detailed consideration of selection interviewing skills is given in Chapter 69). The advantages and disadvantages of interviews are as follows:

Advantages of interviews

- Provide opportunities for interviewers to ask probing questions about the candidate's experience and to explore the extent to which the candidate's competencies match those specified for the job.

- Enable interviewers to describe the job, including its demands (a 'realistic job preview') and the organization in more detail, providing some indication of the terms of the psychological contract.

- Provide opportunities for candidates to ask questions about the job and to clarify issues concerning training, career prospects, the organization and terms and conditions of employment.

- Enable a face-to-face encounter to take place so that the interviewer can make an assessment of how the candidate would fit into the organization and what he or she would be like to work with.

- Give the candidate the same opportunity to assess the organization, the interviewer and the job.

Disadvantages of interviews

- Can lack validity as a means of making sound predictions of performance, and lack reliability in the sense of measuring the same things for different candidates.
- Rely on the skill of the interviewer – many people are poor at interviewing, although most think that they are good at it.
- Do not necessarily assess competence in meeting the demands of the particular job.
- Can lead to biased and subjective judgements by interviewers.

These disadvantages are most common when unstructured interviews are used, but they can be alleviated, first, by using a structured approach as described below and second, by training interviewers. The use of other opinions can also help to reduce bias, especially if the same structured approach is adopted by all the interviewers. Selection tests, especially those measuring intelligence or general ability, can provide valuable information that supplements the interview. In an attempt to rule out stereotyping and discrimination, organizations such as HSBC, the BBC and the civil service are introducing name-blind applications. The big four accounting firms hide details of applicants' school and university from recruiters to eliminate 'unconscious bias'.

Interviews are frequently conducted on a one-to-one basis but there is a case for using a second interviewer to avoid a biased or superficial decision. The alternative is a selection board or panel, which is often used in the public sector. This brings together a number of parties interested in the selection decision. But the drawbacks are that questions tend to be unplanned and delivered at random and the candidates are unable to do justice to themselves because they may not be allowed to expand.

Interviews can be structured or unstructured.

Structured interviews

A structured interview is one based on a defined framework consisting of a set of predetermined questions. All candidates are asked the same questions, which will focus on the attributes and behaviours required to succeed in the job. The answers may be scored through a rating system.

The framework for the interview is provided by a person specification. The aim is to establish the extent to which the candidate has the required knowledge, skills and abilities (KSAs) set out in the specification so as to predict the likelihood of success in the job. This is sometimes referred to as a competency-based interview although, strictly speaking, such an interview is only concerned with behavioural competencies.

A structured interview may include experience-based questions in which candidates are asked to relate how they handled situations in the past requiring skills and abilities necessary for effective performance in the job for which they are applying. And/or it may include situational questions which provide candidates with hypothetical job-relevant situations and ask how they would deal with them. Research by Pulakos and Schmitt (1995) found that experience-based interviews yielded higher levels of validity than situation-based ones. But both types of questions may be incorporated in an interview.

A strengths-based interview is a structured interview in which the objective is to find out what a candidate is good at doing rather than what he or she is capable of doing. It includes questions such as 'What are you good at?' 'What comes easily to you?' and 'What have you done recently that you are proud of?' It is often used with graduates who have little work experience. Strengths-based questions can be incorporated alongside experience-based and situation-based questions as long as the same questions are put to each candidate. The strengths that are important in a job can be identifying the strengths of existing high performers in a similar job.

Unstructured interviews

Unstructured interviews are essentially a general discussion during which the interviewer asks a few questions that are relevant to what he or she is looking for but without any specific aim in mind other than getting an overall picture of the candidate as an individual. Questions are often random and non-specific. Candidates are judged on the general impression they make and the process is likely to be quite subjective. Research quoted later future performance. In these circumstances, it is economical to develop and administer the tests, and a sufficient number of cases can be built up for the essential validation exercise. Tests usually form part of an assessment centre programme. They can be administered online.

Intelligence tests are particularly helpful in situations where intelligence is a key factor and there is no other reliable method of measuring it. Aptitude tests are most useful for jobs where specific and measurable skills are required, such as word processing and skilled repair work. Personality tests can complement structured interviews and intelligence and aptitude tests. Some organizations use them for jobs such as selling, where they believe that 'personality' is important and where it is not too difficult to obtain quantifiable criteria for validation purposes. They may be used to assess integrity and conscientiousness where these characteristics are deemed to be important.

In some situations, a battery of tests may be used, including various types of intelligence, personality and aptitude tests. These may be a standard battery supplied by a test agency, or a custom-built battery may be developed. The biggest pitfall to avoid is adding extra tests just for the sake of it, without ensuring that they make a proper contribution to the success of the predictions for which the battery is being used.

Tests should be administered only by people who have been trained in what the tests are measuring, how they should be used, and how they should be interpreted. Also, it is essential to evaluate all tests by comparing the results at the interview stage with later achievements. To be statistically significant, these evaluations should be carried out over a reasonable period of time and cover as large a number of candidates as possible.

Assessment centres

Assessment centres assemble a group of candidates and use a range of assessment techniques over a concentrated period (one or two days) with the aim of providing a more comprehensive and balanced view of the suitability of individual members of the group. The main features of assessment centres are that:

- exercises are used to capture and simulate the key dimensions of the job; these may include one-to-one role-plays and group exercises; it is assumed that performance in these simulations predicts behaviour on the job;
- candidates are interviewed and tested;
- performance in the centre is measured in several dimensions in terms of a competency framework which defines what is required to achieve success in a career with the organization and possibly to become a member of a talent pipeline (see Chapter 25);
- several candidates or participants are assessed together to allow interaction and to make the experience more open and participative;
- several trained assessors or observers are used in order to increase the objectivity of assessments.

The case for assessment centres is that they obtain much more information about candidates than conventional interviews, even when these are supplemented by tests. But research by Schmidt and Hunter (1998) has shown that on their own, the ability of assessment centres to predict how well someone will perform (predictive validity) is lower than that of intelligence tests combined with structured interviews. Assessment centres are expensive and time-consuming and their use tends to be restricted to large organizations for managerial positions or for graduates.

Choice of selection methods

There is a choice between the selection methods. The most important criterion is the ability of a selection method or combination of methods to predict future performance. Predictive ability is expressed as a coefficient – complete validity would be 1.0; no validity would be 0.0.

The meta-analysis on the validity of different selection methods conducted by Schmidt and Hunter (1998: 265), which covered 85 years of research findings, produced the following predictive validity coefficients:

Intelligence tests and structured interviews	.63
Intelligence tests and unstructured interviews	.55
Assessment centres and structured interviews	.53
Intelligence tests only	.51

Structured interviews only	.51
Unstructured interviews only	.38
Assessment centres only	.37
Graphology only	.02

Robertson and Smith (2001) added personality assessments to this list with a validity coefficient of .37.

Schmidt and Hunter (1998) established that the reason why intelligence (GMA) is such a good predictor of job performance is that intelligent people acquire job knowledge more rapidly and acquire more of it, and it is this knowledge of how to perform the job that causes their job performance to be higher. Their research clearly indicates that the combination of structured interviews and intelligence tests is the most effective in terms of predictive validity. Graphology is useless.

Making the decision

When making the decision, the first step is to identify the candidates who have the abilities and personality which most closely match the specification for the job (person-job fit). Account may also be taken of the extent to which the candidates' personality and values will fit into the organization (person-organization fit).

The next step is to make a choice if there is more than one possible candidate. This choice should be evidence-based but judgement may still be required, which can be difficult. The decision may have to be a balanced one – the match may not be perfect but it may be felt that it will do. However, for the sake of the organization and the individual concerned, what has to be avoided at all cost is the selection in desperation of someone who is not properly qualified to do the job. If there is no one available, it is better to start again. It can happen that no suitable person emerges, even after another attempt or attempts. It could them be necessary to re-think the job specification to make it more realistic. In these circumstances, organizations have been known to resume their internal search, recognizing that some special training may be necessary for an individual with the potential to do the job but who lacks some of the expertise required.

Inevitably, managers and team leaders will want to appoint someone they think they will be able to work with, but great care has to be taken to avoid superficial or prejudiced decisions based on appearances rather than the reality of what the candidate has to offer. It is too easy to make superficial judgements. Managers can also fall into the trap of selecting 'like for like', ie someone they feel is like themselves rather than someone who can do the job well, even if they are different.

To minimize bias, Linos and Reinhard (2015: 22) recommend the following approach:

All forms of assessment should follow structured processes and hiring decisions should be based firmly on the aggregated scores or data, rather than gut feeling. The current weight of evidence suggests that, in general, structured interviews are preferable to unstructured interviews. Assessors of CVs and tests should be as blind as possible to the characteristics of the applicant (gender, age, name, and so on) and should read through tests and CVs in identical circumstances, such as the same time of day, or in the same format (for example paper versus online).

Provisional offers and obtaining references

After the interviewing and testing procedure has been completed, a provisional decision to make an offer by telephone or in writing can be made. This is normally 'subject to satisfactory references' and the candidate should, of course, be told that these will be taken up. If there is more than one eligible candidate for a job, it may be advisable to hold one or two people in reserve. Applicants often withdraw, especially those whose only purpose in applying for the job was to carry out a 'test marketing' operation, or to obtain a lever with which to persuade their present employers to value them more highly.

The main purpose of a reference is to obtain in confidence factual information about a prospective employee. This information is straightforward and essential. It is necessary to confirm the nature of the previous job, the period of time in employment, the reason for leaving (if relevant), the salary or rate of pay and, possibly, the attendance record.

Opinions about character, competence, performance and suitability are unreliable. Referees are reluctant to commit themselves and they are not in any position to assess suitability – only the prospective employer can do that. Personal referees are, of course, entirely useless. All they prove is that the applicant has at least one or two friends.

A written request for a reference could simply ask the previous employer to confirm the candidate's employment record. More precise answers may be obtained if a standard form is provided for the employer to complete. The questions asked on this form should be limited to the following:

- What was the period of employment?
- What was the job title?
- What work was carried out?
- What was the rate of pay or salary?
- How many days' absence were there over the last 12 months?
- Would you re-employ (if not, why not)?

The last question is important, if it is answered honestly or at all.

Telephone references may save time and may be more reliable. They can be used as an alternative or in addition to written references. Ask factual questions only and keep a record of the conversation.

References – legal aspects

The key legal points that should be considered when asking for or giving references are:

- Once the decision has been made to make an offer, the letter should state that 'this is a provisional offer subject to the receipt of satisfactory references'.

- It has been generally held that there is no common law duty on an employer to provide references for a serving or past employee unless there is a term to that effect in the employment contract. But it has been ruled (*Spring* v. *Guardian Assurance* 1994) that there might be a moral duty to provide a reference where it is 'natural practice' to require a reference from a previous employer before offering employment, and where the employee could not expect to enter that type of employment without a reference.

- If a reference contains a false or unsubstantiated statement that damages the reputation of the individual, action for damages may result.

- It is possible to succeed in a claim for damages if it can be shown that the reference provided was negligent because reasonable care had not been taken in preparing it, which includes ensuring that it is factually correct.

Checking applications

It is a sad fact that applicants all too often misinform their prospective employers about their education, qualifications and employment record. This was confirmed by a survey carried out by the CIPD (2008), which found that 25 per cent of employers had to withdraw their offers because applicants had lied or misrepresented their application. It is always advisable to check with universities, professional institutes and previous employers that the facts given by applicants are correct. Other checks can be made, such as:

- interview questions about actual (not hypothetical) experiences, with deep probing to ascertain the extent of the individual's personal involvement, decision making and contribution;

- detailed application forms with open-ended questions about specific learning related to the skills, knowledge and competencies required for the vacancies under consideration;

- identification check;

- electoral register check;

- credit reference agency check (especially appropriate for positions in the financial services sector);

- confirmation of previous employment with HM Revenue and Customs or through the Department of Work and Pensions;

- Criminal Records Bureau check;

- Companies House check (for directors); and

- fraud prevention check, including Cifas staff fraud database check (to prevent an employer unwittingly employing people previously dismissed for fraud somewhere else). Cifas is a not-for-profit fraud prevention service.

Final offers

The final stage in the selection procedure is to confirm the offer of employment after satisfactory references have been obtained, and the applicant has passed the medical examination required for pension and life assurance purposes or because a certain standard of physical fitness is required for the work. The contract of employment should also be prepared at this stage.

Following up

It is essential to follow up newly engaged employees to ensure that they have settled in and to check on how well they are doing. If there are any problems, it is much better to identify them at an early stage rather than allowing them to fester.

Following up is also important as a means of checking on the selection procedure. If by any chance a mistake has been made, it is useful to find out how it happened so that the procedure can be improved. Misfits can be attributed to a number of causes; for example: inadequate person specification, poor sourcing of candidates, weak advertising, poor interviewing techniques, inappropriate or invalidated tests, or prejudice on the part of the selector.

Dealing with recruitment problems

Every experienced HR professional who is responsible for recruitment and selection will occasionally come across a vacancy that is particularly difficult to fill. In this situation, any compromise that involves appointing someone who does not meet the specification must be avoided. To deal with the problem constructively it is necessary to take the following actions:

- Ensure that all the possible sources of candidates have been used.
- Consider any ways in which the website or social media notice or advertisement could be made more attractive.
- Check that the person specification is realistic – that the requirements have not been overstated.
- Consider whether it might be necessary to improve the package offered to candidates – check market rates to ensure that the levels of pay and benefits are competitive.
- In discussion with the line manager, examine the possibility of reshaping the role to increase its attractiveness.
- If the worst comes to the worst, discuss with the manager alternative ways of carrying out the work with existing staff.

CASE STUDY

Recruitment assessment processes at Embarq

Embarq is the largest independent local telecoms provider in the United States. It suffered catastrophic rates of staff turnover in its call centres; then a new assessment process designed by PreVisor reduced turnover from 33.5 per cent in the first 90 days to 12.5 per cent.

The new process begins with an online screening tool that identifies characteristics and motivations that define long-term success in the roles, such as 'customer focus' and 'persistence'. There follows a behaviour-based structured interview and a sales-based role-play exercise. This exercise, which takes place over the phone, tests candidates in the most realistic way possible, and is more convenient and cost-effective.

Sales have since increased by 24 per cent, and customer service has also improved.

Key learning points: Recruitment and selection

Define requirements

Requirements are set out in the form of job descriptions or role profiles and person specifications. These provide the information required to draft advertisements, post vacancies on the internet, brief agencies or recruitment consultants and assess candidates by means of interviews and selection tests.

Analyse recruitment strengths and weaknesses

The analysis should cover such matters as the national or local reputation of the organization, pay, employee benefits and working conditions, the intrinsic interest of the job, security of employment, opportunities for education and training, career prospects, and the location of the office or plant.

Analyse the requirement

- Establish how many jobs have to be filled and by when.
- Set out information on responsibilities and competency requirements.
- Consider where suitable candidates are likely to come from.
- Define the terms and conditions of the job (pay and benefits).
- Consider what is likely to attract good candidates.

Identify sources of candidates

Initially, consideration should be given to internal candidates. An attempt can be made to persuade former employees to return to the organization or obtain suggestions from existing employees (referrals). If these approaches do not work, the main sources of candidates are online recruiting, advertising, agencies and job centres, consultants, recruitment process outsourcing providers and direct approaches to educational establishments.

Selection methods

The aim is to assess the suitability of candidates by predicting the extent to which they will be able to carry out a role successfully. It involves deciding on the degree to which the characteristics of applicants match the person specification and using this assessment to make a choice between candidates. The interview is the most familiar method of selection. The aim is to elicit information about candidates that will enable a prediction to be made about how well they will do the job and thus lead to a selection decision.

Structured interviews

A structured interview is one based on a defined framework. Within the framework there may be a set of predetermined questions. All candidates are asked the same questions and the answers may be scored through a rating system.

Selection tests

Selection tests are used to provide valid and reliable evidence of levels of abilities, intelligence, personality characteristics, aptitudes and attainments.

Choice of selection methods

There is a choice between the selection methods. The most important criterion is the predictive validity of the method or combination of methods. Schmidt and Hunter (1998) found that the best results were obtained by combining intelligence tests with structured interviews.

Making the decision

When making the decision, the first step is to identify the candidates who have the abilities and personality which most closely match the specification for the job (person-job fit). Account may also be taken of the extent to which the candidate's personality and values will fit into the organization (person-organization fit).

References and offers

After the interviewing and testing procedure has been completed, a provisional offer by telephone or in writing can be made. This is normally 'subject to satisfactory references'. It is essential to check the information provided by candidates on qualifications and their work experience.

References

CIPD (2008) *Survey of Recruitment, Retention and Turnover* London, CIPD

CIPD (2013) Resourcing and talent planning survey, *CIPD* [online] http://www.cipd.co.uk/hr-resources/survey-reports/resourcing-talent-planning-2013.aspx [accessed 22 October 2015]

CIPD (2015) Resourcing and talent planning survey, *CIPD* [online] http://www.cipd.co.uk/hr-resources/survey-reports/resourcing-talent-planning-2015.aspx [accessed 22 October 2015]

Headworth, A (2015) *Social Media Recruitment*, London, Kogan Page

Linos, E and Reinhard, J (2015) A head for hiring: The behavioural science of recruitment and selection, *CIPD* [online] http://www.cipd.co.uk/binaries/a-head-for-hiring_2015-behavioural-science-of-recruitment-and-selection.pdf [accessed 25 October 2015]

Pulakos, E D and Schmitt, N (1995) Experience-based and situational interviews: studies of validity, *Personnel Psychology*, **48** (2), pp 289–308

Robertson, I T and Smith, M (2001) Personnel selection, *Journal of Occupational and Organizational Psychology*, **74** (4), pp 441–72

Schmidt, F L and Hunter, J E (1998) The validity and utility of selection methods in personnel psychology: practical and theoretical implications of 85 years of research findings, *Psychological Bulletin*, **124** (2), pp 262–74

Spearman, C (1927) *The Abilities of Man*, New York, Macmillan

Syedain, H (2012) *People Management Guide to Recruitment Marketing*, July, p 19

25
Talent management

LEARNING OUTCOMES

On completing this chapter you should be able to define these key concepts. You should also know about:

- The meaning of talent management
- The process of talent management
- Talent pools
- Talent management strategy
- Talent management policy
- The talent pipeline
- Talent resourcing
- Talent identification
- Talent development

Talent management defined

Talent management is about ensuring that the organization has the capable and well-qualified people it needs to attain its goals. Talent is what people must have in order to perform well in their roles. They make a difference to organizational performance through their immediate efforts, they have the ability to learn and grow, and they have the potential to make an important contribution in the future. Talent management is based on the proposition that 'those with the best people win'. It emerged in the late 1990s when McKinsey and Company coined the phrase 'the war for talent'. It involves the systematic attraction, retention, identification and development of individuals who are of particular value to an organization.

As suggested by Younger *et al* (2007), approaches to talent management include emphasizing 'growth from within', regarding talent development as a key

FIGURE 25.1   The CEMEX model of talent management

element of the business strategy, being clear about the competencies and qualities that matter, maintaining well-defined career paths, taking management development, coaching and mentoring seriously and demanding high performance.

There are many versions of talent management but in one way or another it can cover such traditional HRM activities as workforce planning, recruitment, managing employee retention, performance management, potential assessment, leadership and management development, succession planning and career planning. The difference is that talent management is a wider-reaching approach that 'joins up' these HR practices. A model of talent management produced by CEMEX Ltd is shown in Figure 25.1.

The process of talent management

The purpose of talent management is to establish a 'talent pool' (or talent pools) from which people can be obtained as required to fill key roles. This is achieved by operating a 'talent pipeline' which provides for the flow of talent needed to maintain the talent pool through the processes of resourcing, talent identification and talent development. These activities are initiated by the business strategy which informs workforce plans. Talent management policies and strategies determine the scope of the talent pool and influence workforce plans. The process is modelled in Figure 25.2.

FIGURE 25.2   The process of talent management

The talent pool

A talent pool contains the resources of talented people required by an organization to ensure that vacancies for people in pivotal roles can be filled readily. Talent management policy will define the view of the organization on what constitutes talent and who should be included in a talent management pool. The talent management strategy as informed by workforce planning will indicate the size of the talent pool and the operation of the talent pipeline.

Criteria

Criteria for inclusion in the talent pool in the shape of generic competencies and skills need to be defined. These criteria will be used to identify potential and qualify people for membership of a pool. For its senior posts, a Civil Service department uses the three Corporate Leadership Council (2002) elements:

1 Ability: technical skills, attitudes and behaviour.

2 Aspiration: setting and achieving challenging goals, and seeking opportunities for learning within their subject area.

3 Engagement: emotional and rational commitment to the organization, resulting in discretionary effort.

In the *Harvard Business Review*, Fernandez-Araoz (2014) recommended the following criteria for defining high talent:

- *Motivation*: a fierce commitment to excel in the pursuit of unselfish goals.

- *Curiosity*: a penchant for seeking out new experiences, knowledge, and candid feedback and an openness to learning and change.

- *Insight*: the ability to gather and make sense of information that suggests new possibilities.

- *Engagement*: a knack for using emotion and logic to communicate a persuasive vision and connect with people.

- *Determination*: the wherewithal to fight for difficult goals despite challenges and to bounce back from adversity.

Talent on demand

The existence of a talent pool enables a policy of 'talent on demand' to be adopted, which means that talented people are available as required to meet emerging needs for senior managers or other key staff. This is a more practical approach than the management succession plans that were formerly produced by large bureaucratic organizations. They never worked well and are even less likely to succeed in today's more flexible and rapidly changing organizations, where elaborate succession plans are likely to be out of date as soon as they are made. As McDonnell and Collings (2011: 64) observed:

> Succession planning has evolved from the traditional short-term focus on replacing senior managers if they happened to leave without prior warning. There is now a more long-term aim of developing a cadre of key talent who are able to take on higher-level roles, potentially roles that may not currently exist... The utilization of talent pools consisting of employees with key generic type competencies and skills allows the organization far greater scope when positions become available. Management will be able to select the most suitable candidate from a pool of candidates and train the person into the specific requirements of that particular role.

Talent management policy

An organization developing a talent management programme has initially to make two policy decisions. The first decision is whether to adopt a 'talent on demand' policy as described above. There is much to be said for doing this in any situation in which it is difficult to produce precise definitions of future talent requirements; and today that is a typical situation. The second policy decision is on who should be included in a talent management programme. The choice is between an exclusive and inclusive approach.

An exclusive approach may focus on an elite group of those assessed as having high potential – the 'high flyers'. These will be possible future leaders able to fill senior posts in the organization. Iusclid *et al* (2005) argued that talent management policies should concentrate on the 'A list' people who fall into this category. But a modified form of exclusivity recognizes that there are a number of other key positions with which talent management may be concerned, for example pivotal professional or technical roles or even middle-ranking managers such as departmental heads and team leaders. An inclusive approach means that everyone in the organization is seen as actually or potentially talented, given opportunity and direction.

The most common view seems to be that the aims of talent management are to obtain, identify and develop people with high potential. But it should not be at the expense of the development needs of people generally. A case study of a global management consultancy (Tansley and Tietze, 2013) revealed that the consultancy's approach to talent management was both inclusive (everyone is talented) and exclusive (key people were developed in ways different to those adopted for 'everyday talent'). This was expressed by the company's talent development director as follows:

> Talent in the firm means two things. One, I think that everybody is a talented individual. We recruit bright people intellectually. But our business also has the responsibility to help them realize that. So there is a fundamental belief that everyone is talented, and there is a belief that we do need to identify future leaders who are going to lead key parts or have key roles in the business in the future, and these would be quite senior roles. And that identifying talent to these spaces, and helping people to gravitate towards one of these roles, will be the key challenge for us.

These beliefs were put into effect by the firm through a talent progression sequence of four stages:

1 *Rising talent* – highly educated graduate recruits who are given education and training for core technical or professional roles.

2 *Emerging leaders* – who are given training and education for management under the guidance of sponsors or mentors.

3 *Next generation leaders* – who undertake leadership development programmes and may attend a corporate academy.

4 *Corporate next generation leaders* – who are provided with one-to-one development through coaches and mentors and briefed on corporate/governance strategy.

Talent management strategy

A talent management strategy consists of a view on how the processes involved in creating a talent pool should mesh together with an overall objective – to acquire and nurture talent wherever it is and wherever it is needed by using a number of interdependent policies and practices. Talent management is the notion of 'bundling' in action. The strategy should take into account the future talent requirements of the organization as determined by workforce planning. It should also take account of talent management policies referring to who the talent management programme should cover and definitions of what is meant by talent in terms of competencies and potential.

The aims of a talent management strategy can be expressed as being to:

● develop the organization as an 'employer of choice';

● plan and implement recruitment and selection programmes that ensure good-quality people are recruited who are likely to thrive in the organization and stay with it for a reasonable length of time (but not necessarily for life);

● plan and implement talent retention programmes;

● introduce reward policies that help to attract and retain high-quality staff;

● design jobs and develop roles that give people opportunities to apply and grow their skills and provide them with autonomy, interest and challenge;

● implement talent development programmes;

● provide talented staff with opportunities for career development and growth;

● recognize those with talent by rewarding excellence, enterprise and achievement;

● generate and maintain a talent pool so that 'talent on demand' is available to provide for management succession.

Cappelli (2008) suggested that the signs of a successful talent management strategy are that it is inclusive and that it can address and resolve any incongruity between the supply and demand of talent. He stated that too many firms have more employees than they need for available positions, or a talent shortfall, and always at the wrong times. He argued that talent management should not just be about employee development or succession planning, as many of the commonplace definitions suggest, but should focus on helping the firm attain its strategic objectives. His four principles for 'talent on demand' were:

1 Make and buy talent to manage the demand-side risk.

2 Reduce the uncertainty in talent demand.

3 Earn a return on investment in developing employees.

4 Employee interests should be balanced by creating an internal labour market that offers all the advantages of the external labour market to reduce staff turnover and to avoid the associated costs and loss of talent.

Workforce planning

Workforce planning for talent management (talent planning) estimates the number of talented people needed in the future taking into account the implications of business plans. It also assesses the type of skills that will be required. Workforce planning therefore informs decisions on the size and composition of the talent pool in accordance with talent management policy. It also provides the basis for the resourcing (recruiting) activities required to ensure that the talent needed by the organization is readily available in terms of both numbers and skills. The techniques used were described in Chapter 23.

Resourcing

Resourcing is the first step in the direction of creating a talent pool. It is primarily about ensuring that the organization obtains the right people with the right skills for future roles as well as for immediate vacancies. The Civil Service has a fast-stream entry scheme which is used to attract relatively small numbers of external recruits with the perceived potential to reach senior leadership levels over their career. These entrants have rapid early career progression and a wide range of early experiences to accelerate the early stages of their career development. Organizations in such fields as accountancy, retailing, aerospace engineering and pharmaceuticals recruit graduates who have the potential for a career in management, a professional role or research and development.

The talent resourcing strategy should include the establishment of an employer brand and employee value proposition that will attract high-quality candidates. Role specifications for recruiting purposes should define the competencies required to progress in the organization. Structured interviews should focus on these competencies, intelligence and ability tests should be used and consideration should be given to the use of assessment centres. Interviewers should be trained in how to assess potential.

The implementation of talent resourcing plans may be the responsibility of a talent management function in an organization but it is often carried out by recruitment specialists, leaving those concerned with talent management to concentrate on the pipeline activities of identification and development, the management of the talent pool and, importantly, keeping in touch with those in the talent pipeline (talent relationship management).

It is also necessary to consider what needs to be done to retain as well as to obtain talent. The steps that can be taken include demonstrating that the organization values its talented people, providing ample scope for learning and growth, recognizing and rewarding achievement and high performance, and keeping people informed about their progress (regular feedback). Talent management specialists will be responsible for dealing with talent retention issues.

Identifying talent

Procedures are necessary for identifying people who are qualified now for membership of a talent pool, or who have the potential to become members after completing a talent management development programme. It is usual for assessments of potential to be made initially by the individual's line manager. They may be followed up with additional conversations with a talent management specialist, and possible attendance at an assessment centre for promising individuals.

In the initial assessment by the line manager, a simple three-box method can be used to classify people. For example, 'emerging', 'growing' or 'high' potential, or 'ready now to progress beyond current grade', 'could progress beyond current grade within two years' or 'best suited to current grade'.

As noted by Campbell and Hirsh (2013), a police force uses five categories for talent development:

1 Performance difficulties in their role – remedial action required.

2 Good match now – still room to develop in current role.

3 Lateral development – consistent performer, consider opportunities for individual in other areas.

4 Ready to go now – high performing, one-step progression to the next level.

5 Ones to watch – high performing and high potential, require opportunities to develop quickly to senior level.

There are two problems with this approach to assessing potential. First, line managers may be reasonably good at assessing performance in the present job but they are not so well qualified to judge potential to carry out higher-level jobs because they may not be aware of the requirements for their successful performance. Second, high performance in the current job may contribute to high potential but does not necessarily equate with it.

To deal with these problems it is necessary to do three things. First, clarify the criteria to be used for assessing potential; these should be those adopted for defining the qualifications for membership of a talent pool (see above). Second, train line managers who make potential assessments in how to apply the criteria. And third, consider using the nine-box grid. This is a widely adopted approach to identifying talent – over half of the organizations studied by Campbell and Hirsh (2013) were using it or were planning to introduce it in the future. As illustrated in Figure 25.3, the grid uses two axes – performance and potential – with three levels on each axis, forming nine boxes in total.

FIGURE 25.3   A nine-point performance/potential assessment grid

Performance		
Low	*Medium*	*High*
Shows every sign of the potential to go further but is under-performing in the present role.	Has the potential to go further. Performance is at an acceptable level.	Demonstrates high potential. Regularly achieves challenging and stretching goals.
Capable of taking on greater responsibilities if there is a significant improvement in performance.	Has the potential to keep developing and to deliver more in either scale or complexity. Performance is acceptable.	Capable of growing into a higher-level role in due course. A consistently strong performer, delivering excellent value.
No potential for growth beyond this level. Is seriously under-performing in the present role.	Valued in current role but is not expected to advance beyond this level. Generally meets performance expectations.	Highly valued at this level and in current role. A strong performer who is a core team member.

High

Medium   Potential

Low

Whatever approach to assessing potential is adopted, it is important to ensure that the line manager discusses it with the individual, explaining the reason for the assessment and giving performance feedback. This should be a two-way conversation in which the individual has the opportunity to comment. It should lead to a general discussion on the career prospects of the individual. If there is room for performance improvement, the aim should be to reach an agreement on what needs to be done – by the individual *and* by the manager.

Talent development

Talent development is the process of ensuring that talented employees gain the skills and experience required to fulfil their promise, advance their careers and satisfy the organization's need to fill senior and key posts with high-quality people. As the final part of the pipeline, it enables those with potential to become part of a talent pool but, because there is always room for further growth, qualified members of a talent pool will still benefit from continuing developmental activities. Talent development involves leadership and management development and career development.

Leadership and management development

Leadership and management development programmes ensure that managers have the leadership and managerial qualities required to achieve success. A blended learning approach is used which is based on an analysis of learning needs and combines a number of learning activities. These can include planned experience, self-managed learning, coaching, mentoring, action learning, outdoor learning and formal training courses.

Leadership development programmes prepare people for leadership roles and situations beyond their current experience. The aim is to enhance leadership qualities by getting participants to understand what leadership involves and enabling them to appreciate, practice and develop the skills required for effective leadership. They focus on people management. As suggested by Bolden (2010), the essential elements of leadership development are reflection, practice, self-awareness, personal support and opportunities to apply the learning to work.

Management development programmes aim to enhance the ability of participants to achieve their goals by directing and controlling a whole range of resources, including people. They focus on the hard skills of managing for results as well as softer people management skills. Because managers generally have to work on a day-to-day basis in conditions of variety, turbulence and unpredictability, their development largely takes place by gaining the right sequence of experience through the career development activities described below, although this may be supplemented by self-directed learning and courses on management techniques. Guidance provided by coaching and from mentors can be an important part of a programme. Leadership and management development activities are described in more detail in Chapter 39.

Career development

Career development is concerned with shaping the progression of individuals within an organization in order to provide those with promise a sequence of experience and learning activities that will equip them for whatever level of responsibility they have the ability to reach. It includes career counselling to help people progress their careers to their advantage as well as that of the organization.

Giving breadth of career experience is more difficult for those in specialized roles, as they often have fewer opportunities for movement. To deal with this problem it is necessary to build on what they know, through repeat exposure to similar, but increasingly complex, activities.

Career development includes the following activities:

- a policy of promoting from within wherever possible;
- the definition of career paths that define the routes talented people can take to advance their careers within an organization by moving upwards or laterally as opportunities arise;
- personal development planning to develop each individual's knowledge and skills;
- systems and processes to achieve sharing and development of knowledge across the firm;
- multidisciplinary project teams, with a shifting membership, to offer developmental opportunities for as wide a range of employees as possible.

Key learning points: Talent management

Talent management defined

- Talent management is about ensuring that the organization has the talented people it needs to attain its goals.

- It involves establishing and maintaining a 'talent pool' (or talent pools).

- This is achieved by operating a 'talent pipeline' which provides for the flow of talent needed to maintain the talent pool through the processes of resourcing, talent identification and talent development.

Talent defined

Talent is what people must have in order to perform well in their roles. They make a difference to organizational performance through their immediate efforts, they have the ability to learn and grow, and they have the potential to make an important contribution in the future.

The process of talent management

- The process of talent management involves operating a talent management pipeline in which resourcing, talent identification and talent development activities take place in order to create the talent pool.

- These activities are initiated by the business strategy which informs workforce plans. Talent management policies and strategies determine the scope of the talent pool and influence workforce plans

The talent pool

A talent pool contains the resources of talented people required by an organization to ensure that vacancies for people in pivotal roles can be filled readily.

Talent on demand

The existence of a talent pool enables a policy of 'talent on demand' to be adopted, which means that talented people are available as required to meet emerging needs for senior managers or other key staff.

Talent management policy

An organization developing a talent management programme has initially to make two policy decisions. The first decision is whether to adopt a 'talent on demand' policy. There is much to be said for doing this in any situation in which it is difficult to produce precise definitions of future talent requirements.

The second policy decision is on who should be included in a talent management programme. The choice is between an exclusive (talented people are the high flyers in an organization) and inclusive (everyone is talented) approach.

Talent management strategy

A talent management strategy consists of a view on how the processes involved in creating a talent pool should mesh together with an overall objective – to acquire and nurture talent wherever it is and wherever it is needed by using a number of interdependent policies and practices.

Workforce planning

Workforce planning for talent management (talent planning) estimates the number of talented people needed in the future, taking into account the implications of business plans. It also assesses the type of skills that will be required.

Resourcing

Resourcing is the first step in the direction of creating a talent pool. It is primarily about ensuring that the organization obtains the right people with the right skills for future roles as well as for immediate vacancies.

Identifying talent

- Procedures are necessary for identifying people who are qualified now for membership of a talent pool, or who have the potential to become members after completing a talent management development programme.

- It is usual for assessments of potential to be made initially by the individual's line manager. They may be followed up with additional conversations with a talent management specialist, and possible attendance at an assessment centre for promising individuals.

Talent development

Talent development is the process of ensuring that talented employees gain the skills and experience required to fulfil their promise, advance their careers and satisfy the organization's need to fill senior and key posts with high-quality and capable people.

Leadership and management development

- Leadership and management development programmes ensure that managers have the leadership and managerial qualities required to achieve success.

- A blended learning approach is used which is based on an analysis of learning needs and combines a number of learning activities. These can include planned experience, self-managed learning, coaching, mentoring, action learning, outdoor learning and formal training courses.

Career development

Career development is concerned with shaping the progression of individuals within an organization in order to provide those with promise a sequence of experience and learning activities that will equip them for whatever level of responsibility they have the ability to reach.

References

Bolden, R (2010) Leadership, management and organizational development, in (eds) J Gold, R Thorpe and A Mumford, *Gower Handbook of Leadership and Management Development*, Gower, Farnham, pp 118–32

Campbell, V and Hirsh W (2013) Talent management: A four-step approach, *Institute for Employment Studies* [online] http://www.employment-studies.co.uk/system/files/resources/files/502.pdf, [accessed 14 January 2016]

Cappelli, P (2008) *Talent on Demand: Managing talent in an uncertain age*, Boston MA, Harvard Business School Press

Corporate Leadership Council (2002) Building the high performance workforce [online] http://talentexperiment.com/images/CLC_Building_the_High_Performance_Workforce_A_Quantitative_Analysis_of_the_Effectiveness_of_Performance_Management_Strategies_1_.pdf [accessed 13 January 2016]

Fernandez-Araoz, C (2014) 21st-century talent spotting, *Harvard Business Review*, June, pp 46, 48–56

Huselid, M A, Beatty, R W and Becker, B E (2005) A-players or A-positions? The strategic logic of workforce management, *Harvard Business Review*, December, pp 110–17

McDonnell, A and Collings, D G (2011) Identification and evaluation of talent in MNEs, in H Scullion and D G Collings (eds) *Global Talent Management*, London, Routledge, pp 56–73

Schein, E H (1978) *Career Dynamics: Matching individual and organizational needs, Reading*, MA, Addison-Wesley

Sparrow, P, Hird, M and Cooper C L (2015) *Do We Need HR?* Basingstoke, PalgraveMacmillan

Tansley, C and Tietze, S (2013) Rites of passage through talent management stages: an identity work perspective, *International Journal of Human Resource Management*, 24 (9), pp 1799–815

Younger, J, Smallwood, N and Ulrich, D (2007) Developing your organization's brand as a talent developer, *Human Resource Planning*, 30 (2), pp 21–29

26
Introduction to the organization

Introduction

First impressions matter; getting off to a good start is all-important. If it goes wrong at the beginning, the employee will take too much time to settle down and do a good job. If things go really badly the individual will leave and all the hard work and money put into recruitment will have been wasted. It is essential to take care over introducing people to the organization through effective induction arrangements as described in this chapter.

Induction defined

Induction is the process of receiving and welcoming employees when they first join a company and giving them the basic information they need to settle down quickly and happily and start work. The aims are to:

- smooth the preliminary stages when everything is likely to be strange and unfamiliar to the starter;

- establish quickly a favourable attitude to the organization in the mind of new employees so that they are more likely to stay;

- accelerate progress up the learning curve;

- obtain effective output from the new employee in the shortest possible time;

- reduce the likelihood of the employee leaving quickly;

- save the considerable costs which are incurred when someone leaves;

- enable the process of socialization to take place smoothly – the social aspects of work are very important for most people and if good relationships with colleagues are quickly established, employees are likely to settle in more quickly and enjoy their work.

To achieve these aims the induction arrangements as described below should be concerned with reception, documentation, initial briefing, introduction to the workplace, formal induction course and formal and informal training.

Reception

New starters will be concerned about who they are going to work for (their immediate manager or team leader), who they are going to work with, what work they are going to do on their first day and the geographical layout of their place of work (location of entrances, exits, lavatories, restrooms and the canteen).

Some of this information may be provided by a member of the HR department, or an assistant in the new employee's place of work. But the most important source of information is the immediate manager, supervisor or team leader.

Reception is most likely to go well if:

- the person whom the starter meets first (the receptionist, HR assistant or manager) knows of their pending arrival and what to do next;

- reception staff know that they are expected to be friendly and helpful;

- a guide is provided if the starter has to go to another location unless the route is very straightforward;

- the starter is not kept waiting; steady, unhurried, guided activity is a good antidote to first-day nerves.

Information for new staff

The following information should be made available to new staff:

- a brief description of the company – its history, products, organization and management;

- basic conditions of employment – hours of work, holidays, pension scheme;

- sickness – notification of absence, certificates, pay, insurance, pensions;

- leave of absence;

- company rules and disciplinary, capability and grievance procedures;

- pay – structure or scales and when paid;

- trade union arrangements, where applicable;

- learning and development facilities;

- health and safety arrangements and rules;

- rules for using the internet.

Introduction to the workplace

The departmental induction programme should, wherever possible, start with the departmental manager, not the immediate team leader. The manager may give only a general welcome and a brief description of the work of the department before handing over new employees to their team leaders for the more detailed induction. But it is important for the manager to be involved at this stage so that he or she is not seen as a remote figure. At least this means that the starter will not be simply a name or a number to the manager. The detailed induction in the workplace is probably best carried out by the immediate team leader, who should do six things:

1 Put the new employee at ease.

2 Interest the employee in the job, explaining its purpose, significance and how it relates to the work going on elsewhere in the department or company.

3 Interest the employee in the company, explaining what it is like to work there.

4 Provide basic information about working arrangements.

5 Indicate the standards of performance and behaviour expected of the employee.

6 Tell the employee about training arrangements and how he or she can progress in the company.

The team leader should introduce new starters to their fellow team members. It is best to get one member of the team to act as a guide or 'starter's friend'. There is much to be said for these initial guides being people who have not been long with the organization. As relative newcomers they are likely to remember all the small points that were a source of worry to them when they started work, and so help new employees to settle in quickly.

On-the-job induction training

Most new starters other than those on formal training schemes will learn on the job, although this may be supplemented with special off-the-job courses to develop particular skills or knowledge. But on-the-job learning can be haphazard, inefficient and wasteful. A planned, systematic approach is desirable. This can incorporate an assessment of what the new starter needs to learn, the use of designated and trained colleagues to act as guides and mentors, and coaching by team leaders or specially appointed and trained departmental trainers.

These on-the-job arrangements can be supplemented by self-managed learning arrangements in which individuals take responsibility for meeting their own learning needs, with help and guidance as necessary, offering access to flexible learning packages or providing advice on learning opportunities.

Formal induction courses

Formal induction courses assemble new starters in groups so that members can be given consistent and comprehensive information at the same time, which might not be forthcoming if reliance is placed on the team leader. A formal course provides an opportunity to deliver messages about the organization, its products and services, its mission and its values. A range of media can be used which might not be available in departments. But formal courses cannot replace informal induction arrangements in the workplace, where the most important requirement – settling people down – can best be met.

Decisions will have to be made about who attends an induction course and when. It is usual to mix people from different departments but less common to have people from widely different levels on the same course. In practice, managers and senior professional staff are usually dealt with individually.

Ideally, induction courses should take place soon after starting. If there are sufficient new employees available, this could be a half day in the first week. But the course may have to be delayed until a sufficient number of new starters are available.

The content of the induction course could include some or all of the following subjects:

● information about the organization – its products, services, structure, mission and values;

● learning arrangements and opportunities;

● performance management processes;

● health and safety;

● policies on such matters as diversity and inclusion, equal opportunity, bullying, sexual and racial harassment, use of the internet;

● pension arrangements;

● trade unions and employee involvement.

Key learning points: Introduction to the workplace

First impressions matter, as does the impact of the initial weeks of employment; getting off to a good start is all-important. If it goes wrong to begin with the employee will take too much time to settle down.

Induction defined

Induction is the process of receiving and welcoming employees when they first join a company and giving them the basic information they need to settle down quickly and happily and start work.

Introduction to the workplace

New starters will be concerned about who they are going to work for, who they are going to work with, what work they are going to do on their first day, and the geographical layout of their place of work (location of entrances, exits, lavatories, restrooms and the canteen). Detailed induction in the workplace is probably best carried out by the immediate team leader.

On-the-job induction training

Most new starters other than those on formal training schemes will learn on the job, although this may be supplemented with special off-the-job courses to develop particular skills or knowledge. But on-the-job learning can be haphazard, inefficient and wasteful. A planned, systematic approach is desirable.

Formal induction courses

Formal induction courses assemble new starters in groups so that members can be given consistent and comprehensive information at the same time which might not be forthcoming if reliance is placed on the team leader.

27
Release from the organization

KEY CONCEPTS AND TERMS

Downsizing

Job shop

Outplacement

LEARNING OUTCOMES

On completing this chapter you should be able to define these key concepts. You should also understand:

● What to do about redundancy

● How to handle dismissals

Introduction

The employment relationship may be ended voluntarily by someone moving elsewhere. Or it may finish at the end of a career on retirement. Increasingly, however, people are having to go involuntarily. Some organizations are becoming mean as well as lean. Mean or not, businesses are 'managing costs' by 'downsizing' (a euphemism for redundancy) and

they are tightening up disciplinary procedures to handle cases of incapability as well as misconduct. Resourcing policies and practices covering release from the organization also have to cover voluntary turnover and retirement.

One of the most demanding areas of human resource management in organizations is that of handling arrangements for releasing people through redundancy, dismissal or retirement.

Redundancy

Redundancy takes place when the organization as a whole is reducing the number of employees, when structural changes are being made following mergers and acquisitions, and when individual jobs are no longer needed. If, unfortunately, redundancy has to take place, it is necessary to plan ahead – seeking and implementing methods of avoiding redundancy as far as possible, making arrangements for voluntary redundancy and helping people to find jobs (outplacement). HR usually has the onerous responsibility of handling the redundancy itself.

Redundancy, like the poor, has always been with us. It frequently results from adverse trading conditions, especially during a recession, exacerbated by global competition. Government austerity programmes lead to redundancies in the public sector. The drive for competitive advantage has forced employers 'to take costs out of the business', another euphemism for getting rid of people, employment costs being the ones on which organizations in both the private and public sectors focus as they are usually the largest element in their cost structures. Costs have been reduced by 'delayering' (eliminating what are deemed to be unnecessary layers of management) and outsourcing. Flexibility programmes (see Chapter 31) have led to head-count (number employed) reductions. The pursuit of 'rightsizing' (another egregious euphemism) has resulted in losses. The introduction of new technology (especially computerization) has contributed hugely to the reduction of semi-skilled or unskilled people in offices or on the shop floor. And benchmarking to find out how other organizations 'do more with less' is another factor.

What organizations should do about redundancy

Organizations should:

- plan ahead to achieve headcount reductions without involuntary redundancy;
- adopt other methods of reducing numbers or avoiding redundancy;
- encourage voluntary redundancy if other methods fail;
- introduce a redundancy procedure or ensure that an existing procedure is satisfactory;
- develop fair and considerate methods of handling redundancy;
- help redundant employees through outplacement policies and practices.

Planning ahead

Planning ahead means that future reductions in people needs are anticipated and the normal flow of leavers (natural wastage) is allowed to cater for future requirements to reduce the head count. Recruitment can be frozen in the occupations likely to be affected. Plans to minimize redundancy can also include calling in outsourced work, reducing or eliminating overtime, reducing the number of part-timers and temporary staff, work-sharing (two people splitting one job between them) or, more reluctantly, reduction in working hours or temporary layoffs.

Voluntary redundancy

Asking for volunteers – with a suitable payoff – is another way of reducing compulsory redundancies. The disadvantage is that the wrong people might go, ie the good workers who find it easy to get other work. Such people can be offered a special loyalty bonus if they stay on.

Outplacement

Outplacement is about helping redundant employees to find other work and to cope with the problems they face. It can take place through specialized outplacement consultants and counselling or by setting up 'job shops'.

Outplacement consultants provide counselling on how people can make the best use of what they can offer to other employers. They can be helped to identify their strengths and achievements, the type of job they are qualified to do and the sort of employer that is most likely to want people with their experience and qualifications. Assistance can be provided in preparing what is sometimes called an 'achievement CV', which spells out what the individual has been successful in and prompts the thought in the new employer's mind: 'What the individual has done for them he or she can do for us.'

Counselling involves help and advice in identifying possible moves, preparing CVs and how to make the best impression in interviews. Counselling may be provided by HR staff, but there is much to be said for using specialized outplacement consultants.

Job shops. The staff of the job shop, who may be from HR or are sometimes members of a specialized outplacement consultancy, scour the travel-to-work area seeking job opportunities, match people to jobs and arrange interviews.

Dismissal

Dismissal takes place when an employer terminates the employment of someone with or without notice. A contract can be terminated as a result of demotion or transfer, as well as dismissal. People can be 'constructively dismissed' if they resign because of their employer's unreasonable behaviour.

Approach to dismissal

Dismissals should be handled in accordance with the following principles of natural justice:

- Individuals should know the standards of performance they are expected to meet and the rules to which they are expected to conform.

- They should be given a clear indication of where they are failing or what rules they have broken.

- Except in cases of gross misconduct, they should be given an opportunity to improve before disciplinary action is taken.

Disciplinary procedure

These principles should form the basis of a disciplinary procedure, which is staged as follows:

- An informal discussion on the problem.
- A first written warning.
- A final written warning.
- Dismissal or action short of dismissal such as loss of pay or demotion.

Employees should be reminded of their right to be accompanied by a colleague or employee representative in disciplinary hearings. (An example of a full disciplinary procedure incorporating the stages listed above is given in Chapter 10.)

Managers and team leaders should be made aware of the procedure and told what authority they have to take action. It is advisable to have all written warnings and any final action approved by a higher authority. In cases of gross misconduct, managers and team leaders should be given the right to suspend if higher authority is not available, but not to dismiss. The importance of obtaining and recording the facts should be emphasized. Managers should always have a colleague with them when issuing a final warning and should make a note to file of what was said on the spot.

Key learning points: Release from the organization

Redundancy

Redundancy takes place when the organization as a whole is reducing the number of employees, when structural changes are being made following mergers and acquisitions, and when individual jobs are no longer needed.

What organizations should do about redundancy:

- plan ahead to achieve headcount reductions without involuntary redundancy;

- adopt other methods of reducing numbers or avoiding redundancy;

- encourage voluntary redundancy if other methods fail;

- introduce a redundancy procedure or ensure that an existing procedure is satisfactory;

- develop fair and considerate methods of handling redundancy;

- help redundant employees through outplacement policies and practices.

Dismissal

Dismissal takes place when an employer terminates the employment of someone with or without notice. A contract can be terminated as a result of demotion or transfer, as well as dismissal. People can be 'constructively dismissed' if they resign because of their employer's unreasonable behaviour.

Dismissals should be handled in accordance with the following principles of natural justice:

- Individuals should know the standards of performance they are expected to meet and the rules to which they are expected to conform.

- They should be given a clear indication of where they are failing or what rules they have broken.

- Except in cases of gross misconduct, they should be given an opportunity to improve before disciplinary action is taken.

These principles should form the basis of a disciplinary procedure.

28
Managing employee retention

LEARNING OUTCOMES

On completing this chapter you should be able to define these key concepts. You should also know about:

- Measuring employee turnover
- Estimating the cost of employee turnover
- Retention planning
- Risk of leaving analysis

Introduction

Losing key employees can have a disproportionate impact on the business. The people that organizations wish to retain are often the ones most likely to leave. It has been said that every worker is five minutes away from handing in his or her notice, and 150 working hours away from walking out of the door to a better offer. There is no such thing as a job for life and today's workers have few qualms about leaving employers. Action is required to retain talented people, but there are limits to what any organization can do.

Employees are more likely to stay willingly if they feel valued, and ensuring that this happens is the most important message of this chapter. But actions to increase employee retention will be influenced by data on employee turnover or wastage and this chapter therefore starts with an examination of how turnover can be measured and what can be done with the data. The second part of the chapter covers methods of dealing with employee retention problems in the light of information about its incidence and causes.

Employee turnover

Employee turnover (sometimes known as 'labour turnover', 'labour wastage' or 'attrition') is the rate at which people leave an organization. It can be disruptive and costly. The CIPD (2013) *Survey of Resourcing and Talent Planning* found that the average rate of turnover (the number leaving as a percentage of the number employed) in the UK was 11.9 per cent. It has fallen considerably since 2006 when it was 18.3 per cent.

The cost of employee turnover can be considerable. The CIPD 2008 survey established that the average cost per employee was £5,800, rising to £20,000 for senior managers or directors. Cost estimates are useful as means of backing up a business case for taking action to reduce turnover. The following factors should be considered when calculating costs:

- direct cost of recruiting replacements (advertising, interviewing, testing, etc);
- direct cost of introducing replacements (induction cost);
- direct cost of training replacements in necessary skills;
- leaving costs – payroll and HR administration;
- opportunity cost of time spent by HR and line managers in recruitment, induction and training;
- loss of output from those leaving before they are replaced;
- loss of output because of delays in obtaining replacements;
- loss of output while new starters are on their learning curves acquiring the necessary knowledge and skills.

Research by Phillips (1990) found that the 'visible' (ie direct) costs of recruitment accounted for only 10 to 15 per cent of total costs. By far the highest costs were associated with the inefficiencies arising while the post was vacant (33 per cent) and the inefficiency of new workers (32 per cent). On average, 12.5 months were required for executives to be comfortable in a new position and 13.5 months were required for a new employee to achieve maximum efficiency.

It is necessary to measure employee turnover and calculate its costs in order to identify problems such as adverse trends and forecast future losses for planning purposes. Plans can then be made to reduce unnecessary turnover and its associated costs. There are a number of different methods.

Employee turnover index

The employee turnover index (sometimes referred to as the employee or labour wastage index) shown below is the traditional formula for measuring turnover:

$$\frac{\text{Number of leavers in a specified}}{\text{period (usually 1 year)}} \times 100$$
$$\frac{}{\text{Average number of employees}}$$
$$\text{during the same period}$$

This method is in common use because it is easy to calculate and to understand. It is a simple matter to work out that, if last year 30 out of an average force of 150 employees left (20 per cent turnover) and this trend continues, then the company will have to recruit 108 employees during the following year to increase and to hold the workforce at 200 in that year (50 extra employees, plus 40 to replace the 20 per cent wastage of the average 200 employees employed, plus 18 to replace wastage of the 90 recruits).

The formula is simple, but it can be misleading. The problem is that the percentage may be inflated by the high turnover of a relatively small proportion of the workforce, especially in times of heavy recruitment. Thus, a company employing 1,000 people might have had an annual wastage rate of 20 per cent, meaning that 200 jobs had become vacant during the year. But this could have been spread throughout the company, covering all occupations and long- as well as short-service employees. Alternatively, it could have been restricted to a small sector of the workforce – only 20 jobs might have been affected although each of these had to be filled 10 times during the year. These are different situations and unless they are understood, inaccurate forecasts would be made of future requirements and inappropriate actions would be taken to deal with the problem. The turnover index is also suspect if the average number of employees upon which the percentage is based is unrepresentative of recent trends because of considerable increases or decreases during the period in the numbers employed.

Stability index

The stability index is considered by many to be an improvement on the turnover index. The formula is:

$$\frac{\text{Number with 1 years' service or more}}{\text{Number employed 1 year ago}} \times 100$$

Survival rate

The survival rate is the proportion of employees who are engaged within a certain period who remain with the organization after so many months or years of service. Thus, an analysis of a cohort of 20 trainees who have completed their training might show that after two years, 10 of the original trainees were still with the company, a survival rate of 50 per cent. The distribution of losses for each entry group, or cohort, can be plotted in the form of a survival curve, as shown in Figure 28.1.

The basic shape of this curve has been found to be similar in many situations, although the peak of the curve may occur further along the time scale and/or may be lower when it relates to more highly

skilled or trained entry cohorts. An example of a survival rate analysis is shown in Table 28.1. This indicates that half the number of recruits in any one year may be lost over the next five years, unless something can be done about the factors causing wastage.

The survival rate is useful as a means of tracking a 'cohort' of recruits (eg graduates) to assess the effectiveness of recruitment and retention policies. But it cannot be used as a means of measuring the turnover rates of whole populations in order to allow for future wastage when making supply forecasts.

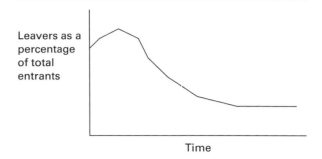

FIGURE 28.1   A survival curve

TABLE 28.1   A survival rate analysis

Entry cohort	Original number	Number surviving to end of year after engagement				
		Year 1	Year 2	Year 3	Year 4	Year 5
A	40	35	28	26	22	20
B	32	25	24	19	18	16
C	48	39	33	30	27	24
D	38	32	27	24	22	19
E	42	36	30	26	23	21
Total	200	167	142	125	112	100
Average survival rate	100%	83%	71%	62%	56%	50%

demands of the work they have to do. Rapid turnover can result simply from poor selection or promotion decisions.

3 Reduce the losses of people who cannot adjust to their new job – the 'induction crisis' – by giving them proper training and support when they join the organization.

4 Design jobs to maximize skill variety, task significance, autonomy, control over work and feedback, and ensure that they provide opportunities for learning and growth. Some roles can be 'customized' to meet the needs of particular individuals.

5 Deal with uncompetitive, inequitable or unfair pay systems. But as Cappelli (2000) pointed out, there is a limit to the extent to which people can be bribed to stay.

6 Encourage the development of social ties within the company. In the words of Cappelli (2000: 108), 'loyalty to companies may be disappearing but loyalty to colleagues is not'.

7 Take steps to improve work–life balance by developing policies, including flexible working, that recognize the needs of employees outside work.

8 Eliminate as far as possible unpleasant working conditions or the imposition of too much stress on employees.

9 Select, brief and train managers and team leaders so that they appreciate the positive contribution they can make to improving retention by the ways in which they lead their teams. Bear in mind that people often leave their managers rather than their organization.

10 Improve arrangements for giving employees a voice on matters that concern them.

11 Pay close attention to communications with employees to explain what is happening and underline improvements to their conditions of employment. Use all forms of media including social media.

12 Ensure that policies for controlling bullying and harassment are in place and are applied.

References

Bevan, S, Barber, I and Robinson, D (1997) *Keeping the Best: A practical guide to retaining key employees*, Brighton, Institute for Employment Studies

Cappelli, P (2000) A market-driven approach to retaining talent, *Harvard Business Review*, January–February, pp 103–11

CIPD (2008) *Survey of Recruitment, Retention and Turnover*, London, CIPD

CIPD (2013) *Survey of Resourcing and Talent Planning* [online] http://www.cipd.co.uk/binaries/resourcing-and-talent-planning_2013.PDF [accessed 26 October 2015]

CIPD (2015) *Survey of Resourcing and Talent Planning* [online] http://www.cipd.co.uk/hr-resources/survey-reports/resourcing-talent-planning-2015.aspx [accessed 26 October 2015]

Holbeche, L (1998) *Motivating People in Lean Organizations*, Oxford, Butterworth-Heinemann

Phillips, J D (1990) The price tag of turnover, *Personnel Journal*, December, pp 58–61

29
Absence management

KEY CONCEPTS AND TERMS

Absence management

The Bradford Factor

LEARNING OUTCOMES

On completing this chapter you should be able to define these key concepts. You should also know about:

- The causes of absences
- Absence management policies
- Controlling short- and long-term absence

Introduction

Absence or attendance management is the development and application of policies and procedures designed to reduce levels of absenteeism. The CIPD (2015) *Survey of Absence Management* revealed that:

- the average length of employee absence was 6.9 days per employee per year;
- larger organizations have higher average levels of absence than smaller organizations;
- on average, two-thirds of working time lost to absence is accounted for by short-term absences of up to seven days; one-fifth is attributed to long-term absences;

- the average cost of absence was £554 per employee per year;
- musculoskeletal injuries and back pain are the more common causes of absence for manual workers, while stress is more common for non-manual workers.

Thirty per cent of respondents to the survey reported that non-genuine absence ('sickies') is one of their top causes of short-term absence for manual workers. Twenty-three per cent stated that this was the top cause for non-manual workers. Some respondents suggested that flexible working arrangements may help reduce non-genuine absence.

To do something about this situation means understanding the causes of absence, adopting comprehensive absence management (or, more positively, attendance management) policies, measuring absence and implementing procedures for the management of short- and long-term absence.

Causes of absence

The causes of absence have been analysed by Huczynski and Fitzpatrick (1989) under three headings: job situation factors, personal factors and attendance factors.

Job situation factors

- Job scope – a high degree of task repetitiveness is associated with absenteeism, although job satisfaction itself is a contributory rather than a primary cause of absence.
- Stress – it is estimated that 40 million working days are lost each year in the UK through stress. This can be attributed to work load, poor working conditions, shift work, role ambiguity or conflict, relationships and organizational climate.
- Frequent job transfers increase absenteeism.
- Management style – the quality of management, especially that of immediate supervisors, affects the level of absenteeism.
- Physical working conditions.
- Work group size – the larger the organization the higher the absence rate.

Personal factors

- Employee values – for some workers, doing less work for the same reward improves the deal made with the employer (the effort-reward bargain). The following positive outcomes of absence have been shown by research to be particularly important to employees: break from routine, leisure time, dealing with personal business and a break from co-workers.
- Age – younger employees are more frequently absent than older ones.

- Personality – some people are absence-prone (studies have noted that between 5 and 10 per cent of workers account for about half of the total absence, while a few are never absent at all).

Attendance factors

- Reward systems – as pay increases attendance improves.
- Sick-pay schemes may increase absenteeism.
- Work group norms can exert pressure for or against attendance.

Absence policies

Absence policies should cover:

- methods of measuring absence;
- setting targets for the level of absence;
- deciding on the level of short-term absence that would trigger action, possibly using the Bradford Factor, as explained below;
- the circumstances in which disciplinary action might be taken;
- what employees must do if they are unable to attend work;
- sick-pay arrangements;
- provisions for the reduction and control of absence such as return-to-work interviews;
- other steps that can be taken to reduce absence, such as flexible working patterns.

The skills required to manage absenteeism are examined in Chapter 76.

Recording and measuring absence

As a basis for action, absence levels need to be recorded so that they can be measured and monitored against targets for minimizing absenteeism.

An HR information system (HRIS) can provide the best means of recording absenteeism. If a self-service approach is in place, managers and team leaders have direct access to absence records showing the incidence of absenteeism (number and lengths of absence). This data can be consolidated for use by HR in compiling absence statistics and monitoring against targets. The most common measurement is the percentage of time available that has been lost due to absence.

The Bradford Factor

The Bradford Factor provides a useful measure. This index identifies persistent short-term absence by measuring the number and duration of spells of absence. Its exact origin is a mystery, although IDS (2007) believes that it has some connection with Bradford University's School of Management. It is calculated using the formula $S \times S \times D$ = Bradford points score, where S is the number of occasions of absence in the last 52 weeks and D is the total number of days' absence in the last 52 weeks. Thus, for employees with a total of 14 days' absence in a 52-week period, the Bradford score can vary enormously depending on the number of occasions involved. For example:

- one absence of 14 days is 14 points: $1 \times 1 \times 14$
- seven absences of two days each is 686 points: $7 \times 7 \times 14$
- 14 absences of one day each is 2,744 points: $14 \times 14 \times 14$

The Bradford index can be used as a trigger to initiate action. It is typically set at 250 points so that action would be initiated if, for example, there had been 10 days' absence over five spells.

Controlling short-term absence

Short-term absence can be controlled by the following:

- return-to-work interviews conducted by line managers, which can identify problems at an early stage and provide an opportunity for a discussion on ways of reducing absence;
- training line managers in methods of controlling absence, including return-to-work interviews;
- use of a trigger period to review attendance and if necessary issue a warning (the trigger period at the UK Department of Work and Pensions is eight days over 12 months); the Bradford Factor can be used as a trigger mechanism;
- invoking disciplinary procedures for unacceptable absence levels;
- extending the scope for flexible working.

Managing long-term absence

The best way to manage long-term absence is to keep in contact with employees by letter, telephone or visits to discuss the situation and, where possible, plan the return to work. This plan may include modified working hours or a modified role for a period.

CASE STUDIES

Controlling sickness absence at Wincanton

Distribution company Wincanton had a problem controlling sickness absence because its large workforce is spread over 285 sites. The solution was to outsource absence management to Active Health Partners, which operates a call centre staffed by nurses – employees must report their absences and can receive medical advice. An online absence recording system is also provided, which provides line managers with information on absences and access to absence statistics.

As soon as an employee calls Active Health Partners an e-mail or text is sent to the employee's line manager via an automated system, informing him or her of the absence and the reason for it and giving an approximate return-to-work date. The system also provides various triggers to line managers. For example, once an employee has been away for more than 15 days, the manager receives a message indicating that contact needs to be made. Managers are expected to conduct return-to-work interviews and have more formal discussions when an absence exceeds 15 days.

They will explore why there has been this amount of time off, if there is an underlying health issue, if an employee should be referred to Occupational Health and if the disciplinary process should be started.

As a result, Wincanton reduced sickness absence by 10,000 days in six months.

Absence management at Westminster City Council

Monitoring

Sickness absence is recorded by line managers on the intranet system.

Return-to-work interviews

A return-to-work interview is held between the manager and the employee after any length of absence, even one day, although this may only take a couple of minutes. Employees are required to complete a self-certification/return to work form. Employees who have been absent for eight days or more are informed that they will be referred to Occupational Health.

Absence trigger points

An employee who has had more than seven days' sickness absence in any rolling 365-day period is dealt with through the 'enhanced sickness management procedure'. If sickness absence exceeds 20 days, the long-term sickness procedure is applied.

The enhanced sickness management procedure

- Line managers complete a referral form that is forwarded to Occupational Health staff who decide to conduct a face-to-face consultation or make a desktop assessment – and in either case provide any advice necessary to the manager or the individual and send a report to the manager and HR.

- Within 10 days of receiving the report the manager meets the employee to review the sickness record, consider any further explanations for the absence, discuss the report from Occupational Health and

agree action to improve attendance and minimize sickness.

- As necessary, especially in cases of disability, Occupational Health will discuss with the manager and the employee any reasonable adaptations to the work environment that may be helpful.

Long-term sickness absence management

- Every four weeks, managers review cases of long-term absence with the Occupational Health service and also contact the employee.

- If an employee has been off work the managers and Occupational Health hold a case conference to assess the situation. The employee is required to meet Occupational Health if this is possible.

- The manager makes an assessment following the case conference covering the nature and likely length of the illness, the impact of the absence on the work and how any impact will be managed.

- Following this assessment a face-to-face meeting is held with the employee to ensure that other relevant factors and personal circumstances are taken into account.

- A sickness absence hearing may be called as a result of this meeting and the case conference.

Employee assistance programme

An employee assistance programme (EAP) is available through an external provider. Employees can raise problems with helpline staff, and face-to-face counselling can be made available.

Key learning points: Absence management

Absence or attendance management is the development and application of policies and procedures designed to reduce levels of absenteeism.

Causes of absence

The causes of absence have been analysed by Huczynski and Fitzpatrick (1989) under three headings: job situation factors, personal factors and attendance factors.

Absence policies

Absence policies should cover:

- methods of measuring absence;
- setting targets for the level of absence;
- deciding on the level of short-term absence that would trigger action, possibly using the Bradford Factor;
- the circumstances in which disciplinary action might be taken;
- what employees must do if they are unable to attend work;
- sick-pay arrangements;
- provisions for the reduction and control of absence such as return-to-work interviews;
- other steps that can be taken to reduce absence, such as flexible working patterns.

Recording and measuring absence

As a basis for action, absence levels need to be recorded so that they can be measured and monitored against targets for maintaining absence at a certain level, or reducing absenteeism.

Controlling short-term absence

Short-term absence can be controlled by the following:

- return-to-work interviews conducted by line managers, which can identify problems at an early stage and provide an opportunity for a discussion on ways of reducing absence;
- use of trigger mechanisms such as the Bradford Factor to review attendance;
- invoking disciplinary procedures for unacceptable absence levels;
- training line managers in methods of controlling absence, including return-to-work interviews;
- extending the scope for flexible working.

Managing long-term absence

The best way to manage long-term absence is to keep in contact with employees by letter, telephone or visits to discuss the situation and, where possible, plan the return to work. This plan may include modified working hours or a modified role for a period.

References

Huczynski, A A and Fitzpatrick, M J (1989) *Managing Employee Absence for a Competitive Edge*, London, Pitman

IDS (2007) Absence Management, HR Study 810, London, IDS

CIPD (2015) *Survey of Absence Management*, CIPD [online] http://www.cipd.co.uk/hr-resources/survey-reports/absence-management-2015.aspx [accessed 27 October 2015]

30
Managing diversity and inclusion

KEY CONCEPTS AND TERMS

Diversity

Inclusion

LEARNING OUTCOMES

On completing this chapter you should be able to define these key concepts. You should also know about:

- The meaning of diversity and inclusion
- The rationale for managing diversity and inclusion
- How to manage diversity and inclusion

Introduction

The management of diversity and inclusion is based on the proposition that everyone should be valued as an individual and treated fairly irrespective of their race, gender, level of disability, religion, sexual orientation or age. A number of personal characteristics are covered by discrimination law to give people protection to ensure that this happens. These 'protected characteristics' are race, disability, gender reassignment, sex, marriage and civil partnership, pregnancy and maternity, religion and belief, sexual orientation and age. But it is not enough to rely on the law. More needs to be done to create and maintain a culture which recognizes that, although people are different, they all need to be treated in ways that are fair and tailored to their individual needs, and which ensure they feel that they belong and that they are important to the organization.

This chapter examines the meaning and significance of managing diversity and inclusion and the ways in which they can be managed.

The meaning and significance of managing diversity and inclusion

Managing diversity in the workplace means bringing together people of different ethnic backgrounds, religions, gender and age groups into cohesive and productive organizational units. It involves formulating and implementing policies and processes that maximize the potential advantages of diversity while minimizing the potential disadvantages. It means developing a culture which spells out that 'this is the way we do things around here about diversity'. It is a concept that recognizes the benefits to be gained from differences. It is not the same as equal opportunity, which aims to legislate against discrimination, assumes that people should be assimilated into the organization and, often, relies on affirmative action.

Managing inclusion is about forming and maintaining a culture in which individuals of all backgrounds – not just members of historically favoured groups – are fairly treated and valued for who they are. Inclusive cultures are characterized by a collective commitment to integrating diverse identities as a source of insight and skill. It is the process of ensuring that people feel they belong and are connected.

The management of diversity and the management of inclusion are closely connected. In fact, they overlap and much of what can be done to improve one will affect the other. But both diversity issues concerning distinct groups of people and more general inclusion issues need to be considered when developing policy and practice and ensuring that everyone knows what they need to do through means such as communications, workshops and training interventions. Stephen Frost, who headed the highly successful diversity and inclusion programme for the London 2012 Olympics, was quoted by the CIPD (2012a: 5) as saying: 'It is important to recognize the easy potential trap of achieving diversity without inclusion, and inclusion without diversity. Only both in unison really add value to the organization.'

As Nishii (2013: 1754–55) pointed out: 'To the extent that diversity management practices that focus specifically on improving the outcomes of historically disadvantaged groups cause resentment or backlash on the part of individuals who do not directly benefit from these practices, they can have the unintended effect of exacerbating negative stereotypes and perceived intergroup competition... To really manage both the problems and the potential benefits associated with diversity, organizations need to create environments that are inclusive of all employees.'

The rationale for managing diversity and inclusion

The case for managing diversity was made by Kandola and Fullerton (1994) as follows:

> The basic concept of managing diversity accepts that the workforce consists of a diverse population of people. The diversity consists of visible and non-visible differences which include factors such as sex, age, background, race, disability, personality and workstyle. It is founded on the premise that harnessing these differences will create a productive environment in which everybody feels valued, where their talents are being fully utilized and in which organizational goals are met.

There is a social justice argument for pursuing diversity and inclusion policies: everyone has the right to be treated fairly in a workplace which values the differences between people and which promotes an environment of fairness, dignity and respect. They will have career development and promotion opportunities based on merit and will be given the opportunity for work–life balance – for example, through working flexible hours.

There is also a business case. The effective management of diversity and inclusion can help to increase levels of engagement, promote cooperation and reduce conflict. It can provide for the best candidates from the widest possible pool of applicants to be selected for jobs.

How to manage diversity and inclusion

The overall aim of a diversity and inclusion programme should be to achieve culture change so that the approach to dealing with diversity and inclusion issues becomes a way of life for all concerned. To manage diversity and inclusion by achieving culture change it is necessary to:

- develop a diversity and inclusion strategy;
- define the values of the organization concerning diversity and inclusion;
- set out the diversity and inclusion policies of the organization;
- implement programmes for communicating the values and policies;
- pay particular attention to potential problem areas – recruitment, appointments and promotions, learning and career development opportunities and pay;
- devise and run training programmes designed to increase awareness and influence behaviour;
- create diversity networks as described later;
- monitor progress and evaluate training.

Diversity and inclusion strategy

When developing a diversity and inclusion strategy it is first necessary to ensure that initiatives will have the support of the board and senior management. This will mean preparing a business case but equal emphasis should be placed on the moral imperative. In preparing the business case, consideration should be given to the areas of diversity and inclusion that should be covered. A survey by the CIPD (2012b) found that the most typical areas included in the programmes of the respondents were gender, ethnicity, age, disability, sexual orientation and religion. These would be appropriate in most organizations.

The strategy should make it plain that the focus will be on fairness and inclusion, ensuring that merit, competence and potential are the basis for all decisions about recruitment and development, and being alert to the influence of conscious and unconscious biases. But it should emphasize that the aim will be to support business goals as well as responding to moral imperatives. The strategy should also cover the need to define the values of the organization concerning diversity and inclusion and it should stress the importance of involving employees both in agreeing those values and, importantly, discussing how they should be put into effect as 'values in use'.

A broad indication of the methods that will be used in a programme for managing diversity and inclusion, such as communications, the creation of diversity networks and training, should be given, bearing in mind that managing diversity and inclusion is a continuous process of improvement, not a one-off initiative. Additionally, the strategy should set out the employment areas that will be covered. These are typically recruitment and selection, performance management, rewards, opportunities for learning and development, career development and talent management, and work–life balance.

Consideration should be given to what needs to be done to deal specifically with diversity and with inclusion. Actions should be planned which will support the management of diversity and other actions proposed which will support the management of inclusion. There will be some planned actions which support both diversity and inclusion.

For example, Northern Rail introduced diversity ambassadors, an inclusion charter, and e-learning on unconscious bias. It reached out to local schools and colleges, and targeted advertising on Asian TV networks to encourage candidates from previously untapped audiences.

Defining the values

The values could be defined under such headings as

- fairness;
- equality;
- inclusion;
- respect for the individual;
- care for the individual;
- valuing individuals;
- developing staff and their careers.

It is important to involve employees in discussing these values.

Diversity and inclusion policy

A policy on managing diversity should be produced to provide guidelines to managers on their role in managing diversity, and information to employees in general on the part they are expected to play. It could:

- acknowledge cultural and individual differences in the workplace;
- state that the organization values the different qualities that people bring to their jobs;
- emphasize the need to eliminate bias in such areas as selection, promotion, performance assessment, pay and learning opportunities;
- indicate the need to promote inclusion, the process of ensuring that people from all backgrounds feel they belong and are connected;
- focus attention on individual differences rather than group differences.

Critical areas

The critical areas where there can be diversity and inclusion issues are recruitment, appointments and promotions, learning and career development opportunities, pay, and bullying and harassment. In each case, policies and definitions of good practice need to be developed to avoid biased and prejudiced decisions. These policies and practices should be communicated extensively and form the base of training programmes.

Communicating

It is essential to let everyone know about the diversity and inclusion values and policies of the organization and what is being done about them. This is a continuous process, not a one-off campaign. All available media should be used, including newsletters, the intranet, enterprise social networks, consultative committees, briefing groups, in-house magazines and notice bards.

Training

The aims of diversity and inclusion training should be to alert people to the importance of dealing with the issues involved, communicate the values and policies of the organization and indicate the sort of behaviours required. This should be part of the induction training programmes for new employees. It should be provided for all existing managers and those who are about to be promoted, and should emphasize the vital part they have to play in creating an inclusive culture and how they should set about doing it. Specifically, the training for managers should cover how to create an inclusive culture, leadership behaviours, interviewing and assessing people, performance management and dealing with bullying and harassment. Briefing programmes for other members of staff should also be held.

The methods used should be participative – the minimum amount of lecturing and the maximum amount of participation in discussions, the analysis of case studies, and role plays illustrating situations where bias might creep in and what can be done about it.

Diversity networks

Diversity networks can be set up which act as support groups for minority staff to share problems and swap tips. But they can additionally help organizations to understand the people who work for them and help the business to perform better. For example:

- At Cisco, the women's network helps business development by hosting events for prospective and existing customers.
- At PwC there are four main networks: for women, ethnic minorities, disabled people and GLEE (an inclusive business network for gays, lesbians and everyone else).
- At BT a disability network focuses on awareness raising about different disabilities to help managers understand them and get the best from people living with a disability. 'Knowledge calls' are provided which consist of presentations done via conference calls and desktop technology with expert speakers on particular subjects such as Parkinson's and migraines. They typically include someone who has experienced the condition, a Q&A session and inputs from HR relating to the condition or disability. There are online forums and sub-groups offering support.

Evaluation

It is essential to monitor and evaluate progress. The key performance indicators that can be used for evaluating progress are representation/demographic data by group of employee, employee survey results, and trend data on demographics by recruitment and by promotions. Actions should be tracked to see if they have had the intended results so that changes can be made if necessary.

CASE STUDY

London 2012 Olympics

Stephen Frost made the following comments about the London 2012 Olympics diversity and inclusion programme in the CIPD 2012(a) publication 'Game on! How to keep diversity progress on track':

- We were able to achieve significant, and in some cases unprecedented, diversity in our workforce of 200,000, increasing a 30 per cent ethnic minority to 49 per cent. This happened because of strong and thoughtful leadership and the achievement of effective delivery with limited resources (in terms of people and money).

- We had to work hard, be bold and, to a certain extent, experiment in order to integrate diversity and inclusion as core to our way of doing business.

- To help everyone to understand diversity and inclusion and its organizational relevance, it is important to provide practical examples of what it means to people.

- Leadership is critical in terms of executing diversity and inclusion, but many people (especially 'management') fail to realize that everyone at all levels can be empowered to lead, and lead on diversity and inclusion issues.

- It is definitely the case that without strong top team leadership backing for diversity and inclusion, progress and traction suffers hugely. Nevertheless, leadership is not only the preserve of the top team. Everyone can be, and should be encouraged to be, a leader. We set in place several frameworks to help everyone act as a leader to drive the diversity and inclusion agenda. The most important frameworks we put in place were our Leadership Pledge and our Diversity Board.

- The Leadership Pledge was launched by Paul Deighton, CEO, Sebastian Coe, Chair, and Archbishop Desmond Tutu. It was a voluntary process that people signed up to which was designed to get them to think about and integrate diversity and inclusion into everything they did and every decision they made. Over 90 per cent of our workforce signed up to the pledge as part of their induction – and it was something which we constantly and consistently reinforced.

- The second important leadership framework we had was our Diversity Board, chaired by Paul Deighton. Membership of this board included directors across the business and each was accountable for leading a stream of diversity and inclusion. The board also included a number of well-known external people recognized for their personal interest and influence in diversity and inclusion.

- The Diversity Board had a crucial role in making sure the Diversity and Inclusion Team and functional management were held to account for progressing diversity and inclusion and maintaining momentum. This leadership mechanism helped to keep people on their toes and to maintain traction.

- To be successful in making diversity and inclusion responses systemic, it is vital that each functional area of an organization takes responsibility for it and is held accountable for driving the agenda, and that everyone involved in the diversity and inclusion team feels empowered to lead.

- Delivering well meant tracking our achievement of results. We did this by carrying out granular, detailed work on diversity and inclusion metrics and indicators across departments and across our total workforce on a monthly basis. We found that the use of different league tables based on this comparative data provided an internal competitive stimulus for the progress of diversity and inclusion.

Key learning points: Managing diversity and inclusion

The management of diversity and inclusion is based on the proposition that everyone should be valued as an individual and treated fairly.

The meaning and significance of managing diversity and inclusion

Managing diversity in the workplace means bringing together people of different ethnic backgrounds, religions, gender and age groups into cohesive and productive organizational units.

Managing inclusion is about forming and maintaining a culture in which individuals of all backgrounds – not just members of historically favoured groups – are fairly treated and valued for who they are.

The rationale for managing diversity and inclusion

There is a social justice argument for pursuing diversity and inclusion policies: everyone has the right to be treated fairly in a workplace which values the differences between people and which promotes an environment of fairness, dignity and respect.

There is also a business case. The effective management of diversity and inclusion can help to increase levels of engagement, promote cooperation and reduce conflict.

How to manage diversity and inclusion

To manage diversity and inclusion it is necessary to:

- develop a diversity and inclusion strategy;
- define the values of the organization concerning diversity and inclusion;
- set out the diversity and inclusion policies of the organization;
- implement programmes for communicating the values and policies;
- pay particular attention to potential problem areas – recruitment, appointments and promotions, learning and career development opportunities and pay;
- devise and run training programmes designed to increase awareness and influence behaviour;
- create diversity networks;
- monitor progress and evaluate training.

References

CIPD (2012a) Game on! How to keep diversity progress on track, *CIPD* [online] http://www.cipd.co.uk/binaries/game-on-how-to-keep-diversity-progress-on-track_2012.pdf [accessed 30 October 2015]

CIPD (2012b) Diversity and inclusion: Fringe or fundamental? *CIPD* [online] www.cipd.co.uk/binaries/diversity-and-inclusion_2012-fringe-or-fundamental.pdf [accessed 30 October 2015]

Kandola, R and Fullerton, J (1994) *Managing the Mosaic: Diversity in action*, London, CIPD

Nishii, L H (2013) The benefits of climate for inclusion for gender-diverse groups *Academy of Management Journal*, **56** (6), pp 1754–74

31
Managing flexibility

LEARNING OUTCOMES

On completing this chapter you should be able to define these key concepts. You should also know about:

- Why flexibility is important
- The nature of the flexible firm

- The different types of flexibility
- Zero-hours contracts

Introduction

Organizations today have to be able to adjust quickly and smoothly to rapidly changing circumstances. They have to be flexible. This was the case in 1984 when John Atkinson wrote his seminal article 'Manpower strategies for flexible organizations'. He stated that: '[Firms] have put a premium on achieving a workforce which can respond quickly, easily and cheaply to workforce changes, which may need to contract as smoothly as they expand, in which worked time precisely matches job requirements, in which unit labour costs can be held down.' This applies as much today as it did then.

The aim of managing flexibility is to satisfy the operational requirements spelled out above and in so doing, improve the use of employees' skills and capacities, increase productivity and reduce employment costs. It was suggested by Atkinson (1984) that, overall, managing flexibly is based on his concept of the flexible firm.

The flexible firm

The flexible firm model was developed by Atkinson (1984) following research by the Institute of Manpower Studies. It makes a distinction between the core and the peripheral workforce. It is sometimes called the 'core-peripheral model.' As illustrated in Figure 31.1 the model consists of:

1 *The core* which consists of workers who have the security of permanent (ie not fixed-term) contracts, and have skills which are very important to the employer. These employees are able to apply their skills across a wide range of tasks. The firm will want to retain these employees even in hard times.

2 *The first peripheral group* comprises workers who are employed on contracts which have some degree of permanence (some part-timers could be included in this category), but due to their lower levels of skills they will not have the same level of security as their colleagues in the core. Typically, their work will be characterized by little responsibility and lower pay. These employees can be laid off relatively easily since people with similar skills can be hired quickly if necessary.

3 *The second peripheral group* consists of workers who are part-timers or are on temporary contracts. They have little employment security and can be taken on or discharged easily.

4 *The external workforce* consists of people who work for another employer or are self-employed. This includes workers in firms to which work has been sub-contracted or outsourced and agency workers.

The flexible firm model is a convenient method of summing up the ways in which firms can achieve flexibility by using various types of peripheral workers while retaining a core of essential employees. But it cannot fully represent the reality of how firms manage flexibility. This is more likely to be on an ad hoc basis, selecting whatever method of dealing with employment problems is readily available rather than consciously and systematically applying the model to their organization. Hunter and MacInnes (1991) found little evidence of a drive towards the flexible

firm in the companies they studied which were selected on the basis of likely fit with the model. However, the model is a help to understanding how the various forms of flexible working can take place. This means reconsidering traditional employment patterns and, as described below, could include operational flexibility, multiskilling, flexible hours, or adopting different working arrangements such as job sharing, homeworking and 'hot desking.'

Operational flexibility

Operational flexibility refers to flexibility in the ways in which work is carried out. The three main forms of operational flexibility are:

● Functional flexibility so that employees can be redeployed quickly and smoothly between activities and tasks. It may require multi-skilling – workers who possess and can apply a number of skills, for example, both mechanical and electrical engineering, or multitasking – workers who carry out a number of different tasks in a work team.

● Structural flexibility in a 'flexible firm' where the core of permanent employees is supplemented by a peripheral group of part-time employees, employees on short- or fixed-term contracts or sub-contracted workers.

● Numerical flexibility, which is associated with structural flexibility and means that the number of employees can be quickly and easily increased or decreased in line with even short-term changes in the level of demand for labour.

In addition, there is financial flexibility which provides for pay levels to reflect the state of supply and demand in the external labour market and also means the use of flexible pay systems that facilitate either functional or numerical flexibility.

Multiskilling

Multiskilling takes place when workers acquire through experience and training a range of different skills they can apply when carrying out different tasks (multitasking). This means that they can be

FIGURE 31.1 The core-periphery model (adapted from Atkinson, 1984)

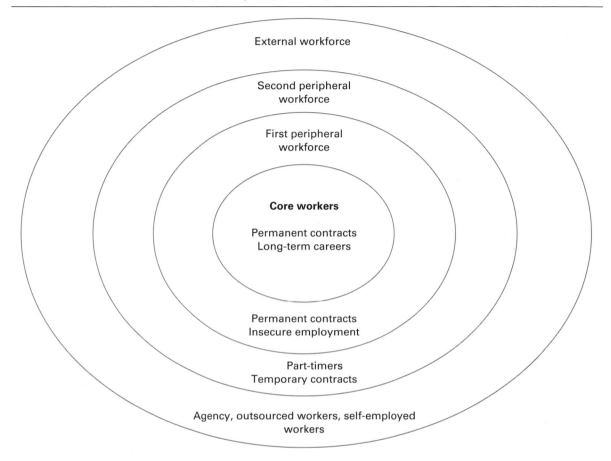

used flexibly, transferring from one task to another as the occasion demands.

A multiskilling strategy will mean providing people with a variety of experience through, for example, moving them between different jobs or tasks (job rotation) and secondments, and by making arrangements for them to acquire new skills through training. It typically includes setting up flexible work teams, the members of which can be deployed on all or many of the team's tasks. A flexible employee resourcing policy can then be established that enables the organization to redeploy people rapidly to meet new demands. This implies abandoning the traditional job description which prescribes the tasks to be carried and replacing it with a role profile which specifies the range of knowledge and skills the role holder needs to achieve the role's objectives.

Flexible hour arrangements

Flexible hour arrangements can be included in a flexibility plan in one or more of the following ways:

- flexible daily hours – these may follow an agreed pattern day by day according to typical or expected workloads;
- flexitime systems – these provide a core period when employees are expected to be at work (for example, between 11 am and 3 pm), while the rest of the working day is 'flexible time', in which employees can choose when they work, subject to achieving total daily, weekly or monthly hours in the region of what the employer expects, and subject to the necessary work being done;

- flexible weekly hours – providing for longer weekly hours to be worked at certain peak periods during the year;
- flexible daily and weekly hours – varying daily or weekly hours or a combination of both to match the input of hours to the required output. Such working times, unlike daily or weekly arrangements, may fluctuate between a minimum and a maximum;
- compressed working weeks in which employees work fewer than the five standard days;
- annual hours – scheduling employee hours on the basis of the number of hours to be worked, with provisions for the increase or reduction of hours in any given period, according to the demand for goods or services;
- zero-hours contracts – these have recently become prominent and controversial and are therefore dealt with separately below.

Zero-hours contracts

The CIPD (2015a) defines a zero-hours contract as 'an agreement between two parties that one may be asked to perform work for another but there are no minimum set contracted hours.' The contract will provide what pay the individual will get if he or she does work and will deal with circumstances in which work may be offered and possibly turned down.

The exact nature of zero-hours contracts may differ from organization to organization. For example:

- Individuals on zero-hours contracts may be engaged as employees or workers.
- In some zero-hours contracts the individual will be obliged to accept work if offered, but in others they will not.
- The pay arrangements and benefits provided may differ.

They are most suited to situations where work fluctuates unexpectedly so that the employer cannot always guarantee work, and are most common in retail, hospitality and restaurants.

Zero-hours contracts have received a very bad press but the CIPD (2015b) takes a more favourable view, summarized as follows:

Zero-hours contracts have sometimes, it seems, been singled out as an especially unfair form of employment. In our view, this is unjustified. Our research shows that zero-hours contracts appear to work well for many of those on them. But they are not for everybody and that's why zero- hours contract workers need to understand their employment rights as well as how these contracts are likely to work in practice. Zero-hours contracts work best when there's an element of give and take, a recognition that flexibility works both ways. A small minority of employers using them don't seem to recognize this, but there are many 'permanent' jobs where the actions of employers can make them anything but secure. There may be too much emphasis at times on the precise terms of the employment contract, with not enough attention given to the spirit in which the employment relationship is conducted.

Other forms of flexible working

Job sharing

This is an arrangement in which two employees share the work of one full-time position, dividing pay and benefits between them according to the time each works. Job sharing can mean splitting days or weeks or, less frequently, working alternate weeks. Because it may suit the needs of individuals, job sharing can reduce employee turnover and absenteeism. There can be greater operational continuity because if one half of the job-sharing team is ill or leaves, the sharer will continue working for at least half the time. Job sharing also means that a wider employment pool can be tapped for those who cannot work full time but want permanent employment. The disadvantages are the administrative costs involved and the risk of responsibility being divided.

Hot desking

Hot desking means that individual desks are shared between several people who use them at different times. Those involved do not therefore have a permanent work station. This is convenient for the organization but not everyone likes it.

Homeworking

Home-based employees can carry out such roles as consultants, analysts, designers or programmers, or they can undertake administrative work. The advantages are flexibility to respond rapidly to fluctuations in demand, reduced overheads and lower employment costs if the homeworkers are self-employed (care, however, has to be taken to ensure that they are regarded as self-employed for Income Tax and National Insurance purposes).

Key learning points: Managing flexibility

Flexibility

Organizations today have to be able to adjust quickly and smoothly to rapidly changing circumstances. The aim of managing flexibility is to satisfy this requirement and in so doing, improve the use of employees' skills and capacities, increase productivity and reduce employment costs.

The flexible firm

The flexible firm model was developed by Atkinson (1984) following research by the Institute of Manpower Studies. It makes a distinction between the core and the peripheral workforce.

Operational flexibility

Operational flexibility refers to flexibility in the ways in which work is carried out. The three main forms of operational flexibility are: functional flexibility, structural flexibility and numerical flexibility.

Multiskilling

Multiskilling takes place when workers acquire through experience and training a range of different skills they can apply when carrying out different tasks (multitasking).

Flexible hour arrangements

Flexible hour arrangements can be included in a flexibility plan in one or more of the following ways: flexible daily hours, flexitime systems, flexible weekly hours, flexible daily and weekly hours, compressed working weeks, annual hours and zero-hours contracts.

Zero-hours contracts

The CIPD (2015) defines a zero-hours contract as 'an agreement between two parties that one may be asked to perform work for another but there are no minimum set contracted hours.' It believes that, used responsibly, zero-hours contracts can provide flexibility that works for both employers and individuals.

Hot desking

Hot desking means that individual desks are shared between several people who use them at different times.

Homeworking

Home-based employees can carry out such roles as consultants, analysts, designers or programmers, or they can undertake administrative work.

References

Atkinson, J (1984) Manpower strategies for the flexible organization, *Personnel Management*, August, pp 28–31

CIPD (2013) Zero-hours contracts: myth and reality, *CIPD* [online] http://www.cipd.co.uk/binaries/zero-hours-contracts_2013-myth-reality.pdf [accessed 29 October 2015]

CIPD (2015a) Fact sheet: zero-hours contracts, *CIPD* [online] http://www.cipd.co.uk/hr-resources/factsheets/zero-hours-contracts.aspx [accessed 29 October 2015]

CIPD (2015b) Zero-hours and Short-hours Contracts in the UK, *CIPD* [online] http://www.cipd.co.uk/binaries/zero-hours-and-short-hours-contracts-in-the-uk_2015-employer-employee-perspectives.pdf [accessed 26 December 2015]

Hunter, L and MacInnes J (1991) Employers' Labour Use Strategies, London, Employment Department Research Paper No 87

PART VII

Learning and development

Introduction

Learning and development (L&D) is defined as the process of ensuring that the organization has the knowledgeable, skilled and engaged workforce it needs and that individual employees have the opportunity to develop their abilities and maximize their potential. It means enabling the acquisition by individuals of knowledge and skills through experience, coaching provided by line managers and others, guidance and self-directed or self-managed learning activities carried out by individuals, and learning events, programmes and facilities provided by the organization.

The components of L&D are:

- *Learning* – the process by which a person acquires and develops knowledge, skills, capabilities, behaviours and attitudes. It involves the modification of behaviour through experience as well as more formal methods of helping people to learn within or outside the workplace.

- *Development* – the growth or realization of a person's ability and potential through the provision of learning and educational experiences.

- *Training* – the systematic application of formal processes to impart knowledge and help people to acquire the skills necessary for them to perform their jobs satisfactorily.

- *Education* – the development of the knowledge, values and understanding required in all aspects of life rather than the knowledge and skills relating to particular areas of activity.

Learning should be distinguished from training. 'Learning is the process by which a person constructs new knowledge, skills and capabilities, whereas training is one of several responses an organization can undertake to promote learning' (Reynolds *et al*, 2002: 9). Learning is what individuals do; training is what organizations do to individuals. The components of learning and development are shown in Figure 1.

The term 'learning and development' (L&D) has largely replaced that of 'human resource development' (HRD), at least for practitioners. Rosemary Harrison (2009: 5) observed that:

> The term human resource development retains its popularity among academics but it has never been attractive to practitioners. They tend to dislike it because they see its reference to people as a 'resource' to be demeaning. Putting people on a par with money, materials and equipment creates the impression of 'development' as an unfeeling, manipulative activity, although the two terms are almost indistinguishable.

The terms are indeed often used interchangeably by commentators and practitioners, although the introduction of 'learning' has emphasized the belief

FIGURE 1 (PART VII)   The components of learning and development

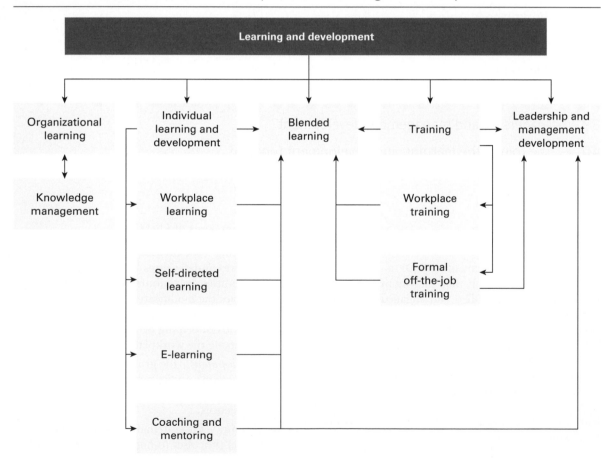

that what matters for individuals is that they are given the opportunity to learn, often for themselves, with guidance and support, rather than just being on the receiving end of what the organization provides.

This part deals with L&D under the following headings:

- strategic learning and development – how L&D is aligned to the business strategy; L&D strategy as affected by the concepts of the learning culture, organizational learning and the learning organization; the nature of individual learning;

- how people learn;

- the process of learning and development – identifying L&D needs, L&D activities (formal and informal learning, the 70\20\10 model, blended learning), evaluating L&D;

- workshop learning – where most learning takes place;

- social learning – the powerful influence of other people on the process of learning;

- e-learning – the use of electronic means to facilitate learning;

- planning and implementing learning events, training courses and development programmes of various kinds;

- leadership and management development – the planning and implementation of processes and programmes for developing leadership qualities and for developing managers generally;

- The often demanding role of the L&D function.

References

Harrison, R (2009) *Learning and Development*, 5th edn, London, CIPD

Reynolds, J, Caley, L and Mason, R (2002) *How Do People Learn?* London, CIPD

32
Strategic learning and development

KEY CONCEPTS AND TERMS

Communities of practice

Individual learning

Learning culture

Learning and development (L&D)

The learning organization

Organizational learning

Strategic L&D

LEARNING OUTCOMES

On completing this chapter you should be able to define these key concepts. You should also know about:

- The meaning and aims of strategic L&D
- The philosophy that underpins L&D strategy and practice
- The business case for L&D
- How L&D impacts on performance
- How to create a learning culture
- The concept of organizational learning
- The concept of the learning organization
- The nature of strategies for promoting individual learning

Introduction

Organizations need people with high and appropriate levels of knowledge, skills and abilities. Steps taken to meet this need are business-led in the sense that they are based on an understanding of the strategic imperatives of the business and support the achievement of its goals. But organizations also need to take account of the personal needs for development and growth of those they employ. This is good in itself but it means that the organization will be a more fulfilling and therefore attractive place in which to work.

The aim of this chapter is to define what is involved in strategic learning and development. It starts with a definition of strategic L&D and then deals with three important aspects of a strategic approach to L&D, namely the underpinning philosophy, the business case for L&D and the impact of L&D on performance.

The chapter continues with a description of the three areas in which fundamental L&D strategies are developed. These are the active components of an overall approach to strategic L&D. They express intentions on how L&D activities will take place and provide guidance on how these activities should be planned and implemented in order to ensure the L&D philosophy of the organization is acted upon. They are concerned with developing a learning culture, promoting organizational learning and providing for individual learning.

Strategic L&D defined

Strategic L&D is an approach to helping people to learn and develop that is concerned with how the organization's goals will be achieved through its human resources by means of integrated L&D strategies, policies and practices. Like strategic HRM, it is based on the fundamental proposition that the human resources of an organization play a strategic role in its success. Strategic L&D policies are closely associated with that aspect of strategic HRM concerned with investing in people and developing the organization's human capital.

The following definition of strategic HRD, produced by Walton (1999: 82), could serve equally well as a definition of strategic L&D:

> Strategic human resource development involves introducing, eliminating, modifying, directing, and guiding processes in such a way that all individuals and teams are equipped with the skills, knowledge and competences they require to undertake current and future tasks required by the organization.

Aims of strategic L&D

Strategic L&D aims to produce a coherent and comprehensive framework for developing people through the creation of a learning culture, the encouragement of organizational learning and the formulation of organizational and individual learning strategies. It exists to enhance resource capability in accordance with the belief that a firm's human resources are a major source of competitive advantage. It is therefore about developing the intellectual capital required by the organization as well as ensuring that people of the right quality are available to meet present and future needs.

The main thrust of strategic L&D is to provide an environment in which people are encouraged to learn and develop. Although it is business-led, its strategies have to take into account the needs of individual employees. The importance of increasing employability outside as well as within the organization is also a concern.

Learning and development philosophy

The philosophy underpinning strategic L&D is as follows:

- Learning and development activities make a major contribution to the successful attainment of the organization's objectives and investment in them benefits all the stakeholders of the organization.

- Learning and development plans and programmes should be integrated with and support the achievement of business and human resource strategies.

- Learning and development should be performance-related – designed to achieve specified improvements in corporate, functional, team and individual performance and make a major contribution to bottom-line results.

- Everyone in the organization should be encouraged and given the opportunity to learn – to develop their skills and knowledge to the maximum of their capacity.

- The framework for individual learning is provided by personal development plans that focus on self-managed learning and are supported by coaching, mentoring and formal training.

- The organization needs to invest in learning and development by providing appropriate learning opportunities and facilities, but the prime responsibility for learning and development rests with individuals, who will be given the guidance and support of their managers and, as necessary, members of the HR department.

The business case for L&D

The business case for learning and development should demonstrate how L&D programmes will meet business needs. Kearns and Miller (1997) go as far as to claim that if a business objective cannot be cited as a basis for designing training and development, then no training and development should be offered.

A cost/benefit analysis is required to compare the benefits, expressed in quantified terms as far as possible, that will result from the learning activity. The business case has to convince management that there will be an acceptable return on the investment (RoI) in learning and training programmes and events. It can be difficult to produce realistic figures, although the attempt is worth making with the help of finance specialists. The case for investing in L&D can refer to all or any of the following potential benefits:

- Improve individual, team and corporate performance.
- Attract high-quality employees by offering them learning and development opportunities, increasing their levels of competency and enhancing their skills, thus enabling them to obtain more job satisfaction, to gain higher rewards and to progress within the organization.
- Improve operational flexibility by extending the range of skills possessed by employees (multiskilling).
- Increase the commitment of employees by encouraging them to identify with the mission and objectives of the organization.
- Help to manage change by increasing understanding of the reasons for it and

providing people with the knowledge and skills they need to adjust to new situations.
- Provide line managers with the skills required to lead, manage and develop their people.
- Help to develop a positive culture in the organization, for example, one that is oriented towards performance improvement.
- Provide higher levels of service to customers.
- Minimize learning costs (reduce the length of learning curves).

The business case for L&D is enhanced by reference to research such as the examples given below.

Impact of learning and development on performance

Research by Benabou (1996) examined the impact of various training programmes on the business and financial results at 50 Canadian organizations. The conclusion reached was that in most cases a well-designed training programme can be linked to improvements in business results and that return on investment in training programmes is very high. Birdi *et al* (2008), in their longitudinal study of 308 companies, found that extensive training produced a gain of nearly 6 per cent in value added per employee. Research by Aragon and Valle (2013) into the impact of training on the performance of managers established that firms that train their managers obtain better results than those that do not, and that the intensive training contributes to improved performance.

Strategies for creating a learning culture

A learning culture is one in which learning is recognized by top management, line managers and employees generally as an essential organizational process to which they are committed and in which they engage continuously. The characteristics of a learning culture are self-managed learning not instruction, long-term capacity building not short-term fixes, and empowerment not supervision.

Reynolds (2004: 9) described a learning culture as a 'growth medium', in which 'employees will commit to a range of positive discretionary behaviours, including learning.' He suggested that to create a learning culture it is necessary to develop organizational practices that 'give employees a sense of purpose in the workplace, grant employees opportunities to act upon their commitment, and offer practical support to learning.' He suggested that the following steps were required to create a learning culture:

1 Develop and share the vision – belief in a desired and emerging future.

2 Empower employees – provide 'supported autonomy'; freedom for employees to manage their work within certain boundaries (policies and expected behaviours) but with support available as required. Adopt a facilitative style of management in which responsibility for decision making is ceded as far as possible to employees.

3 Provide employees with a supportive learning environment where learning capabilities can be discovered and applied, eg peer networks, supportive policies and systems, and protected time for learning.

4 Use coaching techniques to draw out the talents of others by encouraging employees to identify options and seek their own solutions to problems.

5 Guide employees through their work challenges and provide them with time, resources and, crucially, feedback.

6 Recognize the importance of managers acting as coaches, mentors and role models.

7 Encourage networks – communities of practice (groups of people with shared expertise who work together).

8 Align systems to vision – get rid of bureaucratic systems that produce problems rather than facilitate work.

Organizational learning strategies

Organizational learning is concerned with the methods adopted by organizations to promote learning; it is not simply the sum of all the L&D activities that are carried out in an organization. It focuses on collective learning but takes into account the proposition made by Argyris (1992) that organizations do not perform the actions that produce the learning; it is individual members of the organization who behave in ways that lead to it, although organizations can create conditions that facilitate such learning. The concept of organizational learning recognizes that the way in which this takes place is affected by the context of the organization and its culture. It is sometimes associated with the notion of the learning organization but, as suggested later, the concepts are quite different.

The process of organizational learning

Organizational learning can be characterized as an intricate three-stage process consisting of knowledge acquisition, dissemination and shared implementation. As such, it is closely related to knowledge management. Knowledge may be acquired from direct experience, the experience of others or organizational memory.

Argyris (1992) explained that organizational learning occurs under two conditions: first, when an organization achieves what is intended and second, when a mismatch between intentions and outcomes is identified and corrected. He distinguished between single-loop and double-loop learning. These two types of learning have been described as adaptive or generative learning.

Single-loop or *adaptive learning* is incremental learning that does no more than correct deviations from the norm by making small changes and improvements without challenging assumptions, beliefs or decisions. Organizations where single-loop learning is the norm define what Argyris calls the 'governing variables', ie what they expect to achieve in terms of targets and standards, and then monitor and review achievements, taking corrective action as necessary, thus completing the loop.

Double-loop or *generative learning* involves challenging assumptions, beliefs, norms and decisions rather than accepting them. On this basis, learning takes place through the examination of the root causes of problems so that a new learning loop is established that goes far deeper than the traditional learning loop provided by single-loop or

FIGURE 32.1   Single- and double-loop learning

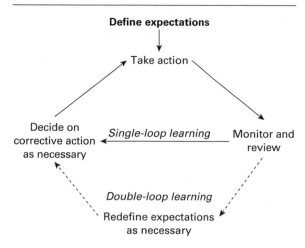

instrumental learning. It occurs when the monitoring process initiates action to redefine the governing variables to meet the new situation, which may be imposed by the external environment. The organization has learnt something new about what has to be achieved in the light of changed circumstances and can then decide how this should be done. This learning is converted into action. The process is illustrated in Figure 32.1.

As Easterby-Smith and Araujo (1999) commented, single-loop learning could be linked to incremental change. In contrast, double-loop learning is associated with radical change, which may involve a major change in strategic direction. It is generally assumed that double-loop learning is superior, but there are situations when single-loop learning may be more appropriate.

Organizational learning strategies

Organizational learning strategies aim to improve organizational effectiveness through the acquisition and development of knowledge, understanding, insights, techniques and practices. This is in accordance with one of the basic principles of HRM, namely that it is necessary to invest in people in order to develop the human capital required by the organization and to increase its stock of knowledge and skills. As stated by Ehrenberg and Smith (1994: 279–80), human capital theory indicates that: 'The knowledge and skills a worker has – which comes from education and training, including the training that experience brings – generate productive capital.'

The concept of the learning organization

A learning organization was described by Senge (1990: 3), who originated the idea, as one 'where people continually expand their capacity to create the results they truly desire, where new and expansive patterns of thinking are nurtured, where collective aspiration is set free, and where people are continually learning how to learn together.' Further definitions of a learning organization were provided by Wick and Leon (1995: 299), who stated that it was one that 'continually improves by rapidly creating and refining the capabilities required for future success', and by Pedler *et al* (1997: 3), who referred to it as an organization that 'facilitates the learning of all its members and continually transforms itself.' Garvin (1993) suggested that learning organizations are good at doing five things:

1 Systematic problem solving – which rests heavily on the philosophy and methods of the quality movement. Its underlying ideas include relying on scientific method rather than guesswork for diagnosing problems – what Deming (1986) called the 'plan-do-check-act' cycle and others refer to as 'hypothesis-generating, hypothesis-testing' techniques. Data rather than assumptions are required as the background to decision making – what quality practitioners call 'fact-based management', and simple statistical tools such as histograms, Pareto charts and cause-and-effect diagrams are used to organize data and draw inferences.

2 Experimentation – this activity involves the systematic search for and testing of new knowledge. Continuous improvement programmes – 'kaizen' – are an important feature in a learning organization.

3 Learning from past experience – learning organizations review their successes and failures, assess them systematically and record the lessons learnt in a way that employees find open and accessible. This process has been called the 'Santayana

principle', quoting the philosopher George Santayana who coined the phrase: 'Those who cannot remember the past are condemned to repeat it.'

4   Learning from others – sometimes the most powerful insights come from looking outside one's immediate environment to gain a new perspective. This process has been called SIS, for 'steal ideas shamelessly'. Another more acceptable word for it is 'benchmarking' – a disciplined process of identifying best-practice organizations and analysing the extent to which what they are doing can be transferred, with suitable modifications, to one's own environment.

5   Transferring knowledge quickly and efficiently throughout the organization – by seconding people with new expertise, or by education and training programmes, as long as the latter are linked explicitly with implementation.

Critical evaluation of the learning organization notion

The notion of the learning organization is persuasive because it provides a rationale for comprehensive learning and development programmes. However, Scarborough *et al* (1999) argued that the learning organization concept is over-concerned with organization systems and design. Little attention seems to be paid to what individuals want to learn or how they learn. The idea that individuals should be enabled to invest in their own development seems to have escaped learning organization theorists, who are more inclined to focus on the imposition of learning by the organization, rather than creating a climate conducive to learning.

Viewing organizations as learning systems is a limited notion. Argyris and Schön (1996) explained that organizations are products of visions, ideas, norms and beliefs, so that their shape is much more fragile than the organization's material structure. People act as learning agents for the organization in ways that cannot easily be systematized. They are not only individual learners but also have the capacity to learn collaboratively. This is described by organization learning theory and leads to the belief that it is the culture and environment that are important, not the systems approach implied by the concept of the learning organization.

The notion of a learning organization is rather nebulous. It incorporates miscellaneous ideas about human resource development, systematic training, action learning, organizational development and knowledge management, with an infusion of the precepts of total quality management. But they do not add up to a convincing whole. Easterby-Smith (1997) contended that attempts to create a single best-practice framework for understanding the learning organization are fundamentally flawed. There are other problems with the concept: it is idealistic; knowledge management models are beginning to supersede it; few organizations can meet the criteria; and there is little evidence of successful learning organizations.

Burgoyne (1999), one of the earlier exponents of the learning organization, has admitted that there has been some confusion about it and that there have been substantial naiveties in most of the early thinking. He believes that the concept should be integrated with knowledge management initiatives so that different forms of knowledge can be linked, fed by organizational learning and used in adding value.

The learning organization and organizational learning

The notion of the learning organization is often associated with the concept of organizational learning. But they are different. Easterby-Smith and Araujo (1999) explained that the literature on organizational learning focuses on the observation and analysis of the processes of individual and collective learning in organizations, whereas the learning organization literature is concerned with using specific diagnostic and evaluative tools that can help to identify, promote and evaluate the quality of the learning processes inside organizations. In other words, organizational learning is about how people learn in organizations, and the learning organization notion attempts to explain what organizations should do to facilitate the learning of their members.

However, as explained above, learning organization theory provides a dubious base for action. The idea of a learning culture supported by the understanding of how organizations learn, as provided by organizational learning theory and knowledge management initiatives, has more to offer.

Individual learning strategies

Individual learning comprises the processes and programmes used to increase the capabilities of individual employees. Strategies for individual learning are driven by the organization's human resource requirements, which are expressed in terms of the skills and behaviours required to achieve business goals. Strategies should cover:

- how learning needs will be identified;
- the role of self-managed learning;
- the facilitation of workplace learning;
- the support that should be provided for individual learning in the form of guidance, coaching, mentoring, learning resource centres, e-learning and internal or external training programmes and courses;
- the evaluation of learning.

CASE STUDY

Developing a learning strategy for Remploy

Remploy is a government-funded organization that provides employment and development opportunities for disabled people. It operates 83 factories. The company's strategy for learning is explicit and well understood in the organization, and was developed from the bottom up rather than top down. Its starting point was recognition that a number of local initiatives in the factories were proving successful and could be developed on a national basis.

The trade unions advocated enhanced opportunities for skill development in basic areas. As a result, a national strategy was developed with learning centres as a major element in all 83 sites. Although the use of each learning centre is locally determined, they all have the following in common: a physical location (with at least some PCs); a relationship with a local college whose tutors will visit the site to advise and facilitate; and access to a suite of e-learning programmes, made available from the LearnDirect library (the national e-learning initiative).

Key learning points: Strategic learning and development

Strategic L&D

Strategic L&D is an approach to helping people learn and develop that is concerned with how the organization's goals will be achieved through its human resources by means of integrated L&D strategies, policies and practices. Strategic L&D aims to produce a coherent and comprehensive framework for developing people through the creation of a learning culture and the formulation of organizational and individual learning strategies.

Learning and development strategies

Learning and development strategies are the active components of an overall approach to strategic L&D. They express the organization's intentions on how L&D activities will take place in the organization and provide guidance on how these activities should be planned and implemented.

Learning culture

A learning culture is one in which learning is recognized by top management, line managers and employees generally as an essential organizational process to which they are committed and in which they engage continuously.

Organizational learning

Organizational learning is about the development and acquisition in organizations of knowledge, understanding, insights, techniques and practices in order to improve organizational effectiveness. It is concerned with the processes adopted by organizations in promoting learning; it is not simply the sum of all the learning and development activities that are carried out in an organization.

The learning organization

Defined by Pedler *et al* (1997) as an organization that 'facilitates the learning of all its members and continually transforms itself.' Learning organization theory provides a dubious base for action. The idea of a learning culture, supported by the understanding of how organizations learn, as provided by organizational learning theory and knowledge management initiatives, has more to offer.

Organizational learning strategies aim to develop a firm's resource-based capability.

Individual learning strategies

The individual learning strategies of an organization are driven by its human resource requirements, the latter being expressed in terms of the sort of skills and behaviours that will be required to achieve business goals.

References

Aragon, I B and Valle, R S (2013) Does training managers pay off? *The International Journal of Human Resource Management*, **24** (8), pp 1671–84

Argyris, C (1992) *On Organizational Learning*, Cambridge, MA, Blackwell

Argyris, C and Schön, D A (1996) *Organizational Learning: A theory of action perspective*, Reading, MA, Addison Wesley

Benabou, C (1996) Assessing the impact of training programs on the bottom line, *National Productivity Review*, **15** (3), pp 91–99

Birdi, K, Clegg, C, Patterson, M, Robinson, A, Stride, C B, Wall, T D and Wood, S J (2008) The impact of human resource and operational management practices on company productivity: a longitudinal study, *Personnel Psychology*, **61** (3), pp 467–501

Burgoyne, J (1999) Design of the times, *People Management*, 3 June, pp 39–44

Deming, W E (1986) *Out of the Crisis*, Cambridge, MA, Massachusetts Institute of Technology Center for Advanced Engineering Studies

Easterby-Smith, M (1997) Disciplines of organizational learning: contributions and critiques, *Human Relations*, **50** (9), pp 1085–113

Easterby-Smith, M and Araujo, J (1999) Organizational learning: current debates and opportunities, in (eds) M Easterby-Smith, J Burgoyne and L Araujo, *Organizational Learning and the Learning Organization*, London, Sage

Ehrenberg, R G and Smith, R S (1994) *Modern Labor Economics*, New York, Harper Collins

Garvin, D A (1993) Building a learning organization, *Harvard Business Review*, July–August, pp 78–91

Harrison, R (2009) *Learning and Development*, 5th edn, London, CIPD

Kearns, P and Miller, T (1997) Measuring the impact of training and development on the bottom line, *FT Management Briefings*, London, Pitman

Pedler, M, Burgoyne, J and Boydell, T (1997) *The Learning Company: A strategy for sustainable development*, 2nd edn, Maidenhead, McGraw-Hill

Reynolds, J (2004) *Helping People Learn*, London, CIPD

Reynolds, J, Caley, L and Mason, R (2002) *How Do People Learn?* London, CIPD

Scarborough, H, Swan, J and Preston, J (1999) *Knowledge Management: A literature review*, London, IPM

Senge, P (1990) *The Fifth Discipline: The art and practice of the learning organization*, London, Doubleday

Walton, J (1999) *Strategic Human Resource Development*, Harlow, Financial Times/Prentice Hall

Wick, C W and Leon, L S (1995) Creating a learning organization: from ideas to action, *Human Resource Management*, **34** (2), pp 299–311

33
How people learn

KEY CONCEPTS AND TERMS

Cognitive learning theory

Experienced workers standard (EWS)

Experiential learning

Neuroscience

Operant conditioning

Progressive parts method of training

Reinforcement theory

Self-directed learning

Social learning theory

LEARNING OUTCOMES

On completing this chapter you should be able to define these key concepts. You should also understand:

- The basis of learning
- The motivation to learn
- Learning theory
- The lessons of neuroscience
- Learning styles

- Learning to learn
- The learning curve
- The implications of learning theory and concepts

Introduction

The aim of this chapter is to describe how people learn in order to create a conceptual framework that can be used when planning and executing learning and development activities as examined in later chapters in this part of the handbook. The framework covers learning theory and the lessons that can be derived from neuroscience. The framework also covers the other factor which affects how people learn, namely the existence of different learning styles.

experiences. To learn effectively, individuals must shift from being observers to participants, from direct involvement to a more objective analytical detachment. Every person has his or her own learning style; one of the most important arts that trainers have to develop is to adjust their approaches to the learning styles of trainees. Trainers must acknowledge these learning styles rather than pursue their own preferred approach.

The Honey and Mumford learning styles

Another analysis of learning styles was made by Honey and Mumford (1996). They identified the following four styles:

1 *Activists* – who involve themselves fully without bias in new experiences and revel in new challenges.

2 *Reflectors* – who stand back and observe new experiences from different angles. They collect data, reflect on it and then come to a conclusion.

3 *Theorists* – who adapt and apply their observations in the form of logical theories. They tend to be perfectionists.

4 *Pragmatists* – who are keen to try out new ideas, approaches and concepts to see if they work.

However, none of these four learning styles is exclusive. It is quite possible that one person could be both a reflector and a theorist and someone else could be an activist/pragmatist, a reflector/pragmatist or even a theorist/pragmatist.

Use of learning style theory

Learning style theory can be used in the design and conduct of learning events or personal development programmes. Learning situations can be set up to fit the learning style of participants. The problem is that people do not necessarily have a single learning style and there certainly will be a large range of styles in any learning group. It may therefore be difficult to fit the approach to the style.

The learning curve

The concept of the learning curve refers to the time it takes an inexperienced person to reach the required level of performance in a job or a task, which is sometimes called the experienced worker's standard (EWS). The existence of the learning curve needs to be taken into account when planning and implementing training or instruction programmes. The standard learning curve is illustrated in Figure 33.2.

But rates of learning vary, depending on the effectiveness of the training, the experience and natural aptitude of the learner and the latter's interest in learning. Both the time taken to reach the EWS and the variable speed with which learning takes place at different times affect the shape of the curve, as shown in Figure 33.3.

Learning is often stepped, with one or more plateaus, while further progress is halted. This may be because learners cannot continually increase their skills or speeds of work and need a pause to consolidate what they have already learnt. The existence of steps such as those shown in Figure 33.4 can be used when planning skills training to provide deliberate reinforcement periods when newly acquired skills are practised in order to achieve the expected standards.

When a training module is being prepared that describes what has to be learnt and the training needed to achieve the required levels of skill and speed, it is often desirable to proceed step by step, taking one task or part of a task at a time, reinforcing it and then progressively adding other parts, consolidating at each stage. This is called the 'progressive parts method' of training.

FIGURE 33.2   A standard learning curve

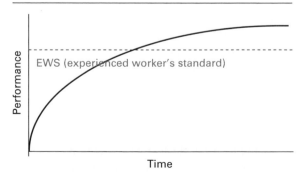

FIGURE 33.3   Different rates of learning

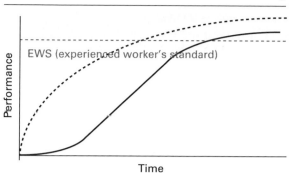

FIGURE 33.4   A stepped learning curve

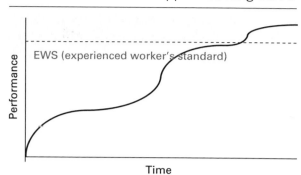

The implications of learning theory and concepts

The practical implications of the learning theories described above are summarized in Table 33.1.

TABLE 33.1   The practical implications of learning theory

Theory/concept	Content	Practical implications
The process of learning	Learning is complex and is achieved in many different ways. The context is important.	Different learning needs require different learning methods, often in combination. Learning effectiveness depends on the extent to which the organization believes in learning and supports it.
The motivation to learn	People need to be motivated to learn effectively.	Learners should be helped to develop learning goals and to understand the benefits to them of achieving them. Performance management processes leading to personal development plans can provide a means of doing this.
Reinforcement theory	Behaviours can be strengthened by reinforcing them with positive feedback (conditioning).	Reinforcement theory underpins training programmes concerned with developing skills through instruction. In these, the learner is conditioned to make a response and receives immediate feedback and progress is made in incremental steps, each directed to a positive outcome.

References

Bandura, A (1977) *Social Learning Theory*, Englewood Cliffs, NJ, Prentice Hall

Chartered Institute of Personnel and Development (Howard-Jones) (2014) Fresh thinking in learning and development Part 1, Neuroscience and learning, *CIPD* [online] http://www.cipd.co.uk/binaries/ fresh-thinking-in-learning-and-development _2014-part-1-neuroscience-learning.pdf [accessed 3 November 2015]

Hendel-Giller, R (2010) The neuroscience of learning: new paradigms for corporate education, *Maritz Institute* [online] http://www.themaritzinstitute. com/Perspectives/-media/Files/MaritzInstitute/ White-Papers/The-Neuroscience-of-learning-The- Maritz- Institute.pdf [accessed 3 November 2015]

Honey, P and Mumford, A (1996) *The Manual of Learning Styles*, 3rd edn, Maidenhead, Honey Publications

Kolb, D A, Rubin, I M and McIntyre, J M (1974) *Organizational Psychology: An experimental approach*, Englewood Cliffs, NJ, Prentice Hall

Lombardo, M M and Eichinger, R W (1996) *The Course Architect Development Planner*, Minneapolis, Lominger

Reynolds, J, Caley, L and Mason, R (2002) *How Do People Learn?* London, CIPD

Royal Society (2011) Brain Waves 2: Neuroscience: implications for education and lifelong learning, *Royal Society* [online] https://royalsociety.org/ topics-policy/projects/brain-waves/education- lifelong-learning/ [accessed 3 November 2015]

Skinner, B F (1974) *About Behaviourism*, London, Cape

Wenger, E (1998) *Communities of Practice: Learning, meaning and identity*, Cambridge, Cambridge University Press

34

The process of learning and development

LEARNING OUTCOMES

On completing this chapter you should be able to define these key concepts. You should also understand:

- How to identify learning needs
- The general approaches to learning and development – formal and informal learning, self-directed and self-managed learning, understanding how to learn,

the use of personal development plans, blended learning and the use of social media

- How to evaluate learning

Introduction

The process of learning and development as described in this chapter starts with the analysis of learning and development needs. This leads to a choice of which of the different types of learning and development activities are appropriate as means of satisfying those needs. Finally, the effectiveness of those activities is evaluated as the basis for making improvements.

Identifying learning needs

All learning activities need to be based on an understanding of what should be done and why it should be done. The purpose of the activities must be defined by identifying and analysing learning needs for the groups and individuals within the organization.

Approaches to learning needs analysis

Learning needs are often established on the basis of general assumptions about what people in particular occupations need to know and be able to do; for example, managers need to learn about leadership. This is an easy approach but it can be facile. The assumptions could be so generalized that the resulting learning process will be all things to everybody and nothing to anyone in particular.

Evidence on learning needs can be collected through a gap analysis and review of corporate, collective and individual needs. These three areas are interconnected, as shown in Figure 34.1. The analysis of corporate needs will lead to the identification of collective learning needs in different departments, functions or occupations, while these in turn will indicate what individual employees need to learn. The process operates in reverse. As the needs of individual employees are analysed separately, common needs emerge, which can be dealt with on a group basis. The sum of group and individual needs will help to define corporate needs, although there may be some overarching learning requirements that can be related only to the company as a whole to attain its business goals. These areas of analysis are discussed below.

Gap analysis

Learning needs analysis is often described as the process of identifying the learning gap – the gap between what is and what should be, as illustrated in Figure 34.2.

Gap analysis involves identifying the gap between what people know and can do and what they should know and be able to do. The learning needed to fill the gap can then be specified. Information on the nature of the gap may be obtained by one or more of the methods described below. But this 'deficiency model' – only putting things right that have gone wrong – is limited. Learning is much more positive than that. It should be concerned with identifying and satisfying development needs – fitting people to take on extra responsibilities, acquire new skills to deal with changing work demands, or develop a range of skills to facilitate multitasking.

FIGURE 34.1   Learning needs analysis – areas and methods

FIGURE 34.2   The learning gap

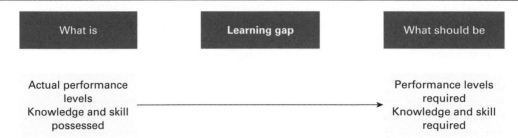

Analysis of business and workforce plans

Business and workforce plans should indicate in general terms the types of skills and competencies that may be required in the future and the numbers of people with those skills and competencies who will be needed. An analysis should also be made of any areas where future changes in work processes, methods or job responsibilities are planned and any additional knowledge or skills that may be required. These broad indicators have to be translated into more specific plans that cover, for example, the outputs from training programmes of people with particular skills or a combination of skills (multiskilling).

Surveys

Special surveys or an interviewing programme can obtain the views of managers and other employees on what they need to learn. However, the material gathered from a survey may be unspecific and, when interviewed, people may find it difficult to articulate what they want. In the latter case it is best to lead with a discussion of the work they do and identify any areas where they believe that their performance and potential could be developed. This could lead to the identification of any additional things they feel they need to know or be able to do. Individual views can be amalgamated to provide a picture of common learning needs.

Role analysis

Role analysis is the basis for preparing role profiles that provide a framework for analysing and identifying learning needs. Role profiles set out the key result areas of the role but, importantly, also define the competencies required to perform it. Performance management should ensure that role profiles are updated regularly, and the review can be built on an analysis of the results achieved by reference to the key result areas and agreed objectives. The competency framework for the role is used to assess the level of competency displayed. An assessment can then be made of any learning required to develop levels of competency. Ideally, this should be a self-assessment by individuals who should be given every encouragement to identify learning needs for themselves. But these can be discussed with the individuals' manager and agreement reached on how the learning needs should be met by the individuals through self-managed learning, and with the help and support of their managers. The output of role analysis could be a learning specification, as illustrated in Figure 34.3.

This method of assessing individual learning needs can generate information on common learning needs. The information can be related to the organization's competency framework and used to inform the design of competency-based learning events.

Skills analysis

Skills analysis, as described in Chapter 70, determines the skills required to achieve an acceptable standard of performance. It is mainly used for technical, craft, manual and office jobs to provide the basis for devising learning and training programmes.

Performance management

Performance management processes, as described in Chapter 41, should be a prime source of information

FIGURE 34.3 A learning specification

LEARNING SPECIFICATION	
Role: Product Manager	**Department:** Marketing

What the role holder must understand	
Learning outcomes	*Learning methods*
• The product market • The product specification • Market research availability • Interpretation of marketing data • Customer service requirements • Techniques of product management	• Coaching: Marketing Manager and Advertising Manager • Coaching: Operations Manager • Coaching: Market Research Manager • Coaching: Market Research Manager • Coaching: Customer Service Manager • Institute of Marketing courses

What the role holder must be able to do	
Learning outcomes	*Learning methods*
• Prepare product budget • Prepare marketing plans • Conduct market reviews • Prepare marketing campaigns • Specify requirements for advertisements and promotional material • Liaise with advertising agents and creative supplier • Analyse results of advertising campaigns • Prepare marketing reports	• Coaching: Budget Accountant • Coaching: Mentor • Coaching: Market Research Department • Read: Product Manager's Manual • Read: Product Manager's Manual • Attachment to agency • Coaching: Mentor, read: analyses • Read: previous reports; observe: marketing review meetings

about individual learning and development needs. Performance management is based on an analysis of role requirements in the shape of knowledge, skills and abilities (KSAs) and the behavioural competencies needed to perform effectively, taking into account any new demands that will be made on the role holder. Performance reviews, which should be held whenever appropriate rather than simply being an annual event, will include discussions on the extent to which the individual would benefit, in career progression as well as performance terms, from some form of learning and development activity. Problems of performance arising from lack of knowledge or skill can be identified so that remedial action can be taken. A joint assessment can then be made of what sort of development programme is required. This can lead to personal development plans and learning contracts, which involve action plans, self-managed learning and an agreement on what support will be provided to the individual by the organization and the manager. An overall analysis of performance and development review reports can reveal any common learning needs that can be satisfied by tailored learning events.

Learning evaluations

Further information should be obtained from learning evaluations, as described at the end of this chapter.

Approaches to learning and development

Approaches to learning and development are influenced by the learning theory presented in Chapter 33, especially experiential learning theory. This emphasizes that people learn mainly from experience and therefore most learning takes place in the workplace. This is expressed in the 70/20/10 model which explains that 70 per cent of learning takes place through experience, 20 per cent through contacts and relationships with other people (social learning) and only 10 per cent through formal training programmes. Learning theory also indicates that people learn best when they are motivated to do it for themselves – self-directed and self-managed learning. But they need support and help.

In general, as discussed below, approaches to learning are concerned with the use of formal and informal learning, self-directed and self-managed learning, learning how to learn, personal development planning, blended learning and the use of social media. The particular learning and development activities of workplace learning, social learning, e-learning and training are considered in chapters 35 to 38 respectively.

Formal and informal learning

People learn both formally and informally. Formal learning is essentially face-to-face (F2F) instruction or classroom or training centre learning. Informal learning is primarily experiential learning and can be self-directed and self-managed, although support may be available from managers, coaches, mentors and social media.

Formal learning presents difficulties. Hoyle (2015: 3) maintains that: 'For a formal programme to result in learning that actually enables people to do different things, training courses must require learners to take some tentative steps to try things out, to experience through trial and error, to reflect on lived experience, and to discuss and connect with others.'

As described by Hoyle, informal learning is not entirely directed and controlled by the learner. He describes it as a continuum, as illustrated in Figure 34.4. In the south-west quadrant there are traditional courses and programmes. But these sessions only work if a degree of informal learning takes place to effect the traditional change in behaviour that improves performance. In the north-west quadrant there is performance support. This may be provided by the organization in the shape, for example, of e-learning programmes. Support may also be available from social networks. The south-east quadrant covers such activities as coaching and learning with colleagues – trying new things and reporting back on experiences. The north-east quadrant refers to work experiences from which people learn by reflecting, drawing conclusions and planning future actions. This model indicates that there are many varieties of informal training and that formal training does have a part to play but not in the old way of relying on classroom training and ignoring everything else. Further learning is required on the job.

Hoyle recommends that the formal training provided on induction courses should be interspersed with on-the-job experience. Following that experience, the employee can return to the classroom for a review of the learning that has been achieved.

Self-directed and self-managed learning

Self-directed learning takes place when individuals set their own learning goals and plan for themselves how they are to be attained through self-managed learning. Self-managed learning is based on a process of recording achievement and action planning, which means that individuals review and reflect on what they have learnt, what they have achieved, what their goals are, how they are going to achieve those goals and what new learning they need to acquire. The learning programme can be 'self-paced'

References

Eraut, M J, Alderton, G, Cole, G and Senker, P (1998) *Development of Knowledge and Skills in Employment*, London, Economic and Social Research Council

Paine, M (2015) *The Learning Challenge*, London, Kogan Page

Reynolds, J (2004) *Helping People Learn*, London, CIPD

Stern, E and Sommerlad, E (1999) *Workplace Learning, Culture and Performance*, London, CIPD

Zuboff, S (1988) *In the Age of the Smart Machine*, New York, Basic Books

36
Social learning

KEY CONCEPTS AND TERMS

Community of practice   Learning community

Connected learning   Social learning

Enterprise social network

LEARNING OUTCOMES

On completing this chapter you should be able to define these key concepts. You should also understand:

- The nature and significance of social learning
- The ways in which social learning can be developed: communities of practice, learning communities, online social learning

The nature and significance of social learning

As defined by Hart (2014): 'Social learning is about people connecting, conversing, collaborating and learning from, and with, one another on a daily basis at work... It's about helping teams learn as they work, rather than taking them out and forcing them to endure a learning "experience".' Social learning theory as formulated by Bandura (1977) regards learning as a series of information-processing steps set in train by social interactions and emphasizes that effective learning requires such interaction.

Wenger (1998) suggested that we all participate in 'communities of practice' (groups of people with shared expertise who work together) and that these are our primary sources of learning. This chapter is concerned with how social learning can be developed as an important part of an organization's learning and development strategy.

A survey conducted by Jane Hart (2014) into how people valued 10 different forms of learning established the following order of preference from respondents:

1 Collaborative working within their team.
2 Web search for resources.

3 General conversations and meetings with people.

4 Personal and professional networks and communities.

5 External blogs and news feeds.

6 Content curated from external sources.

7 Self-directed study of external courses.

8 Internal job aids.

9 Internal documentation.

10 Company training and e-learning.

As she commented, this clearly shows that social and collaborative learning activities – and in particular self-organized activities - are the main ways that the survey respondents preferred to learn. She noted that, in particular, knowledge workers prefer to learn as an integral part of their daily job and like to learn continuously from the constant flow of information they encounter from other people – which may come from both internal and external channels. Knowledge workers want to be able to find answers to their learning and performance problems as soon as they encounter them. They don't want to have to wait to go on a course or get some other response. They want to solve their problems immediately and get on with their jobs. If, when sitting at their desk, they encounter a problem with a task they are working on, they tend either to seek help from their professional network or to go straight to Google and search for a solution. She also noted (ibid 35) that:

> It is in the area of workforce collaboration where there are plenty of new opportunities for L&D to support work teams and groups. Since people learn from one another as a consequence of working together, rather than focusing exclusively on the learning, it is more about helping them work collaboratively and enabling continuous learning to take place as part of that process. It is also important to reiterate that supporting continuous learning in the flow of work is not about providing them with courses as they do their work, helping them to find their own courses, or even helping them to create their own courses for one another – rather it is about helping them share their knowledge, experiences, ideas and resources as part of their daily workflow.

Some form of social learning happens continually in the workplace as individuals and groups work together. Groups solve problems jointly and learn in doing so. Project teams do the same. Individuals observe what their colleagues do and learn from their observations. But it cannot be left to chance. Social learning can be even more effective if it is supported by communities of practice, learning communities and online social learning as described below.

Connected learning

Connected learning addresses the learning needs and interests of individuals and how these can be linked with the opportunities for learning provided by fellow workers through such means as communities of practice and learning communities.

Communities of practice

Communities of practice are groups of people bound together by shared expertise who meet together to share knowledge. They may be set up by individuals or groups, but L&D may support them as an approach to learning which offers more than traditional training.

Learning communities

Learning communities are groups of people who get together to learn from one another. They are usually set up by L&D professionals to support a training course or an online programme. Learning communities might be established before a course to prepare participants and give them some preliminary material to absorb. After the course, community members can get together to discuss what they have learnt and how they are applying it. Problems can be raised and solutions considered. The emphasis is on interaction, sharing and conversations between the participants. In effect, learning communities may become communities of practice in which further learning possibilities can be explored and agreement reached on how they should be pursued by the community itself or with help from L&D. Learning communities can be established and supported by L&D, who may appoint a community facilitator who provides guidance and help but does not dictate what the community members discuss. Communities may be set up by individuals or groups independently but they will benefit from L&D support.

36
Social learning

KEY CONCEPTS AND TERMS

Community of practice

Connected learning

Enterprise social network

Learning community

Social learning

LEARNING OUTCOMES

On completing this chapter you should be able to define these key concepts. You should also understand:

● The nature and significance of social learning
● The ways in which social learning can be developed: communities of practice, learning communities, online social learning

The nature and significance of social learning

As defined by Hart (2014): 'Social learning is about people connecting, conversing, collaborating and learning from, and with, one another on a daily basis at work... It's about helping teams learn as they work, rather than taking them out and forcing them to endure a learning "experience".' Social learning theory as formulated by Bandura (1977) regards learning as a series of information-processing steps set in train by social interactions and emphasizes that effective learning requires such interaction.

Wenger (1998) suggested that we all participate in 'communities of practice' (groups of people with shared expertise who work together) and that these are our primary sources of learning. This chapter is concerned with how social learning can be developed as an important part of an organization's learning and development strategy.

A survey conducted by Jane Hart (2014) into how people valued 10 different forms of learning established the following order of preference from respondents:

1 Collaborative working within their team.
2 Web search for resources.

3 General conversations and meetings with people.

4 Personal and professional networks and communities.

5 External blogs and news feeds.

6 Content curated from external sources.

7 Self-directed study of external courses.

8 Internal job aids.

9 Internal documentation.

10 Company training and e-learning.

As she commented, this clearly shows that social and collaborative learning activities – and in particular self-organized activities - are the main ways that the survey respondents preferred to learn. She noted that, in particular, knowledge workers prefer to learn as an integral part of their daily job and like to learn continuously from the constant flow of information they encounter from other people – which may come from both internal and external channels. Knowledge workers want to be able to find answers to their learning and performance problems as soon as they encounter them. They don't want to have to wait to go on a course or get some other response. They want to solve their problems immediately and get on with their jobs. If, when sitting at their desk, they encounter a problem with a task they are working on, they tend either to seek help from their professional network or to go straight to Google and search for a solution. She also noted (ibid 35) that:

> It is in the area of workforce collaboration where there are plenty of new opportunities for L&D to support work teams and groups. Since people learn from one another as a consequence of working together, rather than focusing exclusively on the learning, it is more about helping them work collaboratively and enabling continuous learning to take place as part of that process. It is also important to reiterate that supporting continuous learning in the flow of work is not about providing them with courses as they do their work, helping them to find their own courses, or even helping them to create their own courses for one another – rather it is about helping them share their knowledge, experiences, ideas and resources as part of their daily workflow.

Some form of social learning happens continually in the workplace as individuals and groups work together. Groups solve problems jointly and learn in doing so. Project teams do the same. Individuals observe what their colleagues do and learn from their observations. But it cannot be left to chance. Social learning can be even more effective if it is supported by communities of practice, learning communities and online social learning as described below.

Connected learning

Connected learning addresses the learning needs and interests of individuals and how these can be linked with the opportunities for learning provided by fellow workers through such means as communities of practice and learning communities.

Communities of practice

Communities of practice are groups of people bound together by shared expertise who meet together to share knowledge. They may be set up by individuals or groups, but L&D may support them as an approach to learning which offers more than traditional training.

Learning communities

Learning communities are groups of people who get together to learn from one another. They are usually set up by L&D professionals to support a training course or an online programme. Learning communities might be established before a course to prepare participants and give them some preliminary material to absorb. After the course, community members can get together to discuss what they have learnt and how they are applying it. Problems can be raised and solutions considered. The emphasis is on interaction, sharing and conversations between the participants. In effect, learning communities may become communities of practice in which further learning possibilities can be explored and agreement reached on how they should be pursued by the community itself or with help from L&D. Learning communities can be established and supported by L&D, who may appoint a community facilitator who provides guidance and help but does not dictate what the community members discuss. Communities may be set up by individuals or groups independently but they will benefit from L&D support.

Although learning communities may sometimes be added on to a traditional training course, they work best if the community itself, with help as necessary from L&D, decides on what they need to learn together and how they will learn it. They can benefit from the use of online learning resources.

Online social learning

Online social learning tools enable people to share with others what they know and what they have learnt. The learning is not structured but it is real – based on the actual experiences of colleagues – and therefore more effective than a formal presentation by a trainer on a course.

Social learning can be encouraged by the use of an enterprise social network (ESN) such as Yammer. ESN technology is similar to public social networking tools like Facebook in that it supports a constant flow of real-time, threaded conversations through user updates and replies. Within an organization, people can share their experiences and thoughts and learn from one another. In using an ESN, an individual's personal activity stream will consist of all their activity streams – from all their learning initiatives as well as from their work teams and communities. Learning is no longer seen as a separate activity from working and it can become a continuous, social experience.

Key learning points: Social learning

The nature and significance of social learning

As defined by Hart (2014): 'Social learning is about people connecting, conversing, collaborating and learning from, and with, one another on a daily basis at work.'

Some form of social learning happens continually in the workplace as individuals and groups work together. Groups solve problems jointly and learn in doing so. Project teams do the same. Individuals observe what their colleagues do and learn from their observations. But it cannot be left to chance. It should be enhanced by the use of communities of practice, learning communities and online social learning.

- *Connected learning* addresses the learning needs and interests of individuals and how these can be linked with the opportunities for learning provided by fellow workers.

- *Communities of practice* are groups of people bound together by shared expertise who meet together to share knowledge.

- *Learning communities* are groups of people who get together to learn from one another.

- *Online social learning tools* such as enterprise social networks enable people to share with others what they know and what they have learnt.

References

Bandura, A (1977) *Social Learning Theory*, Englewood Cliffs, NJ, Prentice-Hall

Hart, J (2014) *The Social Learning Handbook* [online] http://www.c4lpt.co.uk/blog/2014/01/27/social-learning-handbook-pdf-now-available/ [accessed 7 November 2015]

Wenger, E (1998) *Communities of Practice: Learning, meaning and identity*, Cambridge, Cambridge University Press

37
E-learning

KEY CONCEPTS AND TERMS

Blogs	Rapid authoring software
E-learning	Virtual classroom
Gamification	Virtual learning environments (VLEs)
Learning management system	Virtual learning systems
Microblogging	Webinar
MOOC	Wiki
Podcast	

LEARNING OUTCOMES

On completing this chapter you should be able to define these key concepts. You should also understand:

- The nature, uses and advantages and disadvantages of e-learning
- The developments taking place in the use of e-learning

E-learning defined

E-learning is learning that is delivered through electronic Web 2.0 technology. The content of e-learning can consist of a whole programme covering, for example, health and safety compliance, or it can usefully contain small and easily assimilated segments or 'bites' of material dealing with a specific topic such as handling difficult conversations. A Web 2.0 site allows users to interact and collaborate with each other by reference to user-generated content in a virtual community. It can be used to promote organizational learning and knowledge management through intranets and enterprise social networks within organizations.

The aim is to enhance learning. E-learning extends and supplements face-to-face learning rather than replacing it. Reinforcement is provided through post-event reading, help with self-assessment and chatroom support. The emphasis is on self-paced learning – learners control the rate at which they learn, although they may be given targets for completion and guidance from tutors on how they should learn. However, the impact of e-learning is strongly influenced by the quality of the support provided to learners. It is the effectiveness of this support rather than the sophistication of the technology that counts.

E-learning material may be managed by means of a learning management system (LMS), a software application for e-learning administration, curriculum management, documentation, tracking the progress of learners, reporting and delivery. E-learning modules, especially those designed for compliance training, often test participants on what they have learnt by getting them to tick boxes in such formats as multiple-choice questions.

Uses of e-learning

Formal e-learning technology provides content in the form of training courses or 'bite-sized' learning material delivered in small, easily assimilated nuggets lasting up to 10 minutes or so. As established by the CIPD (2011) e-learning survey, it is most commonly used for compliance training (for example, health and safety, hygiene and data protection). It is also often used for induction training. E-learning can also support informal learning in the workplace. It may be blended with other types of learning. For example, the majority of learning content may be delivered through face-to-face lectures or coaching, or through textual material, but the dialogue with other learners, the conduct of collaborative activities and the searching for supporting material are all conducted online.

Advantages and disadvantages of e-learning

E-learning enhances learning by extending and supplementing face-to-face learning rather than replacing it. It enables learning to take place when it is most needed (just-in-time as distinct from just-in-case) and can be accessed at any time from anywhere. Learning can be provided in short segments or bites

that focus on specific learning objectives. It is 'learner-centric' in that it can be customized to suit an individual's learning needs – learners can choose different learning objects within an overall package. E-learning material can reach simultaneously an unlimited number of employees, even in dispersed locations or complex organizational structures.

The drawbacks are the need for learners to be self-motivated, the time and effort required to develop and update e-learning programmes, and the problem of providing adequate support to learners. The CIPD's 2015 Learning and Development Survey found that while e-learning was the fourth most used learning method, after on-the-job training, in-house development programmes and coaching, it was rated as the seventh most effective. The CIPD's 2011 survey of e-learning found that the completion rates of e-learning modules were poor, as was user experience.

Developments in e-learning

It was suggested by Johnson *et al* (2011) that there is a point in an innovation cycle where the 'adjacent possibles' come into play. This means that developments in new technologies or processes to the original product or concept are identified that extend the uses to which the product can be put. The adjacent possibilities in e-learning have included the use of:

- knowledge-sharing technologies such as blogs, podcasts, wikis, rapid authoring software;
- virtual learning environments (VLEs);
- social media;
- online learning;
- mobiles;
- game-based learning or 'gamification'.

The power of cloud computing, which allows massive storage capacity and ready access to content, enhances the use of social networking technologies.

Knowledge sharing

Knowledge-sharing technologies that can be used to extend e-learning include blogs (websites on which individuals or groups post their observations and experiences), podcasts (digital audio files made available on the internet for downloading to a computer or portable media player), wikis (websites which allow collaborative modification of their content and structure directly from a web browser) and rapid authoring software (which enables those without programming skills to design content using programmes such as PowerPoint).

Microblogs can also be used. These are miniature blogs posted on sites such as Twitter. The process of microblogging can be harnessed for corporate learning through knowledge-sharing tools like Yammer. Microblogs can be captured and distilled into learning points.

Virtual learning environment

A virtual learning environment (VLE) or virtual learning system is a set of learning tools designed to enhance an individual's learning experience by including computers and the internet in the learning process. A VLE package will include online support for both trainer and learner, electronic communication such as e-mail, threaded discussions (online discussions initiated by a trainer – contributions are posted on a discussion forum) and internet links to outside resources. VLE tools such as Moodle take learners through a whole system of learning experiences and integrate the online interactions of the learner. It may involve the use of virtual classrooms and webinars.

A virtual classroom is an online learning environment. The environment can be web-based and accessed through a portal, or software-based and therefore require a downloadable executable file. Trainers and individuals are logged into the virtual learning environment at the same time to provide and receive instruction.

Webinars (short for web-based seminar) are presentations, workshops or seminars that are transmitted over the web using video conferencing software. A key feature of a webinar is its interactive elements – the ability to give, receive and discuss information.

Social media

Terms such as 'social media/networking' or 'interactive media' are often used interchangeably with the term 'Web 2.0'. Social media such as Facebook and LinkedIn can be used as platforms for e-learning and act as a source for learning content by locating expertise and information.

As the CIPD (2013: 14) reported:

The main benefit of social media as a learning tool lies not in hosting formally designed tools and programmes, but in supporting informal learning. Through building relationships with new people and joining communities of interest, social media can help us locate the expertise we are looking for or, indeed, lead us to stumble upon useful or interesting information we were not aware of.

Online learning through MOOCS

Online learning can be made available through Massive Open Online Courses (MOOCs). These are online courses accessible to everyone that often have an unlimited number of participants. Some organizations are now offering MOOCs to their employees as a form of e-learning, either by directing them to relevant course content, or developing bespoke 'corporate MOOCs'.

Mobiles

The development of smartphone technology has enabled mobiles to become an important part of the learning environment. This trend has accelerated through the increased use of 'apps'. These can be specifically designed for organizations and will contain learning material, often in 'bites', which facilitates learning in any place and at any time, including 'learning on the move'.

Apps are available for note-taking. The notes function in the iPhone and iPad enables users to take notes in a stylized script, much like writing. Notes and memos can also be recorded, adding to the power of recall. This can help to clarify thought and track learning and assist reflection.

Research by Hird and Sparrow (2012) found that in one organization, apps were used in three ways:

1 Follow-ups to a learning intervention, broadening access out to different 'layers' of sites that provide basic information, and access to broader communities of practice.

2 Awareness-building material, for example enhancing leadership models with provision of additional guidance; support tools that lay out different options for development and provide feedback and progress checks.

3 Process confirmation, where learners can record information, and the L&D function can check for process alignment and behavioural reinforcement.

Game-based learning

Game-based learning involves the use of computer games as part of an e-learning programme or during a more conventional formal course. Games offer 'immersive experiences' in which players can learn about problem solving, collaboration, leadership and communication. Players have to take in information from many sources, as in real life, and make decisions quickly, to deduce a game's rules from playing rather than by being told, to create strategies for overcoming obstacles and to understand complex systems through experimentation.

The unlovely term 'gamification' is used to describe what is claimed to be a different approach to using games for learning purposes. But the only significant difference is that gamification is more concerned with achieving the motivation of learners through competition, incentives and rewards such as the use of 'leader boards' (tables listing game leaders), the award of points for achieving higher levels and the provision of 'badges' (digital indications of the level of skills reached).

Game-based learning is not an easy option. Time and effort are needed to plan and implement its use. The steps required are:

1 Define objectives – the sort of behaviours the game is intended to develop.

2 Select or produce a game, which will focus on those behaviours and fits the people who are going to play it.

3 Decide on any help that can be provided through e-learning.

4 Define to participants how they should analyse their performance in the game under such headings as problem solving, teamwork and leadership.

5 Ensure that participants carry out this analysis and draw up a list of lessons learnt.

6 Get participants to define what action they intend to take at work to apply the lessons learnt.

CASE STUDY

Integrated e-learning at Cable & Wireless

E-learning at Cable & Wireless is based on the establishment and promotion of a single platform for learning. This has been delivered through an outsourcing arrangement with the e-learning company SkillSoft. The core platform is a learning management system that is available to Cable & Wireless colleagues as a portal labelled 'iLEARN'. All training delivery channels are linked to this portal. The library of generic material consists of some 15,000 items, plus about 60 modules commissioned by Cable & Wireless. In the first year since the e-learning system was launched, three-quarters of the workforce used it and this penetration figure is rising. Some 20,000 e-learning activities were accessed and 15,000 hours of e-learning undertaken in total.

Key learning points: E-learning

E-learning defined

E-learning is learning that is delivered through electronic technology.

Uses of e-learning

Formal e-learning technology provides content in the form of training courses or 'bite-sized' learning material delivered in small, easily assimilated nuggets lasting up to 10 minutes or so. As established by the CIPD (2011) e-learning survey, it is most commonly used for compliance (for example, health and safety, hygiene and data protection). It is also often used for induction training.

Advantages and disadvantages of e-learning

E-learning enhances learning by extending and supplementing face-to-face learning rather than replacing it.

The drawbacks are the need for learners to be self-motivated, the time and effort required to develop and update e-learning programmes, and the problem of providing adequate support to learners.

Developments in e-learning

- knowledge-sharing technologies such as blogs, podcasts, wikis, rapid authoring software;
- virtual learning environments (VLEs);
- social media;
- online learning (MOOCs);
- mobiles;
- game-based learning or 'gamification'.

References

CIPD (2011) Focus on E-learning, *CIPD* [online] http://www.cipd.co.uk/hr-resources/survey-reports/focus-e-learning.aspx [accessed 9 November 2015]

CIPD (2013) Social Technology – Social Business, *CIPD* [online] www.cipd.co.uk/binaries/social-technology-social-business_2013.pdf [accessed 10 November 2015]

CIPD (2015) Survey of Learning and Development, *CIPD* [online] http://www.cipd.co.uk/binaries/learning-development_2015.pdf [accessed 10 November 2015]

Hird, M and Sparrow, P (2012) Learning & development: seeking a renewed focus? White Paper 12/01 October 2012 Centre for Performance-Led HR, Lancaster University [online] http://www.lancaster.ac.uk/media/lancaster-university/content-assets/documents/lums/cphr/LDWP.pdf [accessed 11 November 2015]

Johnson, L, Smith, R, Willis, H, Levine, A and Haywood, K (2011) *The 2011 Horizon Report*, Austin, Texas, The New Media Consortium

38
Training

Introduction: training defined

Training is the use of systematic and planned instruction activities to promote learning. The approach can be summarized in the phrase 'learner-based training'. It is one of several responses an organization can undertake to promote learning.

As Reynolds (2004: 45) pointed out, training has a complementary role to play in accelerating learning: 'It should be reserved for situations that justify a more directed, expert-led approach rather than viewing it as a comprehensive and all-pervasive people development solution.' He also commented that the conventional training model has a tendency to 'emphasize subject-specific knowledge, rather than trying to build core learning abilities.'

Types of training

Training programmes or events can be concerned with any of the following:

- manual and administrative skills;
- IT skills;

- team leader or supervisory training;
- leadership and management training;
- interpersonal skills, eg leadership, team building, group dynamics, neurolinguistic programming;
- personal skills, eg assertiveness, coaching, communicating, time management;
- training in organizational procedures or practices, eg induction, health and safety, performance management, equal opportunity or managing diversity policy and practice.

The justification for training

Formal training is indeed only one of the ways of ensuring that learning takes place, but it can be justified in the following circumstances:

- The knowledge or skills cannot be acquired satisfactorily by experiential learning in the workplace or by self-managed learning.
- Different skills are required by a number of people, which have to be developed quickly

to meet new demands and cannot be gained by relying on experience.

- The tasks to be carried out are so specialized or complex that people are unlikely to master them on their own initiative at a reasonable speed.
- When a learning need common to a number of people has to be met that can readily be dealt with in a training event or programme, for example induction, essential IT skills, communication skills.

Systematic training

Training should be systematic in that it is specifically designed, planned, implemented and evaluated to meet defined needs. It is provided by people who know how to train and the impact of training is carefully evaluated. The concept was originally developed for the industrial training boards in the 1960s and, as illustrated in Figure 38.1, consists of a simple four-stage model:

FIGURE 38.1   Systematic training model

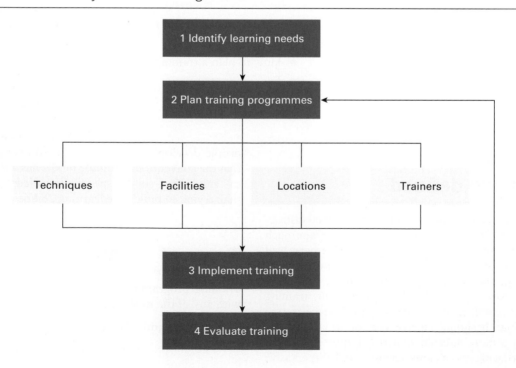

1 Identify training needs (see Chapter 34).

2 Decide what sort of training is required to satisfy these needs.

3 Use experienced and trained trainers to implement training.

4 Follow up and evaluate training to ensure that it is effective (see end of this chapter).

Transferring learning

The problem of transferring learning following a training course was raised by Reynolds (2004: 47) as follows:

> Some types of intervention [can] disrupt self-directed learning by paying insufficient attention to the needs of the learner in the work context. Methods that rely heavily on the transfer of external expertise or content to employees... carry the highest risk in this regard, since their design is often removed from the context in which work is created. As a result, it is impossible to meet learning needs adequately.

This is a fundamental problem and applies equally to externally and internally run training courses where what has been taught can be difficult for people to apply in the entirely different circumstances in their workplace. Training can seem to be remote from reality and the skills and knowledge acquired can appear to be irrelevant. Transfer of learning problems often occur after management or supervisory training, but even the manual skills learnt in a training centre can be difficult to transfer.

Baldwin and Ford (1988: 64) defined 'positive' transfer 'as the degree to which trainees effectively apply the knowledge, skills, and attitudes gained in a training context to the job'. In essence, transfer is the most important of all training effectiveness criteria. They defined two conditions of transfer: 1) the maintenance of material learned in training over time; and 2) the generalization of material from the training environment to the workplace context. This model noted the training input of trainee characteristics, such as the trainee's motivation and ability, as a prerequisite for learning and transfer.

To tackle this problem, it is necessary to make the training as relevant and realistic as possible, anticipating and dealing with any potential transfer difficulties. Individuals are more likely to apply learning when they do not find it too difficult, believe what they have learnt is relevant, useful and transferable, are supported by line managers, have job autonomy, believe in themselves, and are committed and engaged. Transfer is also more likely if 'just-in-time training' approaches are used, as described below.

Just-in-time training

Just-in-time training is training that is closely linked to the pressing and relevant needs of people by its association with immediate or imminent work activities. It is delivered as close as possible to the time when the activity is taking place. The training will be based on an identification of the latest requirements, priorities and plans of the participants, who will be briefed on the live situations in which their learning has to be applied. The training programme will take account of any transfer issues and aim to ensure that what is taught is seen to be applicable in the current work situation.

Bite-sized training

Bite-sized training involves the provision of opportunities to acquire a specific skill or a particular piece of knowledge in a short training session focused on one activity, such as using a particular piece of software, giving feedback, or handling an enquiry about a product or service of the company. It is often carried out through e-learning. It can be a useful means of developing a skill or understanding through a concentrated session or learning activity without diversions, which can then be readily put to use in the workplace. But it can be weak in expanding individuals' intellectual capacity and their understanding of the business – essential qualities to enable employees to respond creatively to the challenges of today's knowledge economy. It can also be facile and too restricted and reliant on the support of line managers, which is not always forthcoming. It is best for training employees in straightforward techniques that they can use immediately in their work.

Effective training practices

Effective training uses the systematic approach defined earlier with an emphasis on skills analysis.

The purpose of the training should be clearly defined in terms of the behaviour required as a result of training. The focus of the training should be to develop transferable skills and it will only be successful if those skills are put to good use in the place of work. The training should be evaluated on the basis of the extent to which it has achieved its purpose.

Instructional design

Instructional design is the process of planning a learning process to ensure that it takes place effectively. The following are the nine conditions for effective instructional design set out by Gagne (1977):

1 Gain attention of learners.
2 Inform learners of learning objectives.
3 Stimulate recall of prior learning.
4 Present the content and break it down into components so as to avoid information overload.
5 Provide learning guidance.
6 Elicit performance.
7 Provide feedback to learners.
8 Assess the performance of learners.
9 Enhance knowledge retention and transfer to real life in the workplace.

Planning and delivering training events and programmes

The process of planning and delivering training or learning events and programmes is described by the ADDIE model, which has five phases: analysis, design, development, implementation and evaluation.

Analysis phase

In the analysis phase the learning goals and objectives are defined as criterion or terminal behaviour (what participants will learn and be able to do as a result of the training), and the learning environment and learners' existing knowledge and skills are identified.

Design phase

The design phase deals with subject matter analysis and the methods to be used. This should be a 'blended learning' approach making appropriate use of presentations, discussions, case studies, role plays and simulations and games. The maximum amount of learner involvement rather than spoon-feeding through lectures should be planned. An 80/20 rule can be adopted, ie about 80 per cent involvement and only 20 per cent direct teaching, although the proportions may vary according to the subject matter of the programme. The programme outline can then be prepared and the use of learning aids and assessment instruments planned.

Development phase

In the development phase the detailed programme is constructed as conceived in the design phase. This covers the session plan, the outline content and learning outcomes of each session, nomination and briefing of the people who will be involved in delivering the programme, methods of delivery, preparation of visual aids, handouts, supporting material, games and exercises and the arrangements for administering the programme. Plans are made to provide the necessary facilities (main lecture room, 'break out' rooms in which small groups can meet for discussions or to tackle case studies, projectors, flip charts, etc). The final version of the programme is prepared for distribution to nominating managers and, later, to participants. This will set out the objectives and benefits of the programme and how these will be achieved. The costs of the programme will be calculated to ensure that they are within budget.

Those conducting the programme prepare the detailed contents of their sessions, decide on their method of delivery, rehearse their sessions and work out how the exercises will fit in. The programme director ensures that the efforts of all those involved are coordinated.

Implementation phase

The programme is implemented as planned.

Evaluation phase

Each session is evaluated by the programme director and, at the end, by participants. The impact of the programme on performance is measured and the degree to which it met expectations assessed.

CASE STUDIES

Training overhaul for Scottish police

A radical overhaul of training for the Scottish police has created more opportunities for promotion and culminated in a prestigious National Training Award. The improved training scheme uses facilitated learning delivery, where trainees pre-read all information before attending sessions and then discuss issues and learn from each other. Responsibility for learning is now firmly placed on the shoulders of the individual – you have got to want to be a police officer and you have got to want to learn. After 15 weeks of initial training, a two-week 'reconvention'

period helps staff with the areas they particularly need to address. This training is tailored to individual requirements: syndicates of recruits with similar needs are put together to receive it. This 'partnership approach' has helped the participants to focus on communication and problem-solving skills. A Certificate of Higher Education in policing, accredited by the University of Stirling, is awarded on completion of the programme. There are also opportunities to take a diploma in management skills.

Training and learning at a customer support centre

The customer support centre employs 300 people. Customer service agents work in a group of five, known as a 'pod'. One of the pod members will be a team coach who provides support and advice to his or her agent colleagues.

A working knowledge of each customer support system is essential to do the job and one of the central tasks of the training department is to bring new entrants up to competence as quickly as possible. The following pattern is adopted. New entrants join in cohorts of 8 to 10 and spend their first week in the training room. As the week progresses,

they spend periods in a pod sitting next to a 'buddy', listening to calls. At the end of that week they are allocated to a pod team and receive close ongoing support from the pod team coach.

Given the emphasis on learning in the workplace, the role of the team coach is critical and there are a number of steps in place to support and enhance their role. A set of skills and needs has been defined and these are delivered to the 30 centre team coaches in 90-minute modules in the training room.

Evaluation of training

It is important to establish the effectiveness of a training course or programme. The four-level system suggested by Kirkpatrick (1994) is often used.

Level 1: Reaction

At this level, evaluation measures how those who participated in the training have reacted to it, ie an assessment of immediate customer satisfaction. Reactions may be recorded on a form (sometimes called a 'happy sheet') and tend to be mainly about the quality of the speakers or trainers. Kirkpatrick

suggested the following guidelines for evaluating reactions:

- determine what you want to find out;
- design a form that will quantify reactions;
- encourage written comments and suggestions;
- get 100 per cent immediate response;
- get honest responses;
- develop acceptable standards;
- measure reactions against standards, and take appropriate action;
- communicate reactions as appropriate.

Research by Warr *et al* (1970) showed that there was relatively little correlation between learner reactions and subsequent measures of changed behaviour. But as Tamkin *et al* (2002) claimed, despite this, organizations are still keen to get reactions to training, and used with caution this can produce some information on the extent to which learning objectives were perceived to be met and why.

Level 2: Evaluate learning

This level obtains information on the extent to which learning objectives have been attained. It will aim to find how much knowledge was acquired, what skills were developed or improved, and the extent to which attitudes have changed in the desired direction. So far as possible, the evaluation of learning should involve the use of tests before and after the programme – written, oral or performance tests.

Level 3: Evaluate behaviour

This level evaluates the extent to which the expected changes in behaviour have happened when people attending the programme return to their jobs. The question to be answered is the extent to which knowledge, skills and attitudes have been transferred from the classroom to the workplace. Ideally, the evaluation should take place both before and after the training. Time should be allowed for the change in behaviour to take place. The evaluation needs to assess the extent to which specific learning objectives relating to changes in behaviour and the application of knowledge and skills have been achieved.

Level 4: Evaluate results in terms of impact on organizational performance

This is the ultimate level of evaluation and provides the basis for assessing the benefits of the training against its costs. The objective is to determine the added value of learning and development programmes – how they contribute to raising organizational performance significantly above its previous level. The evaluation has to be based on before-and-after measures and should determine the extent to which the fundamental objectives of the training have been achieved in areas such as increasing sales, raising productivity, reducing accidents or increasing customer satisfaction. Evaluating results is obviously easier when they can be quantified. However, it is not always easy to prove the contribution to improved results made by training as distinct from other factors and, as Kirkpatrick said, evaluators should be satisfied with evidence, because proof is usually impossible to get.

Application of evaluation

The more care that has been taken in the assessment of needs and the more precise the objectives, the greater will be the possibility of effective evaluation. This is the basis for conducting evaluation at various levels.

It could be argued that the only feedback that matters from evaluation is the results in terms of improved unit or organizational performance that learning brings. But if this is hard to measure, a learning event could still be justified in terms of any actual changes in behaviour that the programme was designed to produce. This is based on the assumption that the analysis of learning needs indicated that the behaviour is more than likely to deliver the desired results. Similarly, at the learning level, if a proper analysis of knowledge, skills and attitude requirements and their impact on behaviour has been conducted, it is reasonable to assume that if the knowledge, etc, has been acquired, behaviour is likely to change appropriately. Finally, if all else fails, reactions are important in that they provide immediate feedback on the quality of training given (including the performance of the trainer), which can point the way to corrective action.

In practice, organizations find it difficult to advance much above Level 1. That is why there have been moves to use overall measures such as return on investment or return on expectations which were described in Chapter 34.

Key learning points: Training

Training defined

Training is the use of systematic and planned instruction activities to promote learning.

Types of training

Training programmes or events can be concerned with any of the following:

- manual skills, including apprenticeships;
- IT skills;
- team leader or supervisory training;
- leadership and management training;
- interpersonal skills, eg leadership, team building, group dynamics, neurolinguistic programming;
- personal skills, eg assertiveness, coaching, communicating, time management;
- training in organizational procedures or practices, eg induction, health and safety, performance management, equal opportunity or managing diversity policy and practice.

Systematic training

Training should be systematic in that it is specifically designed, planned, implemented and evaluated to meet defined needs.

Transferring learning

It may be difficult to transfer the learning acquired on a training course to the workplace. Special efforts need to be made to effect this transfer.

Just-in-time training

Just-in-time training is training that is closely linked to the pressing and relevant needs of people by its association with immediate or imminent work activities.

Bite-sized training

Bite-sized training involves the provision of opportunities to acquire a specific skill or a particular piece of knowledge in a short training session focused on one activity.

The justification of training

Formal training is indeed only one of the ways of ensuring that learning takes place, but it can be justified in the following circumstances:

- The knowledge or skills cannot be acquired satisfactorily by experiential learning in the workplace or by self-managed learning.
- Different skills are required by a number of people, which have to be developed quickly to meet new demands and cannot be gained by relying on experience.
- The tasks to be carried out are so specialized or complex that people are unlikely to master them on their own initiative at a reasonable speed.
- When a learning need common to a number of people has to be met that can readily be dealt with in a training event or programme.

Effective training practices

Effective training uses the systematic approach defined earlier with an emphasis on skills analysis.

Instructional design

The process of planning a learning process to ensure that it takes place effectively.

Planning and delivering training events and programmes

This process of planning and delivering training or learning events and programmes is described by the ADDIE model, which has five phases: analysis, design, development, implementation and evaluation.

Evaluation of training

The Kirkpatrick system is often used but generally only at the basic level of individual reactions to the training.

References

Baldwin, T and Ford, J (1988) Transfer of training: a review and directions for future research, *Personnel Psychology*, **41**, pp 63–105

Gagne, R M (1977) *The Conditions of Learning*, 3rd edn, New York, Rinehart and Winston

Kirkpatrick, D L (1994) *Evaluating Training Programmes*, San Francisco, CA, Berrett-Koehler

Reynolds, J (2004) *Helping People Learn*, London, CIPD

Tamkin, P, Yarnall, J and Kerrin, M (2002) Kirkpatrick and beyond: a review of training evaluation, Report 392, Brighton, Institute for Employment Studies

Warr, P B, Bird, M W and Rackham, N (1970) *Evaluation of Management Training*, Aldershot, Gower

39
Leadership and management development

LEARNING OUTCOMES

On completing this chapter you should be able to define these key concepts. You should also understand:

- The nature of leadership and management development
- The nature of leadership and management
- Leadership and management development compared
- Leadership development
- Management development
- Formal approaches to management development
- Informal approaches to management development
- The role of the organization
- The role of the individual
- The role of HR and L&D specialists
- The criteria for leadership and management

Introduction

This chapter is about what organizations can do to develop effective leaders and managers, bearing in mind the point made by Drucker (1955: 158) that: 'The prosperity if not the survival of any business depends on the performance of its managers of tomorrow.'

The chapter starts with a definition of leadership and management development. This leads to a discussion of the nature of leadership and management as a basis for an analysis of what leadership and management development programmes might cover and an examination of the extent, if at all, to which leadership development and management development programmes are different. The conclusion is reached that while they are closely associated, and indeed may be conducted jointly, they are sufficiently different to justify being examined separately, and this is undertaken in the next two sections of the chapter.

Leadership and management development defined

Leadership and management development programmes provide managers with the leadership and managerial qualities required to achieve success. They form a vital ingredient in talent management, in association with the career planning and career management activities described in Chapter 25. A blended learning approach is used, which combines a number of learning activities such as planned experience, self-directed learning, coaching, mentoring, action learning, outdoor learning and formal education and training in programmes based on an analysis of learning needs.

The nature of leadership and management

There has been much debate on how leadership differs from management. The problem is that leadership involves management and management involves leadership, so it may be difficult to separate the two. There is some consensus on the essential nature of both and the skills involved, as set out below, but there is more disagreement on which is the most important.

Leadership

Leadership means inspiring people to do their best to achieve a desired result. It involves developing and communicating a vision for the future, motivating people and securing their engagement. As defined by Dixon (1994: 214): 'Leadership is no more than exercising such an influence upon others that they tend to act in concert towards achieving a goal which they might not have achieved so readily had they been left to their own devices.' Leadership skills include the ability to:

- inspire others;
- persuade others willingly to behave differently;
- clarify what needs to be done and why;
- communicate a sense of purpose to the team;
- understand, as established by research conducted by Tamkin *et al* (2010), that leaders cannot create performance themselves but are conduits for performance through their influence on others;
- get the team into action so that the task is achieved.

Management

Management is the process of achieving goals by deciding what to do and then getting it done through the effective use of resources. Management has often been defined as 'getting things done through people'. But managers are also responsible for guiding and controlling the business or their part of it by managing their other resources – finance, work systems and technology – as well as people.

Managers are doers. They deal with events as they occur. But they must also be concerned with where they are going. This requires strategic thinking, especially at higher levels. As strategic thinkers, managers develop a sense of purpose and frameworks for defining intentions and future directions. They are engaged in the process of strategic management.

The traditional model of what managers do is a logical and systematic process of planning, organizing, motivating and controlling. But this is misleading. Managers often carry out their work on a day-to-day basis in conditions of variety, turbulence and unpredictability. Managers may have to be specialists in ambiguity, with the ability to cope with conflicting and unclear requirements.

What are the differences?

Are leadership and management the same or different? Some commentators regard leadership as synonymous with management; others see them as distinct but closely linked and equally necessary activities; others consider management to be a subset of leadership; and yet others praise leadership and demonize management. Bennis (1989) viewed managers as those who promote efficiency, follow the rules and accept the status quo, while leaders focus on challenging the rules and promoting effectiveness. Kotter (1991) saw managers as being the ones who plan, budget, organize and control, while leaders set direction, manage change and motivate people. Hersey and Blanchard (1998) claimed that management merely consists of leadership applied to business situations; or in other words, management forms a subset of the broader process of leadership. It can be said that leadership is about managing people while management is about managing all the available resources, including people.

But as Birkinshaw (2010: 23) commented: 'By dichotomizing the work of executives in this way, Kotter, Bennis and others squeezed out the essence of what managers do and basically left them with the boring work that "leaders" don't want.' His view was that: 'To put it simply, we all need to be both leaders and managers' (ibid: 23). Burgoyne (2010: 42) observed that: 'Both [management and leadership] are needed and need to work closely together, often through the same person or team.' Earlier, Mintzberg (2004: 22) summed it all up (as he often did) when he wrote: 'Let's stop the dysfunctional separation of leadership from management. We all know that managers who don't lead are boring, dispiriting. Well, leaders who don't manage are distant, disconnected.'

Leadership and management development compared

In some quarters the term 'leadership development' has replaced 'management development', perhaps because the importance of ensuring that people have leadership qualities has been recognized, while it is believed that they can be safely left to acquire management skills in other ways, eg through experience. However, they are not the same, although they are closely associated.

The difference between them is that leadership development tends to be concerned with nurturing the softer skills of leadership through various educational processes, including formal learning events and programmes and coaching. This is illustrated in the three case studies at the end of the next section of this chapter.

In contrast, management development relies more on ensuring that managers acquire the ability to achieve their goals by managing a whole range of resources, including people. Because, as noted earlier, they have to work on a day-to-day basis in conditions of variety, turbulence and unpredictability, their development largely takes place by gaining the right sequence of experience, although this may be supplemented by self-directed learning and courses on management techniques. Further guidance can be provided by coaching and from mentors.

Leadership development

Leadership development programmes prepare people for leadership roles and situations beyond their current experience. It is sometimes said that leaders are born, not made. This is a rather discouraging statement for those who are not leaders by birthright. It may be true to the extent that some exceptional people seem to be visionaries, have built-in charisma and a natural ability to impose their personality on others. However, even they probably have to develop and hone these qualities when confronted with a situation demanding leadership. Ordinary mortals need not despair; they too can build on their natural capacities and develop their leadership abilities. As defined by Burgoyne (2010: 43):

'Leadership development in the widest sense involves the acquisition, development and utilization of leadership capability or the potential for it.' He observed: 'The will to lead is largely innate but the ability to do it well is largely learnt' (ibid 42).

Yukl (2006) proposed the following conditions for successful leadership development:

- clear learning objectives;
- clear, meaningful content;
- appropriate sequencing of content;
- appropriate mix of training methods;
- opportunity for active practice;

- relevant, timely feedback;
- high trainee confidence;
- appropriate follow-up activities.

But it is not all about subjecting leaders to development programmes. The organization has to play its part in ensuring that leaders are provided with the support and the working conditions they need to carry out their role properly. As Fiedler (1967: 276) emphasized: 'If we wish to increase organizational and group effectiveness we must learn not only to train leaders more effectively but also to build an organizational environment in which the leaders can perform well.'

CASE STUDIES

Cargill

Cargill is an international provider of food, agricultural and risk management products and services. Those in Cargill's different talent pools, such as the 'Next Generation Leaders' and 'Emerging Leaders' undertake both formal and informal development. In Cargill's high-performance Leadership Academy, entrants learn about the fundamentals of leadership and management in the company and work through a number of accelerated leadership modules, gaining the

knowledge to enable them to lead Cargill businesses. All of these courses are interspersed with more challenging projects and work assignments. Cargill corporate leaders also take part in the Leadership Academy, where they learn transformational leadership skills and the essentials of coaching and mentoring in formal programmes and informal learning activities, all of which form an important part of their leadership development.

Diageo

At Diageo, the international beverages company, a series of development strategies, particularly for leadership, have been based on Diageo's five values, which were created as the common heartbeat of all the component businesses. The values – 'Be the best', 'Passionate about consumers', 'Proud of what we do', 'Freedom to succeed' and 'Valuing each other' – have become central to Diageo's success, alongside a comprehensive performance management framework. Conversations about performance are now on a 'partnership' basis, where managers, with their employees, are expected to discuss the latter's aspirations and how their growth needs can be satisfied by the business.

The company's first leadership development programme, 1998's 'Building Diageo talent', was designed to help link strategy and organizational performance with individual performance. This had many components, including coaching and benchmarking for leadership development for 4,000 managers. Over recent years the company's leadership training has evolved to focus more on building 'a core Diageo mindset'. The senior team has prioritized developing a 'total talent strategy' and HR processes have been thoroughly embedded in management thinking worldwide.

HML

At HML (a financial services company) the leadership development programme for middle and senior managers consisted of the following elements:

- individual 360-degree feedback;

- orientation event – introduction and contracting;

- action learning sets (sets of six people, three sets in one programme group);

- four modules: profit, client, effectiveness, engagement;

- big event – transformational residential learning;

- self-directed modules;

- individual 360-degree feedback – benchmark scores;

- accreditation and celebration event.

Interview

Leadership development – the views of Pierre Nanterme, CEO of Accenture, the global professional services firm with 330,000 employees

The following answer was given by Pierre Nanterme to the question: 'You served as Accenture's chief leadership officer at one point. What's your philosophy on the best way to train employees to be better leaders?'

I learned a lot through that role which, frankly, I had to figure out a bit, because it was quite new. My background is around economics and finance; yet of course, in professional services, talent is key. And for many of our clients, whatever the industry, they all are coming to me saying their No. 1 challenge is getting the right talent. So first, I figured out that leadership and talent is the name of the game. Second, it's all about how you motivate people, how you're making sure they're going to stretch their own boundaries.

It's about selecting, hiring the best people, but that's not enough. Performance management is extraordinarily important to get people to their very best. Do you feel good in your role? If yes, that's the perfect time for you to experiment with something new, to get out of your comfort zone. This willingness to learn is probably the most important thing for leaders of today and tomorrow.

Source: Cunningham, 2015.

Management development

Management development is concerned with improving the performance of managers in their present roles, preparing them to take on greater responsibilities in the future and also developing their leadership skills. It was defined by Peters (2010: 28), as: 'A complex process by which individuals learn to perform effectively in a management role.' A systematic approach to management development is necessary to meet the needs of organizations for the talented managers they require and because the increasingly onerous demands made on line managers mean that they have to possess a wider range of developed skills than ever before.

The object of management development is to find ways in which the organization can produce, mainly from within, a supply of managers better equipped for their jobs at all levels. The principal method of doing this is to ensure that managers gain the right sequence and variety of experience, in good time, which will equip them for whatever level of responsibility they have the ability to reach in the course of their career. This experience can be supplemented – but never replaced – by courses carefully timed and designed to meet particular needs. Management development policies involve the use of both formal and informal approaches.

Formal approaches to management development

Formal approaches to management development consist of processes and events that are planned and provided by the organization. These should be based on the identification of development needs. The methods of defining learning needs described in Chapter 34 can be used to determine collective needs. For individuals, performance management reviews are an important means of producing personal development plans and learning contracts, also described in Chapter 34. This can be done more systematically at development centres. These consist of a concentrated (usually one or two days) programme of exercises, tests and interviews designed to identify managers' development needs and to provide counselling on their careers. Competency frameworks can be used as a means of identifying and expressing development needs and pointing the way to self-managed learning programmes or the provision of learning opportunities by the organization.

The formal approaches that can be used are:

- planned experience – which includes job rotation, job enlargement, taking part in project teams or task groups and secondment outside the organization – this is possibly the most effective approach on the grounds that managers learn to manage mainly by managing;

- coaching – a personal and usually one-to-one approach to helping people develop their skills and levels of competence (coaching skills are dealt with in Chapter 71);

- mentoring – the process of using specially selected and trained individuals (mentors) to provide guidance, pragmatic advice and continuing support that will help the person or persons allocated to them to learn and develop (see also Chapter 71);

- action learning – a method of helping managers develop their talents by exposing them to real problems; they are required to analyse them, formulate recommendations and then take action;

- outdoor learning – getting teams of participants to carry out physical activities so that they can learn about how they act under pressure as team leaders or team members;

- the use of performance management processes to provide feedback and satisfy

development needs; these would be competency-based in the sense that they would specify the competencies required and assess the degree to which individuals needed to develop those competencies;

- training by means of internal or external courses or through e-learning;

- structured self-development following a self-managed learning programme set out in a personal development plan and agreed as a learning contract with the manager or a management development adviser.

Informal approaches to management development

Informal approaches to management development make use of the learning experiences managers encounter during the course of their everyday work. Managers are learning every time they are confronted with an unusual problem, an unfamiliar task or a move to a different job. They then have to evolve new ways of dealing with the situation. They will learn if they reflect on what they did, in order to determine how and why it contributed to success or failure. This retrospective or reflective learning will be effective if managers can apply it successfully in the future.

Managers also learn from their managers. This may include how not to do things as well as what to do. Again, they will learn more if they have the capacity to reflect on what they have learnt and apply it to their own circumstances.

Experiential and reflective learning is potentially the most powerful form of learning. It comes naturally to some managers. They seem to absorb, unconsciously and by some process of osmosis, the lessons from their experience, although in fact they have probably developed a capacity for almost instantaneous analysis, which they store in their mental databank to retrieve when necessary.

But many managers either find it difficult to do this sort of analysis or do not recognize the need. This is where informal or at least semi-formal approaches can be used to encourage and help managers to learn more effectively. These comprise:

- emphasizing self-assessment and the identification of development needs by getting managers to assess their own performance against agreed objectives and analyse the factors that contributed to effective or less effective performance – this can be provided through performance management;

- getting managers to produce their own personal development plans – self-directed learning programmes;
- encouraging managers to discuss their problems and opportunities with their manager, colleagues or mentors to establish for themselves what they need to learn or be able to do;
- helping managers to understand their own learning styles so that they can make the best use of their experience and increase the effectiveness of their learning activities (this guidance may have to be provided more formally).

The role of the organization

The traditional view is that the organization need not concern itself with management development. The natural process of selection and the pressure of competition will ensure the survival of the fittest. Managers, in fact, are born not made. Cream rises to the top (but then so does scum). Management development has also been seen as a formal process using management inventories, multicoloured replacement charts, 'Cook's tours' around different departments for newly recruited graduates, detailed job rotation programmes, elaborate points schemes to appraise personal characteristics, and lots of formal courses operating on the 'sheep-dip' principle (ie everyone undergoes them).

The true role of the organization in management development lies somewhere between these two extremes: on the one hand, it is not enough, in conditions of rapid growth (when they exist) and change, to leave everything to chance – to trial and error; on the other hand, elaborate management development programmes cannot successfully be imposed on the organization. A mix of formal and informal methods is required that has to fit the organization's context and specific requirements.

The success of any management development programme depends upon the degree to which there is commitment to it at all levels of management. It

is not a separate activity to be handed over to a specialist and forgotten or ignored. The development of subordinates must be recognized as a natural and essential part of any manager's job. But the lead must come from the top.

The role of the individual

As Drucker perceptively wrote many years ago (1955: 162): 'Development is always self-development. Nothing could be more absurd than for the enterprise to assume responsibility for the development of a man. The responsibility rests with the individual, his abilities, his efforts.' But he went on to say:

> Every manager in a business has the opportunity to encourage individual self-development or to stifle it, to direct it or to misdirect it. He should be specifically assigned the responsibility for helping all men working with him to focus, direct and apply their self-development efforts productively. And every company can provide systematic development challenges to its managers. (ibid: 163)

The ability to manage is eventually something individuals mainly develop for themselves while carrying out their normal duties. But they will do this much better if they are given encouragement, guidance and opportunities by their organization and their managers. In McGregor's (1960: 192) vivid phrase, managers are grown – they are neither born nor made: 'The individual will grow into what he is capable of becoming, providing we can create the proper conditions for that growth.'

The role of HR and learning and development specialists

However, HR and L&D specialists still have an important role to play. They interpret the needs of the business and advise on how management development as a business-led activity can play its part in meeting these needs. They encourage managers to carry out their developmental activities, providing guidance as required, and they act as coaches or mentors. They also, of course, conduct or manage formal learning events and programmes, but their most important role is to help in developing a climate in which managers can grow.

Criteria for leadership and management development

The effectiveness and value of any approach to leadership and management development include the extent to which it:

- links to organizational goals and context – and so has relevance for the organization as well as for individuals;

- builds on and develops the qualities, skills and attitudes of participants;

- is supported by appropriate HR policies to do with recruitment and selection, talent management, succession planning and reward;

- has the full commitment of those responsible for the operation of the process, including line managers;

- is motivating to those encouraged to participate in it.

Key learning points: Leadership and management development

Leadership and management development defined

Leadership and management development programmes ensure that managers have the leadership and managerial qualities required to achieve success.

Leadership

Leadership means inspiring people to do their best to achieve a desired result. It involves developing and communicating a vision for the future, motivating people and securing their engagement.

Management

Defined as deciding what to do and then getting it done through the effective use of resources.

Leadership development compared with management development

Leadership development tends to be concerned with nurturing the softer skills of leadership through various educational processes, including formal learning events and programmes and coaching.

Management development relies more on ensuring that managers have the right sequence of experience, which may be supplemented by self-directed learning and courses on management techniques. Further guidance may be provided by coaching and from mentors. Management development programmes traditionally also cover leadership skills.

Leadership development

Leadership development programmes prepare people for leadership roles and situations beyond their current experience.

Management development

Management development is concerned with improving the performance of managers in their present roles, preparing them to take on greater responsibilities in the future and also developing their leadership skills.

Formal approaches to management development consist of processes and events planned and provided by the organization. They include planned experience, coaching and mentoring, action learning, outdoor learning, performance management, formal training and structured self-development.

Informal approaches to management development make use of the learning experiences that managers encounter during the course of their everyday work.

Responsibility for management development

Individual managers are largely responsible for their own development but need guidance, support and encouragement from their own managers and the HR function.

References

Bennis, W G (1989) *On Becoming a Leader*, New York, Addison Wesley

Birkinshaw, J (2010) An experiment in reinvention, *People Management*, 15 July, pp 22–24

Burgoyne, J (2010) Crafting a leadership and management development strategy, in (eds) J Gold, R Thorpe and A Mumford, *Gower Handbook of Leadership and Management Development*, Farnham, Gower, pp 42–55

Cunningham, L (2015) Accenture CEO explains why he's overhauling performance reviews, Washington Post [online] 2015 https://www.washingtonpost.com/news/on-leadership/wp/2015/07/23/accenture-ceo-explains-the-reasons-why-hes-overhauling-performance-reviews/ [accessed 8 February 2016]

Dixon, N F (1994) *On the Psychology of Military Incompetence*, London, Pimlico

Drucker, P (1955) *The Practice of Management*, Oxford, Heinemann

Fiedler, F E (1967) *A Theory of Leadership Effectiveness*, New York, McGraw-Hill

Hersey, P and Blanchard, K H (1998) *Management of Organizational Behaviour*, Englewood Cliffs, NJ, Prentice Hall

Kotter, J P (1991) Power, dependence and effective management, in (ed) J Gabarro, *Managing People and Organizations*, Boston, MA, Harvard Business School Publications

McGregor, D (1960) *The Human Side of Enterprise*, New York, McGraw-Hill

Mintzberg, H (2004) Enough leadership, *Harvard Business Review*, November, p 22

Peters, K (2010) National and international developments in leadership and management development, in (eds) J Gold, R Thorpe and A Mumford, *Gower Handbook of Leadership and Management Development*, Gower, Farnham, pp 23–38

Tamkin, P, Pearson, G, Hirsh, W and Constable, S (2010) *Exceeding Expectation: The principles of outstanding leadership*, London, The Work Foundation

Yukl, G (2006) *Leadership in Organizations*, 6th edn, Upper Saddle River, NJ, Prentice-Hall

40

The role of the learning and development function

KEY CONCEPTS AND TERMS

Enterprise social network

Social learning

Workplace learning

LEARNING OUTCOMES

On completing this chapter you should be able to define these key concepts. You should also understand:

- The role of the L&D function
- The role of the L&D specialist
- What needs to be done to manage the change
- The overall and specific roles of L&D specialists

Introduction

What might be called the learning and development revolution has taken place over the last few years. Although formal training courses are still provided where appropriate and e-learning is becoming more important, the emphasis is now on workplace, social and self-managed learning. This has also meant changes in the role of the L&D function and its members.

The role of the L&D function

The role of the L&D function is to provide advice, guidance and services in order to develop the capability of employees and thus improve individual and organizational performance. As Harrison (2009: 8) observed, the primary purpose of the L&D function is: 'To aid collective progress through the collaborative, expert and ethical stimulation and facilitation of learning and knowledge that support business goals, develop individual potential, and respect and build on diversity.'

A strategic approach is required. This means supporting the achievement of business goals by aligning L&D strategies to business strategies. These L&D strategies are designed to provide a comprehensive framework for developing people through the establishment of a learning culture and the encouragement of organizational learning. Strategies are also formulated for ensuring that L&D activities support talent management and knowledge management processes.

The L&D function operates as a centre of expertise, providing advice and support to line managers on how they should fulfil their responsibilities for promoting learning in their departments, overseeing the implementation of social learning, developing e-learning, and planning, commissioning, delivering and supervising learning events. In organizations with large numbers of managers to be trained or considerable quantities of apprentices or trainees, members of the function may spend a fairly high proportion of their time organizing education and training programmes.

Research by Hird and Sparrow (2012: 7) led to the conclusion that:

> Traditionally L&D departments have been transactional support functions that supply a range of courses that satisfy requests for support from the business. However, the business is increasingly looking for learning support that fits the requirements of knowledge workers – embedded in day-to-day activity, supporting development of professional networks and ultimately ensuring that the business has the knowledge and skills to deliver the business plan.

They also noted (ibid: 8) that:

> The influence of L&D in the organization was expanding, their learning offerings would grow, online learning was set to take centre stage, the majority of learning would become collaborative, and would be delivered in short timescales using micro-modules to provide more focused learning. This would require a significant change in course design and presentation, a move beyond current primary offerings of mainly foundational skills, and the need to embrace more blended learning (ie combining different learning methods).

The role of the L&D specialist

The old-style training managers were mainly engaged in providing formal courses or supervising formal training programmes. The new-style learning and development specialists have a very different role. They no longer spend most if not all of their time delivering training events or supervising training. Instead, their role is much more that of an internal consultant advising on and promoting workplace and social learning, who may act as a coach but not an old-fashioned trainer.

This was confirmed through research conducted by the CIPD (2015: 3) which noted: 'A key shift is a move away from learning delivery to performance consultancy, underpinned by the need for L&D to be aligned to the business and deliver tangible organizational and individual impact. There is also increasingly a need for L&D to support social learning.' The CIPD also commented (ibid: 15) that: 'L&D roles are becoming more diverse in response to a complex external environment. This represents a challenge for how to best focus roles. Do you build "performance consultants" able to diagnose, develop and curate? Or do you need experts who are focused entirely on data analytics, coaching or online learning?'

L&D specialists analyse learning needs and make proposals on how these can best be satisfied. They advise line managers on the achievement of workplace learning and coach them on the learning and development skills they need. They promote social learning, develop e-learning and the use of social media to aid learning, provide individual coaching, and plan, implement and evaluate training events and programmes, often outsourcing training to external providers.

The following typology of roles for L&D specialists, in broad levels of seniority starting from the top, was produced by Rosemary Harrison (2009: 309):

- A professional adviser – a strategic business partner working to achieve tailored, value-adding solutions to meet clients' needs.

- A knowledge architect – a senior strategic adviser on learning processes and solutions to aid knowledge creation, sharing and transfer.

- A brand manager – shapes and maintains a clear and consistent brand image for all L&D activity and manages the L&D function.
- A commercial lead – creates revenue streams from the organization's L&D processes, selling them to internal and external customers.
- A learning specialist – expert with specialist skills in the design, delivery and evaluation of learning events and processes.
- An administrator – supports L&D activity at all levels.

The role of L&D specialists in workplace learning

Although 70 per cent of learning may occur in the workplace, this does not absolve L&D from any responsibility for its effectiveness; quite the opposite. L&D has to be much more closely involved in what is going on than it was when it lived in a remote learning centre.

What L&D specialists have to do is to brief line managers and their team leaders on their responsibilities for learning and provide coaching on how to fulfil them. L&D specialists can advise on learning arrangements, eg the provision of induction training, mentoring or buddying. They can assist in choosing departmental staff who will be involved in encouraging learning and provide them with coaching on their duties on a one-to-one basis or jointly in workshops. L&D specialists can also monitor the effectiveness of workshop learning arrangements in departments to ensure that advice and help is given to effect improvements where necessary.

The role of L&D specialists in social learning

The role of L&D specialists in social learning is to liaise with work teams to build or enhance existing sharing practices as an integral part of their daily work, not as an extra initiative. 'Supporting social learning in work teams involves working closely with teams – not by designing a programme of instruction for them, but by encouraging team members to share their knowledge and engage in new collaborative work practices' (Hart, 2014: 42).

L&D specialists can also help to build and sustain communities of practice and learning communities. They may be involved in setting up and using an Enterprise Social Network (ESN) as described in Chapter 36 and may develop a stream of short optional learning activities to be hosted on the ESN as small chunks of learning content probably lasting less than 15 minutes.

Skills required

The CIPD (2016) quoted a senior manager, academy development in the finance sector as follows: 'We need social learning and collaboration tools. Ability to facilitate learning rather than deliver learning. Using analytics to understand performance improvement. Curating content that exists already rather than buying new.' The following formidable range of skills required by L&D specialists were listed by the CIPD:

- classroom/F2F learning/training delivery;
- learning management/strategy;
- marketing and stakeholder engagement;
- instructional design;
- implementing blended learning;
- supporting ongoing workplace performance (eg curating assets etc);
- facilitating social and collaborative learning;
- programme evaluation and data analytics;
- live online learning delivery;
- digital content development;
- performance consulting.

Key learning points: The role of the learning and development function

The role of the L&D function

The role of the L&D function is to provide advice, guidance and services in order to develop the capability of employees and thus improve individual and organizational performance.

The role of the L&D specialist

L&D specialists no longer spend most if not all of their time delivering training events or supervising training programmes, although they may still be involved in the development of e-learning programmes. Instead, their role is much more that of an internal consultant advising on and promoting workplace and social learning, who may act as a coach but not an old-fashioned trainer.

As established through research conducted by the CIPD (2015: 3): 'A key shift is a move away from learning delivery to performance consultancy, underpinned by the need for L&D to be aligned to the business and deliver tangible organizational and individual impact.'

The CIPD research (ibid:15) also produced the comment that: 'L&D roles are becoming more diverse in response to a complex external environment. This represents a challenge for how to best focus roles. Do you build "performance consultants" able to diagnose, develop and curate? Or do you need experts who are focused entirely on data analytics, coaching or online learning?'

L&D specialists:

- analyse learning needs and make proposals on how these can best be satisfied;

- advise line managers on the achievement of workplace learning and coach them on the learning and development skills they need;

- promote social learning;

- develop e-learning and the use of social media to aid learning;

- provide individual coaching;

- plan, implement and evaluate training events and programmes, often outsourcing training to external providers.

The following typology of roles for L&D specialists, in broad levels of seniority starting from the top, was produced by Rosemary Harrison (2009: 309):

- a professional adviser;

- a knowledge architect;

- a brand manager;

- a commercial lead;

- a learning specialist;

- an administrator.

The role of L&D in workplace learning

L&D has in effect a consultancy and coaching role – much harder and more demanding than laying on a course but more rewarding. What L&D has to do is to focus on line managers and their team leaders who need to be briefed on their responsibilities for learning and coached in how to fulfil them.

The role of L&D in social learning

The role of L&D in social learning is basically to liaise with work teams to build or enhance existing sharing practices as an integral part of their daily work, not as an extra initiative.

The skills required

L&D specialists need to understand the business, possess insight into the people issues relating to capability and skill in order to establish learning and development needs, have the ability to facilitate workplace and social learning, possess technological capability, especially related to the use of e-learning, and have diagnostic and analytical skills.

References

CIPD (2015) Learning and development: evolving roles, enhancing skills, *CIPD* [online] http://www.cipd.co.uk/binaries/l-d-evolving-roles-enhancing-skills_2015.pdf [accessed 11 November 2015]

CIPD (2016) Preparing for the future of learning: a changing perspective for L&D leaders, *CIPD* [online] http://www.cipd.co.uk/binaries/preparing-for-the-future-of-learning_2016-a-changing-perspective-for-l-and-d-leaders.pdf [accessed 5 June 2016]

Harrison, R (2009) *Learning & Development*, 5th edn, London, CIPD

Hart, J (2014) *The Social Learning Handbook* [online] http://www.c4lpt.co.uk/blog/2014/01/27/social-learning-handbook-pdf-now-available/ [accessed 7 November 2015]

Hird, M and Sparrow, P (2012) Learning & development: seeking a renewed focus? White paper 12/01, October 2012, Centre for Performance-Led HR, Lancaster University [online] http://www.lancaster.ac.uk/media/lancaster-university/content-assets/documents/lums/cphr/LDWP.pdf [accessed 11 November 2015]

PART VIII

Performance management

PART VIII CONTENTS

Introduction

Performance management is a systematic process for improving individual, team and organizational performance. It does this by helping people to understand what good performance means and by providing the guidance and help needed to achieve it. The term performance management has largely replaced that of performance appraisal which should be restricted to a description of the assessment process following a performance review.

The part covers in Chapter 41 a description of the fundamental concepts governing the practice of performance management together with an analysis of how performance management affects organizational performance and how it functions as a rewarding process. Chapter 42 includes a description of the process of performance management, described as sets of interrelated activities and processes which are treated as an integrated and key component of an organization's approach to managing performance through people and developing the skills and capabilities of its human capital. It also covers methods of introducing performance management and reviews the issues that affect how well it functions. Reference is made to new developments in performance management typified by a number of large organizations that have 'reinvented' the process by abandoning the annual performance review and rating.

41
Performance management fundamentals

KEY CONCEPTS AND TERMS

Objectives

Performance appraisal

Performance management

LEARNING OUTCOMES

On completing this chapter you should be able to define these key concepts. You should also know about:

- The meaning of performance
- The theories underpinning performance management
- Principles of performance management

- The aims of performance management
- The impact of performance management on performance
- Performance management and reward

Introduction: performance management defined

Performance management is the continuous process of improving performance by setting individual and team goals which are aligned to the strategic goals of the organization, planning performance to achieve the goals, reviewing progress, and developing the knowledge, skills and abilities of people.

Its four elements are agreement, feedback, positive reinforcement and dialogue. Cappelli (2008: 196) wrote that: 'When employees fail in their jobs, part of the organization also fails.' Performance management aims to eliminate or at least significantly reduce this possibility. Pulakos (2009:3) emphasized that: 'Performance management is the key process through which work gets done. It's how organizations communicate expectations and drive behaviour to achieve important goals; it's also about how organizations identify ineffective performers for development programmes or other personnel actions.'

The basis of performance management

Performance management should be based on an understanding of what the word 'performance' means. Those concerned with introducing and operating performance management should be aware of the underpinning theories and the principles involved.

The meaning of performance

Performance is defined as behaviour that accomplishes results. As noted by Brumbach (1988: 387):

> Performance means both behaviours and results. Behaviours emanate from the performer and transform performance from abstraction to action. Not just the instruments for results, behaviours are also outcomes in their own right – the product of mental and physical effort applied to tasks – and can be judged apart from results.

Brumbach observed that because of the significance of behaviour there was more to success or failure than whether results were achieved: 'Success is not always positive nor failure always negative' (ibid: 388). This concept of performance leads to the conclusion that when assessing and rewarding the performance of individuals a number of factors have to be considered, including both outputs (results) and inputs (behaviour); in other words, not just what is done but how it is done.

Any attempt to manage performance should also bear in mind that it is a complicated notion. Campbell (1990) suggested that performance is the outcome of three determinants:

- knowledge about facts and things (termed declarative knowledge);
- knowledge about how things are done and the skills to do them (termed procedural knowledge and skills);
- motivation to act, to expend effort and to persist (termed motivation).

Underpinning theories

The following three theories underpin performance management.

Goal theory

Goal theory, as developed by Latham and Locke (1979), highlights four mechanisms that connect goals to performance outcomes: 1) they direct attention to priorities; 2) they stimulate effort; 3) they challenge people to bring their knowledge and skills to bear to increase their chances of success; and 4) the more challenging the goal, the more people will draw on their full repertoire of skills. This theory supports the emphasis in performance management on setting and agreeing objectives against which performance can be measured and managed.

Control theory

Control theory focuses attention on feedback as a means of shaping behaviour. As people receive feedback on their behaviour they appreciate the discrepancy between what they are doing and what they are expected to do, and take corrective action to overcome the discrepancy. Feedback is recognized as a crucial part of performance management processes.

Social cognitive theory

Social cognitive theory was developed by Bandura (1986). It is based on his central concept of self-efficacy. This suggests that what people believe they can or cannot do powerfully impacts on their performance. Developing and strengthening positive self-belief in employees is therefore an important performance management objective.

Principles of performance management

The principles governing effective performance management were defined well by Egan (1995):

> Most employees want direction, freedom to get their work done, and encouragement not control. The performance management system should be a control system only by exception. The solution is to make it a collaborative development system in two ways. First, the entire performance management process – coaching, counselling,

feedback, tracking, recognition, and so forth – should encourage development. Ideally, team members grow and develop through these interactions. Second, when managers and team members ask what they need to be able to do to do bigger and better things, they move to strategic development.

Strebler *et al* (2001) suggested that the principles set out below were required for performance management to work effectively. They must:

- have clear aims and measurable success criteria;
- be designed and implemented with appropriate employee involvement;
- be simple to understand and operate;
- play a major part in the achievement of management goals;
- allow employees a clear 'line of sight' between their performance goals and those of the organization;
- focus on role clarity and performance improvement;
- be closely allied to a clear and adequately resourced training and development infrastructure;
- make crystal clear the purpose of any direct link to reward and build in proper equity and transparency safeguards;
- be regularly and openly reviewed against success criteria.

Aims of performance management

Performance management is a means of getting better results by providing the means for individuals to perform well within an agreed framework of planned goals, standards and competency requirements. It involves developing a shared understanding about what is to be achieved and how it is to be achieved. The aim is to develop the capacity of people to meet and exceed expectations and to achieve their full potential to the benefit of themselves and the organization. A further aim is to clarify how individuals are expected to contribute to the achievement of organization goals by aligning

individual objectives with the strategic objectives of the organization.

Performance management provides the basis for self-development but, importantly, it is also about ensuring that the support and guidance people need to develop and improve are readily available. Performance management can play an important role in rewarding employees by providing them with positive feedback and the recognition of their accomplishments.

The impact of performance management on performance

Performance management is expected to improve organizational performance generally by creating a performance culture in which the achievement of high performance is a way of life. More specifically, effective performance management ensures that individual goals are aligned with organizational goals, so that key performance indicators for employees are linked to those of the organization, and the contribution people can make to organizational performance is therefore defined.

A description of what performance management should contribute was defined by Jones *et al* (1995) as follows:

- communicate a shared vision throughout the organization to help to establish and support appropriate leadership and management styles;
- define individual requirements and expectation of all employees in terms of the inputs and outputs expected from them, thus reducing confusion and ambiguity;
- provide a framework and environment for teams to develop and succeed;
- provide the climate and systems which support reward and communicate how people and the organization can achieve improved performance;
- help people manage ambiguity.

It is assumed that managers and their team members working together on a continuing basis throughout the year to use performance management processes such as goal setting, feedback, performance analysis and coaching will create a situation in which continuous improvement in results will be guaranteed. This could be regarded as an unrealistic aspiration – an optimistic belief – but it is the one that underpins the concept of performance management. The holy grail of performance management is to provide evidence that this belief is justified. But it isn't easy – for the reasons given below.

Establishing the impact

Establishing the impact between human resource management (HRM) practices – including performance management – and firm performance is problematic. This is because causality – determining the link between independent and dependent variables (cause and effect) – is a major issue in research, especially in the HRM field. Correlation does not imply causation. It may be relatively easy to establish correlations in the shape of a demonstration that X is associated with Y; it is much more difficult and sometimes impossible to prove that X causes Y.

Evidence from research

Research projects and other analytical studies that deal with the impact of performance management on overall firm performance, or as aspects of individual performance, are summarized below.

Latham and Locke

As reported by Latham and Locke (1979), field research in a logging company involving 292 supervisors established that those who set specific production goals achieved the highest productivity. A further study of 892 supervisors produced the same result.

Another study in a logging company involved setting a difficult but attainable target for loading trucks. Loggers were told that they would receive no reward for achieving the target but that no one would be criticized for failing to do so. After the third month, performance exceeded 90 per cent of the trucks' capacity compared with 58–63 per cent previously. This level has been sustained for the seven years to date.

An analysis of 10 field studies conducted by various researchers for a range of jobs showed that the percentage change in performance after goal setting ranged from 11 per cent to 27 per cent (median 16 per cent).

McDonald and Smith

Research was conducted by McDonald and Smith (1991) covering 437 publicly quoted US companies. The findings were that the 205 respondents with performance management as opposed to the others without had:

- higher profits, better cash flows, stronger stock market performance and higher stock value;
- significant gains over three years in financial performance and productivity;
- higher sales growth per employee;
- lower real growth in number of employees.

The researchers commented that: 'In the successful companies the difference in managing employee performance seems to be that it is regarded as a mainstream business issue, not an isolated "personnel problem".'

This is a classic case of reversed causality. Performance management systems may have helped to generate successful companies but it is just as likely that the successful companies were the ones with the inclination and money to introduce sophisticated practices such as performance management.

Institute of Personnel Management

It was reported by the IPM in 1992 that their extensive research found no evidence that improved performance in the private sector is associated with the pursuit of formal performance management programmes. Poor financial performers were as likely to introduce performance management as good performers. There were no readily available and comparable measures of performance in the public sector to test this link, even though performance management is more likely to be adopted in the public sector.

However, one positive theme that was traced throughout the research was the extent to which performance management raised awareness of the pressures on the organization to perform.

Rodgers and Hunter

A meta-analysis by Rodgers and Hunter (1991) of 70 studies in goal setting, participation in decision making and objective feedback (as included in typical management-by-objectives programmes) found that 68 of them showed productivity gains and only two showed productivity losses. This led to the conclusion that management by objectives programmes, when properly implemented and when supported by top management, had an almost universal positive effect on productivity.

Bernadin *et al*

Bernardin *et al* (1995) found improvement in subordinate and peer ratings following 360-degree feedback, but no changes in customer ratings or sales volume.

Guest and Conway

An analysis by Guest and Conway (1998) covered the 388 organizations with performance management surveyed by Armstrong and Baron in 1998. The key criteria used for determining the effectiveness of performance management were the achievement of financial targets, development of skills, development of competence, improved customer care and improved quality. Against these criteria, over 90 per cent of respondents rated performance management as being moderately or highly effective. The personnel managers, who in the main responded to the survey, believed that others, and more particularly senior managers, are even more positive in their evaluation. Many also believed that the overall performance of their organization, judged by internal criteria such as quality, productivity and cost, and external criteria such as market share and profitability, was at least as good and often better than that of their main competitors.

But there were caveats. The analysis indicated that the views of respondents to the survey should all be viewed with extreme caution since they are often based on a very limited form of formal evaluation, or made in the absence of any formal evaluation. This raises serious questions about the basis for the generally positive assessment of performance management.

Further, more detailed statistical analysis of the replies to the questionnaire failed to demonstrate consistent evidence of any link between the practice of performance management and outcomes such as the achievement of financial targets, achievement of quality and customer service goals and employee development goals. The conclusion reached was that this survey produced no convincing evidence that performance management has an impact on overall organizational performance.

Gallup

As reported by Risher (2005) Gallup has analysed its Q12 survey and found that employers with a formal performance review process have more engaged employees – 33 per cent versus 21 per cent – and fewer disengaged employees – 12 per cent versus 29 per cent.

Sibson and WorldatWork

As reported by Kochanski (2007) a survey by Sibson and WorldatWork found that high-performing firms have strong leadership support for performance management. An analysis of total return to shareholders over a three-year period (2003–05) revealed that 64 per cent of the top-performing companies had performance management systems that were rated as effective, compared to only 36 per cent of the bottom-performing companies. The companies that excelled at performance management: 1) used their systems as the primary way to manage individual performance throughout the company; 2) have strong leadership support; and 3) have more line champions.

Watson Wyatt

As cited by Pulakos *et al* (2009), a recent Watson Wyatt survey found that only 30 per cent of workers felt that their performance management system helped to improve performance. Less than 40 per cent said that the system established clear performance goals or generated honest feedback.

Conclusions

The results of these studies are mixed. But it is still possible to believe in the benefits of performance management to organizations on the assumption that people are more likely to respond positively and are more likely to work to improve their performance and develop their capabilities if they share in the processes of defining expectations and reviewing performance and competency against those expectations, and are involved in creating and implementing plans for developing their skills and competences. If this happens generally (admittedly, often a big if), and if the organization provides the managerial and systems support necessary, then the presumption that this will contribute to overall performance improvement is not unreasonable, even if it cannot be proved.

Performance management as a rewarding process

Performance management, if carried out properly, can reward people by recognition through feed-back, the provision of opportunities to achieve, the scope to develop skills, and guidance on career paths. All these are non-financial rewards that can encourage job and organizational engagement and make a longer-lasting and more powerful impact than financial rewards such as performance-related pay.

Performance management is, of course, also associated with pay by generating the information required to decide on pay increases or bonuses related to performance, competency or contribution. In some organizations this is its main purpose, but performance management is, or should be, much more about developing people and rewarding them in the broadest sense.

Key learning points: Performance management fundamentals

Performance management defined

Performance management is the continuous process of improving performance by setting individual and team goals which are aligned to the strategic goals of the organization, planning performance to achieve the goals, reviewing and assessing progress, and developing the knowledge, skills and abilities of people.

The meaning of performance

Performance is defined as behaviour that accomplishes results.

Underpinning theories

- goal theory;
- control theory;
- social cognitive theory.

Aims of performance management

Performance management is a means of getting better results by providing the means for individuals to perform well within an agreed framework of planned goals, standards and competency requirements.

Impact of performance management

Performance management is expected to improve organizational performance, generally by creating a performance culture in which the achievement of high performance is a way of life.

The results of research studies on the impact of performance management are mixed. But it is still possible to believe in the benefits of performance management to organizations on the assumption that people are more likely to respond positively and are more likely to work to improve their performance and develop their capabilities if they share in the processes of defining expectations and reviewing performance and competency against those expectations, and are involved in creating and implementing plans for developing their skills and competences.

Performance management and reward

Performance management, if carried out properly, can reward people by recognition through feedback, the provision of opportunities to achieve, the scope to develop skills, and guidance on career paths.

References

Armstrong, M and Baron, A (1998) *Performance Management: The new realities*, London, CIPD

Bandura, A (1986) *Social Boundaries of Thought and Action*, Englewood Cliffs, NJ, Prentice-Hall

Bernadin, H K, Kane, J S, Ross, S, Spina, J D and Johnson, D L (1995) Performance appraisal design, development and implementation, in (eds) G R Ferris, S D Rosen, and D J Barnum, *Handbook of Human Resource Management*, Cambridge, MA Blackwell

Brumbach, G B (1988) Some ideas, issues and predictions about performance management, *Public Personnel Management*, Winter, pp 387–402

Campbell, J P (1990) Modeling the performance prediction problem in industrial and organizational psychology, in (eds), M P Dunnette and L M Hugh, *Handbook of Industrial and Organizational Psychology*, Cambridge MA, Blackwell

Cappelli, P (2008) *Talent on Demand: Managing talent in an uncertain age*, Boston, MA, Harvard Business School Press

Egan, G (1995) A clear path to peak performance, *People Management*, 18 May, pp 34–37

Guest, D E and Conway, N (1998) An analysis of the results of the CIPD performance management survey, in M Armstrong and A Baron, *Performance Management: The new realities*, London, CIPD

Institute of Personnel Management (1992) *Performance Management in the UK: An analysis of the issues*, IPM, London

Jones, P, Palmer, J, Whitehead, D and Needham, P (1995) Prisms of performance, *The Ashridge Journal*, April, pp 10–14

Kochanski, J (2007) Sibson reveals secrets of successful performance management, *Employee Benefit News*, September, pp 22–23

Latham, G P and Locke, E A (1979) Goal setting: a motivational technique that works, *Organizational Dynamics*, Autumn, pp 442–47

McDonald, D and Smith, A (1991) A proven connection: performance management and business results, *Compensation & Benefits Review*, January–February, pp 59–64

Pulakos, E D (2009) *Performance management: A new approach for driving business results*, Malden, MA, Wiley-Blackwell

Pulakos, E D, Mueller-Hanson, R A and O'Leary, R S (2008) Performance management in the US, in (eds) A Varma, P S Budhwar and A DeNisi, *Performance Management Systems: A global perspective*, Routledge, Abingdon

Risher, H (2005) Getting serious about performance management, *Compensation & Benefits Review*, November–December, pp 18–26

Rodgers, R and Hunter, J E (1991) Impact of management by objectives on organizational performance, *Journal of Applied Psychology*, 76 (2), pp 322–36

Strebler, M T, Bevan, S and Robertson D (2001) *Performance Review: Balancing objectives and content*, Brighton, Institute for Employment Studies

42
The process of performance management

KEY CONCEPTS AND TERMS

Forced distribution

KSAs

Objectives

Performance management cycle

Performance management system

Personal development planning

Smart goals

360-degree feedback

Vitality curve

LEARNING OUTCOMES

On completing this chapter you should be able to define these key concepts. You should also know about:

- The performance management cycle
- Performance planning
- Managing performance throughout the year
- Reviewing performance
- Assessing performance
- Performance management issues
- 360-degree feedback systems
- Introducing performance management
- Developments in performance management

Introduction

Performance management consists of a number of interrelated activities and processes. These are treated as an integrated and key component of an organization's approach to creating a high-performance culture, managing performance through people and developing the skills and capabilities of its human capital, thus enhancing organizational capability and the achievement of sustained competitive advantage.

Performance management is a natural process of management; it is not an HRM technique or tool. As a natural process of management, performance management can be modelled as a cycle, as shown in Figure 42.1, which corresponds with Deming's (1986) plan-do-check-act model.

The processes of performance planning, managing performance, performance reviews, performance assessment, recording the agreement and review and the use of web-enabled technology are described below.

Performance planning

Performance planning is carried out within the context of the corporate strategy. It is based on performance agreements. These emerge from the analysis of role requirements and from performance

FIGURE 42.1   The performance management cycle

reviews where assessments of performance lead to the definition of future requirements. Agreement is reached during the planning process on how performance will be assessed. Changes to the role profile and objectives can be made as required by changing circumstances.

Expectations are defined generally in role profiles that specify key result areas; the knowledge, skills and abilities (KSAs) required and the behavioural competencies needed to perform well. What has to be accomplished in key result areas can be defined in the form of objectives or targets. The acronym 'SMART' is a popular way of defining a good objective. Traditionally, S stands for specific (sometimes 'stretching'), M for measurable, A for agreed, R for realistic and T for time-related. Line managers and individual employees do indeed require some guidance on setting objectives but not in this simplistic form. Rather than using this facile formula they should be encouraged to focus on the five key requirements of a good objective, namely that it should be:

1 Clear.
2 Challenging.
3 Achievable but not too easily.
4 Measurable either in quantified or in qualitative terms.
5 Agreed.

Methods of measuring performance in the shape of key performance indicators (KPIs) are also agreed.

An important aspect of performance planning is the process of aligning individual goals with the strategic goals of the organization.

The manager and the individual also agree on a development plan which specifies what the latter needs to do with the help of the manager to achieve objectives, raise standards and improve performance.

The plan may incorporate a personal development plan that provides a learning action programme to be actioned by the individual with the support of the manager. This may include formal training but, more importantly, it will cover a wider set of learning and development activities such as self-managed learning, coaching, mentoring, project work and e-learning.

Managing performance throughout the year

Perhaps one of the most important features of performance management is that it is a continuous process which reflects normal good management practices of setting direction, monitoring and measuring performance and taking action accordingly. Performance management should not be imposed on managers as something 'special' they have to do. It should instead be treated as a natural function that all good managers carry out.

The process of managing performance throughout the year needs to take into account that in these turbulent times it is probable that an annual objective-setting exercise will not be appropriate. Objectives need to be reviewed as circumstances and demands change.

Performance reviews

Traditionally, formal performance reviews provided an annual (usually) focal point for the consideration of key performance and development issues. They led to the completion of the performance management process by informing performance agreements and often involved some form of assessment, as examined in the next section of this chapter. The following are some basic guidelines for the satisfactory conduct of a traditional formal review:

● The review should be rooted in the reality of the individual's performance.

● The review should be conducted as a dialogue between partners.

● Individuals should be encouraged to assess their own performance and become active agents for change in improving their results.

● Managers should adopt an enabling role: coaching and providing support and guidance.

● There should be no surprises – performance issues should have been dealt with as they arise throughout the year.

● Positive feedback should be given on the things that the individual did well in addition to areas for improvement.

● The review should be forward looking, focusing on the development needs of the individual and how they can be met by the individual with the help of the manager.

These guidelines may sound straightforward and obvious enough but they can be hard to apply in the traditional formal appraisal review. Too often, this takes the form of a dishonest annual ritual. Its primary purpose is often to inform performance pay decisions (or worse, in some systems, whether or not the individual should be retained). Reviews are backward looking and judgmental rather than looking to the future to establish development needs. Traditional formal reviews can be stressful for both parties. Managers often hate doing them and therefore do them badly, treating them as a ritual to be observed at the behest of HR and dishonestly fudging their judgements. Research by The Society for Human Resource Management in 2012 found that between 60 and 90 per cent of employees (including managers) dislike formal reviews. Mueller-Hanson and Pulakos (2015) noted that: 'Study after study has shown that the performance review is dreaded – it is not only perceived to be of little value but it is highly demotivating to employees.'

The answer to this problem is to abolish the annual formal review and hold less formal performance and development conversations (PDCs). These take place throughout the year as part of the normal process of management. They could be held once a quarter or even more frequently as required. This is the approach adopted by organizations such as Adobe, Deloitte, Gap and IBM. PDCs include feedback from the manager and, possibly, some self-assessment by the individual. They are rooted in the reality of what the individual is doing. PDCs are concrete not abstract. They focus on the goals people set for themselves and how they are progressing toward those goals, along with their contribution, past and present, to the company. They focus on strengths rather than dwelling on shortcomings. Successes are recognized although things that have not gone according to plan will be noted in order to learn lessons for the future. PDCs do not lead to a performance rating or the completion of a report although a note can be taken of any agreed actions. They also provide opportunities for revising or renewing objectives and development plans. Reference may be made to recent events but the emphasis is on the future. They are not post-mortems.

Performance assessment

Performance management schemes usually but not inevitably include an assessment, which is carried out during or after a performance review meeting. This may be carried out by overall assessment, rating or visual assessment, as described below.

Overall assessment

An overall assessment is based on a general analysis of performance under the headings of the performance agreement. The aim is to reach agreement about future action rather than to produce a summarized and potentially superficial judgement. Managers are expected to reach an understanding with each member of their team as a result of the analysis, which will ensure that the latter will appreciate how well or not so well they are doing. The analysis should also identify the high-flyers and those who are failing to meet acceptable standards. An overall assessment is recorded in a narrative consisting of a written summary of views about the level of performance achieved. This at least ensures that managers have to collect their thoughts together and put them down on paper. But different people will consider different aspects of performance and there will be no consistency in the criteria used for assessment, so it is necessary to have a framework for the analysis. This could be provided on a 'what' and 'how' basis. The 'what' is the achievement of previously agreed objectives related to the headings on a role profile. The 'how' is behaviour in relating to competency framework headings. The results for each 'what' and 'how' heading could be recorded following a joint analysis during a review meeting.

One problem with this form of assessment, indeed any form of assessment, is that we can recognize people at either extreme (top performers and inadequate performers) but cannot accurately distinguish performance differences in the bulk of people lying between those extremes. What managers can do is to tell an individual that he or she has done exceptionally well and that they will therefore be included in the talent management programme, or managers can inform another individual that he or she has not done very well and that they must discuss what needs to be done about it. The others can be told that they are doing a perfectly good job and discussions can take place on how they can build on their strengths or on any learning activity (preferably self-directed) that might help them to do even better. Another problem with overall assessments is that they can be bland, superficial and overgeneralized. This is why many schemes use rating.

Rating

However, the most common form of assessment in traditional performance management schemes is rating. Rating summarizes on a scale the views of the rater on the level of performance achieved. A rating scale is supposed to assist in making judgements that inform performance pay decisions, or it simply produces an instant summary for the record of how well or not so well someone is doing.

Rating scales can be defined alphabetically (a, b, c, etc), or numerically (1, 2, 3, etc). Initials (ex for excellent, etc) are sometimes used in an attempt to disguise the hierarchical nature of the scale. The alphabetical or numerical points scale may be described adjectivally, for example, a = excellent, b = good, c = satisfactory and d = unsatisfactory.

The e-reward 2014 survey of performance management found that overall ratings were used by 79 per cent of respondents. The most popular number of levels was five (43 per cent of respondents). However, some organizations settled for three levels. There is no evidence that any single approach is clearly superior to another, although the greater the number of levels the more is being asked of managers in the shape of discriminatory judgement. It is, however, preferable for level definitions to be positive rather than negative and for them to provide as much guidance as possible on the choice of ratings. It is equally important to ensure that level definitions are compatible with the culture of the organization and that close attention is given to ensuring that managers use them as consistently as possible.

The main problem with ratings is that they are largely subjective and it is difficult to achieve consistency between the ratings given by different managers. Because the notion of 'performance' is often unclear, subjectivity can increase. Even if objectivity is achieved, to sum up the total performance of a person with a single rating is a gross oversimplification of what may be a complex set of factors influencing that performance. To do this after a detailed discussion of strengths and weaknesses suggests that the rating will be a superficial and arbitrary judgement. To label people as 'average' or 'below average', or whatever equivalent terms are used, is both demeaning and demotivating.

The whole performance review session may be dominated by the fact that it will end with a rating, thus severely limiting the forward-looking and developmental focus of the meeting, which is all-important. This is particularly the case if the rating governs increases in performance or contribution pay.

Another problem is that managers may inflate ratings to avoid confrontation with the individuals concerned. Some organizations (8 per cent of the respondents to the performance management survey conducted by Armstrong and Baron (2004)) attempted to counter this by using forced distribution, which requires conforming to a laid down distribution of ratings between different levels, for example: A = 5 per cent, B = 15 per cent, C = 60 per cent, D = 15 per cent and E = 5 per cent. This achieves consistency of a sort but managers and staff rightly resent being forced into this sort of straitjacket.

An alternative to forced distribution is forced ranking. It is most common in the United States where the outcome is sometimes known as a 'vitality curve'. Managers are required to place their staff in order from best to worst. The problem with forced ranking, as with forced distribution, is that the notion of performance may not be defined and is therefore not measurable. In the case of ranking it is therefore unclear what the resulting order of employees truly represents.

Some organizations, mainly in the United States, have gone as far as adopting the practice of annually terminating the employment of 5 to 10 per cent of the consistently lowest performers. This is sometimes called 'stack ranking' and may be referred to colloquially as 'rank and yank'. It is claimed that this practice 'raises the bar', ie it is said that it improves the overall level of performance in the business. There is no evidence that this is the case. A mechanistic 'rank and yank' system will only create a climate of fear and will at best inhibit and at worst destroy any possibility that performance management is perceived and used as a developmental

FIGURE 42.3(a)   Performance management form (part 1)

PERFORMANCE AND DEVELOPMENT: AGREEMENT AND PERSONAL DEVELOPMENT PLAN	
Name:	Forename(s):
Job title:	Department:
Reviewer's name:	Job title:

PERFORMANCE AND DEVELOPMENT AGREEMENT	
Objectives	Performance measures
Competencies	Agreed actions

PERSONAL DEVELOPMENT PLAN			
Development need	How it is to be met	Action by whom	Target completion date

FIGURE 42.3(b)   Performance management form (part 2)

PERFORMANCE AND DEVELOPMENT REVIEW	
Objectives	Achievements
Competencies	Actions taken
Development needs	Actions taken

Comments by reviewer:

Signed: Date:

Comments by person reviewed:

Signed: Date:

not interested, or they don't have the skills, or both. It is important to get buy-in from top management so that their leadership can encourage line managers to play their part. Line managers should be involved in planning the scheme and its implementation. They have to be convinced that the time they spend will pay off in terms of improved performance. To encourage buy-in, the process has to be simple (not too much paper). The demanding skills of concluding performance agreements, setting objectives, assessing performance, giving feedback and coaching need to be developed by formal training, supplemented by coaching and the use of mentors.

Requirements for success

Research by Haines and St-Onge (2012) established that performance management is more likely to be successful when:

- there is more performance management training for managers covering performance coaching and constructive feedback;
- employee recognition is emphasized;
- the corporate culture values engagement;
- performance management is strategically integrated with human resource management and the business plans of the organization;
- human capital is valued;
- there is a positive employee relations climate.

To which could be added two further points. First, the comment made by Lawler and McDermott (2003: 55) that:

> Managers at all levels in a hierarchy can play an important role in the operation of the performance management system. If the performance management system is going to be tied into the business strategy, it is critical that senior management take a role and make the tie between business strategy and the performance management system. The behaviour of management is also an indication of how important the performance management system is and as a result is likely to have a strong influence on how the system is actually executed.

Second, performance management systems are more likely to be successful when the culture of the organization is performance-oriented.

Performance management issues

The many-faceted nature of performance was commented on as follows by Cascio (2010: 334): 'It is an exercise in observation and judgement, it is a feedback process, it is an organizational intervention. It is a measurement process as well as an intensely emotional process. Above all, it is an inexact, human process.'

As a human process, performance management can promise more than it achieves. Some years ago Grint (1993: 62), referring to performance appraisal, asserted, famously, that: 'Rarely in the history of business can such a system have promised so much and delivered so little.' More recently, Shields (2007: 6) argued that: 'Ill-chosen, badly designed or poorly implemented performance management schemes can communicate entirely the wrong messages as to what the organization expects from its employees.' Coens and Jenkins (2002: 1) delivered the following judgement:

> Throughout our work lives, most of us have struggled with performance appraisal. No matter how many times we redesign it, retrain the supervisors, or give it a new name, it never comes out right. Again and again, we see supervisors procrastinate or just go through the motions, with little taken to heart. And the supervisors who do take it to heart and give it their best mostly meet disappointment.

Performance management can be modelled convincingly as a system (see above) but the acts or failures to act of fallible human beings prejudice the effectiveness of the system in practice. Duncan Brown (2010) commented that:

> The problems [of performance management] are... not of ambition or intent, but rather practice and delivery. Low rates of coverage and even more frequently low-quality conversations and non-existent follow-up are commonplace in the wake of uncommitted directors, incompetent line managers, uncomprehending employees and hectoring HR with their still-complex and bureaucratic HR processes.

On the basis of research conducted in 2011 by the Institute for Employment Studies, Brown also observed that: 'The main areas of concern [about performance management] were the skills and attitudes of reviewing managers, the consistency and quality of approach across large organizations, the complexity of the paperwork and the value of outputs... Performance management, it appears, isn't working' (2011: 16).

A survey by WorldatWork and Sibson (2010) established that the top three performance management challenges reported by respondents were: 1) managers lack courage to have difficult performance discussions (63 per cent); 2) performance management is viewed as an 'HR process' instead of as a 'business-critical process' (47 per cent); and 3) that they experienced poor goal setting (36 per cent).

However well designed a performance management system is, its effectiveness mainly depends on the commitment and skills of line managers. Postuma and Campion (2008: 47) remarked that:

> One of the most dreaded tasks managers face is meeting with employees to discuss their job performance. These meetings present a dilemma for managers. On one hand, managers need to give constructive criticism so that employees can improve their performance. On the other hand, managers do not like to give negative feedback because of the bad feelings that often result. It is not surprising, then, that managers avoid giving accurate evaluations, give overly generous evaluations or avoid the process altogether.

They also noted that: 'Too much attention has been placed on the design of a [performance management] system and not enough on how it works when implemented' (ibid: 50).

Performance reviews or appraisals are often expected to fulfil numerous functions including performance improvement, feedback, coaching, goal setting, skill development, the identification of potential, pay determination and the identification of under-performers. No performance appraisal system can meet all these ends. Peter Reilly (2015) commented that 'all-singing, all-dancing performance appraisal... requires managers to review a wide range of content (reward, training needs, business alignment, etc) and use of multiple processes (eg personal development planning, performance ranking, potential assessment etc), but also to apply different modes of management – appreciation, evaluation and coaching – which can be very tough on them to deliver.' It is no wonder that line managers do not live up to the expectations of HR or that the perfunctory training in performance management provided by most organizations fails to produce the multiskilled, multitasking paragons the system demands.

This might explain why the e-reward 2014 survey of performance management established that one of the main problems concerning respondents about their performance management processes was line managers who are reluctant to actually conduct performance management reviews.

There is also the issue of the extent to which employees believe that performance management has improved their performance. A survey by the CIPD (2014) found that only 22 per cent of respondents thought that performance management had been effective in improving their performance, while 22 per cent felt that it was ineffective and 16 per cent that it was very ineffective.

A performance management issue identified by neuroscience is that it fosters an incorrect but prevalent view of human growth and learning. Carol Dweck (2006), professor of psychology at Stanford University, has discovered that most people hold one of two implicit theories about human growth and learning. The 'fixed mind-set', as she calls it, holds that intelligence and talent are basically established at birth and remain static throughout life. People are born smart or not, and there's not much anyone can do about it. The 'growth mind-set', by contrast, holds that people learn, grow, and improve all their lives. But they could learn far more effectively, and bring more of a high-performance attitude to everything they did if they weren't held back by the mental paralysis associated with the fixed mind-set. The fixed mind-set is often reinforced by performance management systems and when this happens people will typically strive to avoid difficult challenges. Any demanding objective will be seen as an invitation to fail. When reinventing performance management, it is necessary to encourage managers to adopt a growth mind-set and thus promote continuous development.

Dealing with performance management issues

Respondents to the e-reward (2014) survey on performance management made the following suggestions about how to deal with performance management issues:

- 'Train, communicate, evaluate performance management through employee engagement surveys, and have HR business partners work with line managers. Encourage ongoing performance management; it's more than just an annual administrative hoop – it's a powerful management tool.'

- 'Keep it very, very simple, ensure all managers are capable to deliver performance management; ie have a performance dialogue (this is the key!) at any time and not just at the annual review.'

- 'Ensure the system isn't hampered by bureaucracy and tedious paperwork. Put the focus on having quality open conversations between reviewer and reviewee.'

- 'Consistency – one scheme for all, make it about good conversations, not just a process.'

- 'Clear line of sight between objective setting, performance review and business goals. Regularly review and update in accordance with any changes in business needs.'

But the annual performance review is perhaps the most fundamental issue. Here is what three managers told Dilys Robinson of the Institute for Employment Studies (2013: 4) about how they reviewed performance.

- 'So, the key for me is just one-to-one time, and they know what they're aiming for, and we talk about it regularly. So it never really gets to the situation where there's like a really great big formal sit-down to say let's review everything you've done.'

- 'I think it's regular dialogue… at least once a fortnight for an extended period of time, just one to one and just about them and the work they're doing and what's going on… just so that I understand what they're doing and so I can give a bit of a steer or give them a bit of coaching if they need some coaching;

help them if they want some help and support.'

- 'Every week I have a one-to-one session with people who work for me. And it's half an hour, it's the opportunity to talk things over with people. I say to people, it's your time with me. But, to be honest, it's not just that; it's me getting to talk to them.'

Perhaps the best way to deal with the annual performance review is to encourage managers to act like this.

Reinventing performance management

A number of companies have recently 'seen the light' and introduced radical changes to their performance management systems. They have belatedly come to realize that, in the words of one of them, 'traditional performance management is broken'. This applies to the reliance on the annual performance appraisal rating, especially forced distribution, and the direct link with performance-related pay. Commentators, including the writer, have been saying for years that these practices are dubious but the message has finally got through.

The focus is now on continuous coaching and development rather than one annual and stressful review, the abolition of ratings, and 'de-coupling' performance management from performance-related pay. Accenture has scrapped annual appraisals for its 300,000-plus workforce and has instead instituted a 'continuous feedback' culture. Deloitte is joining the likes of Microsoft, Gap and Expedia in moving towards less formal, more frequent performance reviews. The latter has introduced a 'Passport to Performance' system of regular check-ins which are more coaching oriented. In other words, they are moving towards 'managing performance throughout the year'.

CASE STUDY

Reinventing performance management at Adobe

Background

- 13,000 employees.
- Adobe estimated that managers spend 80,000 hours on PM.
- Had tried to realign and make incremental changes for five years and failed to satisfactorily align to needs for collaboration, creativity and innovation.
- 'Genuine, Exceptional, Innovative and Involved' – Adobe's founding values.
- Super-competitive industry.

The changes

- No annual review, no ratings, no prescribed format, no forms, no PM technology 'system'.
- Manager and employee 'check-ins'.
- Check-in content: expectations, feedback, growth and development agenda.
- Frequency of check-ins – whenever sensible but at least quarterly.
- Employee support centre established.
- Extensive training support for managers – role plays, lectures and online.

- Managers manage pay outcomes and allocated budgets – entirely.
- Regular pulse survey provides insights on decisions and impact.
- Managers able to define their own processes and requirements for HR support.

Results

- Voluntary turnover down 30 per cent in two years.
- Employee engagement up.
- Fear of feedback gone.
- Frequent feedback is the new currency for employees and managers.
- Demand for training on coaching others, difficult conversations, mentoring, career development and managing reward up.
- Focus on process, chasing numbers and ratings wiped out.
- Belief in changes being real and aligned to values up.
- Regularity of 'check-ins', average of one a month per employee.
- Managers' knowledge of performance of individuals significantly greater than ever before.

PART IX

Rewarding people

PART IX CONTENTS

Introduction

Reward management as described in this part is defined as the processes of deciding how people should be paid or rewarded by other means and of ensuring that reward policies are implemented.

The part covers: (a) an analysis of reward management in terms of the basis of reward strategy (strategic reward) and a description of the constitu-ents of a reward system; (b) an examination of the process of reward management dealing with the main reward activities of market pricing, job evaluation, managing grade and pay structures (base pay management), contingent pay, employee benefits and pensions, rewarding special groups (executives, knowledge workers, sales and customer service staff and manual workers), and managing reward (administering the reward system).

43
Reward management

LEARNING OUTCOMES

On completing this chapter you should understand and be able to define these key concepts. You should also understand:

- The meaning and aims of reward management
- The nature of reward philosophy and guiding principles
- Reward management guiding principles

- The operation of reward strategy
- The make-up of a reward system
- The concept of total rewards
- The factors that affect pay levels
- Recognition schemes
- Employee benefits

Reward management defined

Reward management deals with the strategies, policies and processes required to ensure that the value of people and the contribution they make to the achievement of organizational, departmental and team goals is recognized and rewarded. It is concerned with the design, implementation and maintenance of reward systems (interrelated reward processes, practices and procedures covering how jobs and people should be valued, the design and management of grade and pay structures, rewarding and recognizing achievements and performance, providing employee benefits and managing the system). Reward systems aim to satisfy the needs of both the organization and its stakeholders and to operate fairly, equitably and consistently.

But it should be emphasized that reward management is not just about pay and employee benefits. It is equally concerned with non-financial rewards such as recognition, learning and development opportunities, and increased job responsibility.

The aims of reward management are set out below. As discussed later, reward management processes are based on a philosophy, which may be expressed in the form of guiding principles. They function through the reward system as described in this chapter.

Aims of reward management

Reward management provides answers to two fundamental questions: 1) How do we value people? and 2) How are we going to reward them according to their value?

The aims of reward management are to:

- support the achievement of business goals by developing a performance culture and stimulating high performance;
- define what is important in terms of behaviours and outcomes;
- align reward practices with employee needs;
- reward people according to the value they create;
- attract and retain the high-quality people the organization needs;
- motivate and win the engagement of employees;
- add value through the introduction of effective but affordable reward practices.

But Ghoshal and Bartlett (1995) reminded us that reward management is essentially about adding value to people. It is not just about attaching value to them.

Reward philosophy

Reward philosophy consists of the set of values and beliefs that influence reward strategy and the design and operation of the reward system. An organization's reward philosophy may be defined and set out in the form of guiding principles. But it may be implicit – all organizations have a reward philosophy that governs reward practice, even if they do not articulate it. It may be just a crude understanding of what should be done, such as offering competitive rates of pay or paying for performance.

Reward philosophies provide the basis for decisions on how people should be rewarded. The following is an example of a reward philosophy produced by Colt Telecom:

> Colt believes that talented and motivated people make a difference; talented people put us ahead of the competition and deliver the results on which the success of Colt is built. Colt seeks to offer a compensation and benefits package that rewards people for their contribution to the success of the company and ensures that external market competitiveness and internal relativities are taken into account.

Guiding principles

Guiding principles specify the approach an organization intends to use in managing reward. Reward guiding principles may be concerned with such matters as:

- developing reward policies and practices which support the achievement of business goals;
- providing rewards which help to develop a high-performance culture and attract, retain and motivate staff;
- maintaining competitive rates of pay;
- rewarding people according to their contribution;
- recognizing the value of all staff who are making an effective contribution, not just the exceptional performers;
- allowing a reasonable degree of flexibility in the operation of reward processes and in the choice of benefits by employees;
- devolving more responsibility for reward decisions to line managers.

Guiding principles are often agreed by top management with advice from company reward specialists or external consultants. But they will be more acceptable if members of the organization are involved in their definition. Guiding principles can then be communicated generally to increase understanding of what underpins reward policies and practices. However, employees will suspend their judgement of the principles until they experience how they are applied. What matters to them is not the principles themselves but the pay practices emanating from them and the messages about the employment 'deal' that they get as a consequence. It is the reality that is important, not the rhetoric.

The following is an example of reward guiding principles at Diageo:

- *Performance*: rewards are developed that reflect team and individual achievements.

- *Market*: rewards reflect the market in which an employee is based, whether that be geographical or functional, and compare favourably with those of competitors.

- *Communication*: Diageo aims to explain to everyone 'the components and value of their reward package, the criteria that affect it, and how they can influence it'.

- *Effectiveness*: the company seeks 'best practice' and ensures its benefits programmes 'remain effective for the business and our employees'.

Reward strategy

Reward strategy provides the impetus for reward system design and operation in order to achieve three major objectives: performance, competitiveness and fairness. It aims to provide answers to two basic questions: 1) what do we need to do about our reward practices to ensure that they are fit for purpose, and 2) how do we intend to do it? It is a declaration of intent that defines what the organization wants to do in the future to develop and implement reward policies, practices and processes that will further the achievement of its business goals and meet the needs of its stakeholders. The aim is to provide a sense of purpose and direction and a basis for developing reward policies, practices and processes. The strategy is based on an understanding of the needs of the organization and its employees and how they can best be satisfied.

Trevor (2011: 8) observed that strategic reward is:

... a means of enhancing company performance and securing competitive advantage, through the alignment of pay strategies, systems, practices and processes to the organizational strategy. As a management tool, pay is no longer purely a cost of hiring necessary labour, but a means of aligning a company's unique and inimitable asset – their employees – to the strategic direction of the organization.

The content of reward strategy

As Armstrong and Murlis (2007: 33) stated: 'Reward strategy will be characterized by diversity and conditioned both by the legacy of the past and the realities of the future.' All reward strategies are different, just as all organizations are different. Of course, similar aspects of reward will be covered in the strategies of different organizations but they will be treated differently in accordance with variations between organizations in their contexts, business strategies and cultures. But the reality of reward strategy is that it is not such a clear-cut process as some believe. It evolves, it changes and it has sometimes to be reactive rather than proactive.

Reward strategy often has to be a balancing act because of potentially conflicting goals. For example, it may be necessary to reconcile the competing claims of being externally competitive and internally equitable – paying a specialist more money to reflect market rate pressures may disrupt internal relativities. Or the belief that a universally applicable reward system is required may conflict with the perceived need to adopt a policy of segmentation (varying the reward package for different jobs, occupations or people to reflect particular knowledge and skills and the types and levels of contribution they make).

Reward strategy may be a broad-brush affair, simply indicating the general direction in which it is thought reward management should go. Additionally, or alternatively, reward strategy may set out a list of specific intentions dealing with particular aspects of reward management, for example:

- the development of a 'total reward' system;

- the introduction of performance pay;

- replacement of an existing contingent pay scheme;

- the introduction of a new grade and pay structure;
- the replacement of a decayed job evaluation scheme;
- the introduction of a formal recognition scheme;
- the development of a flexible benefits system;
- the conduct of equal pay reviews with the objective of ensuring that work of equal value is paid equally.

Examples of key themes in reward strategies

Airbus: Introduce performance pay for all employees; ensure that its rates are competitive with the external market and deal with anomalies caused by previous rigidities, such as grade drift brought about by people having to be promoted to a higher grade to receive additional pay.

AstraZeneca: Promote a culture that values, recognizes and rewards outstanding performance.

Centrica: Establish a link between pay and performance and align pay with the market.

The Children's Society: Develop flexible and fair reward systems that will support our mission and corporate objectives by recognizing contribution, accountability, teamworking and innovation, and are market sensitive but not market led.

Diageo: Release the potential of every employee to deliver Diageo's performance goals.

Kent County Council: Pay people a fair rate for the job and give additional reward for excellent contribution.

National Union of Teachers: Develop a new broad graded pay structure and introduce a new job evaluation scheme as a basis for the structure.

Tesco: Reward staff for their contribution in a way that enables them to benefit directly from the success they help to create.

Critical evaluation of the concept of reward strategy

The problem with a strategic approach to reward is that it can promise more than it achieves. This contradicts the main message delivered by US writers such as Lawler (1990) in his *Strategic Pay* and Schuster and Zingheim (1992) in their *The New Pay*, which was that it provides a powerful lever for improving business performance. As Thompson (1998: 70) commented:

> The most that companies can hope to do in their approach to reward is to make sure that it does not distort the relationship [between management and employees]. Managing reward is thus a job of damage limitation and perhaps not the 'strategic lever for organizational transformation' that

appears so seductive in the writing of American commentators.

Trevor (2011) posed the question: To what extent can pay be strategic? He claimed that rationalism is limited and pointed out that pay systems tend to be selected for their legitimacy (best practice as advocated by institutions such as the CIPD and by management consultants) rather than for purely economic reasons. He observed (ibid: 35) that: 'What is desired (approach), and what is intended (design), may not be reflected in what is achieved (operation).'

However, it cannot be denied that to have a sense of purpose and direction is a good thing and with all its limitations, this justifies a strategic approach to reward.

CASE STUDY IN REWARD STRATEGY

Reward strategy at BT

Reward strategy at BT (British Telecom) is a fairly broad-brush affair simply indicating the general direction in which it is thought reward management for the 90,000 staff at BT should go, with an emphasis on adopting a more holistic, total reward approach. It is summarized as follows:

> Use the full range of rewards (salary, bonus, benefits and recognition) to recruit and retain the best people, and to encourage and reward achievement where actions and behaviours are consistent with the BT values.

Guiding principles

BT's reward strategy is underpinned by a set of guiding principles defining the approach the organization takes to dealing with reward. These guiding principles are the basis for reward policies and provide guidelines for the actions contained in the reward strategy. They express the reward philosophy of the organization – its values and beliefs about how people should be rewarded. The six guiding principles governing the design of the reward system at BT are as follows:

1 Business linkage.

2 Clarity and transparency.

3 Market competitiveness.

4 Performance differentiation.

5 Choice and flexibility.

6 Equal pay.

Broadly speaking, the three principal elements driving individual reward are:

1 The individual's performance and contribution in the role – what does it mean to have high individual performance?

2 The competitiveness of the individual's existing salary, together with the actual (and anticipated) salary movement in relevant local markets – how does salary align to the external market?

3 The company's business results and ability to pay – can the company afford to invest money in terms of additional reward?

Underpinning these pillars are the principles of clarity (a 'focus on roles'), equal pay and choice.

Reward policies

Reward policies set specific guidelines for decision making and action and therefore provide the framework for managing a reward system. They indicate what the organization and its management are expected to do about managing reward and how they will behave in given circumstances when dealing with reward issues. They can be distinguished from guiding principles, which usually express a more generalized philosophy. The key reward policy areas are described below.

Level of rewards

The policy on the level of rewards indicates whether the company is a high payer, is content to pay median or average rates of pay or even, exceptionally, accepts that it has to pay below the average. Policies on pay levels will also refer to differentials and the number of steps or grades that should exist in the pay hierarchy. This will be influenced by the structure of the company. In today's flatter organizations an extended or complex pay hierarchy may not be required on the grounds that it does not reflect the way in which work is organized and will constrain flexibility. Policies on the level of rewards also cover employee benefits – pensions, sick pay, health care, holidays and perks such as company cars.

TABLE 43.1   Theories explaining pay levels

Name of theory	Summary of theory	Practical significance
The law of supply and demand	Other things being equal, if there is a surplus of labour and supply exceeds demand, pay levels go down; if there is a scarcity of labour and demand exceeds supply, pay goes up.	Highlights the role of labour market factors in affecting rates of pay and therefore emphasizes the importance of market pricing, ie establishing the level of market rates.
Efficiency wage theory	Firms will pay above the market rate because they believe that high levels of pay will increase productivity by helping to motivate and retain employees.	Firms use efficiency wage theory (although they will not call it that) when they formulate pay policies that place them as above the average, eg in the upper quartile of the distribution of market rates.
Human capital theory	Workers have a set of skills developed by education and training that generate a stock of productive capital.	Employers and employees each benefit from investment in creating human capital. Pay should be fixed at a level which supplies both parties with a reasonable return on that investment.
Agency theory (also known as principal agent theory)	The owners of a firm (the principals) are separate from the employees (the agents). The difference can create 'agency costs' because the agents may not be so productive as the principals would like them to be. The latter therefore have to devise ways of motivating and controlling the efforts of the employees.	A system of incentives is needed to motivate and reward acceptable behaviour. This process of 'incentive alignment' consists of paying for measurable results that are deemed to be in the best interests of the owners. (Agency theory is particularly relevant as a means of explaining the high levels of executive pay.)
Tournament theory	The motivation of high-quality staff will be increased by offering lucrative prizes (ie pay) for a small number of people who are promoted to higher-level jobs, with the highest prize of all to the person who wins the tournament by getting the top job.	Provides a rationale for increasingly large pay differentials between jobs in the hierarchy. Is also a justification for high levels of pay for chief executives.
The effort bargain	Workers aim to strike a bargain about the relationship between what they regard as a reasonable contribution and what their employer is prepared to pay to elicit that contribution.	Management has to assess what level and type of inducement it has to offer in return for the contribution it requires from its workforce. Pay negotiations may in effect centre on the effort bargain.

Policies on the level of rewards can be explained in general terms by the theories summarized in Table 43.1.

The process of determining pay levels and the rates of pay for individual jobs within organizations is influenced by all the factors described above. Levels of pay are affected by an implicit belief in efficiency wage theory – that higher rates of pay attract good candidates (the sorting effect), enhance performance (the incentive effect) and help to retain employees. There will be policies and practices on the range or dispersion of pay between different levels in the organization. The organization will have a defined or implicit 'pay stance' policy, ie the relationship desired between the levels of pay within the organization and market rates.

The other factors affecting rates of pay are beliefs about the value of the job and the person, internal relativities, financial considerations (the ability to pay), the influence of trade unions and the minimum or living wage.

Value of the job

The intrinsic value of a job is a measure of what a job (not a person) is worth in terms of what it contributes to achieving the purpose of the organization. An intrinsic value is attached to jobs because of the impact they make on organizational results and by reference to the levels of responsibility and skill required to perform them. Increases in impact and these levels lead to higher rates of pay. This concept provides the theoretical base for job evaluation. However, as an explanation of the value attached to jobs it is limited because it ignores external relativities.

Value of the person

Individuals are valued by organizations for three main reasons: 1) the contribution they make to organizational success; 2) their competencies and skills; and 3) the experience they bring to their jobs. People also have their own value in the market place – their market worth, which has to be taken into account by employers in setting their rates of pay.

Internal relativities

It can be argued that the value of anything, including jobs, is always relative to something else, that is, other jobs. Views on job values within organizations are based on perceptions of the worth of one job compared with others, which may be a matter of opinion but attempts can be made to measure relative worth through job evaluation, which is essentially a comparative process. The aim is to achieve internal equity, which occurs when people are rewarded appropriately in relation to others according to the value of their contribution. The case for equal pay for work of equal value is based on the imperative to achieve internal equity.

Financial circumstances of the organization

Affordability is an important concept in reward management. The aim is to ensure that pay systems do not cost more than the organization can afford and this will influence the level of pay that can be offered to employees. Extra expenditure on pay, eg bonus payments, should add value in the sense that the benefits resulting from improved performance outweigh the cost.

Trade union influence

Pay levels may be determined through collective bargaining with trade unions. They will want their members' pay to keep ahead of inflation, to match market rates and to reflect any increases in the prosperity of the business. The amount of pressure they can exert on pay levels will depend on the relative bargaining strengths of the employer and the union.

The minimum or living wage

Minimum or living wage regulation in the UK sets minimum rates of pay. The amount is increased from time to time.

Example of pay policy

An example of a policy on pay levels is provided by AEGON UK, where the reward system is designed to recognize three core factors which affect the level of pay individuals should receive for their 'personal commitment and consistent contribution within their roles'. These are:

- *Internal job value* – the bigger the job, the higher the reward.

- *External job value* – the level of reward will be influenced by external market rates and the degree to which market forces affect the salaries required to attract and retain quality staff.

- *Value of the person* – individual employees may be rewarded at a higher level because they are making a greater contribution, are performing better, meeting objectives and have achieved a higher level of skill or competence than their colleagues (measured through the performance management process).

External competitiveness versus internal equity

Reward policy is also concerned with the extent to which rewards are market driven (ie primarily influenced by market rate pressures) rather than equitable (ie employees are paid fairly in relation to one another). The policy will be influenced by the culture and reward philosophies of the organization and the pressures on the business to obtain and keep high-quality staff. Any organizations that have to attract and retain staff who are much in demand and where market rates are therefore high, may, to a degree, have to sacrifice their ideals (if they have them) of internal equity to the realism of the market place. They will provide 'market pay'; in other words, they will be 'market driven'.

The pay management process must cope as best it can when the irresistible force of market pressures meets the immovable object of internal equity. There will always be some degree of tension in these circumstances, and while no solution will ever be simple or entirely satisfactory, there is one basic principle that can enhance the likelihood of success. That principle is to make explicit and fully identifiable the compromises with internal equity that are made and have to be made in response to market pressures.

The policy may indicate that market considerations will drive levels of pay in the organization. It may, however, allow for the use of market supplements – a payment that reflects market rates in addition to the rate for a job as determined by internal equity. The policy may lay down that these payments should be reviewed regularly and no longer offered if they are unnecessary. Market supplements for those who have them may not be withdrawn (the people concerned would not lose pay), but adjustments may be made to pay progression to bring their rates more into line with those for comparable jobs. Market pay and market supplements can lead to gender inequalities if, as is often the case, men in comparable jobs are paid more generally or more men get market supplements than women. Equal pay case law has ruled that market pay and market supplements should be 'objectively justified', and the requirement to do this should be included in the pay policy.

The 2007 e-reward survey of grade and pay structures revealed that respondents with market supplements adopted the following policies when such supplements were no longer required:

- remove immediately – 33 per cent;
- retain until upgraded – 30 per cent;
- reduce progressively – 19 per cent;
- protect in line with policy – 18 per cent.

Segmentation

Segmentation involves varying the reward package for different jobs or to reflect the types and levels of contribution people make, or providing rewards that are tailored to meet individual needs.

A policy on segmentation will recognize that parts of the workforce and individuals in the successive stages of their career may be motivated by different combinations of rewards. A total rewards package can be tailored to meet these needs. Rewards may be segmented to take account of key employee differences. This could mean individual performance-related pay for some, team reward for others, and other forms of pay progression and recognition rather than incentives for a third group. This is a flexible approach to reward management, although it should be flexibility within a framework, the framework being provided by guiding principles that apply to all aspects of reward.

The reward system

Strategic reward leads to the design of a reward system. As illustrated in Figure 43.1, This consists of the interrelated processes and practices that combine to ensure that reward management is carried out effectively to the benefit of the organization and the people who work there. The system is driven by the business and HR strategies from which flow the reward strategy. As described below, its major components are financial and non-financial rewards that are combined to form a total reward system. Performance management plays an important part in supporting non-financial rewards and may be used to inform performance or contribution pay decisions. All these components combine to achieve the aims of reward management.

The other main elements of the financial reward system are described in the next five chapters. These are market pricing, job evaluation, the management of grade and pay structures (base pay management), contingent pay (pay for performance, competence or contribution) and employee benefit and pension schemes. Recognition schemes are covered in the penultimate section of this chapter.

The three key elements of a reward system – financial rewards, non-financial rewards and total rewards are described below.

Financial rewards

Financial rewards consist of job-based pay, which provides pay related to the value of the job, and person-based pay, which provides rewards that recognize the individual's contribution. They also include employee benefits and pensions and financial recognition schemes. The management of job- and person-based pay involves:

- *Pay determination* – making decisions on the value of jobs by means of market pricing and

FIGURE 43.1   A reward system

job evaluation. The factors that affect pay levels are examined in chapter 49.

- *Base pay management* – developing and operating pay structures which group jobs into grades, bands or levels in accordance with internal and external relativities and usually provide for pay progression.

- *Contingent pay* – planning and managing schemes which provide for pay progression related to performance, contribution, competence, skill or length of service.

Labour economists distinguish between the incentive effect of financial rewards (generating more engagement and effort) and the sorting effect (attracting better quality employees). The fundamental issue is the extent to which financial rewards provide an incentive effect. The sorting effect is important but creates less controversy, perhaps because it is more difficult to pin down.

The case for and against financial rewards as incentives and a description of the contingent pay schemes that provide such awards are dealt with in Chapter 47.

Non-financial rewards

Non-financial rewards focus on the needs people have to varying degrees for recognition, achievement, personal growth and acceptable working conditions. They include the non-financial recognition of achievements as described in the next section of this chapter, the design of fulfilling jobs, giving people the scope to develop their skills and careers and offering a work environment which provides a high quality of working life and an appropriate relationship between work and private life (work–life balance). Non-financial rewards can be extrinsic, such as praise or recognition, or intrinsic, associated with job challenge and interest and feelings that the work is worthwhile.

Total rewards

Total rewards are the combination of financial and non-financial rewards made available to employees. The various aspects of reward, namely base pay, contingent pay, employee benefits and non-financial rewards, which include intrinsic rewards from the work itself, are linked together and treated as an integrated and cohesive whole.

The concept of total rewards describes an approach to reward management that emphasizes the need to consider all aspects of the work experience of value to employees, not just a few such as pay and employee benefits. A total rewards approach recognizes that it is necessary to get financial rewards (pay and benefits) right. But it also appreciates the importance of providing people with rewarding experiences that arise from their work environment (the job they do and how they are managed) and the opportunity to develop their skills and careers. It contributes to the production of an employee value proposition that provides a clear, compelling reason why talented people should work for a company.

The Towers Perrin model shown in Figure 43.2 can be used as the basis for planning a total rewards approach. It consists of a matrix with four quadrants. The upper two quadrants – pay and benefits – represent transactional or tangible rewards. These are financial in nature and are essential to recruit and retain staff but can be easily copied by competitors. By contrast, the relational or intangible non-financial rewards represented in the lower two quadrants cannot be imitated so readily and therefore create both human capital and human process advantage. They are essential to enhancing the value of the upper two quadrants. The real power comes when organizations combine relational and transactional rewards. The model also makes a useful distinction between individual and communal rewards, particularly, in the latter case, those provided by the work environment.

Recognition schemes

Recognition schemes enable appreciation to be shown to individuals for their achievements either informally on a day-to-day basis or through formal recognition arrangements. They can take place quietly between managers and individuals in their teams or be visible celebrations of success.

A formal recognition scheme can provide scope to recognize achievements by gifts or treats or public applause. Typically, the awards are non-financial but some organizations provide cash awards. Importantly, recognition is also given less formally when managers simply say 'Well done', 'Thank you' or 'Congratulations' face to face or in a brief note of appreciation.

FIGURE 43.2   Model of total rewards: Towers Perrin

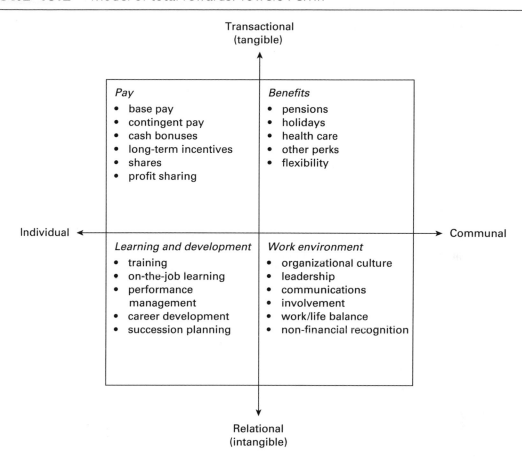

Employee benefits

Employee benefits consist of arrangements made by employers for their employees that enhance the latter's well-being. They are provided in addition to pay and form important parts of the total reward package. As part of total remuneration, they may be deferred or contingent, such as a pension scheme, insurance cover or sick pay, or they may be immediate, such as a company car or a loan. Employee benefits also include holidays and leave arrangements, which are not strictly remuneration. Benefits are sometimes referred to dismissively as 'perks' (perquisites) or 'fringe benefits', but when they cater for personal security or personal needs they could hardly be described as 'fringe'. Flexible benefit schemes give employees a choice, within limits, of the type or scale of benefits offered to them by their employers.

Pension provision has undergone considerable change recently. The traditional defined benefit scheme, which provides a pension based on final salary, is disappearing rapidly (too costly) and is being replaced by defined contribution schemes where the retirement pension is whatever annual payment can be purchased with the money accumulated in the fund for a member (cheaper). The 2013 CIPD survey found that the average employer contribution to a defined contribution scheme was 7.9 per cent of salary, while the average employee contribution was 5.0 per cent of salary.

Employee benefits are a costly part of the remuneration package. They can amount to one-third or more of basic pay costs and therefore have to be planned and managed with care.

CASE STUDIES

Kent County Council: Successful reward

The council attributes success in its reward policies to a strong and united political direction from the top, a long-term consistency of purpose, but with the appropriate phasing of changes and with adaptation to local circumstances, and a high-involvement approach.

McDonald's: Demonstrating reward effectiveness

McDonald's is a company with a strong culture of measurement and has built its own people–profit chain methodology to produce impressive evidence that demonstrates how rewards can enhance employee engagement and thereby business performance. The operational and cost focus in the business means that reward arrangements are reviewed regularly and changed if they are not found to be delivering. But the subtler processes of consultation and change management are equally vital in maintaining and strengthening reward effectiveness.

The NSPCC: Approaches to achieving reward effectiveness

The experience of the NSPCC was that while measures of organizational and reward effectiveness may differ, the delivery of them is every bit as critical, if not more so, in voluntary organizations. It also shows that limited resources need not be a barrier to assessing and demonstrating effectiveness. Establishing links to the core purpose of the organization was the major driver behind the extensive research undertaken into effectiveness. The culture of the organization and its values were important considerations, as was ensuring that the values of the people in the organization were aligned to them.

Changing the pay structure at Marks & Spencer

Prior to 2005 there were 429 different rates for customer assistants, ranging from £4.94 per hour for new staff, up to £10 per hour for long-serving employees. In May 2005, M&S announced that it would reduce these to four standard rates for customer assistants (with regional variations), which would be tied to specific roles – trainee and qualified, which already existed, and two newly created positions: coach and section coordinator. The move was designed to give staff better career progression opportunities.

Key learning points: Reward management

Reward management defined

Reward management deals with the strategies, policies and processes required to ensure that the value of people and the contribution they make to achieving organizational, departmental and team goals are recognized and rewarded.

Aims of reward management

Reward management provides answers to two fundamental questions: 1) How do we value people? and 2) How are we going to reward them according to their value?

Reward strategy

Reward strategy defines what an organization wants to do about reward in the next few years and how it intends to do it.

Reward strategy may be a broad-brush affair, simply indicating the general direction in which it is thought reward management should go. Additionally, or alternatively, reward strategy may set out a list of specific intentions dealing with particular aspects of reward management.

Reward system

A reward system consists of the interrelated processes and practices of financial and non-financial rewards that combine into a total rewards approach to ensure that reward management is carried out to the benefit of the organization and the people who work there.

Financial rewards

Financial rewards consist of job-based pay, which provides pay related to the value of the job, and person-based pay, which provides rewards that recognize the individual's contribution. They also include employee benefits and pensions and financial recognition schemes.

The management of job- and person-based pay involves:

- *Pay determination* – making decisions on the value of jobs by means of market pricing and job evaluation.
- *Base pay management* – developing and operating pay structures which group jobs into grades, bands or levels in accordance with internal and external relativities and usually provide for pay progression.
- *Contingent pay* – planning and managing schemes which provide for pay progression related to performance, contribution, competence, skill or length of service.

Non-financial rewards

Non-financial rewards focus on the needs people have to varying degrees for recognition, achievement, personal growth and acceptable working conditions. Non-financial rewards can be extrinsic, such as praise or recognition, or intrinsic, associated with job challenge and interest and feelings that the work is worthwhile.

Total rewards

Total rewards are the combination of financial and non-financial rewards made available to employees. The various aspects of reward, namely base pay, contingent pay, employee benefits and non-financial rewards, which include intrinsic rewards from the work itself, are linked together and treated as an integrated and cohesive whole.

The concept of total rewards describes an approach to reward management that emphasizes the need to consider all aspects of the work experience of value to employees, not just a few such as pay and employee benefits.

Recognition schemes

Recognition schemes enable appreciation to be shown to individuals for their achievements either informally on a day-to-day basis or through formal recognition arrangements.

Employee benefits

Employee benefits consist of arrangements made by employers for their employees that enhance the latter's well-being. They are provided in addition to pay and form important parts of the total reward package. As part of total remuneration, they may be deferred or contingent such as a pension scheme, insurance cover or sick pay, or they may be immediate such as a company car or a loan.

References

Armstrong, M and Murlis, H (2007) *Reward Management*, revised 5th edn, London, Kogan Page

Chartered Institute of Personnel and Development (2013) *Annual Reward Survey*, London, CIPD

e-reward (2007) *Survey of Grade and Pay Structures*, Stockport, e-reward

Ghoshal, S and Bartlett, C A (1995) Changing the role of top management: beyond structure to process, *Harvard Business Review*, January–February, pp 86–96

Lawler, E E (1990) *Strategic Pay*, San Francisco, CA, Jossey-Bass

Schuster, J R and Zingheim, P K (1992) *The New Pay*, New York, Lexington Books

Thompson, M (1998) Trust and reward, in (eds) S Perkins and St J Sandringham, *Trust, Motivation and Commitment: A reader*, Faringdon, Strategic Remuneration Research Centre

Trevor, J (2011) *Can Pay Be Strategic?* Basingstoke, Palgrave Macmillan

44
Market pricing

LEARNING OUTCOMES

On completing this chapter you should be able to define these key concepts. You should also understand:

- What market pricing involves
- The concept of a market rate

Market pricing defined

Market pricing is the process of making decisions on pay structures and individual rates of pay. A policy decision is required on the relationship between market rate levels and levels of pay within the organization. This is called the 'pay stance', which may be expressed in such terms as matching median (average) rates or paying upper quartile rates (loosely, within the top 25 per cent).

Use of market pricing

Market pricing informs decisions on base of pay, ie, the amount of pay that constitutes the basic rate for the job or the person. The aim is to ensure that the rates are competitive. It also helps to develop the pay structure – the pay ranges attached to grades. Information on market rates may lead to the introduction of market supplements for individual jobs or the creation of separate pay structures (market groups) to cater for particular market rate pressures. It is referred to as 'extreme market pricing' when market rates are the sole means of deciding on internal rates of pay and relativities, and conventional job evaluation is not used. An organization that adopts this method is said to be 'market-driven'.

Acceptability of market pricing

The acceptability of market pricing is dependent on the availability of robust market data and, when looking at external rates, the quality of the job-to-job matching process, ie comparing like with like. Market pricing may be associated with formal job evaluation, which establishes internal relativities and the grade structure.

Market pricing can therefore vary from analysis of data by job titles to detailed matched analysis collected through bespoke surveys focused on real market equivalents. Extreme market pricing can provide guidance on internal relativities. But it may lead to detrimental pay levels for women, where the market has traditionally been discriminatory, and it does not satisfy UK equal pay legislation.

The concept of a market rate

Market pricing attempts to establish the market rate for jobs, but the notion of a market rate is a more elusive concept than it seems. There is no such thing as a definitive market rate for any job, even when comparing identically sized organizations in the same industry and location. Different market information sources for the same types of jobs produce different results because of variations in the sample, the difficulty of obtaining precise matches between jobs in the organization and jobs elsewhere (job matching), and timing (the dates on which the data is collected may differ).

This means that market rate analysis is most unlikely to produce definite information on the rate for the job. The possibly incomplete data from a number of sources, some more reliable than others, has to be interpreted to indicate what the organization should do about it. This may be expressed as a 'derived market rate', which is a sort of average of a range of pay information – a dubious notion. Data may be available for some jobs but not for others that are unique to the organization.

Market rate analysis

Market rate analysis involves the following steps:

1 Identify and define the jobs for which market rate data is required. These are benchmark jobs that are representative of different levels and occupations and can be compared with similar jobs. In conducting the survey, the aim will be to 'match' these jobs as closely as possible with jobs elsewhere.

2 Identify the sources of information. These can include published surveys conducted by a pay consultancy or research organization, surveys conducted specially by the organization, 'pay clubs' (groups of employers who exchange pay information) and advertisements. Published surveys are likely to provide the most convenient source of robust information. Special surveys and pay clubs can produce useful data but they are time consuming. More than one source should be used if possible. Advertisements are useless.

3 Collect, analyse and interpret the information.

4 Present the pay data for jobs in the form of a range of pay from lowest to highest, the median rate (the midpoint in a distribution of rates of pay) and the upper and lower quartiles (the values which, respectively, are exceeded by a quarter of the values in the upper areas of a distribution or by a quarter of the values in the lower areas of a distribution). Interpreting the data may mean producing a derived market rate from the different sources.

5 Apply the information in line with a policy decision on market stance – the pay levels required to be competitive and affordable.

Key learning points: Market pricing

Market pricing defined

Market pricing is the process of making decisions on pay structures and individual rates of pay and obtaining information on market rates (market rate analysis).

Use of market pricing

Market pricing informs decisions on base of pay, ie the amount of pay that constitutes the basic rate for the job or the person. The aim is to ensure that the rates are competitive. It helps to develop the pay structure – the pay ranges attached to grades.

The concept of a market rate

Market pricing attempts to establish the market rate for jobs, but the notion of a market rate is a more elusive concept than it seems. There is no such thing as a definitive market rate for any job, even when comparing identically sized organizations in the same industry and location.

Market rate analysis

Market rate analysis involves the following steps:

1 Identify and define the jobs for which market rate data is required.

2 Identify the sources of information.

3 Collect, analyse and interpret the information.

4 Present the pay data for jobs in the form of a range of pay from lowest to highest, the median rate and the upper and lower quartiles.

5 Apply the information in line with a policy decision on market stance.

45
Job evaluation

KEY CONCEPTS AND TERMS

Analytical job evaluation

Analytical matching

Non-analytical job evaluation

Point-factor rating

LEARNING OUTCOMES

On completing this chapter you should be able to define these key concepts. You should also understand:

- The meaning of job evaluation
- How analytical job evaluation works
- How non-analytical job evaluation works

Job evaluation defined

Job evaluation is a systematic and formal process for defining the relative worth or size of jobs within an organization in order to establish internal relativities. It is carried out through either an analytical or a non-analytical scheme.

Analytical job evaluation schemes

Analytical job evaluation is based on a process of breaking down whole jobs into a number of defined elements or factors and then comparing them factor by factor, either with a graduated scale of points attached to a set of factors, or with grade or role profiles analysed under the same factor headings.

The advantages of an analytical approach are that: first, evaluators have to consider each of the characteristics of the job separately before forming a conclusion about its relative value; second, evaluators are provided with defined yardsticks or guidelines that help to increase the objectivity and consistency of judgements. It can also provide a defence in the UK against an equal pay claim.

The main analytical schemes, as described below, are point-factor rating and analytical matching.

Point-factor rating

Point-factor schemes are the most common forms of analytical job evaluation. The basic methodology is to break down jobs into factors. These are the elements in a job such as the level of responsibility, knowledge and skill or decision making that represent the demands made by the job on job holders. For job evaluation purposes it is assumed that each of the factors will contribute to the value of the job and is an aspect of all the jobs to be evaluated, but to different degrees.

Each factor is divided into a hierarchy of levels, typically five or six. Definitions of these levels are produced to provide guidance on deciding the degree to which the factor applies in the job to be evaluated. A maximum points score is allocated to each factor. The scores available may vary between different factors in accordance with beliefs about their relative significance. This is termed 'explicit weighting'. If the number of levels varies between factors, this means that they are implicitly weighted because the range of scores available will be greater in the factors with more levels.

The total score for a factor is divided between the levels to produce the numerical factor scale. The complete scheme consists of the factor and level definitions and the scoring system (the total score available for each factor and distributed to the factor levels). This comprises the 'factor plan'.

Jobs are 'scored' (ie allocated points) under each factor heading on the basis of the level of the factor in the job. This is done by comparing the features of the job with regard to that factor with the factor level definitions in order to find out which definition provides the best fit. The separate factor scores are then added together to give a total score, which indicates the relative value of each job and can be used to place the jobs in rank order, or allocate them into grades in a graded pay structure that have been defined in terms of job evaluation points.

Analytical job matching

Like point-factor job evaluation, analytical job matching is based on the analysis of a number of defined factors. Profiles of roles to be evaluated that have been analysed and described in terms of job evaluation factors are compared with grade, band or level profiles that have been analysed and described in terms of the same job evaluation factors. The role profiles are then 'matched' with the range of grade or level profiles to establish the best fit and thus grade the job.

Analytical matching can be used to grade jobs or place them in levels following the initial evaluation of a sufficiently large sample of benchmark jobs, ie representative jobs that provide a valid basis for comparisons. This can happen in big organizations when it is believed that it is not necessary to go through the whole process of point-factor evaluation for every job, especially where 'generic' roles are concerned. It takes much less time than using a point-factor scheme and the results can be just as accurate.

Non-analytical job evaluation schemes

Non-analytical job evaluation schemes enable whole jobs to be compared in order to place them in a grade or a rank order – they are not analysed by reference to their elements or factors. They can operate on a job-to-job basis in which a job is compared with another job to decide whether it should be valued more, less, or the same (ranking and 'internal benchmarking' processes).

Alternatively, they may function on a job-to-grade basis in which judgements are made by comparing a whole job with a defined hierarchy of job grades (job classification) – this involves matching a job description to a grade description. Non-analytical schemes are simple to introduce and operate but provide no defined standards of judgement. Differences between jobs are not measured and they do not provide a defence in an equal pay case.

Key learning points: Job evaluation

Job evaluation defined

Job evaluation is a systematic and formal process for defining the relative worth or size of jobs within an organization in order to establish internal relativities. It is carried out through either an analytical or a non-analytical scheme.

Analytical job evaluation schemes

Analytical job evaluation is based on a process of breaking down whole jobs into a number of defined elements or factors and then comparing them factor by factor, either with a graduated scale of points attached to a set of factors, or with grade or role profiles analysed under the same factor headings. The two main types of analytical scheme are point-factor rating and analytical matching.

Non-analytical job evaluation schemes

Non-analytical job evaluation schemes enable whole jobs to be compared in order to place them in a grade or a rank order – they are not analysed by reference to their elements or factors.

46
Grade and pay structures

KEY CONCEPTS AND TERMS

Anchor point

Base pay

Base pay management

Broad-banded pay structure

Broad-graded pay structure

Grade

Grade drift

Job family pay structure

Narrow-graded pay structure

Pay range

Pay spine

LEARNING OUTCOMES

On completing this chapter you should be able to define these key concepts. You should also understand:

- Methods of pay determination – market pricing, job evaluation
- Base pay management – grade and pay structures

Purpose of grade and pay structures

Grade and pay structures provide the framework for base pay management as a means of implementing an organization's pay policies. They enable the organization to determine where jobs should be placed in a hierarchy, define pay levels and the scope for pay progression, and provide the basis upon which relativities can be managed, equal pay achieved and the processes of monitoring and controlling the implementation of pay policies can take place. Grade and pay structures also enable organizations to communicate the career and pay opportunities available to employees.

Grade structures

A grade structure consists of a sequence or hierarchy of grades, bands or levels into which groups of jobs that are broadly comparable in size are placed. There may be a single structure defined by the number of grades or bands it contains. As illustrated in Figure 46.1, such structures can be narrow- or multi-graded with 10 or more grades, broad-graded with six to eight grades, or broad-banded with fewer than six 'bands'. Alternatively, the structure may be divided into a number of job families, consisting of groups of jobs where the essential nature and purpose of the work are similar but it is carried out at different levels. As shown in Figure 46.2, each of the families in such a structure will be divided into grades, the number of which may vary between families. A variety of job family structure is a career family structure where the emphasis is on defining career ladders in terms of a hierarchy of grades.

FIGURE 46.1   Narrow-graded, broad-graded and broad-banded structures

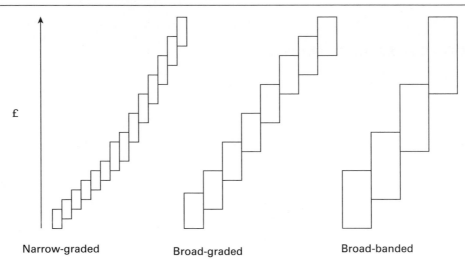

FIGURE 46.2   A job family structure

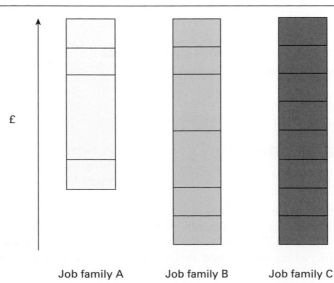

Pay structures

A pay structure consists of pay ranges, brackets or scales that are attached to each grade, band or level in a grade structure. Pay structures are defined by the number of grades they contain and, especially in narrow- or broad-graded structures, the span or width of the pay ranges attached to each grade. 'Span' is the scope that the grade provides for pay progression and is usually measured as the difference between the lowest and the highest point in the range expressed as a percentage of the lowest point. Thus a range of £20,000 to £30,000 would have a span of 50 per cent.

Pay can progress within the grades in a narrow- or broad-graded structure on the basis of performance or merit, or time served in the grade. Broad-banded structures in theory allow more flexibility, but they often contain pay zones that provide an indication of the extent to which the pay of individuals in a particular role, or cluster of roles, can vary around what is known as an 'anchor point' – the rate for a fully competent person in a role that is aligned to market rates. Another form of pay structure is a pay spine (found mainly in the public and voluntary sectors) consisting of an incremental scale that provides progression on the basis of time served.

Some organizations, especially smaller ones, do not have a formal graded structure and rely entirely on 'spot rates', ie the rates for jobs do not define any scope for the progression of base pay in the form of a pay range or salary bracket, although bonuses may be provided on top of the base rate. Senior executives in larger companies are often on spot rates. A less common method is to have 'individual job grades' which are, in effect, spot rates to which a defined pay range of, say, 20 per cent on either side of the rate has been attached to provide scope for pay progression.

Guiding principles

Grade and pay structures should:

- be appropriate to the culture, characteristics and needs of the organization and its employees;
- facilitate the management of relativities and the achievement of equity, fairness, consistency and transparency in managing gradings and pay;
- enable jobs to be graded appropriately and not be subject to grade drift (unjustified upgradings);
- be flexible enough to adapt to pressures arising from market rate changes and skill shortages;
- facilitate operational flexibility and continuous development;
- provide scope as required for pay progression;
- clarify reward, lateral development and career opportunities;
- be constructed logically and clearly so that the basis upon which they operate can readily be communicated to employees;
- enable the organization to exercise control over the implementation of pay policies and budgets.

Criteria for choice

The criteria for choice between the main types of grade and pay structures are set out in Table 46.1.

TABLE 46.1   Criteria for choice

Type of structure	Criteria for choice: the structure may be considered more appropriate when:
Narrow-graded	• the organization is large and bureaucratic with well-defined and extended hierarchies; • pay progression is expected to occur in small but relatively frequent steps; • the culture is one in which much significance is attached to status as indicated by gradings; • some but not too much scope for pay progression is wanted.
Broad-graded	• it is believed that if there is a relatively limited number of grades it will be possible to define and therefore differentiate them more accurately as an aid to better precision when grading jobs; • an existing narrow-graded structure is the main cause of grade drift; • it is considered that pay progression through grades can be related to contribution and that it is possible to introduce effective control mechanisms.
Broad-banded	• greater flexibility in pay determination and management is required; • it is believed that job evaluation should no longer drive grading decisions; • the focus is on rewarding people for lateral development; • the organization has been delayered.
Job family	• there are distinct market groups that need to be rewarded differently; • the range of responsibility and the basis upon which levels exist vary between families; • it is believed that career paths need to be defined in terms of competence requirements.
Pay spine	• this is the traditional approach in public or voluntary sector organizations and it fits the culture; • it is believed to be impossible to measure different levels of contribution fairly and consistently; • ease of administration is an important consideration.

Key learning points: Grade and pay structures

Purpose of grade and pay structures

Grade and pay structures provide the framework for base pay management as a means of implementing an organization's pay policies. They enable the organization to determine where jobs should be placed in a hierarchy, define pay levels and the scope for pay progression, and provide the basis upon which relativities can be managed, equal pay achieved and the processes of monitoring and controlling the implementation of pay practices can take place.

Grade and pay structures also enable organizations to communicate the career and pay opportunities available to employees.

Grade structures

A grade structure consists of a sequence or hierarchy of grades, bands or levels into which groups of jobs that are broadly comparable in size are placed. There may be a single structure defined by the number of grades or bands it contains.

Alternatively, the structure may be divided into a number of job families.

Pay structures

A pay structure consists of pay ranges, brackets or scales that are attached to each grade, band or level in a grade structure.

Pay structures are defined by the number of grades they contain and, especially in narrow- or broad-graded structures, the span or width of the pay ranges attached to each grade.

47
Contingent pay

KEY CONCEPTS AND TERMS

Compa-ratio   Pay matrix

Line of sight   Performance-related pay

Merit pay

LEARNING OUTCOMES

On completing this chapter you should be able to define these key concepts. You should also know about:

- Contingent pay
- Performance-related pay
- Team pay
- Paying for organizational performance

Contingent pay

Contingent pay provides financial rewards that are related to a factor such as performance or service in the job. It can take the form of consolidated increases to base pay and so provide for pay progression. It can also consist of cash non-consolidated bonuses.

For individuals, the most common form of contingent pay is performance-related pay as described below. Individual contingent pay is sometimes called merit pay and this covers pay related to performance, competence, contribution (performance plus competence) or skill. When payments are related to service it is known as service-related pay.

Bonuses can be based on individual, team or organizational performance. Wage earners may receive unconsolidated cash payments in addition to their base pay through an incentive scheme. The CIPD 2013 reward survey found that the most common split between total spend on fixed pay and contingent pay was 90 per cent fixed to 10 per cent variable; 71 per cent of the respondents related pay to individual performance.

Performance-related pay

While performance-related pay (PRP) is the most popular individual contingent pay scheme it is also controversial, largely because, especially in its early days, it was introduced and managed badly and the high expectations of its impact on performance and its ability to change cultures were not fulfilled. How PRP works and arguments for and against it are discussed below.

How performance-related pay works

The basic feature of most PRP schemes is that pay increases are related to the attainment of agreed results defined as targets or outcomes. In some schemes, performance is defined as embracing both results (achieving targets or outcomes) and behaviour (competency, or how the results were obtained). This reference to both the 'what' and the 'how' is in line with a broader definition of performance often used in performance management schemes. If both results and behaviour are taken into account, the scheme may be referred to as contribution-related pay.

In a PRP scheme scope is provided for consolidated pay progression within pay brackets attached to grades or levels in a graded or job family structure or zones in a broad-banded structure. Such increases are permanent.

A formula in the shape of a pay matrix as illustrated in Figure 47.1 is often used to decide on the size of increases. This indicates the percentage increase payable for different performance ratings according to the position of the individual's pay in the pay range. It is sometimes referred to as an individual 'compa-ratio' (short for comparison ratio) and expresses pay as a percentage of the mid-point in a range. A compa-ratio of 100 per cent means that the salary would be at the mid-point.

Pay progression in a graded structure is typically planned to decelerate through the grade for two reasons. First, it is argued in line with learning curve theory that pay increases should be higher during the earlier period in a job when learning is at its highest rate. Second, it may be assumed that the central or reference point in a grade represents the market value of fully competent people. Depending on the pay policy of the organization, this may be at or higher than the median. Especially in the latter case, it may be believed that employees should progress quite quickly to that level but, because beyond it they are already being paid well, their pay need not increase so rapidly. This notion is reasonable but it can be difficult to explain to people why they get smaller percentage increases when they are performing well at the upper end of their scale.

Alternatively, or additionally, high levels of performance or special achievements may be rewarded by cash bonuses that are not consolidated and have to be re-earned. Individuals may be eligible for such bonuses when they have reached the top of the pay bracket for their grade, or when they are assessed as being fully competent, having completely progressed along their learning curve. The rate of pay for someone who reaches the required level of competence

FIGURE 47.1   A pay matrix

Rating	Position in pay range			
	80–90%	91–100%	101–110%	111–120%
Excellent	12%	10%	8%	6%
Very effective	10%	8%	6%	4%
Effective	6%	4%	3%	0
Developing	4%	3%	0	0
Ineligible	0	0	0	0

can be aligned to market rates according to the organization's pay policy.

Another approach is to define performance zones in a pay range as in the following examples.

Xansa

Salary ranges are divided into three levels:

1 Entry level typically represents employees who are new to the job, meeting some objectives and demonstrating some of the skills and competencies at the required level.

2 Market average typically represents employees who either consistently meet their objectives and demonstrate many of the skills and competencies at the required level, or who meet most but not all objectives and consistently demonstrate all of the skills and competencies at the required level.

3 High level typically represents employees who meet all objectives and exceed some, and who demonstrate all of the skills and competencies at the required level and some at a higher level.

Nationwide

The majority of ranges consist of a target rate (100 per cent of the median market rate), a minimum (80 per cent), and a maximum (120 per cent). People tend to enter the range at the minimum. Progression thereafter is solely by means of performance. Each year, pay scales are uplifted by the percentage paid to 'good' performers. The percentage increases paid to individuals are applied to the target, rather than their own salaries, ensuring that everyone on a particular range with the same performance rating receives the same amount of money; that is, the same effort is guaranteed the same reward.

Employees who start on the minimum of a range are guaranteed progression to the target in three years if they receive consistently 'good' performance ratings. Those rated higher receive enhanced progression. Once the target has been reached, employees get the percentage increase resulting from their performance rating based on their target salary. This means that 'good' performers will stay at the target, since this (and the rest of the scales) is uprated by the percentage given to good performers, while better performers will move beyond the target towards the maximum.

Arguments for performance-related pay

The most powerful argument in favour of performance-related pay is that those who contribute more should be paid more. It can be claimed that it is right and proper to recognize achievement with a financial and therefore tangible reward. This is in accordance with the principle of distributive justice, which, while it states that rewards should be provided equitably, does not require them to be equal, except when the value of contribution is equal. The financial rewards provided by PRP can also be used to highlight key performance areas to indicate the behaviours that are valued and generally to emphasize the importance of high performance.

There is plenty of research evidence that financial rewards can improve performance. For example, in the UK this was established by Booth and Frank (1999), Marsden (2004), Prentice et al (2007), and Thompson (1998). In the United States, Gupta and Shaw (1998), Jenkins et al (1998), Lazear (1999) and Prendergast (1999) amongst others, all found positive relationships between financial incentives and performance.

Arguments against performance-related pay

The case for using performance-related pay rests on three assumptions:

- that it acts as an incentive and thus motivates people to improve their performance;
- that individual differences in performance can be accurately and fairly measured;
- that pay differences can be fairly related to performance differences and can be seen to be related.

These assumptions are difficult to justify. The effectiveness of PRP as an incentive is highly questionable. As normally operated it fails to meet the requirements of expectancy theory in three critical ways: 1) people are too often unclear about what they have to do to get a pay increase, ie there is no 'line of sight' between the effort and the reward; 2) people do not necessarily expect that they will get a reward; and 3) they do not expect that the reward will be worthwhile (the IRS 2012 review of pay trends showed that average merit pay increases were worth only 2.9 per cent – increases of less than 10 per cent are unlikely to have any motivating effect). PRP schemes also fail to meet the criterion that the reward should follow as closely as possible the accomplishment that generated it, in that it is usually made annually.

Fair measurement is hard in any situation where outcomes cannot be quantified, and this is the most typical situation. Relating pay fairly to performance can be subject to partiality or prejudice. The success of PRP largely depends on the line managers who make pay recommendations, and they are not necessarily equipped with the information, skills or the powers of judgement required to do so fairly and consistently.

Moreover, they usually rely on potentially subjective and inaccurate ratings. As Murphy and Cleveland (1995) concluded following their extensive review of performance appraisal: 'It is surprisingly difficult to determine whether or not performance ratings provide valid and accurate indications of individuals' performance.'

A vociferous chorus of disapproval has been heard on the incentive effect of the financial rewards provided by performance-related pay. One of the best known and most influential voices was that of Alfie Kohn (1993: 62) who stated in the *Harvard Business Review* that: 'Rewards, like punishment, may actually undermine the intrinsic motivation that results in optimal performance. The more a manager stresses what an employee can earn for good work, the less interested that employee will be in the work itself.' His summary was that 'bribes in the workplace simply can't work' (ibid: 63). Jeffrey Pfeffer (1998: 114) concluded in his equally influential *Harvard Business Review* article, 'Six dangerous myths about pay', that: 'Most merit-pay systems share two attributes: they absorb vast amounts of management time and make everybody unhappy.' A more recent and much-quoted opponent of financial rewards is Daniel Pink (2009). He listed the following seven deadly sins of 'carrots and sticks' as follows:

1 They can extinguish intrinsic motivation.
2 They can diminish performance.
3 They can crush creativity.
4 The can crowd out good behaviour.
5 They can encourage cheating, shortcuts and unethical behaviour.

6 They can become addictive.
7 They can foster short-term thinking.

Pink offered no evidence to support his assertions with the exception of the first deadly sin. This contention that financial rewards reduce intrinsic motivation is the one most commonly referred to by critics. Pink's argument is based on the research of Deci (1975), who is credited with recognizing the importance of intrinsic satisfaction as a powerful source of motivation. Deci's conclusions were based largely on student experiments. The problem is that the research focused on simple tasks in artificial situations that differed substantially from real work settings. This is best illustrated in the introduction to Pink's book, which is largely devoted to a Deci experiment where students rearranged blocks – with their performance rewarded with what today is equivalent to $6.

But there is more convincing evidence about the problems associated with performance-related pay. This has been provided by researchers such as Bowey and Thorpe (1982), Kessler and Purcell (1992), Marsden and Richardson (1994) and Thompson (1992a, 1992b). The points they made were that:

● the extent to which performance pay schemes motivate is questionable – the amounts available for distribution are usually so small that they cannot act as an incentive;

● the requirements for success are exacting and difficult to achieve;

● money by itself will not result in sustained motivation; intrinsic motivation provided by the work itself goes deeper and lasts longer;

● people react in widely different ways to any form of motivation – it cannot be assumed that money will motivate everyone equally, yet that is the premise on which performance pay schemes are based;

● financial rewards may possibly motivate those who receive them but they can demotivate those who don't, and the numbers who are demotivated could be much higher than those who are motivated;

● performance pay schemes can create more dissatisfaction than satisfaction if they are perceived to be unfair, inadequate or badly managed, which can easily be the case;

- employees can be suspicious of schemes because they fear that performance bars will be continuously raised; a scheme may therefore only operate successfully for a limited period;
- schemes depend on the existence of accurate and reliable methods of measuring performance, contribution, competence, or skill, which might not exist;
- individuals are encouraged to emphasize only those aspects of performance that are rewarded;
- performance pay decisions depend on the judgement of managers, which in the absence of reliable criteria can be partial, prejudiced, inconsistent or ill-informed;
- the concept of performance pay is based on the assumption that performance is completely under the control of individuals, when in fact it is affected by the system in which they work;
- performance-related pay can militate against quality and teamwork.

These are powerful arguments. There is plenty of evidence from the researchers mentioned above that performance pay schemes are difficult to manage well. Organizations, including the UK Civil Service, rushed into performance-related pay in the 1980s without really understanding how to make it work. Inevitably, problems of implementation arose. Failures may arise because insufficient attention has been paid to fitting schemes to the context and culture of the organization. But problems are often rooted in implementation and operating difficulties, especially those of inadequate performance management processes, the lack of effective communication and involvement, and line managers who are not capable of or interested in properly carrying out the actions involved. Vicky Wright (1991: 82) remarked that: 'Even the most ardent supporters of performance-related pay recognize that it is difficult to manage well'; Trevor (2011: 201) also questioned the extent to which such systems are manageable.

Critical evaluation of performance-related pay

The argument that people should be rewarded in accordance with the value of their contribution is a strong one. But the evidence that incentives improve performance is conflicting. In some circumstances, as demonstrated by research projects, it works, but in others it doesn't. Most performance-related pay schemes are unlikely to provide a direct incentive, simply because they do not match demanding requirements such as:

- rewards are worth having;
- fair and consistent means are available for measuring or assessing performance;
- people are able to influence their performance by changing their behaviour;
- the reward follows as closely as possible the accomplishment that generated it;
- the scheme fits the culture of the organization;
- the scheme is manageable and cost-effective.

The main purpose of PRP schemes is to recognize the level of contribution, and even this is questionable because of the difficulty of making fair and consistent assessments of performance as a basis for pay decisions. Such schemes can demotivate more people than they motivate. Research by the Corporate Leadership Council (2002) on financial incentives suggested that incentives are more likely to attract and retain employees than drive performance.

But what's the alternative? Should everyone be paid the same rate in a job however well they perform? Or should pay be progressed in line with length of service – paying people for being there? For all its problems, the balance of the argument is in favour of some scheme for relating pay to performance. But the difficulties of doing this should be recognized and every attempt should be made to ensure that pay decisions are fair, consistent and transparent.

Team pay

Team pay links payments to members of a formally established team to the performance of that team. The rewards are shared among the members of the team in accordance with a published formula, or on an ad hoc basis in the case of exceptional achievements. Rewards for individuals may also be influenced by assessments of their contribution to team results.

Team pay can enhance cooperative behaviour, encourage flexible working and multiskilling and clarify team goals. It can also persuade less effective performers to improve in order to meet team standards and help to develop self-managed teams. But there are a number of problems:

- The effectiveness of team pay depends on the existence of well-defined and mature teams and they may be difficult to identify. Even if they can be, do they need to be motivated by a purely financial reward?

- Team pay may seem unfair to individuals who could feel that their own efforts are unrewarded.

- Pressure to conform, which is accentuated by team pay, could result in the team maintaining its output at lowest common denominator levels – sufficient to gain what is thought collectively to be a reasonable reward but no more.

- It can be difficult to develop performance measures and methods of rating team performance that are seen to be fair – team pay formulae may well be based on arbitrary assumptions about the correct relationship between effort and reward.

- There may be pressure from employees to migrate from poorly performing teams to highly performing teams. If allowed, this could cause disruption and stigmatize the teams from which individuals transfer; if refused, it could leave dissatisfied employees in the inadequate teams, making them even worse.

For many organizations, the disadvantages outweigh the advantages. Perhaps this is why the e-reward 2009 reward survey found that only 11 per cent of respondents had team pay.

Pay for organizational performance

Many organizations believe that their financial reward systems should extend beyond individual merit pay, which does not recognize collective effort, or team pay, which is difficult. They believe that their system should help to enhance engagement and commitment and convince employees that they have a stake in the business as well as providing them with additional pay. The response to this belief is to offer financial rewards that are related to business or organizational performance (sometimes known as 'company-wide' or 'factory-wide' schemes).

The three types of formal business performance schemes are:

- *Profit sharing* – the payment of sums in cash or shares related to the profits of the business.

- *Share schemes* – employees are given the opportunity to take out share options or participate in a save-as-you-earn scheme of a share incentive plan.

- *Gain sharing* – the payment of cash sums to employees related to the financial gains made by the company because of its improved performance.

Key learning points: Contingent pay

Contingent pay

Contingent pay provides financial rewards in addition to base pay that are related to a factor such as individual or organizational performance or service in the job. The most common form of individual contingent pay is performance-related pay.

How performance-related pay works

The basic feature of most PRP schemes is that pay increases are related to the achievement of agreed results defined as targets or outcomes.

Arguments for performance-related pay

The most powerful argument in favour of performance-related pay is that those who contribute more should be paid more. The financial rewards provided by PRP can also be used to highlight key performance areas, to indicate the behaviours that are valued and generally to emphasize the importance of high performance.

Arguments against performance-related pay

The effectiveness of PRP as an incentive is highly questionable. It is hard to make fair and consistent assessments of performance as a basis for pay decisions.

Team pay

Team pay links payments to members of a formally established team to the performance of that team. The rewards are shared among the members of the team in accordance with a published formula, or on an ad hoc basis in the case of exceptional achievements.

Pay for organizational performance

Financial rewards can be related to business or organizational performance (sometimes known as 'company-wide' or 'factory-wide' schemes). The three types of formal business performance schemes are *profit sharing*, *share schemes* and *gain sharing*.

References

Booth, A L and Frank, J (1999) Earnings, productivity and performance related pay, *Journal of Labor Economics*, **17** (3), pp 447–63

Bowey, A and Thorpe, R (1982) *The Effects of Incentive Pay Systems*, London, Department of Employment

CIPD (2013) *Reward Management Annual Survey Report*, London, CIPD

Corporate Leadership Council (2002) Building the high performance workforce, [online] http://talentexperiment.com/images/CLC_Building_the_High_Performance_Workforce_A_Quantitative_Analysis_of_the_Effectiveness_of_Performance_Management_Strategies_1_.pdf [accessed 13 January 2016]

Deci, E L (1975) *Intrinsic Motivation*, New York, Plenum Press

e-reward (2009) *Survey of Contingent Pay*, Stockport, e-reward

Gupta, N and Shaw, J D (1998) Financial incentives, *Compensation & Benefits Review*, March–April, pp 26, 28–32

IRS Employment Review (2012) *Annual Review of Pay Trends*, September, p 1

Jenkins, D G, Mitra, A, Gupta, N and Shaw, J D (1998) Are financial incentives related to performance? A meta-analytic review of empirical research, *Journal of Applied Psychology*, **3**, pp 777–87

Kessler, I and Purcell, J (1992) Performance-related pay: objectives and application, *Human Resource Management Journal*, **2** (3), pp 16–33

Kohn, A (1993) Why incentive plans cannot work, *Harvard Business Review*, September–October, pp 54–63

Lazear, E P (1999) Performance pay and productivity, *American Economic Review*, 90, pp 1346–61

Marsden, D (2004) The role of performance-related pay in renegotiating the 'effort bargain': the case of the British public service, *Industrial and Labor Relations Review*, 57 (3), pp 350–70

Marsden, D and Richardson, R (1994) Performing for pay? The effects of 'merit pay' on motivation in a public service, *British Journal of Industrial Relations*, 32 (2), pp 243–61

Murphy, K R and Cleveland, J N (1995) *Understanding Performance Appraisal*, Thousand Oaks, CA, Sage

Pfeffer, J (1998) Six dangerous myths about pay, *Harvard Business Review*, May–June, pp 109–19

Pink, D H (2009) *Drive: The surprising truth about what motivates us*, New York, Riverhead Books

Prendergast, C (1999) The provision of financial incentives in firms, *Journal of Economic Literature*, 37, pp 7–63

Prentice, G, Burgess, S and Propper, C (2007) *Performance Pay in the Public Sector: A review of the issues and evidence*, London, Office of Manpower Economics

Thompson, M (1992a) *Pay and Performance: The employer experience*, Brighton, IMS

Thompson, M (1992b) *Pay and Performance: The employee experience*, Brighton, IMS

Thompson, M (1998) HR and the bottom line, *People Management*, 16 April, pp 38–41

Trevor, J (2011) *Can Pay Be Strategic?* Basingstoke, Palgrave Macmillan

Wright, V (1991) Performance-related pay, in (ed) E Neale, *The Performance Management Handbook*, London, Institute of Personnel Management

48

Managing reward for special groups

KEY CONCEPTS AND TERMS

Agency theory

Commission

Deferred bonus schemes

Measured day work

Piece work

Segmentation

Share option schemes

Time rates

Tournament theory

Work measurement

LEARNING OUTCOMES

On completing this chapter you should be able to define these key concepts. You should also know about:

● Reward policies and practices for directors and senior executives
● Reward policies and practices for sales and customer service staff
● Reward policies and practices for manual workers

Introduction

Many organizations have one reward system applied to all categories of staff below the levels of chief executive and executive directors. However, others find it necessary to cater for the needs of special groups of staff by adopting different reward practices. This is called reward segmentation and, as described in this chapter, frequently applies to the methods used for directors and senior executives, knowledge workers, sales and customer service staff and manual workers.

Rewarding directors and executives

Executives are well paid. A report by the High Pay Centre in 2015 stated that the average pay of a FTSE 100 chief executive in 2014 was £4.9m. The Centre also reported that the pay of the chief executives had grown from 60 times that of the average worker in 1998 to 183 times in 2014.

PwC, the financial services and consultancy firm, commented in 2012 that: 'There is an emerging consensus, at least in Western economies, that there is something deeply flawed about the current model of executive pay. Executive pay has risen dramatically over a period when, in hindsight, the Western economic model has not been at its most successful.'

A non-executive director interviewed by Perkins and Hendry (2005) during their research on top pay remarked: 'There is neither a moral nor a market argument to justify the explosion in pay, but once started, it is hard to stop. You cannot be seen to be left out.'

It has been established by research (Conyon and Leech, 1994; Gomez-Mejia and Balkin, 1992; Gregg *et al*, 1993) that there is no evidence that the huge increases in pay have resulted in improved company performance.

Factors affecting the level of executive rewards

The major factor

The level of executive rewards is primarily affected by how companies react to market forces in order to recruit and retain the executives they want and need. The Hampel Report (1998) stated that British boardroom remuneration will be 'largely determined by the market'.

The way market forces work in executive pay is mainly based on benchmarking – finding out what other chief executives in relevant businesses are paid and responding accordingly.

The following comments on this approach were made by Elson and Ferrere (2013):

> In setting the pay of their CEO, boards invariably reference the pay of the executives at other enterprises in similar industries and of similar size

and complexity. For this, compensation consultants are retained to construct a 'peer group' of such companies and survey the pay practices that are prevalent. Then, in what is described as 'competitive benchmarking', compensation levels are generally targeted to either the 50th, 75th, or 90th percentile. This process is alleged to provide an effective gauge of the 'market wage', which is necessary for executive retention. In essence, this process creates a model of a competitive market for executives where it otherwise does not exist. The model may, in this case, drive the empirical results rather than the other way around. As we describe, this conception of such a market was created purely by happenstance, and by its uniform application across companies, the effects of structural flaws in its design can have potentially compounding macro effects on the level of executive compensation. Both the academic and professional communities have observed that the practice of targeting the pay of executives to median or higher levels will naturally create an upward bias and movement in total compensation amounts.

In essence, what Elson and Ferrere are saying is that this benchmarking process produces an upward ratchet. Firms end up overpaying for executives in order to establish a short-lived advantage that is neutralized by rivals paying more as well.

Data collected by Perkins and Hendry (2005) over 10 years for 81 of the FTSE 100 companies tended to show a relative lack of intra-company movement among executive directors, in particular internationally. This, they commented, undermines the presumption of a market in executives and hence in executive pay. They went on to point out that: 'While the evidence for a market with price as a clearing mechanism remains questionable, therefore, there is certainly no widespread subjective sense of such a market among those who are closest to it. Rather, there are a series of localized bargains.' They quoted a remuneration committee member they interviewed who categorically denied the existence of a recognizable market for executives: 'Certainly not like that for beef or shares'. Instead, he said, there are 'just key people in unique positions at a given moment in time, who are not readily interchangeable'.

Research conducted by the High Pay Commission (2011b), suggested that losing a CEO to a competitor remains very unlikely. In a survey of CEO departures over the last five years in the FTSE 100, it was found that the chance of a CEO being poached by a national competitor in any one year would be 0.2 per cent. The likelihood of a CEO being snatched by a global firm was zero.

Other factors

The level of executive rewards can be explained in general terms by agency theory and tournament theory. Agency theory states that the only way in which owners (principals) can get the performance they want from their managers (agents) is by paying them more. Shareholders must structure the CEO's pay arrangements to reward behaviours that increase shareholder value. Tournament theory explains that the remuneration of a chief executive is in effect a prize and executives expend effort to increase the likelihood of winning it.

High rewards for chief executives are sometimes justified by reference to beliefs on their value to the business as wealth creators – generators of shareholder value. But the High Pay Commission (2011a) found that at its worst, excessive high pay bears little relation to company success and is rewarding failure. The Commission established that between 1998 and 2009, chief executive remuneration quadrupled while share prices declined. The remuneration of chief executives of FTSE 100 companies rose by 6.7 per cent a year, while earnings per share fell by 1 per cent per year over the same period.

It may also be claimed that chief executives are worth more because they are overseeing larger, more complex operations. But it does not necessarily follow that larger firm size should be matched by proportionally larger executive remuneration. A firm that has grown in size by a certain percentage has not necessarily grown in complexity by the same proportion, nor has the contribution of the executive role grown by the same proportion. A firm that is double the size will not necessarily have double the strategic decisions to make.

The elements of executive remuneration

The main elements of executive remuneration are basic pay, short- and long-term bonus or incentive schemes, share option and share ownership schemes, benefits and service contracts. The salary is usually a one-off, negotiated rate and commonly incorporates a golden hello or pay-off deal. It should be set through a remuneration committee that meets good practice guidelines.

Basic pay

Decisions on the base salary of directors and senior executives are usually founded on views about the market worth of the individuals concerned. Remuneration on joining the company is commonly settled by negotiation, often subject to the approval of a remuneration committee. Reviews of base salaries are then undertaken by reference to market movements and success as measured by company performance. Decisions on base salary are important not only in themselves but also because the level may influence decisions on the pay of both senior and middle managers. Bonuses are expressed as a percentage of base salary, share options may be allocated as a declared multiple of basic pay and, commonly, pension will be a generous proportion of final salary.

Bonus schemes

Virtually all major employers in the UK have incentive (bonus) schemes for senior executives. Bonus schemes provide directors and executives with cash sums or shares based on the measures of company and, frequently, individual performance. They are often paid annually but can be deferred for a longer period.

Typically, bonus payments are linked to achievement of profit and/or other financial targets and they are sometimes 'capped'; that is, a restriction is placed on the maximum amount payable. There may also be elements related to achieving specific goals and to individual performance. Bonuses tend to be high – 70 per cent of base salary or more. They are ostensibly intended to motivate directors to achieve performance improvements for the business. A more common although not always disclosed reason for bonuses is to ensure that what is believed to be a competitive remuneration package is available: 'Everyone else is doing it so we must too.'

One of the problems with high bonus expectations is that of the 'moral hazard' involved. For example, directors might be tempted to manipulate reported profits to drive up the share price, frequently an important determinant of bonuses.

TABLE 48.1 Summary of payment and incentive arrangements for sales staff

Method	Features	Advantages	Disadvantages	When appropriate
Salary only	Straight salary, no commission or bonus.	Encourages customer service rather than high-pressure selling; deals with the problem of staff who are working in a new or unproductive sales territory; protects income when sales fluctuate for reasons beyond the individual's control.	No direct motivation through money; may attract under-achieving people who are subsidized by high achievers; increases fixed costs of sales because pay costs are not flexed with sales results.	When representing the company is more important than direct selling; staff have little influence on sales volume (they may simply be 'order takers'); customer service is all-important.
Salary plus commission	Basic salary plus cash commission calculated as a percentage of sales volume or value.	Direct financial motivation is provided related to what sales staff are there to do, ie generate sales, but they are not entirely dependent on commission – they are cushioned by their base salary.	Relating pay to the volume or value of sales is too crude an approach and may result in staff going for volume by concentrating on the easier-to-sell products, not those generating high margins; may encourage high-pressure selling as in some financial services firms in the '80s and '90s.	When it is believed that the way to get more sales is to link extra money to results but a base salary is still needed to attract the many people who want to be assured of a reasonable basic salary which will not fluctuate but who still aspire to increase that salary by their own efforts.

TABLE 48.1 continued

Method	Features	Advantages	Disadvantages	When appropriate
Salary plus bonus	Basic salary plus cash bonus based on achieving and exceeding sales targets or quotas and meeting other selling objectives.	Provides financial motivation but targets or objectives can be flexed to ensure that particular sales goals are achieved, eg high-margin sales, customer service.	No clear line of sight between effort and reward; may be complex to administer; sales representatives may find it hard to understand and resent the use of subjective judgements on performance other than sales.	When flexibility in providing rewards is important; it is felt that sales staff need to be motivated to focus on aspects of their work other than simply maximizing sales volume.
Commission only	Only commission based on a percentage of sales volume or value is paid; there is no basic salary.	Provides a direct financial incentive; attracts high-performing sales staff; ensures that selling costs vary directly with sales; little direct supervision required.	Leads to high-pressure selling; may attract the wrong sort of people who are interested only in sales anc not customer service; focuses attention on high volume rather than profitability.	When sales performance depends mainly on selling ability and can be measured by immediate sales results; staff are not involved in non-selling activities; continuing relationships with customers are relatively unimportant.
Additional non-cash rewards	Incentives, prizes, cars, recognition, opportunities to grow.	Utilizes powerful non-financial motivators.	May be difficult to administer; does not provide a direct incentive.	When it is believed that other methods of payment need to be enhanced by providing additional motivators.

TABLE 48.2 *continued*

Scheme	Main features	For employers		For employees		When appropriate
		Advantages	Disadvantages	Advantages	Disadvantages	
Performance-related pay	Payments on top of base rate are made related to individual assessments of performance.	Reward individual contribution without resource to work measurement; relevant in high-technology manufacturing.	Measuring performance can be difficult; no direct incentive provided.	Opportunity to be rewarded for own efforts without having to submit to a pressured PBR system.	Assessment informing performance pay decisions may be biased, inconsistent or unsupported by evidence.	As part of a reward harmonization (shop floor and staff) programme; as an alternative to work measured schemes or an enhancement of a high day rate system.
Group or team basis	Groups or teams are paid bonuses on the basis of their performance as indicated by work measurement ratings or the achievement of targets.	Encourage team cooperation and effort; not too individualized.	Direct incentive may be limited; depends on good work measurement or the availability of clear group output or productivity targets.	Bonuses can be related clearly to the joint efforts of the group; fluctuations in earnings minimized.	Depend on effective work measurement, which is not always available; individual effort and contribution not recognized.	When team working is important and team efforts can be accurately measured and assessed; as an alternative to individual PBR if this is not effective.
Factory-wide bonuses	Bonuses related to plant performance – added value or productivity.	Increase commitment by sharing success.	No direct motivation.	Earnings increased without individual pressure.	Bonuses often small and unpredictable.	As an addition to other forms of incentive when increasing commitment is important.

Key learning points

Segmentation

Many organizations have one reward system applied to all categories of staff below the level of chief executive. However, others find it necessary to cater for the needs of special groups of staff by adopting different reward practices. This is called reward segmentation.

Executive pay levels

Executive pay is out of control. The reasons are:

- Tournament theory: the increasing demands made on chief executives.
- Star culture: the creation of the celebrity CEO.
- The talent shortage.
- Pay disclosure in annual reports leads to demands from CEOs to achieve parity.

Elements of directors' and senior executives' pay

Basic, pay, bonus schemes, share options, executive restricted share schemes.

Payment and incentive schemes for sales staff

Summarized in Table 48.1.

Pay for customer service staff

Customer service staff usually have the opportunity to progress their base pay on the basis of their performance or competence, either through a range or up a pay spine, or between grades/levels of job.

Pay for manual workers

The pay of manual workers takes the form of time rates, also known as day rates, day work, flat rates or hourly rates. Incentive payments by means of payment-by-results scheme as summarized in Table 45.2 may be made on top of a base rate.

References

Conyon, M J and Leech, D (1994) Top pay, company performance and corporate performance, *Oxford Bulletin of Economics and Statistics*, **56** (3), August, pp 229–47

Elson, C M and Ferrere, C K (2013) Executive superstars, peer groups and overcompensation: Cause, effect and solution, *Journal of Corporation Law*, Spring, pp 98–131

Gomez-Mejia, L R and Balkin, D B (1992) *Compensation, Organizational Strategy, and Firm Performance*, Cincinnati, OH, South Western

Gregg, P, Machin, S and Szymanski, S (1993) The disappearing relationship between directors' pay and corporate performance, *British Journal of Industrial Relations*, **3** (1), pp 1–9

Hampel, R (1998) *Committee on Corporate Governance: Final report*, London, Gee Publishing

High Pay Centre (2015) *Report on Executive Pay* [online] http://highpaycentre.org/pubs/new-high-pay-centre-report-executive-pay-continues-to-climb-at-expense-of-ordinary-workers [accessed 20 November 2015]

High Pay Commission (2011a) *More for Less: What has happened to pay at the top and does it matter?* London, High Pay Commission

High Pay Commission (2011b) Final Report, London, High Pay Commission 29

Perkins, S and Hendry, P (2005) Ordering top pay: interpreting the signals, *Journal of Management Studies*, **42** (7), pp 1443–68

PwC (2012) *Making Executive Pay Work* [online] http://www.pwc.co.uk/human-resource-services/publications/making-executive-pay-work.jhtml 2012 [accessed 12 February 2015]

West, M, Fisher, G, Carter, M, Gould, V and Scully, J (2005) *Rewarding Customer Service? Using reward and recognition to deliver your customer service strategy*, London, CIPD

49
Managing reward systems

KEY CONCEPTS AND TERMS

Compa-ratio analysis

Mid-point management

LEARNING OUTCOMES

On completing this chapter you should be able to define these key concepts. You should also know about:

- Controlling reward through mid-point management and the use of compa-ratios
- Conducting general pay reviews
- Conducting individual pay reviews
- Reward procedures

Controlling reward

The implementation of reward policies and procedures should be monitored and controlled to ensure that value for money is obtained. Control is easier if the grade and pay structure is well defined and clear guidelines exist on how it and the benefits arrangements should be managed.

It is necessary to ensure that policy on levels of pay is achieved. The most typical policy value is the mid-point in the pay structure's ranges, which represents the target rate for a fully competent individual in any job in the grade. This point is aligned with market rates in accordance with the organization's market stance (its policy on the relationship between its levels of pay and market rates). This technique of mid-point management uses compa-ratio (short for comparative ratio) analysis to check on the implementation of pay policy.

Compa-ratio analysis establishes differences between pay policy and practice (variations in levels of pay above or below the mid-point) so that action can be taken to slow down or accelerate increases if compa-ratios are too high or too low compared with the policy level.

Compa-ratios are calculated as follows:

$$\frac{\text{actual rate of pay}}{\text{mid or reference point of range}} \times 100$$

A compa-ratio of 100 per cent means that actual pay and policy pay are the same. Compa-ratios higher or lower than 100 per cent mean that, respectively, pay is above or below the policy target rate. For example, if the target (policy) rate in a range was £30,000 and the average pay of all the individuals in the grade was £27,000, the compa-ratio would be 90 per cent.

Compa-ratios can also be used to measure where an individual is placed in a pay range, and therefore provide information on the size of pay increases when a pay matrix is used, as shown in chapter 47.

General pay reviews

General reviews take place when employees are given a pay increase in response to general market rate movements, increases in the cost of living, or union negotiations. General reviews are often combined with individual reviews, but employees are usually informed of both the general and individual components of any increase they receive. Alternatively, the general review may be conducted separately to enable better control to be achieved over costs and to focus employees' attention on the performance-related aspect of their remuneration.

Some organizations have completely abandoned the use of across-the-board reviews. They argue that the decision on what people should be paid should be an individual matter, taking into account the personal contribution people are making and their 'market worth' – how they as individuals are valued in the marketplace. This enables the organization to adopt a more flexible approach to allocating pay increases in accordance with the perceived value of individuals to the organization.

The steps required to conduct a general review are:

- Decide on the budget.
- Analyse data on pay settlements made by comparable organizations and rates of inflation.
- Conduct negotiations with trade unions as required.
- Calculate costs.
- Adjust the pay structure – by either increasing the pay brackets of each grade by the percentage general increase or by increasing pay reference points by the overall percentage and applying different increases to the upper or lower limits of the bracket, thus altering the shape of the structure.
- Inform employees.

Individual pay reviews

Individual pay reviews determine contingent pay increases or bonuses. Individual awards may be based on ratings, an overall assessment that does not depend on ratings, or ranking, as discussed below.

Individual pay reviews based on ratings

Managers propose increases on the basis of their performance management ratings within a given pay review budget and in accordance with pay review guidelines.

There is a choice of methods. The simplest way is to have a direct link between the rating and the pay increase, for example:

Rating	Increase
A	6
B	4
C	3
D	2
E	0

A more sophisticated approach is to use a pay matrix, as illustrated in Chapter 47 (Figure 47.1). This indicates the percentage increase payable for different performance ratings according to the position of the individual's pay in the pay range. This is sometimes referred to as an individual 'compa-ratio' and expresses pay as a percentage of the mid-point in a range. A compa-ratio of 100 per cent means that the salary would be at the mid-point.

Managers propose increases on the basis of their performance management ratings within a given pay review budget and in accordance with pay review guidelines.

Many people argue that linking performance management too explicitly to pay prejudices the essential developmental nature of performance management. However, realistically, it is accepted that decisions on performance-related or contribution-related increases have to be based on some form of assessment. One solution is to 'decouple' performance management and the pay review by holding them several months apart. There is still a read-across but it is not so immediate. Some try to do without formulaic approaches (ratings and pay matrices) altogether, although it is impossible to dissociate merit pay completely from some form of assessment.

Guidelines to managers on conducting individual pay reviews

Guidelines have to be issued to managers on how they should conduct reviews. The guidelines will stipulate that they must keep within their budgets and may indicate the maximum and minimum increases that can be awarded, with an indication of how awards could be distributed. For example, in happy days when the budget is 4 per cent overall, it might be suggested that a 3 per cent increase should be given to the majority of staff and the others given higher or lower increases as long as the total percentage increase does not exceed the budget. Managers in some companies are instructed that they must follow a forced pattern of distribution (a forced choice system).

Steps required

The steps required to conduct an individual pay review are:

1 Agree the budget.
2 Prepare and issue guidelines on the size, range and distribution of awards and on methods of conducting the review.
3 Provide advice and support.
4 Review proposals against budget and guidelines and agree modifications to them if necessary.
5 Summarize and cost proposals and obtain approval.
6 Update the payroll.
7 Inform employees.

Reward procedures

Grading jobs

The procedures for grading jobs set out how job evaluation should be used to grade a new job or re-grade an existing one. A point-factor evaluation scheme that has defined grades may be used for all new jobs and to deal with requests for re-grading. However, an analytical matching process may be used to compare the role profiles of the jobs to be graded with grade or level profiles or profiles of benchmark jobs. This is likely to be the case in large organizations and for broad-banded structures.

Fixing rates of pay on appointment

The procedure should indicate how much freedom line managers and HR have to pay above the minimum rate for the job. The freedom may be limited to, say, 10 per cent above the minimum or two or three pay points on an incremental scale. More scope is sometimes allowed to respond to market rate pressures or to attract particularly well-qualified staff by paying up to the reference point or target salary in a pay range, subject to HR approval and bearing in mind the need to provide scope for contingent pay increases. If recruitment supplements or premia are used, the rules for offering them to candidates must be clearly defined.

Promotion increases

The procedure will indicate what is regarded as a meaningful increase on promotion, often 10 per cent or more. To avoid creating anomalies, the level of pay has to take account of what other people are paid who are carrying out work at a similar level, and it is usual to lay down a maximum level that does not take the pay of the promoted employee above the reference point for the new range.

Appeals

It is customary to include the right to appeal against gradings as part of a job evaluation procedure. Appeals against pay decisions are usually made through the organization's grievance procedure.

Key learning points: Managing reward systems

Controlling reward

The implementation of reward policies and procedures should be monitored and controlled to ensure that value for money is obtained.

It is necessary to ensure that policy on levels of pay is achieved through mid-point management techniques using compa-ratio analysis.

General pay reviews

General reviews take place when employees are given a pay increase in response to general market rate movements, increases in the cost of living, or union negotiations.

Individual pay reviews

Individual pay reviews determine contingent pay increases or bonuses. Individual awards may be based on ratings, an overall assessment that does not depend on ratings, or ranking.

Reward procedures

Reward procedures deal with grading jobs, fixing rates of pay and handling appeals.

PART X

Employee relations

Introduction

Employee relations, sometimes referred to as employment relations, are concerned with managing the employment relationship and the psychological contract. They consist of the approaches and methods adopted by employers to deal with employees either collectively through their trade unions or individually. This includes providing employees with a voice and developing communications between them and management.

Employee relations cover a wider spectrum of the employment relationship than industrial relations, which are essentially about what goes on between management and trade union representatives and officials involving collective agreements, collective bargaining and disputes resolution. This wider definition of employee relations recognizes the move away from collectivism towards individualism in the ways in which employees relate to their employers.

This part starts with a review of the nature of employee relations, employee relations strategies and policies, and the approaches used by organizations to employee relations including how they manage with or without trade unions. The next two chapters examine the fundamental concepts that affect employee relations, namely the nature of the employment relationship and the psychological contract. These chapters provide the background to Chapter 53 which deals with the practice of industrial relations, covering union recognition and the processes of collective bargaining and dispute resolution. The last two chapters deal respectively with employee voice (participation and involvement) and communications.

50
The basis of employee relations

KEY CONCEPTS AND TERMS

Collectivism

Derecognition

Employee relations

Employee relations climate

Individualism

Industrial relations

Mutuality

Pay–work bargain

Pluralist viewpoint

Single-table bargaining

Union recognition

LEARNING OUTCOMES

On completing this chapter you should be able to define these key concepts. You should also know about:

- The process of employee relations
- The basis of employee relations
- Employee relations policies
- Employee relations strategies
- The employee relations climate
- Managing with and without unions

Introduction

Employee relations are concerned with managing and maintaining the employment relationship, taking into account the implications of the notion of the psychological contract (these concepts are discussed in the next two chapters). This means dealing with employees either collectively through their trade unions or individually; handling employment practices, terms and conditions of employment and issues arising from employment, providing employees with a voice and communicating with them.

The meaning of employee relations

Employee relations are about how managements and employees live together and what can be done to make that work. There are two views about the relationship. The unitary viewpoint is the belief that management and employees share the same concerns and it is therefore in both their interests to cooperate. This was defined by Walton (1985: 64) as the principle of mutuality. A similar belief is expressed in the idea of social partnership, which states that as stakeholders, the parties involved in employee relations should aim to work together to the greater good of all. Partnership agreements try to put this idea into practice.

In contrast, the pluralist viewpoint is that the interests of employees will not necessarily coincide with their employers and that the unitary view is naive, unrealistic and against the interests of employees. People of this persuasion don't believe that partnership agreements can work.

The meaning of employee relations can be described somewhat simplistically in terms of the pay–work bargain – the agreement made between employers and employees whereby the former undertakes to pay for the work done by the latter. According to this notion, many employers simply want employees who will do what they are told without costing too much. They want engagement and commitment on their own terms. But employees want a 'fair day's pay for a fair day's work' and a say in their terms and conditions of employment and the way in which their work is organized. They want security of employment, good working conditions, a healthy and safe working environment and the scope to raise and resolve grievances. Conflicts of interest can arise between employers and employees on these issues, and where there are unions these conflicts are resolved by the various industrial relations procedures described in Chapter 53. Because of this, employee relations need to be managed by reference to understood and communicated policies and strategies.

Employee relations policies

Employee relations policies express the philosophy of the organization on what sort of relationships are wanted between management and employees and, where necessary, their unions, and how the pay–work bargain should be managed. A social partnership policy will aim to develop and maintain a positive, productive, cooperative and trusting climate of employee relations.

Approaches

There are four approaches to employee relations:

1 Adversarial: the organization decides what it wants to do, and employees are expected to fit in. Employees only exercise power by refusing to cooperate.

2 Traditional: a reasonably good day-to-day working relationship but management proposes and the workforce reacts through its elected representatives, if there are any; if not, employees just accept the situation or walk.

3 Partnership: the organization involves employees in the drawing up and execution of organization policies, but retains the right to manage.

4 Power sharing: employees are involved in both day-to-day and strategic decision making.

Adversarial approaches are much less common now than in the 1960s and '70s. The traditional approach is still the most typical but more interest is being expressed in partnership. Power sharing is rare.

Objectives of employee relations policies

The objectives of employee relations policies may include maintaining good relations with employees and their unions, developing a cooperative and constructive employee relations climate, the effective management of the work process, the control of labour costs, and the development of an engaged and committed workforce. When these policies are articulated, they provide guidelines for taking action on employee relations issues and can help to ensure that these issues are dealt with consistently. They provide the basis for defining management's intentions (its employee relations strategy) on key matters such as union recognition and collective bargaining.

Employee relations policy areas

The areas covered by employee relations policies are:

- *Trade union recognition* – whether trade unions should be recognized or derecognized, which union or unions the organization would prefer to deal with, and whether or not it is desirable to recognize only one union for collective bargaining and/or employee representational purposes. The policy will have to consider the factors affecting managing with or without unions, as discussed later in this chapter.

- *Collective bargaining* – the extent to which it should be centralized or decentralized and the scope of areas to be covered by collective bargaining.

- *Employee relations procedures* – the nature and scope of procedures for redundancy, grievance handling and discipline.

- *Participation and involvement* – how far the organization is prepared to go in giving employees a voice on matters that concern them.

- *Partnership* – the extent to which a partnership approach is thought to be desirable.

- *The employment relationship* – the extent to which terms and conditions of employment should be governed by collective agreements or based on individual contracts of employment (ie collectivism versus individualism).

- *Harmonization of terms and conditions of employment for staff and manual workers.*

- *Working arrangements* – the degree to which management has the prerogative to determine working arrangements without reference to trade unions or employees (this includes job-based or functional flexibility).

Policy choices

The following policy options for organizations on industrial relations and HRM have been described by Guest (1995):

- *The new realism* – a high emphasis on HRM and industrial relations. The aim is to integrate HRM and industrial relations.

- *Traditional collectivism* – priority to industrial relations without HRM. This involves retaining the traditional industrial relations arrangements within an unchanged industrial relations system. Management may take the view in these circumstances that it is easier to continue to operate with a union, since it provides a useful, well-established channel for communication and for the handling of grievance, discipline and safety issues.

- *Individualized HRM* – high priority to HRM with no industrial relations. According to Guest, this approach is not very common, except in US-owned firms. It is, he believes, essentially piecemeal and opportunistic.

- *The black hole* – no industrial relations. This option is becoming more prevalent in organizations in which HRM is not a policy priority for managements but where they do not see that there is a compelling reason to operate within a traditional industrial relations system. When such organizations are facing a decision on whether or not to recognize a union, they are increasingly deciding not to do so.

Employee relations strategies

Employee relations strategies set out how employee relations policy aims are to be achieved. The intentions expressed by employee relations strategies may direct the organization towards any of the following:

- Altering the forms of recognition, including single union recognition, or derecognition.

- Changes in the form and content of procedural agreements.

- New bargaining structures, including decentralization or single-table bargaining (ie bringing all the unions in an organization together as a single bargaining unit).

- The achievement of increased levels of commitment through involvement or participation.

- Deliberately bypassing trade union representatives to communicate directly with employees.

- Increasing the extent to which management controls operations in such areas as flexibility.

- Developing a 'partnership' with trade unions, recognizing that employees are stakeholders and that it is to the advantage of both parties to work together.

- Generally improving the employee relations climate, as discussed below, to produce more harmonious and cooperative relationships.

Employee relations climate

The employee relations climate of an organization refers to the perceptions of management, employees and their representatives about the ways in which employee relations are conducted and how the various parties (managers, employees and trade unions) behave when dealing with one another. An employee relations climate may be created by the management style adopted by management (see below) or by the behaviour of the trade unions or employee representatives (cooperative, hostile, militant, etc) or by the two interacting with one another. It can be good, bad or indifferent, according to perceptions about the extent to which:

- management and employees trust one another;

- management treats employees fairly and with consideration;

- management is open about its actions and intentions – employee relations policies and procedures are transparent;

- harmonious relationships are generally maintained on a day-to-day basis that result in willing cooperation rather than grudging submission;

- conflict, when it does arise, is resolved without resort to industrial action and resolution is achieved by integrative processes that result in a 'win-win' solution;

- employees are generally committed to the interests of the organization and, equally, management treat them as stakeholders whose interests should be protected as far as possible.

Improving the climate

Improvements to the climate can be attained by developing fair employee relations policies and procedures and implementing them consistently. Line managers and team leaders who are largely responsible for the day-to-day conduct of employee relations need to be educated and trained on the approaches they should adopt. Transparency should be achieved by communicating policies to employees, and commitment increased by involvement and participation processes. Problems that need to be resolved can be identified by simply talking to employees, their representatives and their trade union officials. Importantly, as discussed below, the organization can address its obligations to the employees as stakeholders and take steps to build trust.

Management style in employee relations

The term 'management style' refers to the overall approach the management of an organization adopts to the conduct of employee relations. Purcell and Sisson (1983) identified five typical styles:

1 Authoritarian – employee relations are not regarded as important and people issues are not attended to unless something goes wrong.

2 Paternalistic – in some ways this resembles the authoritarian style but a more positive attitude to employees is adopted.

3 Consultative – trade unions are welcomed and employee consultation is a high priority.

4 Constitutional – there is a trade union presence but the management style tends to be adversarial.

5 Opportunistic – management style is determined by local circumstances, which in turn determine whether or not unions are recognized and the extent to which employee involvement is encouraged.

Purcell (1987: 535) defined management style as 'a guiding set of principles which delineate the boundaries and direction of acceptable management action in dealing with employees.' He described two major dimensions: 1) individualism, which refers to the extent to which personnel policies are focused on the rights and capabilities of individual workers; and 2) collectivism, which is concerned with the extent to which management policy is directed towards encouraging the development of collective representation by employees and allowing employees a collective voice in management decision making. According to Purcell, style is a deliberate choice linked to business policy. Organizations may choose to focus on one or both aspects. Not all firms have a distinctive preferred management style.

An ethical approach

Businesses aim to achieve prosperity, growth and survival. Ideally, success should benefit all the stakeholders in the organization – owners, management, employees, customers and suppliers. However, the single-minded pursuit of business objectives can act to the detriment of employees' well-being and security. There may be a tension between accomplishing business purposes and the social and ethical obligations of an organization to its employees. But the chances of attaining a good climate of employee relations are slight if no attempt is made to recognize and act on an organization's obligations to its members.

An ethical approach will be based on high-commitment and high-involvement policies. The commitment will be mutual and the arrangements for involvement will be genuine, ie management will be prepared not only to listen but to act on the views expressed by employees or, at least, if it cannot take action, the reasons will be explained. It will also be transparent and, although the concept of a 'job for life' may no longer be valid in many organizations, an attempt will be made to maintain full employment policies.

Managing with unions

Managements and trade unions can learn to live together, often on a give-and-take basis, the presumption being that neither would benefit from a climate of hostility or by generating constant confrontation. It would be assumed in this situation that mutual advantage would come from acting in accordance with the spirit as well as the letter of agreed joint regulatory procedures. However, both parties would probably adopt a realistic pluralist viewpoint. This means recognizing the inevitability of differences of opinion, even disputes, but believing that with goodwill on both sides they could be settled without recourse to industrial action.

Of course, the reality in the 1960s and '70s was often different. In certain businesses, for example in the motor and shipbuilding industries, hostility and confrontation were rife, and newspaper proprietors tended to let their unions hold sway in the interests of peace and profit. Times have changed. Trade union power has diminished in the private sector, if not in the public sector. Managements in the private sector have tended to seize the initiative. They may be content to live with trade unions but they give industrial relations lower priority. They may feel that it is easier to continue to operate with a union because it provides a useful, well-established channel for communication and for the handling of grievance, discipline and safety issues. In the absence of a union, management would need to develop its own alternatives, which would be costly and difficult to operate effectively. The management perspective may be that it is safer to marginalize the unions than formally to derecognize them and risk provoking a confrontation.

The pattern varies considerably but there is general agreement based on studies such as the Workplace Employee Relations Survey (2004) that employers have been able to assert their prerogative – 'management must manage' in the workplace. They seem generally to have regained control over how they organize work, especially with regard to the flexible use of labour and multiskilling. The 'status quo' clause, typical of many agreements in the engineering industry, whereby management could not change working arrangements without union agreement, has virtually disappeared in the private sector.

Four types of industrial relations managements have been identified by Purcell and Sisson (1983):

1 *Traditionalists*, who have unitary beliefs and are anti-union with forceful management.

2 *Sophisticated paternalists*, who are essentially unitary but they do not take it for granted that their employees accept the organization's objectives or automatically legitimize management decision making. They spend considerable time and resources in ensuring that their employees adopt the right approach.

3 *Sophisticated moderns*, who are either constitutionalists – where the limits of collective bargaining are codified in an agreement but management is free to take decisions on matters that are not the subject of such an agreement; or consulters – they accept collective bargaining but do not want to codify everything in a collective agreement, and instead aim to minimize the amount of joint regulation and emphasize joint consultation with 'problems' having to be solved rather than 'disputes' settled.

4 *Standard moderns*, who are pragmatic or opportunist. Trade unions are recognized, but industrial relations are seen as primarily fire fighting and are assumed to be non-problematic unless events prove otherwise. This is by far the most typical approach.

On the whole, pluralism prevails and management and unions will inevitably disagree from time to time on employment issues. The aim is to resolve these issues before they become disputes. This means adopting a more positive partnership approach. Where collective agreements are being made, a cooperative or integrative bargaining philosophy can be adopted, based on perceptions about the mutual interdependence of management and employees and the recognition by both parties that this is a means to achieve more for themselves.

Managing without unions

Some firms, especially larger ones, manage without trade unions by adopting a union substitution policy that offers employment policies and pay packages that employees will see as an attractive alternative to trade union membership. They may focus on communications and information sharing but they will basically deal with people individually rather than collectively. Others, especially smaller firms, simply deal with employees individually – sometimes well, sometimes not – and make no attempt to provide substitute arrangements.

Key learning points: Strategic employee relations

Employee relations

Employee relations are concerned with managing and maintaining the employment relationship, taking into account the implications of the concept of the psychological contract. Employee relations are basically about how managements and employees live together and what can be done to make that work.

Employee relations policies

Employee relations policies express the philosophy of the organization on what sort of relationship between management and employees and their unions is wanted, and how the pay–work bargain should be managed. The areas covered by employee relations policies are trade union recognition, collective bargaining, employee relations procedures, participation and involvement, partnership harmonization and working arrangements.

Employee relations strategies

Employee relations strategies set out how employee relations policy objectives are to be achieved. The intentions expressed by employee relations strategies may direct the organization towards any of the following:

- Altering the forms of recognition, including single union recognition, or derecognition.

- Changes in the form and content of procedural agreements.

- New bargaining structures, including decentralization or single-table bargaining (ie bringing all the unions in an organization together as a single bargaining unit).

- The achievement of increased levels of commitment through involvement or participation.

- Deliberately bypassing trade union representatives to communicate directly with employees.

- Increasing the extent to which management controls operations in such areas as flexibility.

- Developing a 'partnership' with trade unions, recognizing that employees are stakeholders and that it is to the advantage of both parties to work together.

- Generally improving the employee relations climate to produce more harmonious and cooperative relationships.

Employee relations climate

The employee relations climate of an organization refers to the perceptions of management, employees and their representatives about the ways in which employee relations are conducted and how the various parties (managers, employees and trade unions) behave when dealing with one another. An employee relations climate may be created by the management style adopted by management, or by the behaviour of the trade unions or employee representatives (cooperative, hostile, militant, etc), or by the two interacting with one another.

Managing with unions

Ideally, managements and trade unions learn to live together, often on a give-and-take basis, the presumption being that neither would benefit from a climate of hostility or by generating constant confrontation. It would be assumed in this ideal situation that mutual advantage would come from acting in accordance with the spirit as well as the letter of agreed joint regulatory procedures. However, both parties would probably adopt a realistic pluralist viewpoint. This means recognizing the inevitability of differences of opinion, even disputes, but believing that with goodwill on both sides they could be settled without recourse to industrial action.

Managing without trade unions

Some firms, especially larger ones, manage without trade unions by adopting a union substitution policy that offers employment policies and pay packages that employees will see as an attractive alternative to trade union membership. They may focus on communications and information sharing but they will basically deal with people individually rather than collectively. Others, especially smaller firms, simply deal with employees individually – sometimes well, sometimes not – and make no attempt to provide substitute arrangements.

References

Guest, D E (1995) Human resource management: trade unions and industrial relations, in (ed) J Storey, *Human Resource Management: A critical text*, London, Routledge

Purcell, J (1987) Mapping management styles in employee relations, *Journal of Management Studies*, **24** (5), pp 78–91

Purcell, J and Sisson, K (1983) Strategies and practice in the management of industrial relations, in (ed) G Bain, *Industrial Relations in Britain*, Oxford, Blackwell

Walton, R E (1985) From control to commitment in the workplace, *Harvard Business Review*, March–April, pp 77–84

Workplace Employee Relations Survey (2004) HMSO, Norwich

51
The employment relationship

LEARNING OUTCOMES

On completing this chapter you should be able to define these key concepts. You should also understand:

- The nature of the employment relationship
- Employment relationship contracts

- Managing the employment relationship
- Developing a high-trust organization

Introduction

The employment relationship describes how employers and employees work together. A positive employment relationship is one in which management and employees are interdependent and both benefit from this interdependency, and where there is mutual trust. Such a relationship provides a foundation for employment and employee relations policies. This chapter describes the employment relationship, how it is managed and how a climate of trust can be created.

The nature of the employment relationship

The employment relationship can be expressed formally by what Rubery *et al* (2002) regarded as disciplinary procedures and redundancy. The ways in which people are required to carry out their work (including flexibility and multiskilling), how performance expectations are expressed and communicated, how work is organized and how people are managed will also make a significant impact on the employment relationship. HR specialists can contribute to the development of a positive and productive employment relationship in the following ways:

- *during recruitment interviews* – presenting the unfavourable as well as the favourable aspects of a job in a 'realistic job preview';

- *in induction programmes* – communicating to new starters the organization's HR policies and procedures and its core values, indicating to them the standards of performance expected in such areas as quality and customer service, and spelling out requirements for flexibility;

- *by encouraging the maximum amount of contact between managers and team leaders and their team members* – to achieve mutual understanding of expectations and to provide a means of two-way communications;

- *by adopting a general policy of transparency* – ensuring that on all matters affecting them, employees know what is happening, why it is happening and the impact it will make on their employment, development and prospects.

These approaches to managing the employment relationship cover all aspects of people management. It is important to remember, however, that this is a continuous process. The effective management of the relationship means ensuring that values are upheld and that a transparent, consistent and fair approach is adopted in dealing with all aspects of employment. It is also important to remember that perhaps the best way of improving the employment relationship is to develop a climate of trust in the organization.

Developing a climate of trust

Trust, as defined by the *Oxford English Dictionary*, is a firm belief that a person may be relied on. A more complex definition by Rousseau *et al*

(1998: 395) indicated that: 'Trust is a psychological state comprising the intention to accept vulnerability based upon positive expectations of the intentions or behaviour of another.'

A climate of trust in the shape of a high-trust organization is an essential ingredient in a positive employment relationship. It has been suggested by Herriot *et al* (1988) that trust should be regarded as social capital – the fund of goodwill in any social group that enables people within it to collaborate with one another. Searle and Skinner (2011) noted that the benefits of increased trust could include:

- improved employee performance;

- higher levels of motivation and positive attitudes (including employees putting more effort into performing and developing their roles);

- reduced cost due to higher productivity, less wastage, lower staff turnover, fewer stoppages, and so on;

- enhanced pro-social behaviour at work, including desirable work-related behaviour and appropriate discretionary behaviour;

- enhanced knowledge-sharing and increased innovation;

- improved cooperative working.

Building trust

As Thompson (1998: 69) noted, trust is an outcome of good management. He also commented that a number of writers have generally concluded that trust is 'not something that can, or should, be directly managed'. He cites Sako (1994) who wrote that: 'Trust is a cultural norm which can rarely be created intentionally because attempts to create trust in a calculative manner would destroy the effective basis of trust.'

In the end, trust is about relationships and mutual support. Trust is created and maintained by managerial behaviour and by the development of better mutual understanding of expectations – employers of employees, and employees of employers. The sort of behaviour that is most likely to engender trust is when management is honest with people, keeps its word (delivers the deal) and practises what it preaches. Organizations that espouse core values ('people are our greatest asset') and then proceed to ignore them will be low-trust organizations. More specifically, trust will be developed if management acts fairly, equitably and consistently; if a policy of transparency is implemented; if intentions and the reasons for proposals or decisions are communicated both to employees generally and to individuals; if there is full involvement in developing reward processes; and if mutual expectations are agreed through performance management. Leaders have a crucial role. As O'Toole and Bennis (2009: 54) pointed out: 'We won't be able to rebuild trust in institutions until leaders learn how to communicate honestly – and create organizations where that's the norm.'

Renewing trust

As suggested by Herriot *et al* (1988), if trust is lost, a four-step programme is required to renew it:

1 Admission by top management that it has paid insufficient attention in the past to employees' diverse needs.

2 A limited process of contracting whereby a particular transition to a different way of working for a group of employees is done in a form that takes individual needs into account.

3 Establishing 'knowledge-based' trust, which is based not on a specific transactional deal but on a developing perception of trustworthiness.

4 Achieving trust based on identification in which each party empathizes with each other's needs and therefore takes them on board themselves (although this final state is seldom reached in practice).

Key learning points: The employment relationship

The employment relationship describes how employers and employees work together and relate to one another.

Basis of the employment relationship

The basis of the employment relationship is an undertaking by an employee to provide skill and effort to the employer in return for which the employer provides the employee with a salary or a wage. The employer's obligations also include the duty to provide a safe workplace, to act in good faith towards the employee and not to act in such a way as to undermine the trust and confidence of the employment relationship. The employee has corresponding obligations, which include obedience, competence, honesty and loyalty.

Employment relationship contracts

The three types of employment relationship contracts are transactional, relational and psychological.

Managing the employment relationship

The nature of the employment relationship is strongly influenced by HR actions. These cover all aspects of HRM. Of particular importance is how people are treated in such areas as recruitment, performance reviews, promotion, career development, reward, involvement and participation, grievance handling, disciplinary procedures and redundancy. The ways in which people are required to carry out their work (including flexibility and multiskilling), how performance expectations are expressed and communicated, how work is organized and how people are managed will also make a significant impact on the employment relationship.

Developing a high-trust organization

A high-trust organization exists when management is honest with people, keeps its word (delivers the deal) and practises what it preaches. Trust is created and maintained by managerial behaviour and by the development of better mutual understanding of expectations – employers of employees, and employees of employers.

References

Braverman, H (1974) *Labour and Monopoly Capital*, New York, Monthly Review Press

Herriot, P, Hirsh, W and Riley, P (1988) *Trust and Transition: Managing the employment relationship*, Chichester, Wiley

Kessler, S and Undy, R (1996) *The New Employment Relationship: Examining the psychological contract*, London, IPM

Marsden, D (2007) Individual employee voice: renegotiation and performance management in public services, *International Journal of Human Resource Management*, **18** (7), pp 1263–78

Marsden, D and Canibano, A (2010) An economic perspective on employee participation, in (eds) A Wilkinson, P J Gollan, M Marchington and D Lewins, *The Oxford Handbook of Participation in Organizations*, Oxford, Oxford University Press, pp 131–63

O'Toole, J and Bennis, W (2009) What's needed next: a culture of candor, *Harvard Business Review*, June, pp 54–61

Rousseau, D M and Wade-Benzoni, K A (1994) Linking strategy and human resource practices: how employee and customer contracts are created, *Human Resource Management*, **33** (3), pp 463–89

Rousseau, D M, Sitkin, S B, Burt, R S and Camerer, C (1998) Not so different after all: a cross-discipline view of trust, *Academy of Management Review*, **23** (3), pp 393–404

Rubery, J, Earnshaw, J, Marchington, M, Cooke, F L and Vincent, S (2002) Changing organizational forms and the employment relationship, *Journal of Management Studies*, **39** (5), pp 645–72

Sako, M (1994) *The informational requirement of trust in supplier relations: evidence from Japan, the UK and the USA*, unpublished

Searle, R H and Skinner, D (2011) New agendas and perspectives, in (eds) Searle, R H and Skinner, D, *Trust and Human Resource Management*, Cheltenham, Edward Elgar

Thompson, M (1998) Trust and reward, in (eds) S Perkins and St John Sandringham, *Trust, Motivation and Commitment: A reader*, Faringdon, Strategic Remuneration Research Centre, pp 66–71

Thompson, P and Harley, B (2007) HRM and the worker: labour process perspectives, in (eds) P Boxall, J Purcell and P Wright, *Oxford Handbook of Human Resource Management*, Oxford, Oxford University Press, pp 147–65

52
The psychological contract

KEY CONCEPTS AND TERMS

Employability

The psychological contract

Realistic job preview

LEARNING OUTCOMES

On completing this chapter you should be able to define these key concepts. You should also know about:

- The psychological contract defined
- The significance of the psychological contract
- The psychological contract and the employment relationship

- The problem with the psychological contract
- Developing a positive psychological contract

Introduction

The psychological contract underpins the employment relationship. This chapter defines the psychological contract, explains its significance and describes how a positive contract can be developed.

The psychological contract defined

A psychological contract is a set of unwritten expectations that exist between individual employees and their employers. As Guest (2007: 133) explained, it is concerned with: 'The perceptions of both parties to the employment relationship, organization and individual, of the reciprocal promises and obligations implied in that relationship.'

A psychological contract is a system of beliefs that encompasses the actions employees believe are expected of them and what response they expect in return from their employer, and, reciprocally, the actions employers believe are expected of them and what response they expect in return from their employees.

An expanded definition was produced by Rousseau and Wade-Benzoni (1994: 464) as follows:

> Psychological contracts refer to beliefs that individuals hold regarding promises made, accepted and relied upon between themselves and another. (In the case of organizations, these parties include an employee, client, manager, and/or organization as a whole.) Because psychological contracts represent how people interpret promises and commitments, both parties in the same employment relationship (employer and employee) can have different views regarding specific terms.

Within organizations, as Katz and Kahn (1966) pointed out, every role is basically a set of behavioural expectations. These expectations are often implicit – they are not defined in the employment contract. Basic models of motivation such as expectancy theory (Vroom, 1964) maintain that employees behave in ways that they expect will produce positive outcomes. But they do not necessarily know what to expect.

Employees may expect to be treated fairly as human beings, to be provided with work that uses their abilities, to be rewarded equitably in accordance with their contribution, to be able to display competence, to have opportunities for further growth, to know what is required of them and to be given feedback (preferably positive) on how they are doing. Employers may expect employees to do their best on behalf of the organization – 'to put themselves out for the company' – to be fully committed to its values, to be compliant and loyal, and to enhance the image of the organization with its customers and suppliers. Sometimes these assumptions are justified – often they are not. Mutual misunderstandings can cause friction and stress and lead to recriminations and poor performance, or to a termination of the employment relationship. As pointed out by Guest and Conway (1998: ix), the psychological contract lacks many of the characteristics of the formal contract: 'It is not generally written down, it is somewhat blurred at the edges, and it cannot be enforced in a court or tribunal.'

The significance of the psychological contract

The concept of the psychological contract highlights the fact that employee/employer expectations take the form of unarticulated assumptions. Disappointments on the part of management as well as employees may therefore be inevitable. These disappointments can, however, be alleviated if managements appreciate that one of their key roles is to manage expectations, which means clarifying what they believe employees should achieve, the competencies they should possess and the values they should uphold. This is a matter not just of articulating and stipulating these requirements but of discussing and agreeing them with individuals and teams.

The psychological contract and the employment relationship

As described by Guest *et al* (1996), the psychological contract may provide some indication of the answers to the two fundamental employment relationship questions that individuals pose: 'what can I reasonably expect from the organization?' and 'what should I reasonably be expected to contribute in return?' But it is unlikely that the psychological contract, and therefore the employment relationship, will ever be fully understood by either party.

The aspects of the employment relationship covered by the psychological contract will include, from the employees' point of view:

- how they are treated in terms of fairness, equity and consistency;
- security of employment;
- scope to demonstrate competence;

- career expectations and the opportunity to develop skills;
- involvement and influence;
- trust in the management of the organization to keep their promises.

The CIPD (2012: 16) suggested that to build trust leaders need to tell the truth and be willing to admit mistakes. They must share information openly, support transparency and seek information from multiple sources, not merely relying on what they are told by their close advisers. Finally, and importantly, they should be candid in their dealings with followers.

From the employer's point of view, the psychological contract covers such aspects of the employment relationship as competence, effort, compliance, commitment and loyalty. The research conducted by Guest and Conway (2002: 22) led to the conclusion that:

> The management of the psychological contract is a core task of management and acknowledged as such by many senior HR and employment relations managers, and shows that it has a positive association with a range of outcomes within the employment relationship and is a useful way of conceptualizing that relationship.

How psychological contracts develop

Psychological contracts are not developed by means of a single transaction; they evolve over time and can be multifaceted. There are many contract makers who exert influence over the whole duration of an employee's involvement with an organization. Spindler (1994: 326) observed that:

> Every day we create relationships by means other than formal contracts... As individuals form relationships they necessarily bring their accumulated experience and developed personalities with them. In ways unknown to them, what they expect from the relationship reflects the sum total of their conscious and unconscious learning to date.

The problem with psychological contracts

The problem with psychological contracts is that employees are often unclear about what they want from the organization or what they can contribute to it. Some employers are equally unclear about what they expect from their employees.

Because of these factors, and because a psychological contract is essentially implicit, it is likely to develop in an unplanned way with unforeseen consequences. Anything that management does or is perceived as doing that affects the interests of employees will modify the psychological contract. Similarly, the actual or perceived behaviour of employees, individually or collectively, will affect an employer's concept of the contract.

Developing and maintaining a positive psychological contract

As Guest *et al* (1996: v) explained: 'A positive psychological contract is worth taking seriously because it is strongly linked to higher commitment to the organization, higher employee satisfaction and better employment relations. Again, this reinforces the benefits of pursuing a set of progressive HRM practices.' They also emphasized the importance of a high-involvement climate and suggested in particular that HRM practices such as the provision of opportunities for learning, training and development, focus on job security, promotion and careers, minimizing status differentials, fair reward systems and comprehensive communication and involvement processes will all contribute to a positive psychological contract. The steps required to develop such a contract are:

1 Define expectations during recruitment and induction programmes.

2 Communicate and agree expectations as part of the continuing dialogue implicit in good performance management practices.

3 Adopt a policy of transparency on company policies and procedures and on

53
The practice of industrial relations

KEY CONCEPTS AND TERMS

Arbitration

Bargaining power

Collective agreements

Collective bargaining

Conciliation

Employee relations

Mediation

New realism

New style agreement

LEARNING OUTCOMES

On completing this chapter you should be able to define these key concepts. You should also know about:

- Trade union membership
- Union recognition
- Collective bargaining
- Collective agreements
- Disputes resolution
- Informal industrial relations

Introduction

Industrial relations involve managements and trade unions in concluding collective agreements, collective bargaining, disputes resolution and dealing with issues concerning the employment relationship and the working environment. In this chapter the practice of industrial relations is discussed in terms of the approaches, methods and procedures adopted by employers to deal with employees collectively through their trade unions.

This chapter begins with an analysis of trade union membership and the factors affecting union recognition. It continues with a description of the formal procedures and arrangements that take place when unions are recognized. But industrial relations are also conducted on a daily informal and semi-formal basis, and this is considered in the last section. The employee relations processes of providing employees with a voice and communicating with employees, which can take place in either a unionized or a non-unionized environment, are covered in the next two chapters.

Trade union membership

Trade union membership in the UK in 2014 was 6.4 million. Union density (ie the proportion of those in employment who are union members) was 25 per cent of employees – 14.2 per cent in the private sector and 54.3 per cent in the public sector. The overall density in 2014 was down from 32.4 per cent in 1995 (BIS, 2013). According to the 2011 Workplace Employment Relations Survey (WERS), 22 per cent of workplaces with five or more employees recognized at least one trade union.

Overall union membership has declined significantly in the UK from its peak of some 12 million in 1979. This has been largely in the private sector for structural reasons – the demise of large manufacturing firms, the rise in the service industries and the growing numbers of part-time workers. Trade unions remain strong in the public sector.

Union recognition

An employer fully recognizes a union for the purposes of collective bargaining when pay and conditions of employment are jointly agreed between management and trade unions. Partial recognition takes place when employers restrict trade unions to representing their members on issues arising from employment. Full recognition provides unions with negotiating and representational rights; partial recognition only gives unions representational rights. The following discussion of union recognition is only concerned with the much more common practice of full recognition. Unions can be derecognized although, as noted by Blanden *et al* (2006), this is happening less frequently.

Factors influencing recognition or derecognition

Employers in the private sector are in a strong position now to choose whether they recognize a union or not, which union they want to recognize and the terms on which they would grant recognition: for example, a single union and a no-strike agreement.

When setting up on greenfield sites, employers may refuse to recognize unions. Alternatively, they can hold 'beauty contests' to select the union they prefer to work with, one that will be prepared to reach an agreement in line with what management wants.

An organization deciding whether or not to recognize a union will take some or all of the following factors into account:

- the perceived value or lack of value of having a process for regulating collective bargaining;
- if there is an existing union, the extent to which management has freedom to manage; for example, to change working arrangements and introduce flexible working or multiskilling;
- the history of relationships with the existing union;
- the proportion of employees who are union members and the degree to which they believe they need the protection that their union provides; a decision on derecognition has to weigh the extent to which its perceived advantages outweigh the disadvantages of upsetting the status quo;
- any preferences as to a particular union, because of its reputation or the extent to which it is believed that a satisfactory relationship can be maintained.

In considering recognition arrangements, employers may also consider entering into a 'single-union deal', as described later in this chapter.

Collective bargaining

Managing with unions involves collective bargaining – the establishment by negotiation and discussion of agreements on matters of mutual concern to employers and unions covering the employment relationship and terms and conditions of employment. Collective bargaining is a joint regulating process, dealing with the regulation of management in its relationships with work people as well as the regulation of conditions of employment. It was described by Flanders (1970) as a social process that continually turns disagreements into agreements in an orderly fashion.

Collective bargaining can also be seen as a political relationship in which trade unions, as Chamberlain and Kuhn (1965) noted, share industrial sovereignty or power over those who are governed – the employees. The sovereignty is held jointly by management and union in the collective bargaining process.

Above all, collective bargaining is a power relationship that takes the form of a measure of power sharing between management and trade unions (although recently the balance of power has shifted markedly in the direction of management in the private sector). Bargaining power is the ability to induce the other side to make a decision or take a course of action that it would otherwise be unwilling to make. Each side is involved in assessing the bargaining preferences and bargaining power of the other side.

Forms of collective bargaining

Walton and McKersie (1965) made the distinction between distributive bargaining, defined as the complex system of activities instrumental to the attainment of one party's goals when they are in basic conflict with those of the other party, and integrative bargaining, defined as the system of activities that are not in fundamental conflict with those of the other party and which therefore can be integrated to some degree.

Another analysis of collective bargaining forms was made by Chamberlain and Kuhn (1965), who distinguished between conjunctive bargaining, in which both parties are seeking to reach agreement, and cooperative bargaining, in which it is recognized that each party is dependent on the other and can achieve its objectives more effectively if it wins the support of the other.

Collective agreements

The formal outcomes of collective bargaining are agreements between management and unions dealing with terms and conditions of employment or other aspects of the relationships between the two parties. They consist of substantive agreements, procedural agreements, new style agreements, partnership agreements and employee relations procedures.

Substantive agreements

Substantive agreements set out agreed terms and conditions of employment covering pay, allowances and overtime, working hours, holidays and flexibility arrangements and the achievement of single status or the harmonization of terms and conditions. Single status means that there are no differences in basic conditions of employment. Harmonization is the adoption of a common approach to pay and conditions for all employees, for example, placing all employees in the same grade and pay structure.

Procedural agreements

Procedural agreements set out the methods to be used and the procedures or rules to be followed in the processes of collective bargaining and the settlement of industrial disputes. Their purpose is to regulate the behaviour of the parties to the agreement, but they are not legally enforceable and the degree to which they are followed depends on the goodwill of both parties, or the balance of power between them. Like substantive agreements, procedural agreements are seldom broken and, if so, never lightly – the basic presumption of collective bargaining is that both parties will honour agreements that have been made freely between them.

The scope and content of such agreements can vary widely. Some organizations have limited agreements to the provision of representational rights only; others have taken an entirely different line in concluding single-union deals, which, when they first emerged in the 1980s, were referred to as the 'new realism'.

Single-union deals

Single-union deals typically agree that there should be a single union representing all employees, flexible working practices, the harmonization of terms and conditions between manual and non-manual employees, the commitment of the organization to involvement and the disclosure of information, the resolution of disputes by such means as arbitration, a commitment to continuity of production, and a 'no-strike' provision.

New style agreements

The so-called 'new style agreements' emerged in the 1990s. These stipulated that negotiating and disputes procedures should be based on the mutually accepted 'rights' of the parties expressed in the recognition agreement. They typically included provision for single-union recognition, single status, labour flexibility, a company council and a no-strike clause to the effect that issues should be resolved without recourse to industrial action.

Partnership agreements

Partnership agreements are based on the concept of social partnership. Both parties (management and the trade union) agree to collaborate to their mutual advantage and to achieve a climate of more cooperative and therefore less adversarial industrial relations. Management may offer job security linked to productivity and the union may agree to more flexible working.

The perceived benefits of partnership agreements are that management and unions will work together in a spirit of cooperation and mutuality. This is clearly preferable to an adversarial relationship. Provision is made for change to be introduced through discussion and agreement rather than by coercion or power.

An analysis by Guest *et al* (2008) of evidence from the 2004 Workplace Employee Relations Survey suggested that partnership practice remains relatively undeveloped and that it is only weakly related to trust between management and employee representatives and to employees' trust in management. Direct forms of participation generally have a more positive association with trust than representative forms.

However, data gathered by Roche (2009) from a large representative sample of employees in Ireland showed that some mutual gains are associated with partnership. Employees gained from enhancement to the intrinsic aspects of their work, eg autonomy, but did not gain security or more pay and did not seem to be more willing to accept change. Employers gained more commitment, an improved climate of

employee relations and better supervisor/employee relationships. Unions gained influence and more members.

Dispute resolution

The aim of dispute resolution is to resolve differences between management and a trade union. The aim of collective bargaining is, of course, to reach agreement, preferably to the satisfaction of both parties. Grievance or negotiating procedures provide for various stages of 'failure to agree' and often include a clause providing for some form of dispute resolution in the event of the procedure being exhausted. The types of dispute resolution are conciliation, arbitration and mediation.

Conciliation

Conciliation is the process of reconciling disagreeing parties. It is carried out by a third party, in the UK often an ACAS conciliation officer, who acts in effect as a go-between, attempting to get the employer and trade union representatives to agree on terms. Conciliators can only help the parties to come to an agreement. They do not make recommendations on what that agreement should be: that is the role of an arbitrator or a mediator.

The incentives to seek conciliation are the hope that the conciliator can rebuild bridges and the belief that a determined, if last minute, search for agreement is better than confrontation, even if both parties have to compromise.

Arbitration

Arbitration is the process of settling disputes by getting a third party, the arbitrator, to review and discuss the negotiating stances of the disagreeing parties and make a recommendation on the terms of settlement, which is binding on both parties, who therefore lose control over the settlement of their differences. The arbitrator is impartial and the role is often undertaken in the UK by ACAS officials, although industrial relations academics are sometimes asked to act in this capacity. Arbitration is the means of last resort for reaching a settlement, where disputes cannot be resolved in any other way. Procedure agreements may provide for either side unilaterally to invoke arbitration, in which case the decision of the arbitrator is not binding on both parties. The process of arbitration in its fullest sense, however, only takes place at the request of both parties, who agree in advance to accept the arbitrator's findings. ACAS will not act as an arbitrator unless the consent of both parties is obtained, conciliation is considered, any agreed procedures have been used to the full and a failure to agree has been recorded.

The notion of 'pendulum' or 'final offer' arbitration emerged in the 1980s. It increases the rigidity of the arbitration process by allowing an arbitrator no choice but to recommend either the union's or the employer's final offer – there is no middle ground. The aim is to get the parties to avoid adopting extreme positions. But the evidence from the Workplace Employee Relations Survey (2004) is that the full version of pendulum arbitration as defined here was rare.

Mediation

Mediation takes place when a third party (often ACAS) helps the employer and the union by making recommendations that they are not, however, bound to accept. It is a cheap and informal alternative to an employment tribunal and offers a quick resolution to problems, privacy and confidentiality.

Informal employee relations processes

The formal processes of union recognition, collective bargaining and dispute resolution described in this chapter provide the framework for industrial relations in so far as this is concerned with agreeing terms and conditions of employment and working arrangements, and settling disputes. But within or outside that framework, informal employee relations processes are taking place continuously.

Informal employee relationships happen whenever a line manager or team leader is handling an issue in contact with a union representative, an individual employee or a group of employees. The issue may concern methods of work, allocation of work and overtime, working conditions, health and safety, achieving output and quality targets and standards, discipline, or pay – in the latter case especially if a payment-by-results scheme is in operation, which can generate continuous arguments about times, standards, retimings, payments for waiting time or when carrying out new tasks, and fluctuations or reductions in earnings because of alleged managerial inefficiency.

Line managers and supervisors handle day-to-day grievances arising from any of these issues and are expected to resolve them to the satisfaction of all parties without involving a formal grievance procedure or allowing the issue to become a formal dispute. The thrust for devolving responsibility to line managers for HR matters has increased the onus on them to handle employee relations effectively. A good team leader will establish a working relationship with the union representative of his or her staff that will enable issues arising on the shop floor or with individual employees to be settled amicably before they become a problem. The 2011 Workplace Employment Relations Survey found that in 78 per cent of the workplaces covered employment relations issues were part of the wider duties of the owner or general manager.

CASE STUDY

Mediation at the Arts Council of England

When workplace relationships go wrong at the Arts Council of England, staff now turn to TCM, an external provider of mediations services, to manage the conflict and help bring the parties to a workable solution. Mediation will typically be used for a conflict between a line manager and a staff member and, when this happens, a TCM mediator will take over the case until resolution. There is a regular follow-up for a year after that to see how the parties are getting on.

Key learning points: The practice of industrial relations

Union recognition

An employer fully recognizes a union for the purposes of collective bargaining when pay and conditions of employment are jointly agreed between management and trade unions. Partial recognition is when employers restrict trade unions to representing their members on issues arising from employment.

Collective bargaining

Collective bargaining is a joint regulating process, establishing by negotiation and discussion agreements on matters of mutual concern to employers and unions covering the employment relationship and terms and conditions of employment.

Collective agreements

The formal outcomes of collective bargaining are substantive agreements, procedural agreements, new style agreements, partnership agreements and employee relations procedures.

Disputes resolution

The processes of dispute resolution are conciliation, arbitration and mediation.

Informal industrial relations

Informal industrial relations processes take place whenever a line manager or team leader is handling an issue in contact with an individual employee, a group of employees or an employee representative.

References

BIS (Department for Business, Innovation and Skills) (2010) Labour Force Survey, London, BIS

Blanden, J, Machin, S and Reenen, J V (2006) Have unions turned the corner? New evidence on recent trends in union recognition in UK firms, *British Journal of Industrial Relations*, **44** (2), pp 169–90

Chamberlain, N W and Kuhn, J (1965) *Collective Bargaining*, New York, McGraw-Hill

Department for Business, Innovation and Skills (2015) Trade Union Membership 2014 [online] https://www.gov.uk/government/uploads/system/uploads/attachment_data/file/431564/Trade_Union_Membership_Statistics_2014.pdf [accessed 20 November 2015]

Flanders, A (1970) *Management and Unions: The theory and reform of industrial relations*, London, Faber and Faber

Guest, D E, Brown, W, Peccei, R and Huxley, K (2008) Does partnership at work increase trust? An analysis based on the 2004 Workplace Employment Relations Survey, *Industrial Relations Journal*, **39** (2), pp 124–52

Roche, W K (2009) Who gains from workforce partnership? *International Journal of Human Resource Management*, **20** (1), pp 1–33

Walton, R E and McKersie, R B (1965) *Behavioural Theory of Labour Negotiations*, New York, McGraw-Hill

Workplace Employee Relations Survey (2004) *DTI* [online] https://www.gov.uk/government/publications/the-2011-workplace-employment-relations-study-wers

54
Employee voice

LEARNING OUTCOMES

On completing this chapter you should be able to define these key concepts. You should also understand:

- The meaning, purpose and stages of employee voice
- How employee voice can be expressed

Introduction

The term 'employee voice' refers to the say that employees have in matters of concern to them in their organization. Participation and involvement are treated as aspects of employee voice in this chapter, although as Wilkinson and Dundon (2010: 168) noted: 'Employee participation, involvement and voice are somewhat elastic terms with considerable width in the range of definitions.'

The meaning of employee voice

As defined by (Wilkinson and Fay 2011: 65), the term 'employee voice' refers to the extent to which employees are 'able to have a say regarding work activities and decision-making issues within the organization in which they work'. The elements of employee voice are participation and involvement. The difference between them was explained by Brewster *et al* (2007: 1248) as follows:

56
The practice of employee well-being

Introduction

The practice of employee well-being as examined in this chapter deals with creating a satisfactory work environment, managing stress, attending to work–life balance issues, dealing with sexual harassment and bullying problems, providing services for individuals including employee assistance programmes, and providing group services such as restaurants and social/sporting facilities. But it is first necessary to consider why organizations should be concerned with employee well-being.

Reasons for concern

The reasons for being concerned about employee well-being are as follows:

- Employers have a duty of care and this means adopting a socially responsible approach to looking after their people.

- It is in the interests of employers to do so because this will increase the likelihood of their employees being committed to the organization and will help to establish it as a 'best place to work'.

- Employers are responsible for creating a good work environment, not only because it is their duty to do so but also as part of the total reward system.

The work environment

The work environment consists of the system of work, the design of jobs, working conditions and the ways in which people are treated at work by their managers and co-workers. When designing the work system – and the jobs in it – well-being is achieved when account is taken of the needs of the people concerned. Working conditions need to meet health and safety requirements. The way people are treated is affected by managerial behaviour, achieving work–life balance and how issues such as stress, harassment and bullying are dealt with.

Managerial behaviour

Lawler (2003) suggests that what managers have to do is 'treat people right'. This means recognizing them as individuals with different needs and wants, rewarding their achievements, helping them to develop and treating them with consideration as human beings.

Work–life balance

Work–life balance is about the achievement by employees of a satisfactory equilibrium between work and non-work activities (eg parental responsibilities and wider caring duties, as well as other activities and interests). Thus employees can reconcile the competing claims of work and home by meeting their own needs as well as those of their employers.

Work–life balance can be enhanced by what are sometimes called 'family-friendly' policies that facilitate flexible working. This covers homeworking, part-time working, compressed working weeks, annualized hours, job sharing, term-time only working and 'flexitime' (an arrangement for providing flexible hours in which employees are contracted to work for a weekly or monthly number of hours; within limits, they may vary their start or finish times as long as they work the hours required during the defined period). It can also involve special leave schemes that provide employees with the freedom to respond to a domestic crisis or to take a career break without jeopardizing their employment status.

Individual requests for a particular working arrangement generally need to be considered on a case-by-case basis, but the culture should not discourage employees from making such requests. In addition to fearing the reaction of line managers, the risk of career-damage is a common reason for poor take-up of work–life balance arrangements. Line management will need to be convinced that work–life balance measures are important and pay off in terms of increased engagement.

Work–life balance policies can lower absence and help to tackle the low morale and high degrees of stress that can lead to retention problems as employees tire of juggling work and life responsibilities. The research conducted by the Institute for Employment Studies (Kodz *et al*, 2002) identified employees who were staying longer with their firms because of access to flexible working arrangements.

Managing stress

There are four main reasons why organizations should be concerned about stress and should do something about it. First, they should act in a socially responsible way to provide a good quality of working life; second, because excessive stress causes illness; third, because it can result in inability to cope with the demands of the job, which of course creates more stress; and fourth, because excessive stress can reduce employee effectiveness and therefore organizational performance. The ways in which stress can be managed by an organization include the following:

- *Job design* – clarifying roles, reducing the danger of role ambiguity and conflict, and giving people more autonomy within a defined structure to manage their responsibilities.
- *Targets and performance standards* – setting reasonable and achievable targets that may stretch people but do not place impossible burdens on them.
- *Job placement* – taking care to place people in jobs that are within their capabilities.
- *Career development* – planning careers and promoting staff in accordance with their capabilities, taking care not to over- or under-promote.
- *Performance management processes* – allowing a dialogue to take place between managers and individuals about the latter's work problems and ambitions.
- *Counselling* – giving individuals the opportunity to talk about their problems with a member of the HR department, or through an employee assistance programme, as described later in this chapter.
- *Anti-bullying campaigns* – bullying at work is a major cause of stress.
- *Management training* – training in what managers can do to alleviate their own stress and reduce it in others.

'Mindfulness' programmes involving meditation can be used to alleviate the effects of stress but deal with the symptoms, not the causes.

Sexual harassment

Sadly, sexual harassment has always been a feature of life at work. Perhaps it is not always quite as blatant today as it has been in the past, but it is still there, in more or less subtle forms, and it is just as unpleasant. People who are subject to sexual harassment can take legal action, but it must be the policy of the organization to make it clear that it

will not be tolerated and this policy should be backed up by procedures and practices for dealing with harassment.

Problems of dealing with harassment

There are three problems in dealing with harassment. First, it can be difficult to make a clear-cut case. An accusation of harassment can be hard to prove unless there are witnesses, and those who indulge in this practice usually take care to carry it out on a one-to-one basis. In this situation, it may be a case of one person's word against another's. The harasser, usually a man, resorts to two defences: one, that it did not take place ('it was all in her mind'); and two, that if anything did take place it was provoked by the behaviour of the female. When this happens, whoever deals with the case has to exercise judgement and attempt, difficult though it may be, to remove any prejudice in favour of the word of the man, the woman, the boss or the subordinate.

The second problem is that targets of sexual harassment are often unwilling to take action and in practice seldom do so. This is because of the actual or perceived difficulty of proving their case. But they may also feel that they will not get a fair hearing and are worried about the effect that making such accusations will have on how they are treated by their boss or their colleagues in the future, whether or not they have substantiated their accusation.

The third, and perhaps the most deep-rooted and difficult problem is that sexual harassment may be part of the culture of the organization – 'the way we do things around here'; a norm, practised at all levels.

Solutions

There are no easy solutions to these problems. It may be very hard to eradicate sexual harassment completely. But the effort must be made, along the following lines:

- Issue a clear statement by the chief executive that sexual harassment will not be tolerated.
- Back up the statement with a policy directive that spells out in more detail that the

organization deplores harassment, why it is not acceptable and what people who believe they are being subjected to harassment can do about it.

- Reinforce the policy statement by behaviour at senior level that demonstrates it is not merely words but that these exhortations have meaning.

- Ensure that the sexual harassment policy is stated clearly in induction courses and is conveyed to everyone. Reinforce this message with regular reminders.

- Make arrangements for employees subjected to sexual harassment to seek advice, support and counselling without any obligation to take a complaint forward. They could talk informally with someone in HR. Alternatively, a counsellor (possibly engaged as part of an employee assistance programme) can usefully offer guidance on harassment problems; assist in resolving them informally by seeking, with the agreement of the complainant, a confidential and voluntary interview with the person complained against to achieve a solution without recourse to a formal disciplinary procedure; assist in submitting a complaint if the employee wishes to raise it formally; and provide counselling to each of the parties on their future conduct.

- Create a special procedure for hearing complaints about sexual harassment. The normal procedure may not be suitable because, for example, the harasser could be the employee's line manager. The procedure should provide for employees to bring their complaint to someone of their own sex, should they so choose.

- Handle complaints about harassment with sensitivity and due respect for the rights of both the complainant and the accused. Ensure that hearings are conducted fairly and that both parties are given an equal opportunity to put their case.

- Where sexual harassment has taken place, crack down on it. It should be stated in the policy that it is regarded as gross industrial misconduct and, if it is proven, makes the individual liable to instant dismissal. Less severe penalties may be reserved for minor cases but there should always be a warning that repetition will result in dismissal.

- Ensure that everyone is aware that the organization does take action, when required, to punish those who indulge in sexual harassment.

- Provide training to line managers and team leaders to ensure that the policy is properly implemented and to make them aware of their direct responsibility to prevent harassment taking place and to take action if it does.

Bullying

Bullying is a form of harassment and can be very unpleasant. It is perhaps one of the most difficult aspects of employee relationships to control. Like sexual harassment, it can be hard to prove that bullying has taken place and employees may be reluctant to complain about a bullying boss, simply because he or she is a bully. But this does not mean that an organization can ignore the problem. A policy should be published stating that bullying is unacceptable behaviour. People who feel that they are being bullied should have the right to discuss the problem with someone in the HR department or a trained counsellor. Bullies should not be punished automatically. They should initially be helped to acknowledge the impact of their behaviours, and to change. Punishment should be reserved for those who persist in spite of this guidance.

Services for individuals

Services may be provided for individuals to help them deal with their problems. This may involve counselling or personal case work where the aim is, as far as possible, to get individuals to help themselves. The areas where counselling and other forms of help may be provided are:

- *Sickness* – the provision of help and advice to employees absent from work for long periods due to illness; this may include sick visits.

- *Bereavement* – advice on how to cope with the death of a partner or close relative.
- *Domestic problems* – normally they should not be the concern of the employer, but if someone is very distressed, help can be offered through a counselling service.
- *Retirement* – advice can be made available to employees who are about to retire in order to prepare them for their new circumstances; continued counselling and visiting services may be provided for retired employees.

Counselling is a skilled business and is best carried out by trained people. This is where employee assistance programmes (EAPs) can be useful. EAP services are provided by external agencies that enable employees to access counselling through a phone service, although face-to-face counselling may also be offered. Employers can refer employees to the service, which is confidential between the agency and the individual.

CASE STUDY

B&Q's employee assistance programme

The aims of the B&Q employee assistance programme are to:

- Support employees of all ages and backgrounds through the full spectrum of life experiences by offering advice, information, practical help and emotional support free of charge and in confidence.
- Support carers of the chronically sick, disabled or elderly by offering advice and information. Locating care options and community resources.
- Save time for working parents by helping them find and arrange good quality, affordable and reliable care arrangements for children of all ages.
- Support parents through a wide range of parenting issues, including understanding and choosing

education options, and understanding and monitoring behaviour of children.

- Reduce unplanned absence by encouraging employees with personal, practical, emotional and financial problems to seek early help and advice.
- Offer information and support to managers and HR staff with their personal issues, and issues facing their staff.
- Raise employee morale and commitment by showing the caring face of the employer.
- Improve customer service and productivity by saving employees' time and solving and avoiding work–life conflicts.

Group employee services

Group employee services mainly consist of sub-sidized restaurants, sports and social clubs, and child care facilities.

Restaurant facilities are desirable in any large establishment where local facilities are limited. Sports or social clubs should not be laid on because they are 'good for morale' – there is no evidence that they are. They may be provided if there is a real need for them arising from a lack of local facilities. In the latter case, the facilities should be shared with the local community. Child care facilities are one of the most popular forms of group services, if they fill a need that cannot be met easily elsewhere.

Key learning points: The practice of employee well-being

Reasons for concern with well-being

Employers have a duty of care and this means adopting a socially responsible approach to looking after their people.

Employers are responsible for creating a good work environment, not only because it is their duty to do so but also as part of the total reward system. It is in the interests of employers to do so because this will increase the likelihood of their employees being committed to the organization and help to establish it as a 'best place to work'.

The significance of the work environment

The work environment consists of the system of work, the design of jobs, working conditions and the ways in which people are treated at work by their managers and co-workers. When designing the work system – and the jobs in it – well-being is achieved when account is taken of the needs of the people concerned. Working conditions need to meet health and safety requirements. The way people are treated is a matter of managerial behaviour, achieving work–life balance and dealing with issues such as stress, harassment and bullying.

The achievement of work–life balance

Flexible working is the most practical solution to establishing an effective work–life balance. This covers flexitime, homeworking, part-time working, compressed working weeks, annualized hours, job sharing and term-time only working. It also refers to special leave schemes, which provide employees with the freedom to respond to a domestic crisis or to take a career break without jeopardizing their employment status.

Managing stress

Employers have the social responsibility to provide a good quality of working life. Stress can result in inability to cope with the demands of the job, which creates more stress. Excessive stress causes illness and can reduce employee effectiveness and therefore organizational performance.

Sexual harassment

Sexual harassment is difficult to deal with but it is important to make a determined attempt to minimize it through policy statements backed up by special procedures for seeking help and making complaints.

Bullying

A policy should be published stating that bullying is unacceptable behaviour. People who feel that they are being bullied should have the right to discuss the problem with someone in the HR department or a trained counsellor.

Services for individuals

Counselling, possibly through EAP programmes, can be provided for sickness, bereavement, domestic problems and retirement.

Group employee services

These mainly consist of subsidized restaurants, sports and social clubs, and child care facilities.

References

Kodz, J, Harper, H and Dench, S (2002) Work–life Balance: Beyond the rhetoric, Report 384, Brighton, Institute for Employment Studies

Lawler, E E (2003) Treat People Right! How organizations and individuals can propel each other into a virtuous spiral of success, San Francisco, CA, Jossey-Bass

57
Health and safety

LEARNING OUTCOMES

On completing this chapter you should be able to define these key concepts. You should also know about:

- Managing health and safety at work
- Health and safety policies
- Risk assessments
- Health and safety audits
- Health and safety inspections
- Accident prevention

- Occupational health programmes
- Measuring health and safety performance
- Communicating the need for better health and safety practices
- Health and safety training
- Organizing health and safety

Introduction

Health and safety policies and programmes are concerned with protecting employees – and other people affected by what the company produces and does – against the hazards arising from their employment or their links with the company.

Safety programmes deal with the prevention of accidents and with minimizing the resulting loss and damage to people and property. They relate more to systems of work than the working environment, but both health and safety programmes are concerned with protection against hazards, and their aims and methods are clearly interlinked.

Occupational health programmes deal with the prevention of ill-health arising from working conditions. They consist of two elements: 1) occupational medicine, which is a specialized branch of preventive medicine concerned with the identification, diagnosis and prevention of health hazards at work and dealing with any ill-health or stress that has occurred in spite of preventative actions; and 2) occupational hygiene, which is the province of the chemist and the engineer or ergonomist engaged in the measurement and control of environmental hazards.

Managing health and safety at work

The achievement of a healthy and safe place of work and the elimination to the maximum extent possible of hazards to health and safety are the responsibility of everyone employed in an organization, as well as those working there under contract. But the onus is on management to achieve and indeed go beyond the high standard in health and safety matters required by the legislation – the Health and Safety at Work etc Act 1974 and the various regulations and Codes of Practice.

The importance of healthy and safe policies and practices is, sadly, often underestimated by those concerned with managing businesses and by individual managers within those businesses. But the achievement of the highest standards of health and safety in the workplace is important because the elimination, or at least minimization, of health and safety hazards and risks is the moral as well as the legal responsibility of employers – this duty of care is the overriding reason. Close and continuous attention to health and safety is important because ill-health and injuries caused by the system of work or working conditions cause suffering and loss to individuals and their dependents. In addition, accidents and absences through ill-health or injuries result in losses and damage for the organization. This 'business' reason is much less significant than the 'human' reasons, but it is still a consideration, albeit a tangential one.

Health and safety policies

Written health and safety policies are required to demonstrate that top management is concerned about the protection of the organization's employees from hazards at work and to indicate how this protection will be provided. The policies are, therefore: 1) a declaration of intent; 2) a definition of the means by which that intent will be realized; 3) a statement of the guidelines that should be followed by everyone concerned – which means all employees – in implementing the policy.

The policy statement should consist of three parts:

1 The general policy statement.
2 The description of the organization of health and safety.
3 Details of arrangements for implementing the policy.

The general policy statement

The general policy statement should be a declaration of the intention of the employer to safeguard the health and safety of employees. It should emphasize four fundamental points:

- that the health and safety of employees and the public is of paramount importance;
- that health and safety takes precedence over expediency;
- that every effort will be made to involve all managers, team leaders and employees in the development and implementation of health and safety procedures;
- that health and safety legislation will be complied with in the spirit as well as the letter of the law.

Organization

This section of the policy statement should describe the health and safety organization of the business through which high standards are set and achieved by people at all levels in the organization.

This statement should underline the ultimate responsibility of top management for the health and safety performance of the organization. It should then indicate how key management personnel are held accountable for performance in their areas. The role of safety representatives and safety committees should be defined, and the duties of specialists such as the safety adviser and the medical officer should be summarized.

Implementing health and safety policies

The basis for implementing health and safety policies is provided by three review methods:

1 Risk assessments, which identify the existence of hazards.

2 Health and safety audits, which provide for a comprehensive review of all aspects of health and safety policies, procedures and practices.

3 Health and safety inspections, which locate and define any faults in the system, equipment, plant or machines, or any operational errors that might be a danger to health or the source of accidents.

Conducting risk assessments

Risk assessments are concerned with the identification of hazards and the analysis of the risks attached to them. A hazard is anything that can cause harm (working on roofs, lifting heavy objects, chemicals, electricity, etc). A risk is the chance, large or small, of harm being actually done by the hazard.

The purpose of risk assessments is to initiate preventative action. They enable control measures to be devised on the basis of an understanding of the relative importance of risks. Risk assessments must be recorded if there are five or more employees.

Types of risk assessment

There are two types of risk assessment. The first is quantitative risk assessment, which produces an objective probability estimate based upon risk information that is immediately applicable to the circumstances in which the risk occurs. The second is qualitative risk assessment, which is more subjective and is based on judgement backed by generalized data. Quantitative risk assessment is preferable if the specific data is available. Qualitative risk assessment may be acceptable if there is little or no specific data, as long as it is made systematically on the basis of an analysis of working conditions and hazards and an informed judgement of the likelihood of harm actually being done.

Typical hazards that can be identified by risk assessments include:

- lifting and carrying, eg heavy or unwieldy objects;
- stacking and storage, eg falling materials;
- movement of people and materials, eg falls, collisions;
- processing of raw materials, eg exposure to toxic substances;
- maintenance of buildings, eg roof work, gutter cleaning;
- maintenance of plant and machinery, eg lifting tackle, installation of equipment;
- using electricity, eg using hand tools, extension leads;
- operating machines, eg operating without sufficient clearance or at an unsafe speed; not using safety devices;
- failure to wear protective equipment, eg hats, boots, clothing;
- distribution of products or materials, eg movement of vehicles;
- dealing with emergencies, eg spillages, fires, explosions;
- health hazards arising from the use of equipment or methods of working, eg VDUs, repetitive strain injuries from badly designed work stations or working practices.

Most accidents are caused by a few key activities. Assessors should concentrate initially on those that could cause serious harm. Operations such as roof work, maintenance and transport movement cause far more deaths and injuries each year than many mainstream activities.

When carrying out a risk assessment it is also necessary to consider who might be harmed. This means both employees and visitors (including cleaners and contractors and the public when calling in to buy products or enlist services).

Hazards should be ranked according to their potential. A simple three-point scale can be used such as 'low', 'moderate' and 'high', or 'negligible', 'marginal' and 'critical'.

Assessing the risk

When the hazards have been identified it is necessary to assess how high the risks are. This involves answering three questions:

1 What is the worst result?
2 How likely is it to happen?
3 How many people could be hurt if things go wrong?

A probability rating system can be used such as:

1 Probable – likely to occur immediately or shortly.
2 Reasonably probable – probably will occur in time.
3 Remote – may occur in time.
4 Extremely remote – unlikely to occur.

Taking action

Risk assessment should lead to action. The type of action can be ranked in order of potential effectiveness in the form of the following safety precedence sequence:

- *Hazard elimination* – use of alternatives, design improvements, change of process.
- *Substitution* – for example, replacement of one chemical with another that is less risky.
- *Use of barriers* – removing the hazard from the worker or removing the worker from the hazard.
- *Use of procedures* – limitation of exposure, dilution of exposure, safe systems of work (these depend on human response).
- *Use of warning systems* – signs, instructions, labels (these also depend on human response).
- *Use of personal protective clothing* – this depends on human response and is used as a side measure only when all other options have been exhausted.

Monitoring and evaluation

Risk assessment is not completed when action has been initiated. It is essential to monitor the hazard and evaluate the effectiveness of the action in eliminating it or at least reducing it to an acceptable level.

Health and safety audits

Risk assessments identify specific hazards and quantify the risks attached to them. Health and safety audits provide for a much more comprehensive review of all aspects of health and safety policies, procedures and practices.

Who carries out a health and safety audit?

Safety audits can be conducted by safety advisers and/or HR specialists, but the more that managers, employees and employee representatives are involved the better. Audits are often carried out under the auspices of a health and safety committee, with its members taking an active part in conducting them. Some organizations also use outside agencies such as the British Safety Institute to conduct independent audits.

Managers can also be held responsible for conducting audits within their departments and, even better, individual members of these departments can be trained to carry out audits in particular areas. The conduct of an audit will be facilitated if checklists are prepared and a simple form used to record results.

What is covered by a health and safety audit?

A health and safety audit should cover policies, procedures and safety practices, as outlined below.

Policies

The following questions should be asked:

- Do health and safety policies meet legal requirements?

- Are senior managers committed to health and safety?
- How committed are other managers, team leaders and supervisors to health and safety?
- Is there a health and safety committee? If not, why not?
- How effective is the committee in getting things done?

Procedures

How effectively do the procedures:

- support the implementation of health and safety policies?
- communicate the need for good health and safety practices?
- provide for systematic risk assessments?
- ensure that accidents are investigated thoroughly?
- record data on health and safety that is used to evaluate performance and initiate action?
- ensure that health and safety considerations are given proper weight when designing systems of work or manufacturing and operational processes (including the design of equipment and work stations, the specification for the product or service, and the use of materials)?
- provide safety training, especially induction training and training when jobs or working methods are changed?

Safety practices

The following questions should be considered:

- To what extent do health and safety practices in all areas of the organization conform to the general requirements of the Health and Safety at Work etc Act and the specific requirements of the various regulations and Codes of Practice?
- What risk assessments have been carried out? What were the findings? What actions were taken?
- What is the health and safety performance of the organization as shown by the

performance indicators? Is the trend positive or negative? If the latter, what is being done about it?
- How thoroughly are accidents investigated? What steps have been taken to prevent their recurrence?
- What is the evidence that managers and supervisors are really concerned about health and safety?

What should be done with the audit?

The audit should cover the questions above but its purpose is to generate action. Those conducting the audit will have to assess priorities and costs and draw up action programmes for approval by top management.

Health and safety inspections

Health and safety inspections are designed to examine a specific area of the organization – an operational department or a manufacturing process – to locate and define any faults in the system, equipment, plant or machines, or any operational errors that might be a danger to health or the source of accidents. Health and safety inspections should be carried out on a regular and systematic basis by line managers and supervisors with the advice and help of health and safety specialists. The steps to be taken in carrying out health and safety inspections are as follows:

- Allocate the responsibility for conducting the inspection.
- Define the points to be covered in the form of a checklist.
- Divide the department or plant into areas and list the points to which attention needs to be given in each area.
- Define the frequency with which inspections should be carried out – daily in critical areas.
- Use the checklists as the basis for the inspection.

- Carry out sample or spot checks on a random basis.
- Carry out special investigations as necessary to deal with special problems, such as operating machinery without guards to increase throughput.
- Set up a reporting system (a form should be used for recording the results of inspections).
- Set up a system for monitoring that safety inspections are being conducted properly and on schedule.
- Ensure that corrective action is taken where necessary.

Accident prevention

The prevention of accidents is achieved by the following actions:

- Identify the causes of accidents and the conditions under which they are most likely to occur.
- Take account of safety factors at the design stage – build safety into the system.
- Design safety equipment and protective devices and provide protective clothing.
- Carry out regular risk assessments, audits, inspections and checks and take action to eliminate risks.
- Investigate all accidents resulting in damage or harm in order to establish the cause and to initiate corrective action.
- Maintain good records and statistics in order to identify problem areas and unsatisfactory trends.
- Conduct a continuous programme of education and training on safe working habits and methods of avoiding accidents.
- Encourage approaches to leadership and motivation that do not place excessive demands on people.

Occupational health programmes

Occupational health programmes are designed to minimize the impact of work-related illnesses. The control of occupational health and hygiene problems can be achieved by taking the following actions:

- Eliminate the hazard at source through design and process engineering.
- Isolate hazardous processes and substances so that workers do not come into contact with them.
- Change the processes or substances used in order to promote better protection or eliminate the risk.
- Provide protective equipment, but only if changes to the design, process or specification cannot completely remove the hazard.
- Train workers to avoid risk.
- Maintain plant and equipment to eliminate the possibility of harmful emissions, controlling the use of toxic substances and eliminating radiation hazards.
- Adopt good housekeeping practices to keep premises and machinery clean and free from toxic substances.
- Conduct regular inspections to ensure that potential health risks are identified in good time.
- Carry out pre-employment medical examinations and regular checks on those exposed to risk.
- Ensure that ergonomic considerations (ie those concerning the design and use of equipment, machines, processes and work stations) are taken into account in design specifications, establishing work routines and training – this is particularly important as a means of minimizing the incidence of repetitive strain injury (RSI).
- Maintain preventive medicine programmes that develop health standards for each job and involve regular audits of potential health hazards and regular examinations for anyone

at risk. Particular attention needs to be exercised in the control of noise, fatigue and stress. The management and control of stress should be a major part of any occupational health programme.

- Using stress management techniques to deal with the effects of stress at work. These could include 'mindfulness' programmes involving meditation which focus the attention of people on their current experiences.

Measuring health and safety performance

It is essential to measure health and safety performance as a means of identifying in good time where actions are necessary. Account should be taken not only of current and recent figures but also trends. The most common measures are:

The frequency rate:

$$\frac{\text{number of injuries}}{\text{number of hours worked}} \times 100,000$$

The Incidence rate:

$$\frac{\text{number of injuries}}{\text{average number employed during the period}} \times 1,000$$

Some organizations adopt a 'total loss control' approach, which covers the cost of accidents to the business under such headings as 'pay to people off work', 'damage to plant or equipment' and 'loss of production'. A cost severity rate can then be calculated, which is the total cost of accidents per 1,000 hours worked.

Communicating the need for better health and safety practices

It is necessary to deliver the message that health and safety is important; this should supplement rather than replace other initiatives. The following steps can be taken to increase the effectiveness of safety messages:

- *Avoid negatives* – successful safety propaganda should contain positive messages, not warnings of the unpleasant consequences of actions.
- *Expose correctly* – address the message to the right people at the point of danger.
- *Use attention-getting techniques carefully* – lurid images may only be remembered for what they are, not for the message they are trying to convey.
- *Maximize comprehension* – messages should be simple and specific.
- *Messages must be believable* – they should address real issues and be perceived as being delivered by people (ie managers) who believe in what they say and are doing something about it.
- *Messages must point the way to action* – the most effective messages call for positive actions that can be achieved by those who receive them and will offer them a tangible benefit.

Approaches to briefing staff on the importance of health and safety

Advice to a group of staff on the importance of health and safety in the workplace must be based on a thorough understanding of the organization's health and safety policies and procedures and an appreciation of the particular factors affecting the health and safety of the group of people concerned. The latter can be based on information provided by risk assessments, safety audits and accident reports. But the advice must be positive – why health and safety is important and how accidents can be prevented. The advice should not be overweighted by unpleasant warnings. The points to be made include:

- A review of the health and safety policies of the organization with explanations of the reasoning behind them and a positive statement of management's belief that health and safety is a major consideration because:

1) it directly affects the well-being of all concerned; and 2) it can, and does, minimize suffering and loss.

- A review of the procedures used by the organization for the business as a whole, and in the particular area, to assess risks and audit the safety position.

- An explanation of the roles of the members of the group in carrying out their work safely and giving full consideration to the safety of others.

- A reiteration of the statement that one of the core values of the organization is the maintenance of safe systems of work and the promotion of safe working practices.

Health and safety training

Health and safety training is a key part of the preventative programme. It should start as part of the induction course. It should also take place following a transfer to a new job or a change in working methods. Safety training spells out the rules and provides information on potential hazards and how to avoid them. Further refresher training should be provided and special courses laid on to deal with new aspects of health and safety or areas in which safety problems have emerged.

Organizing health and safety

Health and safety concerns everyone in an establishment, although the main responsibility lies with management in general and individual managers in particular. Specific roles should be defined as follows:

- *Management* develops and implements health and safety policies and ensures that procedures for carrying out risk assessments, safety audits and inspections are implemented. Importantly, management has

the duty of monitoring and evaluating health and safety performance and taking corrective action as necessary.

- *Managers* can exert a greater influence on health and safety. They are in immediate control and it is up to them to keep a constant watch for unsafe conditions or practices and to take immediate action. They are also directly responsible for ensuring that employees are conscious of health and safety hazards and do not take risks.

- *Employees* should be aware of what constitute safe working practices as they affect them and their fellow workers. While management and managers have the duty to communicate and train, individuals also have the duty to take account of what they have heard and learnt and apply it in the ways that they carry out their work.

- *Health and safety advisers* advise on policies and procedures and on healthy and safe methods of working. They conduct risk assessments, safety audits and investigations into accidents (in conjunction with managers and health and safety representatives), maintain statistics and report on trends and necessary actions.

- *Health and safety representatives* deal with health and safety issues in their areas and are members of health and safety committees.

- *Medical advisers* have two functions: preventative and clinical. The preventative function is most important, especially on occupational health matters. The clinical function is to deal with industrial accidents and diseases and to advise on the steps necessary to recover from injury or illness arising from work. They do not usurp the role of the family doctor in non-work-related illnesses.

- *Safety committees* consisting of health and safety representatives advise on health and safety policies and procedures, help in conducting risk assessments and safety audits, and make suggestions on improving health and safety performance.

Key learning points: Health and safety

Managing health and safety at work

The achievement of a healthy and safe place of work, and the elimination to the maximum extent possible of hazards to health and safety, is the responsibility of everyone employed in an organization, as well as those working there under contract. But the onus is on the management to achieve and indeed go beyond the high standard in health and safety matters required by the legislation – the Health and Safety at Work etc Act 1974 and the various regulations laid down in the Codes of Practice.

Health and safety policies

Written health and safety policies are required to demonstrate that top management is concerned about the protection of the organization's employees from hazards at work and to indicate how this protection will be provided.

Risk assessments

Risk assessments are concerned with the identification of hazards and the analysis of the risks attached to them. The purpose is to initiate preventative action.

Health and safety audits

Health and safety audits provide for a much more comprehensive review of all aspects of health and safety policies, procedures and practices.

Health and safety inspections

Health and safety inspections should be carried out on a regular and systematic basis by line managers and supervisors, with the advice and help of health and safety advisers.

Accident prevention

Checklist:

- Identify the causes of accidents.
- Take account of safety factors at the design stage.
- Design safety equipment and protective devices and provide protective clothing.
- Carry out regular risk assessment audits and inspections and take action to eliminate risks.
- Investigate all accidents.
- Maintain good records and statistics in order to identify problem areas and unsatisfactory trends.
- Conduct a continuous programme of education and training on safe working habits.

Occupational health programmes

Implementing occupational health programmes can:

- Eliminate the hazard at source through design and process engineering.
- Isolate hazardous processes and substances so that workers do not come into contact with them.
- Change the processes or substances used to promote better protection or eliminate the risk.
- Provide protective equipment, but only if changes to the design, process or specification cannot completely remove the hazard.
- Train workers to avoid risk.

Measuring health and safety performance

This is important as a guide to action using the standard measures of frequency, incidence and severity rate.

Communicating the need for better health and safety practices

It is necessary to deliver the message that health and safety is important as long as this supplements rather than replaces other initiatives.

Health and safety training

Health and safety training is a key part of the preventative programme. It should start as part of the induction course. It should also take place following a transfer to a new job or a change in working methods.

Organizing health and safety

Health and safety concerns everyone in an establishment, although the main responsibility lies with management in general and individual managers in particular. The specific roles should be defined for managers and employees, health and safety advisers, medical advisers and the health and safety committee.

PART XII

International HRM

PART XII CONTENTS

Introduction

International human resource management (international HRM) is the process of managing people across international boundaries by multinational companies (MNCs). It involves the worldwide management of people, not just the management of expatriates.

It was stated by Brewster *et al* (2005: 949) that: 'A critical challenge for organizations from both the public and private sectors in the 21st century is the need to operate across national boundaries.' As Sparrow *et al* (2011: 50) commented: 'The ultimate aim of multinational companies (MNCs) is to build a core competence of being able to transfer capability across multiple countries, which involves monitoring the implementation of relevant policies and practices, ensuring an adequate corporate culture, establishing the necessary networks, and ensuring all parts of the organization are sensitive to the needs of international staff.'

The fundamental differences between international and domestic HRM are that in an international organization:

- HRM is more complex because it involves operating across national boundaries rather than within only one boundary and therefore takes place in different countries each with its own culture and institutions.

- It is necessary to manage a wider mix of people at headquarters and in foreign subsidiaries that employ local staff (home country nationals) and expatriates from either the parent company (parent company nationals) or other countries (third country nationals).

- Choices have to be made on the extent to which parent company HRM policies and practices should be adopted by subsidiaries – the issue of the degree of convergence required and how it is to be achieved.

- Choices have to be made on the extent to which HR decisions on matters such as appointments, promotions, redeployments and talent management should be centralized or decentralized.

- The management of expatriates involves different approaches to selection, training and career management and special concerns about the adjustment of expatriates to working in foreign countries and to the problems of repatriation.

- HR professionals have to exercise a broader range of expertise covering knowledge about foreign countries, their cultures and their institutions.

- Firms become more involved in the personal lives of their expatriate employees.

In this part, the framework of international HRM is dealt with in Chapter 58, which covers the crucial issue of the degree to which international HRM policies and practices should converge or diverge. Chapter 59 deals with the international HRM practices of workforce planning, resourcing, talent management, reward management and performance management. It also refers to multicultural working and the role of an international HR function. Chapter 60 focuses on expatriates – individuals sent by a parent company on foreign assignments. Although the practices of international HRM as described in Chapter 58 will also apply to expatriates working in foreign subsidiaries, there are a number of special considerations regarding their employment, which are considered in Chapter 60.

References

Brewster, C, Sparrow, P and Harris, H (2005) Towards a new model of globalizing HRM, *The International Journal of Human Resource Management*, **16** (6), pp 949–70

Sparrow, P, Scullion, H and Farndale, E (2011) Global talent management: new roles for the corporate HR function? in H Scullion and D G Collings (eds) *Global Talent Management*, London, Routledge, pp 40–55

58
The international HRM framework

KEY CONCEPTS AND TERMS

Centralization

Convergence

Decentralization

Divergence

Ethnocentric orientation

Geocentric orientation

Globalization

Internationalization

Localization

MNC or MNE

Polycentric orientation

Regiocentric orientation

Transnational organization

LEARNING OUTCOMES

On completing this chapter you should be able to define these key concepts. You should also understand:

- The international scene
- International strategies

- Contextual factors
- Convergence and divergence

Introduction

International HRM is concerned with human resource management policies and practices in multinational enterprises. Its aim is to ensure that an international organization attracts, deploys, develops and engages the quality of people it requires to achieve its strategic goals. Dr Michael Dickmann of the Cranfield School of Management believes, as reported by Welfare (2006: 8), that the main contrast between national and global HR practice is the need to see the bigger picture: 'The difference is the higher complexity and the need for sensitivity to different cultures and different business environments.' Dickmann stated that understanding the local context is key and that an international HR person needs to be asking questions such as: What is the business environment here? What is the role of the trade unions? What is the local labour law? Are these people different? Are their motivation patterns different?

As discussed in this chapter, international HRM takes place in a framework consisting of the international scene in general, the implications of the different approaches to international strategy and the specific contextual factors associated with differences in culture and institutions.

A key issue in international HRM also considered in this chapter is the extent to which HR policies and practices should converge or diverge. Bartlett and Ghoshal (2002) proposed that strategies in an international context are characterized by conflicting pressures of global standardization (ie internal consistency with the rest of the multinational company (MNC)) and local differentiation (ie external consistency with local environments). Standardization or convergence refers to the degree to which an international parent company's HR policies and practices are adopted by each of its subsidiaries. Localization or divergence refers to the extent to which subsidiaries operate their own HR policies and practices and act and behave as local firms.

The international scene

Internationalization is the process of international economic integration in worldwide markets. Isidor *et al* (2011: 2167) observed that: 'Internationalization offers firms manifold advantages such as realizing economies of scale and scope, learning from international markets, exploiting interrelations between business segments and geographic areas, achieving risk diversification, and cost reduction.'

According to Theodore Levitt (1983), technological, social and economic developments have combined to create a unified world marketplace in which companies must capture global-scale economies to remain competitive. It encompasses globalization – the development of single international markets for goods or services accompanied by an accelerated growth in world trade. Any company that has economic interests or activities extending across a

number of international boundaries is a global company.

Globalization raises a number of issues not present when the activities of the firm are confined to one country. As Ulrich (1998: 126) contended, it requires organizations:

> to move people, ideas, products, and information around the world to meet local needs. They must add new and important ingredients to the mix when making strategy: volatile political situations, contentious global trade issues, fluctuating exchange rates, and unfamiliar cultures. They must be more literate in the ways of international customers, commerce, and competition than ever before. In short, globalization requires that organizations increase their ability to learn and collaborate and to manage diversity, complexity, and ambiguity.

Brewster *et al* (2005) identified five distinct, but linked, organizational drivers of this process: efficiency orientation, global service provision, information exchange, core business processes and localization of decision making. The outcome has been pressure on international businesses to create a federation of global units (in the sense of working together to achieve global strategic goals) rather than national units (in the sense of taking a parochial interest in local concerns and ignoring global requirements). This in turn has increased the move towards standardization (convergence) of HRM policies and procedures and decreased interest in their localization (divergence). Globalization has encouraged the development of international HRM, enhancing the role and authority of international HR functions.

International HRM strategies

International HRM has to function strategically in order to support the achievement of international business strategies.

International HRM strategies will be affected by the different types of business strategies that MNCs can adopt, as identified by Bartlett and Ghoshal (2002: 18–19):

- Multinational – building strong local presence through sensitivity and responsiveness to local needs.

- Global – building cost advantages through controlled global-scale operations.
- International – exploiting parent company knowledge and capabilities through worldwide diffusion and adaptation.
- Transnational – creating a new organizational model by simultaneously developing global competitiveness, multinational flexibility and worldwide learning capacity.

They suggested that the transnational organization 'is a feasible and necessary response to the changes in the international environment' (ibid: 19) and claimed that adopting the transnational mode allowed companies such as Unilever to deal effectively with these demands. They mentioned that Unilever had developed a strongly held philosophy of management built around independent operating companies whose managers were given maximum responsibility and freedom. The clearly understood role of the Unilever board is to approve plans and budgets, control capital expenditures and appoint and develop executives. At an operating level, local managers have great latitude to develop and implement strategies that reflect the opportunities and constraints of their particular environments. The watchwords that became corporate dogma were 'local initiative and decentralized control'.

In contrast, P&G operations, although regarded by Bartlett and Ghoshal as a transnational organization, were linked back to the parent company in two important respects: not only did foreign subsidiaries depend on the parent for advanced technology and marketing expertise, but they were also structured to operate as replicas of the US company, immersed in the same principles and guided by the same policies.

Contextual factors

All HR activities are affected by the context in which they operate, but the variety of contexts in which international HRM functions is particularly significant. They strongly influence decisions on the dissemination of parent company policies and practices (convergence or divergence) and on the employment of expatriates. As Sparrow *et al* (1994: 269) asserted: 'For global firms to be successful in managing their worldwide workforces, they need to have an understanding and sensitivity to several local environments. They must utilize local information and adapt it to a broader set of human resource policies that reflect the firm itself.' Cultural differences in local environments are often treated as the most significant factor to be taken into account in managing globally, but differences in local institutions and practices such as collective bargaining can also be important.

Cultural differences

Briscoe *et al* (2012: 114) commented that: 'Many of the most important and difficult challenges to the conduct of international human resource management stem from the differences encountered in various countries' and MNEs' (Multinational Enterprise) cultures.' Variations in national cultures are reflected in people's values, beliefs and behaviour patterns.

Hiltrop (1995) noted the following HRM areas that may be affected by national culture:

- decisions of what makes an effective manager (performance management);
- giving face-to-face feedback;
- readiness to accept international assignments;
- different concepts of social justice;
- pay systems (reward management);
- approaches to organizational structuring.

To which could be added employee relations and communications.

Gerhart and Fang (2005: 974) stated that: 'A misfit between national culture and management practice will reduce effectiveness. For example, using a pay for individual performance plan in a country having a highly collectivist culture will not work well.'

The significance of cultural differences was the influential message delivered by Hofstede (1980) based on his research using worldwide data on IBM employees. He suggested that culture consisted of shared values and involved 'the collective mental programming of people in an environment and broad tendencies to prefer certain states of affairs over others' (ibid: 19). One of the conclusions Hofstede reached was that the cultural values within a nation are substantially more similar than the values of individuals from different nations. This view has been taken up by subsequent commentators such as Adler (2002), who claimed that Hofstede's study explained 50 per cent of the difference between countries in employees' attitudes and behaviours.

But this view has been challenged by Gerhart and Fang (2005). They subjected Hofstede's findings to further analysis and established that at the level of the individual, as distinct from the country, Hofstede's results show that: 'Roughly 2 to 4 per cent of the variance in individual values is explained by national differences. And there is nothing in Hofstede's (1980) study that pertains to individual-level "behaviours". Therefore, Hofstede's work should not be interpreted as showing that national culture explains 50 per cent of behaviours' (ibid: 977). They also established from Hofstede's data that culture varies more between organizations than between countries. In their view, cross-country cultural differences, while real, have been overestimated and may well pale in importance when explaining the effectiveness of HR practices compared with other unique country features such as the character of local institutions. But they accepted that national culture differences can be critical and that insensitivity to national culture differences can and does result in business failure (as well as failure and career consequences for individual expatriate managers).

On the basis of research conducted in 30 multinational companies by the Global HR Research Alliance, Stiles (2007: 37) commented that: 'While national cultural differences were not insignificant, they were less important than we had imagined. Organizational culture actually had more influence on HR practice.' The conclusion from the research was that: 'To think there is one best way to manage human resources is simplistic and wrong, but the variation and contextualization of HR, at least for the companies we studied, owes little to national culture' (ibid: 41).

Institutional differences

Institutional differences include the role of the state and financial sectors, employment law, national systems of education and training, and employment expectations. As described by Gerhart and Fang (2005: 971), other local factors in the environment include 'differences in the centrality of markets,

institutions, regulation, collective bargaining and labour-force characteristics'. For example, in Western Europe, collective bargaining coverage is much higher in some countries such as the UK, Germany and Italy than in the United States. Works councils are mandated by law in Western European countries such as Germany, but not in Japan or the United States. In China, Eastern Europe and Mexico, labour costs are lower than in Western Europe, Japan and the United States.

Convergence and divergence

International HRM involves the need to judge the extent to which, on the one hand, an organization should implement similar policies and practices across the world (convergence), or, on the other hand, it should allow overseas subsidiaries to adopt their own practices or at least modify the policies and practices of the parent company to suit local requirements (divergence). Brewster *et al* (2002) noted that the dilemma facing all multinational corporations is that of achieving a balance between international consistency and local autonomy. As Briscoe *et al* (2012: 48) remarked: 'International HRM strategy has to deal with the issue of whether to standardize HRM policies and practices from headquarters, or to localize them to meet local conditions, or do both (eg combination of core policies established by HQ with localized practices to accommodate local culture and practices).'

Festing and Eidems (2011: 163) reported that: 'In the course of increasing globalization, more and more MNEs are being forced to compete globally and simultaneously adapt their business strategies to changing local demands.' They also suggested that 'firms tend not to standardize a whole HRM system but rather focus on single practices' (ibid: 165).

Convergence and divergence are considered below under the following headings:

- the nature of convergence and divergence;
- factors affecting the degree of convergence or divergence;
- the pressure for convergence;
- advantages and disadvantages of convergence;
- achieving convergence.

The nature of convergence and divergence

There is a natural tendency for managerial traditions in the parent company to shape and standardize the nature of key HR policies and practices throughout an international organization. This can be called a 'one-country' approach. But there are arguments for divergence in the form of allowing subsidiaries to apply their own practices as a means of ensuring that local requirements are sufficiently taken into account (localization). Hence the mantra 'think globally but act nationally'. As Brewster *et al* (2005: 951) pointed out:

> Where global integration and coordination are important, subsidiaries need to be globally integrated with other parts of the organization and/or strategically coordinated by the parent. In contrast, where local responsiveness is important, subsidiaries will have far greater autonomy and there is less need for integration.

But the choice is not between total convergence and total divergence. Frenkel and Peetz (1998: 537) described a globalization-induced trend towards increasing convergence, which finds a counterbalance in national culture, the role of the nation state, and national industrialization strategies. Brewster and Suutari (2005) remarked that strategic alignment (convergence) and localization (divergence) can be regarded as opposite extremes on a continuum. And Brewster *et al* (2005: 952) mentioned that: 'The wider convergence-divergence debate also tends to assume that the HRM system as a whole has to converge or remain divergent, rather than considering whether some parts of the overall HR system might be converging, in some regions or geographies, while other parts might be diverging. Moreover, even within a single HR function there might be convergence at one level but divergence at another'. There is no compulsion to do the same thing everywhere.

Dickmann, as reported by Welfare (2006), instanced organizations such as IBM and Oxfam that operate a model based on universal principles or values across the organization, which are then implemented differently at regional or national level. He suggested that the extent of integration or convergence depends on the business model of the organization: if the company is basically a McDonald's, where there are only limited local variations but the product is essentially the same all over the world, then the approach is likely to be different to a company like Unilever, whose products and processes tend to be much more responsive to the local market (ibid: 9).

Pudelko and Harzing (2007: 536) noted that those who favoured convergence assumed that 'in management, best practices can be defined that are universally valid and applicable, irrespective of national culture or institutional context'. But they also observed that: 'We should not expect every subsidiary to be brought into the best practices scheme in the same way. The subsidiary's strategic role may be of some significance' (ibid: 551).

Brewster *et al* (2005: 953) reported approaches to convergence/divergence in three of their case studies as follows: Shell People Services (web-based provision of international HR services and knowledge transfer across four global businesses through the development of communities of practice); Rolls-Royce PLC (a UK-centric company going global and creating a global centre of excellence); and Diageo (convergence around core performance capability management, rewards and talent-development processes, and decentralization of international HR through the use of global networks).

The convergence and divergence of HRM policies are associated respectively with centralization and decentralization – but there are differences. As defined by Huczynski and Buchanan (2007: 474), centralization is the concentration of authority and responsibility for decision making in the hands of managers at the top of an organization's hierarchy, and decentralization involves authority and responsibility for decision making being dispersed more widely downwards and given to the operating units, branches and lower-level managers. Centralization and decentralization are mainly concerned with decision making, degrees of autonomy and organizational structures. In contrast, convergence and divergence are primarily about the dissemination or absence of dissemination of specific policies and practices, although they may be linked to processes of centralization or decentralization.

Factors affecting convergence and divergence

The factors affecting convergence and divergence consist of the orientation of international firms as expressed by their attitudes on the role and place of subsidiaries, the drivers of global integration and the institutional and cultural issues influencing the approach to the dissemination of the policies and practices of the parent company.

The orientation of international firms

As described by Perlmutter (1969) there are four types of orientation in international firms:

- *Ethnocentric orientation* in which fundamental decisions are made at headquarters and foreign subsidiaries possess little autonomy.

- *Polycentric orientation* in which headquarters considers subsidiaries as independent entities and autonomy is granted to a great extent.

- *Regiocentric orientation* in which subsidiaries are interconnected and regulated by a regional centre.

- *Geocentric orientation* in which headquarters and foreign subsidiaries are integrated worldwide and interdependent to a high degree.

More recently, Isidor *et al* (2011: 2171) explained how these orientations developed:

> In the early phase of international firm development, corporations adopt an ethnocentric staffing policy by sending out managers to the host country subsidiaries to transfer parent company culture and to ensure conformity with financial and organizational procedures. After a certain time, they adopt a polycentric staffing policy to management development, promoting, as confidence grows, home country nationals (HCNs) to senior positions in their subsidiaries; yet the polycentric style prevents HCNs from reaching the most senior positions at corporate headquarters. As the company becomes even more international, it adopts a regiocentric and finally a geocentric policy based on developing the best person for the job irrespective of his or her nationality.

Drivers for convergence

Smale (2011) listed three drivers for global integration or convergence:

1 Environmental drivers, which include the removal of trade and investment barriers, the deregulation of markets, the emergence of global customers, the spread of new web-based technologies and the opening up of developing countries such as Brazil, China and India. These drivers force companies to adopt a globally integrated approach to managing the business.

2 Strategic drivers, which capture the business advantages that result from global integration such as global branding, worldwide standardization, and the ability to respond quickly to competitive challenges by redeploying resources.

3 Structural drivers, in the form of global structures based on international product divisions that promote integration (while structures based on national units can inhibit it).

Lertxundi and Landeta (2012: 1788) explained that 'organizational practices should be viewed as valuable resources and capacities that it is useful to replicate and exploit throughout the organization.'

Dissemination of HQ policies and practices

Lertxundi and Landeta (2012: 1791) argued that: 'The transferability of best practices is conditional both on cultural/institutional factors as well as organizational ones.' Institutional theory sees the institutions of a country as the determining agents in this dissemination. The cultural approach addresses the issue of dissemination from the point of view of differences in social values and customs. National management methods may be embedded in their institutional and cultural context, which limits the possibility of cross-national learning from so-called best practices.

Choice of convergence

Harris and Brewster (1999) listed the following factors affecting the choice of convergence:

- The extent to which there are well-defined local norms.

- The degree to which an operating unit is embedded in the local environment.

- The strength of the flow of resources – finance, information and people – between the parent and the subsidiary.
- The orientation of the parent to control.
- The nature of the industry – the extent to which it is primarily a domestic industry at local level.
- The specific organizational competencies, including HRM, which are critical for achieving competitive advantage in a global environment.

The pressure for convergence

Brewster (2004) claimed that convergence may be increasing as a result of the power of the markets, the importance of cost, quality and productivity pressures, the emergence of transaction cost economies, the development of like-minded international cadres and benchmarking 'best practice'. Isidor *et al* (2011: 2167) suggested that: 'Internationalization offers firms manifold advantages such as realizing economies of scale and scope, learning from international markets, exploiting interrelations between business segments and geographic areas, achieving risk diversification, and cost reduction.'

Brewster *et al* (2005) thought that it is quite possible for some parts of an HR system to converge while other parts may diverge. Stiles (2007: 41) noted that common practices across borders may be appropriate: 'Organizations seek what works and for HR in multinational companies, the range of options is limited to a few common practices that are believed to secure high performance.' Reilly and Williams (2012: 29) asserted that 'the reasons for commonality are certainly justifiable and organizations may not have any real choice, especially in protecting corporate reputation.'

Advantages and disadvantages of convergence

Convergence can ensure that established good practice in the parent company, which has demonstrably contributed to success, can also contribute to the success of foreign subsidiaries. It can help to ensure that a global mindset exists that enables distinct units to work together to achieve a common purpose, as expressed in the General Motors mantra – 'One GM one global team'. It can further approaches in each unit that are consistent with the values and beliefs of the parent company. But a misdirected or insensitive policy of convergence can lead to the introduction of inappropriate practices that will fail to operate effectively, alienate local managers and inhibit their willingness and ability to think for themselves.

Research conducted by Reilly and Williams (2012) indicated that the following were the upsides and downsides of what they called a 'one-country' approach by HR, ie convergence:

Upsides:

- promotes common values;
- delivers consistent treatment to staff;
- exports good business practice to all parts of the organization;
- gives greater control over dispersed operations;
- provides cost control.

Downsides:

- harmonization can stifle innovation;
- the centre loses touch with the sharp end of the business;
- ill-conceived policies may be subverted at a local level;
- HR is a focus for frustration as agent of the corporate centre;
- does not easily sit with workforce segmentation.

Perkins and Shortland (2006) noted that strategic choices surrounding employment relationships may be influenced primarily by 'home country' values and practices.

Achieving convergence

If the choice is to adopt convergence to some degree, or in selected areas, it is necessary to remember Tayeb's (2005) proposition that it is generally easier to transfer strategies and policies than practices. Rather than trying to impose central practices, in certain cases it may be preferable simply to set out broad policy guidelines expressing and underpinning the values that the parent company would like to be applied throughout the organization. These could cover, for example, ethical principles on how people should be treated or, more specifically, preferred approaches to the recruitment, selection, induction and reward of employees or to employee participation and communications. It might be necessary to issue guidelines on union recognition and collective bargaining, which recognize that in some countries trade unions will have to be accepted and allowed the rights at least to represent their members and, perhaps, to negotiate on their behalf. It is also necessary to bear in mind that it may not be possible to standardize some aspects of HRM because of local employment law regulations.

Research by Lertxundi and Landeta (2012) found that the practices that reflected the greatest differences between head office and affiliates were those associated with communication and participation. Participation in particular was frequently significantly less in affiliates.

It was established by a Global HR Research Alliance study (Stiles, 2007) that global HR policies and practices were widespread in the areas of maintaining global performance standards, the use of common evaluation processes, common approaches to rewards, the development of senior managers, the application of competency frameworks and the use of common performance management criteria.

Generally, research has indicated that while global HR policies in such areas as talent management, performance management and reward may be developed, communicated and supported by centres of excellence, often through global networking, a fair degree of freedom has frequently been allowed to local management to adopt their own practices in accordance with the local context – as long as in principle these are consistent with global policies.

It was argued by Reilly and Williams (2012: 30) that: 'What HR might need to do is more carefully decide what is common and global, versus what is different and local, against some well thought through criteria. This might mean, for instance, a common HR information system, but local resourcing, or one method of executive reward, yet multiple ways of aligning local pay with the market.' They concluded that: 'It is the essential processes, populations and tools that are the ones to control from the centre, not a crude imposition of one size fits all across the piece' (ibid: 31).

Lertxundi and Landeta (2012) set out two considerations for those making decisions on which HR systems should be exported to their foreign subsidiaries. First, companies with effective HR systems should transfer them to subsidiaries in the same way that they transfer other systems. Second, cultural differences between the parent company's country and the foreign subsidiary should not prevent the export of the general principles of its HR system, although account should be taken of any differences when converting these HR principles into action. HR systems should transfer them to subsidiaries in the same way that they transfer other outstanding systems.

Convergence can be achieved by exercising centralized control; forcing subsidiaries to install the HR policies and practices of the parent company. But managers in subsidiary companies may seek to maintain as much independence as possible and therefore block or at least dilute attempts made by headquarters to enforce its policies. A performance management system complete with standardized forms can readily be installed in foreign companies. But it is easy for local managers to go through the motions and tick the boxes on the forms without conducting performance management properly, in accordance with the precepts of headquarters. Moreover, as reported by Burbach and Royle (2010), when a subsidiary employs a considerable proportion of an MNC's employees it might be able to resist the imposition of an HR system from the centre, simply because the centre could not make it work without the subsidiary's support.

Thus there is a limit to how well compulsion will work. There are other ways of disseminating good practice from headquarters such as information, communication and learning. HR and expatriates can play a major role in these activities. One method of moving practices across boundaries is to establish formal mechanisms to facilitate the transfer of knowledge. For example, Bertelsmann, the German publishing company, has created a number of 'expert committees' for this purpose composed of specialists in such areas as HR, distribution and IT.

Scullion and Starkey (2000: 1074) reported that: 'Our research suggests that MNCs can exert centralized control through the use of expatriates who may be trusted to implement corporate policies and procedures. [This] becomes a de facto centralizing control mechanism. Since network relationships are built and maintained through personal contact, staffing decisions are crucial to the effective management of the linkages that the various subsidiaries have established.' But Edwards *et al* (2011) commented that within a foreign subsidiary of an MNC, home country managers may be able to dilute the influence of expatriates through their greater familiarity with the language and customs of the host country. However, they noted that managers at HQ level also possess sources of power that can be used to overcome resistance at local level and ensure that firms engage in diffusion.

Key learning points: The international HRM framework

International HRM

International HRM is concerned with human resource management policies and practices in multinational enterprises. It has to function strategically in order to support the achievement of international business strategies.

Internationalization and globalization

Internationalization is the process of international economic integration in worldwide markets. Globalization is the development of single international markets for goods or services accompanied by an accelerated growth in world trade. Any company that has economic interests or activities extending across a number of international boundaries is a global company.

Contextual factors affecting international HRM

All HR activities are affected by the context in which they operate, but the variety of contexts in which international HRM functions is particularly significant in the way in which they influence decisions on the dissemination of parent company policies and practices (convergence or divergence) and on the employment of expatriates.

Cultural differences

Briscoe *et al* (2012: 114) commented that: 'Many of the most important and difficult challenges to the conduct of international human resource management stem from the differences encountered in various countries' and MNEs' cultures.'

Institutional differences

Institutional differences include the role of the state and financial sectors, employment law, national systems of education and training, and employment expectations.

Convergence and divergence

International HRM involves the need to judge the extent to which, on the one hand, an organization should implement similar policies and practices across the world (convergence) or, on the other, it should allow overseas subsidiaries to adopt their own practices or at least modify the policies and practices of the parent company to suit local requirements (divergence).

Factors affecting convergence and divergence

The factors affecting convergence and divergence consist of the orientation of international firms as expressed by their attitudes on the role and place of subsidiaries, the drivers of global integration and the institutional and cultural issues influencing the approach to the dissemination of the policies and practices of the parent company and to divergence.

References

Adler, N J (2002) *International Dimensions of Organizational Behaviour*, Cincinnati, OH, South-Western

Bartlett, C A and Ghoshal, S (2002) *Managing Across Borders: The transnational solution*, Boston MA, Harvard Business School Press

Brewster, C (2004) European perspectives of human resource management, *Human Resource Management Review*, 14 (4), pp 365–82

Brewster, C, Harris, H and Sparrow, P (2002) *Globalizing HR*, London, CIPD

Brewster, C, Sparrow, P and Harris, H (2005) Towards a new model of globalizing HRM, *The International Journal of Human Resource Management*, 16 (6), pp 949–70

Brewster, C and Suutari, V (2005) Global HRM: Aspects of a research agenda, *Personnel Review*, 34, pp 5–21

Briscoe, D, Schuler, R and Tarique, I (2012) *International Human Resource Management*, 4th edn, New York, Routledge

Burbach, R and Royle, T (2010) Talent on demand? Talent management in the German and Irish subsidiaries of a US multinational corporation, *Personnel Review*, 39 (4), pp 414–31

Edwards, T, Rees, C and Zhang, M (2011) The diffusion of HR practices in MNCs, in (eds) T Edwards and C Rees, *International Human Resource Management*, Harlow, Pearson Education, pp 120–38

Festing, M and Eidems, J (2011) A process perspective on transnational HRM systems – a dynamic capability-based analysis, *Human Resource Management Review*, 21, pp 162–73

Frenkel, S and Peetz, D (1998) Globalization and industrial relations in East Asia: a three-country comparison, *Industrial Relations*, 3, pp 282–310

Gerhart, B and Fang, M (2005) National culture and human resource management: assumptions and evidence, *The International Journal of Human Resource Management*, 16 (6), pp 971–86

Harris, H and Brewster, C (1999) International human resource management: the European contribution, in (eds) C Brewster and H Harris, *International HRM: Contemporary issues in Europe*, London, Routledge

Hiltrop, J M (1995) The changing psychological contract: the human resource challenge of the 1990s, *European Management Journal*, 13 (3), pp 286–94

Hofstede, G (1980) *Cultural Consequences: International differences in work-related values*, Beverley Hills, CA, Sage

Huczynski, A A and Buchanan, D A (2007) *Organizational Behaviour*, 6th edn, Harlow, FT Prentice Hall

Isidor, R, Scwens, C and Kabst, R (2011) Human resource management and early internationalization: is there a leapfrogging in international staffing? *International Journal of Human Resource Management*, 22 (10), pp 2167–84

Lertxundi, A and Landeta, J (2012) The dilemma facing multinational enterprises: transfer or adaptation of their human resource systems, *International Journal of Human Resource Management*, 23 (9), pp 1788–807

Levitt, T (1983) The globalization of markets, *Harvard Business Review*, May–June, pp 92–102

Perkins, S J and Shortland, S M (2006) *Strategic International Human Resource Management*, London, Kogan Page

Perlmutter, H (1969) The torturous evolution of the multinational company, *Columbia Journal of World Business*, Jan–Feb, pp 9–18

Pudelko, M and Harzing, A W K (2007) Country of origin, localization or dominance effect? An empirical investigation of HRM practices in foreign subsidiaries, *Human Resource Management*, 46 (4), pp 535–59

Reilly, P and Williams, T (2012) The challenges of global HR: one way to go? *People Management*, September, pp 28–31

Scullion, H and Starkey, K (2000) In search of the changing role of the corporate human resource function in the international firm, *International Journal of Human Resource Management*, 11 (6), pp 1061–81

Smale, A (2011) Global integration and international RM, in (eds) T Edwards and C Rees, *International Human Resource Management*, Harlow, Pearson Education, pp 98–119

Sparrow, P, Schuler, R S and Jackson, S E (1994)
Convergence or divergence: human resource
practices and policies for competitive
advantage worldwide, *International Journal
of Human Resource Management*, 5 (2),
pp 267–99

Sparrow, P, Scullion, H and Farndale, E (2011)
Global talent management: new roles for the
corporate HR function? in (eds) H Scullion
and D G Collings, *Global Talent Management*,
London, Routledge, pp 40–55

Stiles, P (2007) A world of difference? *People
Management*, 15 November, pp 36–41

Tayeb, M H (2005) *International Human Resource
Management: A multinational company
perspective*, Oxford, Oxford University Press

Ulrich, D (1998) A new mandate for human
resources, *Harvard Business Review*, January–
February, pp 124–34

Welfare, S (2006) A whole world out there: managing
global HR, *IRS Employment Review*, **862**, 29
December, pp 8–12

59
The practice of international HRM

KEY CONCEPTS AND TERMS

Home country nationals (HCNs)   Talent pool

Parent company nationals (PCNs)   Third country nationals (TCNs)

Talent pipeline

LEARNING OUTCOMES

On completing this chapter you should be able to define these key concepts. You should also understand:

- International workforce planning
- International resourcing
- International talent management
- International reward management

- International performance management
- Multicultural working
- The role of an international HR function

Introduction

The practice of international HRM is concerned with the HR activities conducted by a multinational company (MNC) in managing people throughout the organization. These include headquarters staff, home country nationals (HCNs – employees who are nationals of the country in which the subsidiary is based), third country nationals (TCNs – employees in a subsidiary who are nationals of a country other

than the parent company's country), and expatriates (employees assigned to a foreign subsidiary who are nationals of the parent company's country).

The basic HR practices carried out in subsidiaries for their own nationals – recruitment and selection, training, the payment of junior staff and operatives, day-to-day employee relations and HR administration – are similar to those described in earlier chapters of this book. However, they will be affected by local employment legislation, industrial relations practices, customs and cultures and may be influenced by policy guidelines from the centre. These local activities are not covered in this chapter, although one of the roles of an international HR function will be to be aware of local practices and the local contexts that influence them in order to be in a position to provide advice and guidance, especially where they affect the employment of expatriates. HQs will probably not get involved in detailed employee relations but they may issue policy guidelines on union recognition and negotiations and monitor local decisions to ensure that the guidelines are followed, or that there is good reason to ignore them because of local industrial relations practices.

There are, however, a number of HRM areas in which the parent company may play a major part, as discussed in this chapter. Workforce planning for more senior staff may be centralized, as may be resourcing decisions that affect the deployment of parent company or third country nationals. Talent management processes and the remuneration of senior staff and expatriates may also be centralized. While performance management systems will be administered by subsidiaries, the centre may want to ensure that the processes involved conform to what is regarded as best practice within the organization and provide the information required for talent management and staffing decisions. An international HR function may also be concerned with encouraging the actions required to promote multicultural working throughout the organization.

Workforce planning

International resourcing is based on workforce planning processes, which assess how many people are needed throughout the MNC (demand forecasting), set out the sources of people available (supply forecasting) and, in the light of these forecasts, prepare action plans for recruitment, selection or assignment.

Workforce planning may be carried out by the parent company HR function, although it is likely to focus mainly on managers and professional and technical staff throughout the global organization, and is linked to talent planning and talent management. Workforce planning for junior staff and operatives is more likely to be carried out by

subsidiaries, although the centre may require information on their plans.

In an international organization, estimates of future people needs can be prepared by each subsidiary for their own workforce planning purposes. The basis of such forecasts is the annual budget and longer-term business plan, translated into activity levels. These are in turn converted to specific requirements expressed in terms of numbers of people in different occupations and levels and with different skills. Assessments can also be made by subsidiaries on how anticipated needs will be met. This may be from inside their organization or in their own labour market (national or international) but it could also include information on how many positions will need to be filled by expatriates from the parent company or from other countries (third country nationals). The role of headquarters may be to review the plans of subsidiaries to make sure that they are realistic and to consolidate information on the requirements for expatriates so as to plan for their availability.

Headquarters may also review the corporate business plan to assess the people implications of any proposals for the expansion of existing businesses and the setting up or acquisition of new businesses. Again, the headquarters HR function has to assess sources of people from within the parent company, or elsewhere, as potential expatriates.

Resourcing

Resourcing in an international organization means making policy decisions on how the staffing requirements of headquarters and the foreign subsidiaries can be met, especially for managers, and professionals and technical staff. For managers, resourcing is conducted by talent management processes. Sparrow *et al* 2011: 42) emphasized that: 'MNCs increasingly demand highly skilled, highly flexible, mobile employees who can deliver the required results, sometimes in difficult circumstances.'

Paik and Ando (2011: 3006) suggested, on the basis of their research, that: 'To effectively integrate and coordinate activities of foreign affiliates, MNCs need to maintain a higher level of control at headquarters. MNC headquarters want foreign affiliates to act as if they were the headquarters' agents. In this situation, MNCs are inclined to staff foreign affiliates with managers who understand and appreciate headquarters' directives.' However, they also noted that this policy may evolve to rely more on host country staff as headquarters learns how better to integrate activities of foreign affiliates to achieve global efficiency. Cumulatively, headquarters will learn more about managing in the host country and local practices and will build relationships with local suppliers and recruit more local employees.

The four types of orientation in international firms identified by Perlmutter (1969) can result in the following different approaches to the choice of employees:

- *Ethnocentric orientation.* This means that fundamental decisions are made at headquarters and foreign subsidiaries possess little autonomy. The subsidiaries are likely to be managed by staff from the parent company, ie expatriates. This increases the ability of headquarters to control subsidiary company operations but creates problems in the shape of difficulties in managing expatriates and the frustration of home country nationals.

- *Polycentric orientation.* Headquarters treats subsidiaries as independent entities with considerable autonomy. The subsidiaries are usually managed by local nationals, which provides for continuity (expatriates come and go) and eliminates the problem of using expatriates, including the likelihood that they are more costly. But, as stressed by Dowling *et al* (2008: 82) this might: 'Isolate the corporate headquarters' staff from the various foreign subsidiaries. The result may be that a multinational firm could become a federation of independent national units with nominal links to corporate headquarters.'

- *Geocentric orientation.* Headquarters and foreign subsidiaries are integrated worldwide and are highly interdependent. This results in the creation of a worldwide force of international managers who, as 'global managers', can be deployed in any subsidiary. They can help to develop an international global perspective and to ensure that the MNC operates as a global organization. But it may be difficult to build and maintain an international team of managers.

- *Regiocentric orientation.* Subsidiaries are interconnected and regulated by a regional centre. Staffing policies in regions may resemble those in MNCs with either a polycentric or geocentric orientation.

Whichever orientation exists, an important choice required in staffing subsidiaries in an international firm is between employing parent company or home company nationals or an appropriate combination of the two. Dowling *et al* (2008) listed the advantages and disadvantages of each approach, as shown in Table 59.1.

Additionally, or alternatively, a decision may be made to employ third country nationals (TCNs) in certain posts. TCNs might be easier to obtain than home country nationals and could cost less. But, as pointed out by Dowling *et al* (2008), they might not want to return to their own countries after assignment, the host government may resent the hiring of TCNs, and national animosities (eg India/Pakistan) would have to be considered.

However, there are other ways of meeting staff requirements in foreign subsidiaries. Dowling *et al* (2008) identified the following approaches:

- *Short-term assignments*, which may be for trouble shooting, project management or a stopgap measure until a more permanent arrangement can be made.

- *Extended assignments*, which may last up to one year and involve similar activities as those for short-term assignments.

- *Commuter assignments*, which include special arrangements where the person commutes on a weekly or bi-weekly basis to the place of work in another country.

- *Rotational assignments*, in which employees commute from the home country for a short set period followed by a break in the home country.

- *Virtual assignments*, where the employee does not move to a host location but manages from home some aspect or aspects of the operations in the foreign subsidiary. Use is made of communication technologies such as video conferencing although the home-based employee may have to visit the host country frequently.

These alternatives are becoming increasingly popular, especially in companies finding it difficult to

TABLE 59.1 Advantages and disadvantages of using PCNs and HCNs

Employment of:	Advantages	Disadvantages
Parent company nationals (PNCs)	• Facilitates control and coordination • Provides managers with international experience • Provides people with the best skills for the job • Promotes the dissemination of the MNC's policies and values	• Limits the promotional opportunities of HCNs • Expatriates may find it hard to adapt to the characteristics of the host country's culture and institutions • Expatriates may impose an inappropriate management style based on that of their parent company • The remuneration of PCNs and HCNs may differ • Lack of continuity • The host country may resent and even limit the deployment of foreigners
Home country nationals (HNCs)	• Familiar with local culture, institutions and legal requirements • No language barrier • Provides continuity • Morale improved as HNCs see career potential • Fits local government policy for employing nationals • Reduces employment costs	• Unfamiliar with parent company's practices and systems • Dissemination of HQ practices more difficult • May not have the immediate skills required • More difficult to exercise control from the centre

(Adapted from Dowling *et al*, 2008: 85)

obtain satisfactory expatriates for more conventional assignments. But they can be difficult to manage and stressful for those involved.

International talent management

International talent management uses talent management procedures as described in Chapter 25.

Talent management defined

Talent management is the process of ensuring that the organization has the talented people it needs to attain its business goals. It starts with the business strategy and what it signifies in terms of the talented people required by the organization. The aim is to develop and maintain a pool of talented people. This is done through the talent pipeline, which maintains the flow of talent that the organization needs.

International talent management defined

Mellahi and Collings (2010: 143–44) defined international talent management as:

> The systematic identification of key positions which differentially contribute to the organization's sustainable competitive advantage on a global scale, the development of a talent pool

of high-performing incumbents to fill these roles which reflects the global scope of the multinational enterprise, the development of a differentiated human resource architecture to facilitate filling these positions with the best available incumbent and to ensure their continued commitment to the organization.

The significance of international talent management

Cheese *et al* (2008: 9) argued that: 'Talent has become a precious resource fought over by competitors in a global war for talent.' Isidor *et al* (2011: 2168) claimed that: 'The success of global business depends on recruiting the quality of management [required] in the multinational companies.' Mellahi and Collings (2010: 44) suggested that enabling high-performing HCNs to become senior managers improves the performance of an international business by: 1) being better able to respond effectively to the demands of local stakeholders; 2) legitimizing the firm in the host country; and 3) providing incentives for retaining and motivating talents.

But a study of 40 global organizations by Ready and Conger (2007) found that virtually all the surveyed companies identified a lack of a sufficient talent pipeline to fill strategic positions within the organization. This severely constrained their ability to grow their business.

The process of international talent management

The conduct of international talent management involves basically the same methods as those used in a domestic setting, namely, a pipeline consisting of processes for:

- *Talent planning* – defining what is meant by talent and establishing how many and what sort of talented people are needed now and in the future.

- *Talent pool definition* – on the basis of talent-planning data, deciding what sort of talent pool is required. This would consist of the resources of talent available to an organization in terms of numbers, competencies and skills. As noted by Karaevli and Hall (2003), there is a move towards identifying pools of talent that possess the potential to move into a number of roles. This replaces the traditional objective of succession planning, with its short-term focus on finding replacements for managers who leave. The talent pool is filled mainly from within the organization with additions from outside as required. The pool is not managed rigidly. It can be expanded or contracted as demands for talent change; new members can be included and existing members removed if they are no longer eligible.

- *Identifying talent internally* – by reference to the definitions of talent pool, using assessments of existing staff to decide who is qualified to be included in the talent pool.

- *Recruiting talent* – bringing in talented people from outside the company to supplement internal talent and become additional members of the talent pool.

- *Performance management* – talent is not fixed and therefore needs to be reviewed regularly; performance management also provides information on learning and development needs.

- *Management development and career planning* – a continuous programme of developing the abilities of members of the talent pool and, so far as this is possible, planning their careers.

- *Assignment or promotion* – talent pool members are assigned to positions in headquarters or, as expatriates, in foreign subsidiaries. Alternatively, they may be promoted within headquarters or a subsidiary. Although in a fully formed talent management system the talent pool is considered to be the major source for senior assignments or for promotions, people not actually in the pool may still be eligible. If no one suitable is available in the pool it may be necessary to recruit externally. Those assigned or promoted will still be included in the talent pool.

Computerized talent management systems can be used to take stock of organizational talent, although they cannot show firms how to manage talent. As McDonnell and Collings (2011: 68) pointed out: 'The global nature of MNCs makes talent management a particularly complex issue.' Mellahi and Collings (2010) identified three reasons why global talent management often fails:

1 Subsidiary managers may believe that it is in their interests to keep their own best talent rather than bring them to the attention of headquarters or other subsidiaries.

2 Decision makers at the centre do not always have access to accurate information about the availability of talent elsewhere in the organization.

3 Even when information is available, the sheer volume, diversity and, possibly, unreliability of the data hinders the centre's ability effectively to manage talent in subsidiaries.

Sparrow *et al* (2011: 48) commented that: 'The coordination of international talent management strategies in highly decentralized MNCs is more problematic due to greater tensions between the short-term needs of the operating companies and the long-term strategic needs of the business.'

International talent management in action

As reported by Ready and Conger (2007: 71), HSBC has created a system of talent pools that track and manage the careers of high potentials within the company. After those employees have been identified, they are assigned to regional or business unit talent pools, which are managed by local human resources and business unit leaders. They are then selected initially for new assignments within their region or business and may later be given positions that cross boundaries. Managers of the pools single out people to recommend for the group talent pool, which represents the most senior cadre of general managers and is administered centrally.

Ready and Conger (ibid: 73) reported that at Procter & Gamble, hiring and promotions are the responsibility of local managers, but high-potential prospects are identified globally. People and positions are tracked in a technology-based talent management system that can accommodate all the company's 135,000 employees but is primarily used

to track 13,000 middle- and upper-management employees. Procter & Gamble also conducts a global talent review – a process by which every country, function and business is assessed for its capacity to find, develop, deploy, engage and retain skilled people.

But a case study by Burbach and Royle (2010) revealed that international talent management systems do not always work as well as their sponsors hope. Some employees were unwilling to complete their 'talent profiles' – an essential part of the talent management system used by the company, which were in effect online CVs that every employee was supposed to fill in. The result was that the firm had to force compliance by stipulating that no employees would be promoted unless they completed their profile.

International performance management

Performance management systems in subsidiaries covering home and third country nationals are the area of HRM, where there is likely to be the most convergence. This means that a system based on the one used in the parent company is applied completely or partly worldwide. As Briscoe *et al* (2012: 347) observed: 'There are some valid reasons which suggest that... a standardized approach may be warranted for the sake of global integration, culture cohesiveness, fairness, mobility of global employees, and as a control mechanism.'

Approaches to international performance management

While the arguments in favour of standardization are powerful, and a convergent approach is often adopted, the degree of convergence or divergence in international performance management systems can vary in a number of ways:

● *Total convergence (standardization)* – using the parent company's scheme throughout the international organization.

● *Total divergence (localization)* – foreign subsidiaries use their own systems.

- *Partial convergence* – foreign subsidiaries use a version of the parent company's system, modified to take account of local factors such as culture and work systems. Alternatively, they ensure that their own systems conform to policy guidelines issued by headquarters, possibly including certain requirements such as the design of the forms or methods of rating.

- *Dual system* – using the headquarters scheme for expatriates (parent company nationals), and local, possibly partly converged schemes, for home country and third country nationals (the special considerations affecting performance management for expatriates are dealt with in Chapter 60).

The trend towards convergence was confirmed by the Global HR Research Alliance research, as reported by Stiles (2007: 39), which concluded that: 'In performance management we found little or no difference across the world. We witnessed a concerted effort on the part of group HR departments to maintain global standards supported by global competencies (at foundation, managerial, technical and leadership level), common evaluation processes and common approaches to rewards. It was difficult, therefore, to find many distinctive local practices.'

International performance management systems

International performance management systems basically contain the following elements that correspond to those found in home-based systems, as described in Chapter 42:

- *Performance agreement* – the manager and the individual jointly decide on the goals that the latter is expected to achieve. These may be hard goals that define the results expected, as far as possible expressed in quantitative terms, or soft goals that are qualitative and refer to behaviours or traits such as upholding corporate values, leadership, interpersonal relationships and customer relations. The agreement may also clarify the level of competency required by the individual by reference to a competency framework.

- *Performance management throughout the year* – this involves regular dialogues between the manager and the individual about the latter's performance, coaching, and taking action to improve performance.

- *Performance review* – a formal review of performance in achieving agreed goals and in meeting competency requirements. The review may incorporate ratings of performance and potential and will be summarized on a performance review form. The review provides the basis for a new performance agreement and for a programme of development to enhance abilities and skills. It may also inform performance-related pay decisions.

International performance management issues

The effectiveness of international performance management is affected overall by the sheer complexity of international business and the distance separating headquarters and subsidiaries. Briscoe and Claus (2008) noted that a challenge is provided by 'the major differences that arise between host national perceptions and those of the home office regarding what was being accomplished and the circumstances under which it was being achieved.' Briscoe and Schuler (2004: 354) mentioned the following difficulties:

- problems with the choice of evaluator (eg in the local or parent company) and that person's amount of contact with the ratee;

- the host country's perceptions of performance, which may differ from those in the parent company;

- problems with long-distance communication;

- inadequate contact between parent company rater and subsidiary company rater;

- unclear or contradictory performance objectives for foreign operations;

- lack of understanding by the parent company of the foreign environment and culture;

- indifference to the foreign experience of the expatriate.

The particular issues affecting international performance management are the increased difficulty in influencing and controlling line managers; cultural differences; the problem of achieving consistent rating results; and variable levels of maturity among subsidiaries, which affect relative performance. These issues, as discussed below, need to be taken into account when deciding on the extent to which standardized performance management systems are desirable and, in so far as they are standardized, how they should be managed. There are no easy solutions. Each case has to be decided in accordance with individual circumstances. But it is helpful to be aware of the potential pitfalls so that action can be taken in advance to avoid them, as far as possible.

Line managers

Even in a one-country domestic setting, performance management can easily fail because the line managers on whom the system depends lack the skill or the inclination to do it properly. In an international organization, control over how line managers implement performance management will be even more difficult owing to the diversity of operations, the geographical separation between headquarters and foreign subsidiaries and, possibly, the unwillingness of local managers to take much notice of commands from a remote centre.

Cultural differences

Cultural differences may also affect the ability of an MNC to implement a standardized international system. Shen (2005: 72) noted that: 'For example, in some Asian countries such as China and Japan, feedback is not normally given in order to "save face" and group meetings are often held in performance management processes to achieve group harmony. This aspect of Asian culture is very different from Western culture where individualism is emphasized.'

Rating problems

The achievement of reliable and consistent appraisal ratings in a domestic setting is difficult; in an international operation it is virtually impossible. Care should therefore be taken in designing and interpreting rating systems. It may be best to leave them to the local subsidiary and not try to introduce a suspect universal system.

Variable levels of maturity

The maturity of subsidiaries in terms of their productivity, ability to penetrate markets, availability of skilled employees and work practices will vary and it may be more difficult for some subsidiaries to meet the standards of performance expected by the parent company. Environmental differences such as levels of political stability and standards of living will also affect the results achieved by subsidiaries. Account should be taken of these differences but it is too easy for a remote headquarters to be unaware of how local factors affect performance levels.

International performance management in action

Chartered Standard Bank

The international performance management process used by Chartered Standard Bank is illustrated in Figure 59.1.

Serono SA

As reported by Coleman and Chambers (2005), Serono SA, the Swiss biotechnology company with offices around the world, needed a performance management, pay-for-performance and compensation system that was not only consistent but was also flexible enough to adjust to the laws governing employment in each of its far-flung operations.

Each Serono operating unit has its own objectives, which are aligned to overarching corporate goals. Units in each country tailor their performance management and reward systems for compliance with local laws, customs and budgets. An information technology system was developed to automate performance management and compensation for Serono's global operations. The analytical tools built into this system enable HR at the centre to gain an overview of how the organization as a whole is evaluating its employees. For example, data on assessments presented as bell curves (graphs showing distributions in the form of a curve shaped like a bell), reveal the extent to which appraisal scores are out of line with what is regarded as a normal distribution.

FIGURE 59.1   International performance management system – Standard Chartered Bank

The Process
- Global for all employees
- In transition to accelerate a high-performing organization

Objective Setting (January)
- Financial/business objectives
- 2 core management objectives
- Values objective for all

Performance Coaching (throughout the year)
- Regular open dialogue
- Integrates performance, learning and development, reward and individual engagement
- Addresses performance issues
- Under-performance not tolerated

Final review (Nov/Dec)
- 1–5 financial/business rating scale
- A–D values rating scale
- Effective differentiation
- Additional feedback form
- Cascaded 'level down' rating reviews

Interim Review (July)
- Formal step-back
- 'Tracking' rather than 'rating'

(**SOURCE**: Armstrong and Baron, 2005)

Reward management

International reward management involves the management of all aspects of rewards in organizations operating worldwide, or at least in a number of countries. It is not just the management of expatriate remuneration.

Traditionally, discussions of international reward strategies and practices have tended to focus on an elite of expatriate workers, sourced from headquarter locations and rewarded in isolation from local country staff. Today, a diverse and complex pattern is emerging, requiring a more strategic approach than simply copying the practices of other multinationals.

Stephen Perkins (2006) explained that achieving an appropriate global/local balance between global and local requirements in international staffing and rewards has therefore become a much more strategic and challenging issue for HR and reward managers. Major organizations such as BP and the World Bank have overhauled their policies in recent years to achieve their key strategic reward goals of mobility and affordability in this more demanding global context.

Baeten and Leuven (2010) listed the following main concerns in global compensation:

- the extent of centralization or decentralization of compensation policies and practices;

- balancing corporate and national cultures;

- the sustainability and span of global compensation policies;

- the choice of compensation instruments to be included in global compensation policies;

- global benchmarking;
- measuring the efficiency of a global compensation approach.

Design of international reward systems

The factors that are likely to impact on the design of reward systems, as suggested by Bradley *et al* (1999), are the corporate culture of the multinational enterprise, expatriate and local labour markets, local cultural sensitivities, and legal and institutional factors. They refer to the choice that has to be made between, on the one hand seeking internal consistency by developing common reward policies in order to facilitate the movement of employees across borders and preserve internal equity, and on the other hand, responding to pressures to conform to local practices. But they point out that studies of cultural differences suggest that reward system design and management needs to be tailored to local values to enhance the performance of overseas operations. Although, as Sparrow (1999) indicated, differences in international reward are not just a consequence of cultural differences, but also of differences in international influences, national business systems and the role and competence of managers in the sphere of HRM.

International reward strategy

International reward strategy is concerned with the development of an integrated approach to building reward policies and practices across international boundaries. It should be integrated, in the sense that it takes into account the business goals and drivers of the parent company while at the same time fitting the strategy to the different contexts and cultures across the globe. The issue of the extent to which the reward strategy should be centralized or decentralized (convergence or divergence) needs to be addressed.

As White (2005: 25) stated: 'Best practice tells us that global rewards must not be considered piecemeal.' He explained that:

> The development of any reward programme calls for an integrated approach whereby each individual element of reward supports the others to reinforce organizational objectives. A global

rewards philosophy and total rewards approach can facilitate alignment of an organization's rewards with business strategy, focus employees on the business goals, and reinforce consistent pay practices.

But he also commented that 'different local market practices, regulations and culture are indicators that a one size fits all system will not be truly effective.'

International reward management objectives

Briscoe *et al* (2012: 291–92) gave the following objectives for a typical MNC global compensation and benefits programme:

- Attraction and retention of the best-qualified talent to staff the MNC in all its locations.
- Attraction and retention of employees who are qualified for international assignments.
- Facilitation of transfers between different locations within the MNC.
- Establishment and maintenance of consistent and reasonable relationships between the compensation of employees at home and abroad.
- Maintenance of compensation which is reasonable in relation to the practices of competitors yet minimizes costs to the extent possible.

They noted that national and organizational cultures influence how people perceive the value of the various rewards available and commented that: 'The culture may be performance-driven (and pay-for-performance is an established norm) or it may be entitlement-oriented (with longevity of service rewarded. In some cultures, people are more willing to accept risk in their compensation while in others people are quite risk-averse)' (ibid: 293).

The convergence or divergence of international reward management policy and practice

White (2005: 23) argued that: 'Global consistency in management's messages to employees, as well as in the reward programmes that reinforce these messages is critical in building a cohesive entity that will create shareholder value.'

A consistent approach to international reward management will be developed if a global business strategy exists that encourages similarities in reward management policies and practices amongst MNC subsidiaries. But this might violate local cultural norms or business conditions. International reward management practices are affected by differences in three areas: 1) the labour market, where in each country there will be unique labour demand and supply pattern; 2) institutions such as government regulations, tax systems and trade unions; and 3) national cultures where, for example, there may be difference in the extent to which financial incentives will affect motivation.

As Yanadori (2011: 3867) stated:

> Managing employee compensation in multinational corporations (MNCs) involves carefully balancing two pressures: localization and strategic alignment. On the one hand, the compensation systems in foreign subsidiaries need to be customized to address unique local contexts... On the other hand, MNCs are increasingly interested in establishing, across different subsidiaries, consistent compensation systems that are aligned with their global business strategies.

His research in a multinational finance firm established that different pay rates were adopted to reflect differences in the local labour markets.

Research by Baeten and Leuven (2010) in 31 international companies aimed to provide answers to the issue of centralization versus decentralization of compensation policies and systems. It was established that the degree of centralization was very high for senior management (94 per cent), moderate for middle management (54 per cent) and low for operational employees (12 per cent). Decision making on base pay and incentives was centralized for senior managers. In the case of middle managers, it was centralized for some issues such as grading and criteria for pay reviews, but decentralized for others such as pay ranges and actual base pay increases. It was mainly decentralized for operational employees.

There are four levels of convergence, as set out in Table 59.2.

TABLE 59.2   Levels of convergence in reward management policy and practice

Level 1: Total convergence	Central reward policies and practices have to be followed by each operating unit in accordance with a set of guiding principles. These may include a standard job evaluation scheme, uniform grade and pay structure (with scope for local market differentiation), a common approach to incentives and a common set of benefits.
Level 2: Partial convergence	Central reward policies are applied in some but not all aspects of reward management. Centralization may be limited to senior management or international staff (expatriates or nationals from countries other than the parent company working in the local country – third country nationals). Reward policies and practices for local nationals are decentralized.
Level 3: Partial divergence	Corporate job evaluation schemes and grade structures are recommended but modification is permitted to fit local conditions. However, all locations are expected to comply with the international guiding principles for reward. There may still be centralized policies for senior managers, expatriates, and third country nationals, and some benefits may be standardized. But pay levels and pay progression and incentive arrangements are determined locally.
Level 4: Total divergence	Local companies have complete freedom to develop and apply their own reward policies and practices, although they may be made aware of the international guiding principles.

Briscoe *et al* (2012: 297) listed the following options for establishing a worldwide compensation system:

- Create worldwide salary levels at HQ with differentials for each subsidiary according to their differing costs of living.

- Base pay on local levels (usually excluding executives and globally mobile employees).

- Establish a global base per position where there is a global market for particular occupations or for senior managers and global employees.

- Set up two classifications – local and national – for pay. All local nationals above a certain level are placed on the headquarters scale. The others are paid on a local scale.

International reward management in action

CASE STUDIES

US-owned MNC

A case study by Almond *et al* (2005) of the pay policies of a large US-owned MNC operating in Europe found that over the years the degree of centralization or decentralization changed frequently. Until the 1980s, corporate HQ issued a number of global policies that national managers were expected to implement. Some room was given for the policies to be adapted to fit local circumstances but management in subsidiaries had to justify these changes to headquarters.

During the late 1980s, the firm moved away from this highly centralized approach, allowing more scope for subsidiaries to develop policies that suited their own situation. For example, job evaluation systems could be developed independently of the US system. The decentralizing tendency was reversed in the early 1990s, and there has followed a period during which strong coordination of HR policies between countries and central control has been re-established.

General Motors (GM)

As reported by Mercer Human Resource Consulting (2009), GM moves people around the globe frequently because its products are designed and built on global platforms. The international philosophy of GM is expressed in the mantras 'One GM one global team' and 'Global perspective: local engagement'.

But different locations were using different-level pay structures and job evaluation schemes. A 'leading change' programme involved compensation chiefs around the world. Under the banner of the phrase 'Global compensation takes the approach that what can be should be', the global team:

- analysed the various strategies, structures and practices in place around the world;

- used corporate governance to decide what needed to be global, regional or local;

- identified 'best practices' in compensation to establish a common philosophy, tools and structure for the salaried workforce;

- engaged key stakeholders in the process;

- provided tools, support and education;

- created, with the help of Mercer Consultants, more than 200 benchmarks in 30 job functions and then slotted them into global salary grades.

Multicultural working

A fundamental feature of international operations is that multinational and therefore multicultural teams have to work together in foreign subsidiaries. Haas and Nüesch (2012) conducted research which showed that on the one hand, multinational teams may have access to a greater variety of task-relevant experience, but on the other hand, national diversity may complicate team collaboration and increase team conflict. Evidence was found that multinational teams perform worse than teams with less national diversity. It is therefore necessary for international organizations to develop ways of improving multicultural working.

The following 10 tips for managing a multi-cultural team were devised by Sharon Varney of the Roffey Park Institute (quoted by Craig, 2008):

- Adopt a 'cultural lens'. Be prepared to set aside tried-and-tested management techniques that may have served you well in the past.

- Invest in managing new starters' expectations. Allow more time for team formation, induction and establishing goals.

- Build relationships across cultures. Find time for face-to-face meetings and social activities. However intermittent, time together is of great value.

- Communicate across cultures. Keep in contact and always check that communications are understood in the way that was intended.

- Encourage participation in cross-cultural teams. Vary communication styles and methods. Using visuals can help overcome language barriers.

- Motivate cross-cultural teams. Focus both on team and individual goals. Remember that rewards and incentives can be seen very differently.

- Manage performance across cultures. Take extra care introducing performance management systems, as one size does not fit all.

- Raise cultural awareness and understanding. Bring people from different cultures together for specific projects and assignments to promote greater understanding.

- Manage cross-cultural conflict. Help people clarify their assumptions. Even understanding what the issue is can be difficult.

- Encourage ethical standards in cross-cultural teams. Ways of conducting business can vary across geographies, so provide clear company guidelines and be ready to deal with any ethical issues in a timely manner.

Role of the international HR function

An international HR function is responsible for developing and operating a transnational HR system, which was defined by Festing and Eidems (2011: 162) as 'the sum of HRM policies and practices that a multinational enterprise uses to attract, develop and maintain its human resources including globally standardized and locally adapted structures and processes'. Briscoe *et al* (2012: 413) indicated that the role of an international HR department should be to:

- contribute as an integral partner in formulating the global strategy for the firm;
- develop processes and concepts for top management as they develop the global strategy;
- help top management to understand the people implications of globalization;
- identify the key skills required in the global organization – both line and HR management;
- share the responsibility for HRM with line managers.

To carry out this role, the HR function has to operate strategically and focus on providing advice and support to line executives.

Research by Scullion and Starkey (2000) highlighted a considerable variation in the roles of the HR function in different types of international firms. In centralized global firms, the function undertook a wide range of activities and the key roles were management development, succession planning, career planning, strategic staffing, top management rewards and managing the mobility of international managers. In highly decentralized firms a lower degree of coordination and integration existed and HR executives were more limited in the scope of their roles, focusing on management development and succession planning for senior executives.

On the basis of a survey of 64 companies, Brewster *et al* (2005) observed that global HR professionals are acting as the guardians of culture, operating global values and systems. They referred to the 'greater complexity and strategic importance of the [HR function] international role' (ibid: 951) and commented as follows on the role of a central HR philosophy:

> Also helping the HR function deliver against the organizational strategy was what we have termed a central HR philosophy. This consisted of two elements: centralization of HR decision making and industry-wide convergence of HR practice... The transfer and mutual learning from varied global practice is critically important. However, there was also a drive within organizations to develop some central command and co-ordination over this knowledge. In 21 per cent of firms, the HR-enabling recipe involved a centralized HR philosophy. These elements involve a degree of convergence and assumptions of best practice. (ibid: 964)

In decentralized firms Sparrow *et al* (2011: 48) noted that 'attempts are made to maintain control over the mobility and careers of international managers; however, this is more fragmented and less systematic than in the globally integrated companies... Corporate HR often has less influence on the operating companies and is frequently not responsible for finding re-entry positions for expatriates; and there are less well-developed career and succession planning systems.'

Key learning points: The practice of international HRM

The practice of international HRM

The practice of international HRM is concerned with the HR activities conducted by a multinational company (MNC) in managing people throughout the organization. These include headquarters staff, home country nationals (HCNs – employees who are nationals of the country in which the subsidiary is based), third country nationals (TCNs – employees in a subsidiary who are nationals of a country other than the parent company's country), and expatriates (employees assigned to a foreign subsidiary who are nationals of the parent company's country).

Workforce planning

International resourcing is based on workforce planning processes, which assess how many people are needed throughout the MNC (demand forecasting), set out the sources of people available (supply forecasting) and, in the light of these forecasts, prepare action plans for recruitment, selection or assignment.

Resourcing

Resourcing in an international organization means making policy decisions on how the staffing requirements of headquarters and the foreign subsidiaries can be met, especially for managers, professionals and technical staff.

An important choice required in staffing subsidiaries in an international firm is between employing parent company or home company nationals or an appropriate combination of the two.

Talent management

Talent management is the process of ensuring that the organization has the talented people it needs to attain its business goals.

The conduct of international talent management involves basically the same methods as those used in a domestic setting, namely, a pipeline consisting of processes for talent planning, talent pool definition, identifying talent internally, recruiting talent, performance management, management development and career planning, assignment or promotion.

International performance management systems

International performance management systems basically contain the following elements, which correspond to those found in domestic systems: performance agreement, performance management throughout the year, performance review.

The effectiveness of international performance management is affected overall by the sheer complexity of international business and the distance separating headquarters and subsidiaries.

The particular issues affecting international performance management are the increased difficulty in influencing and controlling line managers, cultural differences, the problem of achieving consistent rating results, and variable levels of maturity among subsidiaries, which affect relative performance.

Reward management

International reward management involves the management of all aspects of rewards in organizations operating worldwide, or at least in a number of countries.

The factors that are likely to impact on the design of reward systems, as suggested by Bradley *et al* (1999), are the corporate culture of the multinational enterprise, expatriate and local labour markets, local cultural sensitivities and legal and institutional factors.

International reward strategy is concerned with the development of an integrated approach to building reward policies and practices across international boundaries.

Multicultural working

A fundamental feature of international operations is that multinational and therefore multicultural teams have to work together in foreign subsidiaries.

Role of the international HR function

An international HR function is responsible for developing and operating a transnational HR system, which was defined by Festing and Eidems (2011: 162) as 'the sum of HRM policies and practices that a multinational enterprise uses to attract, develop and maintain its human resources including globally standardized and locally adapted structures and processes.'

References

Almond, P, Edwards, T, Colling, T, Ferner, A, Gunnigle, P, Müller-Camen, M, Quintanilla, J and Wächter, H (2005) Unravelling home and host country effects: an investigation of the HR policies of an American multinational in four European countries, *Industrial Relations*, 44 (2), pp 276–306

Baeten, X and Leuven, V (2010) Global compensation and benefits management: the need for communication and coordination, *Compensation & Benefits Review*, 42 (3), pp 392–402

Bradley, P, Hendry, C and Perkins, P (1999) Global or multi-local? The significance of international values in reward strategy, in (eds) C Brewster and H Harris, *International HRM: Contemporary issues in Europe*, London, Routledge

Brewster, C, Sparrow, P and Harris, H (2005) Towards a new model of globalizing HRM, *International Journal of Human Resource Management*, **16** (6), pp 949–70

Briscoe, D R and Claus, L M (2008) Employee performance management, in (eds) A Varma, P S Budhwar and A DeNisi, *Performance Management Systems: A global perspective*, Abingdon, Routledge, pp 15–39

Briscoe, D R and Schuler, R S (2004) *International Human Resource Management*, 2nd edn, New York, Routledge

Briscoe, D, Schuler, R and Tarique (2012) *International Human Resource Management*, 4th edn, New York, Routledge

Burbach, R and Royle, T (2010) Talent on demand? Talent management in the German and Irish subsidiaries of a US multinational corporation, *Personnel Review*, **39** (4), pp 414–31

Cheese, P, Thomas, K J and Craig, E (2008) *The Talent Powered Organization*, London, Kogan Page

Coleman, T and Chambers, T (2005) Serono case study: global performance, evaluations and compensation, *Compensation & Benefits Review*, July–August, pp 61–65

Craig, T (2008) Different strokes, Personnel Today, 25 November, pp 25–29

Dowling, P J, Festing, M and Engle, A D (2008) *International Human Resource Management*, 5th edn, Andover, Cengage Learning EMEA

Festing, M and Eidems, J (2011) A process perspective on transnational HRM systems – a dynamic capability-based analysis, *Human Resource Management Review*, **21**, pp 162–73

Haas, H and Nüesch, S (2012) Are multinational teams more successful? *International Journal of Human Resource Management*, **23** (15), pp 3105–13

Isidor, R, Scwens, C and Kabst, R (2011) Human resource management and early internationalization: is there a leapfrogging in international staffing? *International Journal of Human Resource Management*, **22** (10), pp 2167–84

Karaevli, A and Hall, D T (2003) Growing leaders for turbulent times: is succession planning up to the challenge? *Organizational Dynamics*, **32** (1), 2003, pp 62–79

McDonnell, A and Collings, D G (2011) Identification and evaluation of talent in MNEs, in (eds) H Scullion and D G Collings, *Global Talent Management*, London, Routledge, pp 56–73

Mellahi, K and Collings, D G (2010) The barriers to effective global talent management: the example of corporate elites in MNEs, *Journal of World Business*, **45**, pp 143–44

Mercer Human Resource Consulting (2009) A Whole New World, New York, Mercer

Paik, Y and Ando, N (2011) MNC's competitive strategies, experiences, and staffing policies for foreign affiliates, *International Journal of Human Resource Management*, **22** (15), pp 3003–19

Perkins, S (2006) *Guide to International Reward and Recognition*, London, CIPD

Perlmutter, H (1969) The torturous evolution of the multinational company, *Columbia Journal of World Business*, Jan–Feb, pp 9–18

Ready, D A and Conger, J A (2007) Make your company a talent factory, *Harvard Business Review*, June, pp 69–77

Scullion, H and Starkey, K (2000) In search of the changing role of the corporate human resource function in the international firm, *The International Journal of Human Resource Management*, **11** (6), pp 1061–81

Shen, J (2005) Effective international performance appraisals: easily said, hard to do, *Compensation and Benefits Review*, July–August, pp 70–79

Sparrow, P R (1999) *The IPD Guide on International Recruitment, Selection and Assessment*, London, IPD

Sparrow, P, Scullion, H and Farndale, E (2011) Global talent management: new roles for the corporate HR function? in (eds) H Scullion and D G Collings, *Global Talent Management*, London, Routledge, pp 40–55

Stiles, P (2007) A world of difference? *People Management*, 15 November, pp 36–41

Varma, A, Budhwar, P S and DeNisi, A (2008) *Performance Management Systems: A global perspective*, Abingdon, Routledge

Welfare, S (2006) A whole world out there: managing global HR, *IRS Employment Review*, **862**, 29 December, pp 8–12

White, R (2005) A strategic approach to building a consistent global rewards program, *Compensation & Benefits Review*, July–August, pp 23–40

Yanadori, Y (2011) Paying both globally and locally: an examination of the compensation management of a US multinational finance firm in the Asia pacific region, *The International Journal of Human Resource Management*, **22** (18), pp 3867–87

60
Managing expatriates

KEY CONCEPTS AND TERMS

Acculturization

Cross-cultural awareness

Expatriate

Home-based pay

Host-based pay

LEARNING OUTCOMES

On completing this chapter you should be able to define these key concepts. You should also understand:

- Why use expatriates?
- RoI on international assignments
- The process of managing expatriates
- Resourcing policies
- Recruitment and selection policies
- Preparation policy
- Assimilation and support
- Career management
- Expatriate performance
- Re-entry policies
- Pay and allowances policies
- Case studies

Introduction

An expatriate was defined by Lee and Donohue (2012: 1198) as 'any individual who relocates from his/her home base to an international location for business or work purposes and sets up temporary residence in the host country'.

The management of expatriates on international assignments is a major factor determining success or failure in a global business. Expatriates are expensive. They can be difficult to manage because of the problems associated with adapting to and working in unfamiliar environments and cultures, concerns about their development and careers, difficulties encountered when they re-enter their parent company after a foreign assignment, and questions about how they should be remunerated. It is therefore necessary to consider why expatriates should be employed and how the costs and benefits of using them can be evaluated. In this chapter, these issues are dealt with first. The rest of the chapter is devoted to an examination of the various policies and practices required to manage expatriates.

might give rise to double taxation, require particular attention. Some or all of the following allowances may be added to this salary:

- 'incentive to work abroad' premium;
- hardship and location;
- housing and utilities;
- school fees;
- 'rest and recuperation' leave.

Host-based pay

The host-based pay approach provides expatriates with salaries and benefits such as company cars and holidays that are in line with those given to nationals of the host country in similar jobs. This method ensures equity between expatriates and host country nationals. It is adopted by companies using the so-called market rate system, which ensures that the salaries of expatriates match the market levels of pay in the host country.

Companies using the host-based approach commonly pay additional allowances such as school fees, accommodation and medical insurance. They may also fund long-term benefits such as social security, life assurance and pensions from home.

The host-based method is certainly equitable from the viewpoint of local nationals, and it can be less expensive than home-based pay. But it may be much less attractive as an inducement for employees to work abroad, especially in unpleasant locations, and it can be difficult to collect market rate data locally to provide a basis for setting pay levels.

CASE STUDIES

Oxfam

Oxfam is a highly devolved international organization with a strategy of building up local management. Reporting lines for HR staff reflect this devolved approach. Country-based HR staff report to regional HR managers The latter report direct to their regional director but have a 'dotted line' (functional) relationship with Oxfam's head of international HR. This means that they must take account of the principles of Oxfam's international people strategy and its associated policies covering pay, benefits, performance management and other practices that apply to every region.

Thus regions will follow Oxfam's international people strategy, pay and benefits framework and other HR procedures; unless local legislation has to take precedent, they ultimately decide how to implement policies and pay staff within regional budgets. Oxfam recruits locally when it can but it may be necessary to look elsewhere for people with some specialist skills, although this labour pool is from a global labour market rather than a Western one.

IBM

IBM has over 300,000 employees in more than 160 countries. It has evolved in recent years from a predominately IT manufacturing and sales company to become a business services company.

The company is structured into three regions and describes itself as a globally integrated company. Strategy is global but the human front-end of HR is local, staffed with local nationals. A generally integrated approach to HR is adopted, although the extent to which HR policies are tailored to local circumstances varies. This is affected by the need to conform to different legal requirements in each company, which particularly affects employee relations policies. However, total reward and performance management policies and practices are common across the world. The company claims that it acts on its values, for example equal opportunities, even when they may prove controversial locally. Levels of international mobility are high, especially for staff working in HR, finance and IT.

Key learning points: Managing expatriates

Expatriates

An expatriate was defined by Lee and Donohue (2012: 1198) as 'any individual who relocates from his/her home base to an international location for business or work purposes and sets up temporary residence in the host country'.

Managing expatriates

The management of expatriates on international assignments is a major factor determining success or failure in a global business. Expatriates are expensive. They can be difficult to manage because of the problems associated with adapting to and working in unfamiliar environments and cultures, concerns about their development and careers, difficulties encountered when they re-enter their parent company after a foreign assignment, and questions about how they should be remunerated.

Use of expatriates

Organizations use international assignments mainly for: 1) subsidiary control and coordination; 2) skills and knowledge transfer; and 3) managers' development.

RoI on international assignments

International assignments are investments in the use of human capital which involve costs as well as benefits. It is therefore advisable to calculate the return on investment (RoI) that they generate.

The process of managing expatriates

The process of managing expatriates has been summarized by Sparrow *et al* (2004: 145) as a global assignment cycle, the three phases of which are: pre-departure, assignment and post-assignment.

Resourcing

Policies are required on the employment of local nationals and the use of expatriates for long periods or shorter assignments.

Expatriates may be required to provide the experience and expertise that local nationals lack, at least for the time being. But there is much to be said for a long-term resourcing policy which states that the aim is to fill all or the great majority of posts with local people.

Recruitment and selection policies

- People for international assignments can be recruited from within the company from a defined pool, by identifying individuals with the required qualifications, or internal advertisements. It may be necessary to seek recruits outside the firm.

- Other sources of people (locals and self-assigned individuals) and alternative forms of mobility (eg business travel, virtual teams, short-term assignments and commuting) should be considered.

- The critical requirement that expatriates should meet is cross-cultural awareness, ie the ability to understand and work within different national cultures.

Preparation policy

The preparation policy for overseas assignments should include the provision of cultural familiarization for the country in which the expatriate will work, information on how to work in multicultural teams, and the business and HR policies that will apply. A pre-assignment training programme should be provided.

Assimilation and support policies

- Assimilation and support policies provide for the adaptation of expatriates to overseas posts and their progress in them to be monitored and reviewed.

- Progress may be monitored by conventional performance management processes, but additional information may be provided on potential and the ability of individuals to cope with overseas conditions.

- Mentors may be appointed to look after the interests of expatriates.

Career management

Special attention has to be paid to managing the careers of expatriates, either as part of their experience overseas or when they return permanently or for a period to their home country.

Expatriate performance

Standard performance management systems can be used for assessing expatriate performance. But there are unique circumstances surrounding the work of expatriates, including the need for cross-cultural competence, problems of adjustment, and distance from headquarters and the support it can provide.

These combine to suggest that special arrangements should be made for assessing their performance and particular care should be taken to allow for the factors that affect performance.

Pay and allowances policies

The policy of most organizations is to ensure that expatriates are no worse off because they have been posted abroad. In practice, various additional allowances or payments, such as hardship allowances, mean that they are usually better off financially than if they had stayed at home. The basic choice for expatriate pay is whether to adopt a home-based or host-based policy.

References

Altman, Y and Baruch, Y (2012) Global self-initiated corporate expatriate careers: a new era in international assignments, *Personnel Review*, 41 (2), pp 233–55

Briscoe, D and Schuler, R (2004) *International Human Resource Management*, London, Routledge

Briscoe, D, Schuler, R and Tarique, I (2012) *International Human Resource Management*, 4th edn, New York, Routledge

Caligiuri, P (1997) Assessing expatriate success: Beyond just being there, in (ed) Z Aycan, *New Approaches to Employee Management: Theory and research*, Greenwich, JAI Press, pp 117–40

Collings, D and Scullion, H (2006) Global staffing, in (eds) G K Stahl and I Björkman, *Handbook of Research in International Human Resource Management*, Cheltenham, Edward Elgar pp 141–57

Dickmann, M, Doherty, N, Mills, T and Brewster, C (2008) Why do they go? Individual and corporate perspectives on the factors influencing the decision to accept an international assignment, *International Journal of Human Resource Management*, 39 (1), pp 116–34

Doherty, N T and Dickmann, M (2012) Measuring the return on investment in international assignments: an action research approach, *International Journal of Human Resource Management*, 23 (16), pp 3434–54

Farh, C I, Bartol, K M, Shapiro, D L and Shin, J (2010) Networking abroad: a process model of how expatriates form support ties to facilitate adjustment, *Academy of Management Review*, 35 (3), pp 434–54

Haslberger, A and Brewster, C (2009) Capital gains: expatriate adjustment and the psychological contract in international careers, *Human Resource Management*, 48 (3), pp 379–97

Kim, J and Froese, J (2012) Expatriate willingness in Asia: the importance of host-country characteristics and employees' role commitments, *International Journal of Human Resource Management*, 23 (16), pp 3414–33

Kramer, M L and Wayne, S J (2004) An examination of perceived organizational support as a multidimensional construct in the context of an expatriate assignment, *Journal of Management*, 30, pp 209–37

Leblanc, B (2001) European competitiveness – some guidelines for companies, in (ed) M H Albrecht, *International HRM*, Oxford, Blackwell

Lee, L and Donohue, R (2012) The construction and validation of a measure of expatriate job performance, *International Journal of Human Resource Management*, 23 (6), pp 1197–215

Mol, S T, Born, M P, Willemsen, M E, Henk, T V and Derous, E (2009) When selection ratios are high: predicting the expatriation willingness of prospective entry-level job applicants, *Human Performance*, 22, pp 111–29

Pinto, L H, Cabral-Cardoso, C and Werther, W B (2012) Compelled to go abroad: motives and outcomes of international assignments, *International Journal of Human Resource Management*, **23** (11), pp 2295–314

Solomon, C M (1995) Success abroad depends on more than just job skills, *Personnel Journal*, **73** (4), pp 51–54

Sparrow, P, Brewster, C and Harris, H (2004) *Globalizing Human Resource Management*, London, Routledge

Sparrow, P, Scullion, H and Farndale, E (2011) Global talent management: new roles for the corporate HR function? in (eds) H Scullion and D G Collings, *Global Talent Management, London*, Routledge, pp 40–55

Stroh, L K, Black, J S, Mendenhall, M E and Gregersob, H B (2005), *International Assignments: An integration of strategy, research and practice*, Mahwah NJ, Lawrence Erlbaum Associates

Tarique, I and Caligiri, P (1995) Training and development of international staff, in (eds) A W Herzorg and J V Ruyssevelde, *International Human Resource Management*, London, Sage Publications

Wu, P D and Ang, S H (2011) The impact of expatriate supporting practices and cultural intelligence on cross-cultural adjustment and performance of expatriates in Singapore, *International Journal of Human Resource Management*, **22** (13), pp 2683–702

PART XIII

HRM practices

Introduction

This part deals with:

- HR systems that are computer-based processes for managing HRM and providing HR information, also known as e-HRM.

- HR practices that meet employment law requirements.

61
HR information systems

LEARNING OUTCOMES

On completing this chapter you should be able to define these key concepts. You should also know about:

- Reasons for using an HRIS
- Functions of an HRIS

- Features of an HRIS
- Introducing an HRIS

Introduction

An HR information system (HRIS) is a computer-based information system for managing the administration of HR processes and procedures. 'E-HRM' is an alternative term for the use of computer technology within the HR function. Parry and Tyson (2011: 335) defined an HRIS as:

'A way of implementing HR strategies, policies and practices in organizations through a conscious and directed support of and/or with the full use of web technology-based channels.' They listed five goals for e-HRM: efficiency, service delivery, strategic orientation, manager empowerment and standardization (ibid: 335).

Reasons for introducing an HRIS

The CIPD (2007) survey established that the top 10 reasons for introducing an HRIS were:

- to improve the quality of information available;
- to reduce administrative burden on the HR department;
- to improve speed at which information is available;
- to improve flexibility of information to support business planning;
- to improve services to employees;
- to produce HR metrics;
- to aid human capital reporting;
- to improve productivity;
- to reduce operational costs;
- to manage people's working time more effectively.

The functions of an HRIS

The functions that an HRIS can perform (its 'functionality') are set out below. They cover almost every aspect of HRM.

The functions that an HRIS can perform

- absence recording and management;
- employee records;
- employee surveys;
- employee turnover analysis;
- e-learning;
- equal opportunity modelling;
- expenses;
- HR analytics;
- HR planning and forecasting;
- job evaluation;
- knowledge management;
- intranet;
- manage diversity;
- manager and employee self-service;
- metrics and human capital reporting;
- online recruitment;
- online performance management systems and 360-degree feedback;
- payroll administration;
- pay reviews;
- pensions and benefits administration;
- social enterprise networks.

The 2007 CIPD survey found that the 10 most popular uses to which respondents put their HRIS in descending order were:

- absence management;
- training and development;
- rewards;
- managing diversity;
- recruitment and selection;
- other (usually payroll);
- appraisal/performance management;
- HR planning;
- knowledge management;
- expenses.

Features of an HRIS

The features of particular interest in an HRIS system are the use of traditional software packages, cloud computing, enterprise resource planning systems (ERPs), the intranet, enterprise social networks, integration and provisions for self-service.

Traditional software packages

The traditional and still most typical approach is to buy software modules from an external supplier to run in-house applications such as personal records, absence management or payroll. 'Application suites' can be purchased which cover a linked set of modules. There is a choice between buying a 'vanilla system' (ie an 'off-the-shelf' system without any upgrades) or customizing the supplier's system to meet specified business requirements. Extensive customization can make future upgrades problematic and expensive, so it is important to limit it to what is absolutely necessary.

The choice of a supplier should be made as follows:

- research HR software market through trade exhibitions and publications;
- review HR processes and existing systems;
- produce a specification of system requirements;
- send an invitation to tender to several suppliers;
- invite suppliers to demonstrate their products;
- obtain references from existing customers, including site visits;
- analyse and score the product against the specification.

However, organizations are increasingly moving into cloud computing.

Cloud computing

Cloud computing involves providing on-demand shared computing resources and information. Data is stored and processed in separate data centres. Services such as servers, storage and applications are delivered to an organization's computers and devices through the internet. It can replace local arrangements using bought-in software packages.

Cloud computing can be provided by a SaaS (software-as-a-service) system – an on-demand software delivery model in which users are charged for accessing and managing HR IT provision via a network. The system stores and processes data in a standardized form which can then be configured for use in the organization.

The advantages of cloud computing are high computing power – the ability to store and process masses of data – accessibility and, potentially, lower costs. A further benefit provided by using the Cloud is that it is highly adaptive and changes can be made very quickly, although it may be costly to do so.

Integration

In a traditional in-house arrangement, enterprise resource planning (ERP) systems can be used to integrate all data processing processes of an organization into a unified system with the same database. HR systems are not frequently integrated to this extent although they often link payroll administration with other HR functions. Integration of the HR system with IT systems in the wider organization so that they can 'talk to one another' will enable the more effective management of HR data. However, many HR functions retain stand-alone systems, because they believe integration would compromise their own system, and are concerned about potential lack of confidentiality and the cost and perceived risks involved.

Intranet

An intranet system is one where computer terminals are linked so that they can share information within an organization or within part of an organization. The scope of the information that can be shared across terminals can be limited to preserve confidentiality and this security can be enhanced by using passwords. HR intranet systems can be used for purposes such as updating personal details, applications for internal jobs online, requests for training, access to e-learning, administration of queries and communications.

Enterprise social networks

Enterprise social networks (such as those provided by Yammer, Chatter and Jive) function in the same way as social networks such as Facebook. They allow people to post opinions, join in discussions and respond to questions, and are used as employee voice channels and to support social learning.

Self-service

A human resource self-service system (HRSS) allows managers and employees access to information and the facility to interact with the system to input information or make choices of their own. This can operate through an HR portal (a site that functions as a point of access to information on the intranet), which may be specially designed to produce a brand image of the HR function. This is sometimes referred to as a 'business-to-employees' (B2E) portal.

For managers, self-service means that they can access information immediately. This might be HR metrics in such areas as absenteeism, personal details, performance management data, learning and development progress, and pay (as a basis for pay reviews). They can also input data on their staff. This facilitates the devolution of responsibility to line managers and reduces the administrative burden on HR.

Employees can also access information, input data about themselves, request training and apply for jobs online.

E-HRM achievements

Research conducted by Parry and Tyson (2011) in 10 case study organizations established that efficiency goals were achieved by most of them. Service delivery improvements were generally achieved, supporting improved effectiveness of the HR function. The findings showed that a potential goal for e-HRM is to standardize operational procedures across an organization, but they noted that: 'The realization of improved efficiency and effectiveness is dependent on the design and implementation of the system, and increased effectiveness and involvement in delivering the business strategy may depend on appropriate redeployment and up-skilling of HR staff' (ibid: 352).

Below are some case studies, as reported by Parry and Tyson (2011: 341).

CASE STUDIES

AVISA

An Oracle HR system is used with extensive management self-service for performing salary changes, cost centre and allowance changes, processing leavers, updating and reporting absence, processing overtime payments and comparing performance ratings. Employee self-service is available to maintain personal details, look at payslips, request holidays and record absence. In addition, an Ask-Jeeves system to answer generic HR queries has been introduced.

BOC

BOC has used a SAP HR system since 1999 to hold HR data and allow managers to access this data via their desktop to record absence and enter bonus ratings and salary review details. The system drove the payroll process. An e-recruitment system was introduced in 2003 with a recruitment database that sat centrally and was connected to a number of different career centres. The HR intranet has also recently been relaunched.

Marks & Spencer

The range of technological HRM tools includes a main HRIS plus payroll and personnel data, pensions and absence management systems, and an HR portal for information on policies and practices.

Key learning points: HR information systems

Reasons for using an HRIS

The top five reasons are (CIPD, 2007):

- to improve quality of information available;
- to reduce administrative burden on the HR department;
- to improve speed at which information is available;
- to improve flexibility of information to support business planning;
- to improve services to employees.

Functions of an HRIS

Top five uses of an HRIS (CIPD, 2007):

- absence management;
- training and development;
- rewards;
- managing diversity;
- recruitment and selection.

Features of an HRIS

The features of particular interest in an HRIS system are:

- the use of traditional software packages;
- the use of cloud computing;
- integration with other IT systems in the organization;
- use of the intranet;
- use of internal social networks;
- provisions for self-service.

References

CIPD (2007) *HR and Technology: Impact and advantages*, London, CIPD

Parry, E and Tyson, S (2011) Desired goals and actual outcomes of e-HRM, *Human Resource Management Journal*, **21** (3), pp 335–54

62
Employment law

LEARNING OUTCOMES

On completing this chapter you should be able to define these key concepts. You should also know about:

- The objectives of employment law
- The major ways in which the law protects workers
- The ways that employment law is enforced
- The impact of employment law on HRM practice

Introduction

The employment relationship is subject to a great deal of regulation in all industrialized countries and is increasingly a feature of HRM practice in developing economies too. While the details and extent of regulatory protection vary from country to country, as well as the enforcement mechanisms, the aims of employment legislation are remarkably similar (Ashiagbor 2005, Slattery and Broadbent, 2013). It is also the case that in all countries the trend in recent years has been towards greater levels of employment regulation, not least due to the actions of supranational bodies such as the International Labour

Organization (ILO) and the European Union (EU) which have persistently promoted higher standards of employment practice underpinned by law.

For employers in the UK, the adjustment required by the introduction of extensive employment law has often been problematic, as the UK's labour market was historically one of the least regulated in the world. There thus remains a strong tendency for employers and their representatives to resist the introduction of new regulation and to campaign for a reduction in the existing 'regulatory burden' on the grounds that it both deters organizations from taking on new staff, while also making the UK economy as a whole less globally competitive than it would otherwise be. Despite these misgivings, it is clear that employment law is here to stay and that it makes good business sense to comply with its requirements. Most employers have to face employment tribunal claims from time to time and most HR professionals have to deal with their consequences on a fairly regular basis.

The purpose of employment law

There has never been any grand strategy behind the construction of modern employment law. Instead, it has been built up steadily over 50 years, step by step, new laws being introduced in response to political pressure of one kind or another, and only rarely being repealed. Sometimes the impetus for new regulation has come from European institutions, such as the transfer of undertakings regulations which protect employees' terms and conditions when their organizations are acquired by others, outsourced or merged. On other occasions, governments have used employment law to increase their popularity and try to ensure re-election. A good example was the introduction by the government of substantially improved maternity and paternity rights in April 2015 just ahead of the general election. New employment law can be introduced in response to events (eg stricter laws on industrial action following major strikes) or campaigns by trade unions and other groups (eg the National Minimum Wage and disability discrimination laws).

Despite this apparent lack of coherence in its development, it is nonetheless possible to identify a number of key aims that governments hope to achieve by regulating the labour market. In 2013, the UK government issued a progress report on its programme of employment regulation in which three distinct objectives were set out (DBIS 2013a). Here ministers stated that they sought to create a labour market that was:

- flexible – encouraging job creation and making it easy for people to stay in work and find work;
- effective – enabling employers to manage staff productivity; and
- fair – employers competing on a level playing field and workers benefiting from core employment protections.

The idea of a level playing field is particularly important in the context of European Union employment regulation. The aim here is to help ensure that defined minimum standards are observed across all member states so that no one country is able to undercut its labour costs in order to steal an unfair competitive march on the others.

In practice, most employment law exists to protect employees from unjust exploitation or unfair treatment by their employers. It is necessary because, for the vast majority of workers, the employment relationship is very unequal in terms of the power that each side is able to exercise over the other. Employers are vastly more powerful, making it relatively easy for them to abuse that power by treating their employees poorly, by dismissing them or discriminating against them for no good reason, underpaying and overworking them, or causing them to risk their health, safety and welfare while at work. In the early and middle years of the 20th century, trade unions tended to offer employees a much greater level of protection than they are now able to, and so to a considerable extent the state has had to step in to provide protection of the kind that strong unions with high levels of membership once were able to provide.

There are, however, two major further reasons behind employment regulation in today's economic context. First, governments have sought to use employment law to promote good practice in the employment relationship. Ministers are always mindful of the presence of skill shortages and of the presence in our labour market of large numbers of people (typically 20 per cent) who are economically inactive despite being of working age. One aim is to encourage people off welfare and into work; another is to encourage people who could work but who choose not to (eg early retirees) to put their skills at the disposal of the economy. Governments have also wanted to make their countries an attractive destination for highly skilled migrants from overseas who might otherwise choose to settle elsewhere. Ensuring that employers operate fairly and promoting partnership approaches both serve to help meet these objectives. Second, governments are keen to promote flexibility and competition in the labour market. They want to ensure that employees are free to leave their employment and join another organization easily and that they are not prevented from working because of domestic commitments. They also want to ensure that when people persistently perform their jobs poorly or when their jobs are genuinely redundant, employers are able to terminate their contracts swiftly and cheaply. Above all, ministers want to avoid a situation in which employers are deterred from creating new jobs due to fear of employment legislation. There is thus always a need to balance legitimate protection of employees' rights with the need of employers to hire and fire with relative ease.

Employment law also incorporates the regulation of trade unions. And here too the aim is to achieve a balance between the need to protect the right of all workers to form and join trade unions and the need to ensure that trade unions do not become so powerful as to threaten the economic interests of the majority of people. Finding this balance has always been difficult and controversial, and the position varies considerably from country to country. In the UK, for example, our law makes it very difficult for an employer to dismiss someone for a trade union reason or to prevent a union from organizing a strike which its members have voted for in sufficient numbers. On the other hand, the way that unions are governed and the extent to which they can gain power over an employer are limited very effectively by the law.

How are these objectives achieved?

Over many decades, but particularly in more recent years, a large body of employment regulation has been built up in order to achieve the purposes set out above. The precise mechanisms vary a great deal internationally, but there is now considerable convergence across Europe, and we are increasingly seeing examples of similar types of regulation being established in newly industrialized countries. China, for example, introduced three major pieces of new employment regulation in 2008 which aimed both to promote employment and protect the rights of employees (Lee Cooke 2012:156–79). Employment law in the UK is in many respects typical in terms of its scope and impact. From an employer perspective, our regulation is rather less restrictive than that of some jurisdictions (eg France and the Netherlands), but more restrictive than that of others (eg the United States and Australia). In the UK, the objectives of employment regulation are largely met through several distinct bodies of well-established legislation, a number of which have a European origin. The most significant are the following:

Discrimination law

The underpinning principle here is that it is unlawful to cause a detriment to a worker, a job applicant or someone an organization has employed in the past. The term 'detriment' is widely defined to include financial loss, loss of opportunity or any significant injury to someone's dignity or feelings. Much of the relevant law has now been consolidated and, to an extent, harmonized in the Equality Act 2010, which is the main source of law that gives discrimination rights to people who have certain 'protected characteristics', namely, sex, sexual orientation, race, ethnicity, national origin, disability, religion or belief, pregnancy, marital status and age. There are four headings under which an employer's actions can be challenged in court:

- direct discrimination (eg failing to promote a woman because she is a woman);
- indirect discrimination (eg requiring devout employees to work on holy days);
- victimization (eg refusing to give a reference to a former employee who brought a race discrimination claim against the organization);
- harassment (eg teasing someone about their sexual orientation).

The defences available to employers are limited. Direct discrimination and victimization on most grounds are almost always unlawful, although in the cases of discrimination on grounds of disability and age the former can be defended where there is a good, genuine business reason. Direct discrimination is also lawful when the nature of a job requires that it is reserved for members of one sex (eg acting and modelling jobs) or a particular race (eg waiters in ethnic restaurants) or religion (eg clerical roles). Indirect discrimination occurs when an organization has a rule or policy in place which has the effect of causing a disadvantage to one group or another, even though this may be entirely unintentional. This can be defended when the rule can be shown to be 'a proportionate means of achieving a legitimate aim', in other words, an objective business need. Harassment can be defended when an incident occurs outside work and when an employer can show that it:

- acted swiftly and appropriately when it received a complaint; and

- had taken all reasonable steps to prevent such an incident from occurring.

Other statutes give a measure of protection from discrimination to ex-offenders, whistle-blowers, fixed-term employees, part-time workers, agency workers, trade union members and people who do not wish to join a trade union. But in each case the law operates rather differently than is the case for the protected characteristics covered by the Equality Act.

In the UK there are only very limited numbers of situations in which positive discrimination or affirmative action is permitted. In this respect our law varies from that of many jurisdictions in which employers are obliged to take positive steps to improve the position of disadvantaged groups. It is common in many EU countries, for example, for companies to be required to appoint a minimum number of women to senior board positions. Elsewhere in the world, quota systems apply for the employment of different racial or ethnic groups in order to assure fairness, particularly in the public sector. In practice, this means that some jobs are reserved for members of a particular racial origin or caste (Klarsfeld *et al* 2012).

Equal pay law

The Equal Pay Act (1970) ended the previously common practice of employers paying men and women different amounts of money for doing jobs that were either the same or very similar. It became unlawful to operate separate male and female pay scales or to pay men and women differently for doing jobs that should have been paid at the same grade when a job evaluation system was in operation. Later, in 1983, after the UK joined the European Union, it became possible for employees to pursue claims in the Employment Tribunal when they believed that their work, despite being different in nature from that of a comparator of the opposite sex, was nonetheless of 'equal value'. The relevant law is now all found in the Equality Act 2010. It applies equally to men and to women, but in practice, the large majority of cases are brought by women using men as their comparators.

Aside from these three headings under which a claim can be brought (ie like work, work that has been rated as equivalent and work of equal value), the Equality Act sets out the major defences that are available to employers. The most widely deployed is known as the 'material factor defence', which involves satisfying the tribunal that the difference in the level of payment between the claimant and her comparator is genuinely explained by factors that have nothing to do with gender. The most common examples are situations in which a man works longer hours or takes on a less desirable shift pattern than the woman and those in which there are marked differences in relative levels of skill, performance or experience. It is also common for employers to pay more to people who have achieved certain formal qualifications and also to pay London-based employees more than those living elsewhere in the UK. These are both accepted as 'material factors', provided that they genuinely explain the difference in pay. The same is true of situations in which a group of employees enjoys a higher level of 'protected pay' following a merger or acquisition that brings together two groups of people who were previously employed by different employers.

Partly, if not largely as a result of this law, the 'gender pay gap' between male and female workers in the UK has declined from 37 per cent in the early 1970s to around 18 per cent today, depending on how it is measured. The reasons for its persistence despite the presence of equal pay law are widely debated, a number of distinct and plausible explanations having been put forward (see Rubery and Grimshaw, 2014). One possibility is that it simply arises from the requirement that the law places on women to challenge their employers either by threatening or actually taking legal action. This is a difficult path for any employee to take and one which, quite understandably, most are reluctant to embark on. Moreover, in many workplaces, quite strict confidentiality rules have the effect of deterring people from telling their colleagues about the true level of their earnings. As a result, even if someone was willing to challenge unequal payments between men and women, their ability to do so effectively has been seriously curtailed.

Important reforms aimed at reducing this barrier and putting pressure on employers to act proactively with respect to equalizing pay are going to be phased in over a number of years after 2016. These will eventually require all organizations employing more than 250 people to undertake equal pay audits and to publish details of any gender pay gap among their workers on their website. Not only will this make it much harder for employers to hide details of any gender pay gap that they operate, but may in many cases simply serve to alert them when they are paying unlawfully in a manner which is legally difficult to justify. The new law is thus likely to have the effect of further reducing the pay gap between men and women.

Dismissal law

Former employees who have completed more than two years' service are entitled to seek compensation or reinstatement when they have been unfairly dismissed. This means that they have either been sacked for an unfair reason (eg pregnancy, refusal to work in unsafe conditions) or for a lawful reason (eg misconduct, incapability, redundancy) but in an unreasonable manner. In practice, the large majority of cases concern the manner in which someone has been dismissed, and here the law is very helpful from an employer's point of view. The test used to judge 'reasonableness' is known as 'the band of reasonable responses test'. When applying this, a tribunal is required to refrain from judging the matter with reference to what the judge would have done in similar circumstances, or even from making a general judgement as to what most people would consider 'reasonable'. Instead, the requirement is to ask the question: Could the employer's actions in dismissing the employee be said to have been reasonable?

This means that dismissals which 90 per cent of people would consider to have been unreasonable can nonetheless be found to have been reasonable in law, simply because a case for their reasonableness can be put. In practice, this means that many dismissals fall into the 'harsh but fair' category.

That said, in order to be lawful it is essential that any dismissal is managed in accordance with a fair procedure. In a case of poor work performance this means that an employee must be invited to a formal meeting, given a formal warning in writing, allowed an opportunity to appeal, given a reasonable opportunity to improve and, only then, dismissed following a further formal meeting with a right to appeal. Formal warnings are also required in cases of long-term ill health (where disability discrimination law can also be highly relevant) and relatively minor acts of misconduct. Only when an employee is guilty of gross misconduct such as stealing, fighting or serious insubordination, is an employer entitled to dismiss summarily without notice. Here too, though, a fair procedure must always be followed, the employee being given every opportunity to defend themselves and to appeal the dismissal. A further requirement is that employees facing hearings at which they may be dismissed must always be allowed to be accompanied by a work colleague and represented by a trade union official.

Aside from unfair dismissal, UK law provides that employees cannot be wrongfully dismissed or constructively dismissed. Wrongful dismissals occur when the manner of a dismissal breaches the contract of employment. It occurs most commonly when an employee's contract stipulates a notice period which is not then observed when notice is given. So if someone with the right to eight weeks' notice is dismissed with one week's notice, they would be able to bring a claim for compensation.

Constructive dismissals are actually resignations. The law in this area was introduced alongside unfair dismissal law in 1971 in order to prevent employers from circumventing the new rights by treating their employees so badly that they resigned without needing to be dismissed. The test that is now used is contractual. This means that an employee resigns in response to (and soon after) their employer has breached their contract. In such circumstances, the tribunals treat the incident as if it were a dismissal and order that appropriate compensation is paid. Importantly, relevant breaches of contract can involve either express or implied terms.

Express terms are those that the parties agree at the time they first form their relationship. So, for example, if an employer was to cut someone's contractual pay and the employee was to resign in protest, that would generally constitute a constructive dismissal. Implied terms are many and varied, but are deemed to be present in every contract. The most significant is the 'duty to maintain a relationship of mutual trust and confidence'. If that is broken by an employer, as happens, for example, in cases of serious bullying at work, the employee is entitled to resign and claim constructive dismissal.

Health and safety law

UK health and safety law can be divided into two very distinct parts. On the one hand, we have the criminal law which is enforced by health and safety inspectors employed by local authorities and, at national level, by the Health and Safety Executive (HSE). On the other hand, we have personal injury law under which a worker who suffers an injury at work or falls ill as a result of their work can sue their employer for damages.

Health and safety inspectors carry out routine inspections of employers' premises without warning, following which they can issue improvement notices requiring that changes are made to operations, or prohibition notices which prevent the employer from using a piece of equipment or operating a system until recommended changes have been made. In either case, a failure to make the required changes can result in a criminal prosecution. Such prosecutions are also brought when an employer's negligence or recklessness leads either to a death or a serious injury. In the most serious cases, charges of corporate manslaughter can be brought against an organization.

Most personal injury claims also involve demonstrating that an employer or a fellow employee has acted negligently. Importantly, the doctrine of vicarious liability applies here, meaning that employers are deemed to be legally responsible for the actions of their employees while at work. So if an accident is caused as a result of a fellow employee's negligence, the injured person brings the case against the employer rather than the colleague whose fault the accident was. There are a number of defences that employers can deploy when faced with personal injury claims. The most common involves satisfying the court that the accident

'was not reasonably foreseeable'. In practice, this requires an employer to have carried out formal risk assessments and to have recorded these. Managers then need to show that the injury was sustained in spite of the fact that the risks were low, that full training had been provided and that safe systems of work were always observed.

In recent years, many claims of this kind have related to mental breakdowns brought about through stressful work situations. These are not at all easy for workers to win because unless they have suffered two breakdowns, the second after returning to work, it is difficult to show that an excessive workload was the main trigger for the illness.

Hours and wages

A variety of laws regulate working time and the amount of money that workers should be paid. The most important statute covering hours of work is the Working Time Regulations 1998. This is European law which has always been controversial in the UK, where we have a tradition of working long hours and claiming overtime payments in return. The key right here is not to be required to work in excess of 48 hours a week. However, in practice, many employees continue to do so. This is partly because actually the law only limits working time to 48 hours averaged over 17 weeks. So employers can lawfully require their staff to work many more hours in particularly busy weeks, provided on average over any 17-week period the 48-hour rule is observed. In the UK there is also an opt-out system in place, under which employees can remove themselves from the right not to work more than 48 hours a week. This is common because employers can lawfully require new starters to sign opt-out agreements as a condition of being offered a job. There is also a right to opt back in to the regulations without suffering any detriment, but this is not widely known. The Working Time Regulations also provide that minimum rest breaks are provided during a day's work and between shifts. Moreover, they give all workers the right to take 28 days' paid holiday a year (pro rata for part-timers) comprising eight bank holidays and 20 further days' statutory annual leave.

The National Minimum Wage regulations also date from 1998. These require that all workers are paid a minimum amount for every hour that they work, rates being set by the government each year after consulting with the Low Pay Commission. From October 2015, the full adult rate which applies to the vast majority of people is £6.70. This will apply until October 2016 when the rate will rise again. In addition, there is a lower rate for younger workers and workers in training (£5.30 in 2015–16), a youth rate for 16- and 17-year-olds (£3.87) and an apprentice rate (£3.30). Failure to pay the NMW is not only a civil offence which can result in any back pay that is owed being paid to a claimant, but also a criminal offence which can result in large fines being paid as well. From April 2016, the National Minimum Wage will only apply to people aged under 25. Older workers will instead be entitled to receive a higher 'National Living Wage' which will be set at £7.20 an hour, rising to at least £9 an hour by 2020.

Another significant area of employment law concerns the situations in which an employer can and cannot make deductions from a worker's pay packet. These are fairly limited, in most cases requiring prior consent on the part of an employee (eg trade union dues), authorization via statute (eg tax) or a court order (eg in order to pay a fine). Importantly, this means that as a rule, employers cannot deduct wages as part of a disciplinary process. If suspended from work for any reason, an employee must continue to be paid while a matter is investigated. Moreover, if found to have committed an act of misconduct, the employer cannot lawfully fine a worker by way of a punishment.

Family-friendly employment law

In recent years, it is in the area of family-friendly employment rights that the biggest changes in regulations have been made. Every two or three years since the mid-1990s new rights have been introduced, while existing rights have been extended. This step-by-step approach has disguised the radical improvement in employment rights which has occurred over time. The major family-friendly rights that applied in 2016 were as follows for most employees:

- up to one year of shared parental, maternity or adoptive leave;
- nine months of shared parental, maternity or adoptive pay;
- the right to paid time off to attend ante-natal appointments;
- two weeks' statutory paternity leave;
- the right to time off to deal with family emergencies;
- 18 weeks' unpaid parental leave during the first five years of a child's life;
- the right to request a change of contract in order to work more flexibly.

Until April 2014, this last right only applied to employees with children. Since April 2014, all employees with six months' service can request flexible working. Employers can only lawfully turn down a request when one of eight straightforward business reasons apply, and must in any event handle requests reasonably.

In 2015, major reforms were introduced allowing parents to opt for 'shared parental leave' in place of established maternity leave. Under such an arrangement, the allocation of paid and unpaid leave previously available only to mothers can now be shared by both parents. Importantly, this can now be taken concurrently, allowing both a new mother and father to take six months' leave together when their new baby is born. Further extensions of family-friendly employment rights are planned for the future, including a right for grandparents to share some of the 'parental leave' currently allocated to fathers and mothers.

How is employment law enforced?

It is in the area of enforcement and remedies that employment law varies most from country to country (Slattery and Broadbent, 2013). In many countries, including Australia, Germany, India and Japan, specialized employment tribunals are charged with deciding cases that are brought by aggrieved employees or ex-employees who believe that an employer has treated them in an unlawful manner. Sometimes these institutions take an arbitration approach, seeking to promote a settlement to the dispute between the parties. In other jurisdictions, tribunals are more clearly part of a court system, simply deciding cases in favour of one party or the other after hearing evidence. Elsewhere, notably in the United States, cases are heard by standard civil courts with no specialist brief in the field of employment. A rather different type of system operates in countries where the criminal law plays a much greater role in employment matters. Here local labour officials or inspectors have a central place in the administration of the law. In some jurisdictions, such as the Netherlands, employers are obliged to seek their approval before dismissing staff. Elsewhere, officials bring criminal prosecutions when they have evidence that an employer has acted unlawfully. In France, for example, even when an employer settles a discrimination claim with an employee, it can still find itself having to defend its actions in the criminal courts.

In the UK, the inspectorate model is used in the enforcement of health and safety law, in matters concerning the illegal employment of overseas migrants and, to an extent, in the enforcement of the National Minimum Wage. But in most areas of employment law criminal sanctions play no role. The onus is overwhelmingly on aggrieved employees and, more commonly, former employees to bring their cases before the civil courts. When a complaint relates to the alleged breach of an employment statute such as unfair dismissal or unlawful discrimination, claimants bring their cases before their local Employment Tribunal. Here the case will either be heard by an Employment Judge sitting alone, or sometimes by a panel of three in which the judge is assisted by two lay members who have industrial experience. In most cases the burden of proof lies with the claimant (ie the person bringing the case), but on some questions of law it can reverse so that the respondent (ie the employer) must satisfy the tribunal that it did not act unlawfully as is alleged. Employment tribunals then decide cases 'on the balance of probabilities', having weighed the evidence that is presented to them by each party or its representatives.

Employment tribunals operate in a relatively informal way. Anyone can carry out the duty of representing a party, the role being in no way restricted to professional lawyers. Sometimes claimants represent themselves or are represented by a family member or a friend. Trade union officials increasingly carry out this kind of work too. Respondents are more likely to employ lawyers to represent them, but sometimes represent themselves too. As a result, the Employment Tribunal provides a relatively swift and low-cost forum in which a case can be decided. Appeals on questions of law can be taken to the Employment Appeals Tribunal and, subsequently, on to the Court of Appeal, Supreme Court and, if appropriate, the European Court of Justice. But appealing a case is usually more costly. Since 2013, UK claimants whose income is above a set threshold have been obliged to pay fees to the Employment Tribunal when lodging their claims. Despite the fact that these fees are refunded when claimants win their cases, the impact of their introduction has been to reduce the number of claims being brought very significantly.

Employment tribunals do not hear cases that relate to breaches of contract or alleged committing of torts such as negligence. So people wanting to pursue wrongful dismissal cases or personal injury claims must instead take their case to the County Court or High Court. In practice, this requires them to hire lawyers and to be represented by a barrister. Costs are awarded against losing parties too, making this a riskier and potentially expensive route to take.

In practice, awards against losing respondents are rarely very high. Ahead of a case, solicitors representing claimants often set out a schedule of losses which is a good deal inflated and does not realistically represent the actual sum that would be won following a successful hearing in court. This is done in a bid to frighten unwary employers into settling the case for a higher sum than they need to in order to avoid the hassle of defending the case in court. The truth, according to the annual statistics published by the Employment Tribunal Service, is that the sums awarded are typically much lower than claimants might in theory hope to gain (see Table 62.1).

TABLE 62.1 Median awards made in different types of employment tribunal case 2011–12

Unfair dismissal	£6,955
Race discrimination	£8,025
Sex discrimination	£13,500
Disability discrimination	£8,646
Religious discrimination	£1,080
Sexual orientation discrimination	£13,505
Age discrimination	£6,000

(**SOURCE**: ETS Annual Report 2015)

HRM and employment law

The extent to which employment law influences the way that people are managed in organizations varies considerably. Larger corporations with high-profile reputations to defend have a tendency to settle claims ahead of any tribunal hearing in order to avoid negative publicity in the media. The estimated costs associated with defending a claim also typically dwarf the size of the award that the claimant can hope to win. So rather than tie up days of management time defending a case, claimants are simply paid off on condition that they sign a settlement agreement which precludes them from publicizing the case (CBI, 2012: 29). The advantage of such a policy is that it effectively enables managers to run their organizations without taking too much notice of the expectations of employment law. The disadvantage, of course, is that it encourages people whose claims are not strong in law to bring cases in any event in the hope of securing a pay-out.

A very different approach is typically taken in the public and third sectors where considerable efforts are made to comply with employment legislation. Here HR departments often gain a reputation for being over cautious in the way that they handle employee grievances, so great is their wish to avoid having to defend a case in the Employment Tribunal. This means that, in practice, the vast majority of tribunal hearings involve smaller private sector enterprises that neither have the resources available to pay people off as a matter of routine, nor to ensure that they are complying with the requirements of the law. Managers in smaller enterprises also tend to prefer an informal management style which can make legal challenges more likely (DBIS, 2013b).

Published evidence suggests that in practice, employment law has a major impact on the way that HR managers approach their work. As long ago as 2002, when the volume of employment legislation was a good deal less than it is now, the Chartered Institute of Personnel and Development established that two-thirds of HR specialists were spending in excess of 20 per cent of their time 'dealing with employment law issues', while a quarter reported that over 40 per cent of their working days were being spent in this way (CIPD, 2002). A further CIPD survey of HR professionals carried out five years later reported that 40 per cent of respondents rated 'securing compliance with employment regulations' as one of their top five objectives, while 90 per cent saw employment regulation as likely to become more important for their organizations in the future (CIPD 2007). These findings are unsurprising when it is considered that around half a million people are dismissed for one reason or another in the UK each year (DBIS 2012: 23).

Surveys of employer opinion regularly report that managers find the volume of employment regulation that they have to comply with to be burdensome, but it is not generally the principles that cause them to complain. The aims of the law are generally supported by employers. What they dislike is its complexity and the time that they are obliged to devote to keeping up with changes (CIPD 2005). As a result, particularly in the case of smaller firms, managers have a strong tendency to worry that they may be found not to be complying with all expectations of the law. It is the fear of the tribunal that causes them to consider employment law to be a burden as much as their personal experience (DBIS, 2013b).

In fact, the chances that any job applicant, employee or former employee will win a claim against an employer are slim. Employers end up winning four out of five of the claims that are heard in the UK employment tribunals, while over 30 per cent of those that are lodged are withdrawn without a settlement before the case ever comes to court. Avoiding tribunal claims which have any serious prospect of winning is thus not at all difficult. It is really just a question of adhering to the major principles of the law, such as paying staff the National Minimum Wage and avoiding unlawful discrimination, while also taking care to handle dismissals in a procedurally fair manner. Moreover, in 90 per cent of situations that arise in the workplace, there is no need for managers to pay for legal advice. Free guidance is available on numerous websites, including the government's own employment web-pages (**www.gov.uk/browse/employing-people**) and those provided by the Advisory, Conciliation and Arbitration Service (ACAS) (**www.acas.org.uk/index.aspx?articleid=1339**). ACAS also provide a free, confidential telephone helpline staffed by advisers who give excellent advice about all employment law issues.

CASE STUDIES

Jenkins v Legoland Windsor Park Ltd (2003)

Mr Jenkins was employed at the Legoland theme park in Windsor Great Park as an 'attractions team leader'. Due to a motorbike accident he had suffered at the age of 16, Mr Jenkins' left arm was very seriously injured. This required him to use a sling at all times. In March 2001, the company held a ceremony at which long service awards were given to all employees who had completed over three years' service. Mr Jenkins was one of the 58 employees who received awards at this ceremony. Each award took the form of a human model made out of Lego. Most of the employees received models which related directly in some way to their work. Cafe staff, for example, were given models of people eating pizzas or drinking coffee, parking attendants got models of people holding traffic cones, and managers got models holding clipboards. Mr Jenkins, however, was presented with a model of a man with his right arm in a sling. The day after the ceremony Mr Jenkins was absent and never returned to work. He was diagnosed by a consultant psychologist as 'suffering from a depressive episode triggered by an insensitive experience at his place of work'. He then brought a disability discrimination claim to the employment tribunal. He argued that he had suffered a detriment as he had been singled out at a presentation ceremony and identified by a wrongly characterized disability. Mr Jenkins won his case in the Employment Appeals Tribunal (EAT), having lost in the tribunal. It was found that he had been subjected to a detriment for a reason related to his disability. The employer had not been unable to objectively justify its actions. He won damages of over £30,000 to compensate him for financial losses and injury to feelings.

West Bromwich Building Society Ltd v Townsend (1983)

A building society branch in Wolverhampton was subjected to a routine health and safety inspection by a local authority environmental health officer called Mr Townsend. Following his inspection, Mr Townsend took the decision to use the branch as a test case and to issue an improvement notice requiring the building society to install 'anti-bandit screens' to protect staff from the possibility of a violent robbery. The notice stated that it was Mr Townsend's opinion that the employer was contravening the Health and Safety at Work Act (HSWA) 1974 by not providing such screens:

The reasons for my said opinion are that staff engaged in the handling of money and in general office duties in the premises are not protected as far as is reasonably practicable from the risk of attack or personal injury from persons frequenting the area of the premises normally open to the general public and I hereby require you to remedy the said contraventions or, as the case may be, the matter occasioning them by September 22nd 1982, in the manner stated in the schedule which forms part of this notice.

The employer appealed against the improvement notice in the employment tribunal. In doing so it made the following points:

1 The building society had considered how it could best protect its employees and included such considerations in risk assessments that were regularly kept under review.

2 The cost of installing protective screens in all its 86 branches would be over £500,000, yet the amount of cash kept on any one of its premises at any one time was only £3,500 maximum.

3 The improvement notice merely stated that it was Mr Townsend's opinion that the building society was in contravention of the HSWA 1974. No particulars were given about which clause in the Act was being contravened and no justification given to back up the general opinion.

4 The improvement notice was not really concerned with bringing about necessary improvements in health and safety at the particular branch concerned. Its real aim was to create a precedent that would apply to all building society branches across the whole country.

The appeal was successful. The tribunal considered that the costs associated with complying with the order would be disproportionate given the level of risk from a health and safety point of view.

Proctor v British Gypsum Ltd (1992)

Mr Proctor was employed as a foreman by the British Gypsum company. He was summarily dismissed from this job after one of his subordinates claimed to have been assaulted by him. In his defence, Mr Proctor presented evidence to show first that he had been provoked, and second that in the past, employees had not been dismissed for rather more serious incidents of fighting and assault. He therefore claimed that the employer had acted unreasonably in summarily dismissing him – on grounds of inconsistency. Moreover, his previous record of conduct had been impeccable. The employer claimed that the other incidents had occurred some time previously and that their policy on such matters had toughened in the years since. They also claimed that

Mr Proctor's position as a foreman made his case materially different. Mr Proctor lost his case. The EAT took the opportunity to set out the circumstances in which consistency/inconsistency is significant. They said that time was significant as no employer could be expected to act consistently with cases that were some years old – management had the right to tighten up in the way that they had. The main purpose of the inconsistency rule was to stop victimization – employees really being picked on and dismissed for other reasons (eg not getting on with their boss).

Each case had to be looked at on its merits and the employers had acted reasonably in expecting higher standards from this man, given his position.

Key learning points: Employment law

The purpose of employment law

The major purpose of employment law is to deter employers from treating their employees unfairly or from exploiting them unjustly. However, governments also use employment regulation to help make work more attractive to people and to promote flexibility in the labour market.

How are these objectives achieved?

In most jurisdictions, employment laws give employees a strong measure of protection from unfair discrimination and unfair dismissal. Regulation also helps ensure that high levels of health and safety practice are observed and that workers are paid reasonably and are not overworked. Family-friendly employment law helps people to achieve an effective work–life balance.

Enforcing employment law

Enforcement is mainly something employees do for themselves by bringing claims to the Employment Tribunal. However, in the field of health and safety, the government employs inspectors to carry out the main enforcement duties.

Employment law and HRM

Published evidence demonstrates that employment law can have a major impact on the way that employers carry out HRM activities. It consumes a great deal of HR professionals' time and is high on their agendas. A variety of good sources of free advice about the expectations of employment law is available to managers.

References

Ashiagbor, D (2005) *The EuropeanEmployment Strategy: Labour market regulation and new governance*, Oxford, Oxford University Press
CBI (2012) *Facing the Future*, Confederation of British Industry
CIPD (2002) *Employment Law: Survey report*, London, Chartered Institute of Personnel and Development
CIPD (2005) *Employment and the law: burden or benefit?* London, Chartered Institute of Personnel and Development

CIPD (2007) *The Changing HR Function. A survey report*, London, Chartered Institute of Personnel and Development

DBIS (2013a) *Employment law 2013: progress on reform*, London, Department for Business, Innovation and Skills

DBIS (2013b) *Employment regulation: employer perceptions and the impact of employment regulation*, London, Department for Business, Innovation and Skills

ETS (2015) *Annual report and statistics*, London, Employment Tribunals Service

Klarsfeld A, Combs, G M, Susaeta, L and Belizon, M (2012) International perspectives on diversity and equal treatment policies and practices, in (eds) C Brewster and W Mayrhofer, *Handbook of Research on Comparative Human Resource Management*, Cheltenham, Edward Elgar

Lee Cooke (2012) *Human Resource Management in China: New trends and practices*, London, Routledge

Rubery, J and Grimshaw, D (2014) The 40-year pursuit of equal pay: a case of constantly moving goalposts, *Cambridge Journal of Economics*, 2014, pp 1–25

Slattery, E and Broadbent, J (2013) *The International Comparative Legal Guide to Employment and Labour Law*, 3rd edn, London, Global Legal Group

PART XIV

HR skills

Introduction

It can be argued that fully fledged HR professionals have to be able to deploy a range of skills supported by knowledge that is wider than that required by any other professional working in organizations. Even if this claim cannot be substantiated, it is incontrovertible that a very wide variety of skills have to be used by HR specialists on a day-to-day basis.

As business partners, they need strategic and business skills. As professionals constantly faced with the need to gain insight into the organizational and business issues they have to address, they need problem-solving, analytical and critical skills. HR professionals need to know about research methodology to understand the contribution of HR research and, increasingly, to take part in research projects. They must be able to analyse and present information on what is happening in their organizations by using statistical skills.

Another major group of skills that HR professionals need to have are those concerned with HRM practices, especially selection interviewing, job and competency analysis, learning and development techniques and negotiating. Then there are the skills they need because they have a complex role to play within their organizations. They are involved in leading change and exercising leadership in their own functions and, indirectly, in their dealings with line managers – providing guidance and advice. They have to exert influence, not just by using the authority of their position but by the effective exercise of skills in persuading managers to agree to innovations or adopt different courses of action in people management. They will be constantly involved in handling people problems and, from time to time, in managing conflict. Politics is a feature of life in organizations and HR people must know how to cope with political situations.

The purpose of this part is to provide guidance on the application of all the skills mentioned, together with any supporting knowledge required.

63
Strategic HRM skills

KEY CONCEPTS AND TERMS

Business model

Business partner

Competitive advantage

LEARNING OUTCOMES

On completing this chapter you should be able to define these key concepts. You should also know about:

- The strategic role of the HR professional
- The strategic skills required
- HR strategic skills as defined by the CIPD

Introduction

HR professionals are constantly being urged to be strategic. This chapter examines what this means and describes the knowledge and skills required.

The strategic role of the HR professional

HR strategic activities support the achievement of the organization's goals and values by aligning HR strategies with business strategies. HR professionals are involved in the development and implementation of forward-looking HR strategies that are integrated with one another. Importantly, they work with their line management colleagues in the continuous formulation and execution of the business strategy.

HR professionals, especially at the highest level, make a strategic contribution that ensures the organization has the quality of skilled and engaged people it needs. Sparrow *et al* (2010: 88) observed that: 'HR must be fully responsive to the strategy and business model of the business. HR is not a rule to itself. It is not "HR for HR", but HR (as broadly defined across the competing stakeholders whom HR has to satisfy) for the business.'

The strategic skills required

HR professionals who act strategically will think about what the organization wants to be and become and what they can do to ensure this happens. They will have insight into the real needs of the business and its people and will take a broad view of where the business is going. They will be capable of seeing 'the big picture', looking beyond the confines of the immediate problems they and the business face to what lies ahead, how these problems can be solved and what they can do to support the efforts of other people. This means that they need business, problem-solving and analytical skills, as described in the next three chapters of this book.

The HR Profession Map, as issued by the CIPD in 2013, sets out what HR professionals do and need to know in the area of 'strategy, insights and solutions'.

HR strategic activities and skills as defined by the CIPD

In general, according to the CIPD (2013: 9), the strategic role of an HR professional involves the development of 'actionable insights and solutions, prioritized and tailored around a deep understanding of business, contextual and organizational understanding'. In particular, the CIPD (ibid: 10) states that the strategic activities of an HR professional include:

- using a range of analytical tools, personal experience and management information to develop an understanding of what's happening in the organization and externally;
- considering the bigger picture at all times, observing connections, and drawing conclusions about the impact of events and activities on each other;
- developing insights about potential opportunities or risks for the organization from experience;
- using insights to identify opportunities, priorities and potential risks;

- developing and implementing HR solutions that address actions emanating from insights, either to mitigate critical risk or capitalize on opportunity.

The CIPD (ibid: 12–13) also states that to carry out these strategic activities the knowledge required by HR professionals should include the following:

- The vision and purpose of the organization and how to build functional alignment (organization design, strategy and plans) to this vision and purpose. Deep understanding of how things really work in the organization and the barriers to change.
- The rationale for current organization structures and espoused values and behaviour frameworks.
- The differentiating capabilities and skills that drive competitive advantage for the organization – how these can be built, bought or developed.
- What the key organization, commercial and value drivers are and how they impact on HR solutions for the business.

HR as an insight-driven discipline

The CIPD (2010: 4) expanded on what it meant by the use of 'insight' as follows:

> The best HR functions understand exactly how their organization in their market facing their specific challenges can respond in a way unique to it. Indeed, in the same way as marketing has become a consumer insight-driven function, so some HR functions are delivering unique organization insight, helping organizations to find new ways of meeting current and future challenges. In these functions, there is a new relationship to data gathering and analysis – generating true insight.

10 things to do if you want to be strategic

1 Exercise insight – understand the business and its competitive environment, what makes it successful and the external and internal political, social, competitive and economic factors that affect its performance.

2 Be aware of the goals of the business and its plans to attain them and understand the business model – 'how it makes money'.

3 Align what you are doing with the organization's business strategy.

4 Know where you are going and how you are going to get there.

5 Remember that formal strategic plans do not guarantee success; it is the implementation of the plans that delivers results.

6 Know how to plan the use of resources to make the best use of business opportunities.

7 Understand how you can contribute to the achievement of the objectives of the key functions in the business and support the strategic activities of your colleagues.

8 Be able to foresee longer-term developments, envisage options and their probable consequences, and select sound courses of action.

9 Rise above the day-to-day detail and see the broad picture.

10 Challenge the status quo.

Key learning points: Strategic HRM skills

The strategic role of the HR professional

HR strategic activities support the achievement of the organization's goals and values by aligning HR strategies to business strategies. HR professionals are involved in the development and implementation of forward-looking HR strategies that are integrated with one another. Importantly, they work with their line management colleagues in the continuous formulation and execution of the business strategy.

The strategic skills required

HR professionals who act strategically will think about what the organization wants to be and become and what they can do to ensure this happens. They will have insight into the real needs of the business and its people and will take a broad view of where the business is going. They will be capable of seeing 'the big picture', looking beyond the confines of the immediate problems they and the business face to what lies ahead, how these problems can be solved and what they can do to support the efforts of other people.

References

CIPD (2010) *CIPD Next Generation*, London, CIPD

CIPD (2013) HR Profession Map [online] http://www.cipd.co.uk/hr-profession-map-download.aspx [accessed 1 April 2013]

Dyer, L and Holder, G W (1988) Strategic human resource management and planning, in (ed) L Dyer, *Human Resource Management: Evolving roles and responsibilities*, Washington, DC, Bureau of National Affairs, pp 1–46

Sparrow, P, Hesketh, A, Hird, M, Marsh, C and Balain, S (2010) Using business model change to tie HR into strategy: reversing the arrow, in (eds) P Sparrow, A Hesketh, M Hird and C Cooper, *Leading HR*, Basingstoke, Palgrave Macmillan, pp 68–89

Tyson, S (1985) Is this the very model of a modern personnel manager?, *Personnel Management*, May, pp 22–25

64
Business skills

LEARNING OUTCOMES

On completing this chapter you should be able to define these key concepts. You should also understand:

- What it means to be business-like
- How profits are classified
- The meaning of profitability and the key profitability ratios
- The purpose of cash management
- Business models

- How to interpret a balance sheet
- The purpose of trading and profit and loss statements
- How budgeting and budgetary control work
- Methods of costing
- Business model innovation

Introduction

HR professionals need to see themselves – and be seen – as business people with particular expertise in people, rather than HR people who happen to work for a business. To make an effective contribution, they must possess business and financial skills. They need to understand what their business model is – how their organization delivers value to its customers and how the business achieves competitive advantage and makes money. They need to understand and be able to use the language of the business and, because this will generally be expressed in monetary terms, they need to appreciate how the financial systems of the business work. They also need to know about the concepts of the business model and business model innovation in order to understand how the business makes money now and intends to do so in the future so that they can do something about it.

Equipped with this knowledge, HR professionals can develop the skills needed to interpret the organization's business or corporate strategies, to contribute to the formulation of those strategies and to develop integrated HR strategies. This requirement was spelt out by Ulrich (1997: 7) when he wrote that: 'HR professionals must know the business which includes a mastery of finance, strategy, marketing, and operations.' Research by the CIPD (2010: 5) led to the following conclusion:

> It is also evident that for some HR functions, they see HR as an applied business discipline first and a people discipline second. The ability to understand the business agenda in a deep way means that they are then able to help the business see how critical objectives can only truly be delivered if the people and cultural issues are fully factored in – insight into what it would take to truly deliver. In these places HR has a real share of voice and credibility... Where HR is grounded in the business and delivering the fundamentals well, then it is able to engage in higher value-adding 'OD' and talent-related activities that speak to the critical challenges faced in that organization.

Business skills

Business skills are required to adopt a business-like approach to management – one that focuses on allocating resources to business opportunities and making the best use of them to achieve the required results. Managers who are business-like understand and act upon:

- the business imperatives of the organization – its mission and its strategic goals;
- the organization's business model – the basis upon which its business is done (how its mission and strategic goals will be achieved);
- the organization's business drivers – the characteristics of the business that move it forward;
- the organization's core competencies – what the business is good at doing;
- the factors that will ensure the effectiveness of its activities including specific issues concerning profitability, productivity, financial budgeting and control, costs and benefits, customer service and operational performance;
- the key performance indicators (KPIs) of the business (the results or outcomes identified as being crucial to the achievement of high performance) that can be used to measure progress towards attaining goals;
- the factors that will ensure that the firm's resources, especially its human resources, create sustained competitive advantage because they are valuable, imperfectly imitable and non-substitutable (the resource-based view).

Financial skills

A business-like approach means using financial skills to know how to analyse and interpret balance sheets, cash flow and trading statements and profit and loss accounts, and to understand and make use of the financial techniques of budgeting and budgetary control, cash budgeting and costing.

Interpreting balance sheets

A balance sheet is a statement on the last day of the accounting period of the company's assets and liabilities and the share capital or the shareholders' investment in the company. Balance sheet analysis assesses the financial strengths and weaknesses of the company, primarily from the point of view of the shareholders and potential investors, but also as part of management's task to exercise proper stewardship over the funds invested in the company and the assets in its care. With the help of balance sheet ratios, the analysis focuses on the balance sheet equation, considers the make-up of the balance sheet in terms of assets and liabilities, and examines the liquidity position (how much cash or easily realizable assets are available) and capital structure.

The balance sheet equation

The balance sheet equation is: Capital + Liabilities = Assets. Capital plus liabilities shows where the money comes from, and assets indicate where the money is now.

Make-up of the balance sheet

The balance sheet contains four major sections:

- *Assets or capital in use*, which is divided into long-term or fixed assets (eg land, buildings and plant) and current or short-term assets, which include bank balances and cash, debtors, stocks of goods and materials and work in progress.

- *Current liabilities*, which are the amounts that will have to be paid within 12 months of the balance sheet date.

- *Net current assets or working capital*, which are current assets less current liabilities. Careful control of working capital lies at the heart of efficient business performance.

- *Sources of capital*, which comprise share capital, reserves including retained profits, and long-term loans.

Liquidity analysis

Liquidity analysis is concerned with the extent to which the organization has an acceptable quantity of cash and easily realizable assets to meet its needs. The analysis may be based on the ratio of current assets (cash, working capital, etc) to current liabilities (the working capital ratio). Too low a ratio may mean that the liquid resources are insufficient to cover short-term payments. Too high a ratio might indicate that there is too much cash or working capital and that they are therefore being badly managed. The working capital ratio is susceptible to 'window dressing', which is the manipulation of the working capital position by accelerating or delaying transactions near the year end.

Liquidity analysis also uses the 'quick ratio' of current assets minus stocks to current liabilities. This concentrates on the more realizable of the current assets and therefore provides a stricter test of liquidity than the working capital ratio. It is therefore called 'the acid test'.

Capital structure analysis

Capital structure analysis examines the overall means by which a company finances its operations, which is partly by the funds of their ordinary shareholders (equity) and partly by loans from banks and other lenders (debt). The ratio of long-term debt to ordinary shareholders' funds indicates 'gearing'. A company is said to be highly geared when it has a high level of loan capital as distinct from equity capital.

Classification of profits

Profit is basically the amount by which revenues exceed costs. It is classified in trading statements and profit and loss accounts in the following four ways:

1 *Gross profit* – the difference between sales revenue and the cost of goods sold. This is also referred to as gross margin, especially in the retail industry.

2 *Operating or trading profit* – the gross profit less sales, marketing and distribution costs, administrative costs and research and development expenditure.

3 *Profit before taxation* – operating profit plus invested income minus interest payable.

4 *Net profit* – profit minus taxation.

Trading statements

Trading statements or accounts show the cost of goods manufactured, the cost of sales, sales revenue and the gross profit, which is transferred to the profit and loss account.

Profit and loss accounts

Profit and loss accounts provide the information required to assess a company's profitability – the return in the shape of profits that shareholders obtain for their investment in the company. This is the primary aim and best measure of efficiency in competitive business. Profit and loss accounts show:

1 The gross profit from the trading account.
2 Selling and administration expenses.
3 The operating profit (1 minus 2).
4 Investment income.
5 Profit before interest and taxation (3 plus 4).
6 Profit before taxation (5 minus loan interest).
7 Taxation.
8 Net profit (6 minus 7).

Profitability analysis ratios

Profitability is expressed by the following ratios:

- *Return on equity* – profit after interest and preference dividends before tax in relation to ordinary share capital, reserves and retained profit. This focuses attention on the efficiency of the company in earning profits on behalf of its shareholders; some analysts regard it as the best profitability ratio.

- *Return on capital employed* – trading or operating profit to capital employed. This measures the efficiency with which capital is employed.

- *Earnings per share* – profit after interest, taxation and preference dividends in relation to the number of issued ordinary shares. This is an alternative to return on equity as a measure of the generation of 'shareholder value' (the value of the investment made by shareholders in the company in terms of the return they get on that investment). Its drawback is that it depends on the number of shares issued, although it is often referred to within companies as the means by which their obligations to shareholders should be assessed.

- *Price–earnings (P/E) ratio* – market price of ordinary shares in relation to earnings per share. This ratio is often used by investment analysts.

- *Economic value added (EVA)* – post-tax operating profit minus the cost of capital invested in the business. This measures how effectively the company uses its funds.

Financial budgeting

Budgets translate policy into financial terms. They are statements of the planned allocation and use of the company's resources. They are needed to: 1) show the financial implications of plans; 2) define the resources required to achieve the plans; and 3) provide the means of measuring, monitoring and controlling results against the plans.

The procedure for preparing financial budgets consists of the following steps:

1 *Budget guidelines* are prepared that have been derived from the corporate plan and forecasts. They will include the activity levels for which budgets have to be created and the ratios to be achieved. The assumptions to be used in budgeting are also given. These could include rates of inflation and increases in costs and prices.

2 *Initial budgets* for a budget or cost centre are prepared by departmental managers with the help of budget accountants.

3 *Departmental budgets* are collated and analysed to produce the master budget, which is reviewed by top management, who may require changes at departmental level to bring it into line with corporate financial objectives and plans.

4 *The master budget* is finally approved by top management and issued to each departmental (budget centre) manager for planning and control purposes.

Budgetary control

Budgetary control ensures that financial budgets are met and that any variances are identified and dealt with. Control starts with the budget for the cost centre, which sets out the budgeted expenditure under cost headings against activity levels. A system of measurement or recording is used to allocate expenditures to cost headings and record activity levels achieved. The actual expenditures and activity levels are compared and positive and negative variances noted. Cost centre managers then act to deal with the variances and report their results to higher management.

Cash management

Cash management involves forecasting and controlling cash flows (inflows or outflows of cash to or from the company). It is an important and systematic process of ensuring that problems of liquidity are minimized and that funds are managed effectively. The aim is to ensure that the company is not over-trading, ie that the cost of its operations does not significantly exceed the amount of cash available to finance them. The old adage is that whatever else is done, ensure that 'cash in exceeds cash out'.

Cash flow statements report the amounts of cash generated and cash used for a period. They are used to provide information on liquidity (the availability of cash), solvency and financial adaptability.

Cash budgeting

An operating cash budget deals with budgeted receipts (forecast cash inflows) and budgeted payments (forecast cash outflows). It includes all the revenue expenditure incurred in financing current operations, ie the costs of running the business in order to generate sales.

Costing

Costing techniques provide information for decision making and control. They are used to establish the total cost of a product for stock valuation, pricing and estimating purposes and to enable the company to establish that the proposed selling price will enable a profit to be made.

Costing involves measuring the direct costs of material and labour plus the indirect costs (overheads) originating in the factory (factory overheads) and elsewhere in the company (sales, distribution, marketing, research and development and administration). Overheads are charged to cost units – this process is called 'overhead recovery'. It provides information on total costs. There are four main methods of doing this:

- *Absorption costing* – this involves allocating all fixed and variable costs to cost units and is the most widely used method, although it can be arbitrary.
- *Activity-based costing* – costs are assigned to activities on the basis of an individual product's demand for each activity.
- *Marginal costing* – this segregates fixed costs and apportions the variable or marginal costs to products.
- *Standard costing* – is the preparation of predetermined or standard costs, which are compared with actual costs to identify variances. It is used to measure performance.

Business models

HR professionals also need to know about the concept of business models and how this influences their activities. A business model provides a picture of an organization, explaining how it achieves competitive advantage and makes money. As defined by Magretta (2002: 87), business models 'are at heart stories – stories that explain how enterprises work... They answer the fundamental questions every manager needs to ask: How do we make money in this business? What is the underlying economic logic that explains how we can deliver value to customers at an appropriate cost?' She explained that a business model 'focuses attention on how all the elements in a system fit into a working whole' (ibid: 90).

Elements of a business model

Johnson *et al* (2008: 52) stated that: 'A business model, from our point of view, consists of four interlocking elements that, taken together, create and deliver value.'

These are:

- *The customer value proposition*: how the business will create value for its customers; this is the most important element.
- *The profit formula*: the blueprint that defines how the company creates value for itself while providing value to the customer. It consists of the revenue model, cost structure, margin model (the contribution needed from

the following ratios: return on equity, return on capital employed, earnings per share, price–earnings (P/E) ratio and economic value added (EVA).

Financial budgeting

Budgets translate policy into financial terms. They are statements of the planned allocation and use of the company's resources.

Budgetary control

Budgetary control ensures that financial budgets are met and that any variances are identified and dealt with.

Cash management

Cash management involves forecasting and controlling cash flows (inflows or outflows of cash). An operating cash budget deals with budgeted receipts (forecast cash inflows) and budgeted payment (forecast cash outflows).

Costing

Costing techniques provide information for decision making and control. They are used to establish the total cost of a product for stock valuation, pricing and estimating purposes, and to enable the company to establish that the proposed selling price will enable a profit to be made.

Overheads are charged to cost units to provide information on total costs – this is called 'overhead recovery'. There are four methods of doing this: absorption costing, activity-based costing, marginal costing and standard costing.

Business model

A business model provides a picture of an organization that explains how it achieves competitive advantage and makes money. Business model innovation is the process of developing new business models or changing existing ones to deliver better value to customers, achieve competitive advantage and increase profitability.

References

CIPD (2010) *Next Generation*, London, CIPD

Johnson, M (2010) *Seizing the White Space*, Boston, MA, Harvard Business Press

Johnson, M, Christensen, C and Kagermann, H (2008) Reinventing your business model, *Harvard Business Review*, December, pp 52–9

Magretta, J (2002) Why business models matter, *Harvard Business Review*, May, pp 86–93

Schuler, R S and Jackson, S E (2007) Understanding human resource management in the context of organizations and their environments, in (eds)

R S Schuler and S E Jackson, *Strategic Human Resource Management*, Oxford, Blackwell, pp 23–48

Sparrow, P, Hesketh, A, Hird, M and Cooper, C (2010) Introduction: Performance-led HR, in (eds) P Sparrow, A Hesketh, M Hird, and C Cooper, *Leading HR*, Palgrave Macmillan, Basingstoke

Ulrich, D (1997) Judge me by my future not my past, *Human Resource Management*, **36** (1), pp 5–8

65
Problem-solving skills

Introduction

Problem solving is a constant feature of life in organizations and elsewhere. It is something that HR professionals do all the time. A logical approach is desirable but this is not easy – the situations where problems have to be solved are often messy, with conflicting evidence, lack of data and political and emotional issues affecting those involved. But even if it is not possible to apply neat, logical and sequential methods, the principles of getting and analysing what information is available, considering alternatives and making the best choice based on the evidence, an analysis of the context, and an assessment of the possible consequences remain the same.

Problem solving

Problem solving is the process of analysing and understanding a problem, diagnosing its cause and deciding on a solution that solves the problem and prevents it being repeated. You will often have to react to problems as they arise, but as far as possible a proactive approach is desirable, involving anticipating potential problems and dealing with them in advance by taking preventative action using the normal approaches to problem solving set out below. Proactive problem solving may require creative thinking.

Problems and opportunities

It is often said that 'there are no problems, only opportunities'. This is not universally true, of course, but it does emphasize the point that a problem should lead to positive thinking about what is to be done now, rather than to recriminations. If a mistake has been made, the reasons for it should be analysed to ensure that it does not happen again.

Improving your skills

How can you improve your ability to solve problems? There are a few basic approaches you should use, as discussed below.

Improve your analytical ability

A complicated situation can often be resolved by separating the whole into its component parts. Such an analysis should relate to facts, although, as Drucker (1955) points out, when trying to understand the root causes of a problem you may have to start with an opinion. Even if you ask people to search for the facts first, they will probably look for those facts that fit the conclusion they have already reached.

Opinions are a perfectly good starting point as long as they are brought out into the open at once and then tested against reality. Analyse each hypothesis and pick out the parts that need to be studied and tested. (Analytical skills are covered in Chapter 66.) Follett's (1924) 'law of the situation' – the logic of facts and events – should rule in the end.

Be creative

A strictly logical answer to the problem may not be the best one. Creative thinking is often necessary to develop an entirely new approach.

Keep it simple

One of the basic principles of problem solving is known as Occam's razor. It states that 'entities are not to be multiplied without necessity'. That is, always believe the simplest of several explanations.

Focus on implementation

A problem has not been solved until the decision has been implemented. Think carefully not only about how a thing is to be done (by whom, with what resources and by when) but also about what will happen when it is put into effect – its impact on the organization and the people concerned, and the extent to which they will cooperate. Unforeseen consequences can upset the most carefully prepared plans.

Involve people

You will get less cooperation if you impose a solution. The best method is to arrange things so that everyone arrives jointly at a solution, freely agreed to be the one best suited to the situation (the law of the situation again).

Further consideration of the processes of evaluating evidence and options and of the consulting skills used in problem solving is given in the next chapter.

12 problem-solving steps

The 12 steps of problem solving are:

1 Define the situation – establish what has gone wrong or is about to go wrong.

2 Specify objectives – define what is to be achieved now or in the future to deal with an actual or potential problem or a change in circumstances.

3 Develop hypotheses – develop hypotheses about what has caused the problem.

4 Get the facts – find out what has actually happened and contrast this with an assessment of what ought to have happened. This is easier said than done. Insidious political factors may have contributed to the problem and could be difficult to identify and deal with. The facts may not be clear cut. They could be obscured by a mass of conflicting material. There may be lots of opinions but few verifiable facts. Remember that people will see what has happened in terms of their own position and feelings (their framework of reference). Try to understand the political climate and the attitudes and motivation of those concerned. Bear in mind that, as Pfeffer (1996: 36) commented, 'smart

organizations occasionally do dumb things'. Obtain information about internal or external constraints that affect the situation.

5 Analyse the facts – determine what is relevant and what is irrelevant. Diagnose the likely cause or causes of the problem. Do not be tempted to focus on symptoms rather than root causes. Test any assumptions. Distinguish between opinions and facts. Dig into what lies behind the problem.

6 Identify possible courses of action – spell out what each involves.

7 Evaluate alternative courses of action – assess the extent to which they are likely to achieve the objectives, the cost of implementation, any practical difficulties that might emerge and the possible reactions of stakeholders. Consider possible consequences. Critical evaluation techniques, as described in Chapter 66, can be used for this purpose.

8 Weigh and decide – determine which alternative is likely to result in the most practical and acceptable solution to the problem. This is often a balanced judgement.

9 Decide on the objective – set out goals for implementation of the decision.

10 Adopt a 'means–end' approach where appropriate – in complicated situations with long-term implications it may be useful to identify the steps required and select an action at each step that will move the process closer to the goal.

11 Plan implementation – prepare a timetable and identify and assemble the resources required.

12 Implement – monitor progress and evaluate success. Remember that a problem has not been solved until the decision has been implemented. Always work out the solution to a problem with implementation in mind.

Key learning points: Problem-solving skills

Problem solving is a constant feature of life in organizations and elsewhere. It is the process of analysing and understanding a problem, diagnosing its cause and deciding on a solution that solves the problem and prevents it being repeated.

To improve problem-solving skills, it is necessary to improve your analytical ability, be creative, keep it simple and focus on implementation.

The 12 steps of problem solving are:

1 Define the situation.

2 Specify objectives.

3 Develop hypotheses.

4 Get the facts.

5 Analyse the facts.

6 Identify possible courses of action.

7 Evaluate alternative courses of action.

8 Weigh and decide.

9 Decide on the objective.

10 Adopt a 'means–end' approach where appropriate.

11 Plan implementation.

12 Implement.

References

Drucker, P (1955) *The Practice of Management*, London, Heinemann

Follett, M P (1924) *Creative Experience*, New York, Longmans Green

Pfeffer, J (1996) When it comes to 'best practices', why do smart organizations occasionally do dumb things? *Organizational Dynamics*, Summer, pp 33–44

66
Analytical and critical skills

LEARNING OUTCOMES

On completing this chapter you should be able to define these key concepts. You should also understand:

- The meaning of evidence-based management
- The nature of critical evaluation

- The nature of critical thinking
- The nature of logical reasoning
- The use of analytical skills

Introduction

The effectiveness of HR initiatives and the processes of problem solving and decision making in which HR practitioners are constantly involved depend largely on thorough analysis and critical thinking, as covered in this chapter. The basis of all these is provided by evidence-based management, as discussed below.

Evidence-based management

Evidence-based management is a method of informing decision making by making use of appropriate information derived from the analysis of policy and practices and surveys of employee opinion within the organization, systematic benchmarking, and the messages delivered by relevant research. It was defined by Rousseau and Barends (2011: 221) as:

'A decision-making process combining critical thinking with the use of the best available scientific evidence and business information.'

The following comments on evidence-based management were made by Pfeffer and Sutton (2006: 70):

> Nurture an evidence-based approach immediately by doing a few simple things that reflect the proper mindset. If you ask for evidence of efficacy every time a change is proposed, people will sit up and take notice. If you take the time to pursue the logic behind that evidence, people will become more disciplined in their own thinking. If you treat the organization like an unfinished prototype and encourage trial programs, pilot studies, and experimentation – and reward learning from these activities, even when something new fails – your organization will begin to develop its own evidence base.

The need for evidence-based management

Rousseau and Barends (2011: 221) observed that:

> Evidence-based HR is motivated by a basic fact: faulty practices and decision making abound in HR. Companies persist in using unstructured interviews to assess a job candidate's fit even though there is little evidence to support that. HR departments often pursue one-size-fits-all standardization in their policies, despite considerable evidence that programmes promoting flexibility benefit. In all honesty, can you answer 'yes' to the question, 'Do you know the scientific evidence for ANY of the HR practices your company uses?' Recent surveys of HR practitioners lead us to suspect that the frank response from many readers is 'no'.

The approach to evidence-based management

Rousseau (2006: 2012) suggested that at its core, evidence-based management combines four fundamental features in everyday management practice and decision making:

- Use of the best-available evidence from peer-reviewed sources.

- Systematic gathering of organizational facts, indicators and metrics to better act on the evidence.

- Practitioner judgement assisted by procedures, practices and framework that reduce bias, improve decision quality and create more vivid learning over time.

- Ethical considerations weighing the short- and long-term impacts of decisions on stakeholders and society.

A five-step approach was recommended by Briner et al (2009: 23):

1 Practitioners or managers gain understanding of the problem or issue.

2 Internal evidence is gathered about the issue or problem, leading, possibly, to a reformulation of the problem to make it more specific.

3 External evidence is gathered from published research.

4 The views of stakeholders are obtained.

5 All the sources of information are examined and critically appraised.

What is done in organizations with the evidence depends largely on the context in which it is done. Cultural, social and political factors influence perceptions and judgements, and the extent to which people behave rationally is limited by their capacity to understand the complexities of the situation they are in and by their emotional reactions to it – the concept of bounded rationality, as expressed by Simon (1957).

We need to understand the context – its impact on what is happening and how things are done. We need then to understand what actions can be taken to deal with the issues emerging from the situation. We need evidence that tells us what is going on within the organization, what has worked well elsewhere that might fit our requirements and what research has revealed about policies and practices that will guide us in making our decisions. And we need to use that evidence as the basis for our choice of the actions we intend to take. In other words, we need to practice evidence-based management using the analytical, logical reasoning and critical thinking skills described in the rest of this chapter.

Analytical skills

Analysis is the process of breaking down a condition or state of affairs into its constituent parts and establishing the relationships between them. In the Aristotelian sense, analysis involves discerning the particular features of a situation.

Analytical skills are used to gain a better understanding of a complex situation or problem. They involve the ability to visualize, articulate and solve complex problems and concepts and make decisions based on available information. Analytical skills include the capacity to evaluate that information to assess its significance, and the ability to apply logical and critical thinking to the situation. They provide the basis for a diagnosis of the cause or causes of a problem and therefore for its solution. Importantly, they are a means of gaining insight into issues that affect the success of the business and which influence business and HR strategy.

Logical reasoning

If you say people are logical, you mean that they draw reasonable inferences – their conclusions can be proved by reference to the facts used to support them – and they avoid ill-founded and tendentious arguments, generalizations and irrelevancies. Logical reasoning is the basis of critical thinking and evaluation. It takes place when there is a clear relationship (a line of reasoning) between the premise (the original proposition) and the conclusion, which is supported by valid and reliable evidence and does not rely on a fallacious or misleading argument. Logical reasoning is what Stebbing (1959) called 'Thinking to some purpose'. Clear thinking is required to establish the validity of a proposition, concept or idea.

It is necessary to question assumptions, especially when a belief is expressed as a fact. You need to ask yourself – and others – 'What's the evidence for that?' You have to spot fallacious and misleading arguments. A fallacy is an unsound form of argument leading to an error in reasoning or a misleading impression. The most common form of fallacies that need to be discerned in other people's arguments or avoided in one's own are summarized below:

- *Affirming the consequent* – leaping to the conclusion that a hypothesis is true because a single cause of the consequence has been observed.
- *Begging the question* – taking for granted what has yet to be proved.
- *Chop logic* – 'Contrarywise,' said Tweedledee, 'if it was so, it might be, and if it were so, it would be; but as it isn't it ain't. That's logic.' Chop logic may not always be as bad as that, but it is about drawing false conclusions and using dubious methods of argument. For example: selecting instances favourable to a contention while ignoring those that are counter to it; twisting an argument used by an opponent to mean something quite different from what was intended; diverting opponents by throwing on them the burden of proof for something they have not maintained; ignoring the point in dispute; changing the question to one that is less awkward to answer; and reiterating what has been denied and ignoring what has been asserted. Politicians know all about chop logic.
- *Confusing correlation with causation* – assuming that because A is associated with B it has caused B. It may or may not have.
- *False choice* – a situation in which only two alternatives are considered, when in fact there are additional options.
- *Potted thinking* – using slogans and catchphrases to extend an assertion in an unwarrantable fashion.
- *Reaching false conclusions* – forming the view that because some are, then all are. An assertion about several cases is twisted into an assertion about all cases. The conclusion does not follow the premise. This is what logicians call the 'undistributed middle'.
- *Selective reasoning* – selecting instances favourable to a contention while ignoring those that conflict with it.
- *Sweeping statements* – over-simplifying the facts.
- *Special pleading* – focusing too much on one's own case and failing to see that there may be other points of view.

Critical thinking

Critical thinking is the process of analysing and evaluating the quality of ideas, theories and concepts to establish the degree to which they are valid and supported by the evidence and the extent to which they are biased. It involves reflecting on and interpreting data, drawing warranted conclusions and recognizing ill-defined assumptions.

'Critical' in this context does not mean disapproval or being negative. There are many positive uses of critical thinking, for example testing a hypothesis, proving a proposition or evaluating a concept, theory or argument. Critical thinking can occur whenever people weigh up evidence and make a judgement, solve a problem or reach a decision. The aim is to come to well-reasoned conclusions and solutions and to test them against relevant criteria and standards. Critical thinking calls for the ability to:

- recognize problems and establish ways of dealing with them;
- gather and marshal pertinent (relevant) information;
- identify unstated assumptions and values;
- interpret data, to appraise evidence and to evaluate arguments;
- recognize the existence (or non-existence) of logical relationships between propositions;
- draw warranted conclusions and make valid generalizations;
- test assertions, conclusions and generalizations;
- reconstruct ideas or beliefs by examining and analysing relevant evidence.

Critical evaluation

Critical evaluation is the process of making informed judgements about the validity, relevance and usefulness of ideas and arguments. Critical evaluation means not taking anything for granted and, where necessary, challenging propositions. It involves making informed judgements about the value of ideas and arguments. It uses critical thinking by analysing and evaluating the quality of theories and concepts to establish the degree to which they are valid and supported by the evidence (evidence-based) and the extent to which they are biased. The arguments for and against are weighed and the strength of the evidence on both sides is assessed. On the basis of this assessment, a conclusion is reached on which proposition or argument is to be preferred. Critical evaluation is required when testing propositions and evaluating the outcomes of research.

Testing propositions

Propositions based on research investigations and evidence can be tested by using the following checklist.

Checklist

- Was the scope of the investigation sufficiently comprehensive?

- Are the instances representative or are they selected simply to support a point of view?

- Are there contradictory instances that have not been looked for?

- Does the proposition conflict with other propositions for which there are equally good grounds?

- If there are any conflicting beliefs or contradictory items of evidence, have they been put to the test against the original proposition?

- Could the evidence lead to other equally valid conclusions?

- Are there any other factors that have not been taken into account that may have influenced the evidence and, therefore, the conclusion?

Critically evaluating research

Putting the outcomes of research, for example material published in academic journals, to the test requires critical evaluation and the following checklist can be used.

Checklist

1 Is the research methodology sufficiently rigorous and appropriate?

2 Are the results and conclusions consistent with the methodology used and its outcomes?

3 Is the perspective adopted by the researchers stated clearly?

4 Have hypotheses been stated clearly and tested thoroughly?

5 Do there appear to be any misleading errors of omission or bias?

6 Are any of the arguments tendentious?

7 Are inferences, findings and conclusions derived from reliable and convincing evidence?

8 Has a balanced approach been adopted?

9 Have any underlying assumptions been identified and justified?

10 Have the component parts been covered in terms of their interrelationships and their relationship with the whole?

11 Have these component parts been disaggregated for close examination?

12 Have they been reconstructed into a coherent whole based on underlying principles?

It is worth repeating that critical evaluation does not necessarily mean negative criticism; it means reaching a judgement based on analysis and evidence, and the judgement can be positive as well as negative.

Developing and justifying original arguments

An argument as an aspect of critical thinking consists of a presentation of reasons that support a contention. It consists of:

- a proposition or statement that expresses a point of view or belief;

- the reasoning that makes a case for the proposition or point of view;

- a discussion, the aim of which is to get the reader or listener to agree with the case that has been made;

- a conclusion that sums up the argument and its significance.

Developing an argument

An argument is based (predicated) on a premise (the proposition) that sets out the underpinning assumption. There may be more than one proposition or assumption. It could be phrased something like this: 'The argument is that A is the case. It is predicated on the assumption that B and C apply.' In a sense this suggests what conclusion the argument is intended to reach but it also indicates that this conclusion depends on the validity of the assumptions, which will have to be proved (there are such things as false premises).

Justifying an argument

The argument continues by supplying reasons to accept the proposition or point of view. These reasons have to be supported by evidence, which should be based on valid research, rigorous observation, or relevant and verifiable experience, not on hearsay. It involves logical reasoning, which avoids the fallacies referred to earlier and requires critical thinking, which means coming to well-reasoned conclusions and solutions and testing them against relevant criteria and standards. It also demands critical evaluation, which means reflecting on and interpreting data, drawing warranted conclusions and identifying faulty reasoning, assumptions and biases. Assumptions have to be tested rigorously and research evidence has to be evaluated. The checklists set out above can be used for this purpose.

Key learning points: Analytical and critical skills

Basis of the processes of problem solving and decision making

The processes of problem solving and decision making depend largely on effective analysis, critical thinking and evaluation.

Evidence-based management

Evidence-based management is a method of informing decision making by making use of appropriate information derived from the analysis of HR policy and practices and surveys of employee opinion within the organization, systematic benchmarking, and the messages delivered by relevant research.

Analytical skills

Analysis is the process of gaining a better understanding of a complex situation or problem by breaking it down into its constituent parts and establishing the relationships between them.

Logical reasoning

Logical reasoning involves clear thinking to establish the validity of a proposition, concept or idea.

Critical thinking

Critical thinking clarifies goals, examines assumptions, discerns hidden values, evaluates evidence, accomplishes actions and assesses conclusions.

Critical evaluation

Critical evaluation involves making informed judgements about the value of ideas and arguments.

Developing and justifying original arguments

An argument as an aspect of critical thinking consists of a presentation of reasons that support a contention.

References

Briner, R B, Denyer, D and Rousseau, D M (2009) Evidence-based management: concept clean-up time? *Academy of Management Perspectives*, September, pp 19–32

Pfeffer, J and Sutton, R I (2006) Evidence-based management, *Harvard Business Review*, January, pp 62–74

Rousseau, D M (2006) Is there such a thing as evidence-based management? *Academy of Management Review*, **31** (2), pp 256–69

Rousseau, D M and Barends, E G (2011) Becoming an evidence-based HR practitioner, *Human Resource Management Journal*, **21** (3), pp 221–35

Simon, H (1957) *Administrative Behaviour*, New York, Macmillan

Stebbing, S (1959) *Thinking to Some Purpose*, Harmondsworth, Penguin Books

67
Research skills

LEARNING OUTCOMES

On completing this chapter you should be able to define these key concepts. You should also know about:

- The nature of research
- Planning and conducting research programmes

- Research methodology
- Methods of collecting data
- Processes involved in research

Introduction

HRM specialists and those studying for HR professional qualifications may be involved in conducting or taking part in research projects. Postgraduate students frequently do so. Qualified HR specialists should keep up to date as part of their continuous professional development by studying publications that present research findings, such as those produced by the CIPD, or by reading articles in academic journals. Students must extend their understanding of HRM through reading about research findings.

The purpose of this chapter is to describe the skills and techniques used in research and explain what is involved in planning and conducting research projects. This will be done against the background of a brief review of the nature and philosophy of research.

The nature of research

Research is concerned with establishing what is and from this predicting what will be. It does not decide what ought to be; that is for people interpreting the lessons from research in their own context. Research is about the conception and testing of ideas and hypotheses. This is a creative and imaginative process, although new information is normally obtained within the framework of existing theory and knowledge. Logic and rational argument are methods of testing ideas after they have been created.

What emerges from research is a theory – a well-established explanatory principle that has been tested and can be used to make predictions of future developments. Kurt Lewin (1945: 129) wrote that 'Nothing is as practical as a good theory'. A 'good' theory is produced by clear, logical and linear development of argument with a close relationship between information, hypothesis and conclusion. Quality of information is a criterion for good research, as is the use of critical evaluation techniques.

The production of narratives that depict events (case studies) or the collection of data through surveys are elements in research programmes, but they can stand alone as useful pieces of information that illustrate practice. Research can be based on a philosophy of positivism or phenomenology.

Positivism

Positivism is the belief that researchers should focus on facts (observable reality), look for causality and fundamental laws, reduce phenomena to their simplest elements (reductionism), formulate hypotheses and then test them. Researchers are objective analysts. The emphasis in positivism is on quantifiable observations that lend themselves to statistical analysis. It tends to be deductive.

Phenomenology

Phenomenology focuses more on the meaning of phenomena than on the facts associated with them. Researchers adopting this philosophy try to understand what is happening. Their approach is holistic, covering the complete picture, rather than reductionist. Researchers collect and analyse evidence, but their purpose is to use this data to develop ideas that explain the meaning of things. They believe that reality is socially constructed rather than objectively determined. Using a phenomenological approach means that the research unfolds as it proceeds – early evidence is used to indicate how to move on to the next stage of evidence collection and analysis, and so on. It tends to be inductive.

Planning and conducting research programmes

Against this background, the steps required to plan and conduct a research programme are:

1 *Define research area.* This should be one that interests the researcher and has a clear link to an accepted theory or an important issue worth exploring. The research should generate fresh insights into the topic. It is necessary to undertake background reading at this stage by means of a preliminary review of the literature (particularly academic journals but also books, especially those based on research) to identify what has already been achieved in this area and any gaps (academic articles often include proposals on further research). The context within which the research is to be carried out needs to be explained and justified.

2 *Formulate initial research question.* This provides a rationale for the research. It is in effect a statement that answers the questions: 'What is this research project intended to address and what is its potential contribution to increasing knowledge?' At this stage it is based on the outcome of the initial work carried out in step 1, but it will be refined and reformulated at a later stage when more information about the research has been made available.

3 *Review literature.* A literature review will focus mainly on academic journals. The aim is to establish what is already known about the topic, identify existing theoretical frameworks and find out what other relevant research has been carried out.

4 *Develop theoretical framework.* It is necessary to conduct the research within a clear theoretical framework. This will set out the models, concepts and theories that can be drawn on and developed to provide an answer to the research question. If an appropriate framework does not exist, a grounded theory approach may be required in which the researcher uses empirical evidence directly to establish the concepts and relationships that will be contained in the theory adopted as the research framework. It is important to be clear about the assumptions, conditions and limitations that impinge on the investigation.

5 *Finalize the research question.* The initial research question needs to be finalized in the light of the outcome of the earlier steps. The final research question will identify the issues to be explored and the problems to be investigated. It will include a statement of intent, which will set out what the research is to achieve. This statement leads to the formulation of the hypotheses or propositions that will be tested by survey or experiment during the research programme.

6 *Formulate hypotheses or propositions.* A hypothesis provisionally states a relationship between two concepts in such a way that the consequences of the statement being true can be tested. Hypotheses (there may be more than one) indicate the form the research project will take in the shape of obtaining and analysing the evidence required to test them. Hypotheses may be attached to the statement of the research question. A proposition is a proposal put forward as an explanation of an event, a possible situation or a form of behaviour that will be tested by the research.

7 *Design the research.* This means considering initially what research philosophy will be adopted. Is it to be positivist, phenomenological, or both? It is then necessary to establish the methodology. A decision will need to be made as to the extent to which the research will be quantitative, qualitative or, again, a combination of the two and on the methods to be used as described below.

8 *Draw up a research programme.* This will cover how the research will be conducted, the timetable and the resources (funding, people, software, etc) required. Careful project planning is essential.

9 *Prepare and submit proposal.* This will justify the research by setting out the research question, the proposed methodology, and how the research is intended to increase knowledge and understanding. It will also describe the programme and the resources required.

10 *Conduct the research project.* This includes obtaining and analysing the evidence from the various sources needed to answer the research question and prove or disprove hypotheses. The significance of the findings in relation to the research question and the hypotheses will be discussed and reference will be made to relevant information provided in the literature. This involves an extended literary review, data collection, the use of logical, analytical and critical thinking processes and the use of statistical analysis where relevant.

11 *Develop conclusions.* These draw together all the evidence. They provide the answer to the research question and explain why hypotheses have been accepted or rejected. The significance of the findings will also be assessed in terms of how they contribute to the development of existing knowledge and understanding. Any limitations to the study should also be mentioned.

12 *Make recommendations.* These set out any guidelines emerging from the research. They may also indicate any follow-up actions required if the research has been conducted within an organization.

Research methodology

Research methodology involves the collection and analysis of evidence and testing hypotheses or pro-positions. The sources of evidence and how they will be accessed will be identified. This will include the analysis of primary and secondary source documents, further literature reviews, interviews, surveys and field work. The methodology can include the use of triangulation and of quantitative or qualitative research.

Triangulation

Triangulation takes place when information is obtained from more than two sources, for example, surveys, case studies and literature reviews. Greater confidence can be attached to a result if different methods lead to the same answer. If a researcher uses only one source this may be misleading or random. If two sources are used the results may clash. If three sources are used, the hope is that two of the three will produce similar answers, or if three clashing answers are produced, the researcher knows that the question needs to be reframed, methods reconsidered, or both.

Cross-lagged models

Cross-lagged models are longitudinal statistical panel studies in which two or more variables are measured for a large number of subjects at each of several waves or points in time. The variables divide naturally into two sets and the primary purpose of the analysis is to estimate and test the cross-effects between these two sets.

Quantitative research

Quantitative research is empirical – based on the collection of factual data, which is measured and quantified. It answers research questions from the viewpoint of the researcher. It may involve a consid-erable amount of statistical analysis, using methods for collecting the data through questionnaires, sur-veys, observation and experiment. The collection of data is distinct from its analysis.

Qualitative research

Qualitative research aims to generate insights into situations and behaviour so that the meaning of what is happening can be understood. It emphasizes the interpretation of behaviour from the viewpoint of the participants. It is based on evidence that may not be easily reduced to numbers. It makes use of interviews, case studies and observation but it may also draw on the information obtained from sur-veys. It may produce narratives or 'stories' describ-ing situations, events or processes.

Methods of collecting data

The main methods of collecting data are interviews, questionnaires, surveys, case studies, observation, diaries and experimental designs.

Interviews

Interviews are an important research method. They obtain factual data and insights into attitudes and feelings and can take three forms:

1 *Structured*, which means that they obtain answers to a pre-prepared set of questions. This ensures that every topic is covered and minimizes variations between respondents. But they may be too rigid and inhibit spontaneous and revealing reactions.

2 *Unstructured*, which means that no questions have been prepared in advance and the person being interviewed is left free to talk about the subject without interruption or intervention. Such 'non-directive' interviews are intended to provide greater insight into the interviewee's perspective, avoid fitting respondents into pre-determined categories and enable interviewers to explore issues as they arise. But they can be inconsequential and lead to poor data that is difficult to analyse.

3 *Semi-structured*, which means that the areas of interest have been pre-determined and the key questions to be asked or information to be obtained have been identified. The

interviewer may have a checklist but does not follow this rigidly. This approach enables the interviewer to phrase questions and vary their order to suit the special characteristics of each interviewee. It may avoid the problems of the completely structured or unstructured interview but it does require a considerable degree of skill on the part of the interviewer.

Interviews are basically qualitative but they can become more quantitative by the use of content analysis. This records the number of times references are made in an interview to the key issues or areas of interest it was intended to cover.

The advantages of interviews are that they obtain information directly from people involved in the area being researched and can provide insights into attitudes and perspectives that questionnaires and surveys will not reveal, thus promoting in-depth understanding. They enable the interviewer to probe answers and check that questions had been understood. But the disadvantages are that:

- the construction of the interview questions may result in leading questions or bland answers;
- interviewers may influence the interviewees' reactions by imposing their own reference frame;
- respondents may tell interviewers what they want to hear;
- they are time-consuming – to set up, to conduct and to analyse;
- they require considerable interviewing skills, including the abilities to recognize what is important and relevant, to probe when necessary, to listen and to control the interview so that it covers the ground it was intended to cover.

Questionnaires

Questionnaires collect data systematically by obtaining answers on the key issues and opinions that need to be explored in a research project. They are frequently used as a means of gathering information on matters of fact or opinion. They use a variety of methods, namely: closed questions that require a yes or no answer, ranking in order of importance or value, or Likert scales. The latter, named after Rensis Likert, the American sociologist who invented them, ask respondents to indicate the extent to which they agree or disagree with a statement. For example, in response to a statement such as, 'I like my job', the choice may be: 1 – strongly agree, 2 – agree, 3 – disagree, 4 – strongly disagree. Alternatively, an extended scale may be used and respondents asked to ring round the number that reflects their view about the statement (the higher the number the greater the agreement), for example: My contribution is fully recognized – 1 2 3 4 5 6 7. Extended scales facilitate the quantitative analysis of responses to questionnaires.

To construct and use a questionnaire effectively it is necessary to:

1 Identify the key issues and potential questions.
2 Ensure questions are clear.
3 Avoid asking two questions in one item.
4 Avoid leading questions that supply their own answers.
5 Decide on the structure of the questionnaire including its length (not too many items) and the type of scale to be used.
6 Code questions for ease of analysis.
7 Start with simple factual questions, moving on later to items of opinion or values.
8 Add variety and the opportunity to check consistency by interspersing positive statements such as, 'I like working for my boss' with occasional associated negative ones such as, 'I do not get adequate support from my boss'.
9 Pilot test the questionnaire.
10 Code results and analyse. Where rating scales have been used, the analysis can be quantified for comparison purposes. Content analysis can be used to analyse narrative answers to open-ended questions.

Questionnaires can effectively gather factual evidence but are not so useful for researchers who are investigating how or why things are happening. It is also impossible to assess the degree of subjectivity that has crept in when expressing opinions. For example, HR managers may give an opinion of the extent to which a performance-related pay scheme has in fact improved performance, but the evidence to support that opinion will be lacking. This is where interviews can be more informative.

Surveys

Surveys obtain information from a defined population of people. Typically, they are based on questionnaires but they can provide more powerful data than other methods by using a combination of questionnaires and interviews and, possibly, focus groups (groups of people gathered together to answer and discuss specific questions). When developing and administering surveys the issues are:

- The definition of the purpose of the survey and the outcomes hoped for – these must be as precise as possible.
- The population to be covered – this may involve a census of the whole population. Alternatively, if the population is large, sampling will be necessary (see below).
- The choice of methods – relying entirely on questionnaires may limit the validity of the findings. It is better, if time and the availability of finance permit, to complement them with interviews and, possibly, focus groups. Consideration has to be given to the extent to which triangulation (comparing the information obtained from more than two sources) is appropriate.
- The questions to which answers are required, whichever method is used.
- The design of questionnaires and the ways in which interviews or focus groups, if used, should be structured.
- How the outcome of the survey will be analysed and presented, including the use of case studies.

Sampling

In using surveys, and possibly other methods, it may not be feasible to cover the whole population (the sampling frame) and sampling will therefore be necessary. Sampling means that a proportion of the total population is selected for study and the aim is to see that this proportion represents the characteristics of the whole population. The sample must not be biased and that is why in large-scale surveys use is made of random sampling, ie the individuals covered by a survey are not selected in accordance with any criteria except that they exist in the population and can be reached by the survey. It is the equivalent of drawing numbers out of a hat. However, if the sample frame is considered to be already arranged randomly, as in the electoral roll, then structured sampling, that is, sampling at regular intervals, can be employed.

Sampling can produce varying degrees of error depending on the size of the sample. Statistical techniques can be used to establish sample errors and confidence limits. For example, they might establish that a sampling error is 3 per cent and the confidence limit is 95 per cent. This could be reasonably satisfactory, depending on the nature of the research (medical research aims to achieve 100 per cent confidence).

Case studies

A research case study is a description of a situation or a history of an event or sequence of events in a real-life setting which illustrates a particular area of interest, for example, how a performance management system has been developed and works. In learning and development, case studies are analysed by those involved to learn something by diagnosing the causes of a problem and working out how to solve it.

Case studies are used extensively in HRM research as a means of collecting empirical evidence in a real-life context. Information is obtained about a situation, an event or a set of events that establishes what has happened, how it happened and why. Case studies provide information that contributes to the creation of a theory as part of a grounded theory approach or the validation of an established theory. In addition, they can take the form of stories or narratives that illuminate a decision or a set of decisions, why they were taken, how they were implemented and with what result. They can illustrate a total situation and describe the processes involved and how individuals and groups behave in a social setting.

Case study protocol sets out the objectives of the research, how the case study will support the achievement of those objectives, including the evidence required, and how the work of producing the case study will be conducted. The methodology covers:

- sources of evidence – interviews, observation, documents and records;

- the need to use multiple sources of evidence (triangulation) so far as possible;

- the questions to which answers need to be obtained;

- how the case study should be set up, including informing those involved of what is taking place and enlisting their support;

- the schedule of interviews and other evidence collection activities;

- how the case study database recording the evidence will be set up and maintained;

- how the case study will be presented – including the chain of evidence so that the reader can follow the argument and trace the development of events, the headings and report guidelines (these may be finalized during the course of the exercise) and whether or not the name of the organization will be revealed on publication (named cases studies are more convincing than anonymous ones);

- how approval will be sought for the publication of the case study, especially if it reveals the name of the organization.

Case studies are useful ways of collecting information on the reality of organizational life and processes. But there is a danger of them being no more than a story or an anecdote that does not contribute to greater knowledge or understanding. Skill and persistence are required from the researcher in gaining support, ensuring that relevant and revealing information is obtained and presenting the case study as a convincing narrative from which valid and interesting conclusions can be derived. All this must be done without taking a biased view, which can be difficult.

Observation

Observation of individuals or groups at work is a method of getting a direct and realistic impression of what is happening. It can be done by a detached or an involved observer, or by participant observation.

Detached observers who simply study what is going on without getting involved with the people concerned may only get a superficial impression of what is happening and may be resented by the people under observation as 'eavesdropping'. Involved observers work closely with employees and can move around, observe and participate as appropriate. This means that they can get closer to events and are more likely to be accepted, especially if the objectives and methods have been agreed in advance.

Participant observation in the fullest sense means that the researcher becomes an employee and experiences the work and the social processes that take place at first hand. This can provide powerful insights but is time-consuming and requires considerable skill and persistence.

The issues with any form of observation are getting close enough to events to understand their significance and then analysing the mass of information that might be produced in order to come up with findings that contribute to answering the research question.

Diaries

Getting people to complete diaries of what they do is a method of building a realistic picture of how people, especially managers, spend their time.

Experimental designs

Experimental designs involve setting up an experimental group and a control group and then placing subjects at random in one or other group. The conditions under which the experimental group functions are then manipulated and the outcomes compared with the control group, whose conditions remain unchanged. The classic case of an experimental design was the Hawthorne study, the results of which had a major impact on thinking about how groups function and on the human relations movement. But this was exceptional. It is much easier to use experiments in a laboratory setting which has been done many times with students. But there is always the feeling that such experiments do not reflect real-life conditions.

Processes involved in research

This section describes the logical, analytical and critical thinking processes that are used in research: deduction, induction, hypothesis testing, grounded theory, paradigms and critical evaluation.

Deduction

Research involves deduction, which is the process of using logical reasoning to reach a conclusion that necessarily follows from general or universal premises. If the premises are correct, so is the deduction. The conclusion is therefore contained within the evidence. It is not a creative or imaginative argument that produces new ideas.

Induction

Research can also be based on induction, which is the process of reaching generalized conclusions from the observation of particular instances. In contrast to deduction, inductive conclusions may be tentative but they contain new ideas. In research, both deductive and inductive reasoning can be used in hypothesis testing.

Hypothesis testing

Formulating a hypothesis is an important element in a research project in that it provides a basis for the development of theory and the collection and analysis of data. A hypothesis is a supposition – a tentative explanation of something. It is a provisional statement that is taken to be true for the purpose of argument or a study and usually relates to an existing wider body of knowledge or theory. A hypothesis has to be tested and should be distinguished from a theory, which is an explanation of something that has been tested. A good hypothesis contains two concepts and proposes a relationship between the two. A working hypothesis is a general hypothesis that has been operationalized so that it can be tested.

Hypothesis formulation and testing uses the strengths of both deductive and inductive processes;

the former entirely conclusive but unimaginative, the latter tentative but creative. Induction produces ideas and deduction tests them.

To test a hypothesis, data has to be obtained that will demonstrate that its predicted consequences are true or false. Simply leaping to the conclusion that a hypothesis is true because a single cause of the consequence has been observed falls into the trap of what logicians call the 'fallacy of affirming the consequent'. There may be alternative and more valid causes. The preferred method of testing is that of denying the consequent. This is 'falsification' as advocated by Popper (1959). His view was that however much data may be assembled to support a hypothesis, it is not possible to reach a conclusive proof of the truth of that hypothesis. Popper therefore proposed that it was insufficient simply to assemble confirmatory evidence; what must also be obtained is evidence that refutes the hypothesis. Only one instance of refutation is needed to falsify a theory, whereas however many confirmations of the theory exist it will still not be proved conclusively.

Grounded theory

Grounded theory is an inductive method of developing the general features of a theory by grounding the account in empirical observations or evidence. The researcher uses empirical evidence directly to establish the concepts and relationships that will be contained in the theory. Evidence is collected from both primary sources (ie obtained directly by the researcher from the originator of the evidence) and secondary sources (ie information that is already available in the literature or on the internet). Use is made of triangulation.

Paradigm

The term 'paradigm' has become popularized as meaning a way of looking at things. It is often used loosely, but properly it means the philosophical and theoretical framework of a scientific school or discipline within which theories, laws and generalizations and the experiments performed in support of them are formulated. In other words, it is a common perspective that underpins the work of theorists so that they use the same approach to conducting research.

Critical evaluation

Critical evaluation involves making informed judgements about the value of ideas and arguments. It uses critical thinking, which is the process of analysing and evaluating the quality of ideas, theories and concepts to establish the degree to which they are valid and supported by the evidence (evidence-based) and the extent to which they are biased. It means reflecting on and interpreting data, drawing warranted conclusions and identifying faulty reasoning, assumptions and biases. A creative leap may be required to reach a judgement.

Key learning points: Research skills

The nature of research

Research is concerned with establishing what is and from this predicting what will be. It is about the conception and testing of ideas.

Research philosophy

Research design can be based on a philosophy of positivism or phenomenology. Positivism is the belief that researchers should focus on facts (observable reality), look for causality and fundamental laws. Phenomenology is concerned more with the meaning of phenomena than the facts associated with them.

Planning and conducting research programmes

1 Define research area.

2 Formulate initial research question.

3 Review literature.

4 Assess existing theoretical frameworks.

5 Formalize the research question.

6 Formulate hypotheses.

7 Design the research.

8 Draw up research programme.

9 Prepare and submit proposal.

10 Collect and analyse evidence.

11 Develop conclusions.

12 Make recommendations.

Approaches to research

- Research can be quantitative or qualitative.

- It can use inductive or deductive methods.

- It involves the testing of hypotheses and may adopt a grounded theory approach, ie an inductive method of developing the general features of a theory by grounding the account in empirical observations or evidence.

- Use may be made of paradigms – common perspectives that underpin the work of theorists so that they use the same approach to conducting research.

- Informed judgements about the value of ideas and arguments are made through critical evaluation.

- It makes use of critical thinking, which is the process of analysing and evaluating the quality of ideas, theories and concepts to establish the degree to which they are valid and supported by the evidence.

Methods of collecting data

- Interviews obtain factual data and insights into attitudes and feelings and can be structured, unstructured or semi-structured.

- Questionnaires collect data systematically by obtaining answers on the key issues and opinions that need to be explored in a research project.

- Surveys obtain information from a defined population of people.

- Case studies collect empirical evidence in a real-life context.

References

Lewin, K (1945) The research centre for group dynamics at Massachusetts Institute of Technology, *Sociometry*, 8, pp 126–36

Popper, K (1959) *The Logic of Scientific Discovery*, London, Hutchinson

68
Statistical skills

KEY CONCEPTS AND TERMS

KEY CONCEPTS AND TERMS

Average	Mode
Causality	Multi-regression analysis
Chi-squared test	Multi-variant analysis
Correlation	Regression
Dispersion	Reverse causation
Frequency	Scattergram
Frequency distribution	Significance
Line of best fit	Standard deviation
Lower quartile	Trend line
Mean	Upper quartile
Median	Variance

LEARNING OUTCOMES

On completing this chapter you should be able to define these key concepts. You should also know about:

- The use of statistics
- Frequency analysis
- Measures of central tendency
- Measures of dispersion
- Correlation
- Regression
- Tests of significance
- Tests of hypotheses

Introduction

HR professionals need skills in using statistics in order to analyse and present quantitative information (HR analytics) that can be used to guide decisions and monitor outcomes. They are an essential element in human capital management and are also important in such fields as performance management (the analysis of appraisal results and levels of performance) and reward management (the analysis of market rates, pay reviews, the distribution of pay, and equal pay). Statistics play a major part in the analysis of surveys and research evidence.

HR professionals do not need advanced statistical skills unless they are conducting or taking part in detailed research projects. The main statistics they will use regularly, as described in this chapter, are concerned with the analysis of the incidence of events or activities (frequencies), the use of averages (measures of central tendency), how items in a population are distributed (dispersion) and the relationship between two variables (regression). But they should also be familiar with the concepts of correlation, causation and at least understand the meaning of more advanced statistical techniques used by researchers such as tests of significance, the chi-squared test and null-hypothesis testing.

Using statistics

Statistics describe and summarize data relating to a 'population', ie a homogeneous set of items with variable individual values. This involves measuring frequencies, central tendencies and dispersion. Statistics can also measure the relationships between variables (correlation and regression), establish the relation between cause and effect (causality), assess the degree of confidence that can be attached to conclusions (tests of significance) and test hypotheses (the chi-squared test and null-hypothesis testing). A wide variety of software is available to conduct the more sophisticated analyses.

Frequency

Frequency is the number of times individual items in a population or set occur. It is represented in frequency distributions expressed in tabular form or graphically. Commonly used graphs are illustrated in Figure 68.1.

FIGURE 68.1   Examples of charts

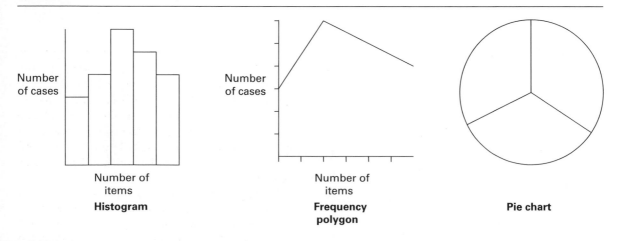

Histogram   Frequency polygon   Pie chart

Measures of central tendency

Measures of central tendency identify the middle or centre of a set of data. There are three types:

- Arithmetic average or mean – the total of items or scores in a set divided by the number of individual items in the set. It may give a distorted picture because of large items at either end of the scale.
- Median – the middle item in a range of items (often used in pay surveys when the arithmetic mean is likely to be distorted).
- Mode – the most commonly occurring item in a set of data.

Measures of dispersion

It is often useful to measure the extent to which the items in a set are dispersed or spread over a range of data. This can be done in five ways:

1 By identifying the upper quartile or lower quartile of a range of data. The strict definition of an upper quartile is that it is the value which 25 per cent of the values in the distribution exceed, and the lower quartile is the value below which 25 per cent of the values in a distribution occur. More loosely, especially when looking at pay distributions, the upper and lower quartiles are treated as ranges rather than points in a scale and represent the top and the bottom 25 per cent of the distribution respectively.

2 By presenting the total range of values from top to bottom; this may be misleading if there are exceptional items at either end.

3 By calculating the inter-quartile range, which is the range between the value of the upper quartile and that of the lower quartile. This can present more revealing information of the distribution than the total range.

4 By calculating the standard deviation, which is used to indicate the extent to which the items or values in a distribution are grouped together or dispersed in a normal distribution, ie one that is reasonably symmetrical around its average. As a rule of thumb, two-thirds of the distribution will be less than one standard deviation from the mean, 95 per cent of the distribution will be less than two standard deviations from the mean, and less than 1 per cent of the distribution will be more than three standard deviations from the mean.

5 By calculating variance, which is the square of a standard deviation.

Correlation

Correlation represents the relationship between two variables. If they are highly correlated they are strongly connected to one another, and vice versa. In statistics, correlation is measured by the coefficient of correlation, which varies between -1 and +1 to indicate totally negative and totally positive correlations respectively. A correlation of zero means that there is no relationship between the variables. Establishing the extent to which variables are correlated is an important feature of HRM research in, for example, assessing the degree to which a performance management system improves organizational performance. But correlations do not indicate causal relationships. Multiple correlation looks at the relationship between more than two variables.

Regression

Regression is another way of looking at the relationship between variables. It expresses how changes in levels of one item relate to changes in levels of another. A regression line (a trend line or line of best fit) can be traced on a scattergram expressing values of one variable on one axis and values of the other variable on another axis, as shown in Figure 68.2.

A trend line like this can be drawn by hand as a line of best fit, but it can be calculated mathematically with greater accuracy. The distances of points from the trend line (the residuals) can be calculated as a check on the reliability of the line.

Multiple regression analysis can be conducted with the aid of a computer to express how changes

FIGURE 68.2   A scattergram with regression (trend) line

in the levels of a number of items relate to changes in levels of other items.

Causality

Causality is the representation of cause and effect, ie the link between independent and dependent variables. To establish causality is to explain how one thing leads to another. Causality is a major issue in research, especially in the HRM field. It may be relatively easy to establish correlations in the shape of a demonstration that X is associated with Y; it is much more difficult and sometimes impossible to prove that X causes Y. There are a number of reasons for this, of which the two set out below are the most important.

First, complications arise because of the phenomenon of multiple causation. There may be a number of factors contributing to a result. Researchers pursuing the holy grail of trying to establish what HRM contributes to an organization's performance are usually confronted with a number of reasons why an organization has done well in addition to adopting 'best practice' HRM, whatever that is. Statistical techniques can be used to 'control' some variables, ie eliminate them from the analysis, but it is difficult if not impossible to ensure that HRM practices have been completely isolated and that their direct impact on the organization's performance has been measured. Multivariate analysis is used where there is more than one dependent variable and where the dependent variables cannot be combined.

Second, there is the phenomenon of reverse causation, when a cause may be pre-dated by an effect – A might have caused B but alternatively, B might have come first and be responsible for A. For example, it is possible to demonstrate that organizations with effective performance management schemes do better than those without. But it might equally be the case that it is high-performing organizations that introduce effective performance management. It can be hard to be certain.

Tests of significance

Significance as a statistical concept refers to the degree to which an event could have occurred by chance. At the heart of statistical science lies a simple idea, which is that the chance or probability of various patterns of events can be predicted. When a particular pattern is observed it is possible to work out what the chances of its occurrence may be, given our existing state of knowledge or by making certain assumptions. If something has been observed that is unlikely to have occurred by chance, this occurrence can be accepted as significant. The problem is that any attempt to reach general conclusions may have to rely on fragmentary data. It is usually necessary to rely on samples of the population being studied and all sampling is subject to experimental error – the result can only be expressed in terms of probability and confidence limits will have to be placed on it. These can be calculated in terms of the standard error that might be expected from a sample. A standard error is the estimated standard deviation of a sample mean from a true mean. This implies that on approximately 95 per cent of occasions the estimate of the mean provided by the sample will be within two standard errors of the true mean.

Testing hypotheses

The chi-squared test uses a statistical formula to assess the degree of agreement between the data actually obtained and that expected under a particular hypothesis.

A null hypothesis is a method of testing a hypothesis frequently used by researchers in which it is assumed that there is no relationship between two or more variables. It asks the question: 'Could the hypothetical relationship have been caused by chance?' If the answer is 'no', then the hypothesis is worth pursuing. However, it does not prove that the hypothesis is correct; it only indicates that something is worth further investigation. It can be associated with the chi-squared test.

Key learning points: Statistical skills

Use of statistics

Statistics are used to describe and summarize data relating to a 'population', ie a homogeneous set of items with variable individual values. This involves measuring frequencies, central tendencies and dispersion.

They are also used to measure the relationships between variables (correlation and regression), to establish the relation between cause and effect (causality), to assess the degree of confidence that can be attached to conclusions (tests of significance) and to test hypotheses (the chi-squared test and null-hypothesis testing).

Statistics are used extensively in HRM to analyse and present quantitative information that can be used to guide decisions and monitor outcomes.

Measures of central tendency

Measures of central tendency identify the middle or centre of a set of data. There are three types: arithmetic average or mean, median and mode.

Measures of dispersion

It is useful to measure the extent to which the items in a set are dispersed or spread over a range of data.

Correlation

Correlation represents the relationship between two variables. If they are highly correlated they are strongly connected to one another, and vice versa.

Regression

Regression is another way of looking at the relationship between variables. It expresses how changes in levels of one item relate to changes in levels of another.

Causality

Determining the link between independent and dependent variables (cause and effect) – is a major issue in research, especially in the HRM field. It may be relatively easy to establish correlations in the shape of a demonstration that X is associated with Y; it is much more difficult and sometimes impossible to prove that X causes Y.

Tests of significance

Significance as a statistical concept refers to the degree to which an event could have occurred by chance.

69
Selection interviewing skills

KEY CONCEPTS AND TERMS

Behavioural-based interview

Closed question

Competency-based interview

Halo effect

Horns effect

Interview

Open question

Situational-based interview

Structured interview

LEARNING OUTCOMES

On completing this chapter you should be able to define these key concepts. You should also know about:

- Selection interviewing skills
- Preparing for the interview
- Planning the interview

- Questioning techniques
- Coming to a conclusion
- Dos and don'ts of selection interviewing

Introduction

The purpose of a selection interview is to establish the extent to which a candidate will be able to do the job. This means finding out how well a candidate's levels of skill, knowledge, abilities and com-

petency fit a person specification for the job that sets out these requirements. Selection interviewing is a skilled process, and this chapter starts with a description of the basic skills required. It then deals with the three areas in which these skills are applied: preparing for the interview, conducting the interview and reaching a conclusion.

Selection interviewing skills

An interview is a conversation with a purpose. It is a conversation because candidates should be given the opportunity to talk freely about themselves and their careers. But the conversation has to be planned, directed and controlled to achieve your aims in the time available. Overall, an effective approach to interviewing can be summed up as the three Cs:

- *Content* – the information you want and the questions you ask to get it.
- *Contact* – your ability to make and maintain good contact with candidates; to establish the sort of rapport that will encourage them to talk freely, thus revealing their strengths and their weaknesses.
- *Control* – your ability to control the interview so that you get the information you want.

This involves using the following interviewing skills: establishing rapport, questioning, listening, maintaining continuity, keeping control and note taking.

Establishing rapport

Establishing rapport means establishing a good relationship with candidates – getting on their wavelength, putting them at ease, encouraging them to respond and generally being friendly. This is not just a question of being 'nice' to them. If you achieve rapport you are more likely to get them to talk freely about both their strengths and weaknesses.

Good rapport is created by the way in which you greet candidates, how you start the interview and how you put your questions and respond to replies. Questions should not be posed aggressively or imply that you are criticizing some aspect of the candidate's career. Some people like the idea of 'stress' interviews but they are counter-productive. Candidates clam up and gain a negative impression of you and the organization.

When responding to answers you should be appreciative, not critical: 'Thank you, that was very helpful; now can we go on to…?' not, 'Well, it seems to me that things did not go according to plan.'

Body language can also be important. If you maintain natural eye contact, avoid slumping in your seat, nod and make encouraging comments when appropriate, you will establish better rapport and get more out of the interview.

Questioning

Questioning is the key skill interviewers need to possess. Their purpose is to draw candidates out and elicit the information the interviewer has decided must be obtained to reach a conclusion. Questioning is a fundamental part of a structured interview. There are a number of different types of questions, described later in the section on questioning techniques.

Listening

If an interview is a conversation with a purpose, listening skills are important. You need not only to hear but also to understand what candidates are saying. When interviewing you must concentrate on what candidates are telling you. Summarizing at regular intervals forces you to listen because you have to pay attention to what they have been saying in order to get the gist of their replies. If you play back to candidates your understanding of what they have told you for them to confirm or amend, it will ensure that you have fully comprehended the messages they are delivering.

Maintaining continuity

So far as possible, link your questions to a candidate's last reply so that the interview progresses logically and a cumulative set of data is built up. You can put bridging questions to candidates such as: 'Thank you, that was an interesting summary of what you have been doing in this aspect of your work. Now, could you tell me something about your other key responsibilities?'

Keeping control

You want candidates to talk, but not too much. When preparing for the interview you should have drawn up an agenda and you must try to stick to it. Don't cut candidates short too brutally but say something like: 'Thank you, I've got a good picture of that, now what about…?'

Focus on specifics as much as you can. If candidates ramble on a bit, ask a pointed question (a 'probe' question) that asks for an example illustrating the particular aspect of their work that you are considering.

Note taking

You won't remember everything that candidates tell you. It is useful to take notes of the key points they make, discreetly, but not surreptitiously. However, don't put candidates off by frowning or tut-tutting when you are making a negative note. It may be helpful to ask candidates if they would mind if you take notes. They can't really object, but will appreciate the fact that they have been asked.

Preparing for the interview

Your first step in preparing for an interview is to familiarize or re-familiarize yourself with the person specification which, as mentioned in Chapter 24, should be set out under the following headings:

- *Knowledge* – what the individual needs to know to carry out the role.

- *Skills and abilities* – what the individual has to be able to do to carry out the role.

- *Behavioural competencies* – the types of behaviour required for successful performance of the role. These should be role-specific, ideally based on an analysis of employees who are carrying out their roles effectively. The behaviours should also be linked to the core values and competency framework of the organization to help in ensuring that candidates will fit and support the organization's culture.

- *Qualifications and training* – the professional, technical or academic qualifications required or the training that the candidate should have undertaken.

- *Experience* – the types of achievements and activities likely to predict success.

- *Specific demands* – anything that the role holder will be expected to achieve in specified areas, eg develop new markets or products, improve sales, productivity or levels of customer service, introduce new systems or processes.

- *Special requirements* – travelling, unsocial hours, mobility, etc.

You should then read the candidates' CVs and, if available, their application forms or letters and refer to any other information about them obtained from the internet. This will identify any special questions you should ask about their career. For example, it may be necessary to fill in any gaps: 'What does this gap between jobs C and D signify?' (Although you would not put the question as baldly as that; it would be better to say something like this: 'I see there was a gap of six months between when you left your job in C and started in D. Would you mind telling me what you were doing during this time?')

Finally, you should consider how you will structure and plan the interview.

Structuring the interview

A structured interview is one that is based on a defined framework within which there is a set of predetermined questions. All candidates are asked the same questions, which will focus on the attributes and behaviours required to succeed in the job. The answers may be scored through a rating system.

The most typical framework is the person specification. Interview questions aim to analyse and build on the information provided by the candidate's CV or application form to establish the extent to which a candidate has the required knowledge, skills and abilities (KSAs). In a so-called competency-based interview the emphasis is on establishing if the candidate has the right level of desirable behavioural competencies. The interview may include experience-based questions in which candidates are asked to relate how they handled situations in the past requiring skills and abilities necessary for effective performance in the job for which they are applying. And/or it may include situational questions which provide candidates with hypothetical job-relevant situations and ask how they would deal with them

Coming to a conclusion

It is essential not to be beguiled by a pleasant, articulate and confident interviewee who is all surface and no substance. Beware of the 'halo' effect, which occurs when one or two good points are seized upon, leading to the neglect of negative indicators. The opposite 'horns' effect of focusing on the negatives should also be avoided.

Individual candidates should be assessed against the criteria. These could be set out under the headings of knowledge and skills, competencies, education, qualifications, training, experience and overall suitability. Ratings can be given against each heading, for example: very acceptable, acceptable, marginally acceptable, unacceptable. If you have used situational or behaviourally based questions you can indicate against each question whether the reply was good, just acceptable or poor. These assessments can inform your overall assessment of knowledge, skills and competencies.

Next, compare your assessment of each of the candidates against one another. You can then make a conclusion on those preferred by reference to their assessments under each heading.

In the end, your decision between qualified candidates could well be judgemental. There may be one suitable candidate but there could be two or three (although sometimes there may be none at all). Where there is a choice, you have to come to a balanced view by reference to your notes and ratings on which particular candidate is more likely to fit the job and the organization and have potential for a long-term career, if this is possible. Don't, however, settle for second best in desperation. It is better to try again.

Remember to make and keep notes of the reasons for your choice and why candidates have been rejected. These, together with the applications, should be kept for at least six months, just in case your decision is challenged as being discriminatory. An example of an interview rating form is given in Figure 69.1.

FIGURE 69.1   Example of an interview rating form

Area	Assessment				Comments
	Very acceptable	Acceptable	Marginally acceptable	Unacceptable	
Experience					
Knowledge and skills					
Competencies					
Education and qualifications					
Training					
Overall suitability					

Dos and don'ts of selection interviewing

TABLE 69.1   Dos and don'ts of selection interviewing

Do	Don't
• Plan the interview.	• Start the interview unprepared.
• Give yourself sufficient time.	• Plunge too quickly into demanding (probe) questions.
• Use a structured interview approach wherever possible.	• Ask multiple or leading questions.
• Create the right atmosphere.	• Pay too much attention to isolated strengths or weaknesses.
• Establish an easy and informal relationship – start with open questions.	• Allow candidates to gloss over important facts.
• Encourage the candidate to talk.	• Talk too much or allow candidates to ramble on.
• Cover the ground as planned, ensuring that you complete a prepared agenda and maintain continuity.	• Allow your prejudices to get the better of your capacity to make objective judgements.
• Analyse the candidate's career to reveal strengths, weaknesses and patterns of interest.	• Fall into the halo effect trap, ie drawing conclusions about a person on the basis of one or two good points, leading to the neglect of negative indicators. Or into the horns trap – focusing too much on one or two weak points.
• Make use of open questions which invite people to talk.	
• Ensure that questions are clear and unambiguous.	• Ask questions or make remarks that could be construed as in any way discriminatory.
• Get examples and instances of the successful application of knowledge, skills and the effective use of capabilities.	• Attempt too many interviews in a row.
• Make judgements on the basis of the factual information you have obtained about candidates' experience and attributes in relation to the person specification.	
• Keep control over the content and timing of the interview.	

Key learning points: Selection interviewing skills

Purpose of an interview

The purpose of a selection interview is to establish the extent to which a candidate will be able to do the job. This means finding out how well a candidate's levels of skill, knowledge, abilities and competency fit a person specification for the job that sets out these requirements.

Nature of an interview

An interview is a conversation with a purpose. It is a conversation because candidates should be given the opportunity to talk freely about themselves and their careers. But the conversation has to be planned, directed and controlled to achieve your aims in the time available.

Interviewing skills

- Establishing rapport – creating a good relationship with candidates – getting on their wavelength, putting them at ease, encouraging them to respond and generally being friendly.

- Questioning is the key skill interviewers need to possess. Their purpose is to draw candidates out and elicit the information the interviewer has decided must be obtained to reach a conclusion.

- If an interview is a conversation with a purpose, listening skills are important. You need not only to hear but also to understand what candidates are saying. When interviewing you must concentrate on what candidates are telling you.

- So far as possible link your questions to a candidate's last reply so that the interview progresses logically and a cumulative set of data is built up.

- You want candidates to talk, but not too much.

- It is useful to take notes of the key points they make, discreetly, but not surreptitiously.

Preparing for the interview

Your first step in preparing for an interview is to familiarize or re-familiarize yourself with the person specification.

Planning the interview

Interviews need to be planned in terms of their three main parts, the structure of questions and how the questions will be sequenced.

The parts of an interview

The content of an interview is in three parts: its beginning, middle and end.

Structuring the interview

A structured interview is one based on a defined framework within which there is a set of predetermined questions. All candidates are asked the same questions and the answers may be scored through a rating system. The most typical framework is the person specification.

Sequencing the interview

When planning interviews, you should give some thought to how you are going to sequence your questions, especially in the middle part. There are two basic approaches. The biographical approach is probably the most popular because it is simple to use and appears to be logical. This approach is often referred to as a 'structured interview'. The targeted approach is based on an analysis of the person specification from which criteria are identified for judging the suitability of the candidate. Interview questions can then 'target' these criteria by asking for specific information on what candidates know, what they can do and how they would typically behave in certain situations.

Questioning techniques

- The interviewer's job is to draw the candidate out, at the same time ensuring that the information required is obtained.

- To this end it is desirable to ask a number of open-ended questions – questions that cannot be answered by 'yes' or 'no' and which promote a full response.

- But a good interviewer will have an armoury of other types of questions to be asked when appropriate.

- Individual candidates should be assessed against the criteria. These could be set out under the headings of knowledge and skills, competencies, education, qualifications, training, experience and overall suitability.

- Ratings can be given against each heading, for example: very acceptable, acceptable, marginally acceptable, unacceptable. If you have used situational or behaviourally based questions you can indicate against each question whether the reply was good, just acceptable or poor. These assessments can inform your overall assessment of knowledge, skills and competencies.

Reference

University of Kent (2015) Strength-based interviews [online] http://www.kent.ac.uk/careers/interviews/ strength-based-interviews.htm [accessed 22 November 2015]

70
Job, role and skills analysis and competency modelling

LEARNING OUTCOMES

On completing this chapter you should be able to define these key concepts. You should also know about:

- Job analysis methodology and techniques

- Job descriptions

- Role analysis methodology

- Competency modelling

Introduction

The analysis of jobs, roles, and skills and competency modelling are some of the key techniques in human resource management. They provide the information required to produce job descriptions, role profiles, and person and learning specifications. They are of fundamental importance in organization and job design, recruitment and selection, performance management, learning and development, management development, career management, job evaluation and the design of grade and pay structures. These constitute most of the key HRM activities.

This chapter starts with definitions of the terms used in job and role analysis and then deals with the skills required to analyse jobs, roles and skills in order to produce job descriptions and role profiles, and to model competencies to produce competency frameworks.

Definitions

Jobs and roles

The terms 'job' and 'role' are often used interchangeably, but they are different. A job is an organizational unit consisting of a group of defined tasks or activities to be carried out or duties to be performed. A role is the part people play in their work – the emphasis is on the expected patterns of behaviour to achieve agreed outcomes. Roles are about people. Jobs are about tasks and duties.

Job description

A job description defines what job holders are required to do in terms of activities, duties or tasks. It is prescriptive and inflexible, giving people the opportunity to say: 'It's not in my job description', meaning that they only need to do the tasks listed there. A job description is more concerned with tasks than outcomes, and with the duties to be performed than the competencies required to perform them (technical competencies covering knowledge and skills, and behavioural competencies).

Job analysis

Job analysis is the process of collecting, analysing and setting out information about jobs in order to provide the basis for a job description and data for recruitment, training, job evaluation and performance management. Job analysis concentrates on what job holders do and achieve. It identifies the tasks job holders undertake and the outcomes and outputs they are expected to produce. Outcomes are the results of performance expressed as something that has been attained, such as a task or a project. Outputs are the results of performance expressed in quantified terms such as sales volume, income generated or units of production.

Role profile

A role profile defines key result areas, accountabilities and competencies for an individual role. It concentrates on outcomes rather than duties and therefore provides better guidance than a job description on expectations. It does not constrain people by prescribing their tasks. Outcomes may be expressed as 'key result areas' – elements of the role for which clear outputs and standards can be defined, each of which makes a significant contribution to achieving its overall purpose. Alternatively, they may be termed 'accountabilities' – areas of the role for which role holders are responsible in the form of being held to account for what they do and what they achieve.

A role profile does not prescribe in detail what has to be done to achieve the required outcomes. It therefore allows for greater flexibility than a job description and is more easily updated to reflect changing demands.

Role profiles are person-oriented. A role can be described in behavioural terms – given certain expectations, this is how the person needs to behave to meet them. Because it identifies knowledge, skill and competency requirements it also provides a better basis for recruitment and selection, performance management and learning and development purposes.

Accountability profile

An accountability profile is a type of role profile that focuses on what role holders will be held to account for in terms of what they do and what they achieve. It may be set out as a list of main accountabilities.

Generic role

A generic role is a role in which essentially similar activities are carried out by a number of people, for example a team leader or a call centre agent. In effect, it covers an occupation rather than a single role. It is described in a generic role profile.

Learning specification

A learning specification defines the knowledge and skills needed to achieve an acceptable level of performance. It is used as the basis for devising learning and development programmes. Learning specifications may be drawn up on the basis of competency and skills analysis.

Person specification

A person specification, also known as a job or role specification, defines the knowledge, skills and abilities (KSAs) required to carry out a role and the education, training, qualifications and experience needed to acquire the necessary KSAs. It may also refer specifically to the competencies required for effective job performance.

Role analysis

Role analysis finds out what people are expected to achieve when carrying out their work and the competencies and skills required to meet those expectations. Role analysis uses similar techniques to job analysis, although the objective of the analysis will be different.

Skills analysis

Skills analysis determines the skills required to achieve an acceptable level of performance.

Competency modelling

Competency modelling is concerned with behavioural analysis to establish the behavioural dimensions that affect job performance, and functional analysis to determine technical or work-based competencies. Behavioural or personal competencies are the personal characteristics of individuals they bring to their work roles. Technical or work-based competencies refer to expectations of workplace performance and the standards and outputs that people carrying out specified roles are expected to attain. They are also described as competences.

Job analysis

Job analysis produces the following information about a job:

- *Overall purpose* – why the job exists and, in essence, what the job holder is expected to contribute.
- *Organization* – to whom the job holder reports and who reports to the job holder.
- *Content* – the nature and scope of the job in terms of the tasks and operations to be performed and duties to be carried out.

If the outcome of the job analysis is to be used for job evaluation purposes, the job will also be analysed in terms of the factors or criteria used in the job evaluation scheme.

Job analysis methodology

The essence of job analysis is the application of systematic methods to the collection of information about job content. It is essentially about data collection and the basic steps are:

1 Obtain documents such as existing organization, procedure or training manuals that give information about the job.
2 Obtain from managers fundamental information concerning the job.
3 Obtain from job holders similar information about their jobs.

There are a number of job analysis techniques used for data collection as described below.

Interviews

The full flavour of a job is best obtained by interviewing job holders and checking findings with their managers or team leaders. The aim of the interview should be to obtain the relevant facts about the job, namely the job title, organizational details (reporting relationships as described in an organization chart) and a list of the tasks or duties performed by the job holder. The interview should also establish outcomes and outputs.

For recruitment, training or job evaluation purposes these basic details can be supplemented by questions designed to elicit from the job holders more information about the level of their responsibilities and the demands made upon them by the job. These can cover the amount of supervision received, the degree of discretion allowed in making decisions, the typical problems to be solved, the amount of guidance available when solving the problems, the relative difficulty of the tasks to be performed and the qualifications and skills required to carry out the work. The following are the steps required to conduct a job analysis interview:

1 Work to a logical sequence of questions that help interviewees to order their thoughts about the job.

2 Probe as necessary to establish what people really do in terms of outputs and outcomes – answers to questions are often vague and information may be given by means of untypical instances.

3 Ensure that job holders are not allowed to get away with vague or inflated descriptions of their work – if, for example, the interview is part of a job evaluation exercise, they would not be human if they did not present the job in the best possible light.

4 Sort out the wheat from the chaff; answers to questions may produce a lot of irrelevant data that must be sifted before preparing the job description.

5 Obtain a clear statement from job holders about their authority to make decisions and the amount of guidance they receive from their manager or team leader. This is not easy: if asked what decisions they are authorized to make, most people look blank because they think about their job in terms

of duties and tasks rather than abstract decisions.

6 Avoid asking leading questions that make the expected answer obvious.

7 Allow the job holder ample opportunity to talk by creating an atmosphere of trust.

It is helpful to use a checklist when conducting the interview. Elaborate checklists are not necessary; they only confuse people. The basic questions to be answered are as follows.

- What is the title of your job?
- To whom are you responsible?
- Who is responsible to you? An organization chart is helpful.
- What is the main purpose of your job in overall terms, ie what are you expected to do?
- What are the key activities you have to carry out in your role? Try to group them under no more than 10 headings.
- What are the results you are expected to achieve in each of those key activities?
- What are you expected to know to be able to carry out your job?
- What skills should you have to carry out your job?

The answers to these questions may need to be sorted out – they can often result in a mass of jumbled information that has to be analysed so that the various activities can be distinguished and refined to seven or eight key areas.

The advantages of the interviewing method are that it is flexible, can provide in-depth information and is easy to organize and prepare. It is therefore the most common approach. But interviewing can be time-consuming, which is why in large job analysis exercises, questionnaires may be used to provide advance information about the job. This speeds up the interviewing process or even replaces the interview altogether, although this means that much of the 'flavour' of the job – ie what it is really like – may be lost.

Questionnaires

Questionnaires about their roles can be completed by role holders and approved by the role holder's manager or team leader. They are helpful when a large number of roles have to be covered. They can also save interviewing time by recording purely factual information and by enabling the analyst to structure questions in advance to cover areas that need to be explored in greater depth. The simpler the questionnaire the better; it need only cover the eight questions listed above.

The advantage of questionnaires is that they can produce information quickly and cheaply for a large number of jobs. But a substantial sample is needed and the construction of a questionnaire is a skilled job, which should only be carried out on the basis of some preliminary fieldwork. It is highly advisable to pilot test questionnaires before launching into a full-scale exercise. The accuracy of the results also depends on the willingness and ability of job holders to complete questionnaires. Many people find it difficult to express themselves in writing about their work.

Observation

Observation means studying role holders at work, noting what they do, how they do it, and how much time it takes. This method is most appropriate for routine administrative or manual roles but it is seldom used because of the time it takes.

Job descriptions

Job descriptions should be based on the job analysis and should be as brief and factual as possible. The headings under which the job description should be written and notes for guidance on completing each section are set out below.

Job title

The existing or proposed job title should indicate as clearly as possible the function in which the job is carried out and the level of the job within that function. The use of terms such as 'manager', 'assistant manager' or 'senior' to describe job levels should be reasonably consistent between functions with regard to grading of the jobs.

Reporting to

The job title of the manager or team leader to whom the job holder is directly responsible should be given under this heading. No attempt should be made to indicate here any functional relationships the job holder might have to other people.

Reporting to job holder

The job titles of all the posts directly reporting to the job holder should be given under this heading. Again, no attempt should be made here to indicate any functional relationships that might exist between the job holder and other employees.

Overall purpose

This section should describe as concisely as possible the overall purpose of the job. The aim should be to convey in one sentence a broad picture of the job that will clearly distinguish it from other jobs and establish the role of job holders and the contribution they should make towards achieving the objectives of the company and their own function or unit. No attempt should be made to describe the activities carried out under this heading, but the overall summary should lead naturally to the analysis of activities in the next section. When preparing the job description, it is often best to defer writing down the definition of overall responsibilities until the activities have been analysed and described.

Main activities, tasks or duties

The following method of describing activities, tasks or duties should be adopted:

1 Group the various activities identified by the job analysis together so that no more than seven or eight areas remain. If the number is extended much beyond that, the job description will become over-complex and it will be difficult to be specific about tasks or duties.

2 Define each activity in one sentence, starting with a verb in the active voice, to provide a positive indication of what has to be done

and eliminate unnecessary wording. Examples are: plan, prepare, produce, implement, process, provide, schedule, complete, dispatch, maintain, liaises with, and collaborates with.

3   Describe what is done as succinctly as possible, for example: test new systems, post cash to the nominal and sales ledgers, dispatch packed output to the warehouse, schedule production, ensure that management accounts are produced, prepare marketing plans.

4   State briefly the purpose of the activity in terms of outcomes, outputs or standards to be achieved. For example: test new systems to ensure they meet agreed systems specifications; post cash to the nominal and sales ledgers in order to provide up-to-date and accurate financial information; dispatch to the warehouse planned output so that all items are removed by carriers on the same day they are packed; schedule production to meet laid-down output and delivery targets; ensure that management accounts are produced that provide the required level of information to management and individual managers on financial performance against budget and on any variances; prepare marketing plans that support the achievement of the marketing strategies of the enterprise, are realistic, and provide clear guidance on the actions to be taken by the development, production, marketing and sales departments; plan and implement sales campaigns to meet sales targets.

An example of a job description is given in Figure 70.1.

Role analysis and role profiles

Role analysis uses the same techniques as job analysis but the focus is on identifying inputs – KSAs (knowledge, skill and abilities), competency requirements and required outcomes (key result areas or accountabilities) rather than simply listing the tasks to be carried out. A role profile is initially set out under the same headings as a job description, ie role title, responsible to, responsible to role holder and the purpose of the role, but it then focuses on the following aspects of the role.

FIGURE 70.1   Example of a job description

Job title:	HR advisor; recruitment
Reports to:	HR Service Centre Manager
Reports to job holder:	None
Overall purpose:	To provide recruitment services to line managers for jobs below management level

Main activities:

1   Respond promptly to requests from line managers to assist in recruiting staff.

2   Produce person specifications that clearly indicate requirements for recruitment purposes.

3   Agree on the use of sources of applicants such as web-based recruitment, agencies or media advertisements that will generate high-calibre candidates at a reasonable cost.

4   Brief and liaise with agencies and/or draft advertisements for jobs for approval by line managers and place advertisements or information on vacancies using the media and/or the internet.

5   Process replies and draw up short lists that enable a choice to be made between well-qualified candidates.

6   Conduct preliminary interviews independently or conduct short-list interviews with line managers that identify candidates who meet the specification.

7   Agree offer terms with line manager, take up references and confirm the offer.

8   Review and evaluate sources of candidates and analyse recruitment costs.

Key result areas

A key result area is an element of a role for which clear outputs and outcomes can be defined, each of which makes a significant contribution to achieving the overall purpose of the role. It may be described as an 'accountability' – an aspect of the role for which the role holder is responsible (held to account for).

The number of key result areas is unlikely to be more than seven or eight, certainly not more than 10. The basic structure of a key result area definition should resemble that of a job description task definition, ie it should be expressed in one sentence starting with an active verb. However, the content of the definition should focus more on the specific purpose of the activity in terms of outputs or standards to be achieved than on describing in detail the duties involved.

Knowledge, skills and abilities required

Knowledge, skills and abilities should be expressed in terms of 'need to know' – the required knowledge of techniques, processes, procedures, systems and the business generally (its products or services and its competitors and customers), and 'need to be able to do' – the skills required in each area of activity. These are the technical competencies required by the job.

Behavioural competencies

Behavioural competencies describe how the role holder is expected to behave when carrying out the role. They may be linked to the organization's competency framework and cover such areas as teamworking, communication, people management and development, and customer relations. An example of a role profile is given in Figure 70.2.

Generic role profiles

Generic role profiles cover occupations rather than individual roles. They tend to be more generalized and may be somewhat simpler than individual role profiles, for example by restricting the profile to lists of key result areas and competency dimensions. An example of a generic role profile is given in Figure 70.3.

Skills analysis

Skills analysis determines the skills required to achieve an acceptable standard of performance. It is mainly used for technical, craft, manual and office jobs to provide the basis for devising learning and training programmes. Skills analysis starts from a broad job analysis but goes into details of not only what job holders have to do but also the particular abilities and skills they need to do it. Skills analysis techniques are described below.

Job breakdown

The job breakdown technique analyses a job into separate operations, processes, or tasks that can be used as the elements of an instruction sequence. A job breakdown analysis is recorded in a standard format of three columns:

1 *The stage column*, in which the different steps in the job are described – most semi-skilled jobs can easily be broken down into their constituent parts.

2 *The instruction column*, in which a note is made against each step of how the task should be done. This, in effect, describes what has to be learnt by the trainee.

3 *The key points column*, in which any special points such as quality standards or safety instructions are noted against each step so that they can be emphasized to a trainee learning the job.

Manual skills analysis

Manual skills analysis is a technique developed from work study. It isolates for instructional purposes the skills and knowledge employed by experienced workers in performing tasks that require manual dexterity. It is used to analyse short-cycle, repetitive operations such as assembly tasks and other similar factory work.

FIGURE 70.2   Example of a role profile

Role title:	Database administrator
Department:	Information systems
Purpose of role:	Responsible for the development and support of databases and their underlying environment

Key result areas

- Identify database requirements for all projects that require data management in order to meet the needs of internal customers.
- Develop project plans collaboratively with colleagues to deliver against their database needs.
- Support underlying database infrastructure.
- Liaise with system and software providers to obtain product information and support.
- Manage project resources (people and equipment) within predefined budget and criteria, as agreed with line manager and originating department.
- Allocate work to and supervise contractors on a day-to-day basis.
- Ensure security of the underlying database infrastructure through adherence to established protocols and to develop additional security protocols where needed.

Need to know

- Oracle database administration.
- Operation of Designer 2000 and oracle forms SQL/PLSQL, Unix administration, shell programming.

Able to

- Analyse and choose between options where the solution is not always obvious.
- Develop project plans and organize own workload on a timescale of 1–2 months.
- Adapt to rapidly changing needs and priorities without losing sight of overall plans and priorities.
- Interpret budgets in order to manage resources effectively within them.
- Negotiate with suppliers.
- Keep abreast of technical developments and trends, bring these into day-to-day work when feasible and build them into new project developments.

Behavioural competencies

- Aim to get things done well and set and meet challenging goals, create own measures of excellence and constantly seek ways of improving performance.
- Analyse information from range of sources and develop effective solutions/recommendations.
- Communicate clearly and persuasively, orally or in writing, dealing with technical issues in a non-technical manner.
- Work participatively on projects with technical and non-technical colleagues.
- Develop positive relationships with colleagues as the supplier of an internal service.

FIGURE 70.3   Example of a generic role profile

Generic role title: Team leader

Overall purpose of role: To lead teams in order to attain team goals and further the achievement of the
organization's objectives.

Key result areas

1   Agree targets and standards with team members which support the attainment of the organization's objectives.

2   Plan with team members work schedules and resource requirements that will ensure that team targets will be reached, indeed exceeded.

3   Agree performance measures and quality assurance processes with team members that will clarify output and quality expectations.

4   Agree with team members the allocation of tasks, rotating responsibilities as appropriate to achieve flexibility and the best use of the skills and capabilities of team members.

5   Co-ordinate the work of the team to ensure that team goals are achieved.

6   Ensure that the team members collectively monitor the team's performance in terms of achieving output, speed of response and quality targets and standards and agree with team members any corrective action required to ensure that team goals are achieved.

7   Conduct team reviews of performance to agree areas for improvement and actions required.

Competencies

- Build effective team relationships, ensuring that team members are committed to the common purpose.
- Encourage self-direction amongst team members but provide guidance and clear direction as required.
- Share information with team members.
- Trust team members to get on with things – not continually checking.
- Treat team members fairly and consistently.
- Support and guide team members to make the best use of their capabilities.
- Encourage self-development by example.
- Actively offer constructive feedback to team members and positively seek and be open to constructive feedback from them.
- Contribute to the development of team members, encouraging the acquisition of additional skills and providing opportunities for them to be used effectively.

The hand, finger and other body movements of experienced operatives are observed and recorded in detail as they carry out their work. The analysis concentrates on the tricky parts of the job which, while presenting no difficulty to the experienced operative, have to be analysed in depth before they can be taught to trainees. Not only are the hand movements recorded, but particulars are also noted of the cues (visual and other senses) that the operative absorbs when performing the tasks. Explanatory comments are added when necessary.

Task analysis

Task analysis is a systematic analysis of the behaviour required to carry out a task with a view to identifying areas of difficulty and the appropriate training techniques and learning aids necessary for successful instruction. It can be used for all types of jobs but is specifically relevant to administrative tasks.

The analytical approach used in task analysis is similar to those adopted in the job breakdown and manual skills analysis techniques. The results of the analysis are usually recorded in a standard format of four columns, as follows:

1 *Task* – a brief description of each element.

2 *Level of importance* – the relative significance of each task to the successful performance of the role.

3 *Degree of difficulty* – the level of skill or knowledge required to perform each task.

4 *Training method* – the instructional techniques, practice and experience required.

Faults analysis

Faults analysis is the process of analysing the typical faults that occur when performing a task, especially the more costly faults. It is carried out when the incidence of faults is high. A study is made of the job and, by questioning workers and team leaders, the most commonly occurring faults are identified. A faults specification is then produced, which provides trainees with information on what faults can occur, how they can be recognized, what causes them, what effect they have, who is responsible for them, what action the trainees should take when a particular fault occurs, and how a fault can be prevented from recurring.

Job learning analysis

Job learning analysis, as described by Pearn and Kandola (1993), concentrates on the inputs and process rather than the content of the job. It analyses nine learning skills that contribute to satisfactory performance. A learning skill is one used to increase other skills or knowledge and represents broad categories of job behaviour which need to be learnt. The learning skills are the following:

- physical skills requiring practice and repetition to get right;
- complex procedures or sequences of activity that are memorized or followed with the aid of written material such as manuals;
- non-verbal information such as sight, sound, smell, taste and touch, used to check, assess or discriminate, and which usually takes practice to get right;
- memorizing facts or information;

- ordering, prioritizing and planning, which refer to the degree to which a role holder has any responsibility for, and flexibility in, determining the way a particular activity is performed;
- looking ahead and anticipating;
- diagnosing, analysing and problem solving, with or without help;
- interpreting or using written manuals and other sources of information such as diagrams or charts;
- adapting to new ideas and systems.

In conducting a job learning analysis interview, the interviewer obtains information on the main aims and principal activities of the job and then, using question cards for each of the nine learning skills, analyses each activity in more depth, recording responses and obtaining as many examples as possible under each heading.

Competency modelling

As defined by Shippmann *et al* (2000: 727):

> Competency modelling approaches typically provide descriptions of the individual-level competencies that are core, or common, for an occupational group, entire level of jobs (eg executive, management, supervisory, hourly), or for the organization as a whole. The focus is on broad applicability and leveraging what is in common or universal. Even when the modelling effort targets a narrowly defined job group (eg sales managers), the resulting descriptions are typically at a fairly high level and general in nature.

Competency modelling is the basis for defining behavioural and technical competencies (see Chapter 13).

Behavioural competency modelling

Behavioural competency modelling is the method used to identify, analyse and describe behavioural competencies. These define the behaviours that organizations expect their employees to practise in their work in order to reach an acceptable level of performance. They have an important part to play in providing information that contributes to a number of HRM activities, for example, recruitment, learning and development, and performance management. Table 70.1 shows guidance on the criteria for a fully rigorous competency definition produced by Shippmann *et al* (2000).

These are exacting criteria. The emphasis is on the systematic collection and analysis of data. There are five approaches to behavioural competency analysis: in ascending order of complexity these are:

1 Expert opinion.
2 Structured interview.
3 Workshops.
4 Critical-incident technique.
5 Repertory grid analysis.

Expert opinion

The basic, crudest and least satisfactory method is for an 'expert' member of the HR department, possibly in discussion with other 'experts' from the same department to draw up a list from their own understanding of 'what counts', coupled with an analysis of other published lists. This is unsatisfactory because the likelihood of the competencies being appropriate, realistic and measurable in the absence of detailed analysis is fairly remote. The list tends to be bland and, because line managers and job holders have not been involved, unacceptable.

Structured interview

This method begins with a list of competencies drawn up by 'experts' and proceeds by subjecting a number of role holders to a structured interview. The interviewer starts by identifying the key result areas of the role and goes on to analyse the behavioural characteristics that distinguish performers at different levels of competence. The basic question is: 'What are the positive or negative indicators of behaviour conducive or non-conducive to achieving high levels of performance?' These may be analysed under headings such as those set out below. Under each heading instances will be sought that illustrate effective or less effective behaviour.

- Personal drive (achievement motivation).
- Impact on results.
- Analytical power.
- Strategic thinking.

- Creative thinking (ability to innovate).
- Decisiveness.
- Commercial judgement.
- Team management and leadership.
- Interpersonal relationships.
- Ability to communicate.
- Ability to adapt and cope with change and pressure.
- Ability to plan and control projects.

One of the problems with this approach is that it relies too much on the ability of the expert to draw out information from interviewees. It is also undesirable to use a deductive approach that pre-empts the analysis with a prepared list of competency headings. It is better to do this by means of an inductive approach, which starts from specific types of behaviour and then groups them under competency headings. This can be done in a workshop by analysing positive and negative indicators to gain an understanding of the competence dimensions of an occupation or job, as described below.

Workshops

Workshops bring a group of people together who have 'expert' knowledge or experience of the role – managers and role holders as appropriate – with a facilitator, usually but not necessarily a member of the HR department or an outside consultant.

The members of the workshop begin by getting agreement to the overall purpose of the role and its key result areas. They then develop examples of effective and less effective behaviour for each area, which are recorded on flipcharts. For example, one of the key result areas for a divisional HR director might be workforce planning, defined as:

> Prepares forecasts of human resource requirements and plans for the acquisition, retention and effective utilization of employees, which ensure that the company's needs for people are met.

The positive indicators for this competency area could include:

- seeks involvement in business strategy formulation;
- contributes to business planning by taking a strategic view of longer-term human resource issues that are likely to affect business strategy;

TABLE 70.1   Criteria for a fully rigorous competency definition (Shippmann *et al*, 2000)

Variable	Conditions required to meet high rigorous criteria
Method of investigation	A logically selected mix of multiple methods is used to obtain information, eg interviews, focus groups, questionnaires.
Type of descriptor content collected	Variable combinations of multiple types of information are collected, eg work activities, KSAs (knowledge, skills and abilities statements) and performance standards.
Procedures for developing descriptors	Information collected from content experts using a structured protocol and a representative sample.
Detail of descriptor content	Use of a number of labels representing discrete categories of content which operationally define each category and leave no room for misinterpretation.
Link to business goals and strategies	Steps taken to ensure that results are aligned with the broader goals and longer-term strategies of the organization.
Content review	Formal review takes place to ensure that: • item level descriptions are clear; • content categories do not overlap, content categories are internally consistent; • items represent measurable content appropriate for the intended application.
Ranking descriptor content	The set of descriptors are prioritized and ranked.
Assessment of reliability	Content category labels are matched with item-level descriptors and rated according to their relative importance for successful job performance.
Item retention criteria	Multiple, clear, logical criteria are consistently applied to items to determine whether content is retained or deleted.
Documentation	Clear definitions are made of the procedures to be employed in applying the competency framework.

- networks with senior management colleagues to understand and respond to the human resource planning issues they raise;
- suggests practical ways to improve the use of human resources, for example, the introduction of annual hours.

Negative indicators could include:

- takes a narrow view of HR planning – does not seem to be interested in or understand the wider business context;
- lacks the determination to overcome problems and deliver forecasts;
- fails to anticipate skills shortages; for example, unable to meet the multiskilling requirements implicit in the new computer-integrated manufacturing system;
- does not seem to talk the same language as line management colleagues – fails to understand their requirements;
- slow in responding to requests for help.

When the positive and negative indicators have been agreed, the next step is to distil the competency dimensions that can be inferred from the lists. In this example they could be:

- strategic capability;
- business understanding;
- achievement motivation;
- interpersonal skills;
- communication skills;
- consultancy skills.

These dimensions might also be reflected in the analysis of other areas of competency so that, progressively, a picture of the competencies is built up, which is linked to actual behaviour in the workplace.

The facilitator's job is to prompt, help the group to analyse its findings and assist generally in the production of a set of competence dimensions that can be illustrated by behaviour-based examples. The facilitator may have some ideas about the sort of headings that may emerge from this process but should not try to influence the group to come to a conclusion it has not worked out for itself, albeit with some assistance from the facilitator.

Workshops can use the critical-incident or repertory grid techniques, as described below.

Critical-incident technique

The critical-incident technique is a means of eliciting data about effective or less effective behaviour related to examples of actual events – critical incidents. The technique is used with groups of job holders and/or their managers or other 'experts' (sometimes, less effectively, with individuals) as follows:

1 Explain what the technique is and what it is used for, ie 'to assess what constitutes good or poor performance by analysing events that have been observed to have a noticeably successful or unsuccessful outcome, thus providing more factual and "real" information than by simply listing tasks and guessing performance requirements.'

2 Agree and list the key results in the role to be analysed. To save time, the analyst can establish these prior to the meeting but it is necessary to ensure that they are agreed provisionally by the group, which can be told that the list may well be amended in the light of the forthcoming analysis.

3 Take each area of the role in turn and ask the group for examples of critical incidents. If, for instance, one of the job responsibilities is dealing with customers, the following request could be made: 'I want you to tell me about a particular occasion at work which involved you – or that you observed – in dealing with a customer. Think about what the circumstances were, eg who took part, what the customer asked for, what you or the other member of the staff did and what the outcome was.'

4 Collect information about the critical incident under the following headings:

- what the circumstances were;
- what the individual did;
- the outcome of what the individual did.

5 Record this information on a flipchart.

6 Continue this process for each key result area.

7 Refer to the flipchart and analyse each incident by obtaining ratings of the recorded behaviour on a scale such as 1 for least effective to 5 for most effective.

8 Discuss these ratings to get initial definitions of effective and ineffective performance for each of the key result areas.

9 Refine these definitions as necessary after the meeting – it can be difficult to get a group to produce finished definitions.

10 Produce the final analysis, which can list the competencies required and include performance indicators or standards of performance for each key result area.

This is a thorough, indeed exhaustive approach, but it is time-consuming and requires skill to manage.

Repertory grid

Like the critical-incident technique, the repertory grid can be used to identify the dimensions that distinguish good from poor standards of performance. The technique is based on Kelly's (1955) personal construct theory. Personal constructs are the ways in which we view the world. They are personal because they are highly individual and they influence the way we behave or view other people's behaviour. The aspects of the role to which these 'constructs' or judgements apply are called 'elements'.

To elicit judgements, a group of people are asked to concentrate on certain elements, which are the tasks carried out by role holders, and develop constructs about these elements. This enables them to define the qualities that indicate the essential requirements for successful performance.

The procedure followed by the analyst is known as the 'triadic method of elicitation' (a sort of three-card trick) and involves the following steps:

1 Identify the tasks or elements of the role to be subjected to repertory grid analysis. This is done by one of the other forms of job analysis, eg interviewing.

2 List the tasks on cards.

3 Draw three cards at random from the pack and ask the members of the group to nominate which of these tasks is the odd one out from the point of view of the qualities and characteristics needed to perform it.

4 Probe to obtain more specific definitions of these qualities or characteristics in the form of expected behaviour. If, for example, a characteristic has been described as the 'ability to plan and organize', ask questions such as: 'What sort of behaviour or actions indicate that someone is planning effectively?' or, 'How can we tell if someone is not organizing his or her work particularly well?'

5 Draw three more cards from the pack and repeat steps 3 and 4.

6 Repeat this process until all the cards have been analysed and there are no more constructs to be identified.

7 List the constructs and ask the group members to rate each task on every quality, using a six- or seven-point scale.

8 Collect and analyse the scores to assess their relative importance.

Like the critical-incident technique, repertory grid analysis helps people to articulate their views by reference to specific examples. An additional advantage is that the repertory grid makes it easier for them to identify the behavioural characteristics or competencies required in a job by limiting the area of comparison through the triadic technique. Although a full statistical analysis of the outcome of a repertory grid exercise is helpful, the most important results that can be obtained are the descriptions of what constitutes good or poor performance in each element of the job.

Like the critical-incident technique, the repertory grid requires a skilled analyst who can probe and draw out the descriptions of job characteristics. It is quite detailed and time-consuming, but even if the full process is not followed, much of the methodology is of use in a less elaborate approach to competency modelling.

Choice of approach

Workshops are probably the best approach They get people involved and do not rely on 'expert' opinion. Critical-incident or repertory grid techniques are more sophisticated and can be associated with workshops but they are time-consuming and considerable expertise is required to run them.

Technical competency modelling

Technical competencies or competences can be modelled through the process of functional analysis, which is used to produce definitions of the competences contained in NVQ (National Vocational

Qualification) frameworks. Functional analysis focuses on the outcomes of work performance. Note that the analysis is not simply concerned with outputs in the form of quantifiable results but deals with the broader results that have to be achieved by role holders. An outcome could be a satisfied customer, a more highly motivated subordinate or a better-functioning team.

Functional analysis deals with processes such as developing staff, providing feedback and monitoring performance as well as tasks. It starts with an analysis of the roles fulfilled by an individual in order to arrive at a description of the separate components or 'units' of performance that make up that role. The resulting units consist of performance criteria, described in terms of outcomes, and a description of the knowledge and skill requirements that underpin successful performance. The techniques used in functional analysis are similar to those used in job analysis, described earlier in this chapter.

Key learning points: Competency and skills analysis

Job analysis methodology and techniques

The essence of job analysis is the application of systematic methods to the collection of information about job content. It is essentially about data collection and the basic steps are:

- obtain documents such as existing organization, procedure or training manuals that give information about the job;

- obtain from managers fundamental information concerning the job;

- obtain from job holders similar information about their jobs.

Job descriptions

Job descriptions should be based on the job analysis and should be as brief and factual as possible. The headings should be: job title, reporting to, reporting to job holder, main purpose of job, main activities, tasks or duties.

Role analysis methodology

Role analysis uses the same techniques as job analysis but the focus is on identifying inputs (knowledge, skill and competency requirements) and required outcomes (key result areas) rather than simply listing the tasks to be carried out.

Behavioural competency modelling

Behavioural competency modelling is used for identifying, analysing and describing behavioural competencies that define the behaviours that organizations expect their staff to practise in their work in order to reach an acceptable level of performance. The emphasis is on the systematic collection and analysis of data. There are five approaches to behavioural competency analysis. In ascending order of complexity these are: expert opinion, structured interview, workshops, critical-incident technique, and repertory grid analysis.

Analysing technical competencies

Functional analysis starts with an analysis of the roles fulfilled by an individual in order to arrive at a description of the separate components or 'units' of performance that make up that role. The resulting units consist of performance criteria, described in terms of outcomes, and a description of the knowledge and skill requirements that underpin successful performance.

Skills analysis

Skills analysis determines the skills required to achieve an acceptable standard of performance. It is mainly used for technical, craft, manual and office jobs to provide the basis for devising learning and training programmes. Skills analysis starts from a broad job analysis but goes into details of what job holders have to do and the particular abilities and skills they need to do it. Skills analysis techniques include job breakdown, manual skills analysis, faults analysis and job learning analysis.

References

Kelly, G (1955) *The Psychology of Personal Constructs*, New York, Norton

Pearn, K and Kandola, R (1993) *Job Analysis: A manager's guide*, London, IPM

Shippmann, J S, Ash, R A and Battista, M (2000) The practice of competency modelling, *Personnel Psychology*, 53 (3), pp 703–40

71
Learning and development skills

KEY CONCEPTS AND TERMS

Coaching

Job instruction

Mentoring

LEARNING OUTCOMES

On completing this chapter you should be able to define these key concepts. You should also know about coaching, mentoring and job instruction skills.

Introduction

HR professionals need skills in coaching and mentoring to fulfil their important responsibilities for enhancing the knowledge and skills of employees and for providing guidance to line managers on conducting their learning and development activities.

Coaching

Coaching is a personal (usually one-to-one) approach that enables people to develop their skills and knowledge and improve their performance. As Whitmore (2002: 8) suggested: 'Coaching is unlocking a person's potential to maximize their own performance. It is helping them to learn rather than teaching them.' Clutterbuck (2004: 23) noted that: 'Coaching is primarily focused on performance within the current job and emphasizes the development of skills.'

Coaching is often provided by specialists from inside or outside the organization who concentrate on specific areas of skills or behaviour, for example leadership. But it is also something that HR professionals have to be prepared to do as part of their normal learning and development duties, and this means deploying the skills described below.

The approach to coaching

To succeed in coaching you need to understand that your role is to help people to learn and ensure that they are motivated to learn. They should be aware of the advantages to them as well as the organization of developing their present level of knowledge or skill or modifying their behaviour. Individuals should be given guidance on what they should be learning and feedback on how they are doing and, because learning is an active not a passive process, they should be actively involved with their coach.

Coaching is sometimes informal but it has to be planned. It is not simply checking from time to time on what people are doing and then advising them on how to do it better. Nor is it occasionally telling people where they have gone wrong and throwing in a lecture for good measure. As far as possible, coaching should take place within the framework of a general plan of the areas and direction in which individuals will benefit from further development. Coaching plans should be incorporated into the personal development plans set out in a performance agreement.

Coaching should provide motivation, structure and effective feedback. As a coach, you should believe that people can succeed and that they can contribute to their own success.

Coaching styles

Clutterbuck and Megginson (2005: 52) identified four coaching styles:

1 *Assessor* – this is akin to instruction and involves telling people the way to do something.

2 *Demonstrator* – this is less directive than the assessor style. It involves showing learners how to do something and then getting them to do it with guidance and comments from the coach as required.

3 *Tutor* – this involves encouraging learners to find out how to do things for themselves. It is still relatively directive as it is the coach who suggests what learners should look for.

4 *Stimulator* – this helps learners to teach themselves by guiding their thinking through the use of insight-provoking questions.

Criteria for effectiveness

The following criteria for evaluating the performance of a coach were listed by Gray (2010: 379):

- establishes rapport;
- creates trust and respect;

- demonstrates effective communication skills;
- promotes self-awareness and self-knowledge;
- uses active listening and questioning techniques;
- assists goal development and setting;
- motivates;
- encourages alternative perspectives;
- assists in making sense of a situation;
- identifies significant patterns of thinking and behaving;
- provides an appropriate mix of challenge and support;
- facilitates depth of understanding;
- shows compassion;
- acts ethically;
- inspires curiosity;
- acts as a role model;
- values diversity and difference;
- promotes action and reflection.

Mentoring

Mentors offer guidance, pragmatic advice and continuing support to help those allocated to them to learn and develop. It is a method of helping people to learn as distinct from coaching, which can be a relatively directive means of increasing people's competence. Mentors may be line managers. They are often appointed and trained by learning and development specialists who therefore need to be aware of the skills required. L&D professionals may act as mentors themselves, although experienced managers are best if they have the skills and enthusiasm required.

Mentors provide people with:

- advice in drawing up self-development programmes or learning contracts;
- general help with learning programmes;
- guidance on how to acquire the necessary knowledge and skills to do a new job;
- advice on dealing with any administrative, technical or people problems individuals meet, especially in the early stages of their careers;

- information on 'the way things are done around here' – the corporate culture in terms of expected behaviour;
- coaching in specific skills;
- help in tackling projects – not by doing it for them but by pointing them in the right direction, helping people to help themselves;
- a parental figure with whom individuals can discuss their aspirations and concerns and who will lend a sympathetic ear to their problems.

Mentors need to adopt a non-directive but supportive approach to helping the person or persons they are dealing with.

Job instruction

When people learn specific tasks, especially those involving basic administrative or manual skills, the learning will be more effective if job instruction techniques are used. HR professionals may possibly be involved in providing direct instruction but their most typical role is that of promoting effective instruction techniques for use by line managers and others involved in workplace learning or running formal training programmes. They should therefore be aware of the sequence of instruction, as described below.

Preparation

Preparation for each instruction period means that the trainer must have a plan for presenting the subject matter and using appropriate teaching methods, visual aids and demonstration aids. It also means preparing trainees for the instruction that is to follow. They should want to learn. They must perceive that the learning will be relevant and useful to them personally. They should be encouraged to take pride in their job and to appreciate the satisfaction that comes from skilled performance.

Presentation

Presentation should consist of a combination of telling and showing – explanation and demonstration. Explanation should be as simple and direct as possible: the trainer explains briefly the ground to be covered and what to look for. He or she makes the maximum use of charts, diagrams and other visual aids. The aim should be to teach first things first and then proceed from the known to the unknown, the simple to the complex, the concrete to the abstract, the general to the particular, the observation to reasoning, and the whole to the parts and back to the whole again.

Demonstration

Demonstration is an essential stage in instruction, especially when the skill to be learnt is mainly a 'doing' skill. Demonstration can take place in three stages:

1 The complete operation is shown at normal speed to show the trainee how the task should be carried out eventually.

2 The operation is demonstrated slowly and in correct sequence, element by element, to indicate clearly what is done and the order in which each task is carried out.

3 The operation is demonstrated again slowly, at least two or three times, to stress the how, when and why of successive movements.

The learner then practises by imitating the instructor and constantly repeating the operation under guidance. The aim is to reach the target level of performance for each element of the total task, but the instructor must constantly strive to develop coordinated and integrated performance – that is, the smooth combination of the separate elements of the task into a whole job pattern.

Follow up

Follow up continues during the training period for all the time required by the learner to reach a level of performance equal to that of the normal experienced worker in terms of quality, speed and attention to safety. During the follow-up stage, the learner will continue to need help with particularly difficult tasks or to overcome temporary set-backs that result in a deterioration of performance. The instructor may have to repeat the presentation for the elements and supervise practice more closely until the trainee regains confidence or masters the task.

Key learning points: Learning and development skills

The requirement

HR professionals need skills in coaching and mentoring to fulfil their important responsibilities for enhancing the knowledge and skills of employees and for providing guidance to line managers on conducting their learning and development activities.

Coaching

Coaching is a personal (usually one-to-one) approach that enables people to develop their skills and knowledge and improve their performance.

The approach to coaching

- To succeed in coaching you need to understand that your role is to help people to learn and to see that they are motivated to learn.

- Coaching is sometimes informal but it has to be planned. It is not simply checking from time to time on what people are doing and then advising them on how to do it better, or occasionally telling people where they have gone wrong and throwing in a lecture.

- Coaching should provide motivation, structure and effective feedback. As a coach, you should believe that people can succeed and that they can contribute to their own success.

Mentoring

Mentors offer guidance, pragmatic advice and continuing support to help those allocated to them to learn and develop. It is a method of helping people to learn as distinct from coaching, which can be a relatively directive means of increasing people's competence. Mentors provide people with:

- advice in drawing up self-development programmes or learning contracts;

- general help with learning programmes;

- guidance on how to acquire the necessary knowledge and skills to do a new job;

- advice on dealing with any administrative, technical or people problems individuals meet, especially in the early stages of their careers;

- information on 'the way things are done around here' – the corporate culture in terms of expected behaviour;

- coaching in specific skills;

- help in tackling projects – not by doing it for them but by pointing them in the right direction, helping people to help themselves;

- a parental figure with whom individuals can discuss their aspirations and concerns and who will lend a sympathetic ear to their problems.

Job instruction

When people learn specific tasks, especially those involving basic administrative or manual skills, the learning will be more effective if job instruction techniques are used. The sequence of instruction is:

1 Preparation for each instruction period means that the trainer must have a plan for presenting the subject matter and using appropriate teaching methods, visual aids and demonstration aids. It also means preparing trainees for the instruction that is to follow.

2 Presentation should consist of a combination of telling and showing – explanation and demonstration.

3 Demonstration is an essential stage in instruction, especially when the skill to be learnt is mainly a 'doing' skill.

4 Follow up continues during the training period for all the time required by the learner to reach a level of performance equal to that of the normal experienced worker in terms of quality, speed and attention to safety.

References

Clutterbuck, D (2004) *Everyone Needs a Mentor: Fostering talent in your organization*, 4th edn, London, CIPD

Clutterbuck, D and Megginson, D (2005) *Making Coaching Work: Creating a coaching culture*, London, CIPD

Gray, D A (2010) Building quality into executive coaching, in (eds) J Gold, R Thorpe and A Mumford, *Gower Handbook of Leadership and Management Development*, Farnham, Gower, pp 367–85

Whitmore, J (2002) *Coaching for Performance*, 3rd edn, London, Nicholas Brealey

72
Negotiating skills

KEY CONCEPTS AND TERMS

Aspiration grid   Negotiating

Bargaining   Zero-sum game

Corridor negotiations

LEARNING OUTCOMES

On completing this chapter you should be able to define these key concepts. You should also know about:

- The process of negotiation
- The stages of a negotiation
- Negotiating and bargaining skills

Introduction

HR practitioners who are involved in industrial relations may conduct or take part in negotiations with trade union representatives or officials. Negotiating is a process that requires considerable skill.

Negotiation involves bargaining, which is reaching the most advantageous position in discussion with another party through a process of offer and counter-offer. It is a process in which two parties – management and the trade union – get together with the aim of getting the best deal possible for their business or their members.

Negotiations involve a conflict of interest. In pay negotiations unions want the highest settlement they can get; management wants the lowest. In negotiations about other terms and conditions, unions will want the best result for their members while management will want to avoid agreeing to anything other than what they think is reasonable from their viewpoint. It can be a zero-sum game – what one side gains the other loses. No one likes to lose, so there is scope for conflict, which has to be managed if an amicable agreement is to be achieved. And negotiators do, or should, try to end up on friendly terms, whatever differences of opinion have occurred on the way. After all, they may well meet again.

The process of negotiation

Negotiating takes place when two parties meet to reach an agreement concerning a proposition, such as a pay claim, that one party has put to the other. Negotiation can be convergent when both parties are equally keen to reach a win-win agreement (in commercial terms, a willing buyer/willing seller arrangement). It can be divergent when one or both of the parties aim to win as much as they can from the other while giving away as little as possible. Negotiations in an industrial relations setting differ from commercial negotiations in the respects shown in Table 72.1.

In negotiations on pay or other terms and conditions of service, management represents the employer's interests and employee representatives represent the interests of employees. Both sides are of equal status. Negotiations take place in an atmosphere of uncertainty. Neither side knows how strong the other side's bargaining position is or what it really wants and will be prepared to accept.

Stages of negotiation

Negotiations are conducted in four stages: initial steps, opening, bargaining and closing.

Initial steps

In a pay negotiation, unions making the claim will define for themselves three things: a) the target they would like to achieve; b) the minimum they will accept; and c) the opening claim they believe will be most likely to achieve the target. Employers define three related things: 1) the target settlement they would like to achieve; 2) the maximum they would be prepared to concede; and 3) the opening offer that will provide them with sufficient room to manoeuvre in reaching their target. The difference between a union's claim and an employer's offer is the negotiating range. If the maximum the employer will offer exceeds the minimum the union will accept the difference will be the settlement range, in which case a settlement will be easily reached. If, however, the maximum the employer will offer is less than the minimum the union will accept, negotiations will be more difficult and a settlement will only be reached if the expectations of either side are adjusted during the bargaining stage. The extent to which this will happen depends on the relative power of the two parties. The strength of the arguments put forward by either party will also be a factor, but the major consideration is usually power.

Preparation for negotiation by either party involves:

- deciding on the strategy and tactics to be used;

TABLE 72.1   Commercial and industrial relations negotiations compared

Industrial relations negotiations	Commercial negotiations
• Assume an ongoing relationship – negotiators cannot walk away.	• Negotiators can walk away.
• The agreement is not legally binding.	• The contract is legally binding.
• Conducted on a face-to-face basis.	• May be conducted at a distance.
• Carried out by representatives responsible to constituents.	• Carried out directly with the parties being responsible to a line manager.
• Make frequent use of adjournments.	• Usually conducted on a continuing basis.
• May be conducted in an atmosphere of distrust, even hostility.	• Usually conducted on a 'willing buyer/willing seller' basis.

- listing the arguments to be used in supporting their case;
- listing the arguments or counter-arguments the other party is likely to use;
- obtaining supporting data;
- selecting the negotiating team, briefing them on the strategy and tactics and rehearsing them in their roles.

Opening

Tactics in the opening phase of a negotiation are as follows:

- open realistically and move moderately;
- challenge the other side's position as it stands; do not destroy their ability to move;
- observe behaviour, ask questions and listen attentively in order to assess the other side's strengths and weaknesses, their tactics and the extent to which they may be bluffing;
- make no concessions at this stage;
- be non-committal about proposals and explanations – do not talk too much.

Bargaining

After the opening moves, the main bargaining phase takes place in which the gap is narrowed between the initial positions. The attempt is made to persuade each other that their case is strong enough to force the other side to close at a less advantageous point than they had planned. Bargaining is often as much about concealing as revealing – keeping arguments in reserve to deploy when they will make the greatest impact.

The following tactics are used:

- Always make conditional proposals: 'If you will do this, then I will consider doing that' – the words to remember are: 'if... then...'.
- Never make one-sided concessions: always trade off against a concession from the other party: 'If I concede x, then I expect you to concede y'.
- Negotiate on the whole package: negotiations should not allow the other side to pick off item by item (salami negotiation).

- Keep the issues open to extract the maximum benefit from potential trade-offs.

There are certain bargaining conventions that experienced negotiators follow because they appreciate that by so doing they create the atmosphere of trust and understanding that is essential to the sort of stable bargaining relationship which benefits both sides. Some of the more generally accepted conventions are as follows:

- Whatever happens during the bargaining, both parties are hoping to reach a settlement.
- Negotiators should show that they respect the views of the other side and take them seriously even if they disagree with them.
- While it is preferable to conduct negotiations in a civilized and friendly manner, attacks, hard words, threats and controlled losses of temper may be used by negotiators to underline determination to get their way and to shake their opponent's confidence and self-possession. But these should be treated by both sides as legitimate tactics and should not be allowed to shake the basic belief in each other's integrity or desire to settle without taking drastic action.
- Off-the-record discussions ('corridor negotiations') can be mutually beneficial as a means of probing attitudes and intentions and smoothing the way to a settlement, but they should not be referred to specifically in formal bargaining sessions unless both sides agree in advance.
- Each side should be prepared to move from its original position.
- It is normal, although not inevitable, for the negotiation to proceed by alternate offers and counter-offers from each side, leading steadily towards a settlement.
- Third parties should not be brought in until both sides agree that no further progress can be made without them.
- Concessions, once made, cannot be withdrawn.
- If negotiators want to avoid committing themselves to 'a final offer' with the risk of devaluing the term if they are forced to make concessions, they should state as positively as they can that this is as far as they can go. But bargaining conventions

allow further moves from this position on a quid pro quo basis.

- Firm offers must not be withdrawn.
- The final agreement should mean exactly what it says. There should be no trickery and the agreed terms should be implemented without amendment.
- So far as possible the final settlement should be framed and communicated in such a way as to reduce the extent to which the other party loses face or credibility.

When bargaining, the parties have to identify the basis for a possible agreement; that is, the common ground. One way of doing this is to use the aspiration grid technique. The grid sets out the parameters for the anticipated outcome of the negotiations. It shows the expected issues one of the parties is prepared to trade as well as the anticipated attitude to the bargaining agenda of the other party. The grid also gives the parameters within which the forthcoming bargaining sessions might be expected to develop. It helps to identify the information required from the other party and the information required to be conveyed by one party to the other party. If the receipt of this information shows expectations as to the behaviour of the other party to be wrong, then the aspiration grid has to be reassessed and modified.

Closing

There are various closing techniques:

- Make a concession from the package, preferably a minor way, which is traded off against an agreement to settle. The concession can be offered more positively than in the bargaining stage: 'If you will agree to settle at x then I will concede y.'
- Do a deal, split the difference or bring in something new, such as extending the settlement timescale, agreeing to back-payments, phasing increases, or making a joint declaration of intent to do something in the future.
- Summarize what has happened so far, emphasize the concessions that have been made and the extent of movement from the original position, and indicate that the limit has been reached.

- Apply pressure through a threat of the dire consequences that will follow if a 'final' claim is not agreed or a 'final offer' is not accepted.

Employers should not make a final offer unless they mean it. If it is not really their final offer and the union calls their bluff, they may have to make further concessions and their credibility will be undermined. Each party will attempt to force the other side into revealing the extent to which they have reached their final position. But negotiators should not allow themselves to be pressurized. They have to use their judgement on when to say 'this is a far as we can go'. That judgement will be based on their understanding that the stage when a settlement is possible has been reached.

Negotiating and bargaining skills

The skills required to be effective in negotiations and bargaining are:

- *Analytical ability* – the capacity to assess the factors that affect the negotiating stance and tactics of both parties.
- *Empathy* – the ability to put oneself in the other party's shoes.
- *Interactive skills* – the ability to relate well with other people.
- *Communicating skills* – the ability to convey information and arguments clearly, positively and logically.
- *Keeping cards close to the chest* – not giving away what you really want or are prepared to concede until you are ready to do so (in the market place it is always easier for sellers to drive a hard bargain with buyers who have revealed somehow that they covet the article).
- *Flexible realism* – the capacity to make realistic moves during the bargaining process to reduce the claim or increase the offer, which will demonstrate that the bargainer is seeking a reasonable settlement and is prepared to respond appropriately to movements from the other side.

Key learning points: Negotiating skills

The process of negotiation

Negotiation is the process of coming to terms and, in so doing, getting the best deal possible. Negotiation involves bargaining, which is reaching the most advantageous position in discussion with another party through a process of offer and counter-offer.

Negotiating takes place when two parties meet to reach an agreement on a proposition, such as a pay claim, that one party has put to the other. Negotiation can be convergent when both parties are equally keen to reach a win-win agreement (in commercial terms, a willing buyer/willing seller arrangement). It can be divergent when one or both of the parties aim to win as much as they can from the other while giving away as little as possible.

Stages of negotiation

Negotiations are conducted in four stages: initial steps, opening, bargaining and closing.

Negotiating and bargaining skills

- *Analytical ability* – the capacity to assess the factors that affect the negotiating stance and tactics of both parties.

- *Empathy* – the ability to put oneself in the other party's shoes.

- *Interactive skills* – the ability to relate well with other people.

- *Communicating skills* – the ability to convey information and arguments clearly, positively and logically.

- *Keeping cards close to the chest* – not giving away what you really want or are prepared to concede until you are ready to do so.

- *Flexible realism* – the capacity to make realistic moves during the bargaining process to reduce the claim or increase the offer, which will demonstrate that the bargainer is seeking a reasonable settlement and is prepared to respond appropriately to movements from the other side.

73
Leading and facilitating change

KEY CONCEPTS AND TERMS

Change agent

Change management

Culture change

Force-field analysis

Organizational capability

Organizational effectiveness

LEARNING OUTCOMES

On completing this chapter you should be able to define these key concepts. You should also know about:

- The role of HR in leading change
- The change process
- Change models

- Reasons for resistance to change
- Overcoming resistance to change
- Implementing change

Introduction

Leading and facilitating change is about initiating and achieving the smooth implementation of new developments and initiatives by planning and introducing them systematically, allowing for the possibility of their being resisted or at least misunderstood. Kotter (1996) emphasized the importance of leading change rather than simply managing it.

The role of HR in leading and facilitating change

Leading and facilitating change is probably the most demanding of all HR roles. If HR is concerned – as it should be – in playing a major part in the achievement of continuous improvement and in the HR processes that support that improvement, then it will need to be involved in facilitating change. Caldwell (2001) stated that the change agent roles that can be carried out by HR professionals are those of change champions, change adapters, change consultants and change synergists.

Leading change

Leading change involves initiating and managing culture change (the process of changing the organization's culture in the shape of its values, norms and beliefs) and the introduction of new structures, systems, working practices and people management processes. The aim is to increase organizational capability (the potential ability of the organization to perform well) and organizational effectiveness (how well the organization actually performs).

Ulrich (1997: 7) observed that HR professionals should be 'as explicit about culture change as they are today about the requirements for a successful training program or hiring strategy'. He later emphasized that, 'HR should become an agent of continuous transformation, shaping processes and a culture that together improve an organization's capacity for change' Ulrich (1998: 125).

Change leadership means:

● identifying where change is required;

● specifying what changes should take place;

● assessing the benefits of the change and what it will cost;

● establishing the consequences of the change;

● assessing any problems the change may create, eg resistance to the change, and any risks involved;

● persuading management and anyone else affected by the change that it is necessary, spelling out the benefits and indicating what will be done to deal with potential problems;

● planning how the change should be implemented, including nominating and briefing change agents (people responsible for achieving change), minimizing potential resistance through communication and involvement, and managing risks;

● facilitating the introduction and management of the change;

● ensuring that the change is embedded successfully – 'holding the gains'.

Facilitating change

Facilitating change is about making it happen. As Hamlin and Davies (2001: 13) observed, one of the major challenges facing HR 'is how to help people through the transitions of change, and how to survive in working conditions that are in a constant state of flux'. Brown and Eisenhardt (1997: 21) noted that managers who were successful in the art of continuous change 'carefully managed the transition between the past and the future. Much like the pit stop in a car race or the baton pass in track, this transition appeared critical'.

The role of HR in facilitating change was described by Vere and Butler (2007: 34) as follows:

● The issue needs to be on the strategic business agenda and managers must see how action will improve business results; that is, there needs to be a sound business case for the initiative. HR managers need to be able to demonstrate the return on the planned investment.

● The change needs to have the active backing of those at the top of the organization, so it is for the HR director to gain the commitment of the top team and engage them in a practical way in taking the work forward.

● HR needs to engage managers in the design of change from the outset (or, if this is a business-driven change, HR needs to be involved at the outset).

● The programme needs to be framed in the language of the business to have real meaning and achieve 'buy in' for all parties; if there is too much HR jargon, this will be a turn-off.

● Project and people management skills are crucial to ensure the programme is well planned and resourced and risks are assessed and managed.

● As in all change programmes, the importance of communication is paramount, to explain, engage and commit people to the programme.

● In this respect, the crucial role that HR can play is to ensure that employees are fully engaged in the design and implementation of the change.

● HR needs to draw on others' experience and learning.

To do all this, Ulrich (1997: 8) pointed out that 'HR professionals need a model of change and the ability to apply the model to a specific situation.' The models described later in this chapter need to be understood and applied as appropriate. The other qualities required are insight – to understand the need for change, courage – to pursue change, and determination – to achieve change.

Leading and facilitating change is hard work. As Alfes *et al* (2010: 111) observed on the basis of their research: 'The role [of HR] is generally constrained and reactive.' They also noted that: 'HR professionals may find their roles circumscribed by expectations of their role, the nature of the change process, capability and capacity' (ibid: 125).

Ulrich (1997) emphasized that one of the key roles of HR professionals is to act as change agents, but it is a difficult role to play. Perhaps, as Thornhill *et al* (2000) noted, the main contribution HR can make is to generate and support change where a core feature is the development and alignment of HRM practices such as culture management, performance management, learning and development, reward management and employee relations.

To lead change it is necessary to understand how the process works. It is important to bear in mind that while those leading change need to be constant about ends, they have to be flexible about means. This requires them to come to an understanding of the various models of change that have been developed and of the factors that create resistance to change and how to minimize such resistance. In the light of an understanding of these models and the phenomenon of resistance to change, they will be better equipped to make use of the guidelines for change set out at the end of this chapter.

The change process

Conceptually, the change process starts with an awareness of the need for change. An analysis of the situation and the factors that have created it leads to a diagnosis of their distinctive characteristics and an indication of the direction in which action needs to be taken. Possible courses of action can next be identified and evaluated and a choice made of the preferred action.

It is then necessary to decide how to get from here to there. Managing change during this transition state is a critical phase in the change process. It is here that the problems of introducing change emerge and have to be managed. These problems can include resistance to change, instability, high levels of stress, misdirected energy, conflict, and loss of momentum. Hence the need to do everything possible to anticipate reactions and likely impediments to the introduction of change.

The final stage, in which the new structure, system or process is installed, can also be demanding, indeed painful. As described by Pettigrew and Whipp (1991: 27), the implementation of change is an 'iterative, cumulative and reformulation-in-use process'.

The next issue is how to 'hold the gains', ie how to ensure that the change is embedded and maintained. This means continuously monitoring the effects and impact of the change and taking corrective action where necessary to ensure that it continues to work well. The change process has been described in the various change models set out below.

Change models

Change models explain the mechanisms for change and the factors that affect its success. The best-known change models are those developed by Lewin (1951) and Beckhard (1969), but other important contributions to an understanding of the mechanisms for change have been made by Thurley (1979) and Beer *et al* (1990).

Lewin

The basic mechanisms for managing change as set out by Lewin (1951) are:

- *Unfreezing* – altering the present stable equilibrium that supports existing behaviours and attitudes. This process must take account of the inherent threats change presents to people and the need to motivate those affected to attain the natural state of equilibrium by accepting change.
- *Changing* – developing new responses based on new information.
- *Refreezing* – stabilizing, supporting and reinforcing the new changed conditions.

Lewin also suggested the following methodology for analysing change, which he called 'force-field analysis':

- Analyse the restraining or driving forces that will affect the transition to the future state – these restraining forces will include the reactions of those who see change as unnecessary or as constituting a threat.
- Assess which of the driving or restraining forces are critical.
- Take steps both to increase the critical driving forces and to decrease the critical restraining forces.

Beckhard

Beckhard (1969) proposed that a change programme should incorporate the following processes:

- Set goals and define the future state or organizational conditions desired after the change.
- Diagnose the present condition in relation to these goals.
- Define the transition state activities and commitments required to meet the future state.
- Develop strategies and action plans for managing this transition in the light of an analysis of the factors likely to affect the introduction of change.

Thurley

Thurley (1979) described the following five approaches to managing change:

- *Directive* – the imposition of change in crisis situations or when other methods have failed. This is done by the exercise of managerial power without consultation.
- *Bargained* – this approach recognizes that power is shared between the employer and the employed and change requires negotiation, compromise and agreement before being implemented.
- *'Hearts and minds'* – an all-embracing thrust to change the attitudes, values and beliefs of the whole workforce. This 'normative' approach (ie one that starts from a definition of what management thinks is right or 'normal') seeks 'commitment' and 'shared vision' but does not necessarily include involvement or participation.
- *Analytical* – a theoretical approach to the change process using models of change such as those described above. It proceeds sequentially from the analysis and diagnosis of the situation, through the setting of objectives, the design of the change process, the evaluation of the results and, finally, the determination of the objectives for the next stage in the change process. This is the rational and logical approach much favoured by consultants – external and internal. But change seldom proceeds as smoothly as this model would suggest. Emotions, power politics and external pressures mean that the rational approach, although it might be the right way to start, is difficult to sustain.
- *Action-based* – this recognizes that the way managers behave in practice bears little resemblance to the analytical, theoretical model. The distinction between managerial thought and managerial action blurs in practice to the point of invisibility. What managers think is what they do. Real life therefore often results in a 'ready, aim, fire' approach to change management. This typical approach to change starts with a broad belief that some sort of problem exists, although it may not be well defined. The identification of possible solutions, often on a trial or error basis, leads to a clarification of the nature of the problem and a shared understanding of a possible optimal solution, or at least a framework within which solutions can be discovered.

Beer, Eisenstat and Spector

Beer *et al* (1990) suggested in a seminal *Harvard Business Review* article, 'Why change programs don't produce change', that most such programmes are guided by a theory of change that is fundamentally flawed. This theory states that changes in attitudes lead to changes in behaviour. 'According to this model, change is like a conversion experience. Once people get religion, changes in their behaviour will surely follow' (ibid: 159). They thought that this theory gets the change process exactly backwards and made the following comment on it:

> In fact, individual behaviour is powerfully shaped by the organizational roles people play. The most effective way to change behaviour, therefore, is to put people into a new organizational context, which imposes new roles, responsibilities and relationships on them. This creates a situation that in a sense 'forces' new attitudes and behaviour on people. (ibid: 159)

They prescribe six steps to effective change that concentrate on what they call 'task alignment' – reorganizing employees' roles, responsibilities and relationships to solve specific business problems in small units where goals and tasks can be clearly defined. The aim of following the overlapping steps is to build a self-reinforcing cycle of commitment, coordination and competence:

1 Mobilize commitment to change through the joint analysis of problems.

2 Develop a shared vision of how to organize and manage to achieve goals such as competitiveness.

3 Foster consensus for the new vision, competence to enact it, and cohesion to move it along.

4 Spread revitalization to all departments without pushing it from the top – don't force the issue: let each department find its own way to the new organization.

5 Institutionalize revitalization through formal policies, systems and structures.

6 Monitor and adjust strategies in response to problems in the revitalization process.

Resistance to change

People resist change because it is seen as a threat to familiar patterns of behaviour as well as to status and financial rewards. Woodward (1968: 80) made this point clearly:

When we talk about resistance to change we tend to imply that management is always rational in changing its direction, and that employees are stupid, emotional or irrational in not responding in the way they should. But if an individual is going to be worse off, explicitly or implicitly, when the proposed changes have been made, any resistance is entirely rational in terms of his own best interest. The interests of the organization and the individual do not always coincide.

Hamlin and Davies (2001: 58) commented that: 'Any change creates stress and anxiety; this is because as human beings we deal individually with uncertainty in different ways.' However, some people will welcome change as an opportunity. These people need to be identified and, where feasible, they can help in the introduction of change as change agents.

Reasons for resisting change

Specifically, the reasons for resisting change are:

- *The shock of the new* – people are suspicious of anything they perceive will upset their established routines, methods of working or conditions of employment. They do not want to lose the security of what is familiar to them. They may not believe statements by management that the change is for their benefit as well as that of the organization, sometimes with good reason. They may feel that management has ulterior motives and, sometimes, the louder the protestations of management, the less they will be believed.

- *Economic fears* – loss of money, threats to job security.

- *Inconvenience* – the change will make life more difficult.

- *Uncertainty* – change can be worrying because of uncertainty about its likely impact.

- *Symbolic fears* – a small change that may affect some treasured symbol, such as a separate office or a reserved parking space, may symbolize big ones, especially when employees are uncertain about how extensive the programme of change will be.

- *Threat to interpersonal relationships* – anything that disrupts the customary social relationships and standards of the group will be resisted.

- *Threat to status or skill* – the change is perceived as reducing the status of individuals or as de-skilling them.

- *Competence fears* – concern about the ability to cope with new demands or to acquire new skills.

Overcoming resistance to change

Resistance to change can be difficult to overcome, even when the change is not detrimental to those concerned. But the attempt must be made. The starting point is an analysis of the potential impact of change by considering how it will affect people in their jobs. The reasons for resisting change set out above can be used as a checklist to establish where there might be problems, with groups or with individuals.

The analysis should indicate what aspects of the proposed change may be supported generally or by specified individuals and which aspects may be resisted. So far as possible, the potentially hostile or negative reactions of people and the reasons for them should be identified. It is necessary to try to understand the likely feelings and fears of those affected so that worries can be relieved and, as far as possible, ambiguities can be resolved. In making this analysis, the individual introducing the change – the change agent – should recognize that new ideas are likely to be suspect and should make ample provision for the discussion of reactions to proposals to ensure complete understanding of them.

Involvement in the change process gives people the chance to raise and resolve their concerns and make suggestions about the form of the change and how it should be introduced. The aim is to get 'ownership' – a feeling amongst people that the change is something that they are happy to live with because they have been involved in its planning and introduction – it has become their change.

A communication strategy to explain the proposed change should be prepared and implemented so that unnecessary fears are allayed. All the available channels should be used, but face-to-face communications direct from managers to individuals or through a team briefing system are best.

Implementing change

The problems of implementing strategic change were summed up by Lawler and Mohrman (2003: 24) as follows:

> Most strategies, like most mergers, fail not because of poor thinking, but because of poor implementation. Implementation failures usually involve the failure to acknowledge and build the needed skills and organizational capabilities, to gain support of the workforce, and to support the organizational changes and learning required to behave in new ways. In short, execution failures are often the result of poor human capital management. This opens the door for HR to add important value if it can deliver change strategies, plans and thinking that aid in the development and execution of business strategy.

Implementing change can indeed be difficult. Research by Carnall (1991) in 93 organizations identified the following explanations for failures to implement change effectively:

- implementation took more time than originally allowed;

- major problems that had not been identified beforehand emerged during implementation;

- coordination of implementation activities was not effective enough;

- competing activities and other crises distracted management from implementing the change decision;

- the capabilities of the employees involved were not sufficient;

- training and instruction to lower-level employees was inadequate;

- uncontrollable factors in the external environment had an adverse effect on implementation.

The following suggestions on how to minimize such problems were put forward by Nadler and Tushman (1980):

- *Motivate* in order to achieve changes in behaviour by individuals.

- *Manage the transition* by making organizational arrangements designed to ensure that control is maintained during and after the transition and by developing and communicating a clear image of the future.

- *Shape the political dynamics of change* so that power centres develop that support the change rather than block it.

- *Build in stability* of structures and processes to serve as anchors for people to hold on to – organizations and individuals can only stand so much uncertainty and turbulence, hence the emphasis by Quinn (1980) on the need for an incremental approach.

As reported by Surowiecki 2013: 44), Professor Michael Roberto of Bryant University suggested that: 'Anytime you're trying to change the ways you do things, small wins are important. Small wins help you build support both internally and externally, and they make it easier for people to buy in.'

The role of change agents

The change process will take place more smoothly with the help of credible internal or external change agents – people who help to manage change by providing advice and support on its introduction and management. A change agent was defined by Caldwell (2003: 139–40) as 'an internal or external individual or team responsible for initiating, sponsoring, managing and implementing a specific change initiative or complete change programme'. As described by Balugon and Hope-Hailey (2004), the role of the change agent is to lead change. Alfes *et al* (2010) noted that change agents establish

what is required, involve people in planning and managing change, advise on how change should be implemented and communicate to people the implications of change.

Keep (2001: 89) listed the following change agent competencies:

- Project management – planning and resource allocation.

- Contracting with clients – defining the task, establishing relationships.

- Team building – defining roles, maintaining good working relationships.

- Analysis and diagnosis – data collection, problem solving, systems thinking.

- Data utilization – qualitative or quantitative data, paper-based review, survey techniques.

- Interpersonal skills – dealing with people, leadership.

- Communication skills – speaking, written presentations/reports, listening.

- Political awareness – sensitivity, influencing.

- Intervention implementation – participation, involvement.

- Monitoring and evaluation – criteria setting and reviewing, measuring effectiveness.

- Technical skills – financial interpretation, psychometrics.

- Process skills – facilitation.

- Insight – reflection, awareness of key issues, critical thinking, intuition.

It is often assumed that only people from outside the organization can take on the change agent role because they are independent and do not 'carry any baggage'. They can be useful, but people from within the firm who are respected and credible can do the job well. This is often the role of HR specialists, but the use of line managers adds extra value.

Guidelines for change management

- The achievement of sustainable change requires strong commitment and visionary leadership from the top.

- Understanding is necessary of the culture of the organization and the levers for change that are most likely to be effective in that culture.

- Those concerned with managing change at all levels should have the temperament and leadership skills appropriate to the circumstances of the organization and its change strategies.

- Change is more likely to be successful if there is a 'burning platform' to justify it, ie a powerful and convincing reason for change.

- It is important to build a working environment that is conducive to change. Learning and development programmes can help to do this.

- It is easier to change behaviour by changing processes, structure and systems than to change attitudes or the organizational culture.

- People support what they help to create. Commitment to change is improved if those affected by change are allowed to participate as fully as possible in planning and implementing it. The aim should be to get them to 'own' the change as something they want and will be glad to live with.

- The reward system should encourage innovation and recognize success in achieving change.

- Change will always involve failure as well as success. The failures must be expected and learnt from.

- Hard evidence and data on the need for change are the most powerful tools for its achievement, but establishing the need for change is easier than deciding how to satisfy it.

- There are always people in organizations who can act as champions of change. They will welcome the challenges and opportunities that change can provide. They are the ones to be chosen as change agents.

- Resistance to change is inevitable if the individuals concerned feel that they are going to be worse off – implicitly or explicitly. The inept management of change will produce that reaction.

- In an age of global competition, technological innovation, turbulence, discontinuity, even chaos, change is inevitable and necessary. The organization must do all it can to explain why change is essential and how it will affect everyone. Moreover, every effort must be made to protect the interests of those affected by change.

Key learning points: Leading and facilitating change

The role of HR in leading and facilitating change

Leading and facilitating change are two of the key roles of HR professionals. In practice, they are probably the most demanding of all HR roles.

Leading change

Leading change involves initiating and managing culture change (the process of changing the organization's culture in the shape of its values, norms and beliefs) and the introduction of new structures, systems, working practices and people management processes.

Facilitating change

Change management is largely about facilitation.

The change process

The change process starts with an awareness of the need for change. An analysis of this situation and the factors that have created it leads to a diagnosis of their distinctive characteristics and an indication of the direction in which action needs to be taken. Possible courses of action can then be identified and evaluated and a choice made of the preferred action.

Change models

The main change models are those produced by Lewin, Beckhard, Thurley and Beer *et al*.

Reasons for resistance to change

The shock of the new, economic fears, inconvenience, uncertainty, symbolic fears, threat to interpersonal relationships, threat to status or skills, competence fears.

Overcoming resistance to change

- Analyse the potential impact of change by considering how it will affect people in their jobs.

- Identify the potentially hostile or negative reactions of people.

- Make ample provision for the discussion of reactions to proposals to ensure complete understanding of them.

- Get 'ownership' – a feeling amongst people that the change is something they are happy to live with because they have been involved in its planning and introduction.

- Prepare and implement a communication strategy to explain the proposed change.

Implementing change

Implementation failures usually involve the failure to acknowledge and build the needed skills and organizational capabilities, to gain support of the workforce, and to support the organizational changes and learning required to behave in new ways.

References

Alfes, K, Truss, C and Gill, J (2010) The HR manager as change agent: evidence from the public sector, *Journal of Change Management*, **10** (1), pp 109–27

Balugon, J and Hope-Hailey, V (2004) *Exploring Strategic Change*, 2nd edn, London, Prentice Hall

Beckhard, R (1969) *Organization Development: Strategy and models*, Reading, MA, Addison-Wesley

Beer, M, Eisenstat, R and Spector, B (1990) Why change programs don't produce change, *Harvard Business Review*, November–December, pp 158–66

Brown, S L and Eisenhardt, K M (1997) The art of continuous change: linking complexity theory and time-paced evolution in relentlessly shifting organizations, *Administrative Science Quarterly*, **42** (1), pp 1–24

Caldwell, R (2001) Champions, adapters, consultants and synergists: the new change agents in HRM, *Human Resource Management Journal*, **11** (3), pp 39–52

Caldwell, R (2003) Models of change agency: a fourfold classification, *British Journal of Management*, **14** (2), pp 131–42

Carnall, C (1991) *Managing Change*, London, Routledge

Hamlin, B and Davies, G (2001) Managers, trainers and developers as change agents, in (eds) B Hamlin, J Keep and K Ash, *Organizational Change and Development: A reflective guide for managers, trainers and developers*, Harlow, Pearson Education, pp 39–60

Keep, J (2001) The change practitioner: perspectives on role, effectiveness, dilemmas and challenges, in (eds) B Hamlin, J Keep and K Ash, *Organizational Change and Development: A reflective guide for managers, trainers and developers*, Harlow, Pearson Education, pp 13–38

Kotter, J J (1996) *Leading Change*, Boston, MA, Harvard University Press

Lawler, E E and Mohrman, S A (2003) HR as a strategic partner: What does it take to make it happen? *Human Resource Planning*, **26** (3), pp 15–29

Lewin, K (1951) *Field Theory in Social Science*, New York, Harper & Row

Nadler, D A and Tushman, M L (1980) A congruence model for diagnosing organizational behaviour, in (ed) R H Miles, *Resource Book in Macro-organizational Behaviour*, Santa Monica, CA, Goodyear Publishing

Pettigrew, A and Whipp, R (1991) *Managing Change for Competitive Success*, Oxford, Blackwell

Quinn, J B (1980) Managing strategic change, *Sloane Management Review*, **11** (4/5), pp 3–30

Surowiecki, J (2013) The turnaround trap, *The New Yorker*, 25th March, p 44

Thornhill, A, Lewis, P, Saunders, M and Millmore, M (2000) *Managing Change: A human resource strategy approach*, Harlow, FT Prentice Hall

Thurley, K (1979) *Supervision: A reappraisal*, London, Heinemann

Ulrich, D (1997) *Human Resource Champions*, Boston, MA, Harvard Business School Press

Ulrich, D (1998) A new mandate for human resources, *Harvard Business Review*, January–February, pp 124–34

Vere, D and Butler, L (2007) *Fit for Business: Transforming HR in the public service*, London, CIPD

Woodward, J (1968) Resistance to change, *Management International Review*, **8**, pp 78–93

74
Leadership skills

LEARNING OUTCOMES

On completing this chapter you should be able to define these key concepts. You should also know about:

- The meaning of leadership
- What leaders do
- The qualities of a good leader
- What makes an effective leader
- The main leadership theories
- The main leadership styles
- The process of leadership development

Introduction

HR professionals need to know about leadership for four reasons: 1) they have to exercise leadership in persuading others to do things; 2) they are, or should be, concerned with the development of leaders in the organization; 3) at a senior level they have to lead their own function; and 4) they are involved in leading change. The purpose of this chapter is to meet this need by analysing the process of leadership and the skills involved.

The meaning of leadership

To lead people is to inspire, influence and guide. Leadership can be described as the ability to persuade others willingly to behave differently. It is the process of getting people to do their best to achieve a desired result. It involves developing and communicating a vision for the future, motivating people and securing their engagement. As Stogdill (1950: 3) explained, leadership is an 'influencing process aimed at goal achievement'.

Leadership theories

Leadership is a complicated notion and a number of theories have been produced to explain it. These theories, as summarized below, have developed over the years and explore a number of different facets of leadership and leadership behaviour. In many ways they complement one another and together they help to gain a comprehensive understanding of what the process of leadership is about.

Trait theory, which explains leadership by reference to the qualities leaders have, is the basic and to many people the most familiar theory. But it has its limitations, and pragmatic research was carried out to identify what types of behaviour characterized leadership rather than focusing on the personalities of leaders. The key leadership behaviour studies conducted by the Universities of Michigan and Ohio State led to the identification of two dimensions of leadership behaviour, respectively: employee as distinct from job-centred behaviour, and the processes of consideration and initiating structure.

The next step in the development of leadership theory was the recognition by researchers that what leaders did and how they did it was dependent or contingent on the situation they were in (Fiedler, 1967). Different traits became important; different behaviours or styles of leadership had to be used to achieve effectiveness in different situations. These studies resulted in the theories of contingent and situational leadership.

Next, traits theory was in effect revived by Goleman (2001) in the notion of emotional intelligence as a necessary attribute of leaders. Most recently, Ulrich put his oar in alongside his colleague Smallwood (2007) with the notion of the leadership brand as a comprehensive approach to leadership by organizations.

The problem with leadership theories

Despite all the research and theorizing, the concept of leadership is still problematic. As Meindl *et al* (1985: 78) commented: 'It has become apparent that, after years of trying, we have been unable to generate an understanding of leadership that is both intellectually compelling and emotionally satisfying. The concept of leadership remains elusive and enigmatic.'

These problems may arise because, as a notion, leadership is difficult to pin down. There are many different types of situations in which leaders operate, many different types of leaders and many different leadership styles. Producing one theory that covers all these variables is difficult, if not impossible. All that can be done is to draw on the various theories that exist to explain different facets of leadership without necessarily relying on any one of them for a comprehensive explanation of what is involved.

Perhaps leadership is best defined by considering what leaders do and how they do it (the different styles they adopt), examining what sort of leaders carry out these activities and practise these styles, and looking at any empirical evidence available on what makes them good leaders. These are all covered in the next four sections of this chapter.

What leaders do

The most convincing analysis of what leaders do was produced by Adair (1973). He explained that the three essential roles of leaders are to:

- *Define the task* – they make it quite clear what the group is expected to do.

- *Achieve the task* – that is why the group exists. Leaders ensure that the group's purpose is fulfilled. If it is not, the result is frustration, disharmony, criticism and, eventually perhaps, disintegration of the group.

- *Maintain effective relationships* – between themselves and the members of the group, and between the people within the group. These relationships are effective if they contribute to achieving the task. They can be divided into those concerned with the team and its morale and sense of common purpose, and those concerned with individuals and how they are motivated.

He suggested that demands on leaders are best expressed as three areas of need which they must satisfy. These are: 1) task needs: to get the job done; 2) individual needs: to harmonize the needs of the

FIGURE 74.1   John Adair's model of leadership

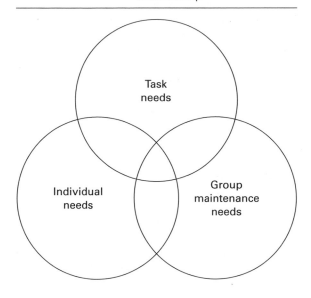

individual with the needs of the task and the group; and 3) group maintenance needs: to build and maintain team spirit. As can be seen in Figure 74.1, he modelled these demands as three interlocking circles.

This model indicates that the task, individual and group needs are interdependent. Satisfying task needs will also satisfy group and individual needs. Task needs, however, cannot be met unless attention is paid to individual and group needs, and looking after individual needs will also contribute to satisfying group needs, and vice versa. There is a risk of becoming so task-oriented that leaders ignore individual and group or team needs. It is just as dangerous to be too people-oriented, focusing on meeting individual or group needs at the expense of the task. The best leaders are those who keep these three needs satisfied and in balance, according to the demands of the situation.

Leadership styles

Leadership style is the approach managers use in exercising leadership when they are relating to their team members. It is sometimes called 'management style'. There are many styles of leadership and no one style is necessarily better than the other in any situation. To greater or lesser degrees, leaders can be autocratic or democratic, controlling or enabling, task-oriented or people-centred. The Hay/McBer research reported by Goleman (2000) identified the following six styles and indicated when they might be used:

1 *Coercive* – demands compliance (use in a crisis or with problem people).
2 *Authoritative* – mobilizes people (use when new vision and direction is needed).
3 *Affiliative* – creates harmony (use to heal wounds and to motivate people under stress).
4 *Democratic* – forges consensus (use to build agreement and get contributions).
5 *Pacesetting* – sets high standards (use to get fast results from a motivated team).
6 *Coaching* – develops people (to improve performance and develop strengths).

In line with contingency and situational theories it should not be assumed that any one style is right in any circumstances. There is no such thing as an ideal leadership style. It all depends. The factors affecting the degree to which a style is appropriate will be the type of organization, the nature of the task, the characteristics of the individuals in the leader's team (the followers) and of the group as a whole and, importantly, the personality of the leader.

Effective leaders are capable of flexing their style to meet the demands of the situation. Normally democratic leaders may have to shift into more of a directive mode when faced with a crisis, but they make clear what they are doing and why. Poor leaders change their style arbitrarily so that their team members are confused and do not know what to expect next.

Good leaders may also flex their style when dealing with individual team members according to their characteristics. Some people need more positive directions than others. Others respond best if they are involved in decision making with their boss. But there is a limit to the degree of flexibility that should be used. It is unwise to differentiate too much between the ways in which individuals are treated or to be inconsistent in one's approach.

Types of leaders

To understand the process of leadership (and, incidentally, provide a basis for leadership development programmes) it is useful not only to analyse the styles that leaders can adopt but also to classify the different types of leaders that apply those styles. As described below, leaders can be charismatic, visionary, transformational, transactional or 'authentic'. However, typical leaders may exhibit any or even all of these characteristics either consistently or in response to the situation in which they find themselves.

Leadership may be exercised by a few selected authoritative individuals and many studies focus on top managers as 'charismatic' or 'visionary' leaders. But it may and indeed should take the form of distributed leadership, which is spread through the organization amongst people working together by processes of influence and interdependencies. As Huczynski and Buchanan (2007: 720) commented: 'leadership is a widely distributed phenomenon. Leadership functions are best carried out by those who have the interest, knowledge, skills and motivation to perform them effectively.' The possibility that people who become managers may not have these qualities to a desirable extent creates a need for systematic leadership development programmes.

Charismatic leaders

Charismatic leaders rely on their personality, their inspirational qualities and their 'aura' to get people to follow them. Burns (1978), who coined the term, suggested that charismatic leaders were set apart from ordinary people and treated as being endowed with exceptional powers or qualities that inspire followers.

Conger and Kanungo (1998) described charismatic leadership as a process of formulating an inspiring vision of the future and then demonstrating the importance of the articulated vision. This may involve unconventional behaviour that conveys important goals that are part of the vision and demonstrates means to achieve these goals. Charismatic leaders also take risks and motivate followers by setting a personal example. In this sense, charismatic leaders operate as visionary and transformational leaders, as described below.

But Carey (1992: 232) charged that: 'when the gifts of charisma, inspiration, consideration and intellectual strength are abused for the self-interest of the leader, the effect on followers ceases to be liberating and moral and becomes instead oppressive and ideological.' And Bennis (2010: 4) commented that: 'the ability to inspire trust, not charisma, is what enables leaders to recruit others to a cause.'

Visionary leaders

Visionary leaders are inspired by a clear vision of an exciting future and inspire their followers by successfully conveying that vision to them. Bennis and Nanus (1985: 89) defined a vision as 'a target that beckons'. Their notion of visionary leadership was explained as follows:

> To choose a direction, a leader must first have developed a mental image of a possible and desirable future state of the organization. This image, which we call a vision, may be as vague as a dream or as precise as a goal or mission statement. The critical point is that a vision articulates a view of a realistic, credible and attractive future for the organization, a condition that is different in some important ways from one that now exists. (ibid: 89)

Kouzes and Posner (2003: 112) claimed that: 'One of the most important practices of leadership is giving life and work a sense of meaning and purpose by offering an exciting vision.'

Transformational leaders

Transformational leaders are able, by their force of personality, to make significant changes in the behaviour of their followers in order to achieve the leader's vision or goals. As described by Burns (1978), what he called 'transforming leadership' involves motivating people to strive for higher goals. He believed that good leadership implies a moral responsibility to respond to the values and needs of people in a way that is conducive to the highest form of human relations. As he put it: 'The ultimate test of moral leadership is its capacity to transcend the claims of the multiplicity of everyday needs, wants and expectations' (ibid: 46).

Another researcher, Bass (1985), extended the work of Burns by explaining the psychological mechanisms that underlie transforming leadership. He pointed out that the extent to which leaders are transformational is measured by their influence on their followers in terms of the degree to which they feel trust, admiration, loyalty and respect for the leader and are willing to work harder than originally expected. According to Bass, this occurs because the leader transforms and motivates through an inspiring mission and vision and gives them an identity. Tichy and Devanna (1986) concluded that the transformational leader has three main roles: recognizing the need for revitalization, creating a new vision and institutionalizing change.

Yukl (1999) advised that transformational leaders should:

- develop a challenging and attractive vision together with employees;
- tie the vision to a strategy for its achievement;
- develop the vision, specify and translate it to actions;
- express confidence, decisiveness and optimism about the vision and its implementation;
- realize the vision through small planned steps and small successes on the path to its full implementation.

Transactional leaders

Transactional leaders trade money, jobs and security for compliance. As Burns (1978: 19) noted: 'Such leadership occurs when a person takes the initiative in making contact with others for the purpose of an exchange of valued things.' Tavanti (2008: 169) stated that: 'Transactional leaders exhibit specific leadership skills usually associated with the ability to obtain results, to control through structures and processes, to solve problems, to plan and organize, and work within the structures and boundaries of the organization.' Put like this, a transactional leader conforms to the stereotype of the manager rather than the leader. Bass (1985) argued that leaders can display both transformational and transactional characteristics. Tavanti (2008) also observed that transactional leadership behaviour is used to one degree or another by most leaders, but that: 'Particular instances of transactional leadership are motivated simply by people's

wants and preferences. This form of leadership uncritically responds to our preferences, that is, even when they are grounded in base motivations or an undeveloped moral sense' (ibid: 171).

Authentic leaders

The concept of the authentic leader was originally defined by George (2003: 12) as follows:

Authentic leaders genuinely desire to serve others through their leadership. They are more interested in empowering the people they lead to make a difference than they are in power, money or prestige for themselves. They lead with purpose, meaning and values. They build enduring relationships with them. Others follow them because they know where they stand. They are consistent and self-disciplined.

Authenticity was described by Harter (2002: 382) as 'owning one's personal experiences, be they thoughts, emotions, needs, preferences, or beliefs, processes captured by the injunction to know oneself and behaving in accordance with the true self.' Authentic leadership is based on a positive moral perspective characterized by high ethical standards that guide decision making and behaviour (May et al, 2003). As Avolio et al (2004) explained, authentic leaders act in accordance with deep personal values and convictions to build credibility and win the respect and trust of followers. By encouraging diverse viewpoints and building networks of collaborative relationships with followers, they lead in a manner that followers perceive and describe as authentic.

George et al (2007: 129) set out the basis of authentic leadership as follows:

We all have the capacity to inspire and empower others. But we must first be willing to devote ourselves to our personal growth and development as leaders... No one can be authentic by trying to imitate someone else. You can learn from others' experiences, but there is no way you can be successful when you are trying to be like them. People trust you when you are genuine and authentic, not a replica of someone else.

Authentic leadership is, in essence, ethical leadership. Walumbwa et al (2008) claimed that it can lead to enhanced trust, job satisfaction and performance.

The reality of leadership

The reality of leadership is that many first-line managers and team leaders are appointed or promoted to their posts with some idea, possibly, of what their managerial or supervisory duties are, but with no appreciation of the leadership skills they need. They see their role as being to tell people what to do and then see that they do it. They may tend to adopt a transactional approach, focusing on getting the job done and neglecting everything else. They may not be charismatic, visionary or transformational leaders because even if they have the latent qualities required, their situation does not seem to require or encourage any of these approaches.

However, the better ones will rely on their know-how (authority goes to the person who knows), their quiet confidence and their cool, analytical approach to dealing with problems. Any newly appointed leader or individual who is progressing to a higher level of leadership will benefit from a leadership development programme (see Chapter 39), which will help them to understand and apply the skills they need.

The qualities of a good leader

As mentioned earlier, the trait theory of leadership has its limitations but there is still some value in studying the qualities required by good leaders. It is generally accepted that one of the key skills a leader or manager needs is an ability to analyse and read situations and to establish order and clarity in situations of ambiguity. Gold *et al* (2010: 6) stated that: 'Leadership demands a sense of purpose, and an ability to influence others, interpret situations, negotiate and express their views, often in the face of opposition'.

Research conducted by the Work Foundation (Tamkin *et al*, 2010), involving 260 in-depth interviews conducted with 77 business leaders from six high-profile organizations, found that outstanding leaders:

- viewed things as a whole rather than compartmentalizing them;
- connect the parts through a guiding sense of purpose;

- are highly motivated to achieve excellence and are focused on organizational outcomes, vision and purpose;
- understand they cannot create performance themselves but are conduits for performance through their influence on others;
- watch themselves carefully and act consistently to achieve excellence through their interactions and their embodiment of the leadership role.

Effective leadership

Effective leaders are confident and know where they want to go and what they want to do. They have the ability to take charge, convey their vision to their team, get their team members into action and ensure that they achieve their agreed goals. They are trustworthy, good at influencing people and earn the respect of their team. They are aware of their own strengths and weaknesses and are skilled at understanding what will motivate their team members. They appreciate the advantages of consulting and involving people in decision making. They can switch flexibly from one leadership style to another to meet the demands of different situations and people. Research by the Hay Group Consultancy into what makes great leaders was commissioned by Firstline, the social work training organization (reported by Brindle, 2016). The finding of the study, which obtained evidence from 169 key figures in the social work sector, was that outstanding leaders create a climate that energizes teams to improve the impact they make, giving them stability, clear direction and definition of role, plus the space and time to reflect on practice and develop their own leadership skills.

They have to answer the following questions about the individuals in the group and the team.

Individuals in the group

- What are their strengths and weaknesses?
- What are their needs, attitudes, perspectives and preferences?
- What are likely to be the best ways of motivating them?

- What tasks are they best at doing?
- Is there scope to increase flexibility by developing new skills?
- How well do they perform in achieving targets and performance standards?
- To what extent can they manage their own performance and development?
- Are there any areas where there is a need to develop skill or competence?
- How can I provide them with the sort of support and guidance that will improve their performance?
- What can be done to improve the performance of any individuals in the group by coaching or mentoring?

The team

- How well is the team organized?
- Is the team clear about what is expected of it?

- Do the members of the team work well together?
- If there is any conflict between team members, how can I resolve it?
- How can the commitment and motivation of the team be achieved?
- Are team members flexible – capable of carrying out different tasks?
- To what extent can the team manage its own performance?
- Is there scope to empower the team so that it can take on greater responsibility for setting standards, monitoring performance and taking corrective action?
- Can the team be encouraged to work together to produce ideas for improving performance?
- What is the team good and not so good at doing?
- What can I do to improve the performance of the team through coaching and mentoring?

Key learning points: Leadership skills

Leadership defined

Leadership is the process of influencing the behaviour of others to achieve results.

Leadership theories

The main leadership theories are trait theory, leadership behaviour theory, contingent and situational theories, emotional intelligence theory and the leadership brand.

What leaders do

Adair (1973) explained that the three essential roles of leaders are to define the task, achieve the task, and maintain effective relationships. Leaders have to satisfy interdependent task, individual and group needs.

Types of leaders

Leaders can be charismatic, visionary, transformational, transactional or 'authentic'.

The qualities of a good leader

Leaders need the ability to analyse and read situations and to establish order and clarity in situations of ambiguity. Leadership demands a sense of purpose and an ability to influence others, interpret situations, negotiate and express their views, often in the face of opposition (Gold *et al*, 2010: 6).

The reality of leadership is that many first-line managers and supervisors are appointed or promoted to their posts with some idea, possibly, of what their managerial or supervisory duties are, but with no appreciation of the leadership skills they need to get the results they want with the help of their team.

Leadership development

Leadership development programmes prepare people for leadership roles and situations beyond their current experience. 'Leadership development in the widest sense involves the acquisition, development and utilization of leadership capability or the potential for it' (Burgoyne, 2010: 43).

References

Adair, J (1973) *The Action-centred Leader*, London, McGraw-Hill

Avolio, B J, Gardner, W L, Walumbwa, F O, Luthans, F and May, D R (2004) Unlocking the mask: A look at the process by which authentic leaders impact follower attitudes and behaviours, *Leadership Quarterly*, **15**, pp 801–23

Bass, B M (1985) *Leadership and Performance*, New York, Free Press

Bennis, W (2010) We need leaders, *Leadership Excellence*, **27** (12), p 4

Bennis, W and Nanus, B (1985) *Leadership: The strategies for taking charge*, New York, Harper & Row

Brindle, D (2016), Leadership in social work: can Firstline be a force for change? *Guardian*, 16 March, pp 8–9

Burgoyne J (2010) Crafting a leadership and management development strategy, in (eds) J Gold, R Thorpe and A Mumford, *Gower Handbook of Leadership and Management Development*, Farnham, Gower, pp 42–55

Burns, J M (1978) *Leadership*, New York, Harper & Row

Carey, M R (1992) Transformational leadership and the fundamental option for self-transcendence, *Leadership Quarterly*, **3**, pp 217–36

Conger, J A and Kanungo, R N (1998) *Charismatic Leadership in Organizations*, Thousand Oaks, CA, Sage

Fiedler, F E (1967) *A Theory of Leadership Effectiveness*, New York, McGraw-Hill

George, B (2003) *Authentic Leadership*, San Francisco, CA, Jossey-Bass

George, B, Sims, P, McLean, A N and Mayer, D (2007) Discovering your authentic leadership, *Harvard Business Review*, February, pp 129–38

Gold, J, Thorpe, R and Mumford, A (2010) *Gower Handbook of Leadership and Management Development*, Farnham, Gower

Goleman, D (2000) Leadership that gets results, *Harvard Business Review*, March–April, pp 78–90

Goleman, D (2001) *What Makes a Leader*, Boston, MA, Harvard Business School Press

Harter, S (2002) Authenticity, in (eds) C R Snyder and S J Lopez, *Handbook of Positive Psychology*, Oxford, Oxford University Press, pp 382–94

Huczynski, A A and Buchanan, D A (2007) *Organizational Behaviour*, 6th edn, Harlow, FT Prentice Hall

Kouzes, J and Posner, B (2003) *The Leadership Challenge*, San Francisco, CA, Jossey-Bass

May, D R, Chan, A, Hodges, T and Avolio, B J (2003) Developing the moral component of authentic leadership, *Organizational Dynamics*, **32** (3), pp 247–60

Meindl, J R, Ehrlich, S B and Dukerich, J M (1985) The romance of leadership, *Administrative Science Quarterly*, **30** (1), pp 78–102

Stogdill, R M (1950) Leaders, membership and organization, *Psychological Bulletin*, **25**, pp 1–14

Tamkin, P, Pearson, G, Hirsh, W and Constable, S (2010) *Exceeding Expectation: The principles of outstanding leadership*, London, The Work Foundation

Tavanti, M (2008) Transactional leadership, in (eds) A Marturano and J Gosling, *Leadership: The key concepts*, London, Routledge, pp 166–70

Tichy, N M and Devanna, M A (1986) *The Transformational Leader*, New York, Wiley

Ulrich, D and Smallwood, N (2007) *Leadership Brand: Developing customer-focused leaders to drive performance and build lasting value*, Boston, MA, Harvard Business School Press

Walumbwa, F O, Avolio, B J, Gardner, W L, Wernsing, T S and Peterson, S J (2008) Authentic leadership: development and validation of a theory-based measure, *Journal of Management*, **34** (1), pp 89–126

Yukl, G (1999) An evaluation of conceptual weaknesses in transformational and charismatic leadership theories, *Leadership Quarterly*, **10**, pp 285–305

75
Influencing skills

LEARNING OUTCOMES

On completing this chapter you should be able to define these key concepts. You should also understand:

- How to persuade
- How to present a case
- How to make a business case
- Facilitating meetings
- Coordinating discussion

Introduction

HR professionals are in the business of influencing people. They have to persuade senior management, line managers and employees generally to accept their advice or proposals. Influencing involves case presentation and submitting business cases. HR professionals can often be concerned with more subtle forms of influencing people by acting as facilitators and leading discussions.

Persuading people

HR specialists spend a lot of time persuading other people to accept their ideas and suggestions. Persuasion is akin to selling. You may feel that good ideas should sell themselves, but life is not like that. People resist change and anything new is usually treated with suspicion. Here are 10 rules for effective persuasion:

1   *Define your objective and get the facts.*
If you are persuading someone to agree to
a proposal, first decide what you want to
achieve and why. Assemble all the facts
you need to support your case. Eliminate
emotional arguments so that you and others
can judge the proposition on the facts alone.

2   *Define the problem.* If there is a problem
to resolve and you are trying to persuade
someone to accept your views on what
should be done about it, first decide whether
the problem is a misunderstanding (a failure
to understand each other accurately) or a
true disagreement (a failure to agree even
when both parties understand one another).
It is not necessarily possible to resolve a true
disagreement by understanding each other
better. People generally believe that an
argument is a battle to understand who is
correct. More often, it is a battle to decide
who is more stubborn.

3   *Find out what the other party wants.*
The key to all persuasion is to see your
proposition from the other person's point
of view. Find out how they look at things.
Establish what they need and want.

4   *Accentuate the benefits.* Present your case
in a way that highlights the benefits to the
other party or at least reduces any
objections or fears.

5   *Predict the other person's response.*
Everything we say should be focused on
that likely response. Anticipate objections
by asking yourself how the other party
might react negatively to your proposition
and thinking up ways of responding to
them.

6   *Create the other person's next move.* It is not
a question of deciding what we want to do
but what we want the other person to do.

7   *Convince people by reference to their own
perceptions.* People decide on what to do on
the basis of their own perceptions, not yours.

8   *Prepare a simple and attractive proposition.*
Make it as straightforward as possible.
Present the case 'sunny side up',
emphasizing its benefits. Break the problem
into manageable pieces and deal with them
one step at a time.

9   *Make the other person a party to your
ideas.* Get them to contribute. Find some
common ground so that you can start with
agreement. Don't try to defeat them in an
argument – you will only antagonize them.

10 *Clinch and take action.* Choose the right
moment to clinch the proposal – don't
prolong the discussion and risk losing it.
But follow up promptly.

Case presentation

Persuasion frequently means making a case for
what you think should be done. You have to convince people to believe in your views and accept
your recommendations. To do this, you must have a
clear idea of what you want, and you have to show
that you believe in it yourself. Above all, the effectiveness of your presentation will depend upon the
care with which you have prepared it.

Thorough preparation is vital. You must think
through not only what should be done and why,
but also how people will react. Only then can you
decide how to make your case: stressing the benefits
without underestimating the costs, and anticipating
objections. The four steps you should take are:

1   Show that your proposal is based on a
thorough analysis of the facts and that the
alternatives were properly evaluated before
the conclusion was reached. If you have
made assumptions, you must demonstrate
that these are reasonable on the basis
of relevant experience and justifiable
projections, which allow for the unexpected.
Bear in mind that a proposal is only as
strong as its weakest assumption.

2   Spell out the benefits – to the company and/
or the individuals to whom the case is being
made. Wherever possible, express benefits
in financial terms. Abstract benefits, such as
customer satisfaction or workers' morale,
are difficult to sell. But don't produce 'funny
numbers' – financial justification that will
not stand up to examination.

3   Reveal costs. Don't try to disguise them in
any way. And be realistic. Your proposition
will be destroyed if anyone can show that
you have underestimated the costs.

4 Remember, senior management decision makers want to know in precise terms what they will get for their money. Most are likely to be cautious, being unwilling and often unable to take much risk. For this reason, it can be difficult to make a case for experiments or pilot schemes unless the decision maker can see what the benefits and the ultimate bill will be.

Making a business case

You may be asked specifically to produce a business case. This will set out the reasons why a proposed course of action will benefit the business, how it will provide that benefit and how much it will cost. A business case is a particular form of persuasion and all the points made above apply to its preparation and presentation. But there are some special features about business cases, as described below.

A business case is typically made either in added-value terms (ie the income generated by the proposal will significantly exceed the cost of implementing it), or on the basis of the return on investment or RoI (ie the cost of the investment, say in training, is justified by the financial returns in such areas as increased productivity). Clearly, a business case is more convincing when it is accompanied by realistic projections of added value or return on investment. When people make out a case for capital expenditure they analyse the cash flows associated with the investment and calculate the benefits – in financial terms as far as possible – that are likely to arise from them. The objective is to demonstrate that in return for paying out a given amount of cash today, a larger amount will be received over a period of time.

It can be more difficult to make out a business case for an HRM innovation in financial terms. The costs can and should be calculated but the benefits may have to be expressed in qualitative terms. A business case will be enhanced if:

- Data is available on the impact the proposal is likely to make on key areas of the organization's operations, eg customer service levels, quality, shareholder value, productivity, income generation, innovation, skills development, talent management.

- It can be shown that the proposal will increase the business's competitive edge, for example enlarging the skill base or multiskilling to ensure that it can achieve competitive advantage through innovation and/or reducing time-to-market.

- There is proof that the innovation has already worked well within the organization (perhaps as a pilot scheme) or represents 'good practice' that is likely to be transferable to the organization.

- It can be implemented without too much trouble, for example not taking up a lot of managers' time, or not meeting with strong opposition from line managers, employees or trade unions (it is as well to check the likely reaction before launching a proposal).

- It will add to the reputation of the company by showing that it is a 'world class' organization, ie what it does is as good as, if not better than, the world leaders in the sector in which the business operates (a promise that publicity will be achieved through articles in professional journals, press releases and conference presentations will help).

- It will enhance the 'employer brand' of the company by making it a 'best place to work'.

- The proposal is brief, to the point and well argued – it should take no more than five minutes to present orally and should be summarized in writing on the proverbial one side of one sheet of paper (supplementary details can be included in appendices).

Making the business case is obviously easier where management is preconditioned to agree to the proposition. For example, it is not hard to convince top managers that performance-related pay is a good thing – they may well be receiving bonus payments themselves and believe, rightly or wrongly, that because it motivates them it will motivate everyone else. Talent management is another process where top management needs little persuasion that things need to be done to enhance and preserve the talent flow, although they will have to be convinced that, in practice, innovations will achieve that aim.

Performance management may be slightly more difficult because it is hard to demonstrate that it can produce measurable improvements in performance, but senior managers are predisposed towards an approach that at least promises to improve the level of performance.

The toughest area for justification in added-value terms can be expenditure on learning and development (L&D) programmes. This is where an RoI approach is desirable. The business case for learning and development should demonstrate how learning, training and development programmes will meet business needs. The following points could be made to support an L&D initiative:

- Improve individual, team and corporate performance in terms of output, quality, speed and overall productivity.

- Attract high-quality employees by offering them learning and development opportunities, increasing their levels of competence and enhancing their skills, thus enabling them to obtain more job satisfaction, to gain higher rewards and to progress within the organization.

- Provide additional non-financial rewards (growth and career opportunities) as part of a total reward policy in order to enhance engagement.

- Improve operational flexibility by extending the range of skills possessed by employees (multiskilling).

- Increase the commitment of employees by encouraging them to identify with the mission and objectives of the organization.

- Help to manage change by increasing understanding of the reasons for change and providing people with the knowledge and skills they need to adjust to new situations.

- Provide line managers with the skills required to manage and develop their people.

- Help to develop a positive culture in the organization, for example one that is oriented towards performance improvement.

- Provide higher levels of service to customers.

- Minimize learning costs (reduce the length of learning curves).

Facilitating

Facilitating in this context is the process of helping a group reach conclusions in the shape of ideas and solutions. Facilitators do not exist to 'chair' the meeting in the sense of controlling the discussion and pressurizing the group to agree to a course of action. The group is there to make up its own mind and the facilitator helps it to do so. The facilitator is exerting influence, but indirectly.

Help in reaching conclusions is provided by asking questions that encourage the group members to think for themselves. These can be challenging and probing questions but the facilitator does not provide the answers – that is the role of the group. Neither do facilitators allow their own opinions to intrude – they are there to help the group marshal its opinions, not to enforce their own ideas. However, by using questioning techniques carefully, facilitators can ensure that the group thoroughly discusses and analyses the issues and reaches conclusions by consensus rather than allowing anyone to dominate the process.

Facilitators ensure that everyone has their say and that they are listened to. They step in quickly to defuse unproductive arguments. They see that the group defines and understands its objectives and any methodology they might use. They summarize from time to time the progress made in achieving the objectives, without bringing their own views to bear. Facilitators are there to ensure that the group makes progress and does not get stuck in fruitless or disruptive argument. They encourage the group rather than drive it forward.

The aim of the facilitator is to guide the group's thinking. He or she may, therefore, be more concerned with shaping attitudes than convincing people about what to do or imparting new knowledge. The facilitator has unobtrusively to stimulate people to talk, guide the discussion along predetermined lines (there must be a plan and an ultimate objective), and provide interim summaries and a final summary.

Coordinating discussions

Coordinating discussions is a matter of getting active participation and then ensuring that the discussion informs people of the issues related to the subject and leads to a conclusion that satisfies the participants. HR practitioners lead discussions when they are taking part in L&D activities. Importantly, discussion is also a means of persuading people to do or accept something by getting them to participate in analysing the issues and reaching a joint and acceptable conclusion.

The following techniques can be used to get active participation and to coordinate the process:

- Ask for contributions by direct questions.
- Use open-ended questions that will stimulate thought.
- Check understanding; make sure that everyone is following the argument.
- Encourage participation by providing support rather than criticism.
- Prevent domination by individual members of the group by bringing in other people and asking cross-reference questions.
- Avoid dominating the group yourself. The leader's job is to guide the discussion, maintain control and summarize from time to time. If necessary, 'reflect' opinions expressed by individuals back to the group to make sure they find the answer for themselves. The leader is there to help the group reach a conclusion, not to do it for them.
- Maintain control – ensure that the discussion is progressing along the right lines towards a firm conclusion.

Key learning points: Influencing skills

Influencing people

HR professionals are often involved in influencing other's thinking and decision making. They must know about persuading people and case presentation.

Persuading people

HR specialists spend a lot of time persuading other people to accept their ideas and suggestions. Persuasion is akin to selling. You may feel that good ideas should sell themselves, but life is not like that. People resist change and anything new is usually treated with suspicion.

Case presentation

Persuasion frequently means making a case for what you think should be done. You have to convince people to believe in your views and accept your recommendations. To do this, you must have a clear idea of what you want, and you have to show that you believe in it yourself.

Making a business case

A business case sets out the reasons why a proposed course of action will benefit the business, how it will provide that benefit and how much it will cost.

Facilitating

Facilitating is the process of helping a group reach conclusions in the shape of ideas and solutions.

Coordinating discussions

Coordinating discussions is a matter of getting active participation and then ensuring that the discussion informs people of the issues related to the subject and leads to a conclusion that satisfies the participants.

76
Handling people problems

Introduction

An important part of the transactional role of HR professionals is handling people problems directly or by providing advice and guidance to line managers. Problem-solving skills, described in Chapter 65, are required but it is also necessary to advise overall on how to handle disciplinary problems and how to deal with absenteeism, poor timekeeping, negative behaviour and under-performance. Dealing with people problems may involve handling challenging conversations and this is dealt with in Chapter 77.

Disciplinary issues

Employees can be dismissed because they are not capable of doing the work, or for misconduct. It is normal to go through a formal disciplinary procedure containing staged warnings, but instant dismissal can be justified for gross misconduct (eg serious theft), which should be defined in the company's disciplinary procedure or employee handbook. Anyone with two years' service or more can claim unfair dismissal if their employer cannot show that one of these reasons applied, if the dismissal was not reasonable in the circumstances, if a constructive dismissal has taken place, or if there has been a breach of a customary or agreed redundancy procedure and there are no valid reasons for departing from that procedure.

Even if the employer can show to an employment tribunal that there was good reason to dismiss the employee, the tribunal will still have to decide whether or not the employer acted in a reasonable way at the time of dismissal. The principles defining 'reasonable' behaviour are in line with the principles of natural justice and are as follows:

- the employee should be informed of the nature of the complaint;
- the employee should be given the chance to explain;
- the employee should be given the opportunity to improve, except in cases of particularly gross incapability or misconduct;
- the employee should be warned of the consequences in the shape of dismissal if specified improvements do not take place;

- the employer's decision to dismiss should be based on sufficient evidence;
- the employer should take any mitigating circumstances into account;
- dismissal should only take place if the offence or misbehaviour deserves it rather than some lesser penalty.

The organization should have a statutory disciplinary procedure (see Chapter 10). Managers need to know what that procedure is and the part they are expected to play in implementing it. Whether or not there is a formal procedure, if it is believed that disciplinary action is necessary the following steps should be taken by the manager, as guided by HR, in planning and conducting a disciplinary interview.

If all the stages in the disciplinary procedure have been completed and the employee has to be dismissed, or where immediate dismissal can be justified on the grounds of gross misconduct, a manager may have to carry out the unpleasant duty of dismissing the employee. This should be as guided by HR and it is advisable that an HR specialist is involved in the dismissal meeting.

Planning and conducting a disciplinary meeting

- Get all the facts in advance, including statements from the people involved.
- Invite the employee to the meeting in writing, explaining why it is being held and that he or she has the right to have someone present at the meeting on his or her behalf.
- Ensure that the employee has reasonable notice (ideally at least two days).
- Plan how to conduct the meeting.
- Line up another member of management to attend the meeting to take notes (they can be important if there is an appeal), generally provide support and witness the proceedings.
- Start the interview by stating the complaint to the employee and referring to the evidence.
- Give the employee plenty of time to respond and state his or her case.
- Take a break as required to consider the points raised and to relieve any pressure in the meeting.
- Consider what action is appropriate, if any. Actions should be staged, starting with a recorded warning followed, if the problem continues, by a first written

warning, then a final written warning and lastly, if the earlier stages have been exhausted, disciplinary action, which would be dismissal in serious cases.
- Deliver the decision, explaining why it has been taken and confirm it in writing.
- If possible, meet when everything is quiet, preferably on a Friday.
- Keep the meeting formal and organized.
- Write down what is going to be said in advance, giving the reason and getting your facts, dates and figures right.
- Be polite but firm – read out what has been written down and make it clear that it is not open for discussion.
- Ensure that the employee clears his or her desk and has no opportunity to take away confidential material or use his or her computer.
- See the employee off the premises – some companies use security guards as escorts; this might be rather heavy-handed, although it could be useful to have someone on call in case of difficulties.

Absenteeism

A frequent people problem managers and HR professionals have to face is absenteeism. It may be necessary to deal with recurrent short-term (one or two days) absence or longer-term sickness absence.

Recurrent short-term absence

Dealing with people who are repeatedly absent for short periods can be difficult. This is because it may be hard to determine when occasional absence becomes a problem or whether it is justifiable, perhaps on medical grounds.

So what can be done about it? Many organizations provide guidelines to managers on the 'trigger points' for action (the amount of absence that needs to be investigated), perhaps based on analyses of the incidence of short-term absence and the level at which it is regarded as acceptable (there may be software to generate analyses and data that can be made available direct to managers through a self-service system). If guidelines do not exist, HR specialists should be available to provide advice.

It is necessary to decide when something needs to be done and then what to do about it. A day off every other month may not be too serious, although if it happens regularly on a Monday (after weekends in Prague, Barcelona, etc?) or a Friday (before such weekends?) you may feel like having a word with the individual, not as a warning but just to let him or her know that you are aware of what is going on. There may be a medical or other acceptable explanation. Return-to-work interviews can provide valuable information and an opportunity to discuss any problems. The individual is seen and given the chance to explain the absence.

In persistent cases of absenteeism an absence review meeting can be held. Although this would be more comprehensive than a return-to-work interview, it should not at this stage be presented as part of a disciplinary process. The meeting should be positive and constructive. If absence results from a health problem it can be established what is being done about it, and if necessary suggest that his or her doctor should be consulted. Or absences may be caused by problems facing a parent or a carer. In such cases it is right to be sympathetic but it would be reasonable to discuss with the individual what steps can be taken to reduce the problem or whether flexible working could be arranged. The aim is to get the employee to discuss as openly as possible any factors affecting his or her attendance and to agree any constructive steps.

If, after holding an attendance review meeting and, it is to be hoped, agreeing the steps necessary to reduce absenteeism, short-term absence persists without a satisfactory explanation, then another meeting can be held that emphasizes the employee's responsibility for attending work. Depending on the circumstances (each case should be dealt with on its merits), at this meeting it can be indicated that absence levels should improve over a defined time-scale (an improvement period). If this does not happen, the individual can expect more formal disciplinary action.

Dealing with long-term absence

Dealing with long-term absence can also be difficult. The aim should be to facilitate the employee's return to work at the earliest reasonable point while recognizing that in extreme cases the person may not be able to come back. In that case, he or she can fairly be dismissed for lack of capability as long as:

- the employee has been consulted at all stages;
- contact has been maintained with the employee – this is something you can usefully do as long as you do not appear to be pressing him or her to return to work before he or she is ready;
- appropriate medical advice has been sought from the employee's own doctor, but the employee's consent is needed and employees have the right to see the report – it may be desirable to obtain a second opinion;
- all reasonable options for alternative employment have been reviewed, as well any other means of facilitating a return to work.

The decision to dismiss should only be taken if these conditions are satisfied. It is a tricky one and it may be advisable to seek advice from an employment law expert.

Handling poor timekeeping

A poor timekeeping record may initially be dealt with by an informal warning. But if in spite of the warning lateness persists, it may be necessary to invoke the disciplinary procedure. This would go through the successive stages of a recorded oral warning, a written warning and a final written warning which would indicate that timekeeping must improve by a certain date (the improvement period) otherwise disciplinary action would take place. If the final warning does not work, such action would be taken; in serious cases this would mean dismissal.

Note that this raises the difficult question of time limits which may be given when a final warning is given. If timekeeping does improve by that date, and the slate is wiped clean, it might be assumed that the disciplinary procedure starts again from scratch if timekeeping deteriorates again. But it is in the nature of things that some people cannot sustain efforts to get to work on time for long, and deterioration often occurs. In these circumstances, is it necessary to keep on going through the warning cycles time after time? The answer ought to be no, and the best approach seems to be to avoid stating a finite end date to a final warning period that implies a 'wipe the slate clean' approach. Instead, the warning should simply say that timekeeping performance will be reviewed on a stated date. If it has not improved, disciplinary action can be taken. If it has, no action will be taken, but the employee is warned that further deterioration will make him or her liable to disciplinary action, which may well speed up the normal procedure, perhaps by only using the final warning stage and by reducing the elapsed time between the warning and the review date. There will come a time, if poor timekeeping persists, when you can say 'enough is enough' and initiate disciplinary action.

Handling negative behaviour

Negative behaviour may take the form of lack of interest in the work, unwillingness to cooperate with team leaders or other members of the team, making unjustified complaints about the work or working conditions, grumbling at being asked to carry out a perfectly reasonable task, objecting strongly to being asked to do something extra (or even refusing to do it) – 'It's not in my job description' – or, in extreme cases, insolence. People exhibiting negative behaviour may be quietly resentful rather than openly disruptive. They mutter away in the background at meetings and lack enthusiasm.

Managers have to tolerate a certain amount of negative behaviour as long as the individual works reasonably well and does not upset other team members. They have simply to say to themselves, 'It takes all sorts...' and put up with it, although they might calmly say during a review meeting, 'You're doing a good job but...'. If, however, they take this line, they have to be specific. They must cite actual instances. It is no good making generalized accusations that will either be openly refuted or internalized by the receiver, making him or her even more resentful.

If the negative behaviour means that the individual's contribution is not acceptable and is disruptive, action has to be taken. Negative people can be quiet but they are usually angry about something; their negative behaviour is an easy way of expressing their anger. To deal with the problem it is necessary to find out what has made them angry.

Causes of negative behaviour

There are many possible causes of negative behaviour, which could include one or more of the following:

- a real or imagined slight from their manager or a colleague;
- a feeling of being put upon;
- a belief that the contribution they make is neither appreciated nor rewarded properly in terms of pay or promotion;
- resentment at what was perceived to be unfair criticism;
- anger directed at the company or their manager because what was considered to be a reasonable request (such as for leave or a transfer) was turned down, or because of an unfair accusation.

Dealing with the problem

It is because there can be such a variety of real or imagined causes of negative behaviour that dealing with it becomes one of the most difficult tasks line managers and HR people have to undertake. If the action taken is crude or insensitive the negative behaviour will only be intensified. This might mean having to invoke the disciplinary procedure, which should be a last resort.

In one sense, it is easier to deal with an actual example of negative behaviour. This can be handled on the spot. If the problem is one of general attitude rather than specific actions, it is more difficult to cope with. Hard evidence may not be available. When individuals are accused of being, for example, generally unenthusiastic or uncooperative, they can simply go into denial and accuse you of being prejudiced. Their negative behaviour may be reinforced.

It is best to deal with this sort of problem informally, either when it arises or at any point during the year when it is felt that something has to be done about it. An annual formal performance review or appraisal meeting is not the right time, especially if it produces ratings that are linked to a pay increase. Raising the issue then will only put individuals on the defensive and a productive discussion will be impossible.

The discussion may be informal but it should have three clear objectives:

1 To review the situation with individuals, the aim being if possible to get them to recognize for themselves that they are behaving negatively. If this cannot be achieved, then the objective is to bring to the attention of individuals your belief that their behaviour is unacceptable in certain ways.

2 To establish the reasons for the individuals' negative behaviour so far as this is feasible.

3 To agree any actions individuals could take to behave more positively, or what you or the organization could do to remove the causes of the behaviour.

Discussing the problem

The starting point should be general questions about how individuals feel about their work. Do they have any problems in carrying it out? Are they happy with the support they get from you or their colleagues? Are they satisfied that they are pulling their weight to the best of their ability?

This generalized start provides the basis for the next two stages – identifying causes and any remedies. It is best if individuals are encouraged to decide for themselves that there is a problem, but in many, if not the majority of cases, this is unlikely to happen. Individuals may not recognize that they are behaving negatively or will not be prepared to admit it.

It is then necessary to discuss the problem. They should be given time to say their piece. The response should spell out how justifiable grievances will be dealt with or why no action is necessary. In the latter case, an explanation should be given as to why the individual's behaviour gives the impression of being negative. This should be specific, bringing up actual instances. For example, a discussion could be based on the following questions: 'Do you recall yesterday's team meeting?', 'How did you think it went?', 'How helpful do you think you were in dealing with the problem?', 'Do you remember saying...?', 'How helpful do you think that remark was?', 'Would it surprise you to learn that I felt you had not been particularly helpful in the following ways...?'

Of course, even if this careful approach is adopted, individuals may still refuse to admit that there is anything wrong with their behaviour. If this impasse is reached, then there is no alternative but to spell out where it is believed they have gone wrong. But this should be done in a positive way: 'Then I think that it is only fair for me to point out to you that your contribution (to the meeting) would have been more helpful if you had...'

Establishing causes

If the negative behaviour is because of a real or imagined grievance about what the manager, colleagues or the organization have done, then the individual has to be persuaded to spell this out as precisely as possible. At this point, the job of the manager or HR practitioner is to listen, not to judge. People can be just as angry about imaginary as real slights. You have to find out how they perceive the problem before you can deal with it.

It may emerge during the discussion that the problem has nothing to do with the manager or the company. It may be family troubles or worries about health or finance. If this is the case, a sympathetic approach is appropriate, which may involve suggesting remedies in the form of counselling or practical advice from within or outside the organization. If the perceived problem is the manager, colleagues or the organization, try to get chapter and verse on what it is so that remedial action can be taken.

Taking remedial action

If the problem rests with the individual, the objective is, of course, to get them to recognize for themselves that corrective action is necessary and what they need to do about it – with help as necessary. In some situations, you might suggest counselling or a source of advice might be recommended. But care needs to be taken: there should be no implication that there is something wrong with them. It is best to go no further than suggesting that individuals may find this helpful – they don't need it but they could benefit from it. Managers or HR specialists should not offer counselling themselves. This is better done by professional counsellors.

If there is anything specific that the parties involved in the situation can do, then the line to take is that the problem can be tackled together: 'This is what I will do', 'This is what the company will do', 'What do you think you should do?' If there is no response to the last question, this is the point where it is necessary to spell out the necessary action. This should be as specific as possible and expressed as suggestions, not commands. A joint problem-solving approach is always best.

10 approaches to handling negative behaviour

1. Define the type of negative behaviour which is being exhibited. Make notes of examples.

2. Discuss the behaviour with the individual as soon as possible, aiming to get agreement about what it is and the impact it makes.

3. If agreement is not obtained, give actual examples of behaviour and explain why you believe them to be negative.

4. Discuss and so far as possible agree reasons for the negative behaviour including those attributed to the individual, yourself and the organization.

5. Discuss and agree possible remedies – actions on the part of the individual, yourself or the organization.

6. Monitor the actions taken and the results obtained.

7. If improvement is not achieved and the negative behaviour is significantly affecting the performance of the individual and the team, then invoke the disciplinary procedure.

8. Start with a verbal warning, indicating the ways in which behaviour must improve and give a time scale and offers of further support and help as required.

9. If there is no improvement, issue a formal warning, setting out as specifically as possible what must be achieved over a defined period of time, indicating the disciplinary action that could be taken.

10. If the negative behaviour persists and continues seriously to affect performance, take the disciplinary action.

Dealing with under-performance

Poor performance can be the fault of the individual but it could arise because of poor leadership or problems in the system of work. In the case of an individual, the reason may be that he or she:

- could not do it – ability;
- did not know how to do it – skill;
- would not do it – attitude; or
- did not fully understand what was expected of him or her.

Inadequate leadership from managers can be the cause of poor performance from individuals. It is the manager's responsibility to specify the results expected and the levels of skill and competence required. As likely as not, when people do not understand what they have to do it is their manager who is to blame.

Performance can also be affected by the system of work. If this is badly planned and organized or does not function well, individuals cannot be blamed for the poor performance that results. This is the fault of management and they must put it right.

If inadequate individual performance cannot be attributed to poor leadership or the system of work, there are seven steps that can be taken to deal with it:

1 Identify the areas of under-performance – be specific.
2 Establish the causes of poor performance.
3 Agree on the action required.
4 Ensure that the necessary support (coaching, training, extra resources etc) is provided to ensure the action is successful.
5 Monitor progress and provide feedback.
6 Provide additional guidance as required.
7 As a last resort, invoke the capability or disciplinary procedure (see Chapter 10), starting with an informal warning.

Key learning points: Handling people problems

The HR role in handling people problems

An important part of the transactional role of HR professionals is handling people problems by providing advice and guidance to line managers or directly.

Disciplinary issues

Employees can be dismissed because they are not capable of doing the work or for misconduct. It is normal to go through a formal disciplinary procedure containing staged warnings, but instant dismissal can be justified for gross misconduct (eg serious theft), which should be defined in the company's disciplinary procedure or employee handbook.

The organization should have a statutory disciplinary procedure. Managers need to know what that procedure is and the part they are expected to play in implementing it.

Absenteeism

A frequent people problem managers and HR professionals have to face is that of dealing with absenteeism. It may be necessary to deal with recurrent short-term (one or two days) absence or longer-term sickness absence.

Many organizations provide guidelines to managers on the 'trigger points' for action (the amount of absence which needs to be investigated), perhaps based on analyses of the incidence of short-term absence and the level at which it is regarded as acceptable. If guidelines do not exist, HR specialists should be available to provide advice.

Handling poor timekeeping

Faced with persistent lateness and when informal warnings to the individual concerned seem to have little effect, it may be necessary to invoke the disciplinary procedure. If timekeeping does not improve, this could go through the successive stages of a recorded oral warning, a written warning and a final written warning. If the final warning does not work, disciplinary action would have to be taken; in serious cases this would mean dismissal.

Handling negative behaviour

Negative behaviour may take the form of lack of interest in the work, unwillingness to cooperate with team leaders or other members of the team, making unjustified complaints about the work or working conditions, grumbling at being asked to carry out a perfectly reasonable task, objecting strongly to being asked to do something extra (or even refusing to do it), or, in extreme cases, insolence.

It is because there can be such a variety of real or imagined causes of negative behaviour that dealing with it becomes one of the most difficult tasks line managers and HR people have to undertake. If the action taken is crude or insensitive, the negative behaviour will only be intensified. This might mean having to invoke the disciplinary procedure, which should be a last resort.

In one sense, it is easier to deal with an actual example of negative behaviour. This can be handled on the spot. If the problem is one of general attitude rather than specific actions, it is more difficult to cope with. It is best to deal with this sort of problem informally, either when it arises or at any point during the year when it is felt that something has to be done about it.

Dealing with under-performance

Poor performance can be the fault of the individual, but it could arise because of poor leadership or problems in the system of work. To deal with it:

1 Identify the areas of under-performance – be specific.

2 Establish the causes of poor performance.

3 Agree on the action required.

4 Ensure that the necessary support (coaching, training, extra resources, etc) is provided to ensure the action is successful.

5 Monitor progress and provide feedback.

6 Provide additional guidance as required.

7 As a last resort, invoke the capability or disciplinary procedure (see Chapter 10), starting with an informal warning.

77
Handling challenging conversations

Many managers find it difficult to have conversations or hold meetings with individuals about performance or discipline issues. In advance, these can look difficult and in practice, they can be challenging if the manager wants to achieve desired changes or improvements in performance. They can be even more challenging in prospect if it is feared that unpleasantness can occur in the shape of lack of cooperation or outright hostility, or in practice when this happens in spite of efforts to prevent it. The following is a 12-point guide to handling challenging conversations.

Handling challenging conversations

1 Don't wait until a formal review meeting. Have a quiet word at the first sign that something is going wrong.

2 Get the facts in advance – what happened, when and why?

3 Plan the meeting on the basis of the facts and what is known about the individual. Define what is to be achieved.

4 Set the right tone from the start of the meeting – adopt a calm, measured, deliberate but friendly approach.

5 Begin the conversation by explaining the purpose of the meeting, indicating to the individual what the issue is and giving specific examples.

6 Focus on the issue and not the person.

7 Ask for an explanation. Ask unloaded questions to clarify the issues and explore them together.

8 Allow people to have their say and listen to them.

9 Keep an open mind and don't jump to conclusions.

10 Acknowledge the individual's position and any mitigating circumstances.

11 Ask the employee for proposals to resolve the situation, discuss the options and if possible agree on action by the individual, the manager or jointly.

12 If agreement cannot be reached, managers may have to define the way forward, with reasons – they are in charge!

78
Managing conflict

Introduction

Conflict is inevitable in organizations because they function by means of adjustments and compromises among competitive elements in their structure and membership. Conflict also arises when there is change, because it may be seen as a threat to be challenged or resisted, or when there is frustration – this may produce an aggressive reaction: fight rather than flight.

Conflict is not to be deplored. It results from progress and change and it can and should be used constructively. Bland agreement on everything would be unnatural and enervating. There should be clashes of ideas about tasks and projects, and disagreements should not be suppressed. They should come out into the open because that is the only way to ensure that the issues are explored and conflicts are resolved.

There is such a thing as creative conflict – new or modified ideas, insights, approaches and solutions can be generated by a joint re-examination of different points of view, as long as this is based on an objective and rational exchange of information and opinions. But conflict becomes counterproductive when it is based on personality clashes, or when it is treated as an unseemly mess to be hurriedly cleared away, rather than as a problem to be worked through. Conflict resolution deals with ways of settling differences between groups, individuals and team members.

Handling intergroup conflict

There are three principal ways of resolving intergroup conflict: peaceful coexistence, compromise and problem solving.

Peaceful coexistence

The aim here is to smooth out differences and emphasize the common ground. People are encouraged to learn to live together, there is a good deal of information, contact and exchange of views, and individuals move freely between groups (for example, between headquarters and the field, or between sales and marketing).

This is a pleasant ideal, but it may not be practicable in many situations. There is much evidence that conflict is not necessarily resolved by bringing people together. Improved communications and techniques such as briefing groups may appear to be good ideas but are useless if management has nothing to say that people want to hear. There is also the danger that the real issues, submerged for the moment in an atmosphere of superficial bonhomie, will surface again later.

Compromise

The issue is resolved by negotiation or bargaining and neither party wins or loses. This concept of splitting the difference is essentially pessimistic. The hallmark of this approach is that there is no 'right' or 'best' answer. Agreements only accommodate differences. Real issues are not likely to be solved.

Problem solving

An attempt is made to find a genuine solution to the problem rather than just accommodating different points of view. This is where the apparent paradox of 'creative conflict' comes in. Conflict situations can be used to advantage to create better solutions.

If solutions are to be developed by problem solving, they have to be generated by those who share the responsibility for seeing that the solutions work. The sequence of actions is: first, those concerned work to define the problem and agree on the objectives to be attained in reaching a solution; second, the group develops alternative solutions and debates their merits; and third, agreement is reached on the preferred course of action and how it should be implemented.

Handling interpersonal conflict

Handling conflict between individuals can be even more difficult than resolving conflicts between groups. Whether the conflict is openly hostile or subtly covert, strong personal feelings may be involved. However, interpersonal conflict, like intergroup conflict, is an organizational reality that is not necessarily good or bad. It can be destructive, but it can also play a productive role. The approaches to dealing with it are withdrawal, smoothing over differences, reaching a compromise, counselling and constructive confrontation.

Withdrawal

The reaction to interpersonal conflict may be the withdrawal of either party, leaving the other one to hold the field. This is the classic win/lose situation. The problem has been resolved by force, but this may not be the best solution if it represents one person's point of view that has ignored counter-arguments, and has, in fact, steamrollered over them. The winner may be triumphant but the loser will be aggrieved and either demotivated or resolved to fight again another day. There will have been a lull in, but not an end to, the conflict.

Smoothing over differences

Another approach is to smooth over differences and pretend that the conflict does not exist, although no attempt has been made to tackle the root causes. Again, this is an unsatisfactory solution. The issue is likely to re-emerge and the battle will recommence.

Reaching a compromise

Yet another approach is bargaining to reach a compromise. This means that both sides are prepared to lose as well as win some points and the aim is to reach a solution acceptable to both sides. Bargaining, however, involves all sorts of tactical and often counterproductive games, and the parties are often more anxious to seek acceptable compromises than to achieve sound solutions.

Counselling

Personal counselling is an approach that does not address the conflict itself but focuses on how the two people are reacting. It gives people a chance to release pent-up tensions and may encourage them to think about new ways of resolving the conflict. But it does not address the essential nature of the conflict, which is the relationship between two people. That is why constructive confrontation offers the best hope of a long-term solution.

Constructive confrontation

Constructive confrontation is a method of bringing the individuals in conflict together with a third party whose function is to help build an exploratory and cooperative climate. Constructive confrontation aims to get the contending parties to understand and explore the other's perceptions and feelings. It is a process of developing mutual understanding to produce a win/win situation. The issues will be confronted but on the basis of a joint analysis, with the help of the third party, of facts relating to the situation and the actual behaviour of those involved. Feelings will be expressed but they will be analysed by reference to specific events and behaviours rather than inferences or speculations about motives. Third parties have a key role in this process, and it is not an easy one. They have to get agreement to the ground rules for discussions aimed at bringing out the facts and minimizing hostile behaviour. They must monitor the ways in which negative feelings are expressed and encourage the parties to produce new definitions of the problem and its cause or causes and new motives to reach a common solution. Third parties must avoid the temptation to support or appear to support either of those in contention. They should adopt a counselling approach, as follows:

- listen actively;
- observe as well as listen;
- help people to understand and define the problem by asking pertinent, open-ended questions;
- recognize feelings and allow them to be expressed;
- help people to define problems for themselves;
- encourage people to explore alternative solutions;
- get people to develop their own implementation plans but provide advice and help if asked.

To conclude, conflict, as has been said, is in itself not to be deplored; it is an inevitable concomitant of progress and change. What is regrettable is the failure to use conflict constructively. Effective problem solving and constructive confrontation both resolve conflicts and open up channels of discussion and cooperative action.

Many years ago, one of the pioneering and most influential writers on management, Follett (1924), wrote something on managing conflict that is as valid today as it was then. She said that differences can be made to contribute to the common cause if they are resolved by integration rather than domination or compromise.

Resolving conflict between team members

To resolve conflict between team members, the following actions can be taken:

1 Obtain an overview of the situation from your own observations.
2 Find out who is involved.
3 Talk to each of the parties to the conflict to obtain their side of the story.
4 Talk to other members of the group to get their views, being careful to be dispassionate and strictly neutral.
5 Evaluate what you hear from both parties and other people against your knowledge of what has been happening, any history of conflict and the dispositions and previous behaviour of the people involved.

6 Reach preliminary conclusions on the facts, the reasons for the dispute and the extent to which either of the parties or both of them are to blame (but keep these to yourself at this stage).

7 Bring the parties together to discuss the situation. The initial aim of this meeting would be to bring the problem out into the open, get the facts and defuse any emotions that may prejudice a solution to the problem. Both parties should be allowed to have their say but, as the facilitator of this meeting, you should do your best to ensure that they stick to the facts and explain their point of view dispassionately. You should not even remotely give the impression that you are taking sides.

8 Try to defuse the situation so that a solution can be reached that on the whole will be acceptable to all concerned. Ideally, this should be an integrated solution reached by agreement on the basis of collaboration along the lines of: 'Let's get together to find the best solution on the basis of the facts.' It may be necessary to reach a compromise or accommodation – something everyone can live with.

9 Only if all else fails or the parties are so recalcitrant in holding an untenable position that no integrated, compromise or accommodating solution can be reached, should you resort to direct action – instructing one or both of the parties to bury their differences and get on with their work. If the worst comes to the worst this may involve disciplinary action, beginning with a formal warning.

Key learning points: Managing conflict

The manifestation of conflict

Conflict is inevitable in organizations because they function by means of adjustments and compromises among competitive elements in their structure and membership. Conflict also arises when there is change, because it may be seen as a threat to be challenged or resisted, or when there is frustration – this may produce an aggressive reaction: fight rather than flight.

Handling intergroup conflict

There are three principal ways of resolving inter-group conflict: peaceful coexistence, compromise and problem solving.

Handling interpersonal conflict

The approaches to dealing with interpersonal conflict are withdrawal, smoothing over differences, reaching a compromise, counselling, and constructive confrontation.

Resolving conflict between team members

- Obtain an overview of the situation.
- Find out who is involved.
- Talk to each of the parties to the conflict to obtain their side of the story.
- Talk to other members of the group.
- Evaluate what you hear.
- Reach preliminary conclusions on the facts and the reasons for the dispute.
- Bring the parties together to discuss the situation.
- Only resort to direct action if all else fails.

Reference

Follett, M P (1924) *Creative Experience*, New York, Longmans Green

79
Political skills

KEY CONCEPTS AND TERMS

Dominant coalition

Networking

Politics

LEARNING OUTCOMES

On completing this chapter you should be able to define these key concepts. You should also know about:

- Typical political approaches
- Using political means to get things done

- Political sensitivity
- Dangers of politics
- Dealing with organizational politics

Introduction

To be politic, according to the *Oxford English Dictionary*, you can be sagacious, prudent, judicious, expedient, scheming or crafty. So political behaviour in an organization could be desirable or undesirable.

Organizations consist of individuals who, while they are ostensibly there to achieve a common purpose, will, at the same time, be driven by their own needs to achieve their own goals. Effective management is the process of harmonizing individual endeavour and ambition to the common good. Some individuals will genuinely believe that using

political means to achieve their aims will benefit the organization as well as themselves. Others will rationalize this belief. Yet others will unashamedly pursue their own ends. They may use all their powers of persuasion to legitimize these ends to their colleagues, but self-interest remains the primary drive. These are the corporate politicians the *OED* describes as 'shrewd schemers, crafty plotters or intriguers'. Politicians within organizations can be like this. They manoeuvre behind people's backs, blocking proposals they do not like. They advance their own reputation and career at the expense of other people's. They can be envious and jealous and act accordingly. They are bad news.

But it can also be argued that a political approach to management is inevitable and even desirable in any organization where the clarity of goals is not absolute, where the decision-making process is not clear-cut and where the authority to make decisions is not evenly or appropriately distributed. And there can be few organizations where one or more of these conditions do not apply.

It was suggested by Kakabadse (1983) that politics in an organization is a process of influencing individuals and groups of people to your point of view, where you cannot rely on authority. In this sense, a political approach can be legitimate as long as the ends are justifiable from the viewpoint of the organization. Whether or not that is the case, political skills and political sensitivity, as described in this chapter, are required to thrive and sometimes even survive in organizations. This applies particularly to HR specialists who may lack the power base others possess and may feel they have to pursue the achievement of their ends and exert influence through political as well as more open means. But it is also essential for them to gain insight into the political situation in their organization in order to understand what is happening, why it is happening and what they need to do about it.

Typical political approaches

Kakabadse (1983) identified seven approaches that organizational politicians adopt, some of which are more legitimate than others:

1 Identify the stakeholders, those who have commitment to act in a particular way.

2 Keep the stakeholders comfortable, concentrating on behaviour, values, attitudes, fears and drives that the individuals will accept, tolerate and manage (comfort zones).

3 Fit the image – work on the comfort zones and align their image to that of the people with power.

4 Use the network – identify the interest groups and people of influence.

5 Enter the network – identify the gatekeepers, adhere to the norms.

6 Make deals – agree to support other people where this is of mutual benefit.

7 Withhold and withdraw – withhold information as appropriate and withdraw judiciously when the going gets rough.

Using political means to get things done

People acting politically get things done by lobbying decision makers and doing deals. This may not always be desirable, but it does happen, and some people rationalize it on the basis that the end justifies the means (always a dubious stance). Other ploys include withholding information, which is not legitimate, but people do indulge in it, which recognizes the fact that knowledge is power. Organizational politicians can go behind people's backs, hatch up plots in dark corners, 'sew things up' before meetings (lobbying) and exert undue influence on weaker brethren. You may not deign to practise these political black arts but it is useful to be aware of the possibility that others will so that you are prepared for that eventuality.

The reality of politics in organizational life means that HR specialists who are proposing new initiatives to managers need to identify the key decision makers before coming to a final conclusion and launching a fully fledged proposal at a committee or in a memorandum. It makes good sense to test opinion and find out how other people may react, especially when it is possible that there will be some opposition or indifference. This testing process enables the anticipation of counter-arguments and the modification of proposals, either to meet legitimate objections or, when there is no alternative, to accommodate other people's requirements.

Political sensitivity

Organizational politicians exert hidden influence to get their way, and 'politicking' in some form takes place in most organizations. A degree of political sensitivity is desirable – knowing what is going on so that influence can be exerted properly. This means that it is necessary to:

- know how 'things are done around here';
- know how key decisions are made and who makes them;
- understand the factors that are likely to affect decisions;
- know where the power base is in the organization (sometimes called the 'dominant coalition') – who makes the running, who are the people who count when decisions are taken;
- be aware of what is going on behind the scenes;
- know who is a rising star and whose reputation is fading;
- identify any 'hidden agendas' – try to understand what people are really getting at beneath the surface by getting answers to the question: 'Where are they coming from?';
- find out what other people are thinking and seeking;
- network – identify the interest groups and keep in contact with them.

Dangers of politics

Much of this behaviour is legitimate, but there are dangers. Politicking can be carried out to excess, and it can then seriously harm the effectiveness of an organization. The signs of excessive indulgence in political behaviour include:

- back-biting;
- buck-passing;
- secret meetings and hidden decisions;

- feuds between people and departments;
- e-mail or paper wars between armed camps – arguing by e-mail or memoranda rather than meeting people face to face is a sign of distrust;
- a multiplicity of snide comments and criticisms;
- excessive and counterproductive lobbying;
- the formation of cabals – cliques that spend their time intriguing.

Dealing with organizational politics

One way to deal with this sort of behaviour is to find out who is going in for it and openly confront them with the damage they are doing. They will, of course, deny that they are behaving politically (they wouldn't be politicians if they didn't), but the fact that they have been identified might lead them to modify their approach. It could, of course, only serve to drive them further underground, in which case their behaviour would have to be observed even more closely and action taken to restrain it.

A more positive approach to keeping politics operating at an acceptable level is for the organization to manage its operations as transparently as possible. The aim should be to ensure that issues are debated fully, that differences of opinion are dealt with frankly and that disagreements are de-personalized, so far as this is possible. Political processes can then be seen as a way of helping to maintain the momentum of the organization as a complex decision-making and problem-solving entity. In their organization development role, HR professionals can exert influence in achieving these aims.

Key learning points: Political skills

Organizational politics

Politics in an organization is a process of influencing individuals and groups of people to your point of view, where you cannot rely on authority (Kakabadse, 1983). In this sense, a political approach can be legitimate as long as the ends are justifiable from the viewpoint of the organization.

Approaches adopted by organizational politicians:

1 Identify the stakeholders.

2 Keep the stakeholders comfortable, concentrating on their comfort zones.

3 Work on the comfort zones and align their image to that of the people with power.

4 Use the network – identify the interest groups and people of influence.

5 Enter the network – identify the gatekeepers, adhere to the norms.

6 Make deals – agree to support other people where this is of mutual benefit.

7 Withhold information as appropriate and withdraw judiciously when the going gets rough.

Using political means to get things done

People acting politically get things done by lobbying decision makers and doing deals. Other ploys include withholding information, which is not legitimate, in recognition of the fact that knowledge is power. Organizational politicians can go behind people's backs, hatch up plots in dark corners, 'sew things up' before meetings and exert undue influence on weaker brethren.

Political sensitivity

To be politically sensitive it is necessary to:

- know how 'things are done around here';
- know how key decisions are made and who makes them;
- understand the factors that are likely to affect decisions;
- know where the power base is in the organization;
- be aware of what is going on behind the scenes;
- know who is a rising star and whose reputation is fading;
- identify any 'hidden agendas' – try to understand what people are really getting at beneath the surface;
- find out what other people are thinking and seeking;
- network – identify the interest groups and keep in contact with them.

Dealing with organizational politicians

To keep politics operating at an acceptable level, the organization should manage its operations as transparently as possible. The aim should be to ensure that issues are debated fully, that differences of opinion are dealt with frankly and that disagreements are de-personalized.

Reference

Kakabadse, A (1983) *The Politics of Management*, Aldershot, Gower

80

Investigating a business issue from an HR perspective

KEY CONCEPTS AND TERMS

Added value

Business case

Business model

Core competencies

Evidence-based approach

Return on investment (RoI)

Triangulation

LEARNING OUTCOMES

On completing this chapter you should be able to define these key concepts. You should also understand how to:

- Identify business issues
- Establish people factors
- Critically analyse relevant HR policy and practice
- Conduct or participate in research

- Analyse quantitative and qualitative information
- Draw conclusions from research and analysis
- Make a business case

Introduction

The *HR Profession Map* of the CIPD (2013) states that an effective HR professional: 'Demonstrates the ability to analyse and understand data and information quickly. Is able to use information, insights and knowledge in a structured way using judgement wisely to identify options and make robust and defendable decisions.'

This specification is directly related to the CIPD's Advanced Diploma module 'Investigating a Business Issue' the purpose and aim of which is defined as:

Key elements of professional competence are strategic awareness, a business orientation and a concern with adding value through human resource (HR) practice. Qualified professionals should be able to research relevant topics and write reports that can persuade key stakeholders in an organization to change or adopt a particular policy and practice.

As set out in the learning outcomes defined for the module and expanded in this chapter, this requirement can be met as follows:

- identify business issues that are of strategic importance to the organization;

- establish the extent and nature of any people factors that affect these issues;

- critically analyse and discuss relevant HR policy and practice by reference to the literature, published research and any other sources of information;

- conduct or participate in research within and outside the organization to find out what factors cause and affect the issues and what remedies have proved to be successful;

- systematically analyse quantitative and qualitative information using HR analytics and statistical methods and present the results in clear and consistent formats;

- draw realistic and appropriate conclusions from analyses and research;

- make recommendations based on costed options and develop and present a persuasive business case for proposals.

Identify business issues

A business issue will be anything occurring in the organization or affecting it that will influence its performance in terms of the achievement of its strategic goals. To identify issues it is necessary to develop qualities of organizational insight defined by the CIPD (2010: 13) as:

The juxtaposition of a deep understanding of what will help make your organization successful – or stop it from being so – in the market within which it operates at this stage in its evolution, together with a deep appreciation of what goes on around here and what really make things happen here (given people, politics and culture). The former derives from understanding the key drivers of the business, the wider market and the context in which it sits. The latter comes from the 'intelligence' generated both systematically through data-gathering and analysis, as well as from the discrete activities and interactions HR engages in across the organization.

At corporate level it is important to understand what the organization exists to do and how it does it. In a commercial business this means knowing how it makes money with particular reference to its development, marketing and operational activities. In a national or local government establishment or a not-for-profit organization it means understanding its key functions – service delivery, administration, research and development. As noted in Chapter 64, this involves finding out:

- the business imperatives of the organization – its mission and its strategic goals;

- the organization's business model – the basis upon which its business is done (how its mission and strategic goals will be achieved);

- the organization's business drivers – the characteristics of the business that move it forward;

- the organization's core competencies – what the organization is good at doing;

- the factors that will affect performance and ensure the effectiveness of its activities including specific issues concerning profitability, productivity, operational performance, quality, financial budgeting and control, costs and benefits and customer service;

- the key performance indicators (KPIs) of the business (the results or outcomes identified as being crucial to the achievement of high performance; eg financial, productivity and quality measures) that can be used to measure progress towards attaining goals;

- the factors that will ensure that the firm's resources, especially its human resources, create sustained competitive advantage because they are valuable, imperfectly imitable and non-substitutable (the resource-based view).

It is particularly important that the head of the HR function and the heads of the key departments, such as talent management, learning and development and reward management, should understand these characteristics of their organization. This will provide the basis for making the strategic contribution expected from those at this level. But any HR practitioner acting as a business partner or delivering a service such as recruitment and selection should also be knowledgeable in each of these areas. And those embedded in divisions or departments need to acquire knowledge of the particular factors in these areas that will affect how the unit operates and performs.

Getting this information cannot be left to chance. To obtain it, the first thing to do is to get hold of as much written or published information as you can: annual reports (see Chapter 64 for guidance on how to read a balance sheet), company websites, sales brochures, articles in the financial pages of newspapers, reports from management consultants. The next thing to do is to talk to people: senior managers (if you can get at them), line managers, team leaders and supervisors and, when the occasion presents itself, people in offices, sales, delivery and on the shop floor. It is necessary to make a deliberate effort to walk about, ask questions and, importantly, listen. Business partners should spend far more time doing this than sitting in their office. So should more senior HR professionals and L&D specialists. Even those who are likely to be office-based for much of the time (eg recruiters and reward specialists) should get out as much as they can. In the experience of the writer (25 years as an HR professional; 12 of them as HR director), understanding takes time and sometimes occurs by a process of osmosis. But it is worth it. HR people earn respect by the quality of their service delivery efforts but, importantly, also by demonstrating that they know what is going on and understand the issues that concern managers and staff generally and base their strategy proposals on them.

Establish people factors

An HR executive reported by the CIPD (2010:13) commented that: 'We need deep employee insights – not just employee engagement surveys which just scratch the surface. As an HR function, we need a deep and segmented understanding of employees' aspirations, motivations and needs in some ways akin to how a customer-facing company thinks about its customers.'

Inevitably, many of the identified business issues will involve people, especially issues concerned generally with performance and particularly with productivity, quality, sales and customer service. People factors can include levels of motivation and engagement, inadequate leadership, poor teamwork, lack of trust, management succession problems, skills (talent) shortages, employee turnover, absenteeism and long-term illness. Sometimes, however, people factors are not so evident. For example, is a fall in productivity due to people not working hard enough or is it because the system of work is failing to deliver? (Although systems of work are deigned and operated by people, so a people factor might still be present.) It may be necessary to drill down to find out what lies behind the people factor; for example, the causes of employee turnover.

Critically analyse relevant HR policy and practice

To address any issues, the first step is to critically analyse any evidence which illustrates good HR practice. There are a number of sources. One of them is the literature. *People Management* contains the most practical and relevant information. Academic journals, particularly *The Human Resource Management Journal*, *The International Journal of Human Resource Management* and *Employee Relations*, should also be consulted. Although many of the articles in these publications are somewhat esoteric – academics writing for academics – some contributions based on rigorous research are relevant for practitioners.

Articles in academic journals are usually based on research but the best and most practical research data is provided by the CIPD, which produces a large number of research reports and surveys every year that are full of relevant information and illustrated by illuminating case studies.

Other sources of information include conferences, networking, for example at CIPD branch meetings, and contacts with organizations that are known to be successfully using a relevant HR practice. Research methods are considered in the next section of this chapter.

An evidence-based management approach is necessary. Five steps were recommended by Briner *et al* (2009: 23):

1 Practitioners or managers gain understanding of the problem or issue.

2 Internal evidence is gathered about the issue or problem leading, possibly, to a reformulation of the problem to make it more specific.

3 External evidence is gathered from published research.

4 The views of stakeholders are obtained.

5 All the sources of information are examined and critically appraised.

Any information obtained should be subject to critical evaluation. As mentioned in Chapter 66, critical evaluation is the process of making informed judgements about the validity, relevance and usefulness of ideas and arguments. Critical evaluation means not taking anything for granted and, where necessary, challenging propositions. It involves making informed judgements about the value of ideas and arguments. It uses critical thinking by analysing and evaluating the quality of theories and concepts to establish the degree to which they are valid and supported by the evidence (evidence-based) and the extent to which they are biased. The arguments for and against are weighed and the strength of the evidence on both sides is assessed. On the basis of this assessment, a conclusion is reached on which proposition or argument is to be preferred. Critical evaluation is required when testing propositions and evaluating the outcomes of research.

Conduct or participate in research

As noted in Chapter 67, research is concerned with establishing what is and from this predicting what will be. It does not decide what ought to be; that is for people interpreting the lessons from research in their own context. Research is about the conception and testing of ideas and hypotheses. This is a creative and imaginative process, although new information is normally obtained within the framework of existing theory and knowledge. Logic and rational argument are methods of testing ideas after they have been created.

It may be useful for HR professionals to conduct formal research within their organization in order to assemble evidence upon which they can base proposals on how to deal with business or HR issues. They may also be involved in research projects outside the organization with fellow HR professionals or academics where these seem likely to produce results of interest to their organization. In either case, they need to know what research methods are available and their relevance in different situations.

A full discussion of research methodology is contained in Chapter 67. A summary of the most used techniques, their advantages and disadvantages, and their relevance in different situations is set out in Table 80.1. These techniques are often combined.

Analyse quantitative and qualitative information

Quantitative business information will be available in the form of financial and operational reports. Quantitative HR data will by generated through HR analytics (see Chapter 11) and by research. Qualitative HR information may be obtained by research but it will also emerge from day-to-day contacts between HR specialists and managers and employees.

TABLE 80.1   Analysis of basic research methods

Research technique	Methodology	Advantages	Disadvantages	Relevance in different situations
Interviews	Interviews are an important research method. They obtain factual data and insights into attitudes and feelings. Direct quotations from individuals can be used to give life and reality to the research.	Interviews obtain information directly from people involved in the area being researched and can provide insights into attitudes and perspectives that questionnaires will not reveal, thus promoting in-depth understanding. They enable the interviewer to probe answers and check that questions had been understood.	• The construction of the interview questions may result in leading questions or bland answers. • Interviewers may influence the interviewees' reactions by imposing their own reference frame. • Respondents may tell interviewers what they want to hear. • They are time-consuming – to set up, to conduct and to analyse. • They require considerable interviewing skills, including the abilities to recognize what is important and relevant, to probe when necessary, to listen and to control the interview so that it covers the ground it was intended to cover. • They are essentially qualitative but can become more quantitative by the use of content analysis techniques.	Can be used to obtain a range of views about a topic as long as when this is required a balanced sample of people are interviewed.
Questionnaires	Questionnaires collect data systematically by obtaining answers, which provide factual information or indicate opinions.	A relatively simple way of assembling data.	• Do not reveal how or why things are happening. • It is impossible to assess the degree of subjectivity that has crept in when expressing opinions.	Useful for collecting basic factual data.

TABLE 80.1 *continued*

Research technique	Methodology	Advantages	Disadvantages	Relevance in different situations
Surveys	Surveys obtain information from a defined population of people. They are usually based on questionnaires but these are best reinforced by interviews and focus groups, a process know as triangulation.	Can provide more powerful data than other methods by using a combination of questionnaires and interviews and, possibly, focus groups.	• If not coupled with interviews, surveys may give only a superficial picture. • It is impossible to assess the degree of subjectivity that has crept in when expressing opinions.	They can be used to provide evidence covering facts and/or opinions. In the latter case triangulation is desirable.
Case studies	A research case study is a description of a situation or a history of an event or sequence of events in a real-life setting which illustrates a particular area of interest.	Case studies are useful ways of collecting information on the reality of organizational life and processes.	There is a danger of them being no more than a story or an anecdote that does not contribute to greater knowledge or understanding. Much skill and persistence are required from the researcher in gaining support, ensuring that relevant and revealing information is obtained and presenting the case study as a convincing narrative from which valid and interesting conclusions can be derived. All this must be done without taking a biased view, which can be difficult.	When it is useful to obtain an illustration of what is actually happening from which conclusions can be drawn on what sort of action can take place. They can reinforce other methods as part of a triangulation process.

Quantitative information

Company annual financial reports (see Chapter 64) containing the balance sheet, profit and loss account and other financial data provide an overall source of information on how well the business is doing. Internal periodical reports will show performance against financial budgets and targets and there are likely to be other reports, depending on the nature of the business, on such matters as sales, output, service levels and quality. They can be analysed to reveal business performance (profitability and productivity) issues expressed in terms of trends and ratios. HR professionals can pursue this analysis in discussions with management to establish the extent and nature of any people problems and consider remedies.

Statistical techniques such as frequency analysis, measures of central tendency, correlation and regression analysis, as described in Chapter 68, can be used when establishing the significance of the data.

Qualitative information

The analysis of qualitative information is inevitably more subjective. But the technique of content analysis can be used to provide a form of measurement. This involves selecting a number of key phrases or words, counting the number of times they are mentioned in interviews or focus groups and then analysing these frequencies.

Draw conclusions

Drawing conclusions from the analysis of the data involves:

- assessing the nature of the issue and its causes;
- considering the HR strategic and operational implications;
- examining and evaluating alternative courses of action;

- deciding on the preferred course of action;
- establishing the costs and benefits of the action.

Prepare and make the business case

A business case should set out the costs and benefits of the proposal. It can be made either in added-value terms (ie the income generated by the proposal will exceed the cost of implementing it) or on the basis of the return on investment or RoI (ie the cost of the investment, say in training, is justified by the financial returns in such areas as increased productivity).

It can be more difficult to make out a business case for an HRM innovation in financial terms. The costs can and should be calculated but the benefits may have to be expressed qualitatively. As described in Chapter 75, a business case will be enhanced if:

- Data is available on the impact the proposal is likely to make on key areas of the organization's operations, for example customer service levels, quality, shareholder value, productivity, income generation, innovation, skills development, talent management.
- It can be shown that the proposal will help to achieve competitive advantage; for example, by enlarging the skill base or multiskilling.
- There is proof that the innovation has already worked well within the organization (perhaps as a pilot scheme) or represents 'good practice' that is likely to be transferable to the organization.
- It can be implemented without too much trouble.
- The proposal is brief, to the point, laid out clearly and well argued.

> ## Key learning points: Investigating a business issue from an HR perspective
>
> When investigating a business issue from an HR perspective, it is necessary to:
>
> - identify business issues that are of strategic importance to the organization;
>
> - establish the extent and nature of any people factors that affect these issues;
>
> - critically analyse and discuss relevant HR policy and practice by reference to the literature, published research and any other sources of information;
>
> - conduct or participate in research within and outside the organization to find out what factors cause and affect the issues and what remedies have proved to be successful;
>
> - systematically analyse quantitative and qualitative information using HR analytics and statistical methods and present the results in clear and consistent formats;
>
> - draw realistic and appropriate conclusions from analyses and research;
>
> - make recommendations based on costed options and develop and present a persuasive business case for proposals.

References

Briner, R B, Denyer, D and Rousseau, D M (2009) Evidence-based management: concept clean-up time? *Academy of Management Perspectives*, September, pp 19–32

Chartered Institute of Personnel and Development (2010) *Next Generation HR*, CIPD, London, http://www.cipd.co.uk/hr-resources/research/ next-generation-hr-time-for-change.aspx [accessed 2 August 2016]

Chartered Institute of Personnel and Development (2013) *HR Profession Map*, http://www.cipd.co. uk/hr-profession-map-download.aspx [accessed 25 January 2013]

AUTHOR INDEX

SUBJECT INDEX

ARMSTRONG'S HANDBOOK OF HUMAN RESOURCE MANAGEMENT PRACTICE

ALSO AVAILABLE BY MICHAEL ARMSTRONG